APPLIED MICROECONOMIC THEORY

ECONOMISTS OF THE TWENTIETH CENTURY

General Editors: David Colander, *Christian A. Johnson Distinguished Professor of Economics, Middlebury College, Vermont, USA* and Mark Blaug, *Professor Emeritus, University of London, UK, Professor Emeritus, University of Buckingham, UK, Visiting Professor, University of Amsterdam, The Netherlands and Visiting Professor, Erasmus University of Rotterdam, The Netherlands*

This innovative series comprises specially invited collections of articles and papers by economists whose work has made an important contribution to economics in the late twentieth century.

The proliferation of new journals and the ever-increasing number of new articles make it difficult for even the most assiduous economist to keep track of all the important recent advances. By focusing on those economists whose work is generally recognized to be at the forefront of the discipline, the series will be an essential reference point for the different specialisms included. Wherever possible, the articles in these volumes have been reproduced as originally published using facsimile reproduction, inclusive of footnotes and pagination to facilitate ease of reference.

A list of published and future titles in this series is printed at the end of this volume.

Applied Microeconomic Theory

Selected Essays of B. Curtis Eaton

B. Curtis Eaton

Professor of Economics, University of Calgary, Canada

ECONOMISTS OF THE TWENTIETH CENTURY

Edward Elgar

Cheltenham, UK • Northampton, MA, USA

Published by
Edward Elgar Publishing Limited
Glensanda House
Montpellier Parade
Cheltenham
Glos GL50 1UA
UK

Edward Elgar Publishing, Inc.
136 West Street
Suite 202
Northampton
Massachusetts 01060
USA

A catalogue record for this book
is available from the British Library

ISBN 1 85898 650 8

Printed and bound in Great Britain by MPG Books Ltd, Bodmin, Cornwall

Contents

Acknowledgements ix
Preface xiii
Intellectual biography xv

PART I STRATEGIC BEHAVIOR

1 'Free Entry in One-Dimensional Models: Pure Profits and Multiple Equilibria', *Journal of Regional Science*, **16** (1), 1976, pp. 21–33. 3
2 'Freedom of Entry and the Existence of Pure Profit' (with Richard G. Lipsey), *Economic Journal*, **88**, September 1978, pp. 455–69. 16
3 'The Theory of Market Pre-emption: The Persistence of Excess Capacity and Monopoly in Growing Spatial Markets' (with Richard G. Lipsey), *Economica*, **46**, May 1979, pp. 149–58. 31
4 'Exit Barriers are Entry Barriers: The Durability of Capital as a Barrier to Entry' (with Richard G. Lipsey), *Bell Journal of Economics*, **11** (2), Autumn 1980, pp. 721–9. 41
5 'Capital, Commitment, and Entry Equilibrium' (with Richard G. Lipsey), *Bell Journal of Economics*, **12** (2), Autumn 1981, pp. 593–604. 50
6 'Asymmetric Equilibria and Strategic Behaviour in Oligopolistic Markets' (with Mukesh Eswaran), 1984, pp. 1–18. 62
7 'Sophisticated Entry in a Model of Spatial Competition' (with Myrna Holtz Wooders), *Rand Journal of Economics*, **16** (2), Summer 1985, pp. 282–97. 80
8 'A Theory of Market Structure with Sequential Entry' (with Roger Ware), *Rand Journal of Economics*, **18** (1), Spring 1987, pp. 1–16. 96
9 'Uncertainty and the Value of Strategic Commitment' (with Roger Ware), 1988, pp. 1–6. 112
10 'Noncooperative Equilibria in One-Shot Games: A Synthesis' (with Mukesh Eswaran), 1991, pp. 1–32. 118
11 'Flexible Manufacturing and Market Structure' (with Nicolas Schmitt), *American Economic Review*, **88** (4), September 1994, pp. 875–88. 150
12 'Supporting Collusion by Choice of Inferior Technologies' (with Mukesh Eswaran), in *Trade, Technology and Economics: Essays in Honour of Richard G. Lipsey* (eds. B. Curtis Eaton and Richard G. Harris), Edward Elgar Press, 1997, pp. 263–83. 164

PART II EFFICIENCY WAGES

13 'Agent Compensation and the Limits of Bonding' (with William D. White), *Journal of Economic Inquiry*, **XX**, July 1982, pp. 330–43. 187

14 'The Economy of High Wages: an Agency Problem' (with William D. White), *Economica*, **50**, May 1983, pp. 175–81. 201

15 'Wealth: The Support of Institutions and the Limits of Control' (with William D. White), 1986, pp. 1–18. 208

16 'The Distribution of Wealth and the Efficiency of Institutions' (with William D. White), *Economic Inquiry*, **29**, April 1991, pp. 336–50. 226

PART III APPLIED PRICE THEORY

17 'Unemployment, Underemployment, and Optimal Job Search' (with Philip A. Neher), *Journal of Political Economy*, **83** (2), April 1975, pp. 355–75. 243

18 'Firm-Specific Human Capital: A Shared Investment or Optimal Entrapment?' (with David Donaldson), *Canadian Journal of Economics*, **9** (3), August 1976, pp. 462–72. 264

19 'Patience, More Than Its Own Reward: A Note on Price Discrimination' (with David Donaldson), *Canadian Journal of Economics*, **14** (1), February 1981, pp. 93–105. 275

20 'Person-Specific Costs of Production: Hours of Work, Rates of Pay, Labour Contracts' (with David Donaldson), *Canadian Journal of Economics*, **17** (3), August 1984, pp. 441–9. 288

21 'Sweezy's Kink: The Original Consistent-Conjectural Equilibrium' (with Jeremiah M. Allen), 1985, pp. 1–7. 297

22 'The Geometry of Supply, Demand, and Competitive Market Structure with Economies of Scope' (with S.Q. Lemche), *American Economic Review*, **85** (4), September 1991, pp. 901–11. 304

23 'Price Versus Quantity Competition in the Gabszewicz–Thisse Model of Vertical Differentiation' (with P. Harrald), in *Market Strategy and Structure* (eds. A. Gee and G. Norman), Harvester/Wheatsheaf, 1992, pp. 217–32. 315

24 'Endogenous Pricing Modes in Markets for Inputs' (with Nicolas Schmitt), in *Does Economic Space Matter: Essays in Honor of Melvin L. Greenhut* (eds. Hiroshi Ohta and Jacques-Francois Thisse), Macmillan, 1993, pp. 352–73. 331

25 'An Address Model of Patent Breadth with Two Countries' (with Patrick van Cayseele and Theon van Dijk), in *The Limits of Patent Protection*, by Theon van Dijk, Maastricht University Press, 1994, pp. 137–55. 353

26 'Image Advertising' (with William D. White), 1995, pp. 1–17. 372

27 'Technology-Trading Coalitions in Supergames' (with Mukesh Eswaran), *Rand Journal of Economics*, **28** (1), Spring 1997, pp. 135–49. 389

28 'Co-specific Investments, Hold-Up, and Self-Enforcing Contracts' (with Patricia Koss), *Journal of Economic Behavior and Organization*, **32**, 1997, pp. 457–70. 404

29 'The Evolution of Type Communication in a Sender/Receiver Game of Common Interest with Cheap Talk' (with Jasmina Arifovic), *Journal of Economic Dynamics and Control*, **22**, August 1998, pp. 1187–207. 418

30 'Endogenous Cartel Formation' (with Mukesh Eswaran), *Australian Economic Papers*, **37** (1), March 1998, pp. 1–13. 439
31 'Know-how Sharing with Stochastic Innovations' (with Mukesh Eswaran), *Canadian Journal of Economics*, **34** (2), May 2001, pp. 525–48. 452

Name index 477

Acknowledgements

The publishers wish to thank the following who have kindly given permission for the use of copyright material.

American Economic Association for articles: 'The Geometry of Supply, Demand, and Competitive Market Structure with Economies of Scope', *American Economic Review*, **85** (4), September 1991, pp. 901–11; 'Flexible Manufacturing and Market Structure', *American Economic Review*, **88** (4), September 1994, pp. 875–88.

Blackwell Publishers for articles: 'Free Entry in One-Dimensional Models: Pure Profits and Multiple Equilibria', *Journal of Regional Science*, **16** (1), 1976, pp. 21–33; 'Freedom of Entry and the Existence of Pure Profit', *Economic Journal*, **88**, September 1978, pp. 455–69; 'The Theory of Market Pre-emption: The Persistence of Excess Capacity and Monopoly in Growing Spatial Markets', *Economica*, **46**, May 1979, pp. 149–58; 'The Economy of High Wages: an Agency Problem', *Economica*, **50**, May 1983, pp. 175–81; 'Endogenous Cartel Formation', *Australian Economic Papers*, **37** (1), March 1998, pp. 1–13.

Canadian Economics Association for articles: 'Firm-Specific Human Capital: A Shared Investment or Optimal Entrapment?', *Canadian Journal of Economics*, **9** (3), August 1976, pp. 462–72; 'Patience, More Than Its Own Reward: A Note on Price Discrimination', *Canadian Journal of Economics*, **14** (1), February 1981, pp. 93–105; 'Person-Specific Costs of Production: Hours of Work, Rates of Pay, Labour Contracts', *Canadian Journal of Economics*, **17** (3), August 1984, pp. 441–9; 'Know-how Sharing with Stochastic Innovations', *Canadian Journal of Economics*, **34** (2), May 2001, pp. 525–48.

Edward Elgar Publishing Limited for excerpt: 'Supporting Collusion by Choice of Inferior Technologies', in *Trade, Technology and Economics: Essays in Honour of Richard G. Lipsey* (eds. B. Curtis Eaton and Richard G. Harris), 1997, pp. 263–83.

Elsevier Science for articles: 'Co-specific Investments, Hold-Up, and Self-Enforcing Contracts', *Journal of Economic Behavior and Organization*, **32**, 1997, pp. 457–70; 'The Evolution of Type Communication in a Sender/Receiver Game of Common Interest with Cheap Talk', *Journal of Economic Dynamics and Control*, **22**, August 1998, pp. 1187–207.

Maastricht University Press for excerpt: 'An Address Model of Patent Breadth with Two Countries', in *The Limits of Patent Protection*, Theon van Dijk, 1994, pp. 137–55.

Macmillan Press Limited for excerpt: 'Endogenous Pricing Modes in Markets for Inputs', in *Does Economic Space Matter: Essays in Honor of Melvin L. Greenhut* (eds. Hiroshi Ohta and Jacques-Francois Thisse), 1993, pp. 352–73.

Oxford University Press for articles: 'Agent Compensation and the Limits of Bonding', *Economic Inquiry*, **XX**, July 1982, pp. 330–43; 'The Distribution of Wealth and the Efficiency of Institutions', *Economic Inquiry*, **29**, April 1991, pp. 336–50.

Pearson Education Limited for excerpt: 'Price Versus Quantity Competition in the Gabszewicz–Thisse Model of Vertical Differentiation', in *Market Strategy and Structure* (eds. A. Gee and G. Norman), Harvester/Wheatsheaf, 1992, pp. 217–32.

Rand for articles: 'Exit Barriers are Entry Barriers: The Durability of Capital as a Barrier to Entry', *Bell Journal of Economics*, **11** (2), Autumn 1980, pp. 721–9; 'Capital, Commitment, and Entry Equilibrium', *Bell Journal of Economics*, **12** (2), Autumn 1981, pp. 593–604; 'Sophisticated Entry in a Model of Spatial Competition', *Rand Journal of Economics*, **16** (2), Summer 1985, pp. 282–97; 'A Theory of Market Structure with Sequential Entry', *Rand Journal of Economics*, **18** (1), Spring 1987, pp. 1–16; 'Technology-Trading Coalitions in Supergames', *Rand Journal of Economics*, **28** (1), Spring 1997, pp. 135–49.

University of Chicago Press for article: 'Unemployment, Underemployment, and Optimal Job Search', *Journal of Political Economy*, **83** (2), April 1975, pp. 355–75.

Every effort has been made to trace all the copyright holders but if any have been inadvertently overlooked the publishers will be pleased to make the necessary arrangements at the first opportunity.

Dedication

To David Donaldson, Dick Lipsey, Jasmina Arifovic, Jay Allen, Mukesh Eswaran, Myrna Wooders, Nic Schmitt, Patricia Koss, Paul Herrald, Phil Neher, Roger Ware, Soren Lemche, Theon van Dijk and Will White.

Preface

I have organized the papers in this volume into three sections, and within each the papers are ordered chronologically. In the section titled *Strategic Behavior* I include 12 papers, most of which were written in the 1970s and 1980s with a number of co-authors, that deal with various aspects of the theory of strategic behavior in oligopoly markets. These papers represent the major thrust of my intellectual activity over this 20 year period, and in my view they constitute a quite significant contribution to this important subject. In the section titled *Efficiency Wages* I include four papers written in collaboration with William White in the 1980s and 1990s on the efficiency wage idea, and extensions of it. Here too I think the papers represent a major contribution to a significant body of literature. The last section, titled *Applied Price Theory*, includes 15 papers written with a number of co-authors on a variety of topics, primarily in the broad area of industrial organization.

I have included in this volume six papers that have not been published elsewhere, all of which seem to me to be worthy of publication. The first is a paper that Mukesh Eswaran and I wrote in 1984 that synthesizes much of the literature on strategic positioning (Chapter 6). The second is a paper in which Roger Ware and I examine the value of strategic positioning in an environment in which there is demand uncertainty (Chapter 9). This interesting little paper, that develops a clever model of the trade-off between commitment and flexibility, somehow was never finalized, and I am pleased to have the opportunity to publish it in this volume. The third is a paper in which Mukesh Eswaran and I synthesize a very large literature on two-person games in which each player's strategy space is a segment of the real line (Chapter 10). I have found it to be an immensely useful teaching tool in a variety of undergraduate and graduate courses. The fourth is a paper that William White and I wrote in 1986 in which we use insights from the efficiency wage literature to reconsider a variety of interesting and, as it turns out, currently topical crime and punishment issues (Chapter 15). The fifth is a history of thought paper that Jeremiah Allen and I wrote on Sweezy's kinky demand model in which we argue that Sweezy deserves some credit for the consistent-conjectural variation idea (Chapter 21). The sixth is a paper that William White and I wrote on image advertising (Chapter 26). Like the Eaton–Ware paper mentioned above, this paper somehow slipped through the cracks. In my estimation, it is an extremely good paper – among other things, we provide a precise definition of image advertising and develop some surprising results that are consistent with the anecdotal evidence we found on the subject.

Intellectual biography

One of the difficulties in tracing out an intellectual biography is deciding where to begin. On looking back, it seems that the very deepest roots are in my family traditions and early school experiences. Like so many able people of their generation, my parents had relatively little formal education. My mother proudly earned her high school equivalency at age 57, about the same time that I completed my undergraduate studies. My father, who was exceptionally intelligent, left school after grade nine to make his way in the world and never gave formal education another thought. They were determined to give their children the educational advantages they never had, however, and from a very young age I knew that I was university bound. Indeed, it was clear to me from about the age of nine that my *job* was to develop my intellectual abilities. And it was very much *my* job – they set high, but not unreasonable, standards and expected me to meet them. I can't recall even one occasion when they tried to manage my progress through the educational system. An important consequence of this hands-off policy was that I learned to manage my own affairs. I mention this because in raising my own children on the same model, I saw many parents who – because they thought it was their job to manage their children's progress – denied their children an important opportunity to grow and mature.

I spent my formative years in Grand Junction, a town of 12 000 people in western Colorado, where I had the benefit of a first-rate high school education. Two very talented and dedicated math teachers, Lois Baufman and particularly Gunhilde Swanson, had a significant influence on my intellectual development. I entered high school the year after the Russians launched their Sputnik satellite. The response to Sputnik was a revolution in the teaching of science and math in many American high schools. In that very first post-Sputnik year, I had the enormous privilege of taking a plane geometry course, taught by Gunhilde Swanson and pitched at the best and the brightest students in the grade 10 class. There was no textbook. Instead, under the guiding and demanding hand of Ms Swanson, we re-created large chunks of Euclid's *Elements*. Each day she would begin by going over the day's homework assignment with us and end by writing down a set of problems to occupy us until we met the next day. These problems kept many of us up until the wee hours, and often we made very limited progress on them. But when we did manage to prove – all on our own – one of Euclid's theorems it was intensely satisfying. I am quite sure that this extraordinary experience played a huge role in forming my taste for applied economic theory. Not all the students in that class were as enthusiastic as I, and many of the parents were outraged that a teacher would challenge their little darlings to spend hours and hours re-creating for themselves the subject of plane geometry. In response to the concerns of these parents, the accelerated math program did not offer quite the same challenge in subsequent years, and therefore was not so satisfying nor captivating. In my last year at Grand Junction High School, I had the considerable advantage of taking a social studies course from Isabelle Benson. Current events played a big part in this course, and Ms Benson's ability to lure students into the events of the day, often leaving us with many more questions than answers, led me to pursue social science in my undergraduate days at the University of Colorado.

At the University of Colorado, political science and economics grabbed my attention. The person who most influenced me as an undergraduate was Richard Wilson, from whom I took two constitutional law courses and a course on regulation. He was, I believe, the first person I ever encountered with a truly dazzling intellect. Seen through his eyes, constitutional law was nearly as captivating as plane geometry. To my surprise it seemed to involve similar analytical skills, and because he, like Ms Swanson, was very demanding of his students, it was almost as satisfying. It was Clifton Grubbs, a student of Clarence Ayers, who enticed me to study economics. His passion for teaching, his expansive irreverence for the conventional wisdom of economics, his willingness to encourage my own efforts at theorizing and the applied math flavor of the course itself led me to a career in economics. In my last summer as an undergraduate, I took a course from Kenneth Boulding which used as the textbook Boulding's *Conflict and Defense*. Because the book and the course took a small set of familiar tools from oligopoly theory and intermediate economics and adapted them for the study of a variety of analogous problems, we students could see quite clearly how applied theory evolves in the hands of a master such as Boulding. Boulding's course was immensely stimulating, and the first piece of original theory that I wrote came out of this course. Fascinated by the fact that the credibility of the threat to use nuclear weapons seemed to be directly related to the distance separating the two countries involved, I developed a theoretical model of deterrence that incorporated this observation.

At about the same time, I decided that I wanted to pursue an academic career. Given both a fellowship from the Ford Foundation and the fact that Diane, my wife, was still an undergraduate when I finished my bachelor's degree, the path of least resistance to the PhD was to stay at the University of Colorado. Although he did not supervise my thesis, Wesley Yordon was my mentor during my years of graduate study at the University of Colorado. Like Clifton Grubbs, Yordon was an institutionalist. He taught me industrial organization, and – consistent with his institutionalist approach – his course was idiosyncratic. He always referred to what then passed for the theory of the firm as the 'theory of the farm' because, in his view, only on the farm could one actually find the almost continuous divisibility and homogeneity of inputs and outputs and the lack of market power that were so much a part of the received theory of the firm. Looking back, it is clear that the seeds of much of the work I did in the 1970s and 1980s in collaboration with Richard Lipsey and others were sown in Wesley Yordon's courses. I always knew that Yordon had had an influence on my own approach to economics, but I did not understand just how large it was until I spent a couple of hours talking about economics with him in the summer of 1995 – it had been more than 25 years since I had had any significant contact with him, yet our interests were still quite similar.

My thesis work at Colorado grew out of a project funded by the Arms Control and Disarmament Agency on the re-employment experiences of several large groups of defense workers who had been laid off in connection with contract cancellation or project completion. Leslie Fishman was the principal investigator, and the contract – worth something like $300,000 – was a large one by the standards of the 1960s. Just after I finished my PhD comprehensive exams, Fishman hired me, Jeremiah Allen and Byron Bunger to assist him. Shortly thereafter, Fishman left the University of Colorado for a position in the United Kingdom, more or less leaving the three of us to complete this project. As I recall, I became the de facto manager of the project. One of my fellow graduate students, Jerry Hunt, suggested that Markov processes could be used to model the re-employment process, and this was the approach I adopted in my thesis. When I had what I thought was an acceptable draft in hand I asked Fred Glahe if he would supervise my thesis. He asked what I intended to do, and I gave him the draft. A few days later he gave it back to me with a few suggested changes and we set the date for the final examination. I learned an enormous amount from this experience, most especially that I was not interested in contract research. So, when I took my first job as a labor economist at the University of British Columbia, I struck out in quite a different direction.

The academic job market of the late 1960s was the kind of market to delight any applicant. The market was so tight that by early November 1968 I had offers in hand from Pennsylvania State University, San Diego State University and the University of British Columbia. The UBC offer was based solely on a letter of application, some letters of reference and a couple of papers that I had written. So, the day after Richard Nixon was elected President, I accepted the UBC offer, just to see if the world looked better from the perspective of another country. When I called Anthony Scott to accept the UBC offer, he asked if I wanted to visit the campus of UBC, and I said no, thinking they might change their minds once they saw me. Eventually I decided that I did prefer Canadian society and so made my career in Canada.

I have often wondered whether my choice to get my PhD at Colorado was a mistake. As I learned within days of my arrival in June 1969 at UBC, my fellow assistant professors – all but one of whom had attended better known universities including Harvard, Northwestern, Pennsylvania, MIT and Brown – knew a lot more economics than I did. But not having studied under the masters of the discipline, I had a naive sense of my own capacity to do original work and a willingness to question the work that other economists were doing. In addition, my pedigree meant that my senior colleagues at UBC did not expect a great deal of me. I still don't know whether my choice was a mistake, but it is clear to me that today a fresh PhD from a university outside the top 30 would have extreme difficulty getting the attention of a top-ranked department in North America.

The contrast between the economics departments at the University of Colorado and the University of British Columbia was very striking. Although there were a number of very productive people at Colorado, the intellectual atmosphere was sleepy. Seminars were few and far between, virtually all of them were presented by visiting scholars, and rarely was anything critical ever said about the seminar paper. In contrast, at UBC there was a sense of activity, excitement and contention. Most of the younger faculty were talking about their own research in the departmental seminar at regular intervals, and the seminar atmosphere was, to me at least, intimidating. The venue for the departmental seminar was the Angus Penthouse, the time Friday afternoon at 3 pm, and the sport was shooting holes in the seminar paper. In my cohort at UBC there were eight tenure-track assistant professors, and we were, of course, expected to make at least one presentation during the first year. Having seen the reception that some of my colleagues received when they presented empirical papers, I chose a date late in the year and an obscure theoretical topic: the introduction of price-sensitive demand into the Hotelling model of spatial competition. The tactic worked; no one found any errors in my presentation, and no one, including me, noticed that Arthur Smithies had written the same paper 30 years earlier. I had carried the analysis somewhat further than Smithies, however, and managed to publish the paper (Eaton 1972).[1] This tactical choice led to a fascination with product differentiation that shaped much of my career.

I was profoundly influenced by those early years at UBC. I had the pleasure of watching Erwin Diewert develop his ideas on index numbers; watching David Donaldson and later Donaldson and Charles Blackorby develop their ideas on justice and distribution; Alan Woodland apply duality techniques to international trade theory; Philip Neher develop his ideas on the muggery and fisheries economics; Knick Harley exercise and develop his extraordinary skills as an economic historian; and so on. As I watched, and as I began to collaborate with my UBC colleagues, I developed my abilities as a theorist. In this regard, my collaborations with Philip Neher and David Donaldson were particularly important. Neher and I adapted the ideas of Harris and Todaro on migration and unemployment in the context of developing economies to fashion a general equilibrium macro model featuring unemployment, underemployment and job search (Eaton and Neher 1975, reprinted here in Chapter 17). Donaldson and I wrote three papers in the mid to late 1970s. In our first paper, we used dynamic programming techniques and what in retrospect is an information theoretic approach to argue that the back-loaded wage profile associated with firm-specific human capital was not, as Becker had argued, evidence of a shared investment in human capital, but rather a strategy to manage turnover (Donaldson and Eaton 1976, reprinted here as Chapter 18). In our second paper, we used an information theoretic approach to develop a theory of price discrimination, which we called 'queue discrimination' (Donaldson and Eaton 1981, reprinted here as Chapter 19). We used this theory to explain the periodic and quite predictable sales in large department stores in which goods are offered at significant price discounts, accompanied by queues and congestion. In our third paper, we explored the implications of person-specific costs of production for hours of work and rates of pay; we argued that the only way to economize on such costs is to induce employees to work long hours, which requires premium wage rates (Donaldson and Eaton 1984, reprinted here as Chapter 20). Both Donaldson and Neher are elegant thinkers who hold very high standards for their own work and, in working with them, I learned much of what I know about the art of modeling and the value of working to a high standard.

In the departmental newsletter which announced my appointment to the Economics faculty at UBC, I noticed that Richard Lipsey was to join the Department as a Visiting Professor for the academic year 1969–70. I first met Lipsey in August 1969, and we almost immediately struck up a friendship that endures to this day. Soon after, we began a collaboration that lasted more than 20 years and produced 16 papers. In Richard Lipsey I found someone with whom I could communicate extraordinarily well, someone who shared many of my intellectual passions, someone with an enormous curiosity, always willing to rethink any proposition and, as a mutual friend put it, someone with a mind like a bear trap. Four of our joint papers are included in this volume, and the entire collection of our joint work is published in another volume of the *Economists of the Twentieth Century* series, entitled *On the Foundations of Monopolistic Competition and Economic Geography* (Eaton and Lipsey 1997).

In the autumn of 1969, we began to work on a paper on the theory of the second best, but we quickly abandoned the effort. Soon after my departmental seminar on the Hotelling/Smithies model, we began a collaboration on Hotelling's principle of minimum differentiation. This collaboration proved more fruitful, leading to a pair of papers finished in 1972 (Queens' University Discussion Papers numbers 87 and 88) and published three and four years later (Eaton and Lipsey 1975, 1976). In the first of these we did an exhaustive analysis of the principle of minimum differentiation in one- and two-dimensional models of spatial competition with a parametric mill price, discovering that minimum differentiation was a very special case. To study minimum differentiation in two dimensions, we found that we needed to use numerical techniques and we developed a computer simulation model for this purpose. In the second paper we adapted the simulation model to examine the Loschian location model. Among other things, we explored in some detail the problem of entry into regular lattices of established firms, including those in which the market areas of established firms are hexagonal and rectangular, and discovered that if entrants took the locations of existing firms as given, their expected profit was discretely less than the pre-entry profit of established firms. Accordingly, we argued in that paper that pure profit was possible in free-entry equilibrium in standard models of spatial competition.

Encouraged by our success with these two papers, and fascinated by the possibilities that the pure profit result seemed to offer, we spent the 1974–75 academic year at the University of Colorado working on a closely related set of ideas. The work begun in that year led to four important discussion papers in the Queen's University Discussion Paper series, three in 1976 (numbers 207, 208 and 226) and another in 1978 (number 327). All of these papers were eventually published (Eaton and Lipsey 1978, 1979a, 1979b, 1982). In this series of papers, we constructed a monopolistic vision of the economy in which indivisibilities, sunk costs, product differentiation, market power, the possibility of pure profit in free-entry equilibrium, strategic behavior, market pre-emption, multiple equilibria, hysteresis and the clustering of economic activity all played important roles. This vision – much of which is now standard fare in applied microeconomics, industrial organization and economic geography – was first drawn together in a paper that was presented in April 1976 at the annual meetings of the Association of University Teachers of Economics in Edinburgh and in May 1976 at the meetings of the Canadian Economics Association in Quebec City, and was published in the AUTE Proceedings Volume (Eaton and Lipsey 1977).

The following line of reasoning is at the core of our monopolistic vision of the economy. In any consumer goods industry, goods are points in some characteristic space and consequently the set of possible goods is a continuum. The preferences of consumers are diverse: different consumers prefer different goods in the continuum. The production of any good, and particularly the production of any new good, involves significant sunk costs associated with product development, marketing and the acquisition of specific capital goods needed to produce the good. Because they are largely independent of quantity produced, these costs imply significant economies of scale, and because they are to a significant degree product specific and sunk, they create barriers both to exit and to relocation of products in the characteristic space. Faced with these sunk costs and associated barriers to exit and relocation, any new firm – or any firm contemplating the introduction of new products – will perceive that the products currently offered balkanize the market. Recognizing that destructive price competition is a real danger if they choose a cloning strategy, firms instead choose to produce goods that are differentiated from those of their competitors. In equilibrium, each product is unique and is in direct competition with a small number of neighboring products. Consequently, in free-entry equilibrium each product is in a position that looks very much like the position of the classical natural monopolist. In particular, entry and the threat of entry do not necessarily drive profit to zero. As Nicolas Kaldor, the pioneer of this particular vision, would have put it, the economy is composed of a series of *overlapping oligopolies*. And just as Wesley Yordon had put it, the competitive theory of the firm really is reduced to the theory of the farm.

The key to this vision is the result that free entry does not drive profit to zero when goods are differentiated in a continuous attribute space. I first discovered this result in a paper that appeared in the UBC Discussion Paper series in 1972 (number 70) and after a series of rejections at first-tier journals was eventually published in the *Journal of Regional Science* (Eaton 1976, reprinted here as Chapter 1). There I used simulation techniques to show that in a one-dimensional product attribute space in which each product was owned by a separate firm, if entrants take the location and prices of existing products as given (subject only to the caveat that entrants are not so naive as to think that they can capture all of an existing firm's market without inducing that firm to make a price cut sufficient to recapture at least some of its former market), substantial pure profit is possible in free-entry equilibrium and the free-entry equilibrium is not unique. Building on the notion of limit pricing, in that paper I also explored a pre-emption strategy in which the would-be monopolist chooses the number, price and attributes of its products to maximize profit subject to the constraint that entry be unprofitable. When I compared this pre-emption equilibrium with the most profitable of the free-entry equilibria when each product is owned by a separate firm, I found them to be almost identical; naturally the pre-emptive monopolist earned more profit, but just 1 percent more, it established fewer products, but just 2 percent fewer, and it charged a lower price, but just 1 percent lower. Remarkably, the discipline of potential entry produced in this model a monopoly equilibrium that was virtually indistinguishable from the most profitable of the free-entry equilibria that I found when I arbitrarily imposed the restriction that no firm could own more than one product.

One of the papers that came out of my joint work with Lipsey at the University of Colorado in 1974–75 (Eaton and Lipsey 1978, reprinted here as Chapter 2) generalizes and buttresses the result that pure profit is possible in free-entry equilibrium in a number of important respects. Most importantly, it provides a justification of the assumption that potential entrants regard the attributes of existing products as given. The justification is based on attribute-specific (or location-specific) sunk costs associated with product development and marketing; in particular, we show that if these costs are large enough, firms will never choose to alter their product attribute. Building on the Eaton and Lipsey analysis of free-entry equilibrium in a one-dimensional product attribute space, Myrna Wooders and I examined the subgame perfect equilibrium of the entry game in a paper written in 1983 and published in 1985 (Eaton and Wooders 1985, reprinted here as Chapter 7). We showed that if entrants correctly anticipate the post-entry price equilibrium, the potential for pure profit in free-entry equilibrium is even larger than the two previous papers indicated, because established firms do react to entry and they react by lowering their prices. Wooders and I showed that, in free-entry equilibrium, the rate of return on product development costs can be more than three times the competitive rate of return. In addition, we showed that there is no general welfare bias in the number of goods that are produced in equilibrium – in some cases, there are inevitably too many goods in free-entry equilibrium, in others there are inevitably too few, and in yet others the surplus-maximizing configuration of goods is itself a free-entry equilibrium.

In working through the nuts and bolts of the monopolistic vision of the economy in the mid 1970s, particularly as regards the theory of entry, Lipsey and I found we had to think from back to front as one does in finding a subgame perfect equilibrium. Although we did not know it at the time, in our analysis of pre-emption begun at the University of Colorado in 1974–75, printed in the Queen's University Discussion Paper series in 1976 (number 208) and finally published in 1979 (Eaton and Lipsey 1979a, reprinted here as Chapter 3), we were in fact using Selten's concept of subgame perfection. In the late 1970s, we gradually came to see that the back-to-front reasoning we first began to use in 1974–75 opened a window on a more general theory of strategic behavior and positioning, and we spent the academic year 1979–80 at Yale refining our understanding of a variety of strategic positioning issues. In the spring of 1980, we finally recognized, thanks to Jon Riley, that we were using Selten's celebrated equilibrium concept. Richard Caves had invited us to present a paper in the Harvard IO seminar and we chose a paper on the durability of capital as a barrier to entry (Chapter 4), which drew on some earlier work by Caves and Porter. When Riley asked me if we were using subgame perfection in the paper we presented that day, I responded with some nonsense that made it perfectly clear that I had no idea what he was talking about. Lipsey noticeably cringed at my response to Riley, and I think recognized immediately that we had at last stumbled upon the equilibrium concept we were using.

The two papers on strategic behavior we wrote that year at Yale (Eaton and Lipsey 1980 and 1981, reprinted here as Chapters 4 and 5) were both concerned with the issue of commitment via sunk costs, and in particular how the depreciation of a particular sunk asset affects its commitment value and the firm's optimal management of its commitments. Commitment has everything to do with staying power; hence the commitment created by any particular asset is inextricably linked to the asset's depreciation characteristics. We illuminated some interesting possibilities in these papers but did not by any stretch of the imagination exhaust the subject. Curiously, the frontier regarding these issues is still not far beyond the contributions in these two papers.

The idea of a contestable market has an interesting connection to the monopoly pre-emption problem in our 'Exit Barriers are Entry Barriers' paper (Chapter 4). In that paper, we consider the monopoly pre-emption problem in a setting where the commitment to the market is embodied in a product-specific capital good with exogenous durability. In the limit as exogenous durability goes to zero the monopolist's ability to commit to the market vanishes, and one might guess that the model would converge to the equilibrium suggested in the contestability literature. That it does not converge to that equilibrium led me to be very skeptical about contestability. In our model, even though as durability goes to zero, profit goes to zero, this is not indicative of a convergence to an efficient result. Rather, profit is being dissipated through premature replacement of capital to maintain a lock on the market, and the equilibrium price in all periods is the full monopoly price.

By the late 1970s and early 1980s, pre-emption and more generally strategic positioning via the management of sunk assets was clearly an idea whose time had come. Michael Spence, Richard Schmalensee, Daniel Spulber, Avinash Dixit, Steven Salop and my student Douglas West were all writing about the subject. In fact West began in 1977 an empirical thesis under my direction in which he tests the pre-emption via product proliferation idea, a thesis he completed in 1979 and published in the *Bell Journal* in 1980. Lipsey and I were certainly among the first to explore these important ideas in depth, and it is my view that we were in fact the very first. The core ideas are clearly there in both my 1972 UBC Discussion Paper (the published version of which is reprinted here as Chapter 1) and in the Eaton and Lipsey 1972 Queen's Discussion Paper on the Loschian model (finally published as Eaton and Lipsey 1975); they were carefully developed in the three Eaton and Lipsey 1976 Queen's University Discussion Papers, and they were integrated into a comprehensive vision of the economy in the paper that was presented at the 1976 meetings of the Association of University Teachers of Economics and the Canadian Economics Association (Eaton and Lipsey 1977). If it is human nature to feel that one's contributions are never adequately recognized, I have to confess that I am human, for it is my perception that Lipsey and I have not received the credit we deserve for our substantial original contributions to the theory of strategic behavior.

William D. White was also visiting Yale in 1979–80 and Brian Wright suggested that we might have some interests in common. White had a wonderful efficiency wage idea that he was having a tough time selling to the profession. He observed that investment bankers and others in positions of trust were paid large salary premiums and argued that the premiums served, in effect, as bonds to ensure their ethical behavior. Similarly, he observed that truck drivers who hauled valuable loads over long distances were also paid a significant wage premium, and again he interpreted the premium as a bond to ensure their good behavior. The idea had immense appeal to me, but because the model White had developed did not effectively convey his efficiency wage idea I developed another in the spring of 1980. This model of the efficiency wage was published in 1982 (Eaton and White 1982, reprinted here as Chapter 13). This paper is, I believe, the very first of a number of important efficiency wage papers published in the 1980s. Steven Soft, then a graduate student at Berkeley, was working on similar ideas in a macro context in this period but they were never published. In the spring of 1981, White and I wrote another efficiency wage paper which emphasized that monitoring and the wage rate were substitutes in the employer's effort to induce employees to perform, and that an employer might well find it attractive to offer a wage higher than the employee's reservation wage in order to economize on resources devoted to monitoring (Eaton and White 1983, reprinted here as Chapter 14).

In both of our efficiency wage papers, the basic idea is that because people who have nothing to lose are difficult to control, in some circumstances it makes sense to make them better off than they otherwise would be in order to induce them to behave themselves. It is a small step from this insight to another: the efficacy of a society's property institutions is jointly determined by the level and the distribution of wealth in the society. We explored this idea in some depth in a paper written in 1986 when I was a National Fellow at the Hoover Institution (Eaton and White 1986, printed here as Chapter 15). Among other things, we nicely articulate in this paper some of the problems that arise when legal sanctions are excessive and those whom society wishes to control have desperate options that enable them to avoid legal sanctions. As some pundits have observed, the 'third strike laws' that are now in place in many US jurisdictions have the potential to induce criminals to choose desperate and, from a social perspective, extremely undesirable options such as killing witnesses. In 1991 we published a related paper that focuses on the interaction of the distribution of wealth and the efficacy of property institutions in a simple general equilibrium model (Eaton and White 1991, reprinted here as Chapter 16). Among other things, we discover situations in which the redistribution of wealth is Pareto improving because it creates the institutional support needed to induce individuals to honor the law of property.

Following the sabbatical at Yale, I taught a special topics graduate course at UBC in which I covered the ground that Lipsey and I had been cultivating for the last few years. There were two exceptional students in the class, Bentley MacLeod and Mukesh Eswaran. In the autumn of 1981 I moved to the University of Toronto, joining a superb group of IO economists. Ralph Winter and Frank Mathewson were in the thick of their pathbreaking work on vertical relations among firms, Nancy Gallini and Roger Ware were exploring various strategic issues, and Yehuda Kotowitz's keen intellect was keeping all of us honest. For one year in the early 1980s we had the pleasure of Mukesh Eswaran's company and intellect, and in 1984 Eswaran and I wrote a very nice paper synthesizing the growing literature on commitment strategies in duopoly models, a paper that was never published but is included in this volume (Eaton and Eswaran 1984, printed here as Chapter 6). In addition to synthesizing the literature, we developed a model in which product durability is the vehicle of commitment.

While working on these problems of strategic commitment, it became clear to me that the approach was not just about pre-emption and monopoly: it contained the seed of a full-blown theory of market structure. Roger Ware had the same insight, and we teamed up to use the strategic choice algorithm to tease out an equilibrium market structure for an industry in which firms produced an undifferentiated good (Eaton and Ware 1987, reprinted here as Chapter 8). In our model, demand and cost conditions are exogenous, firms create commitments by investing in capacity, firms make their commitment choices in sequence and, given their commitments, they compete in quantities. At the time I saw this paper as the final step in a sequence of ideas on oligopoly and market structure that began with Cournot and included contributions by Stackelberg, Bain, Modigliani, Spence, Dixit and Ware. A curious and quite unexpected result in the Eaton and Ware paper is that equilibrium profit is not monotonically decreasing in order of entry.

Subsequently, Ware and I created a very nice model in which we could explore the relative advantages of making commitments in a world of demand uncertainty, on the one hand, and of keeping one's options open until the uncertainty is resolved, on the other. Although we did all the work on the model and wrote a lucid first draft, we never finished the paper. Surprisingly, the intervening years have not rendered our contribution obsolete, and so I have included the paper in the current volume (Eaton and Ware 1988, printed here as Chapter 9).

The graphic techniques that were developed in the strategic positioning literature turn out to be quite useful in the study of a wide variety of two-player games with continuous strategies. In 1991 Eswaran and I produced a paper intended for classroom use in which we showed just how widely applicable the techniques are. I wanted to call it 'the elementary economics of almost everything' but Eswaran objected. I have found the paper to be immensely useful for thinking about a variety of apparently disparate problems in a number of sub-disciplines, including industrial organization, political economy, public finance and environmental economics. We never sent this paper out for review, but it is included in this volume (Eaton and Eswaran 1991, printed here as Chapter 10). In this paper we identify and use two concepts, *plain substitutability* and *complementarity*, that together with the now very familiar concepts of strategic substitutability and complementarity, allow one to grasp the essence of an enormous range of problems. In December 1992 I had the pleasure of discussing a paper by Theon van Dijk, then a graduate student at the University of Maastricht, on patent breadth. Drawing on the insights in Eaton and Eswaran 1991 I was able to see immediately some interesting possibilities that van Dijk had missed. My remarks eventually led to an address model of patent breadth that became part of his thesis (Eaton, van Cayseele and van Dijk 1994, reprinted here as Chapter 25).

In the early 1980s a number of oligopoly models with consistent conjectural variations were published, and more recently some of these models have been used in empirical work on oligopoly behavior. In 1986, my friend Jeremiah Allen, whom I first met when we were undergraduates at the University of Colorado, observed that Paul Sweezy's kinky demand model, published in 1939, was the very first consistent-conjectural variation model of oligopoly. Since none of the consistent-conjectural variation papers acknowledged Sweezy's contribution, it seemed to us to be a point worth making and we produced a paper on the subject (Allen and Eaton 1986, reprinted here as Chapter 21). We found that historians of economic thought were uninterested in this paper – amusingly, one referee observed that Sweezy's model was now *just history*.

At Toronto I had the delightful privilege of teaching the intermediate micro course for students who wanted to specialize in economics. The students were very able and eager, and included Dwayne Benjamin, Andrew Dyck and John Wooders. I found that they were really interested in the art of model building, and I spent a lot of time developing special-purpose models to talk about a variety of topics, including product differentiation, common access, patents, and so on. Diane Eaton, a writer who is also my wife, and I used these special-purpose models as the basis for writing an intermediate micro textbook, the fifth edition of which is now in press (Eaton, Eaton and Allen 1999). The most recent editions, to which Douglas Allen has contributed enormously, retain the textbook's original emphasis on model building as the key to economic understanding.

Although I thoroughly enjoyed the IO group at Toronto, after spending the academic year 1985–86 at the Hoover Institution in Palo Alto, California, my wife and I realized that we wanted to live in western North America. So I accepted a position at Simon Fraser University in 1987 and we moved to Vancouver, British Columbia, where I continued to write and think about IO issues. In my first year at SFU, Paul Harrald, then a graduate student, and I wrote a paper in which we examined the Bertrand versus Cournot issue in the context of the Gabszewicz–Thisse model of vertical differentiation, and the paper was eventually published in 1992 (Eaton and Herrald 1992, reprinted here as Chapter 23). A curious feature of many models in the vertical differentiation literature is that maximal quality is preferred by all consumers when prices reflect the marginal cost of quality. We show that, in this sort of model, if firms compete in quantities they often choose not to differentiate their products, and that if they compete in prices a firm that has no other option to differentiate its product from that of a rival will spend good money to adulterate its good product in order to avoid the ruinous price competition that would otherwise occur.

In my years at Simon Fraser I happily spent a lot of time working with a number of very good graduate students. In addition to Paul Herrald, Patricia Koss, William Morrison, Laura Meriluoto, Weiqiu Yu and Bretton Isaacs all contributed substantially to my enjoyment and learning. In connection with her thesis work, Koss and I produced a nice model in which we explore familiar issues related to co-specific investments, hold-up and self-enforcing contracts (Eaton and Koss 1997, reprinted here as Chapter 28). These students had a liveliness and creativity that seemed to be lacking in many of the graduate students I had encountered in better known graduate programs at UBC and Toronto. This experience, in combination with my own experience as a graduate student at Colorado, leads me to the view that in the better graduate programs too much technical virtuosity is demanded of many students. Clearly this highly technical training serves many students very well, but I think it leads many others who are not technically adept to sell themselves short as economists. In economics, technical virtuosity is not a necessary component of creative work.

Nicolas Schmitt, whose dissertation I had supervised at Toronto, joined the SFU department in the early 1990s and we found that we worked well together. In a paper published in a volume in honor of Melvin Greenhut, Schmitt and I examine the choice of pricing modes (mill price versus delivered price) in a model of spatial competition (Eaton and Schmitt 1993, reprinted here as Chapter 24). Among other things, we show that in equilibrium it is not necessarily the case that the party who is most efficient at transport actually does the job. In addition, we discover a novel variant of the delivered pricing mode in which delivered prices are constrained, not by the transport costs of rivals, but by transport costs of customers. We think this paper cracks open a window on an important set of issues that have received very little attention.

As I began to read about flexible manufacturing in the early 1990s, it occurred to me that most of the literature on market structure was based on the sort of technology that was familiar to Henry Ford, in which economics of scale play a dominant role and economies of scope no role, and therefore that this literature, like Henry Ford's technology, was perhaps obsolete. Schmitt and I reinterpreted a familiar model of spatial price discrimination, originally created by Edgar Hoover and revisited by a number of other investigators over the years, most notably by Bentley MacLeod, George Norman and Jacques Thisse. Our reinterpretation involves the idea of a basic product and a technology for customizing the basic product to produce variants in a continuum of product attributes (Eaton and Schmitt 1994, reprinted here as Chapter 11). The reinterpretation encompasses both economies of scale and scope. We used the model to examine a number of propositions concerning market structure that are part of the economist's received wisdom and found that *none* of them were true in our model of flexible manufacturing. In particular we discovered that the forces which typically inhibit concentration are not at work in this model. Here, too, we think we have cracked open a window that will eventually lead to a significant reformulation of the theory of market structure. In another paper that is also motivated by the realization that Henry Ford's technology is perhaps not a sound foundation on which to build a theory of market structure, Soren Lemche and I explore market structure in a competitive environment in the presence of economies of scope (Eaton and Lemche 1991, reprinted here as Chapter 22).

The move back to Vancouver allowed me to continue my collaboration with Mukesh Eswaran, who had left the University of Toronto to return to UBC. During my years at SFU we produced a series of four papers on cartels. The first of the four papers arose from Eswaran's insight into the role that capacity plays in the no-defection condition for cartels operating in the context of a supergame (Eaton and Eswaran 1997a, reprinted here as Chapter 12). As the capacity of a firm decreases, it becomes progressively easier to satisfy the firm's no-defection constraint because the firm's ability to exploit the market in the defection period is constrained by its capacity. Following this insight, it seemed to us that if firms colluded in choosing their technologies, there would be circumstances in which they would choose inferior technologies. The remaining cartel papers are inspired by Eric von Hippel's work on know-how sharing. One of them focuses on the issues raised by the fact that technological innovations are often driven by unforeseeable, random forces (Eaton and Eswaran 2001, reprinted here as Chapter 31). We adapt the techniques used to study collusion in supergames to discern the circumstances in which know-how sharing can and cannot be supported as a subgame perfect equilibrium. We discover that the dispersion of the distribution of innovations plays a central role – if the distribution is tight, it is relatively easy to support sharing and if it is sufficiently flat, it is impossible to support sharing. Another paper builds on an observation of Baumol's that for know-how-sharing cartels, the usual tension between the severity of the punishment for defection and its plausibility or credibility does not exist; that is, the strategy that maximizes the profit of non-defectors in a know-how-sharing cartel subsequent to defection by some member of the cartel also imposes the maximal damage on the defector (Eaton and Eswaran 1997b, reprinted here as Chapter 27). The strategy itself involves ejection of the defector and continued know-how sharing among the remaining members of the cartel. The form of the strategy in this paper is suggestive of a general approach to cartels that we pursue in the last of our four papers on cartels (Eaton and Eswaran 1998, reprinted here as Chapter 30). In this paper we suppose that, subsequent to defection, the remaining non-defectors in the cartel make the best of a bad situation and choose the strategy that is best for them, producing what we argue is a more sophisticated notion of cartel stability. We show that in the standard framework this more sophisticated notion of stability makes it more difficult to support collusion. Although our collaboration continues, Eswaran and I seem to be moving away from IO issues.

In 1991 White and I started to think about image advertising, and we began by asking ourselves what the word *image* means in the context of advertising. We came to the view that image advertisers were telling consumers that they can send messages about what type of person they are by using their products. For example, owning a Lexus not only provides its owners with transportation services but also allows them to communicate to others that they earn a six-figure income; a high school athletic letter jacket provides not only warmth but also sends a message about the wearer's athletic prowess. As a platform for our theory of image advertising, White and I developed a very nice sender/receiver game in which visible consumption goods can be used to convey information about one's type, and we produced a very good draft of the image advertising paper in 1995. Like the Eaton and Ware paper on flexibility versus commitment, this paper somehow vanished until I started to put this volume together. It is included here, and it represents, we think, a considerable contribution to the theory of image advertising (Eaton and White 1995, printed here as Chapter 26). We show that, to be effective, an image advertising campaign must be pitched broadly to include not only the targeted buyers of the advertised product, but also the group of people the targeted buyers want to impress. Relatedly, we show that to have any effect an image advertising campaign must reach a substantial portion of the relevant population – a little bit of image advertising has absolutely no effect.

Jasmina Arifovic and I used the sender/receiver game that is the core of the image advertising paper to explore the evolution of communication (Arifovic and Eaton 1998, reprinted here as Chapter 29). In this paper we employ the genetic algorithm to evolve communication. There are many equilibria in the model, distinguished by the number of player types who manage successfully to communicate their identity, and the equilibria are Pareto ranked by the number of player types who do communicate effectively. Interestingly, our results suggest that type communication evolves by, in effect, moving from one equilibrium to another, better, equilibrium in which one more player type is able to communicate effectively. When the model is far from equilibrium, the force of selection quickly drives it close to an equilibrium, and when the model is near an equilibrium, genetic drift eventually creates an opportunity to move to a higher-level equilibrium.

My fascination with social interaction and the way in which it interacts with more traditional economic issues and problems continues. It is, in fact, my major focus at the moment. Krishna Pendakur, Clyde Reed and I have completed one paper on the subject which builds on the observations that socializing is an important, even essential, human activity, and that shared experiences are an important input into this activity. We use these observations to construct an explanation of a variety of phenomena, including fads, superstars and cultural imperialism (Eaton, Pendakur and Reed 2000).

When we lived in Toronto, my wife and I learned that we preferred the West to the East. After 12 years back in the Vancouver area, we discovered that we were ready for more sunshine in our lives. So I accepted a job at the University of Calgary, and we moved to Calgary, Alberta in 1999. The Economics Department at the University of

Calgary is young and very lively, and I have already discovered several kindred spirits, including Aidan Hollis, Ken McKenzie, Robert Oxoby, J.F. Wen and Lasheng Yuan, with whom I hope to continue my lifelong exploration of whatever idea strikes my fancy. My former colleague Herb Grubel often remarked that our job was perhaps the best job in the history of the world, and I very much agree with him. The opportunity to go where one's curiosity leads, as I have done for the last 30 years and hope to do for at least a few more, is a rare and precious privilege for which I am truly thankful.

Note

1. In writing an essay of this sort it would seem to be essential to provide detailed references to my own work. Although it would be desirable to provide equally detailed references to the literally hundreds of papers and books on which my work draws, it is not feasible. I have therefore chosen to provide no references to the work of others, asking the reader to rely instead on the references found in the individual papers that follow this introductory essay.

References

Allen, Jeremiah M. and B. Curtis Eaton (1986), *Sweezy's Kink: The Original Consistent-Conjectural Equilibrium*, 10 page manuscript.

Arifovic, Jasmina and B. Curtis Eaton (1998), 'The Evolution of Communication in a Sender/Receiver Game of Common Interest with Cheap Talk', *Journal of Economic Dynamics and Control*, **22**, August, pp. 1187–207.

Donaldson, David and B. Curtis Eaton (1976), 'Firm-Specific Human Capital: A Shared Investment or Optimal Entrapment?', *Canadian Journal of Economics*, **9** (3), August , pp. 462–72.

Donaldson, David and B. Curtis Eaton (1981), 'Patience, More Than Its Own Reward: A Note on Price Discrimination', *Canadian Journal of Economics*, **14** (1), February, pp. 93–105.

Donaldson, David and B. Curtis Eaton (1984), 'Person-Specific Costs of Production: Hours of Work, Rates of Pay, Labour Contracts', *Canadian Journal of Economics*, **17** (3), August, pp. 441–9.

Eaton, B. Curtis (1972), 'Spatial Competition Revisited', *Canadian Journal of Economics*, May, pp. 268–77.

Eaton, B. Curtis (1976), 'Free Entry in One-Dimensional Models: Pure Profits and Multiple Equilibria', *Journal of Regional Science*, **16** (1), pp. 21–33.

Eaton, B. Curtis and Mukesh Eswaran (1984), *Asymmetric Equilibria and Strategic Behaviour in Oligopolistic Markets*, 25 page manuscript.

Eaton, B. Curtis and Mukesh Eswaran (1991), *Noncooperative Equilibria in One-Shot Games: A Synthesis*, 49 page manuscript.

Eaton, B. Curtis and Mukesh Eswaran (1997a), 'Supporting Collusion by Choice of Inferior Technologies', in *Trade, Technology and Economics: Essays in Honour of Richard G. Lipsey* (eds. B. Curtis Eaton and Richard G. Harris), Edward Elgar Press, pp. 263–83.

Eaton, B. Curtis and Mukesh Eswaran (1997b), 'Technology-Trading Coalitions in Supergames', *Rand Journal of Economics*, **28** (1), Spring, pp. 135–49.

Eaton, B. Curtis and Mukesh Eswaran (1998), 'Endogenous Cartel Formation', *Australian Economic Papers*, **37** (1), March, pp. 1–13.

Eaton, B. Curtis and Mukesh Eswaran (2001), 'Know-how Sharing with Stochastic Innovations', *Canadian Journal of Economics*, **34** (2), May, pp. 525–48.

Eaton, B. Curtis and Paul Herrald (1992), 'Price Versus Quantity Competition in the Gabszewicz–Thisse Model of Vertical Differentiation', in *Market Strategy and Structure* (eds. A. Gee and G. Norman), Harvester/Wheatsheaf, pp. 217–32.

Eaton, B. Curtis and Patricia Koss (1997), 'Co-specific Investments, Hold-Up, and Self-Enforcing Contracts', *Journal of Economic Behavior and Organization*, **32**, pp. 457–70.

Eaton, B. Curtis and Soren Lemche (1991), 'The Geometry of Supply, Demand, and Competitive Market Structure with Economies of Scope', *American Economic Review*, **85** (4), September, pp. 901–11.

Eaton, B. Curtis and Richard G. Lipsey (1975), 'The Principle of Minimum Differentiation Reconsidered: Some New Developments in the Theory of Spatial Competition', *Review of Economic Studies*, January, pp. 27–49.

Eaton, B. Curtis and Richard G. Lipsey (1976), 'The Non-Uniqueness of Equilibrium in the Loschian Location Model', *American Economic Review*, March, pp. 77–93.

Eaton, B. Curtis and Richard G. Lipsey (1977), 'The Introduction of Space into the Neo-classical Model of Value Theory', in *Studies in Modern Economic Analysis* (eds. M.J. Artis and A.R. Nobay), Basil Blackwell, pp. 59–96.

Eaton, B. Curtis and Richard G. Lipsey (1978), 'Freedom of Entry and the Existence of Pure Profit', *Economic Journal*, **88**, September, pp. 455–69.

Eaton, B. Curtis and Richard G. Lipsey (1979a), 'The Theory of Market Pre-emption: The Persistence of Excess Capacity and Monopoly in Growing Spatial Markets', *Economica*, **46**, May, pp. 149–58.

Eaton, B. Curtis and Richard G. Lipsey (1979b), 'Comparison Shopping and Clusters of Homogeneous Firms', *Journal of Regional Science*, pp. 421–35.

Eaton, B. Curtis and Richard G. Lipsey (1980), 'Exit Barriers are Entry Barriers: The Durability of Capital as a Barrier to Entry', *Bell Journal of Economics*, **11** (2), Autumn, pp. 721–9.

Eaton, B. Curtis and Richard G. Lipsey (1981), 'Capital, Commitment, and Entry Equilibrium', *Bell Journal of Economics*, **12** (1), Autumn, pp. 593–604.

Eaton, B. Curtis and Richard G. Lipsey (1982), 'An Economic Theory of Central Places', *The Economic Journal*, March, pp. 56–72.

Eaton, B. Curtis and Richard G. Lipsey (1997), *On the Foundations of Monopolistic Competition and Economic Geography: The Selected Essays of B. Curtis Eaton and Richard G. Lipsey*, Edward Elgar Publishing Limited.

Eaton, B. Curtis and Philip A. Neher (1975), 'Unemployment, Underemployment, and Optimal Job Search', *Journal of Political Economy*, **83** (2), April, pp. 355–75.

Eaton, B. Curtis and Nicolas Schmitt (1993), 'Endogenous Pricing Modes in Markets for Inputs', in *Does Economic Space Matter: Essays in Honor of Melvin L. Greenhut* (eds. Hiroshi Ohta and Jacques-Francois Thisse), Macmillan, pp. 352–73.

Eaton, B. Curtis and Nicolas Schmitt (1994), 'Flexible Manufacturing and Market Structure', *American Economic Review*, **88** (4), September, pp. 875–88.

Eaton, B. Curtis and Roger Ware (1987), 'A Theory of Market Structure with Sequential Entry', *Rand Journal of Economics*, **18** (1), Spring, pp. 1–16.

Eaton, B. Curtis and Roger Ware (1988), *Uncertainty and the Value of Strategic Commitment*, 10 page manuscript.

Eaton, B. Curtis and William D. White (1982), 'Agent Compensation and the Limits of Bonding', *Journal of Economic Inquiry*, **XX**, July, pp. 330–43.

Eaton, B. Curtis and William D. White (1983), 'The Economy of High Wages: an Agency Problem', *Economica*, **50**, May, pp. 175–81.

Eaton, B. Curtis and William D. White (1986), *Wealth: The Support of Institutions and the Limits of Control*, Working Paper E-86-26, Domestic Studies Program, Hoover Institution, Stanford University, 29 pages.

Eaton, B. Curtis and William D. White (1991), 'The Distribution of Wealth and the Efficiency of Institutions', *Economic Inquiry*, **29**, April, pp. 336–50.

Eaton, B. Curtis and William D. White (1995), *Image Advertising*, 19 page manuscnpt.

Eaton, B. Curtis and Myrna Holtz Wooders (1985), 'Sophisticated Entry in a Model of Spatial Competition', *Rand Journal of Economics*, **16** (2), Summer, pp. 282–97.

Eaton, B. Curtis, Diane F. Eaton and Douglas W. Allen (1999), *Microeconomics* (fourth edition), Prentice Hall.

Eaton, B. Curtis, Krishna Pendakur and Clyde Reed (2000), *Socializing, Shared Experience, and Popular Culture*, May, 45 page manuscript.

Eaton, B. Curtis, Patrick van Cayseele and Theon van Dijk (1994), 'An Address Model of Patent Breadth with Two Countries', in *The Limits of Patent Protection*, by Theon van Dijk, Maastricht University Press, pp. 137–55.

PART I

STRATEGIC BEHAVIOR

[1]

JOURNAL OF REGIONAL SCIENCE, VOL. 16, NO. 1, 1976

FREE ENTRY IN ONE-DIMENSIONAL MODELS: PURE PROFITS AND MULTIPLE EQUILIBRIA*

B. Curits Eaton†

1. INTRODUCTION

This paper analyzes the process of spatial competition in a one-dimensional model under conditions of free entry. The market is defined as the perimeter of a circle, and is an unbounded, one-dimensional space. In location theory it is well recognized that the existence of boundaries to a spatial market present some special problems not encountered in an unbounded space. In order to avoid these problems it is frequently convenient to develop a model in an unbounded space. We analyze an unbounded model to avoid the problem of the possible nonexistence of equilibrium in a bounded spatial market. For a discussion of the problem of nonexistence of equilibrium in a bounded, spatial market see Eaton [2] and Eaton and Lipsey [4].

We maintain the following set of assumptions:

(i) In each unit of length let there be a consuming unit with a linear demand function

$$q = (P^d - P_0)/b \tag{1}$$

where q is quantity demanded per unit of time, P^d is delivered price, b ($b < 0$) is the slope of the individual's demand function, and P_0 is the price intercept of the demand function.

(ii) Transport costs are assumed to be constant at a per unit distance, and we assume that the consumer bears the full burden of transport costs, and that the producer charges all consumers, regardless of location, the same mill price. Delivered price, P^d, is then mill price plus transport costs from the mill to the site of consumption.

(iii) Cost conditions for the firm are assumed to take the following form

$$C = K + cQ \tag{2}$$

where K represents overhead costs, c marginal costs of production, and Q quantity produced. We can, without loss of generality, take marginal costs to be zero—

* The author is indebted to G. C. Archibald, Harry Bloch, C. K. Harley, and Philip Neher for insights into the nature of the problems discussed in this paper. Two referees have provided valuable suggestions for the revision and reorganization of the paper. A particularly heavy debt is owed to Richard Lipsey. Many of the insights of this paper were developed jointly with him in connection with other joint work.

† Associate Professor of Economics, University of British Columbia.

Date received: June, 1974; revised, April, 1975 and November, 1975.

nonzero marginal costs simply change the scale of the problem.[1] These cost conditions imply that the firm's plant is indivisible. If it were not, demand in any spatial market would be served by production at the site of consumption since transport is costly; there would be an infinite number of firms. Accordingly, virtually all of the literature on spatial competition assumes some sort of plant indivisibility.

(iv) In choosing a location and a price each firm (an existing firm or a new entrant) takes the price and location of all other firms as given—a zero conjectural variation (ZCV) with respect to price and location. We qualify this conjectural variation assumption by the condition that no firm will adopt a policy which will immediately cause the total revenue of another firm to be zero.

Assumption (iv) requires some elaboration. It means that we are analyzing spatial competition as a noncooperative game. It is well known that the possibility of a competitive, socially optimal equilibrium in space is at least questionable (see Koopmans and Beckmann [9]). Yet many models of spatial competition continue to *impose*, as conditions of equilibrium in spatial models, conditions which are appropriate to the competitive model. For example, the zero profit assumption is imposed in most spatial models as a condition of equilibrium. In the present model we make competitive behavioral assumptions and deduce certain properties of equilibrium. The focus of the model is then on the question: if firms behave in a competitive, noncooperative manner what will be the equilibrium configuration? In particular will equilibrium be unique and will it be characterized by zero profits?

Assumption (iv), however, rules out the possibility that one firm will adopt a policy which will cause the total revenue of another to be zero—it eliminates price undercutting. The ZCV behavioral assumption is appropriate where any firm does not expect its competitors to react to its policy. This assumption, for example, seems appropriate to location problems where relocation generally takes place with a long time lag. It is obviously not appropriate in the price undercutting case. No firm could reasonably believe that a competitor whose very existence was threatened (zero total revenue) by his price undercutting would fail to react. This suggests that we must rule out price undercutting as a reasonable strategy.[2]

Then assumption (iv) appears to be internally inconsistent. We assume a zero price conjectural variation, but only up to the point where the price behavior of one firm threatens the existence of its competitor. What we are interested in demon-

---

[1] The critical factor is the relationship between P_0 and c. If we simultaneously increase both P_0 and c by the same absolute amount, Δ, the location problem is unchanged. By virtue of the increase in P_0, total revenue associated with any arbitrary quantity sold by a firm is increased by the factor Δ. Marginal cost is, by hypothesis, increased by the same amount and therefore the profit maximizing quantity for any firm is unchanged. The comparative statics on c are therefore simply the negative of the comparative statics on P_0.

[2] The qualification that there be no price undercutting is also necessary to prevent hopeless instability in the model. In the absence of the qualification the most profitable move for a new entrant is generally to locate at the same point as an already existing firm and to charge a slightly lower price. In this manner the new entrant thinks that he can earn virtually the same level of profits as the already existing firm, in the process he of course reduces that firm's total revenue to zero. If the two firms engage in price competition at this location, eventually one will charge a price consistent with only zero profits and the other will exit. The remaining firm will now increase his price and earn positive profits, thus inducing entry and the cycle begins again.

strating is that zero profits are not a condition of equilibrium when firms behave in a competitive fashion and entry is free. In this context, it seems appropriate to make the strongest assumption about price competition that seems reasonable, for if we can demonstrate that zero profits are not a condition of equilibrium with strong price competition, it seems reasonable that the demonstration will generalize to situations in which price competition is less virulent. It seems to us that the strongest reasonable assumption with respect to price competition is a ZCV subject to a no undercutting restriction.

The model is most closely related to one-dimensional models of free entry developed by Beckmann [1] and Telser [11]. Both Telser and Beckmann conclude that a unique equilibrium exists, and that in equilibrium all firms earn zero profits.[3] The results reported in this paper are quite different from the Telser and Beckmann results. Multiple equilibria exist and, in general, zero profits are not a condition of equilibrium. For purposes of comparison we also develop the full monopoly and entry-preventing models.

We use numerical techniques to analyze the model. Using analytical techniques in the analysis of spatial models can become quite complex. The mathematical conception of the problem is simple enough, but the burden of calculation can be overpowering. For this reason we choose to use numerical techniques. These techniques have proved useful in the analysis of a wide range of location theory problems (see Eaton and Lipsey [3] and [4], and Hartwick and Hartwick [7] for examples).

2. THE MODEL

In order to implement the numerical approach we must be able to determine the optimal location and price for a firm located between two other firms. Figure 1 will be useful in developing the demand function facing such a firm; in terms of that figure we want to develop a demand function for the *i*th firm, $Q_i(P_i, X_i)$. To the left of X_i, the *i*th firm's delivered price, P_i^d, is $P_i + aX_i - aX$, where P_i is the firm's mill price and X_i its location. At any point between the boundary with the $(i - 1)$st firm, B_{i-1}, and X_i, quantity demanded is, from Equation (1), $1/b(P^d - P_0)$, or $1/b(P_i + aX_i - aX - P_0)$. Similarly, for any point between X_i and B_{i+1}, quantity demanded is $1/b(P_i - aX_i + aX - P_0)$. Hence the *i*th firm's demand function is

$$Q_i(P_i, X_i) = \int_{B_{i-1}}^{X_i} 1/b(P_i + aX_i - aX - P_0)\,dx + \int_{X_i}^{B_{i+1}} 1/b(P_i - aX_i + aX - P_0)\,dx \qquad (3)$$

[3] Although Telser's model is nominally developed on a line segment, I prefer to regard it as an unbounded one-dimensional model. Telser eliminates the phenomena of multiple prices and unequal markets by arguing that if all firms were not located in the transport minimizing configuration of locations then it would be profitable for an entrepreneur to purchase all firms and relocate them in the transport minimizing configuration. In the context of Telser's model, I find this argument unconvincing because it is not consistent with the process of spatial competition he is analyzing. If one firm could purchase all existing plants then that firm could be logically expected to pursue an entry preventing strategy which would result in an equilibrium which is quite different from the equilibrium of Telser's model (see the analysis of the entry preventing strategy in Section 2).

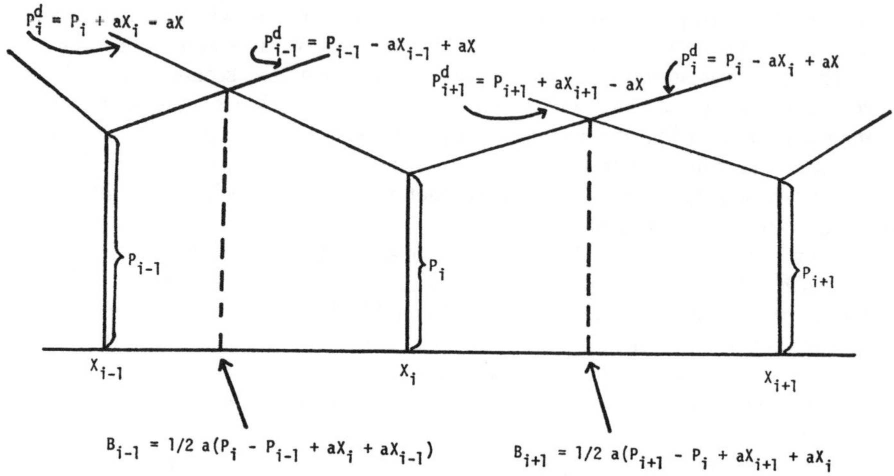

FIGURE 1: Price and Location Decision of a Firm Located Between Two Other Firms.

Evaluating the integrals, eliminating B_{i-1} and B_{i+1} (their values are given in Figure 1), and collecting terms, we obtain Equation (4).

$$(4)\quad Q_i = (1/16b)[(-12P_i^2/a) + (P_i/a)(16P_0 + 4P_{i+1} + 4aX_{i+1} + 4P_{i-1} - aX_{i-1}) + (2P_{i+1}^2/a) + 4aX_i^2 + 2aX_{i+1}^2 - (8P_0P_{i+1}/a) - 8P_0X_{i+1} - 4P_{i+1}X_i + 4P_{i+1}X_{i+1} - 4aX_iX_{i+1} + (2P_{i-1}^2/a) + 2aX_{i-1}^2 - (8P_0P_{i-1}/a) + 8P_0X_{i-1} - 4P_{i-1}X_{i-1} - 4aX_iX_{i-1} + 4P_{i-1}X_i]$$

Setting the partial derivatives of total revenue with respect to P_i and X_i equal to zero yields two conditions for profit maximization (in two unknowns) which can be solved simultaneously to yield the price and location which maximize the *i*th firm's profits, given the location and price of the two neighboring firms. The two equations can be reduced to

$$(5)\quad (-36P_i^2/a) + (P_i/a)(32P_0 + 8P_{i+1} + 8aX_{i+1} + 8P_{i-1} - 8aX_{i-1}) + (P_{i+1}^2/a) + (P_{i-1}^2/a) + aX_{i+1}^2 + aX_{i-1}^2 - (8P_{i+1}P_0/a) - 8X_{i+1}P_0 + 8X_{i-1}P_0 - (8P_{i-1}P_0/a) + 2P_{i+1}X_{i+1} - 2P_{i-1}X_{i-1} + (2P_{i+1}P_{i-1}/a) - 2aX_{i+1}X_{i-1} - 2P_{i+1}X_{i-1} + 2P_{i-1}X_{i+1} = 0$$

$$(6)\quad X_i = (1/2a)(P_{i+1} + aX_{i+1} + aX_{i-1} - P_{i-1})$$

Equation (5) is a quadratic in P_i and can be solved to obtain the profit maximizing price for a firm located (or thinking of locating) between two other firms. The optimal location is obtained from Equation (6). Since we are using numerical methods, it is a simple matter to check to see that Equations (5) and (6) yield a local maximum and not a local minimum.

Before turning to a precise statement of the numerical algorithm some definitions are necessary.

Limited equilibrium: A single firm is in limited equilibrium when there exists no change of price or location (including exit) which will increase the firm's level of expected profits. The model is in limited equilibrium when each firm is in limited equilibrium.

Free entry equilibrium: The model is in free entry equilibrium when each firm is in limited equilibrium *and* when the profits a new entrant expects to earn are less than zero.

We first show that, for a given number of firms, limited equilibrium will be characterized by equal intervals between all pairs of adjacent firms and by a price common to all firms. Let the circumference of the circle be measured from 12:00 in the clockwise direction and let the firms be numbered in the same manner. The length of the market is L. The equal spacing of firms would dictate that in limited equilibrium the ith firm will be located at $L(2i - 1)/2n$, the $(i - 1)$st at $L(2i - 3)/2n$, and the $(i + 1)$st at $L(2i + 1)/2n$. Let the common price of the three firms be P_E. Equation (5) gives the first-order condition with respect to price for maximum profits for a firm located between two others. If we set $P_{i-1} = P_{i+1} = P_i = P_E$ in Equation (5) and also let $X_i = L(2i - 1)/2n$, $X_{i-1} = L(2i - 3)/2n$, and $X_{i+1} = L(2i + 1)/2n$, it reduces to a quadratic in P_E.

$$(7) \quad (-4P_E^2/a) + (P_E/a)[4P_0 + (6aL/n)] + (aL^2/n^2) - (4LP_0/n) = 0$$

Equation (7) has the following solution

$$(8) \quad P_E = (P_0/2) + (3La/4n) - (a/8)[(16P_0^2/a^2) + (52L^2/n^2) - (16P_0L/an)]^{1/2}$$

The proof that this is a limited equilibrium pattern is straightforward. Equations (5) and (6) represent the conditions for a maximum of profits for a firm locating between two other firms. Let $X_{i-1} = L(2i-3)/2n$, $X_{i+1} = L(2i+1)/2n$, and $P_{i-1} = P_{i+1} = P_E$ in Equation (5). Solve the resulting quadratic for P_i; its solution is $P_i = P_E$. Then, Equation (6) gives $X_i = L(2i-1)/2n$. Thus if n firms were in the configuration described in this section, and if we let the ith firm consider a change of price or location, he would choose *not* to change either; he is in limited equilibrium. Since all firms are in a position exactly analogous to that of the ith, none of them want to move, and the model is in limited equilibrium.

For a given number of firms the limited equilibrium price is given by Equation (8), and the locational pattern has the firms arranged at equal intervals around the circle. Making these same substitutions in Equation (4), the demand function for the firm in limited equilibrium is

$$(9) \qquad Q_E = (1/4b)[(4P_EL/n) + (aL^2/n^2) - (4LP_0/n)]$$

For given values of K, n, L, P_0, a, and b, Equations (8) and (9) determine the market price, quantity, and profit in limited equilibrium.

Building on this information about the equilibrium configuration, the free entry algorithm can be stated.

(1) Initial conditions: If one firm were serving a very long market, and if it were limited to one plant, quantity demanded would be limited by transport costs

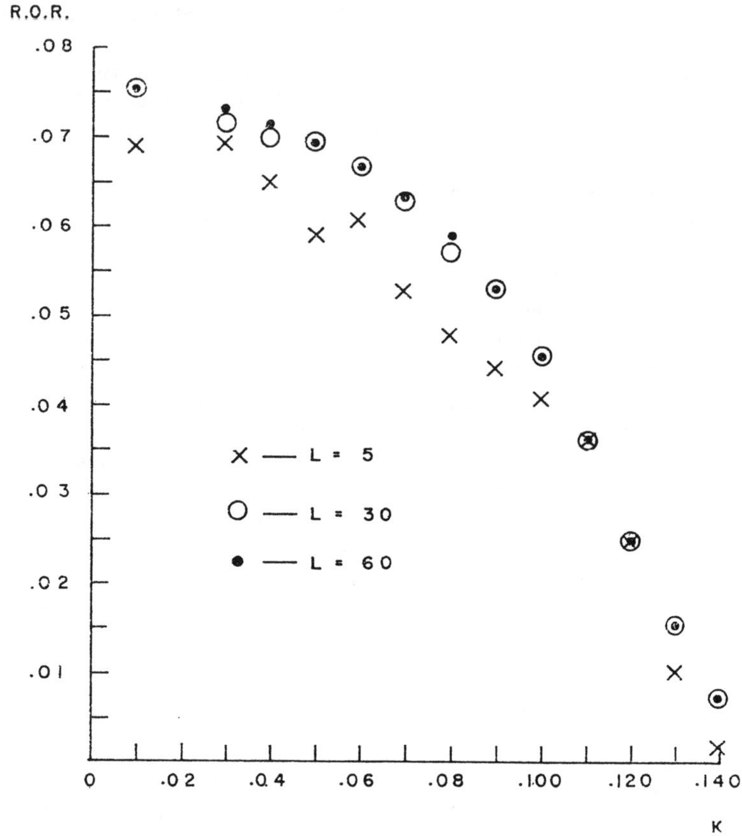

FIGURE 2: Rates of Pure Profit With Single Firm Entry Dynamic.

and the nature of the individual demand function. That is, the firm, even if it had no competitors, would not be able to serve the entire market. It can be shown that such a monopolist's demand function is $-(P - P_0)^2/ab$, where P is the firm's price.[4] Maximum total revenue associated with this demand function is $-4P_0^3/27ab$; the firm serves a market which is $4P_0/3a$ wide; the profit maximizing price is $P_0/3$. Set N, the initial number of firms, at the largest integer in $3aL/4P_0$. N is the maximum number of "monopolists" which can serve this market, since the market of a single plant monopolist is $4P_0/3a$. Let each of them charge a price of $P_0/3$ and

[4] This result can be obtained in the following manner. Let one firm be located at the origin of a very long linear market, and let the market extend in both directions from the firm. The firm's demand function is $Q = 2\int_{x=0}^{x|P^d=P_0} [1/b](P^d - P_0)\, dx$. The upper limit of integration is x such that delivered price has risen to P_0—if the delivered price is higher than P_0, nothing is demanded. Letting P represent the firm's price, the upper limit is $(P_0 - P)/a$, and delivered price as a function of distance is $P + aX$. Making these substitutions and evaluating the integral we obtain the result in the text.

let them locate at equal intervals along the circle. Viability in the initial configuration requires that $K \leq | 4P_0^3/27ab |$ (the total revenue of a single plant monopolist).

(2) Entry: Given the firms in limited equilibrium, use Equations (5) and (6) to calculate the price and location which would maximize profits for a firm considering entry between any pair of adjacent firms. If the maximum profits for the potential entrant are nonnegative, let him enter and proceed to stage 3. If maximum profits are negative, we have reached a free entry equilibrium.

(3) Limited equilibrium: Given an increment of 1 in the number of firms from entry, use Equations (8) and (9) to calculate the new limited equilibrium price, profit, and rate of profit. Return to stage 2 for a consideration of further entry.

The results of this simulation exercise are quite easy to report. We report the results from a particular specification of the model's parameters. The pattern of the results is the same for a wide variation in the parameters of the model, and we will be happy to supply the basic simulation routine to the reader interested in exercising the model for himself. Let P_0 be \$1, let a be \$1 per mile, and let b be -1. We let K and L vary. With these values of P_0, a and b, the maximum revenue which a single plant monopolist could generate is \$.148. Hence, we will let K vary from \$.01 to \$.148.

In Figure 2 we report the results of pure profit on capital (the vertical axis) and values of overhead costs (the horizontal axis). The dots represent the relationship between K and the rate of profit when L equals 60 miles. Any value of K is equivalent to an infinitely lived capital outlay of K/d, where d is the rate of interest. Thus the rate of profit is total revenue minus K divided by K/d. We take d as .10 for convenience.

When K is \$.01 the rate of pure profit is 7.5 percent, and as we increment K the rate of profit steadily declines until the rate of profit is less than 1 percent when K is \$.140. The relationship between the rate of profit and K is reported for two other values of L. When L is 30 miles the relationship is virtually the same as for an L of 60 miles, the differences being attributable to the fact that an integral number of firms must serve the market.[5]

It is simple enough to understand why zero profits are not a condition of equilibrium. Capital is indivisible, and thus average costs must decline over some range, and we have assumed that entry would cease when the profits a potential entrant would anticipate, given the price and location of the two neighboring firms,

[5] It thus appears that the essential features of the model are independent of the size of the market. When L is doubled the number of firms in free entry equilibrium is also doubled, and the individual firms in the two situations charge the same price, sell the same quantity, make the same level and rate of profits. However, changing the density of demand along the market, as opposed to the length of the market, will alter the free entry equilibrium. Given the cost conditions we have adopted, an increase in the density of demand pushes the rate of return asymptotically toward 7.7 percent. This result reflects the increasing returns that our cost function exhibits. If we impose a maximum output on the cost function (or constant returns subject to "indivisibility"), increasing the density of demand drives the profit rate to zero. But this represents a perfectly competitive solution, not a monopolistic competition solution. Impose the constraint on the cost function in Equation (2) that $Q \leq Q_{max}$. Then as density increases, the equilibrium tends to a zero profit equilibrium with each firm producing Q_{max}.

are negative. Since the new entrant takes some profits away from each of his two neighbors, entry stops when the existing firms still earn profits. Putting the same point another way, since the new entrant competes with only two of the existing firms in the market, it must be true that a new entrant will anticipate profits which are substantially less than the profits enjoyed by existing firms. This being true, zero profits are not a condition of equilibrium.

It has been argued that the failure of the zero profit condition to hold in this model is due to the fact that the market is of finite length and yet an integral number of plants must serve the market. That this is not the case can be seen by examination of Figure 2. The relationship between K and the rate of pure profit is approximately the same for market sizes of 5, 30, and 60. The critical variable is the number of firms per unit of length, since new entrants must enter between two existing firms. The failure of the zero profit result to hold is due to the fact that in a spatial market, a new entrant must expect a market (and hence profits) which are substantially less than the market of existing firms (for example, if a new entrant charges the same price as the two firms between which he enters, his market is only one-half that of the existing firms before entry). Since average costs decline with output, it must be possible for existing firms, which have a larger market than new entrants, to earn pure profits while entry is unprofitable.

The results reported thus far have been derived from a particular assumption with respect to the dynamics of entry. We have assumed that if entry is profitable *one* firm enters and all firms completely adjust to the new limited equilibrium before another firm considers entry. We will refer to this dynamics of entry as the "single firm entry dynamic".

Grace [6] suggests a different type of free entry dynamic which deserves attention. He suggests that if two firms are serving a circular market, one located at 12 o'clock, the other at 6 o'clock, and if a third firm finds it profitable to enter (at 3 o'clock, for example), a fourth will also enter (at 9 o'clock). Thus Grace suggests that the number of firms would follow the sequence 1, 2, 4, 8, · · · . We can easily introduce a variant of the Grace entry dynamic into our simulation model. Substitute the following alternate rules in the algorithm.

(A-2) Entry: If entry appears to be profitable between an arbitrary pair of firms, let a firm enter between each pair of firms.

(A-3) Equilibrium: Given a doubling of the number of firms, use Equation (8) to calculate the new equilibrium price (no locational changes are called for) and then calculate profits and the rate of profit at this new equilibrium. Return to A-2 for a consideration of further entry.

This entry rule introduces some interesting new wrinkles into the model. First, the possibility of disequilibrium is introduced into the circular model. The lines in Figure 3 denoted by 0's represent the rates of profit associated with varying levels of K for a given market length under the Grace entry dynamic. ($L = 60.0$ in this case, but as with previous results of this nature, the results are independent of market size). The line denoted by Δ's represents the relationship between profit rates and K for the single firm entry dynamic. For certain ranges of K, the possibility of negative rates of pure profit emerges under the Grace dynamic. In these cases the competitive price reactions occasioned by the doubling of the number of

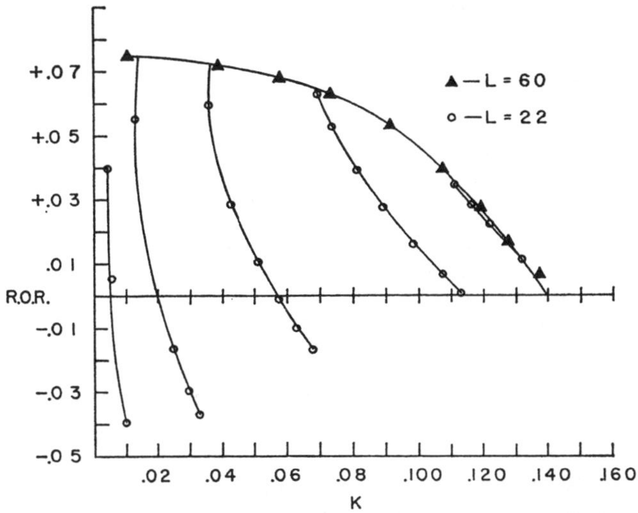

FIGURE 3: Rates of Profit for Single Firm and Grace Entry Dynamics Compared.

firms result in negative profits. The negative returns, of course, imply exit Without some assumption as to which firms will exit, we have no hope of arriving at a determinate solution. In those cases where the equilibrium rate of profit is nonnegative, the Grace entry dynamic generally produces a greater number of firms serving a particular market at a lower, but in general positive, rate of profit. The two solutions are coincident at a number of points as can be seen from the figure.

The divergence between the free entry equilibria associated with the Grace and the single firm entry dynamics suggests that a variety of free entry equilibria are possible. Consider for a moment the "monopolistic competition" solution; that is, consider the solution which results if we impose zero profits on the basic model. In Table I this solution for L equal to 60 miles is presented in the last column. When K is \$.0099, the monopolistic competition solution has 537 firms charging a price of \$.102, and as we increment K the number of firms declines and the price increases until, when K is \$.1284, the price is \$.347 and the number of firms is 72. The monopolistic competition solution represents a limited equilibrium because all existing firms satisfy the first-order conditions for a maximum of profits, and it represents a free entry equilibrium because a new entrant would anticipate negative profits.

In Column 4 of Table 1 we present the equilibria associated with the single firm entry dynamic for L equal to 60 miles. The single firm entry and the monopolistic competition equilibria represent the extremes of the range of free entry equilibria. If the number of firms were greater than the number associated with the monopolistic competition solution all firms would earn negative profits and hence the configuration would not represent a free entry equilibrium. If the number of firms were less than the number associated with the single firm entry dynamic, entry would appear to be profitable between any pair of firms, and hence the

TABLE 1: Alternative Equilibria

	Monopoly				Entry Preventing				Single Firm Entry Dynamic				Monopolistic Competition	
K	N	P	ROR	Aggregate Profits	N	P	ROR	Aggregate Profits	N	P	ROR	Aggregate Profits	N	P
.0099	205	.463	.536	10.86	382	.135	.077	2.907	388	.136	.076	2.885	537	.102
.0395	98	.423	.178	6.888	147	.265	.073	4.258	151	.270	.071	4.248	228	.207
.0691	71	.394	.090	4.423	89	.340	.063	3.876	88	.335	.063	3.858	148	.273
.0988	58	.371	.044	2.516	58	.775	.044	2.513	55	.346	.046	2.484	104	.319
.1284	49	.347	.015	.931	49	.345	.015	.930	45	.333	.015	.889	72	.347

configuration would not represent a free entry equilibrium. As can be seen from a comparison of Columns 3 and 4 of Table 1, the range of free entry equilibria is quite large. For a given value of K the monopolistic competition equilibrium involves one and a half to two times as many firms as does the single firm entry equilibrium.

Thus multiple equilibria characterize the model. The particular equilibrium which emerges will depend upon the assumption with respect to the dynamic of entry. We have presented two dynamics of entry which converge to different equilibria, and we have delimited the range of free entry equilibria. Further speculation as to the nature of free entry equilibrium does not seem fruitful. We evidently have a situation illustrating Samuelson's correspondence principle. The equilibrium which emerges in the market is dependent upon the assumed dynamic of entry. All that can be said here is that the free entry equilibrium is not unique.

It is also instructive to analyze the behavior which might be expected if a multiplant monopolist or a group of colluding firms were to serve the circular market and to compare that behavior with the blindly competitive behavior analyzed above. Two variants of collusive behavior will be developed—unconstrained profit maximizing behavior and an entry preventing or "limit pricing" model. Joint profit maximization will have the firms equally spaced around the circle charging a common price. Thus, if we set $P_i = P_{i-1} = P_{i+1} = P_m$ and $X_i = L(2i-1)/2n$, $X_{i+1} = L(2i+1)/2n$, and $X_{i-1} = L(2i-3)/2n$ in Equation (4), we obtain the demand function for one of the colluding firms, or one plant of the multi-plant monopolist. (In order to maintain comparability with the examples above we also set b at -1, a at \$1 per mile, P_0 at \$1.0, and L at 60 miles.)

$$Q_m = (L^2/4n^2) - (L/n) + (P_m L/n) \tag{10}$$

Maximum total profits are obtained by maximizing (11) with respect to n and P_m.

$$V(P_m, n) = nP_mQ_m - nK \tag{11}$$

The two conditions which maximize $V(P_m, n)$ can be written as

$$P_m = \tfrac{1}{2} - L/8n \tag{12}$$

$$32Kn^3 + 4L^2n - L^3 = 0 \tag{13}$$

Since we suspect that the unconstrained maximization of profits will induce entry, we are led to consider an entry preventing strategy—or, more precisely, a strategy which will maximize profits subject to the constraint that entry will not appear to be profitable. A potential entrant is forced to enter between two existing firms—thus, in order to express mathematically the necessary constraint, set $X_{i+1} + L(2i+1)/2n$, and $X_{i-1} = L(2i-1)/2n$ in Equation (4) and also set $P_{i+1} = P_{i-1} = P_R$ in Equations (4) and (6) where P_R represents the entry preventing price. Having made these substitutions, combine (4) and (6) to obtain

$$(14) \quad \begin{aligned} Q_i = (1/16)[-12P_i^2 + P_i(16 + 8P_R + 4L/n) + 4P_R^2 - 16P_R + L^2/n^2 \\ + 4P_RL/n - 8L/n] \end{aligned}$$

For given n and P_R, Equation (14) defines the demand function facing a potential entrant. If PI_I represents the maximum profits which can be generated from Equation (14) given our cost conditions, then $PI_I < 0$ is the desired constraint. The entry preventing strategy is then to maximize profits with respect to n and P_R subject to $PI_I < 0$.

The results of the joint maximization and entry preventing strategies are reported in Columns 1 and 2 of Table 1. In the absence of the threat of entry, the joint maximizing solution yields profits which are in general much greater than those associated with the entry preventing strategy. Perhaps the most interesting result emerges from a comparison of Columns 2 and 3. The entry preventing strategy yields a configuration which is very similar to the equilibrium which emerges from the single firm entry dynamic. The entry preventing strategy naturally leads to a higher level of aggregate profits for any value of K, but the rate of profit is not necessarily larger nor is the number of firms necessarily smaller. The entry preventing strategy in this example yields an equilibrium which borders on the range of free entry equilibria.

3. CONCLUSIONS

The model is characterized by a multiplicity of equilibria, and in general zero profits are not a condition of equilibrium. This result is in sharp contrast to the accepted analysis of free entry in which the equilibrium is unique and zero profits are a condition of equilibrium. A review of Telser's reasoning is illuminating. Telser reduced the bounded, one-dimensional model to an unbounded, one-dimensional model by reasoning that locations will be efficient (equal market shares) along the line. "Suppose the plants are inefficiently located; then it would pay an entrepreneur to purchase all existing plants and relocate them efficiently." Having imposed equal spacing by this device, he argues that all mill prices will then be equal. He continues (Telser [11, p. 948]): "Nevertheless, the free entry of firms to the road would prevent such an entrepreneur from obtaining a monopoly return. Therefore, there would be that number of plants in business on the road such that each firm maximizes its net revenue with respect to the quantity it sells, and the value of the maximum net revenue would be zero . . . Together these two conditions constitute Chamberlin's well known tangency solution." He does not deduce the zero-profit condition from assumptions about the behavior of entrants, he simply imposes it as a condition of equilibrium with the remark that "the free entry of firms would prevent . . . a monopoly return." The imposition of zero profits as a condition of equilibrium is a common, almost ubiquitous practice in free entry models of spatial competition. For examples, see Beckmann [1] and Mills and Lav [10]. For a more complete consideration of this important methodological point see Eaton and Lipsey [3].

The pure profits in our model arise from the interaction of two factors—average costs are declining due to the indivisibility of capital, and given our behavioral assumptions, the demand curve facing a new entrant lies below the demand curve of an existing firm. Then it is possible that the existing firm's demand curve lies above the declining cost curve over some range of output while the new entrant's demand curve lies below the common average cost curve for all levels of output. In this situation we obviously cannot deduce zero profits as a condition of equilibrium.

It seems obvious that, at least over some initial range of output, average costs do decline in retailing industries. Given that transport is costly, if average costs did not decline over some range of output we would not, in equilibrium, observe any economic unit which we could identify as a firm because all retailing would take place at the point of consumption. Most spatial theorists would not dispute this proposition.

The conjectural variation assumptions on which we base our result are, however, open to question. We believe that the pure profit result will generalize to a large class of conjectural variations.[6] On this point of faith, it is interesting to extract the implicit behavioral assumptions which we believe to be necessary to the Beckmann [1] and Telser [11] papers. A new entrant must be able to anticipate all of the relocation and price adjustments throughout the entire market occasioned by its entry. In addition, all of these adjustments must be instantaneous. If the new entrant expected just a normal rate of return on its capital after all of the adjustments, it must expect a rate of return less than normal over the period of adjustment. This implies that, if the adjustment process is time consuming, the new entrant must expect a return which is less than the return earned by existing firms, and zero profits will not be a condition of equilibrium. Of course, these are simply intuitive speculations and further research on the relationship between pure profits and the behavioral assumptions of new entrants is called for.

It is of some interest to ask if there are any real world analogues of the model other than the standard example of the perimeter of a volcanic island. In the spatial realm there seem to be at least two nontrivial examples. Historically, the medieval walled city seems to approximate the conditions of the model. Traveling merchants were forbidden to sell within the city and were thus forced to sell along the perimeter of the city. Zoning plays a similar role in the modern city. Residential zoning creates an area in which no retailing is allowed and hence retail firms can locate only on the perimeter of the market area. As an anonymous referee has pointed out, the model may also be appropriate for some scheduling problems since time of day can be regarded as a circular space. The scheduling of transport services or television

---

[6] For an illuminating analysis of the role of conjectural variations of the spatial duopoly situation, see Gannon [5].

programs might, for example, be fruitfully analyzed in the context of the circular model.

The evidence which comes out of theoretical simulation models, is, of necessity, in the nature of examples. That is, in order to pursue the problem using numerical methods, specific values must be assigned to the parameters of the model. Thus generalizations are hard to come by using simulation techniques. However, simulation techniques facilitate proof by counter-example. Thus the proposition that zero profits are, in general, a condition of free entry equilibrium is disproved by one example in which equilibrium is characterized by nonzero profits.

The relationship of spatial models of competition to Chamberlin's theory of monopolistic competition deserves attention. It is frequently alleged that the theory of monopolistic competition is applicable to spatial competition. In one-dimensional models such as those developed in this paper each firm has at most only two neighbors, and his perceived demand function is dependent upon his own price and location, and upon the prices and locations of the two neighboring firms. Such situations represent spatial oligopoly—they are examples of linked or overlapping competition. A basic condition which must be fulfilled if Chamberlin's analysis is to apply is that each firm's demand function be dependent upon the decision variables of a large number of other firms. If this condition is met a new entrant will be able to attract customers from a very large number of competitors and the zero profit result follows. This condition is never met in models of spatial competition—spatial competition is an oligopoly problem. Kaldor [8] made this point very forcefully as long ago as 1935, but it is a point which we seem to periodically lose sight of.

REFERENCES

[1] Beckmann, M. J. "Equilibrium versus Optimum: Spacing of Firms and Patterns of Market Areas," *Northeast Regional Science Review*, 1 (1971), 1–20.

[2] Eaton, B. C. "Spatial Competition Revisited," *Canadian Journal of Economics*, 5 (1972), 268–278.

[3] ——— and R. G. Lipsey. "The Non-Uniqueness of Equilibrium in the Löschian Location Model," *American Economic Review* (forthcoming).

[4] ——— and ———. "The Principle of Minimum Differentiation Reconsidered: Some New Developments in the Theory of Spatial Competition," *Review of Economic Studies*, 42 (1975), 27–49.

[5] Gannon, C. A. "Consumer Demand, Conjectural Interdependence, and Location Equilibria in Simple Spatial Duopoly," *Papers, Regional Science Association*, 28 (1972), 83–107.

[6] Grace, S. H. "Professor Samuelson on Free Enterprise and Economic Efficiency: A Comment," *Quarterly Journal of Economics*, 84 (1970), 337–345.

[7] Hartwick, J. M. and P. G. Hartwick. "Duopoly in Space," *Canadian Journal of Economics*, 4 (1971), 485–506.

[8] Kaldor, N. "Market Imperfection and Excess Capacity," *Economica*, 2 (1935), 33–50.

[9] Koopmans, T. and M. Beckmann. "Assignment Problems and the Location of Economic Activity," *Econometrica*, 25 (1957), 53–76.

[10] Mills, E. S. and M. R. Lav. "A Model of Market Area with Free Entry," *Journal of Political Economy*, 72 (1964), 278–288.

[11] Telser, L. G. "On the Regulation of Industry," *Journal of Political Economy*, 77 (1969), 937–952.

[2]

The Economic Journal, **88** (*September* 1978), 455–469
Printed in Great Britain

FREEDOM OF ENTRY AND THE EXISTENCE OF PURE PROFIT[1]

The neoclassical model of perfect competition is spaceless, and assumes constant returns to scale. Since real economies are spatially extended and most production technologies display an initial region of increasing returns due to capital indivisibilities,[2] the applicability of the neoclassical model requires that abstracting from space and scale effects does not seriously affect its properties.

It is well known that *either* space[3] *or* "minor" scale effects[4] can be added to the neo-classical model without serious consequences. It is our contention, however, that the *simultaneous* introduction of space and any range of increasing returns significantly alters the properties of the model. Zero profit is no longer a property of free-entry equilibrium. Furthermore, even as the number of firms in the market is increased without limit, the behaviour of the model remains stubbornly oligopolistic.

A survey of the literature shows that zero-profit is imposed as a condition of free-entry equilibrium in the vast majority of spatially extended models.[5] Thus our contention in this paper is in direct opposition to the assumption usually made, either explicitly or implicitly, that the neoclassical zero-profit result survives the introduction of space and some scale effects.

Kaldor (1935, pp. 42–3) gives a classic statement of the non-zero profit result:

> Let us now introduce indivisibilities and economies of scale. The movement of new firms into the field will then not continue until the elasticities of demand for the individual producers become infinite; it will be stopped long before that by the increase in costs as the output of producers is reduced. *But there is no reason to assume that it will stop precisely at the point where the demand*

[1] The present paper is a revision of Queen's Study Paper No. 207, Eaton and Lipsey (1976*b*). The work was done while the authors held visiting appointments at the University of Colorado at Boulder during the session 1974–5. We are grateful to the Killam Foundation and the Canada Council for support for Professors Lipsey and Eaton respectively.

[2] See Kaldor (1972, p. 1242) for a theoretical discussion and Johnston (1960) for some empirical evidence.

[3] If space is added to the constant-returns, neo-classical model, its main features are unaffected. The minimisation of transport costs will require, however, that production is spread smoothly over space so that there will be no economic unit recognisable as a firm. For an excellent discussion see Koopmans (1957).

[4] If production non-convexities are introduced into the spaceless neoclassical model, no insuperable difficulties are caused as long as the scale effects are "small" (see, for example, Starr, 1969).

[5] Reactions to other papers of ours that have presumed the non-zero profit characteristic of the model presented in this paper (see, for example, Eaton and Lipsey, 1976*a*) have convinced us that we are not dealing with a straw man. Examples in which the zero-profits condition is imposed in spatial models include Beckman (1971, 1974), Böventer (1969), Chamberlin (1933), Denike and Parr (1970), M. Greenhut (1952), M. L. Greenhut (1975), Greenhut and Ohta (1975), Losche (1954), Mills and Lav (1964), Ohta (1976), Southey (1974), and Telser (1969). Examples of models in which a zero profit condition is specifically ruled out are Eaton (1976), Tullock (1965), Kaldor (1935), and Zeuthen (1933). Beckman (1968) makes one of the basic points that market areas of new entrants are significantly smaller than those of existing firms, but he does not there go on to consider the consequences for profits while elsewhere he has imposed a zero profit condition. Eaton and Lipsey (1976*a*) derived the non-zero profit result but assumed a parametric price.

> ***and cost curves are tangential.*** For, on account of the very reason of economies of scale, the potential producer cannot hope to enter the field profitably with less than a certain magnitude of output; and that additional output may reduce demand, both to his nearest neighbours and to him, to such an extent that the demand curves will lie *below* the cost curves and all will be involved in losses. The interpolation of a third producer in between any two producers may thus transform profits into losses. *The same reason therefore which prevents competition from becoming perfect – i.e. indivisibility – will also prevent the complete elimination of "profits"*. It will secure a "monopolistic advantage" to anybody who is first in the field and merely by virtue of priority. The ultimate reason for this is that it is not the original resources themselves, but the various uses to which they are put that are indivisible – you can divide "free capital" but you cannot invest *less* than a certain amount of it in a machine – and consequently the investment of resources cannot be so finely distributed as to equalise the level of marginal productivities.

There are at least three problems with Kaldor's intuitively appealing argument. First, as our survey of the literature reveals, the great majority of writers either reject it, or are unaware of it. Second, the argument is not based on an explicitly formulated model and thus there is no way of dealing with such counter assertions as "once price competition is allowed for pure profit will be driven to zero". Third, Kaldor provides no way to study the potential quantitative significance of his qualitative result. Our work provides an analytical underpinning for Kaldor's argument. It rigorously demonstrates that pure profit will not necessarily be driven to zero by price competition and/or free entry of new firms,[1] it allows the conditions that contribute to the non-zero profit result to be explored; it allows further consequences of these conditions to be deduced; and it permits quantitative estimates of the magnitude of positive profits in equilibrium when specific cases are studied.

I. THE MODEL

We now outline our basic model and in section VII we consider the consequences of relaxing its more restrictive assumptions.

(*a*) The market is a one-dimensional line of infinite length over which customers are spread at a constant density.

(*b*) Average total cost is $ATC = K/Q + c$, where Q is quantity produced, c is a constant marginal cost, and K is the fixed cost associated with a minimum indivisible unit of capital. This cost function is the most convenient way to capture the empirical phenomenon that ATC declines over some initial range. We do not impose a capacity constraint because, as we argue in section VII, it is only the declining portion that is relevant to our argument.

(*c*) Fixed capital is geographically immobile and its value in any other use is less than its replacement cost, i.e. there are sunk costs.

(*d*) No firm owns two adjacent plants. This assumption is used to avoid the

[1] For a survey of all our work on the consequences of introducing space and scale effects into the neo-classical model see Eaton and Lipsey (1977).

possibility of monopolistic behaviour on the part of adjacent plants, and thus to ensure that firm behaviour is as competitive as possible. (See Eaton and Lipsey (1976*c*) for a discussion of the use by multi-plant firms of locational configurations as barriers to entry.)

(*e*) Transport costs are borne by customers and are t per unit of distance per unit of product.

(*f*) Each customer patronises the firm with lowest delivered price.

(*g*) Demand at each point is $q = f(p_d)$, where p_d is delivered price and $f' < 0$. The function f has no price intercept and its elasticity $\to -\infty$ as $p_d \to \infty$. f has either a quantity intercept or is asymptotic to the quantity axis (i.e. customers face a budget constraint).

(*h*) In selecting price and location all firms, existing firms as well as new entrants, seek to maximise profits subject to the same set of conjectural variations. They also have static expectations with respect to the flow of future profits. We refer to a firm's conjectural variations concerning other firms' price and location decisions as *PCV* and *LCV* respectively.

(*i*) In selecting its location, each firm takes the location of all other firms as given (*ZLCV*). We show in section VII that this assumption is not as restrictive as it might at first appear.

(*j*) The price any firm expects a neighbouring firm to charge, V, is dependent upon its own price, p, the price currently charged by the neighbouring firm, v, and the distance between the two firms, D:

$$V = g(p, v, D) \quad (0 \leqslant g_1 \leqslant 1,\ g_3 \geqslant 0,\ g_{33} \leqslant 0). \tag{1}$$

The restriction on g_1 assures that V is non-decreasing in p, and that firms do not expect their neighbours to "overreact" to their price changes. The restrictions on g_3 and g_{33} assure respectively that firms expect a neighbour's price not to decrease with distance between the firms, and that the rate of increase is non-increasing with distance. We qualify our *PCV* by ruling out ***mill-price undercutting***: no firm, i, assumes that any other firm, j, will allow i to charge a mill price such that i's delivered price at j's mill door is less than j's mill price. Our reasons for imposing this qualification are explored in section II.

There is a problem with the *PCV* in (1) because, without further restriction, there is no guarantee that a firm's price expectations will be realised in equilibrium. One way out is to further restrict (1) to ensure that price expectations are fulfilled in equilibrium. We do not consider this problem further but simply note, first, that it arises out of a difficult problem of oligopolistic interdependence, and second, that many specific functions within the general class of (1), including the linear *PCV*, $V = ap + (1-a)\, v\ (0 \leqslant a \leqslant 1)$, do have the desired property. The linear case includes the two cases which have received the most attention in the literature: when $a = 1$ each firm assumes that competitors will match any price (denoted *UPCV*) and when $a = 0$ each firm assumes that its competitors will not alter their price (denoted *ZPCV*). If we can prove our non-zero-profit contention for even this linear *PCV* case we will have dealt with the majority of cases in the literature in which a zero-profit condition has been imposed.

Constant-numbers equilibrium refers to an equilibrium when the number of firms is fixed, and *free-entry equilibrium* refers to an equilibrium when there is freedom of entry and exit. We use the terms *pure profit* and *gross profit* to refer respectively to total revenue minus long run total cost and to total revenue minus variable cost.

There is one condition that is necessary and sufficient for constant-numbers equilibrium: (i) *no firm can find a combination of location and price that offers it a larger anticipated gross profit than that obtained with its present combination of location and price.* Free entry equilibrium requires, in addition to the above: (ii) *all possible combinations of location and price for a potential new entrant offer anticipated gross profit of less than K*; and (iii) *no existing firm earns actual gross profit of less than K.*

II. MILL-PRICE UNDERCUTTING

We now pass to a consideration of the basic question: Is zero profit a condition of equilibrium in this model? One frequently encountered argument for answering this question in the affirmative follows. Assume that any existing firm, *A*, is making positive pure profit. Any new firm, *B*, can enter right beside *A*, undercut *A*'s price ever so slightly, and capture all of *A*'s market. Hence *B* can expect to have profit virtually as large as *A*'s. If any firm is earning positive pure profit entry will occur, and hence positive pure profit is not consistent with free-entry equilibrium.

Notice, first, that this argument is based on the unqualified *ZPCV*. To see the importance of this assume instead *UPCV*: *B* assumes that *A* will match any price that *B* charges. Now *B* cannot expect to capture all of *A*'s market and profit. As long as *ATC* is falling over some range of output and as long as *B* does not expect to capture all of *A*'s market, there will be a range of positive pure profit for *A* that will cause *B* to anticipate negative pure profit if it were to enter alongside *A* with a *UPCV* assumption.

Many *PCV*s are, of course, quite arbitrary. One firm is trying to foresee another's profit-maximising reactions. Arbitrary rules such as *ZPCV* and *UPCV* are used because these reactions are difficult to foresee. Where, however, the reactions can be foreseen we should allow for them, and we now consider one particular reaction that is easily foreseeable.

Firm *B*, considering locating anywhere in *A*'s market – whether right next to *A* or elsewhere – may be uncertain what *A*'s precise reactions will be, but *B* can be certain of one thing: *A* will not voluntarily leave the market as long as there exists any price greater than average variable cost (*AVC*) at which *A* can sell goods. Thus *B* can expect *A* to set its mill price, p^A, in relation to *B*'s mill price, p^B, as follows: $AVC < p^A < p^B + tD$ (where *D* is the distance between the two firms).

Since *B* has not actually entered the market, all of its costs are avoidable; *A*, however, has some fixed costs. Thus $ATC > AVC$ and it follows that there is *no* price that *B* can choose such that, after *A*'s reaction, both of the following are true: (i) $p^B + tD < p^A$, i.e. *A* allows itself to be driven from the market; and (ii) $ATC \leqslant p^B$, i.e. *B* does not make negative pure profit. *If B has even the most elementary foresight B will never assume that it can drive A out of the market, and also earn non-negative pure profit.* Indeed, if *B* tries to capture all of *A*'s market by undercutting A's mill price, B can expect A to follow it all the way down to a price ($p = AVC$) at which B's entry looks decidedly unprofitable. This is our reason for ruling out mill price undercutting.

III. LOCATION AND PRICE DECISIONS

The next step in our analysis is to study the price and location decisions of a firm, B, locating between two other firms, A and C. Locate A at $-L$, C at L and let both charge a common price, v.

Let b_C denote B's anticipated market boundary with C – the point at which B expects the two firms to have the same delivered price. Then b_C must satisfy

$$p+t(b_C-x) = g(p,v,L-x)+t(L-b_C), \tag{2}$$

where x is B's location, and from (1), $g(p,v,L-x)$ is the mill price B expects C to charge. Solving for b_C yields

$$b_C = \frac{1}{2t}[g(p,v,L-x)-p+t(L+x)]. \tag{3}$$

The delivered price, P_C, that B anticipates at b_C is

$$P_C = \tfrac{1}{2}[p+g(p,v,L-x)+t(L-x)]. \tag{4}$$

Aggregate expected quantity demanded from firm B from x to b_C is

$$\int_x^{b_C} f[p+t(z-x)]\,dz, \tag{5}$$

where f is the individual demand function, z is distance measured from the origin, and hence $p+t(z-x)$ is delivered price. Letting $u = p+t(z-x)$, the above expression is easily reduced to

$$\frac{1}{t}\int_p^{P_C} f(u)\,du = \frac{1}{t}[F(P_C)-F(p)], \tag{6}$$

where F is an indefinite integral of f.

Obtaining the expressions analogous to (3)–(6) for the market segment to the left x allows us to derive firm B's expected demand:

$$Q(x,p) = \frac{1}{t}[F(P_A)+F(P_C)-2F(p)], \tag{7}$$

where P_A is the delivered price at its anticipated market boundary with A and is equal to $[p+g(p,\ v,\ L+x)+t(L+x)]/2$.

Firm B must choose price and location so as to maximise profit. It can, however, make these decisions sequentially. For any price that B chooses, B will wish to maximise quantity demanded at that price: if it pays B to sell anything at all it will pay B to sell as much as possible since marginal cost is constant. To maximise sales at any price we require as a necessary condition that

$$\frac{\partial Q}{\partial x} = \frac{1}{2t}\{f(P_A)\,[t+g_3(p,v,L+x)]-f(P_C)\,[t+g_3(p,v,L-x)]\} = 0. \tag{8}$$

Notice first that when $x = 0$, $P_A = P_C$ and condition (8) is satisfied.

Then consider

$$\frac{\partial^2 Q}{\partial x^2} = \frac{1}{2t}\{(\tfrac{1}{2})f'(P_A)\,[t+g_3(p,v,L+x)]^2 + f(P_A)\,g_{33}(p,v,L+x) + (\tfrac{1}{2})f'(P_C)\,[t+g_3(p,v,L-x)]^2 + f(P_C)\,g_{33}(p,v,L-x)\}. \tag{9}$$

The first and third terms in the braces are negative since f' is negative, and the second and fourth are non-positive by the restriction on g_{33} in (1). Then Q is strictly concave with respect to x, and since equation (8) is satisfied when $x = 0$ the global maximum of quantity demanded occurs at $x = 0$, i.e. B will locate at the midpoint of the interval between the two firms.

Letting $x = 0$ in (4) yields the common anticipated delivered price at the two market boundaries, P:

$$P = \tfrac{1}{2}[p+g(p,v,L)+tL]. \tag{10}$$

From (7) B's expected demand curve when it locates at the origin is

$$Q(0,p) = \frac{2}{t}[F(P)-F(p)]. \tag{11}$$

The first-order condition for a maximum of B's gross and pure profits (which differ only by a constant, K) is derived by differentiating $(p-c)\,Q-K$ with respect to p. The first-order condition is easily reduced first to

$$F(P)-F(p)+(p-c)\left[f(P)\frac{\partial P}{\partial p}-f(p)\right] = 0 \tag{12}$$

and second, using $\partial P/\partial p = (g_1+1)/2$ from (10), to

$$\frac{p-c}{F(P)-F(p)}\left[\frac{f(P)\,(g_1+1)}{2}-f(p)\right] = -1. \tag{13}$$

Thus a firm locating between two other firms which charge a common price will maximise its anticipated profits by locating at the midpoint of the interval between the two firms and charging a price which satisfies (13).

IV. POSITIVE PURE PROFIT IN CONSTANT-NUMBERS EQUILIBRIUM

It is often argued that if positive pure profit is being earned, any existing firm will necessarily be tempted to cut its price in an effort to gain a larger share of the profitable market (particularly if it makes a *ZPCV* assumption). This would imply that positive pure profit is inconsistent with equilibrium.

In the Appendix we prove the existence of an equilibrium in which firms are evenly spaced throughout the market charging a common price, p^*, which is independent of fixed costs, K. Given a value of K, assume that by chance pure profit is zero at price p^*. Now reduce K. This produces positive pure profit but causes no competitive price cutting since it leaves p^* unchanged.

The importance of this demonstration is in showing that price competition between existing firms in the market will not necessarily drive pure profit to zero. Our general *PCV* includes the special case of *ZPCV*, which is very conducive to price cutting since any firm feels it can cut its price without *any* retaliation from other firms. Even in this case, an equilibrium p^* exists in which pure profit may be earned but in which each firm is not motivated to cut price.

V. PURE PROFIT IN FREE-ENTRY EQUILIBRIUM

Having shown that price competition among existing firms will not necessarily drive pure profit to zero, even when they adopt *ZPCV*, the remaining question is whether or not *entry* (in addition to the price competition that is an integral part of the model) will do so. To show that it will not we argue as follows.

Let the existing firms be in constant-numbers equilibrium, spaced L units apart charging the common equilibrium price, p^*. Equation (11) in conjunction with (10), yields the demand curve facing an existing firm in constant numbers equilibrium:

$$Q^E = \frac{2}{t}\left\{F\left[\frac{p}{2}+\frac{g(p,p^*,L)}{2}+\frac{tL}{2}\right]-F(p)\right\},$$
$$g(p,p^*,L)+tL > p > g(p,p^*,L)-tL. \qquad (14)$$

The constraints on p are required because if p were above the upper limit, quantity demanded would be zero since the firm's neighbours would undersell the firm at every point in the market; while if p were below the lower limit the "no-mill-price undercutting" restriction would be violated.

Now consider entry of a new firm between any two of the existing firms. Since the existing firms are charging a common price, the new entrant would locate at the midpoint between the existing firms which leaves it only $L/2$ units from each of its neighbours. The new entrant's expected demand function, Q^{NE}, will then be

$$Q^{NE} = \frac{2}{t}\left\{F\left[\frac{p}{2}+\frac{g(p,p^*,L/2)}{2}+\frac{tL}{4}\right]-F(p)\right\},$$
$$g(p,p^*,L/2)+tL/2 > p < g(p,p^*,L/2)-tL/2. \qquad (15)$$

Comparison of (14) and (15) shows that

$$Q^{NE} < Q^E \quad \text{since} \quad \tfrac{1}{2}(p+g(p,p^*,L)+tL) > \tfrac{1}{2}(p+g(p,p^*,L/2)+tL/2).$$

It follows from this that if all firms have the same costs it is possible for the expected demand curve for new entrants to lie everywhere below *ATC*, which is the condition for no new entry, while the demand curves for existing firms lie above *ATC* at p^*, which is the condition for positive pure profit.[1]

[1] The argument in the last paragraph of the text appeals to geometric intuition. A formal proof proceeds by contradiction. (1) Assume a fixed-numbers equilibrium with gross profits of existing firms of $\Pi^E(p^*) > 0$. (2) Assume there exists some p^{**} for which $\Pi^{NE}(p^{**}) \geqslant \Pi^E(p^*)$. From the text we know that $Q^E(p^{**}) > Q^{NE}(p^{**})$. Given constant marginal costs this implies that $\Pi^E(p^{**}) > \Pi^{NE}(p^{**})$. But by (2) above $\Pi^{NE}(p^{**}) \geqslant \Pi^E(p^*)$ so that $\Pi^E(p^{**}) > \Pi^E(p^*)$, which contradicts (1) above. Thus we know that when (1) holds we also have $\Pi^{NE}(p^{**}) < \Pi^E(p^*)$ where p^{**} is the price that maximises Π^{NE}. Now choose K such that $\Pi^E(p^*) > K > \Pi^{NE}(p^{**})$ and positive pure profits exist in free-entry equilibrium.

VI. AN EXAMPLE

The qualitative result proved above would be unimportant if the quantitative divergence from the competitive rate of return on capital were insignificant. We can, however, show by example that the divergence from the competitive rate of return may be substantial.

Let the individual demand function be

$$q = e^{-pd}. \qquad (16)$$

Let all firms adopt a *UPCV*. If existing firms are L units apart, aggregate quantity demanded from any firm is, using equation (11),

$$Q = \frac{2}{t}\left(-e^{-(p+tL/2)} + e^{-p}\right) = \frac{2e^{-p}}{t}\left(1 - e^{-tL/2}\right). \qquad (17)$$

Application of the profit-maximising condition in equation (13) yields the profit-maximising price, $p^* = 1 + c$, which is the constant-numbers equilibrium price. Gross profit for existing firms at price p^* is

$$\Pi^{*E} = \frac{2e^{-(1+c)}}{t}\left(1 - e^{-tL/2}\right). \qquad (18)$$

A new entrant would have neighbours a distance of $L/2$ away and maximum gross profit for the new entrant would be

$$\Pi^{*NE} = \frac{2e^{-(1+c)}}{t}\left(1 - e^{-tL/4}\right), \qquad (19)$$

since the profit maximising price for the new entrant is also $1 + c$.

Entry will not occur if $\Pi^{*NE} < K$, or, substituting for Π^{*NE} (from (14)) in the inequality and rearranging terms, entry will not occur if

$$e^{-tL/4} > 1 - \frac{tKe^{1+c}}{2}. \qquad (20)$$

Inspection of (18) reveals that if the market is to be served at all, K must be less than $2e^{-(1+c)}/t$, since with a market of infinite length gross profits are $2e^{-(1+c)}/t$. If this restriction is satisfied, the right side of (20) is positive, and, squaring both sides, entry will not occur if

$$e^{-tL/2} > 1 - tKe^{1+c} + \left(\frac{tKe^{1+c}}{2}\right)^2. \qquad (21)$$

Maximum profit for existing firms will occur when the left side of (21) is just greater than the right. Thus the supremum of profit of existing firms will occur when (21) holds with equality. Then substituting the right side of (21) for $e^{-tL/2}$ in (18) we obtain the supremum of Π^{*E}, $\hat{\Pi}^E$.

$$\hat{\Pi}^E = 2\left(K - \frac{tK^2e^{1+c}}{4}\right). \qquad (22)$$

It is convenient to express K as a proportion of $2e^{-(1+c)}/t$, the maximum value of K at which the market will be served.

$$K = 2\delta e^{-(1+c)}/t \quad (0 < \delta \leqslant 1). \tag{23}$$

Combining (22) and (23) we obtain

$$\hat{\Pi}^E = \frac{2e^{-(1+c)}}{t}(2\delta - \delta^2). \tag{24}$$

If we assume for convenience that capital has an infinite life, fixed costs of K would arise from a capital expenditure of K/i, where i is the normal rate of return on capital. Then the rate of return on capital associated with $\hat{\Pi}^E$ is $i\hat{\Pi}^E/K$, which yields,

$$r = i(2-\delta). \tag{25}$$

As δ approaches 1, r approaches i and as δ approaches zero r approaches $2i$. *Thus the rate of return consistent with free entry equilibrium in this model can be as much as twice the normal rate of return on capital.*[1]

It is fairly easy to understand the reason for the limits on r. As $\delta \to 1$, one firm can just cover its costs in a market of infinite length and hence $r \to i$. The maximum value of r is approached as $\delta \to 0$. Letting $\delta \to 0$ means that the density of packing of firms per unit of market length, Δ, $\to \infty$. As $\Delta \to \infty$, the difference between mill price and price at the firm's market boundaries approaches zero. Thus the difference between sales at these two points also approaches zero. As this occurs, the advantage in sales that a new entrant gets from having the customers in its market segment closer to its plant than they were to the plant that served them before entry goes to zero. The only remaining influence on the relation between sales of a potential new entrant and the sales of an existing firm is the *number* of customers served (since virtually the same amount is sold to all customers). Since a new firm always gets one half the number of customers that were served by an existing firm before entry, sales and hence profits of the new firm go to half those earned by existing firms before entry as $\Delta \to \infty$. Thus $r \to 2i$.

VII. SOME RESTRICTIVE ASSUMPTIONS REMOVED

In this section we discuss how several of the restrictive assumptions of our basic model might be relaxed. We conjecture that for a more general class of models than we have considered so far *if a fixed numbers equilibrium exists, zero profit is not a condition of free-entry equilibrium.* We thus do not consider existence of equilibrium in this section, but merely note that the position we are assailing, that zero profit is a condition of equilibrium, has no meaning in any model in which equilibrium does not exist.[2]

Demand Conditions. In order to prove the existence of equilbrium we assume that the individual demand function has no price intercept and that its elasticity

[1] Eaton (1976) develops a model based on *ZPCV* in which the maximum rate of return is $1{\cdot}7i$.

[2] Indeed there is some reason to believe that equilibrium may not exist in some otherwise sensible-looking models of spatial competition in bounded two-dimensional space. See Eaton and Lipsey (1975) and Shaked (1975).

goes to infinity as price goes to infinity. Neither of these assumptions has any real bearing on the question of zero profit. As long as firms are in equilibrium and equally spaced along the linear market with all points in the market being served, the expected sales, and hence profit, of a potential new entrant must be substantially lower than those of existing firms, irrespective of the precise shape of the demand curve.[1]

Locational Conjectural Variation. It is often argued that the positive profit result depends on the *arbitrary assumption* that new entrants base their decisions on the expectation that existing firms will not move. Indeed we have used this assumption so far. In this section we examine conditions under which this expectation is the correct one. Our analysis takes us some way towards developing a theory of appropriate *LCV*'s and thus away from arbitrarily assuming some particular *LCV*. We first study the example of the previous section and then, in an intuitive fashion, explore the problem in a more general context.

The immobility of firms must arise either because there are location-specific fixed costs, or because there are costs of moving fixed capital. We capture both of these sources of immobility by postulating that a proportion, λ, of the firms' fixed costs are "location specific". We then ask when it is appropriate for a new entrant to regard the location of existing firms as fixed.

Let there be a constant-numbers equilibrium in the example of the previous section with all firms located L units apart. Suppose a new entrant thinks of entering at the midpoint of the interval between two firms. If neither of the two existing firms move, the excess of an existing firms' revenue over avoidable costs would be

$$\frac{e^{-(1+c)}}{t}[(1-e^{-tL/2})+(1-e^{-tL/4})] > \frac{3e^{-(1+c)}}{2t}(1-e^{-tL/2}) = G, \tag{26}$$

since its profit maximising price would still be $1+c$ and its market would extend $L/2$ units in one direction and $L/4$ in the other. To simplify the arithmetic we will assume that the excess of revenues over avoidable costs is G. Without further assumptions we do not know what profits the existing firm would expect if it were to move. For the purpose of argument let us make the strongest assumption: if the existing firm moves, it believes that it will set off an instantaneous process of adjustment which will leave it with a market of the same size as its market before entry. This clearly biases the analysis towards the movement of the existing firm. On this assumption the excess of revenues over avoidable costs will be

$$H = \frac{2e^{-(1+c)}}{t}(1-e^{-tL/2}) - \lambda K. \tag{27}$$

[1] Assuming that elasticity goes to infinity as price goes to infinity is sufficient to avoid such problems as the non-existence of equilibrium if demand is everywhere inelastic. The existence proof is actually easier if the individual demand curve has a price intercept. In this case the aggregated demand curve will also have a price intercept and it is obvious that as p goes to the price intercept, the left-hand side of equation (30) goes to $-\infty$. However, the positive-profit argument is quite tedious if the individual demand function has a price intercept. The difficulty arises because for very high prices (for existing firms and for the new entrant) the two demand curves in (14) and (15) are coincident because price is so high there are unserved gaps in the market.

The existing firm will not move if $G > H$. Using (26) and (27) and substituting for K from (23) the condition that $G > H$ is easily reduced to

$$e^{-tL/2} > 1 - 4\lambda\delta = \theta_1. \tag{28}$$

It is then quite clear that if λ and/or δ are sufficiently large the existing firm will never move, even if it believes it could regain its whole market by moving. If $\lambda\delta > \frac{1}{4}$ the existing firm will never move regardless of how large L is. Accordingly it would be rational for the new entrant to regard the location of existing firms as fixed. This is sufficient to show that there are circumstances under which a new entrant, rationally calculating the location policies of existing firms, would regard their locations as fixed.

But we can say more. Combining (21) and (23) we can rewrite the conditions under which entry is not profitable if new entrants adopt a *ZLCV*:

$$e^{-tL/2} > 1 - 2\delta + \delta^2 = \theta_2. \tag{29}$$

Imagine a market in which L is very large, large enough so that neither inequality (28) nor (29) holds and hence entry occurs reducing L. (For (28) not to hold $\lambda\delta < \frac{1}{4}$ is necessary.) If $\theta_1 < \theta_2$, then as we decrease L (28) will bind before (29) does, and L will eventually become small enough so that (28) holds while (29) does not – existing firms will not move but entry on a *ZLCV* will still be profitable. In this case the analysis of the previous section, based on *ZLCV*, tells us all there is to know about equilibrium in the model. When $\theta_1 > \theta_2$, L will eventually become small enough so that (29) holds while (28) does not – *ZLCV* is then not always appropriate, given that any existing firm believes that it can recapture its whole market by moving. In this case entry will continue until the rate of return in the market is just i, or until L is small enough so that (28) holds and existing firms will no longer move. The second possibility will occur if $\lambda > \frac{1}{4}$, and the supremum of Π^{*E} will occur when (28) holds with equality, which yields a maximum rate of return of $4\lambda i$. In this case *ZLCV* is not initially appropriate but entry proceeds until it becomes appropriate.

The range of possibilities is outlined in Fig. 1. For any combination of λ and δ above the line $\theta_1 = \theta_2$, *ZLCV* is always appropriate and the maximum rate of return is $i(2-\delta)$. In the triangular region bounded by the vertical axis, and the lines $\theta_1 = \theta_2$ and $\lambda = \frac{1}{4}$, *ZLCV* eventually becomes appropriate but the possibility of pure profit persists, $r = 4\lambda i$. For $\lambda < \frac{1}{4}$, *ZLCV* is inappropriate and $r = i$. Recall that this argument is based on inequality (26); it should be noted that the argument significantly understates the conditions under which *ZLCV* is appropriate. *ZLCV* is in fact always appropriate for combinations of λ and δ above the line, $\lambda = (1-\delta)/2$.

It is fairly easy to understand at least some of the forces contributing to these results. Let us ignore the elasticity of the individual demand function and assume that all firms charge the same price. Then, when faced with a new entrant in the middle of one of its market segments an existing firm will not move if

$$3\Pi(L)/4 > \Pi(L) - \lambda K,$$

or if $\Pi(L) < 4\lambda K$, where $\Pi(L)$ is gross profit which declines with L. There will be no entry on *ZLCV* if $\Pi(L)/2 < K$, or if $\Pi(L) < 2K$. As L decreases existing firms will not move while entry on a *ZLCV* is still profitable if $4\lambda K > 2K$, or if $\lambda > \frac{1}{2}$. Thus when we ignore elasticity of demand, *ZLCV* is always appropriate when $\lambda > \frac{1}{2}$ and questionable when $\lambda < \frac{1}{2}$. Even when $\lambda < \frac{1}{2}$, the possibility of pure profits in free entry equilibrium exists – zero profits will characterise equilibrium only if $\Pi(L) > 4\lambda K$ (existing firms are still willing to move) when L is small enough so that $\Pi(L) - K = 0$. This implies that *ZLCV* is inappropriate and that zero profits will characterise equilibrium only if $\lambda < \frac{1}{4}$.

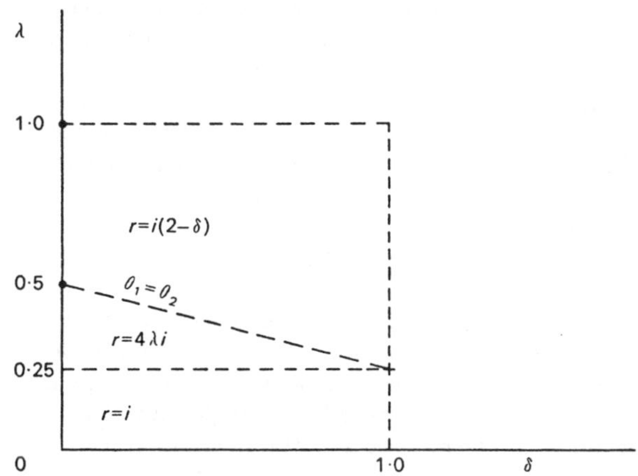

Fig. 1.

Cost Conditions. The key result in our model is that the expected demand curve of a new entrant lies strictly, and in most cases very far, to the left of the demand curve of an existing firm. This will bring entry to a halt before profits of existing firms are reduced to zero as long as average total costs are initially declining. To see why *ATC* only needs to decline initially we alter our cost assumption to make *ATC* constant or rising beyond an arbitrary positive output $\bar{Q}$. As long as the potential demand curve of a new entrant, Q^{NE}, lies somewhere above *ATC*, entry will continue. This is necessarily the case if Q^{NE} intersects *ATC* in the latter's flat or rising portion. As entry proceeds, however, Q^{NE} must finally be pushed everywhere to the left of *ATC*. At this point entry stops even though Q^{E}, the demand curve for an existing firm, lies above *ATC* (because Q^{E} lies substantially to the right of Q^{NE}). Entry thus proceeds until a situation akin to the classical natural monopoly is created in each segment of the market. In each segment one firm faces a demand curve that lies above *ATC* over part of its range, while a second firm considering entry into that market faces an expected demand curve that lies everywhere below its potential *ATC* curve. Thus it is obvious that the introduction of a capacity constraint into our cost function would change nothing.

VIII. SUMMARY AND CONCLUSIONS

We have demonstrated that zero pure profit is not a necessary condition of free-entry equilibrium in a model in which the market is spatially extended and long-run cost curves decline over some initial range. We have shown that neither price competition among existing firms nor the entry of new firms will necessarily drive profits to zero. This is true even when firms assume that they can cut their own price without reaction from their competitors, and when new entrants rationally calculate whether or not their entry will force existing firms to relocate. We have further shown, in a specific example, that rates of return on capital of up to *twice* the competitive rate are possible in free-entry equilibrium.

It is interesting to speculate on the proportion of the economy to which the positive-pure-profit result may apply. Some intuitive feel for the range of applicability may be developed by considering the conditions that are critical for the result: (i) the average total cost curve is declining over some initial range;(ii) customers are geographically spread out, and are intermingled with firms; (iii) transport is costly;[1] and (iv) once the firm enters the market it has location-specific sunk costs.

We believe that condition (i) captures a phenomenon that is nearly ubiquitous. Condition (ii) describes a large number of markets, but not those in which all producers are concentrated in a single geographical location, nor those in which geographically dispersed producers sell in a single centralised market. Conditions (iii) and (iv) would seem to be almost universally true.

The model of this paper is formulated in terms of geographical differentiation among firms. There would seem, however, to be significant applications to product differentiation, where firms sell products with different locations in characteristics space, and a new product fitting in between two established ones must expect a market significantly smaller than those obtained by "neighbouring" products before entry. For a discussion of some of the issues involved in handling monopolistic competition in characteristic space see Archibald and Rosenbluth (1975) and for a practical application that uses some of the properties developed in our model see Schmalensee (1977).

It would thus appear that the positive-profit result applies to a significant range of spatially dispersed activities in both the manufacturing and the retailing sectors of the economy, as well as to some cases of product differentiation. Evidently the neoclassical proposition that profits tend to zero under conditions of

[1] Demsetz (1971) argues that quantity demanded will not be a declining function of delivered prices because the rent gradient for residential sites will adjust so as to make all consumers have the same real income and, since there is only one good on which to spend this income, demand will be the same everywhere in the market, and will vary only with mill price. Demsetz's discussion assumes only one argument in household's utility functions; but if land enters the utility function as well the rent gradient will ensure equal real incomes and hence no income effects throughout the market. But there will be a substitution effect: households close to their nearest firm will face higher rents and a lower delivered price than will households more distant from their nearest firm. The substitution effect will then guarantee that firms face a downward-sloping demand curve in terms of delivered price. Even if Demsetz's argument were correct it would not upset our conclusion since if customer demand is insensitive to delivered price a new firm entering a segment of the market would not only expect to get exactly half the number of customers, it would also expect exactly half the sales enjoyed by existing firms before its entry.

free-entry requires serious amendment when account is taken of the geographical intermingling of producers and consumers and of capital indivisibilities.

University of British Columbia B. CURTIS EATON
Queen's University, Canada RICHARD G. LIPSEY
Date of receipt of final typescript: November 1977

APPENDIX

The existence of constant numbers equilibrium

Place firms A, B, and C at $-L$, 0, and L respectively. We must prove that there exists a common price, v^*, charged by A and C that leads B to charge the same price. Let $v = p$ in (10) to obtain $P = [p+g(p,p,L)+tL]/2$. With P so defined we show that (13) can always be satisfied for some positive finite value of p.

Since $0 \leqslant g_1 \leqslant 1$ the term in brackets in (13) is always negative and as $p \to 0$ the first term in (13) is also negative. Hence the left side of (13) goes to some positive limit as $p \to 0$.

To see what happens to the left side as $p \to \infty$ rewrite (13) as

$$(p-c)\left[\frac{f(P)-f(p)}{F(P)-F(p)}\right]+(p-c)\left[\frac{f(P)\,(g_1-1)/2}{F(P)-F(p)}\right] = -1. \tag{30}$$

As $p \to \infty$ the second term on the left in (30) will either decrease without bound or will approach some non-positive limit. Using the Cauchy mean value theorem write the first term on the left in (30) as

$$(p-c)\left[\frac{f(P)-f(p)}{F(P)-F(p)}\right] = (p-c)\frac{f'(\hat{p})}{f(\hat{p})} \quad (p < \hat{p} < P). \tag{31}$$

Then consider

$$\lim_{p\to\infty}\frac{(p-c)f'(\hat{p})/f(\hat{p})}{\hat{p}f'(\hat{p})/f(\hat{p})} = \lim_{p\to\infty}\left(\frac{p}{\hat{p}}-\frac{c}{\hat{p}}\right) = 1. \tag{32}$$

So the limits on the top and bottom on the left in (32) are identical, but by assumption (g) the limit in the bottom is $-\infty$ since the bottom is the elasticity of the individual demand function. We have then established that as $p \to \infty$, the numerator in (32), the left side of (31) and the left side of (30) go to $-\infty$. Then since the left side of (13) is continuous, and since it approaches a positive limit as $p \to 0$, and $-\infty$ as $p \to \infty$ there exists at least one positive finite p which satisfies (13), call it p^*. Now let all firms be placed L units apart charging price p^*. No firm will wish to move and no firm will wish to change its price. Thus the constant-numbers equilibrium condition is satisfied.

REFERENCES

Archibald, G. C. and Rosenbluth, G. (1975). "The "New" Theory of Consumer Demand and Monopolistic Competition." *Quarterly Journal of Economics*, vol. 89, no. 4, pp. 569–90.

Beckmann, M. (1968). *Location Theory*. New York: Random House.

—— (1971). "Equilibrium Versus Optimum: Spacing of Firms and Patterns of Market Areas." *Northeast Regional Science Review*, vol. 1, no. 1, pp. 1–20.

—— (1974). "A Theorem on Perfect Competition in Spatial Markets." *Regional Science Association Papers and Proceedings*, vol. 33, pp. 3–12.

Böventer, E. von (1969). "Walter Christaller's Central Places and Peripheral Areas: The Central Place Theory in Retrospect." *The Journal of Regional Science*, vol. 9, no. 1, pp. 117–24.

Chamberlin, J. (1933). *The Theory of Monopolistic Competition*. Cambridge: Harvard University Press.

Denike, K. G. and Parr, J. B. (1970). "Production in Space, Spatial Competition, and Restricted Entry." *Journal of Regional Science*, vol. 10, no. 1, pp. 49–63.

Demsetz, H. (1971). "On the Regulation of Industry: A Reply." *Journal of Political Economy*, vol. 79, pp. 356–63.

Eaton, B. C. (1976). "Free Entry in One-Dimensional Models: Pure Profits and Multiple Equilibria." *Journal of Regional Science*, vol. 16, no. 1, pp. 21–33.

—— and Lipsey, R. G. (1975). "The Principle of Minimum Differentiation Reconsidered: Some New Developments in the Theory of Spatial Competition." *Review of Economic Studies*, vol. 42 (1), no. 129, pp. 27–49.

—— (1976*a*). "The Non-Uniqueness of Equilibrium in the Löschian Location Model." *American Economic Review*, vol. 56.

—— (1976*b*). "Freedom of Entry and the Existence of Pure Profits." Queen's University Discussion Paper, no. 207. Kingston, Ontario.

—— (1976*c*). "The Theory of Spatial Pre-Emption: Location as a Barrier to Entry." Queens' University Discussion Paper, no. 208. Kingston, Ontario.

—— (1977). "The Introduction of Space into the Neo-Classical Model of Value Theory." In *Studies in Modern Economics* (ed. M. J. Artis and A. R. Nobay), pp. 59–96. Oxford: Basic Blackwell. (Also printed as Queen's University Discussion Paper, no. 239. Kingston, Ontario.)

Greenhut, M. (1952). "The Size and Shape of the Market Area of a Firm." *Southern Economic Journal*, vol. 17, no. 4, pp. 526–38.

Greenhut, M. L. (1975). "A Theoretical Mapping from Perfect Competition to Imperfect Competition." *Southern Economic Journal*, vol. 42, no. 2, pp. 177–92.

—— and Ohta, H. (1975). *The Theory of Spatial Pricing and Market Areas*. North Carolina: Duke University Press.

Johnston, J. (1960). *Statistical Cost Analysis*. New York: McGraw-Hill.

Kaldor, N. (1935). "Market Imperfections and Excess Capacity." *Economica*, vol. 2, pp. 35–50.

—— (1972). "The Irrelevance of Equilibrium Economics." ECONOMIC JOURNAL, vol. 82, no. 328, pp. 1237–55.

Koopmans, T. C. (1957). *Three Essays on the State of Economic Science*. Essay No. 1. New York: McGraw-Hill.

Lösch, A. (1954). *The Economics of Location*. New Haven: Yale University Press.

Mills, E., and Lav, M. (1964). "A Model of Market Areas with Free Entry." *Journal of Political Economy*, vol. 72, no. 3, pp. 278–88.

Ohta, H. (1976) ."On Efficiency of Production Under Conditions of Imperfect Competition." *Southern Economic Journal*, vol. 43, no. 2, pp. 1124–35.

Shaked, A. (1975). "Non Existence of Equilibrium for the 2-Dimensional 3-Firm Location Problem." *The Review of Economic Studies*, vol. 42, no. 129, pp. 51–6.

Schmalensee, R. (1977). "Entry Deterrence in the RTE Cereal Industry" Working Paper 961–77, Alfred P. Sloan, School of Management MIT, Cambridge, Mass.

Southey, C. (1974). "Spatial Rents, Spatial Competition and Efficiency." *Canadian Journal of Economics*, vol. 52, no. 2, pp. 260–72.

Starr, R. (1969). "Quasi-Equilibrium in Markets with Non-Convex Preferences." *Econometrica*, vol. 37, pp. 25–38.

Telser, L. (1969). "On the Regulation of Industry: A Note." *Journal of Political Economy*, vol. 77, pp. 937–52.

Tullock, G. (1965). "Optimality with Monopolistic Competition." *Western Economic Journal*, vol. 4, pp. 41–8.

Zeuthen, F. (1933). "Theoretical Remarks on Price Policy: Hotelling's Case with Variations." *Quarterly Journal of Economics*, vol. 49, pp. 231–53.

[3]

Economica **46**, 149–158

The Theory of Market Pre-emption: The Persistence of Excess Capacity and Monopoly in Growing Spatial Markets

By B. Curtis Eaton and Richard G. Lipsey

University of British Columbia and Queen's University

There is a substantial literature on the use of excess capacity as a means of preventing entry into monopolistic or oligopolistic markets. Some of the interest in this issue stems from the famous anti-trust judgment against the Aluminum Company of America (Alcoa) written by Judge Learned Hand:

> It was not inevitable that it [Alcoa] should always anticipate increases in demand for ingot and be prepared to supply them. Nothing compelled it to keep doubling and redoubling its capacity before others entered the field. It insists that it never excluded competitors, but we can think of no more effective exclusion than progressively to embrace each new opportunity as it opened, and to face each new comer with new capacity already geared into a giant organization . . . .[1]

Much of the subsequent debate among economists on the issue of excess capacity as a possible barrier to entry was in a static framework, and virtually all of it has been in the standard spaceless context.[2]

In the present paper we consider a spatial market in which demand is increasing. We demonstrate that, if the growth of the market is foreseen, it will *always* pay existing firms to pre-empt the market by establishing new plants before the time when it would first pay new firms to enter. In such markets, monopolies or oligopolies will persist; plants will be built well before their outputs are required and even when current receipts and costs yield losses. Such markets will exhibit the excess capacity that many investigators have thought they discerned;[3] and this excess capacity will occur as a result of the early building of new capacity to which Judge Hand referred.

We also show that, if the existing monopoly firm will not pre-empt—or is prevented from pre-empting—the market by building capacity before it is needed, competition among potential new entrants will lead to the establishment of the unneeded capacity at virtually the same time that it would have been established by the profit-maximizing monopolist.

I. A Model of Market Pre-emption

We begin by specifying assumptions with respect to the nature of the market, the cost conditions of firms and the behaviour of firms and customers. Next we construct a set of *initial* conditions which guarantee that an *existing* firm with one plant is in a position of natural monopoly. We then allow the number of customers to increase at some future date, and demonstrate two propositions:

(a) if the existing monopolist does not establish new capacity to meet the increased demand, competition among potential new entrants will lead to the establishment of new capacity some time *before* the date at which demand increases; and

(b) the existing monopolist will always find it profitable to pre-empt the market by establishing new capacity at a time just earlier than the earliest date at which any potential new entrant would find it profitable to do so.

The first proposition, which we call *pre-emption by new entrants*, ensures that there will be temporal excess capacity in this market—capacity that is installed before it is needed. The second proposition, which we call *monopoly pre-emption*, ensures that, unless the monopoly firm either misjudges the situation or is in some way restrained, it will always maintain its monopoly even though the market grows large enough to sustain many plants. In this section we confine ourselves to cases in which there are only a few firms in the market. In Section II we investigate behaviour when the number of firms in the market is large.

(a) *Assumptions*

We consider a one-dimensional market, two units in length, with a uniform density of customers, D. Each customer has the same downward-sloping demand curve, $q = f(w)$, where w is delivered price, the firm's mill price plus transport costs. Transport costs per unit of product, $t(Z)$, are an increasing function of distance, Z, from firm to customer. Each customer buys from the plant with the lowest delivered price.

All firms have the same cost curves. Their production exhibits increasing returns to scale over a limited range of output at the plant level owing to capital indivisibilities; and, hence, average total costs of production (ATC) decline over some initial range of output. Once the firm's capital is installed it has no opportunity cost and is immobile. (All that we require is that firms have some sunk costs but it is convenient to assume that all capital costs are sunk.)

Firms maximize profits and we assume that *firms are capable of accurately calculating the flows of costs and revenues that will be associated with any plant*; that is, we adopt the assumption of perfect foresight with respect to the flow of profits. (In Section (e) below we examine in some detail the role that this assumption plays in our model.)

We assume that no firm entertains the strategy of *mill-price undercutting*. That is, no firm will charge a mill price low enough so that its delivered price at a competitor's mill door is lower than the competitor's mill price. Elsewhere we have outlined in detail our reasons for adopting this assumption.[4]

(b) *Initial conditions*

Initially let firm A serve the entire market with a plant located in the centre of the market at a_1 in Figure 1. The aggregated demand curve faced by the plant will be

$$Q = 2D \int_0^1 f\{p_A + t(Z)\}\, dZ$$

where p_A is A's mill price. Since the market is symmetrical about the plant and the density of customers is D, we integrate from 0 to 1 and multiply by $2D$. There will be some density, $D = D_0$, such that the aggregated demand curve is just tangent to the ATC curve in the declining portion of that curve.

Now consider the situation that would face a plant owned by another firm, B, and located at an arbitrary point b_1 in the market segment from -1 to a_1 in Figure 1. The *no-mill-price-undercutting* assumption implies that B's market would be

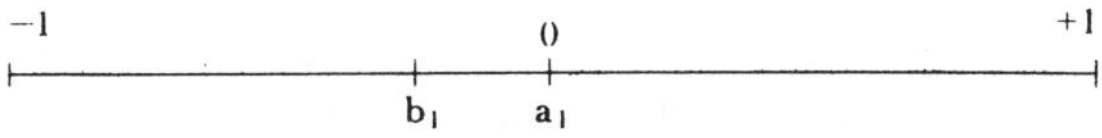

FIGURE 1

confined to some part of the interval from -1 to a_1. Thus the number of customers in B's market would be less than half the number of customers that would be in A's market in the absence of B's plant at b_1. From this it follows that the density of customers, D_2, that would allow the plant at b_1 just to cover its costs must be greater than D_0, the density that allows the single plant serving the whole market from its location at a_1 to cover its costs.

We adopt as an *initial condition* a density of customers, D_1, such that $D_0 < D_1 < D_2$, and we let firm A serve the market with a plant located at a_1. Firm A is thus earning pure profits, but given the initial density of customers, D_1, entry of other firms will not occur. We have thus specified our initial conditions so that firm A is in a position of profitable natural monopoly.

(c) *Market pre-emption*

We now consider entry when the market grows. We use comparative static analysis of a market that undergoes a single, once-for-all increase in density. It would of course be possible to consider a market that was growing continuously. While this would make it necessary to use more complicated analytical techniques than the ones we do employ, it seems to us that it would add very little to the results in which we are interested.

We assume that at some time in the future, T_2, density will increase discretely to $D_3 > D_2$. This increase in density is foreseen and, since $D_3 > D_2$, the increase is sufficient to ensure that a new firm (or firms), if given the opportunity at time T_2, would enter each of the intervals $(-1:0)$ and $(0:1)$ in Figure 1. For simplicity, we further assume that D_3 is not large enough to permit *two* new plants to be profitably operated in each of these intervals.

We ask, first: when will the two new plants be established *if firm A does nothing to pre-empt the market?* By hypothesis the new density, D_3, which occurs at T_2 is great enough so that one new plant in each interval could earn revenues in excess of costs after T_2, but neither plant could cover costs prior to T_2. Since the increase in density is foreseen, competition among potential new entrants will ensure that the opportunity to establish these plants at T_2 will not present itself. There exists some time $T_1 < T_2$ such that the present value of each of the two new plants will be zero. If at time T_1 the two new plants were established at their individual, profit-maximizing locations (say b_1 and b_2 in Figure 2), each plant would earn only a normal rate of return because the present value of profits earned after T_2 would be just offset by the losses incurred from T_1 to T_2. The existence of many would-be entrants will push the actual date of entry back in time to T_1.

This establishes the proposition concerning pre-emption by new entrants: if firm A does nothing to block entry, then some new entrant will pre-empt the

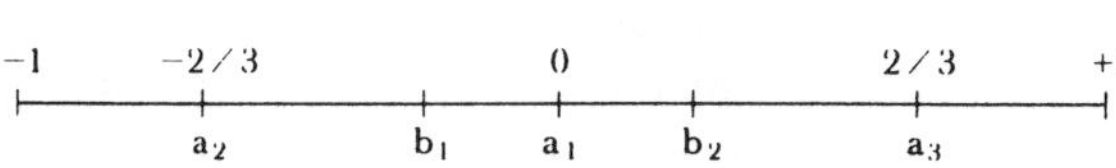

FIGURE 2

market by establishing plants at time T_1 in anticipation of the growth in density at T_2. Intertemporal excess capacity then arises in the sense that new capital is established in the market before the increase in density that justifies its existence.

The interval of time, $T_2 - T_1$, over which excess capacity exists is a function of the flow of profits that a new entrant into each half of the market could earn after T_2. This depends on customer density, which determines demand, and on costs. If ATC is declining or constant over the relevant range, then profits, and hence the size of $T_2 - T_1$, approach an upper limit as D_3 approaches D_4, where D_4 is the customer density that would allow two new plants in each of the intervals $(-1:0)$ and $(0:1)$ to cover costs.

It is useful for future arguments to define two terms:

(i) R_1 is the discounted present value at T_1 of A's plant at a_1 when new entrants establish two new plants at b_1 and b_2 at T_1.

(ii) R_2 is the discounted present value at T_1 of all three plants when A owns the plant at a_1 and new entrants establish two new plants at b_1 and b_2 at T_1.

We have of course chosen T_1 such that $R_2 = R_1$.

We ask, second: what will happen if firm A considers pre-empting the market for itself? It could, of course, effectively prevent the entry of any new firm by establishing a plant of its own in each of the intervals $(-1:0)$ and $(0:1)$ prior to time T_1. If A did this, there would be no entry of new firms at T_1. Is it in firm A's own interest to block entry in this manner, assuming that A foresees the potential for entry at T_1? Consider the consequences if A were to replicate the configuration of locations and prices that would be brought about by other firms entering the market. Just before T_1 let A establish plants at b_1 and b_2 and let A charge the prices that would emerge if new entrants owned the plants at b_1 and b_2. If there were no possibility of entry, the sales and profits that A's new plants at b_1 and b_2 take away from the old plant at a_1 could not be regarded as net additions to firm A's sales and profits. But if A does not pre-empt, new firms will enter at T_1, and firm A's stream of profits and sales from its plant at a_1 will fall abruptly at T_1. *Thus all of the sales and profits of A's new plants at* b_1 *and* b_2 *represent net additions to the stream of sales and profits that A could expect if it did not build these plants*. Since the plants add the same amount to A's profits as they would to those of a new entrant, the plants have the same value to A as to new entrants.

But A will not replicate the configuration of locations and prices that would be brought about by other firms entering the market. In the first place A will choose different locations for the new plants than would new entrants. Firm A will locate the new plants at $-2/3$ and $2/3$, points a_2 and a_3 in Figure 2, so that each plant will serve one-third of the market. This puts the three plants in their joint profit-maximizing locations. New entrants would not, however, adopt these locations; rather, they would locate plants nearer to a_1. The force that leads new entrants to locate nearer to a_1 than $-2/3$ and $2/3$ is the one analysed by Hotelling (1929) and Smithies (1941): the new entrants have no competitors to worry about on their outside flanks and they can gain customers by crowding in towards their competitor at a_1. In addition, firm A can charge the joint profit-maximizing price when it owns all three plants. Normally when there is more than one firm in the market we would expect price competition to result in prices for each plant that differed from the joint profit-maximizing prices.

We now need one further definition:

(iii) R_3 is the discounted present value at T_1 of the three plants when firm A chooses the joint profit-maximizing locations and prices.

Monopolistic pre-emption is now easily proven. The value to A of establishing two new plants in the market at T_1 is $R^A = R_3 - R_1$. The value to new entrants of the two plants (located at b_1 and b_2) is $R^B = R_2 - R_1 = 0$. Since $R_3 > R_2$ (for the two reasons stated above) it follows that $R^A > 0$. It will thus pay firm A to establish new plants just prior to T_1. This proves the monopoly pre-emption result. The value to A of monopoly pre-emption depends on the difference between the profitability of the market when three plants are owned by A and two of the plants are owned by new entrants.

(d) *Extensions of the argument*

The argument of the previous section is easily extended to interior segments of the linear market. Suppose that at T_0 firm A owns two adjacent plants and that at some time in the future, T_2, density will increase sufficiently to allow a new entrant to earn revenues in excess of costs in the market segment bounded by A's plants. There will exist a time $T_1 < T_2$ such that a new entrant would expect only a normal return on its investment and, if A does nothing, some new entrant will pre-empt the market at T_1. Monopoly pre-emption will, however, occur since the new plant will be worth more to A than to the new entrant. In this case A's advantage stems only from joint profit-maximizing prices. A enjoys no locational advantage since both A and a new entrant would locate their new plants at the midpoint of the interval between existing plants. The absence of a locational advantage for A is, however, an artefact of the one-dimensional market. In a two-dimensional spatial market an independent firm entering a hexagonal or a rectangular lattice of firms would not choose the joint profit-maximizing location (see Eaton and Lipsey, 1976b). If one firm owned all adjacent plants in the lattice it would, of course, choose the joint profit-maximizing location. Thus in two-dimensional space A again has both a locational and a price advantage over new competitors in interior market segments.

The analysis is also easily extended to a market that grows in length, holding the density of customers constant. Beginning with the initial conditions in Section (b) let the length of market increase at time T_2 sufficiently to allow a new entrant to earn revenues in excess of costs. If A does nothing, some new entrant will pre-empt the market at some time $T_1 < T_2$, but since A will choose the joint profit-maximizing prices and locations while new entrants will not do so (for reasons similar to those in Section (c)), A itself will establish the new plants just before T_1.

(e) *The role of expectations*

Expectations play a critical role in a model such as ours and there is, of course, some expectations assumption that will yield virtually any conceivable result. We wish to confine our expectations assumptions to the class that may be called *consistent expectations*: those expectations that are consistent with realizations. It seems to us that this is a desirable property to require of expectations in our model since it avoids outcomes that are caused by a mistaken view of market conditions and market processes.

In our model we have employed the strongest form of consistent expectations, *perfect* foresight. Our two basic results on competitive and monopoly pre-emption will hold, however, with weaker forms of consistent expectations. We consider below two cases of imperfect foresight.

First, firms may be uncertain of the outcome of the competitive process and hence of the equilibrium prices that will emerge should new firms enter the market. If the entrant's equilibrium price is a random variable with a distribution that is known to all firms, and if all firms are risk-neutral, then our argument goes through as before. We merely replace the perfectly foreseen values of revenues and profits with expected values. The gap between T_1 and T_2 will be unchanged whenever the expected value of the profits is identical to the perfectly foreseen value. When the existing monopoly firm A values the market at T_1 on the assumption that A pre-empts it, A has no uncertainty since A can set any prices it wishes. Hence A's valuation is unaffected by the uncertainty over the outcome of the competitive process. Thus neither the time at which pre-emption by new entrants would occur nor the incentive for monopoly pre-emption is affected by this uncertainty.

Second, assume that T_2, the time at which demand will increase, is a random variable with a known distribution. New entrants again perform the appropriate expected-value calculations, and again there will exist a $T_1 < \bar{T}_2$ such that the present value of expected profits is zero, where $\bar{T}_2$ is the mathematical expectation of the time of market growth.

The monopolist's problem is, however, slightly more complex than when T_2 was certain. As long as the realization of T_2 is later than T_1 then his pre-emptive strategy of building new capacity just before T_1 works as before. But if there is an "unlucky" realization that yields $T_2 < T_1$, then at T_2 there will be a scramble to establish capacity to meet the *existing* extra demand. The monopolist may then lose its monopoly position. To reduce the probability of this happening the monopolist may pre-empt the market by building new capacity discretely before T_1. This strategy will not, of course, eliminate the possibility that the market will actually grow before the monopolist pre-empts, and our pre-emption results must be cast in probabilistic terms when there exists uncertainty with respect to growth in the market.

The above examples show that, although perfect foresight is sufficient, it is not necessary for our results. All that we require is consistent expectations: that firms correctly apprehend the nature of any uncertainties that they face.

II. Comparisons with Spaceless Models

The pre-emption arguments developed above obviously apply, with modification, to spaceless natural monopoly, the situation in which the minimum efficient scale of production is large relative to market demand. When there is an anticipated increase in demand at some future time, (a) competition among potential entrants will ensure that if the monopolist does nothing entry will occur before the increase in demand occurs, while (b) if the monopoly firm anticipates entry, it will be led to pre-empt the market by establishing the new capacity at a time just earlier than the earliest time at which it would be profitable for a new entrant to do so. In the spaceless case the monopolist's incentive to pre-empt the market arises only from the ability to avoid price competition. One important difference between the two models then is that in a spatial model the monopolist has an added incentive to pre-empt the market since he can increase the total profit that can be extracted from the market; he does this by choosing joint profit-maximizing locations as well as prices.

The really important differences between the two models emerge when initially the number of customers is large enough so that there are many plants in the market. In spaceless models the potential for profits owing to a range of increasing returns to scale is quickly dissipated as the number of plants serving the market increases. That is, the problem of natural monopoly in spaceless models arises only where the ratio of minimum efficient scale to market demand is large. In spatial models the problem of natural monopoly is undiminished when the market is served by a large number of plants. Since the potential for profit remains in spatial models and vanishes in spaceless models as the market grows, the incentive for new entrants or existing firms to pre-empt the market via premature entry remains in spatial models and vanishes in spaceless models. It is after all the possibility of earning profits after an anticipated market growth occurs that leads firms to create capacity before the growth occurs. These arguments are elaborated below.

The propositions we wish to argue are the following. The interval $T_2 - T_1$ falls rapidly to zero as the number of plants initially serving the market is increased in the spaceless model, but does not fall at all as the number of plants initially serving the market is increased in a spatial model.

We first turn to the spaceless model and, for concreteness, consider a limit pricing strategy. Let the market demand arise from the aggregation of demands of identical individuals. As the number of individuals over which we aggregate increases, the absolute value of the slope of the market demand curve at any price decreases towards zero. As this occurs the limit price converges to the minimum cost of production, and the pure rate of return on capital goes to zero.

Now let the number of customers be large enough so that the divergence of the market price, the limit price, from the minimum cost of production is arbitrarily small. Take this as an initial condition and assume that, at some future point in time, T_2, the number of customers will grow enough so that one new entrant could earn pure profits while two would earn losses. The pure profits earned by a single new entrant will be arbitrarily small since the divergence of current price from costs of production is arbitrarily small. Since the profits anticipated subsequent to T_2 are arbitrarily small, the time T_1 comes arbitrarily close to T_2. It follows then that, as the number of customers in the spaceless model increases, T_1 goes to T_2 and excess capacity owing to pre-emption by new entrants disappears. It also follows that the monopolist's incentive to pre-empt vanishes as the market grows. The key to this asymptotic result is that the potential in static equilibrium for pure profit, which is due to barriers to entry arising solely from decreasing unit costs over an initial range of output, vanishes as the market grows through an increase in the number of customers.[5]

Now consider a spatial model. As we have shown elsewhere (Eaton and Lipsey, 1978), the potential for pure profit in free-entry equilibrium in a spatial market does not diminish as the number of customers, and hence the number of plants, is increased. We give here a very brief summary of this argument.

Consider a segment of a linear spatial market with a large number of plants spread out over the market equidistant from each other. If a firm enters a slot between any two existing plants, it will serve, at any common price, half the number of customers as are served by existing plants before its entry. If we assume for simplicity that profits are proportional to customers served, then each existing plant would need to be earning a rate of return on capital of at least $2i$ before a new firm would enter and expect a return of i (where i is the minimum rate of return on capital that will induce entry). Given a uniform increase in density over the whole market, if entry is profitable in one interval between two existing plants, it will be profitable in every interval. Thus plants per unit of space will tend to double on each successive 'round of entry' as density increases. After each round of entry, however, the disadvantage of any new entrant compared with existing firms remains the same: expected customers of the former are only half those of the latter before entry. Thus the rate of profits that can be earned by existing plants without inducing entry does not diminish as density increases.[6]

Now adopt a high initial customer density with a monopolist owning plants spread evenly throughout the market and all charging the joint profit-maximizing price, and let the monopolist have enough plants so that entry is unprofitable. Then let an increase in density at some future time, T_2, be foreseen, the increase being the maximum that would support one but not two new plants in each segment between two existing plants. Since the rate of profit that will be foreseen on a new unit of capacity at T_2 does not diminish as initial customer density is increased, it follows that $T_2 - T_1$, the interval over which competitive pre-emption would create excess capacity, will also not diminish as initial density is increased. It further follows that the incentive for an existing monopolist to pre-empt the market does not diminish as customer density is increased.

III. Summary and Conclusion

The underlying cause of the results in this paper is that large positive pure profits can persist in free-entry equilibrium in spatial models. This result, stated in Eaton and Lipsey (1978), arises because any potential new entrant can expect a demand of the order of only half that enjoyed by existing firms before entry. Thus if an anticipated future increase in demand makes it profitable to install new plants, those plants may earn (depending on the initial density of customers and plants and the amount of the increase in demand) up to twice the competitive rate of return. Competition among potential entrants for the opportunity to earn the pure profits occasioned by the increase in demand will push new entry backwards in time until the present value of the flow of all future profits is zero. In such markets the capacity will be installed well before it is needed. Because the monopolist can extract more profits from the market by locating in a joint profit-maximizing location and charging joint profit-maximizing prices, it will always pay the monopolist to pre-empt the market by installing new capacity just earlier than the earliest point in time that it would be profitable for a new entrant to do so.[7]

We have analysed only the case in which an existing monopolist pre-empts the market by building new plants and operating them at a price less than ATC until market demand increases. Other forms of spatial pre-emption are obviously possible. The firm might build the plant and leave it idle (this would make sense if marginal costs were greater than the current profit-maximizing price). The firm could announce its plans to build in the market and then find its plans subject to a series of "unexpected" delays. Provided that new entrants believed that the existing firm's plans were serious, new entry might be deterred at low cost. If only a few sites were available (a situation not allowed for in our present model) the monopolist could buy them up and put them to other uses and then use one for its new plant when the market did expand.

What public policies could prevent the excess capacity from emerging? The case is similar to a common property problem: premature entry occurs because there exists no property right to establish new capacity in the market, so that the only effective means for establishing such a right is premature entry. The State could, of course, establish property rights by auctioning off the rights to establish new capacity in various segments of a growing market. This would prevent premature entry and would allow the State to appropriate the pure profits available in the market. In order to prevent the monopolist from buying the right and then simply not exercising it, the right, if not acted upon by some specified date, would revert to the State.

Finally, we might wonder if we have proven too much. We have shown that it will always pay an existing firm to blockade entry by locating new plants in an expanding market at a time before it will pay a new firm to enter. We know, however, that new firms do sometimes enter expanding markets. How is this? Our proof employed the assumption of perfect foresight. There are many ways in which imperfect foresight can cause entry of new firms. If either the market grows unexpectedly, or the change comes to be expected only at a time at which new entry is already profitable, the market is "up for grabs" and a scramble may ensue between new entrants and existing firms. It is also possible that either existing or new firms may make mistakes. On the one hand, if the market is very large, local knowledge of one part of it may give a potential new entrant foresight that is superior to that of the distant head office(s) of the existing multi-plant firm(s). On the other hand, new firms may enter the market on false expectations. Once built, the plants will be operated by someone as long as variable costs can be covered. This leads to the general conclusion that, the more stable and easily predictable is market growth, the more will the expanding market be served by new branches of existing firms, while the more erratic and unpredictable is market growth, the greater the possibility of new firms entering to serve part of the expanding market.

Our model is not designed to explain what number of multi-plant firms inhabit a market. Should the market come to be served by more than one firm for whatever reasons, including those sketched above, these firms will, individually and jointly, have the incentive and the ability to block further entry into the market by building new branch plants at a time when it will not pay new entrants to do so.

ACKNOWLEDGMENTS

This paper is a revised version of Eaton and Lipsey (1976c). The research for it was done while the authors were Visiting Professors at the University of Colorado at Boulder during 1974–1975. We acknowledge the generous support of the Killam Foundation for Professor Lipsey and the Canada Council for Professor Eaton. For a general survey of our work in spatial economics see Eaton and Lipsey (1976a).

NOTES

[1] U.S. *vs.* Aluminum Company of America *et al.*, 44F. Supp. 97(1941) 148F, 2d 416(1945), p. 431.

[2] See, e.g., Pashigian (1968), Needham (1971), and Wenders (1971).

[3] See, e.g., Esposito and Esposito (1974).

[4] The argument is detailed in Eaton and Lipsey (1978). It focuses on the fact that existing firms have sunk costs while all costs of potential new entrants are avoidable. Thus the lowest price that

will allow an existing firm to cover avoidable costs is lower than the lowest price that will allow a potential new entrant to cover avoidable costs. It then follows that a new entrant would be forced to charge a price lower than its avoidable cost if it wished to undercut the existing firm's mill price. This is clearly not profitable since all the new entrant's costs are avoidable.

[5] Another way of seeing this result is to note that, as the demand curve gets flatter, the fall in price needed to sell the output of one more indivisible unit of capital operated at its least-cost output gets smaller and smaller. Thus the excess of price over costs that can occur when N plants sell their optimal outputs without allowing an $N + 1$th plant to cover its costs diminishes to zero. Hence the rate of pure profit that can be earned by existing units of capacity in free-entry equilibrium also diminishes to zero in a spaceless model.

[6] The intuitive argument in the text is based on the simplifying assumption that the firm's revenues are proportional to the number of customers. Actually in this model a new entrant will expect to have the same number of customers but more than half the revenues as are enjoyed by an existing firm before entry given any common price. Although the new entrant has only half the customers, it is closer to them and thus will have a lower delivered price over its market than would the original firm for any common mill price. Thus for every common price the ratio of *sales of a new plant to sales of an existing plant before entry* is more than half. Interestingly enough, however, as density of customers and hence density of plants is increased this price effect diminishes, since the distance to a firm's market boundary diminishes. Thus the difference between a firm's mill price and the delivered price at its market boundary diminishes as well. For this reason, as density increases, the ratio defined above *diminishes* towards one-half. This means that the profits that can be earned by existing plants without inducing entry *increases*. Thus in a spatial model the maximum possible duration of the interval $T_2 - T_1$ *increases* as density increases—the opposite result to the one in a spaceless economy (see Eaton and Lipsey, 1978, expecially Section VI).

[7] See Schmalensee (1977) for an interesting case to which the analysis of our paper seems to apply.

REFERENCES

EATON, B. C., and LIPSEY, R. G. (1976a). The introduction of space into the neoclassical model of value theory. In *Studies in Modern Economics* (M. J. Artis and A. R. Nobay, eds.). Oxford: Basil Blackwell.

—— (1976b). The non-uniqueness of equilibrium in the Löschian location model. *American Economic Review*, **66,** 77–93.

—— (1976c). The theory of market pre-emption: location as a barrier to entry. Queen's University Discussion Paper No. 208.

—— (1978). Freedom of entry and the existence of pure profit. *Economic Journal*, **88,** 455–469.

ESPOSITO, FRANCES FERGUSON and ESPOSITO, LOUIS (1974). Excess capacity and market structure. *Review of Economics and Statistics*, **56,** 188–194.

HAND, LEARNED (1941). U.S. *vs.* Aluminum Company of America *et al.*, 44 F. Supp. 97(1941), 148 F. 2d 416(1945).

HOTELLING, H. (1929). Stability in competition. *Economic Journal*, **29,** 41–57.

KALDOR, N. (1935). Market imperfections and excess capacity. *Economica*, **2,** 35–50.

MODIGLIANI, F. (1958). New developments on the oligopoly front. *Journal of Political Economy*, **66,** 215–232.

NEEDHAM, D. (1971). *Economic Analysis and Industrial Structure.* New York: Holt, Rinehart & Winston.

PASHIGIAN, B. P. (1968). Limit price and the market share of the leading firm. *Journal of Industrial Economics*, **16,** 165–177.

SCHMALENSEE, RICHARD (1977). Entry deterrence in the RTE cereal industry. Working Paper 961–77, Alfred P. Sloan School of Management, M.I.T., Cambridge, Mass.

SMITHIES, A. (1941). Optimum location in spatial competition. *Journal of Political Economy*, **49,** 423–439.

WENDERS, JOHN T. (1971). Excess capacity as a barrier to entry. *Journal of Industrial Economics*, **20,** 14–19.

[4]

Reprinted from The Bell Journal of Economics
Vol. 11, No. 2, Autumn 1980

Exit barriers are entry barriers: the durability of capital as a barrier to entry

B. Curtis Eaton*

and

Richard G. Lipsey**

We argue that the effectiveness of capital as an entry barrier depends critically on its durability and that this aspect of capital has been largely ignored. We examine strategic decisions with respect to capital durability in two models. In a broad range of cases an active policy with respect to durability and replacement of capital is necessary to maintain a position of market power. Such policies will result in capital that is "too durable" or "too soon replaced" or "too well maintained" relative to the cost minimizing solution (for a given time path of output).

1. Introduction

■ In his seminal essay on bargaining, Thomas Schelling (1956) distinguishes threats and commitments. Both are designed to influence a competitor by impressing him with the consequences of his actions. Both take the same form: "If you take action X, I shall take action Y, which will make you regret X." The distinguishing characteristic of a threat is that the actor has no incentive to carry out action Y either before or after action X. The distinguishing characteristic of a commitment is that, X having occurred, it is in the actor's self-interest to take action Y. A fanatic may carry out a threat, and may thus make "credible threats." A maximizer would not carry out his threats and thus cannot make his threats credible. There would seem, therefore, to be little place for threats in maximizing models.

In this paper we examine the use of product-specific capital goods as vehicles for entry-deterring *commitments*. It may seem surprising that there is anything left to say on this subject in view of such works as Caves and Porter (1977), Dixit (1979, 1980), Eaton and Lipsey (1978, 1979), Schmalensee (1978), and Spence (1977, 1979). These papers deal, however, with what may be called the atemporal aspect of capital as a barrier to entry: a monopolist strategically commits a quantity of capital which is sufficient to produce a negative *flow* of profits to a new entrant. This may be called a *type-A artificial monopoly* (*A*

* University of British Columbia and Yale University.
** Queen's University and Yale University.
This is a shortened version of Eaton and Lipsey (1980), in which proofs may be found of results asserted in the present article. We are indebted to G. C. Archibald, Y. Kanemoto, and J. Roemer for comments and suggestions.

for "atemporal"). *Type-A natural monopoly* occurs when nonstrategic profit-maximizing behavior commits enough capital to produce a negative flow of profits to an entrant. Capital indivisibilities and decreasing costs are at the heart of this analysis. One firm can profitably serve such a market but two cannot.

The point of this paper is that it is not indivisibilities and decreasing costs *per se* which create barriers to entry. Rather, it is the intertemporal commitment of specific capital to a market, in combination with decreasing costs which creates an entry barrier. We thus focus on the durability of capital in the creation of entry barriers. We define a *type-T natural monopoly* (*T* for "temporal") to be one in which *cost minimizing* decisions with respect to durability, replacement, and maintenance of capital imply that there is no point in time at which entry is profitable, and a *type-T artificial monopoly* to be one in which *strategic decisions* with respect to capital prevent there being any point in time at which entry is profitable.

To see the potential importance of durability as an entry barrier, first consider two extreme cases under static demand and cost conditions. At one extreme is a type-*A* natural monopolist who has no sunk costs. (This would arise, for example, if capital were not product-specific and could be bought, sold, and rented on perfect markets.) Although only one firm can serve this market profitably, there exists no vehicle for commitment to the market. With no sunk costs the market is "up for grabs" at each instant. The absence of capital fixity and associated fixed costs thus seems to imply chaos. At the other extreme, the durability of capital (plant) is exogenous and infinite. Now a type-*A* natural monopolist has a permanent commitment to the market: as long as he can cover his avoidable costs he will remain in the market. As a result, he need never consider the possibility of the entry of new firms.

Second, consider the intermediate case in which a type-*A* natural monopolist's plant has an exogenous and finite durability, $0 < H < \infty$. When unconcerned about entry, the monopolist replaces his plant every H years. But a potential new entrant could establish plant just as the monopolist was about to renew his plant. The market would then belong to the new entrant. But foreseeing that strategy, the existing monopolist would renew his plant a little sooner. But foreseeing this, a potential new entrant would establish his plant sooner yet, and so on. In this case it is clear that the type-*A* natural monopolist must concern himself with the threat of entry; he is not a type-*T* natural monopolist.

In this article we study the strategic use of capital to create a type-*T* artificial monopoly. It is useful in analytical studies to separate strategic decisions with respect to the creation of the two types of monopoly. To isolate the creation of type-*A* artificial monopoly, it is convenient to assume type-*T* *natural* monopoly by letting the durability of capital be infinite (Spence, 1979; Dixit, 1980). Similarly, to isolate the creation of type-*T* artificial monopoly, it is convenient in this article to assume a type-*A* *natural* monopoly. (Our results extend in a fairly obvious way to a firm that has erected entry barriers to create a type-*A* artificial monopoly as well as to oligopolists who wish to maintain their place in the market.)

Our analysis shows that the textbook, type-*A* natural monopoly is not necessarily a type-*T* natural monopoly and that it is impossible for the monopolist to separate cost-minimizing decisions from profit-maximizing ones.

This results because capital produces a revenue to the firm by acting both as a factor of production and as a barrier to entry.

2. Model 1: one-hoss shay capital

■ The basic assumptions of model 1 are as follows. There is an indivisible, product-specific capital good, called plant, which is large enough that a monopolist would require only one unit of it. There are constant returns to the variable factor up to plant capacity.

If there were two firms in the market, each with one unit of plant, their common capacity and common short-run marginal costs would imply a symmetric resolution of the duopoly problem. The symmetric resolution might be Cournot-Nash, or it might be based on some conjectural-variation formulation. Indeed any symmetric resolution will allow us to define what we require: R_1 *is the rate of flow of revenues over variable costs when one firm serves the market;* R_2 *is the rate of flow of revenues over variable costs for either firm when two firms serve the market*. We assume that R_1 and R_2 are time invariant, that firms know them with certainty, and that $R_1 > 2R_2 > 0$. These inequalities imply that the resolution of the duopoly pricing problem is not joint profit maximizing and that duopolists cover variable costs.

In model 1 plant of durability H costs $C(H)$ and requires no maintenance. We assume that

$$\lim_{H\to 0} C(H) > 0, \qquad C'(H) > 0, \qquad \text{and} \qquad C''(H) \geq 0 \text{ for } H > \hat{H}. \tag{1}$$

These restrictions guarantee that H will always be chosen to be positive and finite. The deterioration of this "one-hoss shay" capital depends on its age and is independent of intensity of use. Since R_2 is positive, a firm which has plant is committed (in Schelling's sense of the word) to stay in the market until its plant expires.

If a monopolist replaced plant of durability H every $H - \Delta$ periods, its minimum commitment to the market would be Δ. The discounted present value of this policy to a monopolist would be

$$V(\Delta,H) = \frac{R_1}{r} - \frac{C(H)}{1 - \exp[-r(H - \Delta)]} . \tag{2}$$

It is, of course, Δ that is the deterrent to entry and, given Δ, H will be chosen to maximize profits. Define

$$\tilde{V}(\Delta) = \frac{R_1}{r} - \frac{C(h(\Delta))}{1 - \exp[-r(h(\Delta) - \Delta)]} , \tag{3}$$

where $h(\Delta)$ is the profit-maximizing (or cost-minimizing) value of H, given Δ. It can be shown that $h'(\Delta) > 0$. Let $\check{H} = h(0)$. Type-*A* natural monopoly requires that

$$\tilde{V}(0) = \frac{R_1}{r} - \frac{C(\check{H})}{1 - \exp[-r\check{H}]} > 0 > \frac{R_1}{2r} - \frac{C(\check{H})}{1 - \exp[-r\check{H}]} . \tag{4}$$

The first inequality implies that one firm could more than cover costs and the second implies that two could not.

We assume that entry will occur if and only if the discounted present value of an entrant's profits is greater than zero, and thus we adopt the following definitions. An entry-preventing policy (EPP) is a policy such that the discounted present value of an entrant's profits is always less than or equal to zero. An optimal, entry-preventing policy (OEPP) is an EPP that maximizes the monopolist's present value evaluated at any point in time when he is replacing his plant.

To provide an intuitive explanation of the problem we *assume* that an OEPP exists, denoted by Δ^*, and that potential entrants consider only this policy. Subsequently we show directly the existence of an OEPP with $0 < \Delta^* < h(\Delta^*)/2$. The present value of an entrant's pursuing policy Δ^* is

$$E(\delta,\Delta^*) = -C(h(\Delta^*)) + R_2 \int_0^{\delta} \exp[-rt]dt + R_1 \int_{\delta}^{h(\Delta^*)-\Delta^*} \exp[-rt]dt + V(\Delta^*) \exp[-r(h(\Delta^*) - \Delta^*)],$$

where δ is the length of time until the sitting monopolist's plant expires. To interpret this expression let the origin in time be the time of entry. The entrant's initial plant would cost $C(h(\Delta^*))$ and he would earn R_2 from time 0 to δ. Since Δ^* is, by assumption, an EPP, the sitting monopolist would not renew plant and entry would be deterred at all future times. Thus the entrant would earn R_1 from δ to $h(\Delta^*) - \Delta^*$ at which time he would renew his plant and his present value would be $V(\Delta^*)$. $E(\delta,\Delta^*)$ can be rewritten as

$$E(\delta,\Delta^*) = \bar{V}(\Delta^*) - (R_1 - R_2) \int_0^{\delta} \exp[-rt]dt. \quad (5)$$

The second term is the new entrant's "price of admission": the difference between profits when the market is served by two firms rather than one firm for the length of time until the sitting monopolist exits. This is also, of course, the measure of the barrier to entry at any point in time. Let Δ be the sitting monopolist's policy. Then

$$E(\Delta,\Delta^*) = \max_{\delta} E(\delta,\Delta^*) = \bar{V}(\Delta^*) - (R_1 - R_2) \int_0^{\Delta} \exp[-rt]dt, \quad (6)$$

which is the maximum present value of an entrant.

Thus the monopolist's problem is

$$\left.\begin{array}{l} \max_{\Delta} \bar{V}(\Delta) \\ \text{subject to} \quad E(\Delta,\Delta^*) \leq 0. \end{array}\right\} \quad (7)$$

Both $\bar{V}(\Delta)$ and $E(\Delta,\Delta^*)$ are decreasing in Δ, and thus the maximization problem posed in (7) is solved by finding $\bar{\Delta}$ such that $E(\bar{\Delta},\Delta^*) = 0$. But Δ^* is an OEPP by assumption and thus $\bar{\Delta} = \Delta^*$. So, if it exists, Δ^* must satisfy $E(\Delta^*,\Delta^*) = 0$. $E(0,0) = \bar{V}(0)$, which is positive by the first inequality in (4). $E(\Delta,\Delta)$ is decreasing in Δ and goes to $-\infty$ as Δ goes to ∞. Thus, there exists a unique $\Delta^* > 0$ such that $E(\Delta^*,\Delta^*) = 0$. It can be shown that the second inequality in (4) implies that $\Delta^* < h(\Delta^*)/2$. Intuitively, if Δ^* were greater than $h(\Delta^*)/2$, costs of plant would exceed the costs of having two units of plant in the market at all times, which could not be profitable, given our definition of natural monopoly.

At the outset we assumed existence of Δ^*, and thus the argument above is only an intuitive argument. We can however use the result that Δ^* is the unique value of Δ such that $E(\Delta,\Delta)$ is equal to zero to show directly that Δ^* is the unique OEPP. Note first that $E(\Delta_m,\Delta_e)$ is the maximum present value of an entrant with policy Δ_e, if Δ_e is an EPP, when the sitting monopolist's policy is Δ_m. Note that the first derivatives of E with respect to Δ_m and Δ_e are negative. We use a proof by contradiction to demonstrate that Δ^* is the unique OEPP.

Proof: (i) Assume $\Delta_1 < \Delta^*$ is an EPP and that the sitting monopolist's policy is Δ_1. Then, since Δ_1 is an EPP, $E(\Delta_1,\Delta_1) \leq 0$, otherwise an entrant adopting policy Δ_1 would not be deterred. But we have shown that for $\Delta_1 < \Delta^*, E(\Delta_1,\Delta_1) > 0$, which contradicts our assumption that Δ_1 is an EPP. Thus $\Delta_1 < \Delta^*$ is not an EPP. (ii) Now assume that Δ^* is not an EPP and that the sitting monopolist's policy is Δ^*. Since Δ^* is not an EPP, there exists an EPP, Δ_2, such that $E(\Delta^*,\Delta_2) > 0$. But since $E(\Delta^*,\Delta^*) = 0$ and E is decreasing in its second argument, $\Delta_2 < \Delta^*$. But, by the argument in (i), $\Delta_2 < \Delta^*$ cannot be an EPP, a contradiction. Thus Δ^* is an EPP.[1] (iii) The argument in (ii) implies that any policy, $\Delta > \Delta^*$, is an EPP. But since $\bar{V}(\Delta)$ is decreasing in Δ, Δ^* is the unique OEPP. *Q.E.D.*

For completeness we must show that the monopolist prefers the OEPP to the policy of "graceful exit": allowing entry to occur and then exiting when his plant expires. In the absence of entry prevention, entry would occur $\Delta^* - \epsilon$ periods before the sitting monopolist's plant expired, where ϵ is arbitrarily small. As ϵ goes to zero, the present value of graceful exit approaches

$$G(\Delta^*) = R_2 \int_0^{\Delta^*} \exp[-rt]dt > 0. \tag{8}$$

Note that

$$\bar{V}(\Delta^*) - E(\Delta^*,\Delta^*) = (R_1 - R_2) \int_0^{\Delta^*} \exp[-rt]dt.$$

But since $E(\Delta^*,\Delta^*) = 0$, we have

$$\bar{V}(\Delta^*) = (R_1 - R_2) \int_0^{\Delta^*} \exp[-rt]dt, \tag{9}$$

and since $R_1 > 2R_2$, we have $V(\Delta^*) > G(\Delta^*) > 0$.

We have shown in model 1 that an active policy of entry prevention is necessary—that type-*A* natural monopoly does not imply type-*T* natural monopoly—and that this strategy is profitable. Protecting this monopoly position involves the dissipation of monopoly rents and is wasteful of scarce resources, since the monopolist replaces plant before it is economically obsolete. The dissipation of monopoly rents through early replacement of capital and the resulting resource waste will be smaller the stronger is duopoly price competition, and the smaller are the monopoly profits (*ceteris paribus* the smaller is

---

[1] This argument assumes that the entrant considers only entry-preventing policies. We show in Eaton and Lipsey (1980), footnote 2, that nonentry-preventing strategies are never profitable.

R_2 or R_1). Regulation that reduces monopoly profits may thus reduce the social waste analyzed in this paper.

Since $\Delta^* > 0$ and $h'(\Delta) > 0$, it follows that $h(\Delta^*) > \bar{H}$. In other words, the strategy of entry deterrence leads the monopolist to choose plant which is more durable than the cost-minimizing durability. This result does not reflect an additional burden since, given Δ^*, durability is chosen to minimize costs.

3. Model 2: maintaining plant

■ In model 2 we assume that plant costs K, $K > 0$, and that maintenance costs, m, are a convex function of age of plant, a:

$$m = g(a), \qquad g'(a) > 0, \qquad g''(a) \geq 0. \tag{10}$$

Notice that we have three categories of costs in this model: sunk costs of plant; costs of maintaining plant which are avoidable only by not producing and which are invariant with respect to output; and the constant marginal costs of production. Define $C(S)$ to be the discounted present cost of a new plant over a service life of S periods. Then

$$C(S) = K + \int_0^S g(a)\exp[-ra]da. \tag{11}$$

The restrictions on $g(a)$ imply that $C'(S) > 0$ and $C''(S) > 0$.

$C(S)$ satisfies the restrictions on the cost function in model 1, and it follows immediately that the monopolist could create a minimum commitment to the market, Δ, by replacing plant, *with a prepaid maintenance contract of S periods*, every $S - \Delta$ periods. By analogy with model 1 there exists a Δ^* which maximizes profits, subject to entry's being unprofitable. Further, it is easily demonstrated that the optimal service life associated with Δ^* is less than the cost-minimizing service life, so that plant is replaced before its economic life is over.

Our purpose in model 2 is to explore another entry-preventing strategy when plant is maintainable. Accordingly, define S to be the policy of replacing plant every S periods. The present value to a monopolist of this policy is

$$V(S) = \frac{R_1}{r} - \frac{C(S)}{1 - \exp[-rS]}. \tag{12}$$

$V(S)$ is pseudoconcave in S, decreases without bound as S goes to zero and as S goes to infinity, and therefore has a unique maximum.[2] Let $\bar{S}$ be the value of S which maximizes $V(S)$.

We wish to argue that, in the event of entry, the sitting monopolist would stay in the market until his maintenance costs rose to R_2. We argue as follows: if $g(a)$ were less than R_2, and if the monopolist paid $g(a)$, then he and the entrant would face identical avoidable costs, the resolution of the duopoly problem would be symmetric, and the monopolist would enjoy the flow R_2; therefore, the monopolist will incur the maintenance costs if and only if $g(a) \leq R_2$. Alternatively, in the event of entry the monopolist could sign a binding maintenance contract with a third party, and his avoidable costs would then be just

[2] Pseudoconcavity of $V(S)$ requires that when $V'(S) = 0$, $V''(S) < 0$, which is easily verified. See Diewert, Avriel, and Zang (1977) for a useful taxonomy of concavity.

the marginal costs of production. An optimal maintenance contract would run until $g(a) = R_2$.

Let A be the age of plant such that $g(A) = R_2$. Then if the monopolist chooses a policy $S \leq A$, his minimum commitment to the market is $A - S$. If he chooses $S > A$, his minimum commitment to the market is zero.

Then we seek the existence of a policy S^* which solves

$$\left.\begin{array}{ll} & \max_S V(S) \\ \text{subject to} & E(S,S^*) \leq 0, \end{array}\right\} \quad (13)$$

where

$$E(S,S^*) = \begin{cases} V(S^*) - (R_1 - R_2)\displaystyle\int_0^{A-S} \exp[-rt]dt, & \text{if} \quad S \leq A, \\ V(S^*), & \text{if} \quad S > A. \end{cases} \quad (14)$$

$E(S,S^*)$ is interpreted as the present value of an entrant's pursuing policy S^* when the monopolist's policy is S.

Several cases require attention. First, suppose the monopolist adopts policy $\bar{S}$. It is clear from (14) that if A is large enough relative to $\bar{S}$, the monopolist need not pursue an active policy of entry prevention. Let $\bar{A}$ be the value of A in (14) such that $E(\bar{S},\bar{S}) = 0$. Then, if $A \geq \bar{A}$, $S^* = \bar{S}$, and entry prevention is costless. This is a case of type-T natural monopoly.

Denote by S_1 and S_2 the minimum and maximum values of S such that $V(S) = 0$. Pseudoconcavity of $V(S)$ then implies that $V(S) > 0$ in the open interval (S_1,S_2) and $V(S) < 0$ for $S < S_1$ and for $S > S_2$. When $A \leq S_1$, the constraint in (13) cannot be satisfied in the profitable range of production. Thus $S^* = S_1$ and $S^* = S_2$ are the only solutions to the problem posed in (13) and $V(S^*) = 0$. In this case it is clear that the use of a prepaid maintenance contract to deter entry is the preferred strategy.

Finally, consider the case when $S_1 < A < \bar{A}$. $E(S_1,S_1) < 0$, since $S_1 < A$, and $E(\bar{S},\bar{S}) > 0$, since $A < \bar{A}$. Both $V(S)$ and $E(S,S^*)$ are increasing in S when $S_1 < S < \bar{S}$, and thus S^* must satisfy $E(S^*,S^*) = 0$. Since $E(S,S)$ is increasing in S in this interval, there exists a unique S^*, $S_1 < S^* < \bar{S}$ such that $E(S^*,S^*) = 0$. An argument parallel to that in model 1 shows that S^* is the unique OEPP. Since $S^* < \bar{S}$, plant is replaced before its economically useful life is over.

We have shown that when plant is maintainable, there exist circumstances where entry deterrence is costless, the case of type-T natural monopoly. When an active policy of entry deterrence is necessary, the monopolist has two options, both of which require the replacement of plant before its economically useful life is over. Since a potential entrant has the same options, the monopolist must choose the more profitable option.

4. Conclusions

■ Our analysis suggests a need for revision of the concept of natural monopoly. A fully insulated natural monopoly must have both type-A and type-T natural monopoly. If it has only the former, it may be able to use specific capital to create a type-T artificial monopoly.

Profit maximization does not imply cost minimization in our models. Thus, when one is considering the creation of artificial barriers to entry, taking minimized costs as a primitive can be misleading. Product-specific capital is a natural vehicle for commitment, and firms who so use it will violate cost minimization.

It may be useful to consider the argument that a successful entry-preventing strategy must be based on commitment, not threat, in the context of the creation of a type-T monopoly. To make an entry-deterring threat in model 1, the sitting monopolist must threaten that in the event of entry, he will stay in the market *long enough* that the entrant's present value at time of entry will be nonpositive. "Long enough" is Δ^* periods. If the sitting monopolist's plant has at least Δ^* periods of remaining economic life, then the threat is a commitment, because the sitting monopolist's plant can more than cover its variable costs. If his plant has less than Δ^* periods of remaining economic life, the threat is not a commitment: fulfilling it would require building new plant at a time when it promises a negative present value. Δ^* can be interpreted as the monopolist's minimum commitment to the market or as the minimum *barrier to his exit*. It is in this sense that barriers to exit are barriers to entry.

The intuitive appeal of our results suggests to us that they will survive generalization of our assumptions with respect to capital. Two obvious possibilities are capital that decays exponentially or capital that decays only with use. Specific capital is a natural vehicle for commitment to the market, and commitment is valuable to the firm, since it inhibits entry. Accordingly a profit-maximizing firm will choose the specifications of specific capital (its durability and/or time of replacement and/or level of maintenance, etc.), so that marginal cost is equal to a positive marginal value in inhibiting entry. This choice will often result in specific capital that is "too durable" or "too soon replaced" or "too well maintained" relative to the unconstrained cost-minimizing solution.

The entry-deterring strategies that we have analyzed would be relatively easy to detect in a world of static demand and technology. They would, however, be much harder to detect in the real world of changing demand and technology. The entry-preventing firm may then appear as the "alert" firm, establishing capacity to meet growing demand, and as the "progressive" firm, investing early in new technologies.

Application to policy is clearly premature. The purpose of this article is to reveal a gap in our present theories of natural and artificial monopoly. To do this we use stark concepts of capital. At a minimum, analysis of more "realistic" assumptions with respect to capital and corroborating empirical work are necessary before the social waste that occurs in our models can be held to be likely and/or significant. In this context it is important to note that although waste of capital always occurs in model 1, it may be unnecessary in model 2.[3]

References

CAVES, R.E. AND PORTER, M.E. "Barriers to Exit" in R.T. Masson and P.D. Qualls, eds., *Essays on Industrial Organization in Honor of Joe S. Bain*, Cambridge: Ballinger, 1976.

——— AND ———. "From Entry Barriers to Mobility Barriers: Conjectural Decisions and Contrived Deterrence to New Competition." *Quarterly Journal of Economics* (May 1977), pp. 241–261.

[3] Since writing this paper, our attention has been drawn to Caves and Porter (1976), in which the issues discussed in this paper are foreshadowed. See especially their pages 44–45.

DIEWERT, W.E., AVRIEL, M., AND ZANG, I. "Nine Kinds of Quasi Concavity and Concavity." Discussion Paper 77-31, University of British Columbia, 1977.

DIXIT, A. "A Model of Duopoly Suggesting a Theory of Entry Barriers." *Bell Journal of Economics* (Spring 1979), pp. 20–32.

———. "The Role of Investment in Entry Deterrence." *Economic Journal* (March 1980), pp. 95–106.

EATON, B.C. AND LIPSEY, R.G. "The Theory of Market Preemption: The Persistence of Excess Capacity and Monopoly in Growing Spatial Markets." *Economica* (May 1977).

——— AND ———. "Freedom of Entry and the Existence of Pure Profit." *Economic Journal* (September 1978), pp. 455–469.

——— AND ———. "Exit Barriers Are Entry Barriers." University of British Columbia Discussion Paper No. 80-3, February 1980.

SCHELLING, T.C. "An Essay on Bargaining." *American Economic Review* (June 1956), pp. 281–306.

SCHMALENSEE, R. "Entry Deterrence in the Ready-to-Eat Breakfast Cereal Industry." *Bell Journal of Economics* (Autumn 1978), pp. 305–327.

SPENCE, A.M. "Entry, Capacity, Investment, and Oligopolistic Pricing." *Bell Journal of Economics* (Autumn 1977), pp. 534–544.

———. "Investment Strategy and Growth in a New Market." *Bell Journal of Economics* (Spring 1979), pp. 1–19.

[5]

Reprinted from The Bell Journal of Economics
Vol. 12, No. 2, Autumn 1981

Capital, commitment, and entry equilibrium

B. Curtis Eaton*

and

Richard G. Lipsey**

A primary concern of recent oligopoly literature has been the use of product-specific capital to impose asymmetric market solutions, including the deterrence of entry. This article explores the surprisingly neglected topic of the correspondence between the nature of product-specific capital (PSC) and the properties of entry equilibrium. The nature of PSC determines the type of entry with which firms must be concerned (predatory entry, where the entrant replaces an existing firm, or augmenting entry, where the entrant does not), the instruments available to effect asymmetry, the ability to impose asymmetric solutions, and their profitability.

1. Introduction

■ A recent focus of research on entry barriers has been on sunk capital as a vehicle by which existing firms can make entry-barring commitments (Caves and Porter, 1976, 1977; Dixit, 1979, 1980; Eaton and Lipsey, 1979, 1980; Spence, 1977, 1979). In this article we briefly review two of the models from this literature and add another. Our purpose is to explore the relationship between the nature of capital and entry equilibrium.

The value of entry is the discounted present value of the flow of profits expected by an entrant. Since entry will occur when this value is positive, an established firm that seeks to deter entry must pursue a course of action that makes the value of entry nonpositive. As the problem is usually formulated, the course of action is to promise to produce a postentry stream of output large enough to have the desired effect on the value of entry.

The equilibrium concepts in Dixit (1980) and in Eaton and Lipsey (1980) rely on Schelling's (1956) distinction between threats and commitments. Both take the same form: "If you take action X, I shall take action Y, which will make you regret X." The distinguishing characteristic of a threat is that the actor has no incentive to carry out action Y, while the distinguishing characteristic of a commitment is that, X having occurred, it is in the actor's self-interest to take action Y. We rely on commitment in our equilibrium concept. Entry

* University of Toronto.

** Queen's University.

The work on this article was done while the authors held visiting appointments at Yale University. We acknowledge the helpful comments of Drew Fudenberg and Andrew Mueller on an earlier draft.

deterrence then requires that the established firm unambiguously *commit* itself to a course of action which will deter entry.

The essence of commitment in our model is the ability to create irreversibilities, to "tie one's own hands" in Schelling's words. If capital is to be used as a vehicle for commitment, it is then clear that the capital must be *product-specific* in some degree; otherwise, past expenditures on capital are recoverable, and incurring such expenditures does not "tie one's own hands." We use PSC to denote "product-specific capital." In this article we focus on product-specific plant, equipment, and entry capital. We define the degree of product specificity by the index $1 - R$, where R is the ratio of *value of existing capital in its best alternative use to replacement cost of existing capital*. In the formal analysis we assume for convenience that R is zero. The range of items included in PSC could be expanded to include informational advertising, brand image advertising, firm-specific human capital, and any other items that represent nonrecoverable costs to existing firms, but avoidable costs to new entrants. Our definition of an index of specificity would, however, require amendment in some of these cases (e.g., brand-image advertising).

Given the sunk capital of the existing firm or firms, it is apparent that a model of duopoly, or oligopoly, is required to determine the value of entry. This basic insight, which turns Bain's fundamental insight around, can be found in Dixit (1980) and in Eaton and Lipsey (1979). Bain observed that *we cannot meaningfully analyze oligopoly problems without explicit attention to the possibility of entry*. Dixit (1980) and Eaton and Lipsey (1979) observe that as long as we insist on commitment and not threat, *we cannot analyze entry deterrence without an underlying model of oligopoly*. Thus, there is a correspondence between models of oligopoly and entry equilibrium.

Although the existing literature emphasizes PSC as the vehicle by which a flow of capital services, and hence of output, can be committed to the market by existing firms, surprisingly little attention has been paid to the nature of the PSC that does the job. Two important aspects of PSC are its durability and its divisibility. The title of this article, "Capital, Commitment, and Entry Equilibrium," reflects our basic purpose, which is to explore the correspondence between the nature of capital and entry equilibrium when the equilibrium concept is based on commitment. We demonstrate that the properties of entry equilibrium vary dramatically as the durability and divisibility of PSC change, and that definition cannot be given to the concept of entry equilibrium in the absence of knowledge of the nature of PSC.[1]

2. Variations on a theme

■ **Assumptions of convenience.** For simplicity, we assume that the market is not large enough to support three firms, and that demand and cost conditions are time-invariant and known with certainty. We then examine the behavior

[1] Our first attempt to deal with the correspondence between the nature of capital and entry equilibrium can be found in Eaton and Lipsey (1977), where we consider the problem in a model of spatial competition. In a recent paper, Schmalensee (1980) argues that capital cannot be a significant barrier to entry where the ratio of minimum efficient scale to market demand is small. In models of spatial competition and in some models of product differentiation, the location of firms serves to segment the market. Each firm is then in localized competition with a small number of other firms, and capital acts as a significant barrier to entry even when there is a large number of firms in the whole market.

of an established firm, referred to as ONE, to determine the circumstances in which it is possible and profitable to deter entry of a second firm, referred to as TWO.

We capture decreasing unit costs by assuming that there is a fixed cost of entry associated with *entry capital*, which is product-specific. Production involves the services of a completely product-specific capital good, *production capital*, and a composite input. We assume a fixed-proportions technology involving the services of production capital and the composite input. We choose the unit of production capital so that one unit is required to produce a unit of output. With these assumptions, average total costs of production for any output $x \leq k$ can be written as

$$C = f + wx + rk, \tag{1}$$

where k is quantity of production capital or the firm's capacity, r is the cost of the flow of services of a unit of production capital, w is the cost of the variable input per unit of output, and f is the flow of fixed costs associated with entry capital.

Entry barriers may arise in the natural course of events or they may be the result of conscious strategies. To clarify this distinction, we define *nonstrategic behavior* to be behavior unconstrained by the threat of entry, and *strategic behavior* to be behavior with entry deterrence as its objective. Correspondingly, we define a *natural monopoly* to be one in which the monopolist makes nonstrategic decisions and the value of entry is nonpositive and an *artificial monopoly* to be one in which the monopolist makes strategic decisions so as to make the value of entry nonpositive at all points in time (and where it would be positive, given nonstrategic decisions). We turn now to an examination of entry equilibrium in circumstances which are distinguished by assumptions with respect to the divisibility and durability of capital.

□ **Immortal capital.** Assume that production capital is infinitely durable and perfectly divisible. Assume that entry capital is infinitely durable and completely indivisible. By completely indivisible, we mean that the services of a second unit of this capital are never required for any of the outputs considered by any of the firms in our model. Assume that the underlying duopoly model is the Cournot model and that firms foresee the Cournot quantity-setting equilibrium. By making strategic decisions with respect to production capital, ONE can alter its reaction function and hence the duopoly solution. This yields a simplified version of Dixit's (1980) model. In Figure 1 the line $M'M$ is ONE's "full-cost reaction function"—the reaction function when *avoidable* incremental unit costs are $w + r$. The line $N'N$ is ONE's "variable-cost reaction function"—the reaction function when *avoidable* incremental unit costs are w.

ONE's actual reaction function is dependent on k_1, ONE's capacity. First suppose that $k_1 \leq M$. ONE's reaction function is $N'N$ for $x_1 < k_1$, $M'M$ for $M \geq x_1 > k_1$, the horizontal axis for $x_1 > M$, and the vertical line from $M'M$ to $N'N$ for $x_1 = k_1$. Second, suppose $k_1 > M$. ONE's reaction function is $N'N$ for $x_1 < k_1$, the horizontal axis for $x_1 > k_1$, and the vertical line from $N'N$ to the horizontal axis for $x_1 = k_1$. The line RR' in Figure 1 is TWO's full-cost reaction function. This is the only reaction function we need to consider for TWO, since all its costs are avoidable.

FIGURE 1

ENTRY DETERRENCE WITH IMMORTAL CAPITAL

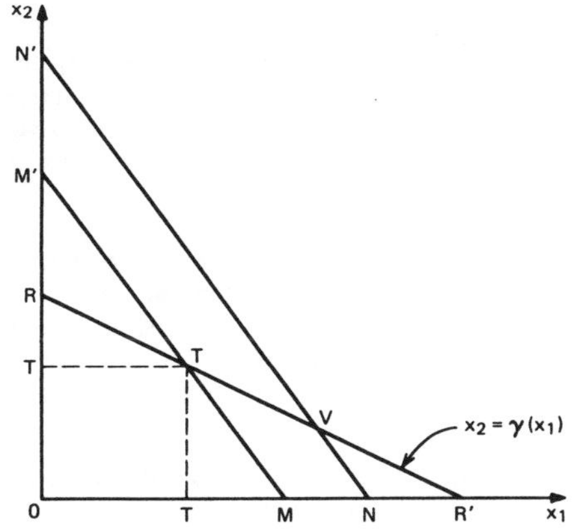

Suppose TWO incurs the fixed cost of entry. The resolution of the duopoly problem then depends on ONE's capacity, k_1. Denote equilibrium values by a hat, TWO's reaction function by $\gamma(x_1)$, the coordinates of point V in Figure 1 by (V_1, V_2), and the coordinates of point T by (T, T) (since the point T is on the line $x_2 = x_1$). Then

$$\hat{x}_1 = \min (k_1, V_1), \quad (2a)$$

$$\hat{x}_2 = \gamma(\hat{x}_1). \quad (2b)$$

Now define $\pi(x_i, x_j)$ $(i = 1, 2; j = 2, 1)$ to be the ith firm's flow of revenue net of variable costs. Assume that $\pi(x_i, x_j)$ is concave. Define $\bar{\pi}(x_i, x_j)$ $(i = 1, 2; j = 2, 1)$ to be

$$\bar{\pi}(x_i, x_j) = \pi(x_i, x_j) - rx_i. \quad (3)$$

Concavity of $\pi(x_i, x_j)$ implies that $\bar{\pi}(x_i, x_j)$ is also concave.

Let $B = (B_1, B_2)$ be the point on RR' such that $\bar{\pi}(B_2, B_1) - f = 0$. B_1 is thus ONE's "limit quantity." Define S to be the value of x_1 which maximizes $\bar{\pi}(x_1, \gamma(x_1))$. S is then ONE's output at the von Stackelberg solution. Define $\bar{S} = \min (S, V_1)$. We can now examine ONE's profit-maximizing behavior.

Case (i): $B_1 > V_1$. ONE cannot create an artificial monopoly. Suppose $k_1 = B_1$. TWO will realize that, should he enter, the duopoly solution would be at V, which promises him positive profits. Thus, $k_1 > V_1$ does not create a commitment to produce $x_1 > V_1$ after entry. Given that he cannot deter entry, ONE will choose $k_1^* = \bar{S}$ and TWO will enter, producing $x_2^* = \gamma(\bar{S})$.

Case (ii): $M < B_1 \leq V_1$. ONE can create an artificial monopoly by setting $k_1 = B_1$. TWO will realize that the duopoly solution would be at B, which promises TWO nonpositive profits. Entry deterrence may not be preferred, however, since ONE's net worth as an artificial monopolist may be less than his net worth in the best duopoly solution ($x_1 = \bar{S}, x_2 = \gamma(\bar{S})$). If ONE does choose to deter entry by setting $k_1^* = B_1$, ONE's output will also be B_1, and ONE will not hold excess capacity.

Case (iii): $B_1 \leq M$. The limit output is less than the monopoly output, and ONE has a natural monopoly.

The influence of the discount rate on the ability to prevent entry is of interest. As the discount rate falls, the limit output, B_1, increases since the opportunity cost of entry and production capital is diminished. The diminished cost of production capital also shifts TWO's full-cost reaction function, RR', upward. As a result, V, decreases. For interest rates below the level such that $B_1 = V_1$, entry deterrence is impossible.

☐ **Radioactive capital.** In this subsection, we amend the model by assuming that production capital decays with time at some continuous rate, z, which is subject to choice. The model of the preceding subsection is then the special case of the radioactive model when $z = 0$. Let $\alpha(z)$ be the cost of producing one unit of capital with rate of decay z. We assume that $\alpha(z)$ is twice continuously differentiable and that

$$\alpha'(z) < 0, \qquad \alpha''(z) \geq 0, \qquad \lim_{z \to 0} \alpha(z) = \infty, \qquad \lim_{z \to \infty} \alpha(z) > 0. \tag{4}$$

Let $\beta(z, i)$ be the present discounted cost to the firm of *maintaining* one unit of capital forever, where i is the appropriate discount rate. Then

$$\beta(z, i) = \alpha(z) + \frac{z\alpha(z)}{i}. \tag{5}$$

The second term on the right is the present discounted cost of the stream of replacement expenditures. The restrictions in (4) on the limits of $\alpha(z)$ ensure that z will always be chosen to be positive and finite. The cost-minimizing value of z, $\hat{z}$, will then satisfy $\beta_1(\hat{z}, i) = 0$ and $\beta_{11}(\hat{z}, i) \geq 0$. For convenience, we assume that $\beta_{11}(z, i) > 0$ for all $z > 0$. Then $\hat{z}$ is unique. Define r to be the cost of the flow of services of a unit of capital,

$$r = i\beta(z, i). \tag{6}$$

The minimum value of r, $\hat{r}$, is $i\beta(\hat{z}, i)$. Average total costs are given by equation (1) above, where r is now defined by (6).

ONE's optimal entry-deterring problem is to choose a time path of committed production-capital services to maximize net worth, subject to the constraint that TWO's value of entry be nonpositive at all points in time. Since revenues and costs are time invariant, the problem reduces to choosing a capital stock, k_1, and a rate of decay, z_1, that will be maintained forever. ONE's monopoly net worth can be written as

$$\phi(k_1, z_1) = \int_0^\infty \pi(x_1^*, 0)e^{-it}dt - k_1\beta(z_1, i) - F,$$

where $x_1^* = \min(k_1, N)$ is the profit-maximizing value of x_1, given k_1, and F is the cost of the entry capital. Evaluating the integral,

$$\phi(k_1, z_1) = \frac{\pi(x_1^*, 0)}{i} - k_1\beta(z_1, i) - F. \tag{7}$$

In Figure 2 QQ' is the locus of values of k_1 which maximize ϕ, given z_1. On this locus the iso-net-worth contours are horizontal. The slope of QQ' is

FIGURE 2

ENTRY DETERRENCE WITH RADIOACTIVE CAPITAL

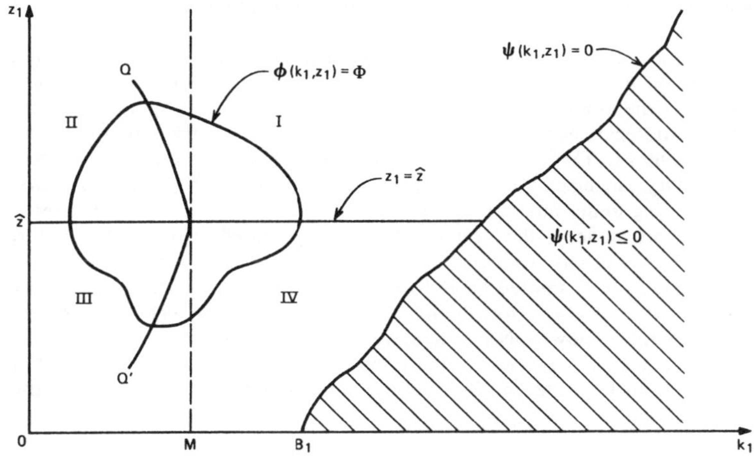

positive for $z_1 < \hat{z}$ and negative for $z_1 > \hat{z}$, since r increases with $|z_1 - \hat{z}|$. The locus of values of z_1 which maximize ϕ, given k_1, is the horizontal line $z_1 = \hat{z}$, and on this locus the iso-net-worth contours are vertical. The two lines intersect at the unconstrained maximum of ϕ: at $z_1 = \hat{z}$ and $k_1 = M$. Differentiating ϕ, we have

$$\left.\frac{dz_1}{dk_1}\right|_{\phi(k_1,z_1)=\bar{\Phi}} = \frac{\partial x_1^*/\partial k_1 \pi_1(x_1^*, 0)/i - \beta(z_1, i)}{k_1\beta_1(z_1, i)}. \tag{8}$$

At points to the right (left) of QQ', the numerator in (8) is negative (positive). At points below (above) the line $z_1 = \hat{z}$, the denominator in (8) is negative (positive). Thus, in quadrants II and IV of Figure 2, the iso-net-worth contours are positively sloped, and in I and III they are negatively sloped. ϕ is concave when $z_1 > \hat{z}$, but when $z_1 < \hat{z}$, it is not necessarily so. Thus the iso-net-worth contours in quadrants III and IV are not necessarily convex.

To evaluate TWO's value of entry and hence write the constraint for the entry-deterring problem, we must determine the resolution of the duopoly problem through time. If TWO considers entering at some point in time, $t = 0$ for convenience, when ONE's stock of production capital is k_1, ONE's *minimum* commitment of capital services at time $t > 0$ is $k_1e^{-z_1t}$, and TWO must foresee this minimum commitment. ONE might commit more—particularly if he engaged in strategic investment decisions after TWO entered—but he cannot commit less. We assume that after TWO enters, both ONE's and TWO's short-run output and long-run investment decisions are determined in Cournot fashion and are foreseen—i.e., we rule out postentry strategic behavior. Then we have

$$x_1^t = \min\,[V_1, \max\,(k_1e^{-z_1t}, T)], \tag{9a}$$

$$x_2^t = \gamma(x_1^t), \tag{9b}$$

where γ is TWO's *minimized* full-cost reaction function. This process of adjustment will follow some portion of line segment VT in Figure 1. If $k_1 > V_1$, it will trace out the entire segment, and the duopoly will remain at V for a positive period of time.

This is not the only possible assumption either about behavior after entry or about the final equilibrium, but this one has a number of desirable features. First, it is the assumption that is most conducive to TWO's entry, since any rational strategic behavior on ONE's part after TWO's entry must reduce the value of entry to TWO. Second, it follows from the first point that any strategy that is entry barring on these assumptions about postentry behavior is *a fortiori* entry barring under alternative assumptions. Third, since the only barrier to entry in this model is the capital ONE has committed to the market before TWO's entry, this is the case that isolates exactly what we wish to study: the effect of precommitted capital as a barrier to entry. If we were to allow postentry strategic behavior, the long-run duopoly solution which is least conducive to entry allows ONE to achieve the von Stackelberg solution. In this case the adjustment process would trace out the segment of TWO's reaction function from V to the von Stackelberg point (provided, of course, that this lies to the left of V).

Now define

$$\hat{\pi}(x_i, x_j) = \pi(x_i, x_j) - \hat{r}x_i. \tag{10}$$

Then the value of entry is

$$\psi(k_1, z_1) = \int_0^{t_1} \hat{\pi}(x_2^t, x_1^t)e^{-it}dt + \frac{\hat{\pi}(T, T)}{i}e^{-it_1} - F, \tag{11}$$

where t_1 satisfies

$$k_1 e^{-z_1 t_1} = T. \tag{12}$$

When $k_1 > T$, $\psi_1(k_1, z_1) < 0$ and $\psi_2(k_1, z_1) > 0$. Redefine B_1 to be the value of x_1 such that

$$\hat{\pi}(\gamma(B_1), B_1) - f = 0. \tag{13}$$

When $B_1 < V_1$, the entry constraint, $\psi(k_1, z_1) = 0$, is positively sloped and intersects the k_1-axis at $k_1 = B_1$. In addition, the value of k_1 on the constraint goes to infinity as z_1 goes to infinity, since for any given value of k_1, sunk capital services at any point in time go to zero as z_1 approaches infinity. In Figure 2, we illustrate the constraint for the case when $M < B_1 < V_1$. For future reference, denote by $\bar{k}_1$ and $\bar{z}_1$ the values (if any) which solve the optimal entry-deterring problem: maximize $\phi(k_1, z_1)$ subject to $\psi(k_1, z_1) \leq 0$.

In the event that TWO does enter, ONE will allow its capital to decay to the amount T and will then begin replacing it. ONE's net worth is then

$$\theta(k_1, z_1) = \int_0^{t_1} \pi(x_1^t, x_2^t)e^{-it}dt - k_1\alpha(z_1) + \frac{\pi(T, T)}{i}e^{-it_1} - \alpha(\hat{z}) \int_{t_1}^{\infty} [z_1 k_1^t + \hat{z}(T - k_1^t)]e^{-it}dt. \tag{14}$$

The last term, which represents the present discounted cost of capital replacement after the duopoly has converged to T, requires explanation. ONE will then choose the cost-minimizing rate of decay, $\hat{z}$, and the unit cost of replacement capital will be $\alpha(\hat{z})$. At any instant the firm will hold k_1^t units of its original capital stock which decays at rate z_1, and it will hold $(T - k_1^t)$ units of capital which decays at rate $\hat{z}$. Denote by $\check{k}_1$ and $\check{z}_1$ the values which maximize $\theta(k_1, z_1)$. It can be shown that $\check{k}_1 > \tilde{S}$ and $\check{z}_1 < \hat{z}$.

We now outline the possible solutions to ONE's profit-maximizing problem. We use k_1^* and z_1^* to denote ONE's profit-maximizing choices.

Case (i): $B_1 > V_1$. Entry deterrence is impossible since TWO could earn positive profit at V, and $k_1^* = \check{k}_1$, $z_1^* = \check{z}_1$. The long-run duopoly solution is the symmetric Cournot solution at T, but the duopoly does not immediately go to T. Rather ONE pursues what might be thought of as a dynamic von Stackelberg strategy. Recall that $\check{k}_1 > \tilde{S}$ and $\check{z}_1 < \hat{z}$. Thus on TWO's entry the instantaneous duopoly solution is asymmetric, but as ONE's capital decays, the duopoly converges to the symmetric solution.

Case (ii): $M < B_1 < V_1$. In this case, illustrated in Figure 3, there are three notable features of the optimal entry deterring strategy. First, $\bar{k}_1 > B_1$, so that the optimal entry-deterring capacity always exceeds what would be the optimal entry-deterring capacity if capital were immortal. Second, $\bar{k}_1$ may exceed N, in which case ONE would hold excess capacity as a barrier to entry. Third, $\bar{z}_1 < \hat{z}$ and ONE's capital is more durable than the cost-minimizing durability. ONE may or may not choose to deter entry in case (ii), since $\phi(\bar{k}_1, \bar{z}_1)$ may or may not exceed $\theta(\check{k}_1, \check{z}_1)$.

Case (iii): $T < B_1 \leq M$. Two possibilities require attention. First, if $\hat{z}$ is sufficiently small, the point $(M, \hat{z})$ will lie below $\psi(k_1, z_1) = 0$, and we have a case of natural monopoly: $k_1^* = M$, $z_1^* = \hat{z}$. When production capital is immortal we necessarily have natural monopoly when $B_1 \leq M$. Second, if $\hat{z}$ is large enough, strategic behavior is required to deter entry. Again $\bar{z}_1 < \hat{z}$ and $\bar{k}_1$ may exceed N, so that excess capacity is a possibility. (Curiously, we have not been able to show that $\bar{k}_1$ is necessarily larger than M.) Again ONE may or may not find strategic entry deterrence preferable to the dynamic von Stackelberg duopoly strategy.

Case (iv): $B_1 \leq T$. This is another case of natural monopoly: $k_1^* = M$, $z_1^* = \hat{z}$.

When strategic entry deterrence is the preferred strategy, the artificial monopolist will *always* choose capital that is more durable than the cost-minimizing durability, and he may or may not hold excess capacity as a barrier to entry. When the dynamic von Stackelberg strategy is preferred, the first firm in the market will choose to make its initial capital stock more durable than the cost-minimizing durability, but all capital subsequently devoted to the market by either firm will have the cost-minimizing durability.

In model 2 the interest rate influences the ability to prevent entry. A decline in the interest rate moves B_1 right and V left, just as in model 1, but it also raises the present value of the distant profits proportionately more than it raises the present value of the early losses. This also makes entry more attractive and diminishes the scope for entry prevention.

□ **One-hoss-shay capital.** Assume that there are no product-specific production inputs and hence that there is no production capital. Assume also that the indivisible entry capital now has a finite life of H years. (Alternatively, we

FIGURE 3

EXCESSIVE DURABILITY AND ENTRY DETERRENCE

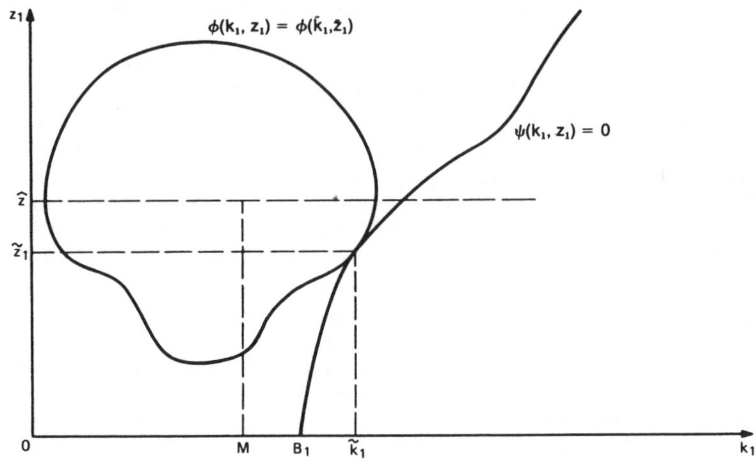

could assume that there is no entry capital and that production capital is completely indivisible with a finite lifetime of H years.) We then have a special case of Eaton and Lipsey (1980) which we summarize briefly below.

In this model ONE cannot (by the definition of an indivisible unit of capital) increase the flow of output it is committed to produce after TWO's entry by precommitting itself to a second unit of indivisible capital. Thus, if a duopoly is profitable, there is no strategic investment decision ONE can make to bar TWO's entry.

This kind of entry, which has been our sole concern up to this point, may be called *augmenting entry*—entry by TWO in the expectation of creating a duopoly. Now consider ONE's situation if the market is not large enough to support a profitable duopoly. With one-hoss-shay capital, ONE must now worry about what may be called *predatory entry*—entry by TWO in the expectation of replacing ONE as the sitting monopolist. This possibility arises because as the age of ONE's capital approaches H, the time over which ONE has capital committed to the market (*ONE's temporal commitment to the market*) approaches zero. If ONE behaves nonstrategically, planning to replace its capital after H periods, TWO could enter the market just before ONE's capital reached age H. ONE would then find himself in the position of a potential new entrant, and replacement of his capital would no longer be profitable.

ONE can affect the value of TWO's entry by replacing his capital h periods before it wears out, thus maintaining a minimum temporal commitment to the market of h periods. If TWO now enters the market with the intention of replacing ONE, TWO must suffer losses for at least h periods until ONE exits. ONE's optimal entry-barring strategy is to maximize his profits, subject to choosing h such that TWO's value of entry is never positive. In Eaton and Lipsey (1980) we show that whenever the market will not support two firms, the optimal predatory entry-barring strategy always exists and is always profitable for ONE. Such a strategy clearly involves deadweight loss, since capital is replaced before it is physically worn out.

A decrease in the rate of interest decreases costs, thereby increasing potential monopoly profits. This forces the artificial monopolist to increase h. However, as the interest rate continues to decrease, the duopoly solution will eventually offer positive profit and augmenting entry will occur. (Notice, however, that the duopolists will need to guard against predatory entry.)

3. Conclusions

■ The importance of the nature of PSC in determining entry barriers is best seen by comparing the results of the three models considered in this article. In the first, featuring immortal capital, the divisibility of production capital implies that ONE has an instrument to affect the value of TWO's entry. The infinite durability of PSC implies that ONE need only worry about augmenting entry, and that the entry-deterring problem is reducible to a static problem. To deter entry, ONE chooses a quantity of production capital (which is committed forever) so that the *flow* of profits to a new entrant is nonpositive.

We considered three possible entry equilibria: the artificial monopoly equilibrium where $k_1^* = x_1^* = B_1$; the natural monopoly equilibrium where $k_1^* = M$; and the duopoly equilibrium where $k_1^* = x_1^* = \hat{S}$. We know that at any instant, holding excess capacity ($k_1^* > N$) cannot create a commitment to use that capacity in that instant should entry occur; and since capital does not decay, excess capacity is not an entry barrier. This is Dixit's no-excess-capacity result. This implies that the artificial monopoly equilibrium (where it is possible) is socially preferred to franchise monopoly; since $k_1^* = x_1^* > M$, entry deterrence involves a transfer of some monopoly rent from the monopolist to his customers and a net increase in social rent relative to the franchise monopoly. The artificial monopoly equilibrium may or may not be socially preferable to the duopoly solution, since in the duopoly solution two units of entry capital are devoted to the market, while output need not be larger than in the monopoly solution—and where it is, the extra output may or may not be enough to compensate for the extra capital devoted to the market.

In the second model, featuring radioactive production capital, the infinite durability of entry capital again dictates that ONE need not be concerned about predatory entry, and the divisibility of production capital again implies that ONE has an instrument to affect the value of augmenting entry. However, the radioactive nature of capital implies that ONE's profit-maximizing problem can no longer be reduced to a static exercise. Whenever augmenting entry is a concern in this model, the profits in the long-run duopoly solution at T are positive. Thus ONE's entry-deterring problem is to create losses during the early stages of the adjustment process which exceed the present value of the profits earned during the later stages of the adjustment, and in the long-run equilibrium. If the duopoly solution is preferred, it converges to the symmetric Cournot solution in our model. However, the established firm still finds it profitable to impose asymmetric initial conditions and thus an asymmetric process of convergence. This process can be thought of as a dynamic von Stackelberg process. Again three equilibria are possible: a natural monopoly equilibrium with $k_1^* = x_1^* = M$; an artificial monopoly equilibrium with $x_1^* \leq k_1^*$; and the duopoly equilibrium at T.

With radioactive capital, it is apparent that artificial monopoly may or may not be preferred to franchise monopoly. Artificial monopoly involves an output which ordinarily exceeds the franchise monopoly output, and this tends to reduce the standard monopoly distortion. However, it also involves the deadweight loss associated with production capital that is excessively durable, and it may involve excess capacity as well. As in Dixit's model, holding excess capacity at any instant cannot create a commitment to use that capacity in that instant should entry occur. It does, however, increase the time at which ONE's output will remain at V_1 after TWO's entry, because it increases the time taken for ONE's capacity to decay to V_1. Excess capacity is thus a barrier to entry when capital is less than infinitely durable. It is also apparent that *artificial* monopoly may or may not be socially preferable to duopoly, since duopoly again involves an extra unit of entry capital.

The third model features indivisible, one-hoss-shay capital, which may be interpreted as either entry or production capital. The absence of divisibility implies that ONE has no instrument to affect the value of augmenting entry; and if the duopoly solution offers pure profit, then the equilibrium will be a duopoly. However, the finite durability of capital implies that predatory entry must be a concern and that premature replacement is an instrument that can prevent predatory entry. In this model, natural monopoly is impossible, and there are thus two possible equilibria: an artificial monopoly equilibrium and a duopoly equilibrium. Franchise monopoly is socially preferred to artificial monopoly, since output is the same and since the artificial monopoly involves the deadweight loss associated with premature replacement. Note that the duopoly equilibrium will also involve a deadweight loss, since the duopolists must concern themselves with predatory entry.

This review demonstrates that the properties of entry equilibrium are dependent upon the nature of PSC and apparently minor changes in the nature of PSC can produce dramatic changes in the properties of equilibrium. As a corollary, knowledge of the nature of PSC is necessary to determine whether entry deterrence is possible, is profitable, and is socially wasteful.

Seen from the vantage point of the neoclassical model, where long-run equilibrium is independent of short-run specificity of capital, giving PSC a key role in a theory of entry equilibrium appears dubious. Consideration of another model may give further insight into the significance of PSC for long-run equilibrium. Assume that there are no product-specific inputs and that the market will profitably support only one firm. Profits of the sitting firm provide an incentive for predatory entry, while the absence of PSC implies that a sitting firm has no way to protect itself against predatory attackers. The essence of entry deterrence is the creation of asymmetries between existing firms and potential new entrants, and without PSC, asymmetries are not possible. Since there is no way any sitting firm can secure a hold on the market, there is no way to stabilize the identity of the one firm that profitably serves it. The chaos of this model belongs, we believe, to the world of economic fiction, and we can be sure that if such conditions did ever exist in our world, some firm would invent a form of PSC that allowed it to create the required asymmetry. Far from being an unnecessary encumbrance, PSC is thus the stabilizing force in any world where a range of falling long-run costs makes it possible for a small number of firms to earn positive profits in a situation where the value of augmenting entry is nonpositive.

In the models we consider there are four possible market structures: natural monopoly, artificial monopoly (where the monopolist must strategically deter augmenting and/or predatory entry), natural duopoly, and artificial duopoly (where the duopolists must strategically deter predatory entry). These exhaust the possibilities in our model, since the market will not support three firms. However, the basic insights for extension of these ideas to a theory of endogenous market structure, driven by the nature of PSC, seem clear enough; and this is a task of major importance.

References

CAVES, R. AND PORTER, M. "From Entry Barriers to Mobility Barriers: Conjectural Decisions and Contrived Deterrence to New Competition." *Quarterly Journal of Economics*, Vol. 91 (May 1977), pp. 241–261.

——— AND ———. "Barriers to Exit" in R. Marson and P. Qualls, eds., *Essays in Industrial Organization in Honor of Joe Bain*, Cambridge, Mass.: Ballinger, 1976, pp. 39–70.

DIXIT, A.K. "A Model of Duopoly Suggesting a Theory of Entry Barriers." *Bell Journal of Economics*, Vol. 9 (Spring 1979), pp. 20–32.

———. "The Role of Investment in Entry Deterrence." *Economic Journal*, Vol. 90 (March 1980), pp. 95–106.

EATON, B. AND LIPSEY, R. "Spatial Monopoly, Natural Monopoly, Pure Profits, and Land Rents." Queen's University Discussion Paper No. 265, 1977.

——— AND ———. "The Theory of Market Preemption: The Persistence of Excess Capacity and Monopoly in Growing Spatial Markets." *Economica*, Vol. 46 (May 1979), pp. 149–158.

——— AND ———. "Exit Barriers Are Entry Barriers: The Durability of Capital as a Barrier to Entry." *Bell Journal of Economics*, Vol. 10 (Autumn 1980), pp. 721–729.

SCHELLING, T. "An Essay on Bargaining." *American Economic Review*, Vol. 46 (June 1956), pp. 557–583.

SCHMALENSEE, R. "Economies of Scale and Barriers to Entry." M.I.T. Working Paper No. 1130, 1980.

SPENCE, A.M. "Entry, Capacity, Investment, and Oligopolistic Pricing." *Bell Journal of Economics*, Vol. 8 (Autumn 1977), pp. 534–544.

———. "Investment Strategy and Growth in a New Market." *Bell Journal of Economics*, Vol. 9 (Spring 1979), pp. 1–19.

[6]

Asymmetric equilibria and strategic behaviour in oligopolistic markets: a synthesis*

with Mukesh Eswaran**

Abstract
This paper offers a synthesis of the application of the commitment paradigm to industrial organization. In a general duopoly model, the incentives of the incumbent to use commitments to effect asymmetric outcomes are examined. Using product durability as a vehicle of commitment, the mechanics of solution by backward induction and the endogenization of market structure are illustrated. The evolution of the paradigm is briefly traced.

1. Introduction

A major thrust of the recent literature in oligopoly theory has been the examination of the incentives and abilities that firms have to rig market structure. There has been a growing awareness that market structure cannot be taken as exogenous, and its endogenization has been seen as an important area of research in the theory of industrial organization. As a necessary step in this direction, the solution to the problem of a single incumbent firm faced with a potential entrant has been vigorously pursued. It has become apparent that, in order to develop a rational theory to predict the possible outcomes in this circumstance, what is needed is a paradigm that eliminates arbitrariness in the conjectured behaviour of the incumbent in the post-entry situation. This need has been filled by Schelling's (1956) fundamental idea of commitment. Quite simply, commitments are activities entailing sunk costs which, having been undertaken, alter *real economic circumstances*, for example by reducing costs or changing demand conditions. Thus commitments can be exploited to lend credibility to an announced or implied course of future actions. The so-called 'new' industrial organization is a body of literature which requires theory to be based on credible strategies, and hence on commitments. We shall refer to this paradigm as the commitment paradigm. In this paper, we offer a synthesis of the voluminous literature in industrial organization that employs the paradigm.[1] We do not attempt a survey. Instead, we seek to lay bare the essence of the paradigm, demonstrate the mechanics of its operation, and elaborate on some of the implications we must accept if we espouse the paradigm.

Even if all firms face identical conditions *ex-ante*, once commitments are incurred a fundamental asymmetry is introduced between firms that have incurred them and those that have not. It is from this fact that commitments derive their strategic value. Much of the existing literature has focused attention on irreversible investment in fixed capital as the vehicle of commitment. In general, however, there are as many

*This paper was written in 1984.

** The University of British Columbia, Canada.

vehicles of commitment as there are ways to sink one's costs in a manner relevant to the problem at hand. Broadly, there are four ways in which firms can choose to exploit commitments. These are:

1. the irrevocable alteration of one's own cost function (e.g. irreversible investment in fixed capital[2]).
2. the irrevocable alteration of the cost functions of rivals (e.g. binding contracts for deliveries of a product-specific input in a market in which one has monopsony power[3]).
3. the irrevocable alteration of one's own revenue function (e.g. advertising[4]).
4. the irrevocable alteration of the revenue functions of rivals (e.g. choice of product durability, to be considered in this paper).

A distinction fundamental to the literature on commitment is the distinction between variables whose values can be irreversibly determined prior to the production (or marketing) of goods and those which cannot be irreversibly determined. We will refer to the former as *pre-committed* variables and to the latter as *non-committed* variables. Brander and Spencer (1983) make a somewhat stronger, and quite illuminating, distinction. Many pre-committed variables *must* necessarily be determined prior to production. Product development costs, for example, must be incurred prior to production; the creation of capital goods to be used in production necessarily precedes their use in production; advertising, the purpose of which is to alter demand conditions, must occur prior to the sale of goods.

An important implication of this partitioning of variables into pre-committed and non-committed variables is that it imposes some strong restrictions on the form of any oligopolistic game. Consider the game played by competing firms when they produce goods, a game we shall call the *market game*. Pre-committed variables are fixed for the market game and the choices open to firms are restricted by their prior decisions with respect to these variables. Thus the market game is preceded by a game in pre-committed variables, the *commitment game*. Costs are incurred in the commitment game but revenues are generated only in the downstream market game. Thus oligopolistic situations which involve pre-committed variables must necessarily be modelled as a sequence of interrelated games.

In Section 2 of this paper we develop a model which exhibits the incentives, created by the existence of pre-committed variables, of firms to rig market structure. Our purpose here is to convey, in the simplest possible way, the fundamental insights which arise from the commitment paradigm. In Section 3 we consider the commitment paradigm in an explicitly intertemporal example, and one in which pre-commitment works through the revenue side. Our purpose here is to illustrate the mechanics of solution by backward induction, which is fundamental to the implementation of the paradigm, and to demonstrate how market structure may be endogenized. We elaborate on the nature of the paradigm in Section 4 and also briefly trace its historical development.

2. Strategic pre-commitment – a general formulation

In this section we develop a simple, but general model of duopoly which conveys the basic insights which follow from the existence of pre-committed variables. We largely ignore the possibility that one firm may have the ability and the incentive to deter entry of the other. We do this to emphasize the fact that one important implication of the existence of pre-committed variables is the asymmetry of the ensuing equilibria, even when *ex-ante* revenue and cost conditions are symmetric. Entry deterrence can then be seen as the most extreme manifestation of asymmetry. The model allows us to focus on the causal mechanisms through which pre-commitments operate, and to contrast the equilibrium of this sequential game with the equilibrium which would obtain if firms did not recognize the sequential structure of the game.

2.1. The role of commitment in the market game

We envisage a situation in which each of the duopolists must choose the value of a pre-committed variable prior to a market game.[5] Let $R_i\,(q_1, q_2, \Delta_1, \Delta_2)$ denote the revenue of firm i in the market game, where q_i is output and Δ_i the value of the pre-committed variable for firm i, $i = 1, 2$. Let $C_i\,(q_i, \Delta_i)$ denote the avoidable costs of production of firm i in the market game. Then the objective function of firm i, $i = 1, 2$, is

$$V_i\,(q_1, q_2, \Delta_1, \Delta_2) = R_i\,(q_1, q_2, \Delta_1, \Delta_2) - C_i\,(q_i, \Delta_i) - F_i\,(\Delta_1, \Delta_2) \tag{1}$$

where $F_i\,(\Delta_1, \Delta_2)$ is the cost to firm i of commitment Δ_i, with $\partial F_i/\partial\Delta_i \geq 0$, $\partial^2 F_i/\partial\Delta_i^2 \geq 0$. We include Δ_j, $j \neq i$, as an argument of F_i to allow for monopsony effects, and assume that $\partial F_i/\partial\Delta_j \geq 0$, $\partial^2 F_i/\partial\Delta_i\partial\Delta_j \geq 0$ for $j \neq i$.

We consider three cases, distinguished by the manner in which the pre-committed variables enter the market game:

Case (i) In this case Δ_i is quantity of a pre-committed factor of production. Thus the partial derivatives of the revenue functions with respect to Δ_1 and Δ_2 are zero. Further, $C_i\,(q_i, \Delta_i)$ can be interpreted as a restricted cost function:

$$C_i\,(q_i, \Delta_i) \equiv \min_{L_i}\,\{wL_i \mid g_i\,(L_i, \Delta_i) \geq q_i\} \tag{2}$$

where L_i is a non-committed factor of production, w is its price, and $g_i\,(L_i, \Delta_i)$ is the (assumed) production function of firm i.

Case (ii) In this case Δ_1 and Δ_2 affect the revenue functions, but not the avoidable cost functions (i.e. $\partial C_i/\partial\Delta_i = 0$) . For concreteness, it may be convenient to interpret Δ_i as quantity of advertising. We assume that $\partial R_i/\partial\Delta_i > 0$ and $\partial R_i/\partial\Delta_j \neq 0$ for $i \neq j$.

Case (iii) In this case we interpret Δ_i as an index of product quality or, more generally, as some product attribute. Here we let $\partial F_i/\partial\Delta_j \equiv 0$ for $i \neq j$. Further we assume that $\partial C_i/\partial\Delta_i > 0$ (quality is costly) and that $\partial R_i/\partial\Delta_i > 0$ (quality is valued by consumers). In contrast to the previous cases, here the pre-committed variables affect both revenues and costs in the market game.

Quantities q_1 and q_2 will be determined in the market game. We denote the solution to the market game by $[\hat{q}_1\,(\Delta_1, \Delta_2),\ \hat{q}_2\,(\Delta_1, \Delta_2)]$ to emphasize that this solution will depend on the variables which are pre-committed in an earlier commitment game and are thus parametric to the market game. We need not tie ourselves to any particular equilibrium concept for the market game. However, we do assume that, at an equilibrium, $\partial R_i/\partial q_i - \partial C_i/\partial q_i \geq 0$, $i = 1, 2$. That is, at an equilibrium, marginal revenue is not less than marginal cost. If the market game is played non-cooperatively in quantities with Cournot conjectures, then $\partial R_i/\partial q_i - \partial C_i/\partial q_i = 0$, $i = 1, 2$.

2.2. The commitment game

In order to make rational decisions in the commitment game, firms necessarily must form conjectures about the solution to the market game. In particular, they must speculate about the dependence of the solution to the market game on the values of the pre-committed variables, since these values are to be chosen in the commitment game. Such conjectures are necessary since the costs which are incurred in the commitment game will generate revenues only in the market game; that is, decisions in the commitment game are in essence *investment* decisions. We assume that firms' conjectures are *rational*. In other words, we assume that both firms know the form of the dependence of the market game solution on Δ_1 and Δ_2: they know $[\hat{q}_1(\Delta_1, \Delta_2), \hat{q}_2(\Delta_1, \Delta_2)]$.

Given the above rationality assumption, the objective functions of firm i in the commitment game can be rewritten

$$V_i[\hat{q}_1(\Delta_1, \Delta_2), \hat{q}_2(\Delta_1, \Delta_2), \Delta_1, \Delta_2] = R_i[\hat{q}_1(\Delta_1, \Delta_2), \hat{q}_2(\Delta_1, \Delta_2), \Delta_1, \Delta_2] - C_i[\hat{q}_i(\Delta_1, \Delta_2), \Delta_i] - F_i(\Delta_1, \Delta_2). \tag{3}$$

The only endogenous variables in the commitment game are Δ_1 and Δ_2.

To highlight the mechanisms through which pre-commitment operates we impose, in this sub-section, a sequential structure on the commitment game. In stage 1, Firm One chooses Δ_1; in stage 2, Firm Two chooses Δ_2. In other words, Firm One has the first mover advantage.

First, we consider Firm Two's profit maximizing choice of Δ_2. Assuming differentiability and an interior solution, Δ_2 will satisfy a standard first order condition:

$$\left[\frac{\partial R_2}{\partial \Delta_2} - \frac{\partial C_2}{\partial \Delta_2} - \frac{\partial F_2}{\partial \Delta_2}\right] + \left[\left(\frac{\partial R_2}{\partial q_2} - \frac{\partial C_2}{\partial q_2}\right)\frac{\partial \hat{q}_2}{\partial \Delta_2}\right] + \left[\frac{\partial R_2}{\partial q_1}\frac{\partial \hat{q}_1}{\partial \Delta_2}\right] = 0. \tag{4}$$

We interpret this condition for the three cases defined above.

Case (i) If Δ_2 is a factor of production, condition (4) can be written as:

$$-\left[\frac{\partial C_2}{\partial \Delta_2} + \frac{\partial F_2}{\partial \Delta_2}\right] + \left[\left(\frac{\partial R_2}{\partial q_2} - \frac{\partial C_2}{\partial q_2}\right)\frac{\partial \hat{q}_2}{\partial \Delta_2}\right] + \left[\frac{\partial R_2}{\partial q_1}\frac{\partial \hat{q}_1}{\partial \Delta_2}\right] = 0. \tag{5.1}$$

Observe that cost minimization would imply that the first term in square brackets is equal to zero, since total costs of production are just $C_2 + F_2$. However, if $\partial \hat{q}_2/\partial \Delta_2$ and $\partial \hat{q}_1/\partial \Delta_2$ are not both equal to zero at the profit maximizing solution, Firm Two will not minimize the cost of producing its equilibrium output because Δ_2 acts as a control on relative market shares. The marginal value to Firm Two of this control on market shares is captured by the second and third terms in square brackets in equation (5.1). Thus Δ_2 is valuable to the firm directly as a factor of production and indirectly, through its influence on $\hat{q}_1$ and $\hat{q}_2$, as a determinant of market shares. Is it plausible that $\partial\hat{q}_1/\partial\Delta_2$ and $\partial\hat{q}_2/\partial\Delta_2$ are both zero at the profit maximizing value of Δ_2? Not in general, since Δ_2 is a determinant of Firm Two's costs of production in the market game. To argue that they are zero in general is to argue that the solution to the market game is independent of Firm Two's costs of production in that game. Thus a major implication of the commitment paradigm is that firms will not, in general, minimize costs.

We can say a bit more if we adopt what appear to be the relevant assumptions with respect to signs of partial derivatives. If the two goods are gross substitutes these assumptions are that $\partial\hat{q}_2/\partial\Delta_2 > 0$, $\partial\hat{q}_1/\partial\Delta_2 < 0$ and $\partial R_2/\partial q_1 < 0$; the last two inequalities would be reversed if the two goods are gross complements. In either case, the profit maximizing value of Δ_2, as determined by equation (5.1), exceeds the value which minimizes the cost of producing $\hat{q}_2(\Delta_1, \Delta_2)$: Firm Two uses 'too much' of the pre-committed factor. Of course, these salient assumptions are just assumptions: the signs of $\partial\hat{q}_2/\partial\Delta_2$ and $\partial\hat{q}_1/\partial\Delta_2$ are determined by the comparative statics of the market game equilibrium.

Case (ii) In this case, Δ_1 and Δ_2 enter only the revenue functions and condition (4) reduces to

$$\left[\frac{\partial R_2}{\partial \Delta_2} - \frac{\partial F_2}{\partial \Delta_2}\right] + \left[\left(\frac{\partial R_2}{\partial q_2} - \frac{\partial C_2}{\partial q_2}\right)\frac{\partial \hat{q}_2}{\partial \Delta_2}\right] + \left[\frac{\partial R_2}{\partial q_1}\frac{\partial \hat{q}_1}{\partial \Delta_2}\right] = 0. \tag{5.2}$$

The first term in square brackets again captures the marginal direct value of Δ_2 and the second and third terms capture the marginal indirect (or strategic) value to the firm of Δ_2. This strategic value arises because, as in case (i), Δ_2 is a control on market shares if $\partial\hat{q}_2/\partial\Delta_2$ and $\partial\hat{q}_1/\partial\Delta_2$ are not both zero. Again it is implausible that these terms are zero: in this case, to argue that they are is to argue that the solution to the market game is independent of Firm Two's revenue function.

Case (iii) When Δ is an index of quality, condition (4) is the relevant first order condition. Again direct effects are captured in the first term and strategic effects in the last two terms.

Condition (4) implicitly determines Δ_2 as a function of Δ_1, since Δ_1 is pre-committed. Thus we may write $\Delta_2 = \hat{\Delta}_2(\Delta_1)$, and turn to the consideration of Firm One's choice of Δ_1. We assume that Firm One's conjectures with respect to the evolution of the entire game subsequent to its choice of Δ_1 are rational: Firm One knows $\hat{\Delta}_2(\Delta_1)$, $\hat{q}_1(\Delta_1, \Delta_2)$ and $\hat{q}_2(\Delta_1, \Delta_2)$. Given this rationality assumption, we rewrite Firm One's objective function as

$$\hat{V}_1(\Delta_1) \equiv V_1\left[\hat{q}_1(\Delta_1, \hat{\Delta}_2(\Delta_1)), \hat{q}_2(\Delta_1, \hat{\Delta}_2(\Delta_1)), \Delta_1, \hat{\Delta}_2(\Delta_1)\right]. \tag{6}$$

Assuming differentiability and an interior solution, the profit maximizing value of Δ_1 will satisfy

$$\left[\frac{\partial R_1}{\partial \Delta_1} - \frac{\partial C_1}{\partial \Delta_1} - \frac{\partial F_1}{\partial \Delta_1}\right] + \left[\left(\frac{\partial R_1}{\partial q_1} - \frac{\partial C_1}{\partial q_1}\right)\frac{\partial \hat{q}_1}{\partial \Delta_1}\right] + \left[\frac{\partial R_1}{\partial q_2}\frac{\partial \hat{q}_2}{\partial \Delta_1}\right]$$
$$+ \left[\left(\frac{\partial R_1}{\partial q_1} - \frac{\partial C_1}{\partial q_1}\right)\frac{\partial \hat{q}_1}{\partial \Delta_2} + \frac{\partial R_1}{\partial q_2}\frac{\partial \hat{q}_2}{\partial \Delta_2} + \frac{\partial R_1}{\partial \Delta_2} - \frac{\partial F_1}{\partial \Delta_2}\right]\frac{\mathrm{d}\hat{\Delta}_2}{\mathrm{d}\Delta_1} = 0. \tag{7}$$

The first three terms in equation (7) are analogous to those of condition (4), which characterize Firm Two's choice of Δ_2. Thus the mechanisms which determine Firm Two's choices of the pre-committed variable influence Firm One's choice as well. In addition Firm One has added leverage since Δ_2 is determined by Δ_1. The marginal value of this leverage to Firm One is captured in the last term on the left-hand side of condition (7), which is largely self-explanatory. It is probably worth noting, however, that

$$-\frac{\partial F_1}{\partial \Delta_2}\frac{\mathrm{d}\hat{\Delta}_2}{\mathrm{d}\Delta_1}$$

is a monopsony effect; to the extent that a higher Δ_1 induces Firm Two to choose a smaller Δ_2, Firm One will exploit its monopsony power through its first mover advantage.

If we assume that the revenue functions are symmetric and the cost functions are identical, we can make one further point. The equilibrium will, in general, be asymmetric. This point follows trivially from the observation that conditions (4) and (7) are not identical, even when there is no *ex-ante* asymmetry between the two firms. Although we do not pursue the algebra here, it can be demonstrated that under a Nash resolution of the market game and some reasonable assumptions on the comparative statics of the equilibrium, Firm One's profit will exceed Firm Two's. The non-strategic equilibrium, that is, the equilibrium that obtains if the firms ignore the sequential nature of the game, however, will be symmetric and here Firm One's profits will equal Firm Two's. Hence the explicit recognition of the strategic value of commitments enables Firm One to implement an asymmetric equilibrium and increase his profits at the expense of Firm Two's.

2.3. *Multiple equilibria*

By allowing Firm One to move first we produced an equilibrium in this model that is presumably unique. Since Δ_2 is determined by Δ_1, Firm One is simply playing a Stackelberg game in commitments. That is, it is choosing Δ_1 to maximize V_1, as defined in equation (3), subject to $\Delta_2 = \hat{\Delta}_2(\Delta_1)$. Of course, if Firm Two were to move first, then Δ_1 would be determined by Δ_2 and we could write $\Delta_1 = \hat{\Delta}_1(\Delta_2)$.

In Figure 1 we display both of these 'reaction' functions. If large values of Δ_1 are not credible, $\hat{\Delta}_2(\Delta_1)$ will be insensitive to Δ_1 for large values of the latter. The reaction curves in Figure 1 are drawn under this presumption. The equilibrium we illuminated in the previous sub-section – the so-called perfect equilibrium – is represented by the point (Δ_1^*, Δ_2^*). It is a standard Stackelberg equilibrium, but in commitments. The usual objection to the Stackelberg equilibrium does not apply in this model since Firm One's

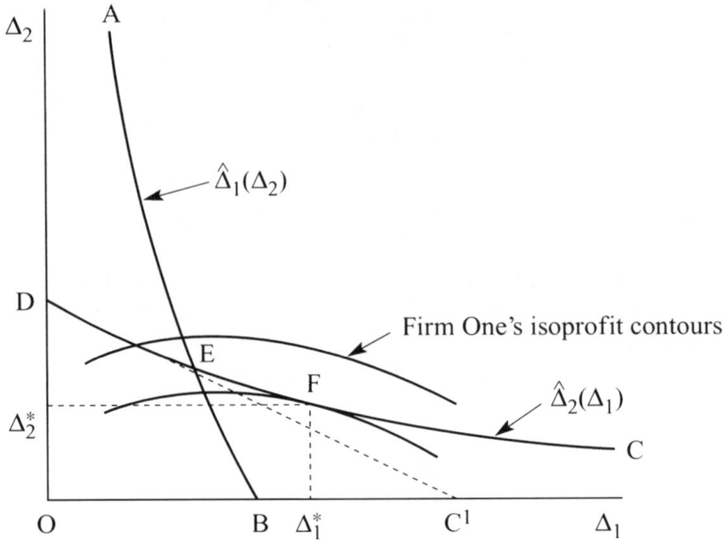

Figure 1. Determination of the perfect equilibrium in the space of pre-committed variables.

choice of Δ_1 is *irreversible*. If Firm One can move first, then (Δ_1^*, Δ_2^*) is the appropriate equilibrium point in this model. By assuming that a positive level of commitment is essential to profitable operation, we can illustrate the deterrence equilibrium in Figure 1. If Firm Two's reaction function is like the dashed curve *DC′*, and if Firm One's preferences over the (Δ_1, Δ_2) space are such that the point on Firm Two's 'reaction' function that affords Firm One the highest profits is *C′*, Firm One would deter Firm Two's entry by enforcing the equilibrium at *C′*.

Note, however, that owing to the irreversibility of pre-committed variables there are clearly other possible equilibria. Indeed any point on or above *AEC* is an equilibrium: neither firm has any incentive to increase its commitment nor can its commitment be reduced. In many circumstances, sequential choices of commitments seem reasonable, and in such cases the perfect equilibrium is the appropriate equilibrium. Where choices are simultaneous, the matter is clearly more complex.

2.4. *Common sense of commitment*

There are three essential features of this model and indeed of the commitment paradigm: the existence of pre-committed variables, the non-trivial dependence of solutions to subsequent games (including market games) on the values of pre-committed variables, and the recognition of this dependence by firms when they choose commitments. Owing to the necessity of solution by backward induction, the paradigm is considerably more complex than the standard, static, profit maximization paradigm of traditional oligopoly theory. We must then ask if the added complexity is worthwhile. The answer will, of course, depend upon the circumstances surrounding any particular oligopoly problem. However, the paradigm itself suggests some more specific queries which are useful in addressing the larger question. Are the sunk costs associated with pre-committed variables significant? If they are not, then perhaps the paradigm is not useful. If they are, then there is an obvious presumption that the solution to the subsequent games will be responsive to the magnitude of the commitments. The remaining query is then whether firms do or do not perceive this dependence. This is obviously an empirical question, which theory cannot answer. However, the fact that the creation of commitments is an investment decision does suggest that rational firms will attempt to form judgements about this dependence.

3. Strategic choice of product durability

In this section we apply the commitment paradigm to the choice of product durability with three goals in mind. First, we wish to illustrate the extension of the paradigm to an intertemporal setting. By its very nature, product durability has potential strategic value only in an intertemporal setting. Second, we seek to demonstrate how the paradigm can be used to endogenize market structure. Third, we wish to examine the nature of the bias, if any, in product durability which strategic choice of durability entails.

3.1. The model

We choose the simplest analytical framework consistent with the above objectives. We examine a duopoly in a two period model. The endogenous variables are (Δ_1, q_1^1, q_1^2) and (Δ_2, q_2^1, q_2^2), where q_i^j is the quantity of good X produced by firm i in period j and Δ_i is an index of the durability associated with the product of firm i. Let x^j denote the quantity of services of good X available in period j. Then, by choice of units,

$$x^1 = q_1^1 + q_2^1 \tag{8.1}$$

$$x^2 = \Delta_1 q_1^1 + \Delta_2 q_2^1 + q_1^2 + q_2^2. \tag{8.2}$$

Thus q_i^1 yields q_i^1 units of service in period 1 and $\Delta_i q_i^1$ units of service in period 2.

The demand for services of X arises from a representative consumer with utility function:

$$U = y + x^1 - \tfrac{1}{2}(x^1)^2 + x^2 - \tfrac{1}{2}(x^2)^2 \tag{9}$$

where y is the quantity of a Hicksian composite commodity. We let the price of the composite commodity and the consumer's income be 1, and we assume a zero rate of interest for convenience. The solution of the representative consumer's choice problem yields the following inverse demand functions:

$$p_1^1 = 1 - q_1^1 - q_2^1 + \Delta_1(1 - \Delta_1 q_1^1 - \Delta_2 q_2^1 - q_1^2 - q_2^2) \tag{10.1}$$

$$p_2^1 = 1 - q_1^1 - q_2^1 + \Delta_2(1 - \Delta_1 q_1^1 - \Delta_2 q_2^1 - q_1^2 - q_2^2) \tag{10.2}$$

$$p^2 = 1 - \Delta_1 q_1^1 - \Delta_2 q_2^1 - q_1^2 - q_2^2, \tag{10.3}$$

where p_i^1, $i = 1, 2$ is the price of a unit of firm i's product in period 1. In period 2 the products of the two firms are perfect substitutes since there is no third period and any durability embodied in products purchased in period 2 is valueless. Thus p^2 is the common price at which products produced in period 2 can be sold. In period 1 durability (potentially) differentiates the products of the two firms and their products will accordingly command different prices. Observe that we can write $p_i^1 = 1 - q_1^1 - q_2^1 + \Delta_i p^2$, for $i = 1, 2$. Note also that $1 - q_1^1 - q_2^1$ is the marginal value of a unit of q_i^1 for use in period 1, and $\Delta_i p^2$ is the marginal value of a unit of q_i^1 for use in period 2. Thus the period 1 price premium associated with durability is simply the value in use in period 2.

In deriving these demand relations we have endowed our representative consumer with knowledge of prices in both periods. This is, of course, necessary if we wish to ensure intertemporal consistency of consumer behaviour. It is also necessary if we are to examine the strategic choice, or indeed any rational choice, of product durability. Durable products allow producers to capture tomorrow's demand today. If we are to analyse the rational choice of durability, we must allow prices today to reflect value in use tomorrow.[6]

The cost side of our model is very simple. The only cost of production is the cost of physical plant, $C(\Delta)$, which depends on durability:

$$C(\Delta) = a + c\,(\Delta - b)^2, \quad a > 0, 0 < b < 1, c > 0. \tag{11}$$

Costs are a minimum when Δ is equal to b. Relative to b, there is a cost penalty associated with 'too much' and with 'too little' durability. The parameter c determines the magnitude of the cost penalty. The cost of physical plant is assumed to be sunk; once Δ has been chosen it cannot be changed.

3.2. Monopoly solution

As a point of reference it is useful to consider the monopoly solution in this model when the monopolist is unconcerned with entry. In this sub-section, we shall drop the subscripts. Suppose the monopolist sets $\Delta = b$ to minimize costs, and chooses $q^1 = 1/2$ and $q^2 = 1/2 - bq^1 = (1 - b)/2$. This will maximize revenues from the two period market for X since services available in each period are 1/2, the monopoly level. This strategy is clearly the profit maximizing strategy, and the monopolist chooses the cost minimizing durability. However, it may not be available to the monopolist.

The difficulty arises from the monopolist's inability to commit himself to produce $q^2 = (1 - b)/2$ in period 2. In period 2 it is in the monopolist's self-interest to choose q^2 to maximize revenues in period 2, given q^1 and Δ. If our representative consumer reads the monopolist's incentives in this fashion, then the price in period 1 will necessarily reflect this reading, and the best available strategy for the monopolist will involve choosing q^2 to maximize revenues in period 2, given q^1 and Δ. That is, the durability premium in period 1 will reflect the presumption that the monopolist will choose q^2 to maximize revenues in period 2 (given Δ and q^1), and then the monopolist's best choice will be to choose q^2 in precisely this fashion.

In these circumstances the monopolist must solve his problem by backward induction. Revenues in period 2 are just p^2q^2. Maximized revenues, R^2, are then determined by q^1 and Δ since p^2 depends on q^1 and Δ:

$$R^2(\Delta, q^1) = \left[\frac{1 - \Delta q^1}{2}\right]^2. \tag{12}$$

In period 1, given Δ, q^1 will be chosen to maximize $q^1p^1 + R^2(\Delta, q^1)$, which implies that maximized revenues over both periods, R, are determined by Δ alone. It is easily verified that

$$R(\Delta) = \frac{1}{4} + \frac{1}{4 + \Delta^2}. \tag{13}$$

Finally, Δ will then be chosen to maximize $R(\Delta) - C(\Delta)$. In the monopoly solution, Δ^* is necessarily less than b, the durability which minimizes costs. Consider Figure 2. $R(\Delta)$ is a concave, strictly decreasing function of Δ on [0, 1], and $C(\Delta)$ is a convex function which attains its minimum at $\Delta = b$. Then Δ^* will be chosen so that the marginal decrease in $R(\Delta)$ from added durability is just offset by the marginal decrease in cost of plant. It is clear from Figure 2 that the optimal Δ must be less than b.

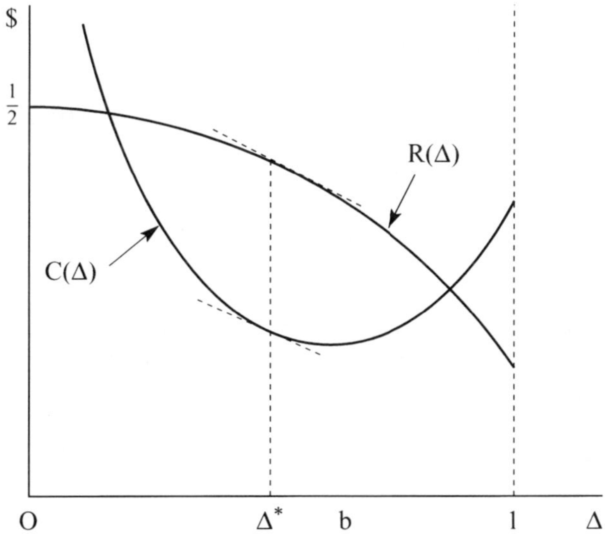

Figure 2. Determination of the monopolist's optimal choice of durability.

3.3. Strategic choice of durability

We now turn our attention to the duopoly. The value of firm j in this duopoly is

$$V_j(\Delta_1, \Delta_2, q_1^1, q_1^2, q_2^1, q_2^2) = q_j^1 p_j^1 + q_j^2 p^2 - C(\Delta_j), \quad j = 1, 2 \tag{14}$$

where we again assume a zero rate of interest for convenience. Before period 1, we allow Firm One to choose Δ_1; that is, Firm One commits itself to Δ_1 by creating the physical plant necessary to produce goods with durability Δ_1. Given Δ_1 , Firm Two subsequently chooses Δ_2. In period 1, q_1^1 and q_2^1 are chosen, given Δ_1 and Δ_2. Finally, in period 2, q_1^2 and q_2^2 are chosen, given the pre-committed variables q_1^1, q_2^1, Δ_1 and Δ_2.

The essential features of the paradigm of strategic choice are: (1) that choice of current variables is conditioned by the values of pre-committed variables; and (2) that commitments are undertaken with full knowledge of their implications. As we have laid the problem out, there are three points in time at which decisions are made in the presence of pre-committed variables: in period 2, when q_1^2, q_2^2 are chosen, and Δ_1, q_1^1, Δ_2, q_2^1 are pre-committed; in period 1, when q_1^1, q_2^1 are chosen, and Δ_1, Δ_2 are pre-committed; and in the beginning of period 1, when Δ_2 is chosen and Δ_1 is pre-committed. At each of these points in time we assume that the rules of the game are Nash and are understood by the firms to be so.

In period 2, then, q_1^2 and q_2^2 are determined as the solution to

$$\max_{q_j^2} \; q_j^2 p_2, \quad j = 1, 2. \tag{15}$$

Solving equation (15), we can express revenues and quantities for each firm in period 2 as functions of the pre-committed variables:

$$\hat{R}^2 = \frac{1}{9}\,(1 - \Delta_1 q_1^1 - \Delta_2 q_2^1)^2 \tag{16.1}$$

$$\hat{q}_1^2 = \hat{q}_2^2 = \frac{1}{3}\,(1 - \Delta_1 q_1^1 - \Delta_2 q_2^1). \tag{16.2}$$

In period 1, q_1^1 and q_2^1 are then obtained by solving

$$\max_{q_j^1} \; q_j^1 p_j^1 + \hat{R}^2, \quad j = 1, 2. \tag{17}$$

Thus quantity decisions made in period 1, which are carriers of the durability commitment into period 2, are determined by taking into account the effects they have on current and future revenues. The maximization in equation (17) yields

$$q_j^1 = \frac{1}{G}\Big[(9 - \Delta_j)\,(18 + 4\,(\Delta_i)^2) - (9 - \Delta_i)\,(9 + \Delta_1\Delta_2)\Big], j = 1, 2, i = 1, 2, i \neq j \tag{18}$$

where

$$G \equiv [18 + 4\,(\Delta_1)^2]\,[18 + 4\,(\Delta_2)^2 - (9 + \Delta_1\Delta_2)^2].$$

Equations (16.2) and (18) allow us to write the four endogenous quantities (q_j^i, $i = 1, 2$, $j = 1, 2$) as functions of Δ_1 and Δ_2, and hence we can express the value function of Firm Two in terms of Δ_1 and Δ_2:

$$\overline{V}_2\,(\Delta_1, \Delta_2) = R_2\,(\Delta_1, \Delta_2) - C\,(\Delta_2). \tag{19}$$

Given Δ_1, Firm Two will choose Δ_2 to maximize $\overline{V}_2\,(\Delta_1, \Delta_2)$. In principle this allows us to express Δ_2 and the four quantities as functions of Δ_1 alone; and hence to write

Firm One's value in terms of Δ_1 alone: $\bar{V}_1(\Delta_1)$. Firm One, of course, chooses Δ_1 to maximize $\bar{V}(\Delta_1)$.

Although we have purposely devised a very simple model, we are unable to obtain a closed form expression for Δ_2 as a function of Δ_1 and are, therefore, unable to provide a complete analytical solution to our model. One can nevertheless acquire an intuitive understanding of the nature of the solution by examining the problem numerically, as we have done. Observe, first, that $R_2(\Delta_1, \Delta_2)$ is decreasing in Δ_1. Then ask: under what conditions is it possible for Firm One to deter Firm Two's entry? Clearly $\Delta_1 = 1$ maximizes the adverse impact which Firm One can exert on Firm Two's value. Let us set $\Delta_1 = 1$ and observe that $R_2(1, \Delta_2)$ is a strictly concave function of Δ_2, as illustrated in Figure 3. The parameter a of the cost function in equation (11) is a set-up cost which is independent of Δ_2, and determines the minimum cost which Firm Two must incur if it enters. From Figure 3 several observations are clear. First, if $a > a_1$ then entry deterrence of Firm Two is always possible. On the other hand, if $a < a_3$ entry deterrence is never possible since Firm Two can limit its costs of production to a by setting $\Delta_2 = b$.

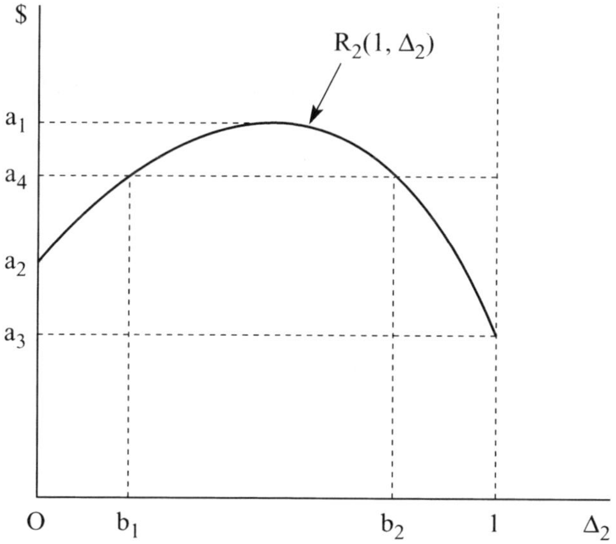

Figure 3. Firm Two's revenue as a function of its choice of durability when $\Delta_1 = 1$.

If $a_2 < a \leq a_1$ the situation is more complex and also more interesting. (As we observe below, this case effectively covers the remaining possibility: $a_3 \leq a \leq a_2$.) Consider the case where $a = a_4$ in Figure 3. If the parameter b of the cost function satisfies $b_1 < b < b_2$ then again entry deterrence is impossible since Firm Two can limit costs to a_4 by choosing $\Delta_2 = b$. However, if $b < b_1$ (or $b > b_2$) the ability of Firm One to deter entry depends on the parameter c. In Figure 4, suppose $b = b_3$. It is clear that there exists some c, say c_3, such that $C(\Delta_2)$ is just tangent to $R_2(1, \Delta_2)$. If $c > c_3$ Firm One can always deter Firm Two's entry and if $c < c_3$ it cannot. Thus, holding $a = a_4$, we infer that (b_3, c_3) is on the boundary of the 'deterrence region' in Figure 5. Now suppose

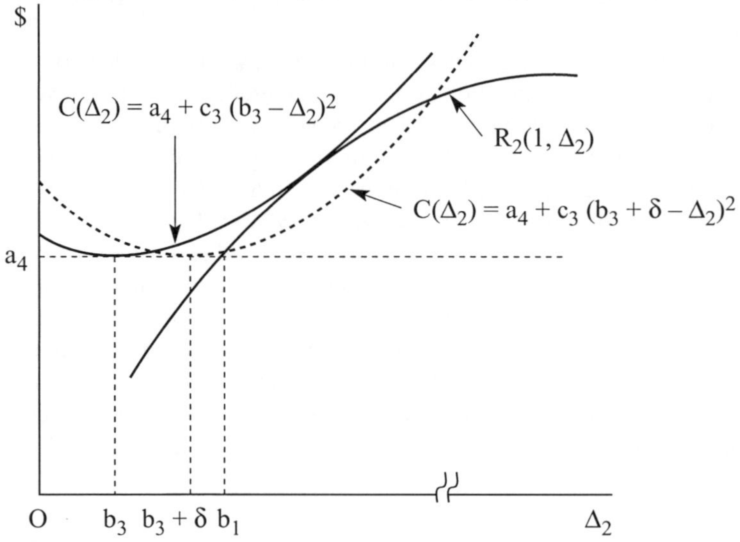

Figure 4. Determination of the (b, c) *combinations that barely deter Firm Two's entry, given that* a = a_4.

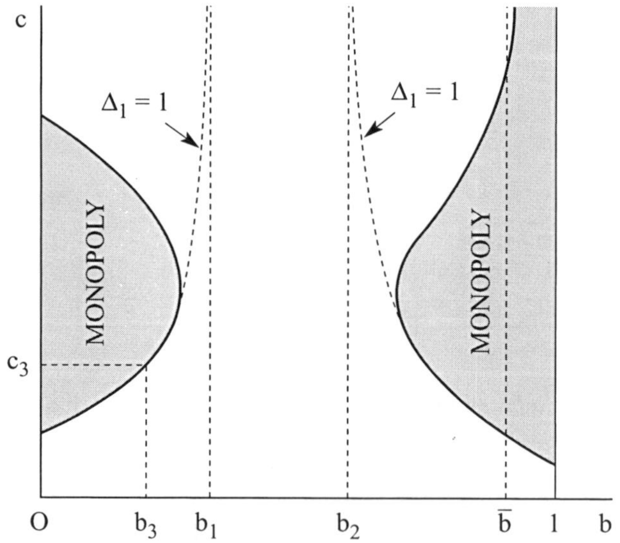

Figure 5. Partitioning of the (b, c) *parameter space (for given* a) *according to the endogenously determined market structure.*

we increase b by a small amount δ to $b = b_3 + \delta$. Then, as we can see from Figure 4, if $c = c_3$ Firm One cannot deter entry. Given $b = b_3 + \delta$, the minimum c which will allow

Firm One to deter entry exceeds c_3 and we conclude that the boundary of the deterrence region in Figure 5 is positively sloped when $b < b_1$. An analogous argument establishes that the boundary of the deterrence region is negatively sloped when $b > b_2$.

Thus we can partition the (b, c) parameter space into regions where deterrence is and is not possible. In Figure 5 deterrence is possible above the lines labelled $\Delta_1 = 1$, that is, above the boundary of the deterrence region. (Figure 5 is drawn on the presumption that $a_2 < a < a_1$. When $a_3 < a < a_2$ we obviously have only the right-hand deterrence region.) There remains the question of whether deterrence is profitable, even if feasible. Along the boundary of the deterrence region we know that $\Delta_1 = 1$, and as we move up along this boundary there must exist a point beyond which deterrence is increasingly costly since c increases without bound. Thus there exists some point on the boundary at which Firm One is indifferent between deterrence and allowing entry; in the latter case Firm One will choose a substantially smaller value for Δ_1. This establishes that the region where deterrence is profitable as well as possible is a proper subset of the deterrence region. The shaded portion of Figure 5 represents the region where Firm One chooses to deter entry.

The upper boundary of the shaded area to the right of Figure 5 asymptotically approaches the vertical line at $b = \bar{b}$. The reason for this can be seen by recognizing that, when c is very large, both firms will be forced to set the durabilities of their products at b. (Although durability is no longer available as a vehicle for pre-commitment, Firm One still has the first mover advantage.) Firm Two's revenues in this case, when $\Delta^1 = \Delta^2 = b$, are seen to be a strictly declining function of b, as shown in Figure 6. As is apparent from the figure, associated with the set-up cost a there is a critical value of b, call it $\bar{b}$, such that, for $b > \bar{b}$, Firm Two's profits would be negative and its entry is blockaded. Thus for large c and for $b > \bar{b}$, Firm One is a natural

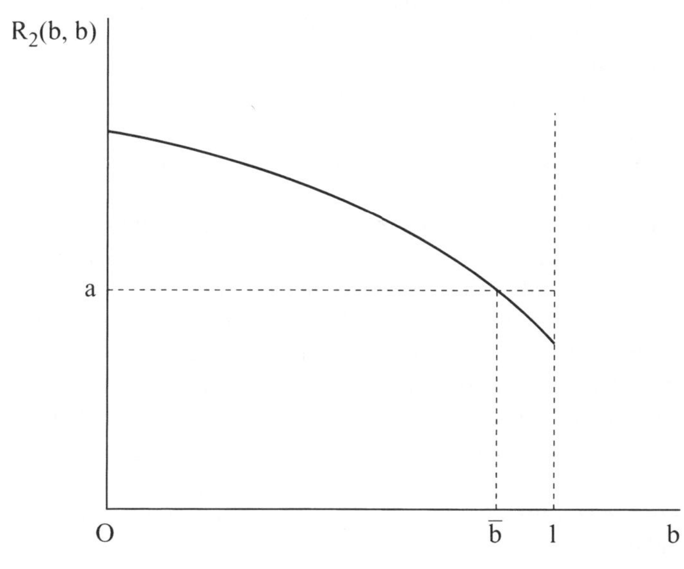

Figure 6. Firm Two's revenues as a function of the cost maximizing durability.

monopolist. In view of the monotone declining nature of Firm Two's revenues in b, there is, however, no corresponding region of natural monopoly in the shaded area to the left of Figure 5. For $b < b_1$ there is always a sufficiently large c for which Firm One prefers the duopoly outcome.

Our simulation results reveal that in the monopoly region on the left in Figure 5, the monopolist chooses Δ_2 substantially greater than b and in the monopoly region on the right the opposite is true, so long as c is not too large. In the duopoly region of Figure 5 neither firm chooses Δ equal to b, in general, but the divergences from b are relatively small. Cost minimization clearly requires that Δ be equal to b. Since durability has strategic value in our model, firms do not choose the socially desirable durability. Interestingly, we may have too much or too little durability in equilibrium.

The received doctrine on a monopolist's choice of durability seems to be that there is no incentive for a monopolist to choose a durability which diverges from the socially optimal durability (see Schmalensee (1979) for a recent survey on this issue). Our analysis indicates that there are two forces which lead the monopolist to choose non-optimal durability. Even where entry is not an issue, as in sub-section 3.2 above, incentive compatibility may force the monopolist to choose too little durability. If durability is used to rig market structure, as is true here, then one cannot expect socially optimal durability.

4. The paradigm

In this section we discuss the essential ingredients of the commitment paradigm and briefly trace its historical development.[7] While it may be convenient to cast the oligopoly problem in a static framework for analytical simplicity, it is conceptually more appropriate to envisage it as a multi-stage game with incumbent firms and potential entrants as the players. In particular, if pre-committed variables *must* be chosen prior to production and marketing, oligopoly games are necessarily sequential, and firms will necessarily see them as such. The analytical framework, therefore, must reflect the sequential nature of the problem.

A central feature of the commitment paradigm is the requirement that acceptable oligopoly equilibria be temporally consistent. In other words, equilibria must be based on the premise that what is perceived as being the optimal future course of action for every player under certain contingencies must indeed be pursued if these contingencies arise. Since the game in any period is generally conditioned by what has transpired in previous periods, to correctly anticipate the optimal responses of his rivals in the future, each player must work through the future consequences of his present actions. Myopic behaviour, then, has no place in a theory based on the commitment paradigm. Further, a necessary condition for intertemporal consistency is that an announced future course of actions by any player must be credible to the other players. As Schelling (1956) has emphasized, credibility is inspired not by threats but rather by commitments – where the two are distinguished by the fact that commitments entail sunk costs that render them essentially irreversible.

The implementation of the commitment paradigm owes much to Selten's (1975) solution concept of subgame perfectness.[8] An equilibrium is subgame perfect if it is an equilibrium for every subgame of the original game. Suppose the game is stopped at the current stage of its evolution and then restarted after reinitializing all the stock variables to their levels prior to the interruption. Then, loosely speaking, an equilibrium of the original game is subgame perfect if it remains an equilibrium in the latter half of its evolution. In effect, subgame perfectness eliminates threats as allowable strategies and accomplishes precisely what the commitment paradigm demands. It is interesting that, while this solution concept is forward-looking in that it requires of players that they embody the optimal responses of the future into their current decision-making, its computation requires backward induction – as demonstrated in the previous sections. For, if future decisions are conditioned by current commitments, it is inevitable that we must first examine the optimal future actions when parameterized on current actions.

Typically, in each period only a subset of the choice variables would represent commitments. The computation of an equilibrium entails a resolution of the (market) game in each period by choice of the variables that are not pre-committed. Each player, given his conjectures, thus 'maximizes out' the latter from his value function in terms of parametrically given commitments. The crux of the problem then boils down to the optimal choice of the commitments – and these are chosen in the commitment game in the foresighted fashion described above. We thus come to the view that an oligopoly equilibrium based on the new paradigm of industrial organization is a subgame perfect equilibrium of a game that is essentially played out in commitments.

It is important to note that the commitment paradigm requires only intertemporal consistency. It says nothing about the rules according to which the one period market games are resolved. Selten (1975) assumed a Nash resolution of these games. However, there is no compelling reason why this must be so, and indeed we did not require this assumption in the general model of Section 2. Conceptually, there is no difficulty with replacing Nash behaviour by any other that seems reasonable.[9] With respect to pre-committed variables, however, the paradigm implies that the appropriate conjectures to posit are Nash: pre-committed variables are irreversibly fixed, by definition.

Explicit recognition of commitments and their role in oligopoly theory has brought to the foreground the importance of the so-called 'first mover advantage' – the privilege of being able to commit oneself before one's rivals. If entry into the industry and the moves in the ensuing game are sequential, the existence of vehicles of commitment confers on firms the privilege of being Stackelberg leaders *vis-à-vis* those whose moves are later. Thus although *ex-ante* all the players may face symmetric demand conditions and have access to identical technologies, commitments facilitate the exploitation of first mover advantages to implement asymmetric outcomes. In this view, entry deterrence emerges as one particular – and a rather extreme – asymmetric equilibrium. In general, first movers will seek to utilize commitments to enforce the most profitable asymmetric outcome within the set of feasible equilibria.

Historically, the first use of the commitment paradigm may be traced to Hotelling (1929). In a linear spatial model in which firm locations, once chosen, were unchangeable, he obtained the Nash duopoly equilibrium (in prices), parameterized on the commitments (i.e. locations) of the two firms. What Hotelling failed to do was to have the firms choose their locations in a foresighted fashion; this was accomplished by Hay (1976) and by Prescott and Visscher (1977). Eaton and Lipsey (1979) applied the paradigm to propose the idea of market pre-emption in a spatial model – bringing to focus the first mover advantage in forestalling entry. Schmalensee (1978) utilized the same principle in an attempt to explain the observed proliferation of brands in the ready-to-eat cereals market, using a one-dimensional characteristics model.

In the context of homogeneous markets, Spence (1977) was the first to apply the idea of irreversibility of capital investment as a vehicle to deter entry. Dixit (1980) pursued the idea and delineated the nature of the perfect equilibria that can obtain when an existing monopolist is faced with a single potential entrant. Ware (1983) has recently analysed the logical structure of the commitment paradigm and has re-examined the perfect equilibria that can obtain in capital-commitment models. Becker and Spulber (1980), Dixit (1980) and Eaton and Lipsey (1980) observed that, since commitments have strategic value in addition to value in production, firms will not minimize costs with respect to pre-committed variables. Brander and Spencer (1983) made the important observation that, when pre-commitments must be chosen prior to production, oligopolistic games are unavoidably sequential.

What purpose has the commitment paradigm served and what has it yet to accomplish? Primarily, it has imposed rationality on solution concepts used in oligopoly theory and has consequently eliminated a great deal of 'adhockery'. The stringent requirements of dynamic consistency and credibility of strategies have narrowed down the set of equilibria that are deemed acceptable. Secondly, the new paradigm affords the possibility of a theory of endogenous market structure. Given the vehicles of commitment available to the players, the rules of behaviour, and the sequence of their moves, the paradigm enables us, in principle, to obtain the market structure endogenously. However, the research agenda suggested by the paradigm is far from complete. There is, to date, no algorithm that systematically applies the paradigm to throw up the equilibrium market structure when the said equilibrium has more than two firms; the commitment paradigm still awaits operationalization.

Acknowledgement
We would like to thank Yehuda Kotowitz for useful comments on an earlier draft.

Notes

1. For a recent overview of the field, see Dixit (1982).
2. Spence (1977) and Dixit (1980) focus on this mechanism.
3. See Salop and Scheffman (1983) on this.
4. Of course, advertising could also affect the revenue function of rivals. See Schmalensee (1983) for an application of this idea.
5. We allow for only one pre-committed variable for ease of exposition; there is no analytical difficulty in allowing for many.
6. We abstract from the possibility that the goods could conceivably be rented rather than sold, since this is an issue separate from the one on which we wish to focus. Bulow (1982) and Bucovetsky and Chilton (1983) consider this possibility.
7. Since the exisiting literature is voluminous, our discussion of the historical development must necessarily be broad.
8. We restrict ourselves to games of perfect information for simplicity.
9. See Brander and Harris (1983) for a treatment of the capital-commitment game when the resolution of the market game is collusive.

References

Becker, R.A. and D.F. Spulber (1980), 'Entry, Strategic Investment and Factor Biases', Brown University Working Paper no. 80-10 (July).

Brander, J.A. and R.G. Harris (1983), 'Anticipated Collusion and Excess Capacity', Queen's University Discussion Paper no. 530.

Brander, J.A. and B.J. Spencer (1983), 'Strategic Commitment with R & D: The Symmetric Case', *Bell Journal of Economics*, pp. 225–35 (Spring).

Bucovetsky, S. and J. Chilton (1983), 'Concurrent Renting and Selling in a Durable-Goods Monopoly Under Threat of Entry', University of Western Ontario Discussion Paper no. 83-17.

Bulow, J.I. (1982), 'Durable-Goods Monopolists', *Journal of Political Economy*, pp. 314–32 (April).

Dixit, A. (1980), 'The Role of Investment in Entry-Deterrence', *Economic Journal*, pp. 95–106 (March).

Dixit, A. (1982), 'Recent Developments in Oligopoly Theory', *American Economic Review*, pp. 12–17 (May).

Eaton, B.C. and R.G. Lipsey (1979), 'The Theory of Market Pre-emption: The Persistence of Excess Capacity and Monopoly in a Growing Market', *Economica*, pp. 149–58 (May).

Eaton, B.C. and R.G. Lipsey (1980), 'Exit Barriers are Entry Barriers: The Durability of Capital as a Barrier to Entry', *Bell Journal of Economics*, pp. 721–9 (Autumn).

Hay, D.A. (1976), 'Sequential Entry and Entry-Deterring Strategies in Spatial Competition', *Oxford Economic Papers*, pp. 240–57 (July).

Hotelling, H. (1929), 'Stability in Competition', *Economic Journal*, pp. 41–57.

Prescott, E.C. and M. Visscher (1977), 'Sequential Location Among Firms with Foresight', *Bell Journal of Economics*, pp. 378–93 (Autumn).

Salop, S.C. and D.T. Scheffman (1983), 'Raising Rivals' Costs', *American Economic Review*, pp. 267–71 (May).

Schelling, T.C. (1956), 'An Essay on Bargaining', *American Economic Review*, pp. 281–306 (June).

Schmalensee, R. (1978), 'Entry Deterrence in the Ready-to-Eat Breakfast Cereals Industry', *Bell Journal of Economics*, pp. 305–27 (Autumn).

Schmalensee, R. (1979), 'Market Structure, Durability and Quality: A Selected Survey', *Economic Inquiry*, pp. 177–96 (April).

Schmalensee, R. (1983), 'Advertising and Entry Deterrence: An Exploratory Model', *Journal of Political Economy*, pp. 636–53 (August).

Selten, R. (1975) , 'Re-examination of the Perfectness Concept for Equilibrium Points in Extensive Games', *International Journal of Game Theory*, pp. 25–55 (January).

Spence, A.M. (1977), 'Entry, Capacity, Investment and Oligopolistic Pricing', *Bell Journal of Economics*, pp. 534–44 (Autumn).

Ware, R. (1983), 'Sunk Costs and Strategic Commitment: A Proposed Three Stage Equilibrium', University of Toronto Working Paper no. 8306.

[7]

Rand Journal of Economics
Vol. 16, No. 2, Summer 1985

Sophisticated entry in a model of spatial competition

B. Curtis Eaton*

and

Myrna Holtz Wooders*

We analyze free-entry equilibrium in a model of spatial competition in which locations of established firms are fixed and entrants' profit expectations are rational. Our most interesting results concern large economies—economies in which the number of firms is arbitrarily large. When the average cost function is U*-shaped, free-entry equilibrium is unique, socially optimal, and characterized by zero profit. In contrast, when there are no diseconomies of scale, even large economies are stubbornly imperfect. Firms can earn substantial pure profit and free-entry equilibrium is neither unique nor socially optimal.*

1. Introduction

■ In this article we explore the properties of free-entry equilibrium in a partial equilibrium model of product differentiation. The model can be interpreted as a model of spatial competition of the sort developed by Eaton and Lipsey (1978), Salop (1979), and Novshek (1980), or more generally as a model of competition in some space of possible brands. Our model differs from these in a number of technical ways and, more importantly, in the concept of free-entry equilibrium. To define free-entry equilibrium we assume that entrants are "sophisticated"—they enter only if their profit in the postentry equilibrium would be positive. That is, we model the entrant as a player in a game of perfect information.

The issue we see in defining the concept of free-entry equilibrium concerns the behavior of entrants. In most of the literature on free-entry equilibrium, potential entrants suppose that established firms will not alter prices in response to entry. (See Eaton (1976) and Novshek (1980) for examples and Salop (1979) for an exception.) This assumption leads to disappointment of the entrant's profit expectations since established firms ordinarily set prices in the postentry equilibrium which are lower than their preentry prices. Accordingly, the entrant's realized profit is less than his expected profit. Our view is that if entrants incur significant sunk costs, this property (that entrant's profit expectations are inaccurate) is undesirable and the price-taking assumption which drives it is naive. (See Archibald, Eaton, and Lipsey (1982) for a discussion of this view.)

---

* University of Toronto.

We are indebted to G.C. Archibald, Russell Davidson, Larry Epstein, Murkesh Eswaran, Larry Jones, Eric Kaltofen, and Richard Lipsey. Ken Judd provided an especially helpful referee's report. We gratefully acknowledge the financial support of the Social Sciences and Humanities Research Council of Canada.

Indeed, as Novshek (1980) argues, if we do not restrict this price expectation assumption, a free-entry equilibrium will ordinarily not exist, and where it does, it must exhibit zero profits. Suppose that some firm earns pure profit. Then an entrant who adopts that firm's location and shaves price will expect to appropriate virtually all of that firm's profit. Thus, zero-profit is a condition of equilibrium. But, the zero-profit condition can now be used to argue that free-entry equilibrium will not ordinarily exist since there may exist no *integer* number of firms—each earning zero profit—serving a finite market. Observe that the price-shaving entrant's price expectation is indeed naive. The firm whose very existence is threatened by this price shaving will respond with a price reduction, and the entrant can foresee this. Thus, Novshek (1980), following Eaton and Lipsey (1978), argues for the imposition of a "no-mill-price-undercutting" restriction on firms' price expectations. This can be seen as an attempt to rule out expectations that are wildly inconsistent with realizations.

In this article we take the next step: we require that expectations be consistent with realizations. Potential entrants, having perfect information, foresee the price equilibrium that would prevail if they were to enter. This allows them to calculate accurately their profits in any postentry equilibrium. Free-entry equilibrium then requires that the number of established firms be large enough that entry of another is not profitable.

In Salop (1979) entrants' expectations are consistent with realizations. In that article established firms respond to entry by changing their locations to establish a symmetric configuration of locations after entry. For this reason, Salop needs only to consider symmetric price equilibria to characterize free-entry equilibrium. In contrast, we assume that firms incur a location-specific sunk cost. Hence, established firms do not relocate in response to entry. To evaluate the profit an entrant would obtain at any location, and thus to characterize free-entry equilibrium, we must consider price equilibria which are asymmetric. This is the major analytical task in our article.

Not surprisingly, when the number of firms in a free-entry equilibrium is "small," firms may earn substantial pure profit, the equilibrium is not unique, and it may diverge from the social optimum. Relative to the social optimum, equilibrium in these small economies may involve an excessive or an insufficient number of firms. There can then be no general presumption whatever that the existence of profit in markets for differentiated goods implies that insufficient resources are being devoted to the market. Indeed, in our model, when there are a sunk set-up cost and constant marginal costs, the number of firms in free-entry equilibrium always exceeds the socially optimal number. It follows that the "best" of the free-entry equilibria in this case is the one that *maximizes* profit.

Our asymptotic results for "large" economies are perhaps more surprising. If firms have *U*-shaped average cost functions, asymptotically the free-entry equilibrium is unique and socially optimal, and pure profits disappear. On the other hand, if there are a sunk set-up cost and constant marginal costs, substantial pure profit persists, the free-entry equilibrium does not converge to the social optimum, and it is not asymptotically unique.

Our asymptotic results are, in what we think is a very interesting way, general results. They are independent in a significant sense of the conjectures entrants make about the price-setting behavior of existing firms in the postentry equilibrium. They hold even when entrants' conjectures are the most pessimistic conjectures in the class of conjectures restricted only by the assumption that established firms will never set a price less than marginal cost.

This suggests the conjecture that the properties of large economies are crucially dependent upon the nature of production costs. If there exists a minimum efficient scale of production, then large economies are essentially perfectly competitive. If there is no minimum efficient scale of production (if costs are composed of a lumpy set-up cost and a constant marginal cost, for example), then even large economies are imperfectly competitive.

In the next two sections we describe the model and characterize the optimal distribution of firms. In Section 4 we define more carefully what we mean by free-entry equilibrium. The analysis is contained in Sections 5 through 9. We conclude in Section 10.

2. The model

■ As we observed above, our model can be interpreted either as a model of spatial competition or as a model of competition in some brand or characteristic space. For simplicity, we shall lay it out as a model of spatial competition. Salop (1979) shows how models of spatial competition can be interpreted more generally.

The continuum of possible locations is the real line. We assume that each established firm produces some good at just one location. From the consumers' perspective, firm i is then completely characterized by its location on the real line, x_i, and by its price, p_i. We use the real line here to avoid tedious and well-known problems associated with the existence of market boundaries.

We assume that there is a uniform density of consumers, D, along the real line, that each consumer has a perfectly price inelastic demand for one unit of the good, and that the consumer incurs transportation costs which are a quadratic function of distance. Specifically, the consumer's cost of transporting a unit of the good from some firm located at x_i to the consumer's location at x is $(x - x_i)^2$. The price to the consumer inclusive of transport costs is then

$$p_i + (x - x_i)^2,$$

which we can regard as a *delivered price.* Consumers purchase their one unit from the firm offering the lowest delivered price. We use this quadratic transport cost function to ensure that price equilibrium always exists. The nonexistence problem in this type of model is articulated by d'Aspremont, Gabsezwicz, and Thisse (1979), and it is from them that we get the quadratic "fix."

Each firm's cost of producing Q units of the good is

$$C(Q) = K + aQ^2 + cQ, \qquad a \geq 0, \qquad K > 0, \qquad c \geq 0. \tag{1}$$

The parameter K is a sunk cost arising from a location-specific investment by the firm. Let J denote the magnitude of this investment. Then K is equal to rJ, where r is the appropriate interest rate. In a more general setting it is natural to interpret J as a product development cost. Since J is location-specific, established firms cannot relocate unless they reincur this cost. We assume, therefore, that after a firm has chosen a location, the location is fixed.

When the parameter a in this cost function is zero, we have the cost function that is ordinarily used in this literature. When a is positive, marginal costs increase linearly with output, and average costs are U-shaped. Without loss of generality we let the parameter c be zero. Thus, we use the following cost function:

$$C(Q) = K + aQ^2. \tag{2}$$

3. Optimality

■ Since consumers' demand is perfectly price inelastic in our model, the obvious optimality criterion is the minimization of the total resource cost of meeting this demand. It is intuitive and easy to show that optimality requires that each consumer patronize the nearest firm and that firms be equally spaced throughout the market. Denoting the distance between firms by L, we write the total resource cost of serving one firm's market segment as

$$DL^3/12 + aD^2L^2 + K.$$

The first term is transportation costs, the second, variable costs, and the third, the sunk cost. Per unit of market area, the total resource cost, which we denote by $RC(L)$, is

$$RC(L) = DL^2/12 + aD^2L + K/L. \tag{3}$$

Differentiating with respect to L and rearranging yield the following characterization of the optimal distance between firms, L^*:

$$DL^{*3} + 6aD^2L^{*2} - 6K = 0. \tag{4}$$

4. The concept of free-entry equilibrium

■ Before we plunge into the analysis of the model, it is useful to be more precise about the exercises we have in mind. Our objective is to examine the symmetric, free-entry equilibria of this model. By *symmetric* we mean equilibria in which established firms, each charging the same price, are evenly spaced along the real line. Let L denote the distance between any two adjacent firms. Let firms 1, 2, 3, . . . be located at $L/2$, $3L/2$, $5L/2$, . . . , and let firms -1, -2, -3, . . . be located at $-L/2$, $-3L/2$, $-5L/2$, ... Let zL denote the location of a potential entrant, where z satisfies $-½ < z < ½$. That is, the potential entrant's location is somewhere in the interval between firms -1 and 1. This configuration of locations is illustrated in Figure 1.

Now let

$$(\ldots, \bar{p}_{-3}, \bar{p}_{-2}, \bar{p}_{-1}, \bar{p}_0, \bar{p}_1, \bar{p}_2, \bar{p}_3, \ldots)$$

be the Nash price equilibrium associated with this configuration of locations. (Notice that we denote the entrant's price by p_0.) This price equilibrium is, of course, a postentry price equilibrium—it is the price equilibrium that would prevail if the potential entrant did, in fact, enter at location zL.

It is intuitive that the most profitable location for the entrant is at the origin in Figure 1. That is, z equal to zero maximizes the entrant's profit. Denote the entrant's profit in the postentry price equilibrium when z is zero by $\pi_0(L, K, D, a)$. Of course, K, D, and a are parameters of the model, while L is endogenous.

By the term (symmetric) *free-entry equilibrium* we mean a value of L such that each established firm earns nonnegative profit, and such that $\pi_0(L, K, D, a)$ is nonpositive. Not surprisingly, the entrant's profit in the postentry equilibrium is increasing in L. Denote by $\bar{L}$ the value of L such that $\pi_0(L, K, D, a)$ is zero. Then L must be less than or equal to $\bar{L}$ in free-entry equilibrium.

The condition that each established firm's profit be nonnegative provides a lower bound, denoted by $\underline{L}$, for L. Let L^e denote the distance between established firms in a free-entry equilibrium. Then,

$$\underline{L} \leq L^e \leq \bar{L}. \tag{5}$$

These bounds are, of course, determined by the parameters of the model, K, D, and a.

In small economies we discover that $\bar{L}$ exceeds $\underline{L}$. As a consequence, pure profit, which can be significant, is possible in free-entry equilibrium since the profit of established firms is zero at $\underline{L}$ and increasing in L. Further, it is impossible to make any general statement about the relationship of the equilibrium distance between firms, L^e, to the optimal distance, L^*; there may be an excessive number of firms, an insufficient number, or just the right number in small economies.

FIGURE 1

POSTENTRY CONFIGURATION OF LOCATIONS

We examine two asymptotic exercises. As K approaches zero or as D approaches infinity, both $\bar{L}$ and $\underline{L}$ approach zero and create a large economy. The properties of free-entry equilibrium in these exercises are dependent upon a. When a is positive and average costs are therefore U-shaped, both $\bar{L}/L^*$ and $\underline{L}/L^*$ approach one. Accordingly, in the large-economy limits the free-entry equilibrium is unique and socially optimal.

When a is zero, the model is stubbornly imperfect, even in large economies. The ratios $\bar{L}/L^*$ and $\underline{L}/L^*$ are, in fact, independent of K and D in this case. There are always an excessive number of firms in free-entry equilibrium since $\bar{L}/L^*$ is less than one (and bounded away from one), and the profit any established firm earns at $\bar{L}$ is significant relative to K.

5. The preentry price equilibrium

■ In this section we derive the preentry price equilibrium—the price equilibrium that prevails when the distance between any two adjacent firms is L. This configuration is illustrated in Figure 2. In the preentry price equilibrium firm i will be in direct competition with precisely two firms, $i - 1$ and $i + 1$.[1] The market boundary between firms i and $i - 1$, which we denote by $\bar{x}$, satisfies

$$p_i + (x_i - \bar{x})^2 = p_{i-1} + (x_{i-1} - \bar{x})^2,$$

where x_i and x_{i-1} are the locations of firms i and $i - 1$. The point $\bar{x}$ is the point where the delivered prices of the two firms are identical. Solving for $\bar{x}$ and using the fact that $x_i - x_{i-1} = L$, we have

$$\bar{x} = p_i/2L - p_{i-1}/2L + x_i - L/2.$$

Similarly, the market boundary between firms i and $i + 1$, call it $\hat{x}$, is

$$\hat{x} = p_{i+1}/2L - p_i/2L + x_i + L/2.$$

The extent of i's market is just $(\hat{x} - \bar{x})$, and quantity demanded from firm i is $D(\hat{x} - \bar{x})$. We then have the demand function for firm i:

$$Q_i = D[p_{i-1} + p_{i+1} + 2L^2 - 2p_i]/[2L]. \quad (6)$$

The gross profit of firm i, the excess of revenues over variable costs, will then be

$$R_i = p_iQ_i - aQ_i^2.$$

FIGURE 2

PREENTRY CONFIGURATION OF LOCATIONS

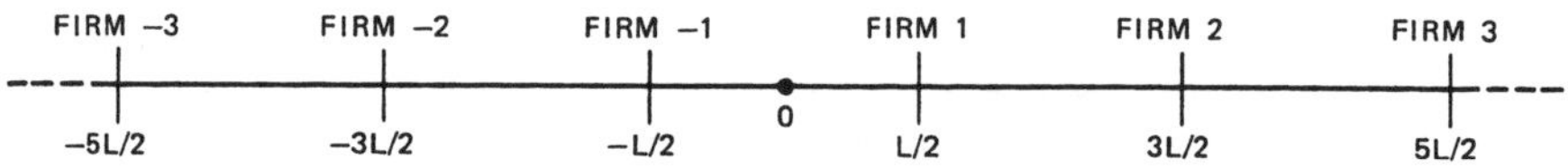

[1] To see that firm i will be in direct competition with its two nearest neighbors in the price equilibrium, assume that it is not. For concreteness, assume that it is in direct competition with $i + 2$ in a price equilibrium. Then the boundary between firms i and $i + 2$ will be at

$$\tilde{x} = L + (p_{i+2} - p_i)/4L + x_i.$$

The delivered price of $i + 1$ at $\tilde{x}$ must be greater than or equal to the delivered price of firm i at $\tilde{x}$, which implies the following inequality:

$$p_{i+1} \geq L^2 + (p_i + p_{i+2})/2.$$

Any such price could not be an equilibrium price for $i + 1$. It sells nothing at this price—i dominates $i + 1$ to the left of $\tilde{x}$ and $i + 2$ dominates it to the right of $\tilde{x}$—and its gross profit is therefore zero. Now evaluate the derivative of R_{i+1} with respect to p_{i+1} at p_{i+1} equal to $L^2 + (p_i + p_{i+2})/2$. It is negative, and $i + 1$ will choose a lower price. At any lower price, firm i is in direct competition with $i + 1$, but not $i + 2$.

Observe that R_i is a strictly concave function of p_i, and thus in the Nash price equilibrium the partial derivative of R_i with respect to p_i must vanish. Setting this derivative equal to zero, we obtain the first-order condition:

$$0 = p_{i+1} - Ep_i + p_{i-1} + 2L^2, \qquad E = [4L + 4aD]/[L + 2aD]. \tag{7}$$

To find the preentry price equilibrium in which each firm chooses the same price, say $\hat{p}$, we can set all three prices in (7) equal to $\hat{p}$, and solve for $\hat{p}$:

$$\hat{p} = L(L + 2aD). \tag{8}$$

Using (8), we can then write the gross profit of a representative firm in the preentry price equilibrium, $\hat{R}$, as

$$\hat{R} = DL^3 + aD^2L^2. \tag{9}$$

6. The postentry price equilibrium

■ We now turn to the more difficult task of finding the Nash price equilibrium for the configuration of locations illustrated in Figure 1. We refer to this price equilibrium as the postentry price equilibrium. In this price equilibrium each firm will be in direct competition with its two neighbors for the reason outlined in footnote 1. Then, using the method for spatial aggregation of demand described above, we have:

$$Q_0 = D[2(1 - 2z)p_{-1} + 2(1 + 2z)p_1 + (1 + 2z)(1 - 2z)L^2 - 4p_0] \div [2L(1 + 2z)(1 - 2z)] \tag{10a}$$

$$Q_{-1} = D[4p_0 + 2(1 + 2z)p_{-2} + (1 + 2z)(3 + 2z)L^2 - 2(3 + 2z)p_{-1}]/[4L(1 + 2z)] \tag{10b}$$

$$Q_1 = D[4p_0 + 2(1 - 2z)p_2 + (1 - 2z)(3 - 2z)L^2 - 2(3 - 2z)p_1]/[4L(1 - 2z)] \tag{10c}$$

$$Q_i = D[p_{i-1} + p_{i+1} + 2L^2 - 2p_i]/[2L], \qquad i = \ldots - 3, -2, 2, 3, \ldots. \tag{10d}$$

Using these demand functions, we can define gross profit functions. We observe that these are strictly concave in own prices. Thus, we can characterize the postentry price equilibrium by one first-order condition for each firm. The first-order conditions are

$$0 = 2(1 - 2z)p_{-1} + 2(1 + 2z)p_1 + (1 + 2z)(1 - 2z)L^2 - 4p_0[2L(1 + 2z)(1 - 2z) + 4aD]/[L(1 + 2z)(1 - 2z) + 4aD], \tag{11a}$$

$$0 = 4p_0 + 2(1 + 2z)p_{-2} + (1 + 2z)(3 + 2z)L^2 - 2p_{-1}(3 + 2z)[2L(1 + 2z) + (3 + 2z)aD]/[L(1 + 2z) + (3 + 2z)aD], \tag{11b}$$

$$0 = 4p_0 + 2(1 - 2z)p_2 + (1 - 2z)(3 - 2z)L^2 - 2p_1(3 - 2z)[2L(1 - 2z) + (3 - 2z)aD]/[L(1 - 2z) + (3 - 2z)aD], \tag{11c}$$

$$0 = p_{i+1} - Ep_i + p_{i-1} + 2L^2, \qquad i = \ldots, -3, -2, 2, 3, \ldots. \tag{11d}$$

The first three of these, respectively, are the profit-maximizing conditions for the entrant, for firm -1, and for firm 1, respectively. Equation (11d) is, of course, identical to (7), and E is defined in (7).

To solve this system of first-order conditions for the postentry price equilibrium we observe that embedded in the system are two second-order difference equations. That is, $i = 2, 3, 4, \ldots$ in (11d) defines a second-order difference equation, and $i = -2, -3, -4, \ldots$ defines an equivalent one. We shall use standard methods for solving second-order difference equations and a restriction on the price equilibrium to collapse the first-order conditions in (11) to a system involving only five equations and five prices, p_{-2}, p_{-1}, p_0, p_1, and p_2.

The restriction we impose is that prices be bounded in the postentry price equilibrium. We discuss this restriction below.

The difference equation defined by the profit-maximizing conditions for firms 2, 3, . . . is

$$p_{i+1} - Ep_i + p_{i-1} = -2L^2.$$

(We use Chiang's (1974) terminology in describing the solution.) The particular integral is $\hat{p}$, the preentry equilibrium price defined in (8). The characteristic equation is

$$b^2 - Eb + 1 = 0,$$

which has two distinct real roots,

$$b_1, b_2 = [E \pm (E^2 - 4)^{1/2}]/2, \tag{12}$$

since E exceeds two, and, therefore, $E^2 - 4$ is positive. The general solution then has the following form,

$$p_i = \hat{p} + A_1 b_1^{i-1} + A_2 b_2^{i-1},$$

where A_1 and A_2 are as yet undetermined constants.

The dominant root of the characteristic equation is b_1. Its value exceeds one (b_2 is positive and less than one). As a consequence, as i increases, p_i increases without bound so long as A_1 is positive. Hence, if prices are to be bounded, A_1 must be zero.

The condition that A_1 be zero determines a relationship between p_1 and p_2 which must hold in the price equilibrium, and it also determines A_2. From the general solution we know that

$$p_1 = \hat{p} + A_1 + A_2,$$

$$p_2 = \hat{p} + A_1 b_1 + A_2 b_2.$$

Using these relationships to express A_1 and A_2 in terms of p_1, p_2, and $\hat{p}$, we have

$$A_1 = [(p_1 - \hat{p})b_2 - (p_2 - \hat{p})]/[b_2 - b_1] \tag{13a}$$

$$A_2 = [p_2 - \hat{p} - b_1(p_1 - \hat{p})]/[b_2 - b_1]. \tag{13b}$$

But A_1 must be zero, which implies that

$$p_2 = p_1 b_2 + \hat{p}(1 - b_2). \tag{14a}$$

Analogously, we see that

$$p_{-2} = p_{-1} b_2 + \hat{p}(1 - b_2). \tag{14b}$$

The collapsed system then consists of (11a), (11b), (11c), (14a), and (14b). These relationships determine five postentry equilibrium prices, which we denote by $\bar{p}_{-2}$, $\bar{p}_{-1}$, $\bar{p}_0$, $\bar{p}_1$, and $\bar{p}_2$. The closed-form expressions for these prices are very complex and therefore uninformative, so we omit them. Using standard techniques, in Eaton and Wooders (1983) we show that these prices are unique and, of course, positive. To determine the remaining postentry equilibrium prices we must determine A_2. From (13b) and (14a) we see that

$$A_2 = (p_1 - \hat{p}).$$

From this and the fact that A_1 is zero, we obtain the particular solution to the difference equation:

$$\bar{p}_i = \hat{p} + (\bar{p}_1 - \hat{p})b_2^{i-1}, \qquad i = 3, 4, 5 \ldots. \tag{15a}$$

Similarly,

$$\bar{p}_i = \hat{p} + (\bar{p}_{-1} - \hat{p})b_2^{-1-i}, \qquad i = -3, -4, -5, \ldots. \tag{15b}$$

By insisting that A_1 be zero we can identify the solution to the first-order conditions in equations (11) in which prices are bounded. Solutions to (11) exist in which prices are unbounded. We claim such solutions are economically meaningless. Suppose that A_1 is positive. (If A_1 were negative, we would clearly have nonsense.) Then, using the general solution, we can compute the extent of firm i's market. It is

$$L + [b_1^{i-2}A_1(1 - b_1)^2 + b_2^{i-2}A_2[1 - b_2]^2]/[2L].$$

Since b_1 exceeds one, we infer that individual firms' markets as well as prices are unbounded. If we want to interpret our results as an approximation to what would happen in a large but finite space of products, the unboundedness of prices and markets is nonsense. In addition, unbounded prices require that individual consumers' incomes be unbounded. For these reasons, we consider the unique solution in which prices are bounded.

In principle we can use these postentry equilibrium prices to write the entrant's gross profit in the postentry price equilibrium as a function of z, a, D, and L:

$$R_0 = R_0(z, a, D, L). \tag{16}$$

Consider now the choice of location (that is, the choice of z) that maximizes the entrant's gross profit. It is easy to see that the derivative of this gross profit function with respect to z is zero when z is zero, since the function is symmetric about z equal to zero: it is an even function of z. To show that the entrant's gross profit is maximized at this location is more difficult. We obtained the result by using a computer algebra program (VAXIMA). See Eaton and Wooders (1983) for details.

When z is zero, $\bar{p}_{-1} = \bar{p}_1$ and $\bar{p}_{-2} = \bar{p}_2$. These results follow from the fact that when z is zero, the entrant is located symmetrically with respect to firms -1 and 1, and also with respect to -2 and 2. We can use these results to characterize the postentry price equilibrium more simply. From (11a) and (11b) (or (11c)) we have

$$0 = 4p_1 - 8p_0[L + 2aD]/[L + 4aD] + L^2, \tag{17a}$$

$$0 = 4p_0 + 2p_2 - 6p_1[2L + 3aD]/[L + 3aD] + 3L^2. \tag{17b}$$

These two equations and (14a) determine $\bar{p}_2$, $\bar{p}_1$, and $\bar{p}_0$ (when z is zero). Equation (15a) determines equilibrium prices for firms 3, 4, ... Finally, $\bar{p}_{-i} = \bar{p}_i$ for all i.

7. Properties of free-entry equilibria: $a = 0$

■ When a is equal to zero, the model is quite manageable. The postentry price equilibrium is

$$\bar{p}_0 = L^2X \tag{18a}$$

$$\bar{p}_1 = L^2Y, \tag{18b}$$

$$\bar{p}_i = L^2[1 - Z(2 - \sqrt{3})^{i-1}], \qquad i = 3, 4, \ldots, \tag{18c}$$

where

$$X = [27 + 16\sqrt{3}]/[72 + 40\sqrt{3}],$$

$$Y = [36 + 22\sqrt{3}]/[72 + 40\sqrt{3}],$$

$$Z = [36 + 18\sqrt{3}]/[72 + 40\sqrt{3}].$$

From (8) we see that the preentry equilibrium price, $\hat{p}$, is equal to L^2. Since $\bar{p}_1$ is less than $\hat{p}$, from (15a), we see that postentry equilibrium prices converge monotonically to $\hat{p}$ from below. How rapid is the convergence? Dividing the postentry price for the entrant and firms 1, 2, 3, and 4 by the preentry price, we obtain the following price ratios: .387, .525, .87, .97, and .99. Thus, competition created by entry is *fierce*—firm 1's price after entry is roughly half its price before entry—but decidedly *local*—firm 4's price is virtually unaffected by entry.

The gross profit of the entrant in the postentry equilibrium is

$$\bar{R}_0 = 2DL^3X^2. \tag{19}$$

Recall that X is defined in (18). The gross profit of any firm in the preentry equilibrium is, from equation (9),

$$\hat{R} = DL^3. \tag{20}$$

Free-entry equilibrium requires that $\bar{R}_0 \leq K$ and that $\hat{R} \geq K$. These conditions imply that

$$\underline{L} = (K/D)^{1/3} \leq L^e \leq (K/2DX^2)^{1/3} = \bar{L}. \tag{21}$$

When a is zero, our welfare criterion is also simplified:

$$L^* = (6K/D)^{1/3}. \tag{22}$$

From (21) and (22) we have

$$.55 \cong (1/6)^{1/3} \leq L^e/L^* \leq (1/12X^2)^{1/3} \cong .82. \tag{23}$$

Thus, relative to the social optimum, there are always an excessive number of firms in free-entry equilibrium. This result—excessive diversity—is consistent with Salop's (1979). As we shall see in the following section, it is not a general result. Salop's cost function is the same as ours, however, with a equal to zero. This suggests the conjecture that when there are no diseconomies of scale, there is always excessive diversity in free-entry equilibrium.

Letting L equal $\bar{L}$, we maximize an established firm's gross profit in free-entry equilibrium, since its gross profit is an increasing function of L. We can express this gross profit as a rate of return on the location-specific investment, J, which is equal to K/r. Doing so, we have

$$\max_{L^e} \hat{R}/J = r/2Z^2 \cong 3.33r. \tag{24}$$

Thus, pure profit is possible in free-entry equilibrium. Since there is inevitably an excessive number of firms in equilibrium, the best of the free-entry equilibria is the one that maximizes the distance between firms, that is, the one that maximizes the profit of established firms. Observe that the results reported in (23) and (24) are independent of K and D.

We can create large economies by letting K get small or by letting D get large. In either case, both $\underline{L}$ and $\bar{L}$ converge to zero. Hence, L^e converges to zero. Further, the price of each established firm approaches marginal cost since from (8) the (common) price in free-entry equilibrium is just $(L^e)^2$ and the marginal cost is zero. These results appear to be competitive results.

Because the results in (23) and (24) are independent of both K and D, however, it is apparent that these asymptotic results are not, in fact, competitive. Even in large economies, the maximum rate of return on the location-specific investment is approximately 3⅓ times the competitive rate of return, and L^e/L^* is bounded above by .82 and below by .55. In this sense our model, when a is zero, is imperfect even in large economies.

We get a different perspective on these results by focusing on the magnitude of the inefficiency in large economies. Using (22) and (3), we can compute *minimized* total resource costs, which we denote by $RC(L^*)$:

$$RC(L^*) = .83D^{1/3}K^{2/3}.$$

Total resource costs in free-entry equilibrium are a maximum when L^e is equal to $\underline{L}$. Using (21) and (3), we can also compute $RC(\underline{L})$:

$$RC(\underline{L}) = 1.08D^{1/3}K^{2/3}.$$

The ratio of $RC(L)$ to $RC(L^*)$, which is obviously independent of K and D, is approximately 1.30. Thus, in *relative* terms the magnitude of inefficiency can be substantial, even in large economies. It is not necessarily large since $RC(\bar{L})/RC(L^*)$ is (approximately) 1.03.

Now let K approach zero. Both $RC(L^*)$ and $RC(\underline{L})$ approach zero, and we see that, in absolute terms, the magnitude of inefficiency is vanishingly small in this large economy limit. As we let D get large, it is informative to consider inefficiency on a *per capita* basis. Dividing $RC(L^*)$ and $RC(\underline{L})$ by D, we have the appropriate *per capita* measure. As D gets large, both $RC(L^*)/D$ and $RC(\underline{L})/D$ approach zero, and again the absolute magnitude of inefficiency is vanishingly small. Thus, in the sense in which Hart (1979) and Jones (1985) use the term, these asymptotic results are *approximately competitive.*

8. Properties of free-entry equilibria: $a > 0$

■ When the average cost function is U-shaped, that is, when a is positive, the closed-form expressions for equilibrium prices and gross revenue of the entrant are so complex that staring at them produces no insight. We shall therefore illustrate the results, many of which are intuitive, and relegate proofs to the Appendix.

In the postentry price equilibrium we have

$$\hat{p} > \bar{p}_2 > \bar{p}_1 > \bar{p}_0.$$

From (15a) we then see that postentry equilibrium prices again monotonically converge to $\hat{p}$ (the preentry equilibrium price) from below. Again the ratio of $\bar{p}_i$ to $\hat{p}$ converges rapidly to one.

To focus discussion of the properties of free-entry equilibrium, we devised a computer program to calculate essential features of the equilibrium. We report typical results in Tables 1 and 2. To generate the results in Table 1, we fixed the values of a and D (a is 10 and D is 1), and varied the remaining parameter, K, over 16 orders of magnitude to create small and large economies. In column 2 we report the potential for pure profit in free-entry equilibrium—we report the gross profit of an established firm when L is equal to $\bar{L}$ divided by J, which is equal to K/r. This ratio is then the maximum rate of return, that an established firm could earn on its location-specific investment. In columns 3 and 5 we report $\bar{L}/L^*$ and

TABLE 1 **Free-Entry Equilibrium, $a = 10$, $D = 1$***

K	max R/J	$\bar{L}/L^*$	$T(\bar{L}, L^*)$	$\underline{L}/L^*$	$T(\underline{L}, L^*)$	L^0/L^*	$T(L^0, L^*)$
10^{11}	3.33r	.82	1.036	.55	1.31	2.56	1.40
10^7	3.22r	.84	1.025	.57	1.26	2.50	1.40
10^5	2.87r	.92	1.005	.63	1.14	2.27	1.39
10^4	2.50r	.99	1.000	.71	1.07	2.04	1.37
10^3	2.03r	1.08	1.003	.81	1.02	1.75	1.31
10^2	1.61r	1.12	1.007	.90	1.01	1.45	1.19
10^1	1.37r	1.10	1.005	.99	1.00	1.23	1.08
10^0	1.18r	1.07	1.003	.99	1.00	1.11	1.03
10^{-1}	1.10r	1.04	1.001	1.00	1.00	1.06	1.01
10^{-4}	1.02r	1.01	1.000	1.00	1.00	1.00	1.00

* Variables:
L^* = optimal L.
$\bar{L}$ = largest L in free-entry equilibrium.
$\underline{L}$ = zero-profit L.
L^0 = largest L in free-entry equilibrium with cautious entrants.
$T(L^i, L^j)$ = ratio of total resource costs at $L = L^i$ to total costs at $L = L^j$.

$\underline{L}/L^*$. In column 4 we report the ratio of total resource costs when L is equal to $\bar{L}$ to total resource costs when L is equal to L^*. In column 5 we report the corresponding ratio when L is equal to $\underline{L}$. (The results reported in the last two columns of the table are relevant to the next section.)

When K is large and therefore the number of firms per unit of market area is small, significant profit is possible in free-entry equilibrium. Since $\bar{L}/L^*$ is less than one, there is inevitably an excessive number of firms in free-entry equilibrium. Also, resource misallocation may be significant since total resource costs in the zero-profit, free-entry equilibrium are as much as 30% higher than they are at L^*. Observe that the results reported in the first row of Table 1 are virtually identical to the results in the case where a is zero. That is, when K is large, the two versions of our model are equivalent in essential respects.

As we decrease K, the potential for pure profit decreases, and both $\bar{L}/L^*$ and $\underline{L}/L^*$ increase. When K is less than 10^3, $\bar{L}/L^*$ exceeds one and $\underline{L}/L^*$ is less than one. Hence, there may be an excessive or an insufficient number of firms in free-entry equilibrium. Correspondingly, the limits on the potential for resource misallocation narrow.

Finally, as K approaches zero, the potential for pure profit vanishes, and both $\bar{L}/L^*$ and $\underline{L}/L^*$ converge to one. That is, in the large economy limit, free-entry equilibrium is unique and socially optimal, and established firms just cover their costs. These large economy results are general results in the sense that they do not depend on the values of D and a. That is, for any D and any positive a, as K approaches zero, free-entry equilibrium is unique and socially optimal, and firms earn zero profit. Proofs appear in the Appendix.

In Table 2 we report the results of an analogous computer exercise. In this exercise we fixed the value of K (100) and again the value of a (100), and created large or small economies by varying D. Qualitatively, the results are identical to those presented in Table 1. Small economies are decidedly imperfect (pure profit is possible and there are inevitably an excessive number of firms in free-entry equilibrium) and large economies are perfect (firms earn no profit and the free-entry equilibrium is unique and socially optimal). Again, the large-economy results are general—they hold for any values of K and positive a. The proof appears in the Appendix.

As we argued in the Introduction, a major reason for exploring the implications of sophisticated behavior on the part of entrants is that naive entrants systematically overestimate the profit available to them. They may enter when entry is not in fact profitable, thereby biasing the free-entry equilibrium toward a zero-profit equilibrium. Nevertheless, in our model with sophisticated entrants, we discover a zero-profit result in the large economy limits when a is positive. This suggests that the large-economy results are, in some sense, independent of the conjectures entrants hold about the response of existing firms to their entry. We explore this possibility in the next section.

TABLE 2 Free-Entry Equilibrium, a = 100, K = 100*

D	max R/J	$\bar{L}/L^*$	$T(\bar{L}, L^*)$	$\underline{L}/L^*$	$T(\underline{L}, L^*)$	L^0/L^*	$T(L^0, L^*)$
10^2	1.00r	1.00	1.000	1.00	1.00	1.00	1.000
10^1	1.01r	1.00	1.000	1.00	1.00	1.00	1.000
10^0	1.10r	1.04	1.001	.99	1.00	1.15	1.010
10^{-1}	2.03r	1.08	1.003	.81	1.00	1.75	1.309
10^{-2}	3.22r	.85	1.025	.57	1.26	2.50	1.395
10^{-3}	3.33r	.82	1.036	.55	1.31	2.56	1.398
10^{-4}	3.33r	.82	1.036	.55	1.31	2.56	1.399
10^{-5}	3.33r	.82	1.036	.55	1.31	2.56	1.399

* Variables are as defined in Table 1.

9. The cautious entrant

■ What is the most pessimistic or cautious view the entrant could entertain about the response of rivals to his entry? Might the entrant entertain the notion that an existing firm would choose price less than its marginal cost? Apparently not. By assumption, each firm owns one and only one plant, and each firm's specific capital is sunk forever. Therefore, firms cannot be driven from the market. In particular, the entrant could not be driven from the market, and minimal foresight allows the entrant and existing firms to see this result.

Therefore, firms will never choose a price that is less than marginal cost since this conflicts with both their short- and long-run self-interest. It then seems to us that the most pessimistic or cautious view the entrant could reasonably entertain must satisfy the restriction that the expected price of each firm must be greater than or equal to that firm's marginal cost.

Not surprisingly, among the set of price expectations that satisfy this restriction, the one that generates the lowest expected profit for the entrant is the one in which the price of each firm is equal to its marginal cost. In this section we examine symmetric free-entry equilibria when entrants adopt this cautious approach (and when the symmetric price equilibrium of existing firms is again a Nash equilibrium). Our purpose in doing so is to examine the robustness of the asymptotic results for the large economy that were discussed in the preceding section. Once again, we discover a striking divergence between the case where the parameter a is zero and the case where it is positive.

When a is zero, the cautious entrant expects his rivals to charge a zero price. His best price response to this conjecture is easily shown to be $L^2/8$, which generates gross profit equal to $DL^3/32$. Before entry existing firms generate gross profit equal to DL^3, and we infer that free-entry equilibrium, *policed only by cautious entrants,* is consistent with a rate of return on the location-specific investment of 32 times the competitive rate of return. This result is independent of D and K. The qualitative nature of this result is not surprising. We showed above that the free-entry equilibrium, driven by sophisticated entrants, was consistent with substantial pure profit. When the free-entry equilibrium is driven by cautious entrants, it is clear that the potential for profit in free-entry equilibrium must increase.

When a is positive, the solution of the cautious entrant's problem requires that we resort to procedures similar to those used in the preceding analysis for the postentry price equilibrium. Since they are directly analogous to the procedures used to analyze the basic model, we omit the details. They are, however, presented in Eaton and Wooders (1983).

We illustrate some features of the free-entry equilibrium with cautious entry in Tables 1 and 2. Define L^0 to be the value of L such that the cautious entrant expects zero profit. In column 7 of both tables we report L^0/L^*. It is immediately clear that our conjecture about the robustness of the results for the large economy is confirmed. In the large-economy limits L^0/L^* converges to one, and therefore L^e converges to L^*. This is a striking result: in large economies, when a is positive, L^e is independent of the conjectures entrants make with respect to the behavior of existing firms after entry. From above we have the additional result that, if the price equilibrium of the established firms (before entry) is a Nash equilibrium, then there can be no profit in the large economy limits. These limiting results are again general in the sense that they do not depend on the parameters of the model as long as a is positive.

It is relatively easy to see why the asymptotic results are identical when a is positive. Consider first the case where D increases without bound. In this case the inverse demand functions become perfectly elastic since D enters multiplicatively in the demand aggregation. Therefore, in the postentry price equilibrium with sophisticated entrants (Section 6), each firm's price approaches its marginal cost as D increases without bound. Hence, in the large-economy limit, the cautious entrant's price expectations are accurate or rational, and the asymptotic results are the same when entrants are cautious as they are when entrants are sophisticated. In the concluding section we show that as K approaches zero, inverse demand functions also become horizontal. Hence, as K approaches zero, the cautious entrant's expectations are again rational.

10. Conclusions

■ The asymptotic results for large economies are crucially dependent on whether the cost function is U-shaped or L-shaped. When a is positive, asymptotically the free-entry equilibrium is unique and socially optimal, and pure profits disappear. When a is zero, the free-entry equilibrium does not converge to the social optimum, it does not become unique, and the potential for pure profit persists. Here we attempt an intuitive explanation of these divergent results.

First, observe that in the postentry price equilibrium, the entrant's price is the lowest, and prices monotonically increase with distance from the entrant and rapidly converge to the preentry equilibrium price. These results are intuitive—price competition in this model of "overlapping oligopolies" is *localized.*

Second, observe that as density increases without limit, the demand functions of all firms become vertical (the inverse demand functions become horizontal) since density enters multiplicatively in the demand aggregation. This implies that each firm's price (in the pre- and postentry price equilibria) asymptotically approaches its marginal cost. It is intuitive that the equilibrium prices of neighboring firms in the postentry equilibrium must converge. In particular, the price of the entrant converges to the prices of his neighbors (firms 1 and -1), which in turn converge to the prices of firms 2 and -2, and so on. But, since competition is localized (the prices of firms not in the immediate vicinity of the entrant are virtually unaffected by entry), all postentry equilibrium prices converge to the preentry equilibrium price.

When the cost function is U-shaped, this implies that all postentry quantities must approach the preentry quantities since all prices approach their own marginal cost. But this implies that gross profits of the entrant in the postentry equilibrium approach gross profits of existing firms in the preentry equilibrium. Hence, zero-profit is a property of free-entry equilibrium in large economies (when a is positive), and all firms produce at minimum average cost. This is efficient since each consumer can purchase his most preferred brand at minimum unit cost in the limiting economy and will incur virtually no transport cost.

When the average cost curve is L-shaped (a is equal to zero), the result that all quantities in the postentry equilibrium converge to the preentry quantities does not follow, even though all prices in the postentry equilibrium converge to the preentry price and all inverse demand functions become horizontal. This is so since the condition that each firm's price approach its own marginal cost does not imply finite quantities in the limiting economy—there are no diseconomies of scale. The persistence of pure profit as density increases is driven by an ever decreasing mark-up on an ever increasing quantity.

The intuitive understanding of the asymptotic results when the set-up cost, K, approaches zero is identical in all respects except one. The difference concerns the force that makes the inverse demand functions become horizontal. As K approaches zero, the distance between firms or brands approaches zero. Any consumer is then choosing between brands which are close in the brand space and those which are close to the consumer's most preferred brand. The rate of change of transport costs with respect to distance is virtually zero when distance is small. This implies that a small reduction in the price of one brand will cause a large proportion of the consumers of competing brands to switch.

We conclude with some observations about cautious entry. Surprisingly, the basic properties of our results for the large economy are independent of the conjectures made by the entrant concerning the postentry behavior of established firms, as long as these conjectures are at least as optimistic as those of the cautious (and pessimistic) entrant. Our approach here is clearly *ad hoc*, but serves our purpose well; it illustrates the robustness of our asymptotic results to the entrant's conjectures. To our knowledge, in the literature concerning free-entry equilibrium in an oligopolistic market, ours are the only results that are independent of the conjectures of the entrant.

Appendix

■ In this Appendix we provide proofs of the central claims of the article. For the convenience of the reader, we repeat the three equations describing the postentry equilibrium (given that the entrant locates at the origin):

$$0 = 4p_1 - 8Fp_0 + L^2, \tag{A1}$$

where

$$F = [L + 2aD]/[L + 4aD];$$

$$0 = 4p_0 + 2p_2 - 6p_1G + 3L^2, \tag{A2}$$

where

$$G = [2L + 3aD]/[L + 3aD];$$

$$p_2 = \hat{p} + b(p_1 - \hat{p}), \tag{A3}$$

where

$$b = b_2 = E - [E^2 - 4]^{1/2}, \qquad \hat{p} = L(L + 2aD), \qquad E = [4L + 4aD]/[L + 2aD].$$

These are simply equations (14a), (17a), and (17b). Throughout the Appendix p_i denotes a postentry equilibrium price (for all i).

Proposition 1. In a postentry equilibrium

$$\hat{p} > p_2 > p_1 > p_0 > (L/2)[(L/2) + 2aD].$$

Proof. We first show that $p_1 < \hat{p}$ by supposing the contrary. Using (A1) and (A3), we solve for p_0 and p_2 as functions of p_1 and substitute these solutions into (A2). We obtain

$$(1/2F)(4p_1 + L^2) + 2\hat{p} + 2b(p_1 - \hat{p}) + 3L^2 - 6Gp_1 = 0, \tag{A4}$$

and by rearranging,

$$p_1[(2/F) + 2b - 6G] + (L^2/2F) + 3L^2 + 2\hat{p}(1 - b) = 0.$$

Now the coefficient of p_1 in (A5) is negative. Therefore, by substituting $\hat{p}$ for p_1 and by supposing that $\hat{p} < p_1$, we obtain

$$\hat{p}[(2/F) + 2b - 6G] + (L^2/2F) + 3L^2 + 2\hat{p}(1 - b) \geq 0. \tag{A6}$$

Simplifying yields

$$\hat{p}[(2/F) - 6G + 2] + (L^2/2F) + 3L^2 \geq 0. \tag{A7}$$

Substituting into (A7) for $\hat{p}$, F, and G by their expressions in terms of a, D, and L and simplifying, we obtain

$$-9L^4 - 31aDL^3 - 24a^2D^2L^2 \geq 0, \tag{A8}$$

which is clearly a contradiction.

To show $p_1 < p_2 < \hat{p}$, simply observe that p_2 is a convex combination of p_1 and $\hat{p}$. (Recall that $0 < b < 1$.)

Now we shall show that $p_0 < p_1$ by supposing the contrary. Using (A2) and substituting p_1 for p_0 and p_2, we obtain

$$6p_1 - 3L^2 - 6Gp_1 < 0, \tag{A9}$$

where the direction of the inequality arises because $p_2 > p_1$ and, by supposition, $p_0 \geq p_1$ (so $4p_0 + 2p_2 > 6p_1$). Substituting into (A9) for G, we obtain

$$6p_1 + 3L^2 - 6p_1[(2L + 3aD)/(L + 3aD)] < 0, \tag{A10}$$

and simplifying, we have

$$L(L + 3aD) < 2p_1. \tag{A11}$$

Using (A1), substituting p_1 for p_0, and supposing $p_0 \geq p_1$, we have

$$4p_1 + L^2 \geq 8p_1[(L + 2aD)/(L + 4aD)], \tag{A12}$$

and simplifying, we obtain

$$L(L + 4aD) \geq 4p_1.$$

Therefore, from (A11) and (A13), we have

$$L(L + 4aD)/4 \geq p_1 > L(L + 3aD)/2, \tag{A14}$$

which implies that

$$L(L + 4aD) > 2L(L + 3aD), \tag{A15}$$

which is a contradiction.

Finally, to show that

$$p_0 > (L/2)(L/2 + 2aD), \tag{A16}$$

observe that since $p_1 > p_0$, from (A1) we have

$$4p_0 + L^2 - 8Fp_0 < 0. \tag{A17}$$

Simplifying and substituting for F yield (A16). *Q.E.D.*

Proposition 2. Assume a is greater than zero. Let (D_j, L_j) be a sequence of pairs of positive numbers representing densities of consumers and distances between established firms, respectively. We consider two cases:

(i) D_jL_j converges to a nonnegative constant, say c, as $D_j \rightarrow \infty$;
(ii) $D_j = D_0$ for all j, and L_j converges to zero.

In both cases, $p_0^j/\hat{p}^j$ converges to one as $j \rightarrow \infty$, where p_0^j and $\hat{p}^j$ denote the postentry equilibrium price of the entrant and the preentry equilibrium price of an established firm, respectively.

Proof. To prove this result we first simply (but laboriously) calculate $p_0/\hat{p}$ as a function of D and L from equations (A1), (A2), and (A3). (For ease in notation, we omit the "j" subscripts and superscripts here.) We obtain

$$p_0/\hat{p} = (L + 4aD)X_1/(L + 2aD)X_2, \tag{A18}$$

where

$$X_1 = 27L^4 + 93aDL^3 + 72a^2D^2L^2 + 16L^3w + 47aDL^2w + 24a^2D^2Lw,$$

$$X_2 = 72L^4 + 248aDL^3 + 192a^2D^2L^2 + 40L^3w + 112aDL^2w - 48a^2D^2Lw,$$

$$w = (3L^2 + 4aDL)^{1/2}.$$

We note that when D_jL_j converges to a constant c as $j \rightarrow \infty$ and $D_j \rightarrow \infty$, then $D_j^nL_j^k$ goes to infinity if $n > k$ and to zero if $k > n$. Therefore, as $D_jL_j \rightarrow c$, the dominant term in X_1 is $24a^2D^2Lw$, and the dominant term in X_2 is $48a^2D^2Lw$. All other terms in X_1 and X_2 go to constants. We conclude that in this case $p_0^j/\hat{p}^j$ converges to one as $j \rightarrow \infty$.

In case (ii) again the dominant terms in X_1 and X_2 are $24a^2D^2Lw$ and $48a^2D^2Lw$, so $p_0^j/\hat{p}^j$ converges to one. *Q.E.D.*

Proposition 3. Assume $a > 0$. In free-entry equilibrium, as D becomes large or K becomes small, $\bar{R}_0(0, a, D, L)/\hat{R}(a, D, L)$ converges to one, where $\bar{R}_0$ represents the maximum gross profits of the entrant in the postentry equilibrium at $z = 0$ and $\hat{R}$ represents the gross profits of an established firm in the preentry equilibrium (defined in (16) and (9), respectively). (Formally, we should write L as a function of D and, for K becoming small, of K; however, this increases notational complexity without any apparent gain in clarity.)

Proof. We first show that we can write $\bar{R}_0$ as

$$\bar{R}_0 = 2p_0^2D[(L + 2aD)/(L + 4aD)^2], \tag{A19}$$

where p_0 is the postentry equilibrium price of the entrant. This expression is obtained from (11a), evaluated at $z = 0$, which yields

$$4p_0(2L + 4aD)/(L + 4aD) = 2p_{-1} + 2p_1 + L^2, \tag{A20}$$

and then from (10a), evaluated at $z = 0$, and with (A20) to eliminate $(2p_{-1} + 2p_1 + L^2)$, which yields

$$Q_0 = D[4p_0(2L + 4aD)/(L + 4aD) - 2p_0]/[2L], \tag{A21}$$

which when simplified becomes

$$Q_0 = 2Dp_0/(L + 4aD). \tag{A22}$$

The entrant's gross profit is then

$$\bar{R}_0 = p_0Q_0 - aQ_0^2,$$

and substituting for Q_0 from (A22), we have

$$\bar{R}_0 = 2Dp_0^2/(L + 4aD) - 4aD^2p_0^2/(L + 4aD)^2. \tag{A23}$$

Simplifying (A23) yields (A19).

Substituting $(L/2)(L/2 + 2aD)$ for p_0 into (A19) and using Proposition 1 we have

$$\bar{R}_0 > DL^2(L + 2aD)/8. \tag{A24}$$

It is now obvious that if we allow D to grow larger, DL^e must be bounded; otherwise $\bar{R}_0$ becomes arbitrarily large as $D \rightarrow \infty$. Suppose, without loss of generality, that $DL^e \rightarrow c$, a constant, which implies that $L^e \rightarrow 0$.

Now consider the expression

$$\bar{R}_0/\hat{R} = [2p_0^2 D(L + 2aD)/(L + 4aD)^2]/(DL^3 - aD^2L^2), \tag{A25}$$

obtained from (9) and (A19). Since $DL^e \rightarrow c$ as $D \rightarrow \infty$, this expression becomes arbitrarily close to

$$[4p_0^2 aD^2/16a^2D^2]/aD^2L^2 = p_0^2/a^2D^2L^2. \tag{A26}$$

(We remind the reader that for ease in notation we sometimes suppress the dependence of L^e on D.) But, since $p_0/\hat{p} \rightarrow 1$ as $D \rightarrow \infty$ by Proposition 2, and $\hat{p}$ becomes arbitrarily close to aDL as $D \rightarrow \infty$, we have (A25) converging to one as $D \rightarrow \infty$.

Now if K goes to zero (given D but with $L^e = L$ depending on K), we must have $\bar{R}_0$ converging to zero; otherwise profitable entry could occur. Since $\bar{R}_0 \rightarrow 0$ from (A24), we must have $L^e \rightarrow 0$. Since D is now fixed and (A25) involves expressions with L raised to a power greater than or equal to two, eventually (A25) again becomes arbitrarily close to (A26), and the analysis of the first case applies.

We remark that in the above proof, since $\bar{R}_0/\hat{R}$ converges to one and $p_0/\hat{p}$ converges to one, we must have $Q_0/\hat{Q}$ converging to one, where $\hat{Q}$ denotes the quantity of a firm in a preentry price equilibrium. Therefore, the unique constant to which DL^e converges as $D \rightarrow \infty$ or $K \rightarrow 0$ is $(K/a)^{1/2}$, the average-cost-minimizing quantity. *Q.E.D.*

Proposition 4. Assume $a > 0$. In free-entry equilibrium as D becomes large or K becomes small, $\bar{L}/L^*$ and $\underline{L}/L^*$ both converge to one; i.e., the equilibrium approaches the social optimum.

Proof. Consider equation (3). Since marginal cost goes to infinity as the output of a firm goes to infinity, it is intuitive (and also can be easily verified) that DL^* is bounded as $D \rightarrow \infty$. Suppose, without loss of generality, that DL^* converges to c, a constant, as $D \rightarrow \infty$; then it follows that $D(L^*)^3 \rightarrow 0$ as $D \rightarrow \infty$ so $(DL^*)^2$ converges to $(K/a)^{1/2}$.

Since in free-entry equilibrium $\bar{R}_0/\hat{R}$ converges to one as $D \rightarrow \infty$, we must have the quantity of each firm converging to the average-cost-minimizing quantity; i.e., DL^e converges to $(K/a)^{1/2}$ for any L^e (in the interval $[\underline{L}, \bar{L}]$). Therefore, $\bar{L}/L^*$ and $\underline{L}/L^*$ both converge to one.

The argument for the case of K's becoming small is similar and therefore omitted. *Q.E.D.*

References

ARCHIBALD, G.C., EATON, B.C., AND LIPSEY, R.G. "Address Models of Value Theory" in J. Stiglitz, ed., *New Developments in the Analysis of Market Structure,* London: MacMillan, 1985.

CHIANG, A.C. *Fundamental Methods of Mathematical Economics,* 2nd ed. New York: McGraw-Hill, 1974.

D'ASPREMONT, C., GABSZEWICZ, J.J., AND THISSE, J.F. "On Hotelling's Stability in Competition." *Econometrica,* Vol. 47 (1979), pp. 1145–1150.

EATON, B.C. "Free Entry in One-Dimensional Models: Pure Profits and Multiple Equilibria." *Journal of Regional Science,* Vol. 16 (1976), pp. 21–33.

——— AND LIPSEY, R.G. "Freedom of Entry and the Existence of Pure Profit." *Economic Journal,* Vol. 88 (1978), pp. 455–469.

——— AND WOODERS, M.H. "Sophisticated Entry in an Address Model of Monopolistic Competition." University of Toronto Discussion Paper, 1983.

HART, O. "Monopolistic Competition in a Large Economy with Differentiated Commodities." *Review of Economic Studies,* Vol. 46 (1979), pp. 1–30.

JONES, L.E. "The Efficiency Properties of Monopolistically Competitive Equilibria in Large Economies: Commodity Differentiation with Gross Substitutes." Mimeo, 1985.

NOVSHEK, W. "Equilibrium in Simple Spatial (or Differentiated Product) Models." *Journal of Economic Theory,* Vol. 22 (1980), pp. 313–326.

SALOP, S. "Monopolistic Competition with Outside Goods." *Bell Journal of Economics,* Vol. 10 (1979), pp. 141–156.

Rand Journal of Economics
Vol. 18, No. 1, Spring 1987

A theory of market structure with sequential entry

B. Curtis Eaton*

and

Roger Ware*

This article sets out a theory of market structure with sequential entry. We characterize the perfect Nash equilibrium to the entry game in several propositions. First, equilibria never involve excess capacity. Second, a sufficient statistic for the entry of any firm is that its profits are positive when computed myopically, i.e., with no further entry. Third, the equilibrium number of firms is the smallest number that can deter entry. Fourth, aggregate output in equilibrium is no smaller than the limit output. We calculate some explicit solutions to the model and examine comparative static properties.

1. Introduction

■ Beginning with the limit-pricing models of Bain (1956), Modigliani (1958), and Sylos-Labini (1962), the modern theory of strategic entry deterrence has grown increasingly sophisticated, but has not achieved its purpose (at least as intended by Bain): the endogenization of market structure. Although today's students of industrial organization are told that conduct feeds back on to structure, and that the two are determined simultaneously, there are few, if any, formal models describing how this determination occurs. The early models of limit pricing cited above restricted attention to a monopolist incumbent's (or collusive oligopoly's) trying to deter a single entrant. This one incumbent-one entrant framework has dominated the theoretical literature. Recent work within this framework has concentrated on refining the concept of strategic investment to deter entry, for example, by the introduction of the concept of perfectness, or credibility into the entry game (Dixit, 1980; Eaton and Lipsey, 1981; Spence, 1977; Fudenberg and Tirole, 1983; Gilbert, 1986; Ware, 1984). Gilbert (1986) provides an enlightening synthesis of this literature. The next step on the theoretical agenda is to use this strategic framework to develop a model in which tastes and technology, but not market structure, are exogenous.

This article accomplishes that task for a restrictive, but not uninteresting, set of demand and cost conditions. The number of firms, aggregate output, and the size distribution of producing firms are determined as the solution to a sequential entry game of perfect information. Although firms enter in sequence, all firms have perfect foresight about the pattern

---

* University of Toronto.

The authors would like to thank Mukesh Eswaran for his considerable input into the early stages of this work. Comments from an anonymous referee have also been valuable. Eaton gratefully acknowledges the support of the Hoover Institution and Ware the support of the Social Sciences and Humanities Research Council of Canada.

of future entry and the equilibrium price (the equilibrium is subgame perfect). The equilibrium is entry deterring in that the next firm in sequence after the last successful entrant cannot enter and earn positive profits.

Some attempts have been made to extend the modern theory of entry deterrence beyond the one incumbent-one entrant framework. An early and important article that pioneered the ideas of sequential entry and endogenous market structure is Prescott and Visscher (1977). Bernheim (1984) considers a sequence of potential entrants and shows that making entry conditions easier may, perversely, lower the scope for entry, because any potential entrant anticipates greater subsequent entry, and hence lower available rents in the final equilibrium. Gilbert and Vives (1984) examine a model with several incumbents and entrants, in which firms incur a sunk entry fee but no sunk production costs. Incumbents move simultaneously in making strategic production decisions toward a sequence of potential entrants. McLean and Riordan (1985), in a paper with a motivation similar to ours, consider the perfect equilibrium to a sequential entry game in which firms choose irreversibly a production technology at the time of entry, and market structure is determined endogenously.

We have been careful to match the strategic structure of the game to the technology, in a way that many previous articles in the area have failed to do. The strategic advantage of earlier movers is conferred only by sunk investments; the later movers use the same technology and are able, in fact obliged, to make sunk investments in the same way to enter the industry. Thus, games of this type are properly modelled in two phases—first, a phase in which all strategic (sunk) investments are committed, and second, a production phase that is nonstrategic and in which a quantity equilibrium (in our case Cournot) is realized, conditioned on the vector of strategic investments made in phase one. The recognition that later movers also incur sunk investment costs gives the earlier movers less strategic power than in models in which this point is ignored. Ware (1984) discusses the distinction in detail for a one incumbent-one entrant model. Our article can be viewed as an extension of the framework developed there to the case in which the number of potential firms is large.

In Section 2 we present our model and develop some useful propositions characterizing the quantity equilibrium, given any vector of strategic investments. In Section 3 we develop three propositions that characterize the perfect Nash equilibrium of the sequential entry game. First, equilibrium never involves excess capacity. Second, a necessary and sufficient statistic for entry of any firm is that its maximal profit, computed on the assumption of no further entry, be positive. As a corollary, aggregate output is no smaller than the limit output. Finally, the equilibrium number of firms is the smallest number that can deter further entry.

In Section 4 we present and discuss some simulation results. Using a computer algorithm, we are able to vary parameters of the model, such as the degree to which the technology is sunk, and to analyze the effect on the equilibrium configuration of firms. This allows us to assess the impact of strategic behavior on the industry. Perhaps surprisingly, we find that strategic entry deterrence is ordinarily welfare improving in our model, because equilibrium output does not change significantly, but the number of firms, and hence the sunk costs associated with entry, are reduced.

The reason for the relative constancy of equilibrium output is that a form of limit pricing is embodied in the entry-deterring equilibrium. It has been clear that limit pricing behavior might work to the benefit of consumers since the work of Bain. In expanding capacity and output to deter entry, a monopolist will lower price and reduce the social cost of monopoly. In our model there is an additional benefit to entry-deterring behavior: a shift in the equilibrium market structure toward the efficient structure, which with globally increasing returns is just a single firm.

Curiously, we discover that the equilibrium profit of firms is not monotonically decreasing in the order of entry: the privilege of being an early entrant is not necessarily valuable. In Section 5 we briefly comment on the possible significance of our results.

2. The model

■ We begin by making four assumptions.

Assumption 1. All firms produce an undifferentiated product with inverse demand function $p = f(\tilde{X})$, where $\tilde{X}$ is aggregate output.

Assumption 2. The function $f(\tilde{X})$ is twice differentiable, and, for $f(\tilde{X}) > 0, f'(\tilde{X}) < 0$. Further, $f'(\tilde{X}) + \tilde{x}_i f''(\tilde{X}) < 0$, for all $\tilde{x}_i \leq \tilde{X}$, where $\tilde{x}_i$ is output of firm i.

The second restriction in Assumption 2 is that the marginal revenue of any firm is decreasing in any other firm's output. As we observe below, this property is crucial for the results we obtain, and the assumption is therefore not innocuous.[1]

There are n potential firms.

Assumption 3. For any firm i the cost function is $C(\tilde{x}_i, k_i) = F(k_i) + V\tilde{x}_i, \tilde{x}_i \leq k_i$.

$F(k_i)$ is the cost of capacity k_i. We suppose that, once incurred, capacity costs are sunk. Output can be produced at constant variable cost V per unit, up to capacity k_i. We further assume the following.

Assumption 4. $F(0) = 0$; $F(k_i) > 0$, for $k_i > 0$; $F(k_i) > F(k_0)$, for $k_i > k_0$; and $F(k_i)/k_i < F(k_0)/k_0$, for $k_i > k_0$.

Notice that capacity costs are increasing in k_i, but average capacity costs are decreasing in k_i.[2]

We analyze an $(n + 1)$-stage game of perfect information (Kuhn, 1954) in which firms 1 through n sequentially choose capacities $k^n = (k_1, \ldots, k_n)$ in the first n stages. In the $(n + 1)$st stage, they play a capacity-constrained Cournot game in quantities. An equilibrium to a game of perfect information is, of course, subgame perfect in the sense of Selten (1975).

□ **Properties of the constrained Cournot equilibrium.** Given $k^n = (k_1, k_2, \ldots, k_n)$, the quantity equilibrium, which we denote by $x^n = (x_1, x_2, \ldots, x_n)$, is the solution to

$$x_i = \min (k_i, Z(X_{-i})), \qquad i = 1, \ldots, n,$$

where $X_{-i} = \sum_{j \neq i} x_j$ and $Z(X_{-i})$ is $\underset{x_i}{\text{argmax}}\, x_i f(X_{-i} + x_i) - Vx_i$. That is, $Z(\cdot)$ is the Cournot reaction function for the quantity-setting game in stage $(n + 1)$. Notice that the symbols x_i and X refer to Cournot *equilibrium* quantities, given capacities.

In Figure 1 we illustrate the solution to the quantity game where there are two firms, one and two, with positive capacities in stage $(n + 1)$. There are four regions in the figure: in I, both firms are unconstrained by their capacities; in II both are constrained; in III (IV), one (two) is constrained and two (one) is unconstrained. The boundary between regions II and IV is $Z(x_2)$ and the boundary between II and III is $Z(x_1)$.

In the Cournot equilibrium there are potentially three types of firms, which are described in the following definition.

Definition 1. If $x_i < Z(X_{-i})$, firm i is *constrained.* If $x_i = Z(X_{-i})$, firm i is: (a) *semiconstrained* if $x_i = k_i$; (b) *unconstrained* if $x_i < k_i$.

Notice that the output of any firm which is either constrained or semiconstrained is equal to its capacity ($x_i = k_i$), and that the output of an unconstrained firm is less than its capacity.

---

[1] A defense of this assumption that has been cited commonly by other authors is that it is sufficient for stability of a Cournot equilibrium.

[2] This seems to be a reasonable simplification of observed cost functions in many manufacturing industries.

FIGURE 1

THE FOUR PHASES OF CONSTRAINED COURNOT EQUILIBRIUM FOR DUOPOLY

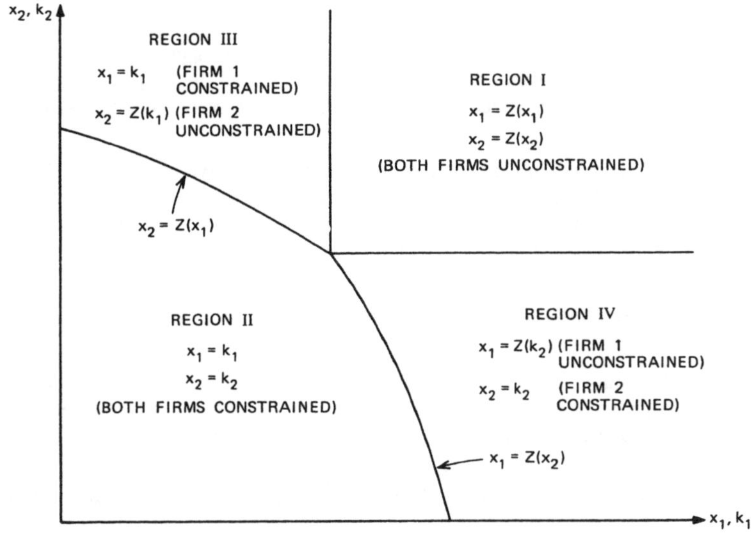

To analyze the sequential entry game we need some properties of the Cournot equilibrium, which are summarized in the following four propositions.

Proposition 1. Given $k^n = (k_1, \ldots, k_n)$, the Cournot equilibrium $x^n = (x_1, \ldots, x_n)$ is unique.

The proof of uniqueness is a direct application of the Rosen (1965) uniqueness theorem. The theorem requires that the game is strictly smooth (Friedman, 1986, p. 44); second, that the Jacobian of the system of first-order conditions, which will not be simultaneously satisfied at boundary equilibria, be negative quasi-definite (Friedman, 1986, p. 45).

Proposition 2. (a) x_i and X $(=\sum x_i)$ are continuous in k^n. (b) Given $(k_1, \ldots, k_{i-1}, k_{i+1}, \ldots, k_n)$, there exists a $\hat{k}_i > 0$ such that firm i is constrained if $k_i < \hat{k}_i$, semiconstrained if $k_i = \hat{k}_i$, and unconstrained if $k_i > \hat{k}_i$. (c) If firms i and j are either semiconstrained or unconstrained, then $x_i = x_j$. (d) If firm i is constrained and firm j is either semiconstrained or unconstrained, then $x_i < x_j$. (e) x_i is decreasing in k_j if i is unconstrained and j is constrained, and nonincreasing otherwise. (f) x_i and X are increasing in k_i if i is constrained, and nondecreasing otherwise.

Proofs of parts (a), (b), (c), and (d) are trivial. Proofs of parts (e) and (f) are straightforward but tedious, and have been omitted for the sake of brevity.

Definition 2. Let $H_i(k^n) = x_i f(X) - Vx_i$ denote the *gross profit* of firm i in Cournot equilibrium.

Proposition 2 has immediate consequences for these gross profit functions that we record in Proposition 3.

Proposition 3. (a) $H_i(\cdot)$ is continuous in k^n. (b) $H_i(\cdot)$ is decreasing in k_j, $j \neq i$, if j is constrained. (c) For any $k_i > 0$, $\bar{k}_j = 0$, and $\tilde{k}_j > 0$, $H_i(k_1, \ldots, \bar{k}_j, \ldots, k_n) > H_i(k_1, \ldots, \tilde{k}_j, \ldots, k_n)$, $j \neq i$. (d) For any pair $\bar{k}_j$, $\tilde{k}_j$ such that j is either semiconstrained or unconstrained, $H_i(k_1, \ldots, \bar{k}_j, \ldots, k_n) = H_i(k_1, \ldots, \tilde{k}_j, \ldots, k_n)$ for all i.

There are some immediate and useful implications of Propositions 2 and 3 concerning the effect of adding or subtracting firms, which we loosely call the entry and exit corollaries.

Entry Corollary. Suppose initially that m firms, $m < n$, have positive capacities. Now suppose one or more additional firms enter with positive capacities. Then aggregate output increases, aggregate output of the m original firms does not increase, and the output of any firm that was originally unconstrained decreases. Finally, the gross profit of each of the m original firms decreases.

Exit Corollary. Suppose again that m firms initially have positive capacities and that one or more of them exit. Then aggregate output decreases, aggregate output of the remaining firms does not decrease, the output of any firm that was initially unconstrained increases, and the output of any firm that was initially constrained remains constant. Finally, the gross profit of each of the remaining firms increases.

Assumption 4 implies a useful proposition concerning net profits of firms in Cournot equilibrium.

Proposition 4. If firms i and j are constrained or semiconstrained, then $[H_i(\cdot) - F(k_i)] - [H_j(\cdot) - F(k_j)]$ has the sign of $(k_i - k_j)$. In words, net profits in a Cournot equilibrium are ranked in order of capacities, provided that the firms being ranked are not unconstrained.

Proof. Since $x_i = k_i$, $H_i(\cdot) - F(k_i) = \left[f(X) - V - \frac{F(k_i)}{k_i}\right]k_i$, which, from Assumption 4, is increasing in k_i.

We are interested in the free-entry equilibria of the $(n + 1)$-stage game—the equilibria in which not all of the n firms choose a positive capacity. Hence, we assume that n is so large that if $k_i > 0$ for all i, then some firm (or firms) earns negative profit. For technical reasons, we assume that n is finite.

Assumption 5. The number of firms, n, is finite and is such that if $k_i > 0$ for all i, then $H_j(k_1, \ldots, k_n) - F(k_j) < 0$ for some j.

3. Properties of perfect equilibrium

■ **Preview of results.** Before turning to the analysis of perfect equilibrium, it is useful to preview the main results that we shall establish. We first show that in perfect equilibrium no firm holds excess capacity. This reflects among other things the fact that excess capacity is not a barrier to entry in this model. From the entry corollary we see why. If a firm is unconstrained before entry—if it holds excess capacity—, then not only will it not use the excess capacity after entry, but it will, in fact, hold even more excess capacity. It is clear that the "no-excess-capacity result" depends critically on the demand restriction that marginal revenue of any firm is decreasing in the output of other firms. Bulow, Geanakoplos, and Klemperer (1985) provide an example in which relaxing this restriction can lead to excess capacity in the perfect equilibrium of a simple entry game.

Next we derive a necessary and sufficient statistic for entry. That is, we determine a necessary and sufficient condition for entry of some firm i, given the predetermined capacities of the first $(i - 1)$ firms. The ith firm will enter if and only if its maximized profit, given that firms $(i + 1)$ through n hold zero capacity, is positive. Firm i will not, of course, actually choose capacity in this myopic fashion if it does enter. The condition simply tells us when a firm will enter, and moreover what it means in this model to say that entry is deterred, or that we have a free-entry equilibrium.

The entry proposition also tells us something about the identity of firms in perfect equilibrium and their aggregate output. Suppose there are i firms in perfect equilibrium:

they will be firms 1 through i, the first i firms in the sequence of potential firms. Further, their aggregate output will be no less than the Bain-Labini-Modigliani limit output.

We then come to perhaps the major result characterizing perfect equilibrium. Suppose the first i firms had infinite capacities, which maximizes their leverage with respect to entry of firm $(i + 1)$. It is clearly possible that firm $(i + 1)$ will not be deterred from entering since excess capacity is no barrier to entry. Given Assumption 5, however, there is some *minimum* value of i, less than n, such that if the first i firms held infinite capacities, firm $(i + 1)$ would be deterred from entering. We show that this minimum number of firms that could deter entry is the number of firms that will, in fact, enter in perfect equilibrium.

Finally, we remark that when the number of firms that enter (choose a positive capacity) is "large," for all practical purposes the output is the limit output. Thus, in a sense we are resurrecting the limit-output model. What our analysis adds is a theory of market structure—the number of firms and their market shares are endogenous in our model.

□ **Nonexistence of equilibrium.** Before we can prove these results we must confront a nonexistence problem. To see the problem, illustrated in Figure 2, we focus on a case in which there are just two potential firms: firm one chooses k_1, firm two chooses k_2, and the firms then play a capacity-constrained quantity game. Firm two's reaction correspondence in Figure 2 comprises two segments—BA and $A'G'$. Given $k_1 = \bar{k}_1$, firm two is indifferent between $\tilde{k}_2$ and $\bar{k}_2$. The line BAG is the ordinary (full-cost) Cournot reaction function—the locus of profit-maximizing values of $x_2 = k_2$, given $x_1 = k_1$. The reaction correspondence is coincident with this reaction function to the left of A. For $k_1 > \bar{k}_1$, firm two's best capacity response is $\bar{k}_2$, which is discretely larger than $\tilde{k}_2$. The discontinuity in firm two's reaction correspondence is defined by the condition that its isoprofit locus through point A be tangent to firm one's variable-cost Cournot reaction function—at point T in the figure. This reaction function is, of course, the boundary between regions II and IV in Figure 1. Hence, in the quantity equilibrium corresponding to any point on $A'G'$, firm one holds excess capacity, but firm two does not. That is, for all (k_1, k_2) on $A'G'$, $x_1 = \bar{k}_1 < k_1$ and $x_2 = \bar{k}_2$. It then follows that firm one's net profit in any Cournot equilibrium corresponding to a point on $A'G'$ is less than its net profit in the Cournot equilibrium corresponding to point A. Hence, firm one will not present firm two with a capacity larger than $\bar{k}_1$.

FIGURE 2

FIRM 2's REACTION CORRESPONDENCE

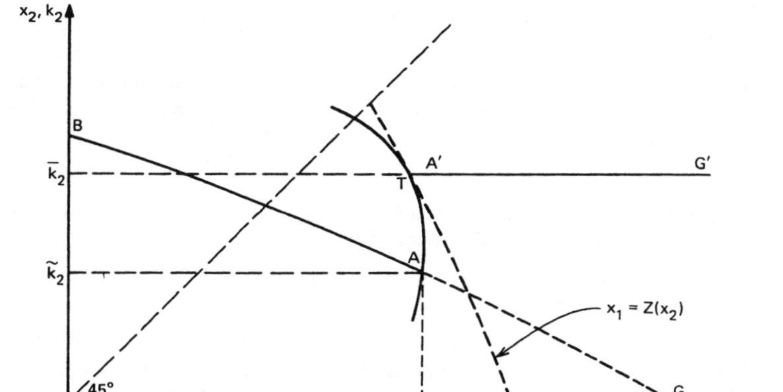

To see the nonexistence problem, suppose that as we move from left to right along *BAG*, firm one's profit is still increasing at point *A*. If, given $k_1 = \bar{k}_1$, there is any positive probability that firm two would choose $\bar{k}_2$ instead of $\tilde{k}_2$, then firm one will choose $k_1 < \bar{k}_1$. But then there is no equilibrium, since firm one's profit is increasing on the half-open interval, $[0, \bar{k}_1)$. This problem potentially occurs in any case where n exceeds 1. To avoid it we assume the following.

Assumption 6. If in any subgame any firm is indifferent between two or more capacities, the firm chooses the smallest capacity.

Note that Assumption 6 ensures that all reaction correspondences are reaction *functions*.

□ **No excess capacity.** In examining the case of no excess capacity we offer the following proposition.

Proposition 5. In perfect equilibrium the output of each firm is equal to its capacity.

The argument proceeds as follows. Consider the subgame (defined by) $(k_1, \ldots, k_i)$, and suppose that $x_i < k_i$ in the ensuing subgame-perfect equilibrium. We show that for k_i set equal to the quantity x_i, aggregate output in the corresponding subgame-perfect equilibrium is no larger (and price no smaller) than it was in the equilibrium of the original subgame, and hence that i's output is identical in both. Therefore, firm i's profit increases if it eliminates excess capacity, and excess capacity is inconsistent with perfect equilibrium.

Proof. Consider the subgame $(k^{i-1}, \bar{k}_i)$, where k^{i-1} denotes the vector of capacities $(k_1, \ldots, k_{i-1})$, and denote the subgame-perfect responses of firms $(i + 1)$ through n by $(\bar{k}_{i+1}, \ldots, \bar{k}_n)$ and the aggregate output in the corresponding equilibrium by $\bar{X}$. Suppose that firm i's output in the equilibrium, $\bar{x}_i$, is less than its capacity, $\bar{k}_i$. Now consider the subgame $(k^{i-1}, \tilde{k}_i = \bar{x}_i)$—the subgame in which firm i's capacity, $\tilde{k}_i$, is equal to $\bar{x}_i$—and denote subgame-perfect responses and aggregate output in the corresponding equilibrium by $(\tilde{k}_{i+1}, \ldots, \tilde{k}_n)$ and $\tilde{X}$. We must show that $\tilde{X} \leq \bar{X}$.

Define

$$S = \{k^{i-1}, k_i, \ldots, k_n | X \geq \bar{X}\},$$

and

$$\bar{S} = \{k^{i-1}, k_i, \ldots, k_n | X < \bar{X}\}.$$

If $(k^{i-1}, \tilde{k}_i, \ldots, \tilde{k}_n) \in \bar{S}$, then $\tilde{X} < \bar{X}$, and we are done.

Suppose then that $(k^{i-1}, \tilde{k}_i, \ldots, \tilde{k}_n) \in S$. Observe that for any $(k^{i-1}, \bar{k}_i, k_{i+1}, \ldots, k_n) \in S$ and any $(k^{i-1}, \tilde{k}_i, k_{i+1}, \ldots, k_n) \in S$, $H_j(k^{i-1}, \bar{k}_i, k_{i+1}, \ldots, k_n) = H_j(k^{i-1}, \tilde{k}_i, k_{i+1}, \ldots, k_n)$ for all $j > i$, since i is either unconstrained or semiconstrained (see Proposition 3(d)). This implies that firm n's reaction functions are identical in the two subgames, which in turn implies that firm $(n - 1)$'s reaction functions are also identical, and so on. Hence, $(\tilde{k}_{i+1}, \ldots, \tilde{k}_n) = (\bar{k}_{i+1}, \ldots, \bar{k}_n)$, and therefore $\tilde{X} = \bar{X}$. *Q.E.D.*

□ **The entry statistic.** Next we find the condition that determines whether a firm will enter, given the capacity choices of all previous firms.

Definition 3. Let $G_i(k^{i-1}) = \max_{k_i > 0} [H_i(k^{i-1}, k_i, 0, \ldots, 0) - F(k_i)]$.

$G_i(k^{i-1})$ is the maximum profit firm i could earn by entering (by choosing $k_i > 0$), given predetermined capacities, k^{i-1}, and given that the capacities of all subsequent firms are zero. That is, $G_i(\cdot)$ is a "myopic" entry signal for firm i, because it is conditioned on no subsequent entry. Proposition 3 implies that $G_i(\cdot)$ is continuous and nonincreasing in

$k_j, j < i$, and strictly decreasing in k_j if k_j is sufficiently small. We show in the following proposition that despite the fact that firm i actually makes its entry decision with perfect foresight about subsequent entry, this myopic calculation yields a statistic that is both necessary and sufficient for entry.

Proposition 6. It is necessary and sufficient for the entry of firm i that $G_i(k^{i-1}) > 0$.

Proof. Necessity is trivial to establish since firm i's profit is nonincreasing in k_j, $j > i$. (We assume for convenience, that a firm anticipating exactly zero profit will not enter.)

To prove sufficiency, let $k_i = \infty$, and consider two cases. If $G_{i+1}(k^{i-1}, k_i = \infty) \leq 0$, then firm i can deter entry. Denote by $\underline{k}_i$ the smallest value of k_i that deters entry, and denote $\underset{k_{i+1}>0}{\operatorname{argmax}} H_{i+1}(k^{i-1}, \underline{k}_i, k_{i+1}, 0, \ldots, 0) - F(k_{i+1})$ by $\underline{k}_{i+1}$. Then, by continuity we have

$$G_{i+1}(k^{i-1}, \underline{k}_i) = H_{i+1}(k^{i-1}, \underline{k}_i, \underline{k}_{i+1}, 0, \ldots, 0) - F(\underline{k}_{i+1}) = 0.$$

Let $\tilde{k}_i = \max(\underline{k}_i, \underline{k}_{i+1})$, and let $\hat{k}_{i+1} = \min(\underline{k}_i, \underline{k}_{i+1})$. Then, from Proposition 4 we have

$$H_i(k^{i-1}, \tilde{k}_i, \hat{k}_{i+1}, 0, \ldots, 0) - F(\tilde{k}_i) \geq G_{i+1}(k^{i-1}, \underline{k}_i) = 0.$$

But $\tilde{k}_i$ deters entry, and firm i's net profit in the subgame $(k^{i-1}, \tilde{k}_i)$ is

$$H_i(k^{i-1}, \tilde{k}_i, 0, \ldots, 0) - F(\tilde{k}_i),$$

which from the preceding inequality and Proposition 3(c) is positive. Thus, $\tilde{k}_i$ is a profitable entry-deterring strategy for firm i.

If $G_{i+1}(k^{i-1}, k_i = \infty) > 0$, we have the second case. In the subgame defined by $(k^{i-1}, k_i = \infty)$, at least one of the perfect responses, denoted by $(\dot{k}_{i+1}, \ldots, \dot{k}_n)$, will be positive. For example, if $\dot{k}_j = 0$ for all $i < j < n$, then $\dot{k}_n > 0$, since n is the last firm. Let $\dot{x}_i$ denote firm i's output and $\dot{X}$ aggregate output in this subgame-perfect equilibrium, and let j denote a firm, $j > i$, such that $\dot{k}_j > 0$. Observe that

$$H_i(k^{i-1}, k_i = \infty, \dot{k}_{i+1}, \ldots, \dot{k}_n) - F(\dot{x}_i) \geq H_j(k^{i-1}, k_i = \infty, \dot{k}_{i+1}, \ldots, \dot{k}_n) - F(\dot{k}_j) > 0.$$

The first inequality follows from the fact that no firm has an output larger than $\dot{x}_i$ and from Proposition 4. Now consider the subgame $(k^{i-1}, k_i = \dot{x}_i)$, and denote the corresponding subgame-perfect responses by $(\hat{k}_{i+1}, \ldots, \hat{k}_n)$ and aggregate output by $\hat{X}$. The "eliminate excess capacity argument" used to prove Proposition 5 implies that $\hat{X} \leq \dot{X}$ and hence that

$$H_i(k^{i-1}, k_i = \dot{x}_i, \hat{k}_{i+1}, \ldots, \hat{k}_n) \geq H_i(k^{i-1}, k_i = \infty, \dot{k}_{i+1}, \ldots, \dot{k}_n).$$

The last three inequalities imply that $k_i = \dot{x}_i$ is a profitable entry strategy for firm i. *Q.E.D.*

Two corollaries deserve attention.

Corollary 1. If there are i positive capacities in the perfect equilibrium of the $(n + 1)$-stage game, then $k_j > 0$ for $j \leq i$, and $k_j = 0$ for $j > i$.

Corollary 2. Let $\underline{X}$ be the value of aggregate output such that

$$\max_x \{xf(\underline{X} + x) - Vx - F(x)\} = 0.$$

Then, letting X^* denote aggregate output in perfect equilibrium, we see that $X^* \geq \underline{X}$.

That is, in perfect equilibrium output is no smaller than the Bain-Labini-Modigliani limit output. The proof of Corollary 2 is quite simple. From Proposition 5 we know that in perfect equilibrium $\sum_{i=1}^{n} k_i = X^*$, and from Corollary 1 we know that $k_n = 0$. Suppose that $X^* < \underline{X}$; then $G_n(k^{n-1}) > 0$, and hence firm n would enter, which is a contradiction.

□ **Determining the equilibrium number of firms.** Now that we have necessary and sufficient conditions for the entry of firm i, we want to determine the number of firms that will enter in perfect equilibrium. Suppose for the moment that i firms had entered and that each of them had an infinite capacity. Denote this vector of capacities by k^i_∞. It is clear that this maximizes their leverage with respect to the entry of $(i + 1)$, and further that k^i_∞ will not necessarily deter entry. Let u be the smallest value of i such that $G_{i+1}(k^i_\infty) \leq 0$. The integer u is then the smallest number of firms that could deter entry. We show that in the perfect equilibrium of the $(n + 1)$-stage game, the first u firms will enter and that no other firm will.

Proposition 7. In perfect equilibrium the number of firms entering (choosing positive capacity levels) is the smallest number that can deter the entry of an additional firm.

We present the proof in the Appendix. The structure of the argument is as follows. We consider all subgames (defined by k^i) in which $G_{i+1}(k^i) > 0$: all subgames in which firm $(i + 1)$ enters. We partition these subgames into sets, indexed by $z \geq 1$ and defined as follows:

$$z = \max_{j \in I^+} j \,|\, G_{i+j}(k^i, k_{i+1} = \infty, k_{i+2} = \infty, \ldots, k_{i+j} = \infty) > 0,$$

where I^+ is the set of positive integers. If $z = 1$, entry will be deterred when k_{i+1} is sufficiently large. If $z = 2$, entry will be deterred when k_{i+1} and k_{i+2} are sufficiently large, and so on. We show that the number of firms entering in the perfect equilibrium of any such subgame is z, the index of the subgame. This proves Proposition 7, since the index of the subgame in which no firm has entered is the integer u—the smallest number of firms that can deter the entry of an additional firm.

Consider first the case $z = 1$, and let $\underline{k}_{i+1}$ be the smallest value of k_{i+1} that deters the entry of firm $(i + 2)$. We show that any "accommodation" strategy $k_{i+1} < \underline{k}_{i+1}$ implies a subgame equilibrium that makes firm $(i + 1)$ worse off. We then consider the case $z = 2$, and let $\underline{k}_{i+1}$ denote the smallest value of k_{i+1} such that firm $(i + 2)$ can deter entry. We know from the $z = 1$ case that firm $(i + 2)$ *will* deter entry if $k_{i+1} \geq \underline{k}_{i+1}$. We show that for $z = 2$, any $k_{i+1} < \underline{k}_{i+1}$ will again make firm $(i + 1)$ worse off than it is with $k_{i+1} = \underline{k}_{i+1}$, and hence exactly two firms will enter any subgame in which $z = 2$. The case $z = 3$ is then proved by using the results for $z = 1, 2$, and so on, recursively.

4. Explicit solutions to the model: the case of linear demand

■ Proposition 7 implies a corollary that greatly simplifies the task of finding solutions to explicit parameterizations of the model. The proposition states that the equilibrium number of firms will be the smallest number that can deter entry. But this number is independent of the capacities of firms that do enter. Thus, the process of finding a solution to the model can be decomposed into two stages, first finding the equilibrium number of firms u, and then solving, conditional on u and on the fact that firm $(u + 1)$ is deterred from entering, for the equilibrium vector of capacities, quantities, and the equilibrium price.

In this section we suppose that the inverse demand function is linear:

$$p = 2 - X.$$

Let $F(k_i) = F + \alpha k_i$ and $V = (1 - \alpha)$, so that

$$C(\tilde{x}_i, k_i) = F + \alpha k_i + (1 - \alpha)\tilde{x}_i, \qquad \tilde{x}_i \leq k_i,$$

where $0 \leq \alpha \leq 1$. The parameter α represents the proportion of production costs that are sunk, with unit production costs held constant at unity. A change in α has no effect on total costs, but does affect the degree of strategic advantage that is conferred by the ability to sink capacity in advance of production. The parameter F represents a fixed (and sunk) cost of entry.

□ **The equilibrium number of firms.** We obtain the equilibrium number of firms by deriving in explicit form the boundaries of the (index) partition of the subgame described in the previous section. These boundaries are equivalent to the equations $G_2(k^1_\infty) = 0$, $G_3(k^2_\infty) = 0$, $G_4(k^3_\infty) = 0 \ldots$, where k^i_∞ is the vector of infinite capacities for the first i firms. The subgame partition is derived in the parameter space (F, α), and is illustrated in Figure 3. Note that Figure 3 identifies equilibrium "n-opolies," without having solved for the full perfect equilibrium to the model. It is instructive to hold F constant in Figure 3 and to observe what happens to the number of firms as we vary α. An increase in α increases the relative importance of the sunk component of unit production costs. This increases the strategic advantage of earlier entrants, and at discrete values of α will reduce the number of firms in perfect equilibrium. When $\alpha = 1$, all production costs are sunk, and the equilibrium consists of a single firm, for all values of F. That is, the first entrant is able credibly to install sufficient capacity to deter any further entry.

Solutions to the model can be further subdivided into one of two kinds—*blockaded* solutions and *strategic* solutions. To see the nature of the distinction, consider the following exercise. Given u, the number of firms that enter in perfect equilibrium, consider a sequential game of perfect information in which there are exactly u firms. If the solution to this game is identical to the perfect equilibrium solution, we say that the perfect equilibrium solution is *blockaded*. If they are different, which implies that the perfect equilibrium is materially influenced by the potential for entry, we say that the perfect equilibrium solution is *strategic*.

The intuition behind the blockaded solution is elementary and traditional; it is a direct extension of Bain's concept of blockaded monopoly. In a blockaded n-opoly, the incumbent firms can ignore the possibility of entry, although there is strategic interaction among them. The division of all solutions into either blockaded or strategic solutions implies a further subpartition of the technology parameter space, which we illustrate in Figure 4.

Obviously, the threat of *additional* entry has no effect in the parameter regions corre-

FIGURE 3

EQUILIBRIUM NUMBER OF FIRMS

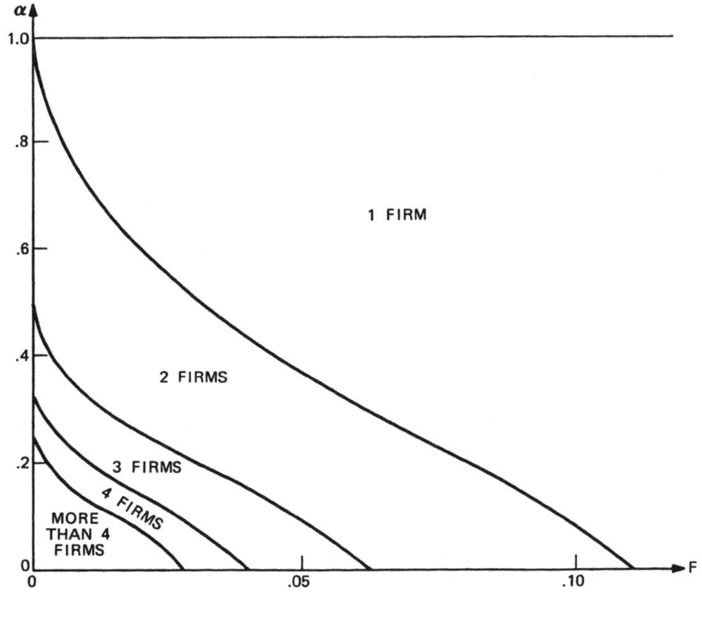

FIGURE 4

BLOCKADED AND STRATEGIC "n–OPOLIES"

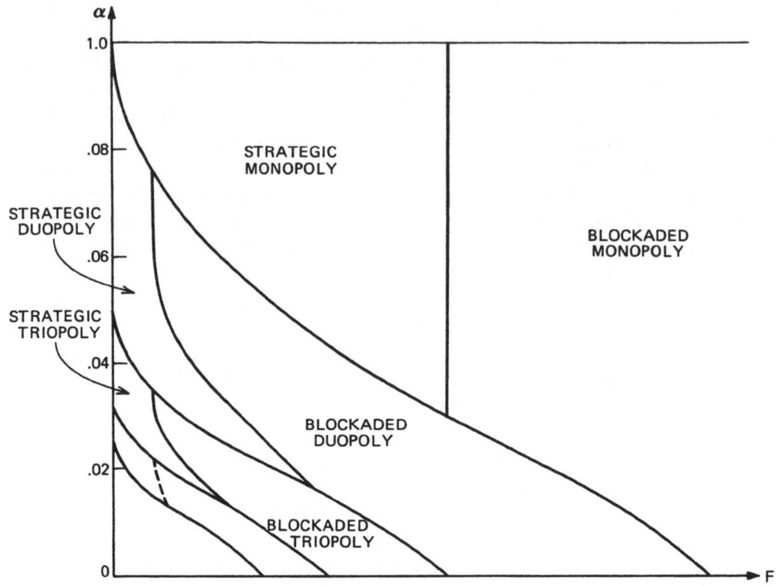

sponding to blockaded solutions. These regions cover a large part of the parameter space, and we conjecture that as the number of producing firms increases, the "likelihood" of blockaded solutions becomes progressively larger. This observation suggests at least a different perspective on the idea that potential entry disciplines the market. In our model the strategic interaction between *actual* entrants often has more impact on the final equilibrium than does the need to deter *potential* entrants.

A complete solution to the model requires that each firm's choice of capacity be profit maximizing, given the vector of capacity choices of earlier entrants, and given the subgame equilibrium conditioned by that firm's capacity choice. The monopoly case is simple. In the blockaded case the monopolist's choice is unconstrained. In the strategic case the monopolist installs just enough capacity to deter entry.

We may also obtain analytic solutions to the duopoly case, albeit with some tedious computation.[3] To derive equilibria involving larger numbers of producing firms, we have written a computer algorithm that computes the (approximate) perfect equilibrium to the entry game for parameter values leading to two or three producing firms.[4] Figure 5 reports approximate perfect equilibria to the entry game for technology parameters leading to one, two, or three producing firms.

□ **Size distributions and the threat of entry.** From the results reported in Figure 5, we can analyze the effect on the equilibrium of varying the technology parameters α and F. We begin with the blockaded equilibria. Starting from any blockaded equilibrium, a decrease

[3] The blockaded duopoly solutions are derived in full in Ware (1984).

[4] The computer algorithm mimics the recursive structure of the sequential game by first finding firm u's best response function, then $(u - 1)$'s, and so on. Details are available from the authors on request.

FIGURE 5

PERFECT EQUILIBRIUM IN F – α SPACE

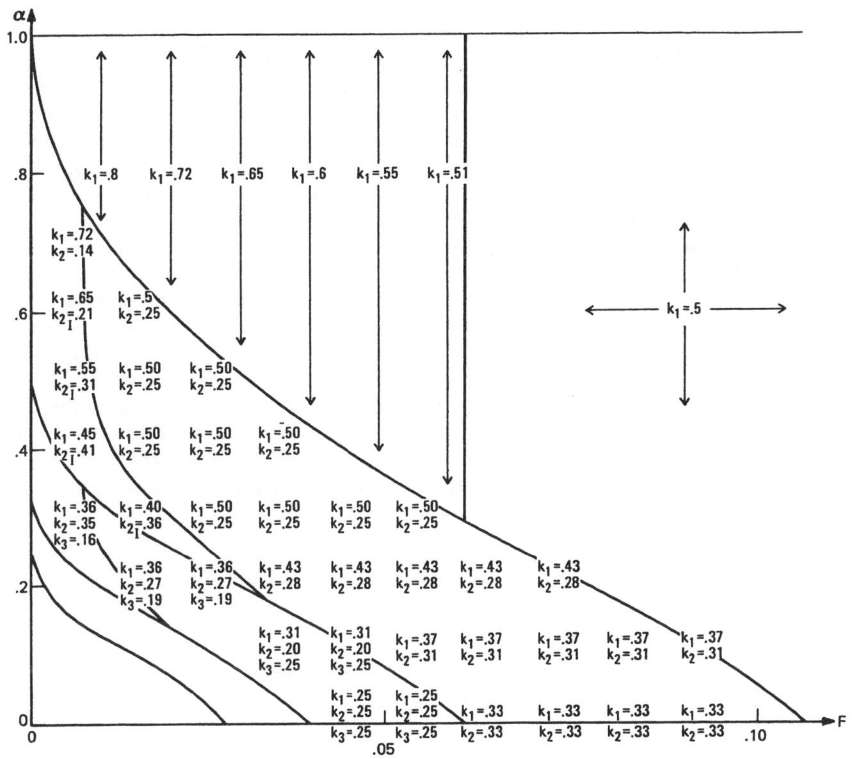

in *F*, the sunk cost of entry, has no effect on the equilibrium (providing that *F* does not change sufficiently to permit entry or to produce a strategic equilibrium). The parameter α, the proportion of production costs that are sunk, is a measure of the degree of strategic advantage held by early movers in the sequential game. The effect on the blockaded equilibrium of varying α is as expected: for a given number of firms, a decrease in α leads to a reduced variance of equilibrium firm sizes. Firms that move early are unable to capture so large a share of the market when the strategic advantage of moving early, in the form of sunk production costs, is reduced.

A general result is that the threat of entry reduces the variance of firm sizes. This can be seen in Figure 5, either moving from right to left across a blockaded-strategic boundary, or from right to left within a strategic region. The issue here is the credibility of the incumbents' capacity in deterring entry. Given aggregate industry capacity, greater symmetry of capacities lowers the minimum fixed cost of entry for which deterrence is feasible. Thus, lowering the fixed costs of entry within any strategic region leads to reduced variance of firm sizes in market equilibrium.

□ **Nonmonotonic market shares.** The results in Spence (1977), Dixit (1980), and Ware (1984) establish that the privilege of being a *first mover* is a valuable one in this type of sequential entry game. An obvious conjecture, consistent with the results in McLean and

Riordan (1985), is that the privilege of being an *early mover* is likewise valuable. Surprisingly, in our model the profit of a firm early in the sequence of entrants is not necessarily larger than (or equal to) the profit of firms later in the sequence. For example, as Figure 5 reveals, when $F = .045$ and $\alpha = .1$, firm three is larger and more profitable than firm two.

To understand this curious result, focus first on firm three's capacity decision, given (k_1, k_2). In this particular case ($F = .045$ and $\alpha = .1$) the existence of a fourth potential firm has no bearing on the equilibrium, since it is a three-firm blockaded equilibrium. This allows us to compute in a straightforward, if tedious, manner the perfect equilibrium for all subgames (k_1, k_2). We record the results in Figure 6.[5] In region I all three firms are constrained, in region IV both firm one and firm two are unconstrained, and in region II (III) firm one (firm two) is unconstrained and firm two (firm one) is constrained.

Now focus on firm two's reaction function. In region I firm two's profit is increasing in k_2 for all k_1. As k_2 passes through the line *ABCDE*, firm two's profit drops discretely, since subgames (k_1, k_2) in regions II, III, and IV induce firm three to choose a capacity discretely larger than the capacity it chooses on *ABCDE*. In regions III and IV, firm two is unconstrained (it holds excess capacity), and hence its reaction function for $k_1 \leq \bar{k}_1$ is *ABC*. For subgames in which $k_1 > \bar{k}_1$, firm two must choose between an equilibrium on *CDE* in region I and the best equilibrium in region II. In region II its best response is on the line *CD'E'*. For $k_1 \leq .311$, its profit on *CDE* is larger, and for $k_1 > .311$, its profit on *CD'E'* is larger. Hence, its reaction function comprises two segments—*ABCD* and *D'E'*.

Finally, consider firm one's choice. It will choose the point on firm two's reaction

FIGURE 6

REACTION FUNCTION OF FIRM 2 IMPLICIT IN A NONMONOTONIC PERFECT EQUILIBRIUM (AT POINT D)

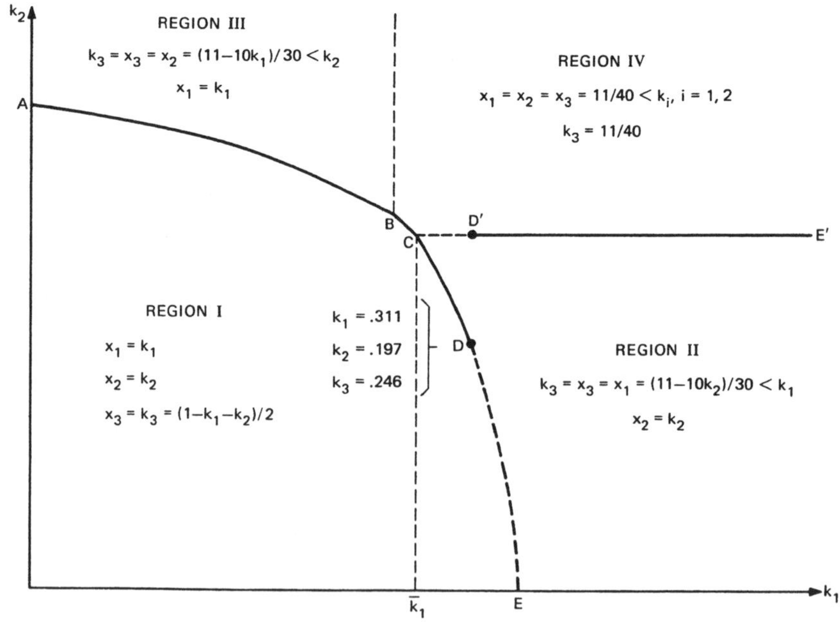

---

[5] In Figure 6 the locus *AB* is defined by $(1 - k_1 - k_2)^2/4 = (11 - 10k_1)(8 - 10k_1)/900$, the locus *BC* by $(1 - k_1 - k_2)^2/4 = 77/1600$, and the locus *CE* by $(1 - k_1 - k_2)^2/4 = (11 - 10k_2)(8 - 10k_2)/900$.

function that offers it the largest profit. Moving from left to right along *ABCDE*, firm one's profit is still increasing at *D*, and its profit at *D* is larger than its profit at any point on *D'E'*, since it holds excess capacity in region II. Hence, firm one chooses $k_1 = .311$ and induces firms two and three to choose $k_2 = .197$ and $k_3 = .246$.

The key to the intuitive understanding of this result is the observation that the equilibrium profit of firm two (and of firm one) in any subgame (k_1, k_2) is discontinuous along *ABCDE*. Below the line, small changes in k_1 or k_2 induce small changes in k_3. Beginning at any point on the line, a small increase in k_1 or k_2 induces firm three to increase its capacity discretely, which action discretely reduces the profit of firm two. That is, on the line *ABCDE* small increases in k_1 or k_2 induce a large increase in k_3 and a discrete decrease in firm two's profit. It is this discontinuity that allows firm one to force the solution at *D*. In moving to the right along *ABCD*, firm one is squeezing firm two and knows that firm two will reduce k_2 to avoid the discrete drop in its profit that any subgame above *ABCDE* promises. At point *D* firm two has been pushed to the limit, and any further increase in k_1 would induce firm two to increase its capacity discretely, and thus to reduce firm one's profit.

The result that profits are not invariably decreasing in the order in which firms enter calls into question the applicability of our model. At a minimum, it suggests that one should incorporate the possibility that firms will attempt to manipulate the order of entry by refusing to enter when their turn comes. Any model that allows for this sort of "wait and see" strategy will, of course, be more complex.

5. Conclusions

■ Recent contributions in theoretical industrial organization, notably those of Spence (1977) and Dixit (1980), have pointed the way toward the development of a theory of market structure. Although these models do not offer a complete theory of market structure, because the entry game is restricted to a single incumbent facing a single potential entrant, it is clear that a theory of market structure is embedded in their assumptions of strategic behavior and sequential entry.

In this article we have developed a theory of market structure suggested by the work of these earlier authors. Firms enter the market in sequence, each computing the reaction of all subsequent entrants to its own strategic investment decision. Only demand and cost conditions and the structure of the entry game are specified exogenously; the number of firms, their size distribution, and the market price are determined as the equilibrium to this entry game.

In a sense, the theory is an elaboration of the Bain-Labini-Modigliani limit-output or limit-price model. Aggregate output in equilibrium is always approximately equal to the limit output. The fact that output is never less than the limit output also has implications for efficiency. Roughly, firms use their power of strategic commitment to obtain as large a share of the market equilibrium quantity as they can. Thus, each firm acts to minimize the number of subsequent entrants. By reducing the number of firms in equilibrium, and hence economizing on entry costs, such behavior tends to improve welfare.

A reservation concerning the model is the artificial "order of entry," which is essential to determining equilibrium market structure. The most spectacular rivalry in many markets—the scramble to establish priority—is ignored in our analysis. Our model is perhaps least useful in understanding the evolution of market structure in such industries.

Our model seems most applicable to explaining entry into an established industry. Any potential entrant must obviously confront the irreversible decisions made by his predecessors, and it must take into account the possibility of subsequent entry by other firms. Indeed, a question that naturally arises is whether such an industry is in entry equilibrium. To answer this question, we believe that one must adopt the analytical framework (broadly defined) used in this article. Entry by its very nature is sequential, and rational entry requires analysis of a sequential game of the kind we develop.

From this perspective, Proposition 6 is particularly interesting. It says that one can answer the "entry equilibrium" question by putting oneself in the frame of reference of a *myopic* entrant—an entrant who makes his entry decision on the basis that there will be no subsequent entry.

Appendix

■ The proof of Proposition 7 follows.

Proof of Proposition 7. We consider all subgames in which $G_{i+1}(k^i) > 0$. We partition these subgames into sets indexed by $z \geq 1$ and defined as follows:

$$z = \max_{j \in I^+} j | G_{i+j}(k^i, k_{i+1} = \infty, k_{i+2} = \infty, \ldots, k_{i+j} = \infty) > 0,$$

where I^+ is the set of positive integers. We must show that in the perfect equilibrium of any such subgame, exactly z firms enter.

Case z = 1. Consider the case $z = 1$, and let $\underline{k}_{i+1}$ be the smallest value of k_{i+1} such that $G_{i+2}(k^i, k_{i+1}) \leq 0$. By continuity, $G_{i+2}(k^i, \underline{k}_{i+1}) = 0$. Let $\underline{k}_{i+2}$ be the value of k_{i+2} implied by the maximization that defines $G_{i+2}(\cdot)$. If $\tilde{k}_{i+1} < \underline{k}_{i+1}$, then there will be $m > i + 1$ firms in the perfect equilibrium of the subgame $(k^i, \tilde{k}_{i+1})$. Denote this equilibrium by $(k^i, \tilde{k}_{i+1}, \ldots, \tilde{k}_m, 0, \ldots, 0)$. We consider four equilibria of the Cournot game in stage $(n + 1)$ associated with the following capacity vectors: $(k^i, \underline{k}_{i+1}, 0, \ldots, 0)$, $(k^i, \underline{k}_{i+1}, \underline{k}_{i+2}, 0, \ldots, 0)$, $(k^i, \tilde{k}_{i+1}, \ldots, \tilde{k}_m, 0, \ldots, 0)$, and $(k^i, \tilde{k}_{i+1}, \ldots, \tilde{k}_m, k_{m+1} = \underline{k}_{i+2}, 0, \ldots, 0)$. The first of these has $(i + 1)$ firms with positive capacity, the second $(i + 2)$, the third m, and the fourth $(m + 1)$. Let X^v_u denote the aggregate output of the first u firms in the v-firm Cournot equilibrium and let x^v_j denote the output of firm j in the v-firm Cournot equilibrium.

To show that $(i + 1)$ will deter entry (that is, choose $k_{i+1} \geq \underline{k}_{i+1}$), it is sufficient to show that $X^m_m \geq X^{i+1}_{i+1}$, since price in the $(i + 1)$-firm equilibrium is then no smaller than it is in the m-firm equilibrium, and since $x^m_{i+1} \leq \tilde{k}_{i+1} < \underline{k}_{i+1} = x^{i+1}_{i+1}$. Assume the opposite:

$$X^m_m < X^{i+1}_{i+1}. \tag{A1}$$

Then

$$X^m_i \geq X^{i+1}_i, \tag{A2}$$

since the marginal revenue of each of the first i firms is greater in the m-firm Cournot equilibrium than it is in the $(i + 1)$-firm equilibrium. Moreover,

$$X^{m+1}_{m+1} \geq X^{i+2}_{i+2}, \tag{A3}$$

and

$$X^{m+1}_m \geq X^{i+2}_{i+1}. \tag{A4}$$

Otherwise, firm $(m + 1)$ would not be deterred, and $(\tilde{k}_{i+2}, \ldots, \tilde{k}_m, 0, \ldots, 0)$ would not be subgame perfect responses to $(k^i, \tilde{k}_{i+1})$. By the same reasoning that led to (A2), inequality (A3) implies that

$$X^{m+1}_i \leq X^{i+2}_i. \tag{A5}$$

From Proposition 2, inequalities (A4) and (A5), and the fact that $\underline{k}_{i+1}$ is the minimum value of k_{i+1} that deters entry, we have

$$x^m_{i+1} + \ldots + x^m_m \geq x^{m+1}_{i+1} + \ldots + x^{m+1}_m \geq x^{i+2}_{i+1} = \underline{k}_{i+1} = x^{i+1}_{i+1}. \tag{A6}$$

The first inequality follows from Proposition 2, the second from subtracting (A5) from (A4), and the equalities from the definition of $\underline{k}_{i+1}$. From (A6) we have

$$x^m_{i+1} + \ldots + x^m_m \geq x^{i+1}_{i+1}. \tag{A7}$$

Adding (A7) and (A2), we have $X^m_m \geq X^{i+1}_{i+1}$, which contradicts (A1). Hence, in any subgame with index $z = 1$, precisely one firm will enter.

Case z = 2. Now consider the case $z = 2$. Let us, we hope without confusion, redefine $\underline{k}_{i+1}$ as the smallest value of k_{i+1} such that $G_{i+3}(k^i, \underline{k}_{i+1}, k_{i+2} = \infty) \leq 0$. That is, $\underline{k}_{i+1}$ is the smallest value of k_{i+1} such that firm $(i + 2)$ *can* deter the entry of firm $(i + 3)$. If $k_{i+1} \geq \underline{k}_{i+1}$, the index of the implied subgame, (k^i, k_{i+1}), is 1, and from above we know that firm $(i + 2)$ *will* deter entry. We shall show that firm $(i + 1)$ prefers $\underline{k}_{i+1}$ to any $\tilde{k}_{i+1} < \underline{k}_{i+1}$, and hence that precisely two firms enter in any subgame with index $z = 2$.

Denote the subgame-perfect responses to $(k^i, \underline{k}_{i+1})$ by $(\underline{k}_{i+2}, 0, \ldots, 0)$. First, we establish that $G_{i+3}(k^i, \underline{k}_{i+1}, \underline{k}_{i+2}) = 0$. To see this switch $\underline{k}_{i+1}$ and $\underline{k}_{i+2}$ in the investment sequence. This makes no difference to firm $(i + 3)$'s opportunity set. Observe that since $\underline{k}_{i+1}$ is the smallest value of k_{i+1} that allows firm $(i + 2)$ to deter entry, then, given $k_{i+1} = \underline{k}_{i+2}$, $k_{i+2} = \underline{k}_{i+1}$ is the smallest value of k_{i+2} that will deter entry, so that $G_{i+3}(k^i, \underline{k}_{i+1}, \underline{k}_{i+2}) = 0$.

Let $\underline{k}_{i+3}$ be the value of k_{i+3} implied by the maximization that defines $G_{i+3}(\cdot)$. If $\tilde{k}_{i+1} < \underline{k}_{i+1}$, then there will be $m > (i + 2)$ firms in the perfect equilibrium of the subgame $(k^i, \tilde{k}_{i+1})$. Denote this equilibrium by $(k^i, \tilde{k}_{i+1}, \ldots, \tilde{k}_m, 0, \ldots, 0)$. We again consider four equilibria of the Cournot game in stage $(n + 1)$ associated with the following capacity vectors:

$$(k^i, \underline{k}_{i+1}, \underline{k}_{i+2}, 0, \ldots, 0), \qquad (k^i, \underline{k}_{i+1}, \underline{k}_{i+2}, \underline{k}_{i+3}, 0, \ldots, 0),$$

$$(k^i, \tilde{k}_{i+1}, \ldots, \tilde{k}_m, 0, \ldots, 0), \qquad \text{and} \qquad (k^i, \tilde{k}_{i+1}, \ldots, \tilde{k}_m, k_{m+1} = \underline{k}_{i+3}, 0, \ldots, 0).$$

To show that firm $(i + 1)$ prefers $\underline{k}_{i+1}$ to $\tilde{k}_{i+1} < \underline{k}_{i+1}$ it is sufficient to show that $X_m^m \geq X_{i+2}^{i+2}$, where X_u^v again denotes the aggregate output of the first u firms in the v-firm Cournot equilibrium. Suppose the contrary,

$$X_m^m < X_{i+2}^{i+2}. \tag{A8}$$

By the reasoning used to establish (A2), we have

$$X_i^m \geq X_i^{i+2}. \tag{A9}$$

By the reasoning used to establish (A6), we have

$$x_{i+1}^m + \ldots + x_m^m \geq x_{i+1}^{m+1} + \ldots + x_m^{m+1} \geq \underline{k}_{i+1} + \underline{k}_{i+2} = x_{i+1}^{i+2} + x_{i+2}^{i+2}. \tag{A10}$$

Adding (A9) and (A10), we have $X_m^m \geq X_{i+2}^{i+2}$, which contradicts (A8). Hence, in any subgame with index $z = 2$, precisely two firms will enter.

Replication of this argument establishes that in any subgame, with index z, exactly z firms enter in perfect equilibrium. The index of the subgame in which there is no committed capacity is, of course, the smallest number of firms that can deter entry of an additional firm. *Q.E.D.*

References

BAIN, J.S. *Barriers to New Competition.* Cambridge: Harvard University Press, 1956.

BERNHEIM, B.D. "Strategic Deterrence of Sequential Entry into an Industry." *Rand Journal of Economics,* Vol. 15 (1984), pp. 1–11.

BULOW, J., GEANAKOPLOS, J., AND KLEMPERER, P. "Holding Idle Capacity to Deter Entry." *Economic Journal,* Vol. 95 (1985), pp. 178–182.

DIXIT, A.K. "The Role of Investment in Entry Deterrence." *Economic Journal,* Vol. 90 (1980), pp. 95–106.

EATON, B.C. AND LIPSEY, R.G. "Capital, Commitment, and Entry Equilibrium." *Bell Journal of Economics,* Vol. 12 (1981), pp. 593–604.

FRIEDMAN, J.W. *Game Theory with Applications to Economics.* New York: Oxford University Press, 1986.

FUDENBERG, D. AND TIROLE, J. "Capital as Commitment: Strategic Investment to Deter Mobility." *Journal of Economic Theory,* Vol. 31 (1983), pp. 227–250.

GILBERT, R.J. "Preemptive Competition" in J.E. Stiglitz and G. F. Mathewson, eds., *New Developments in the Analysis of Market Structure,* Cambridge: MIT Press, 1986, pp. 90–123.

——— AND VIVES, X. "Noncooperative Entry Deterrence and the Free Rider Problem." University of Pennsylvania Discussion Paper, 1984.

KUHN, H. "Extensive Games and the Problem of Information" in H. Kuhn and A. Tucker, eds., *Contributions to the Theory of Games,* Vol. 2, Princeton: Princeton University Press, 1953, pp. 193–216.

MCLEAN, R. AND RIORDAN, M.H., "Industry Structure with Sequential Technology Choice." Preliminary Working Paper, Stanford University, 1985.

MODIGLIANI, F. "New Developments on the Oligopoly Front." *Journal of Political Economy,* Vol. 66 (1958), pp. 215–232.

PRESCOTT, E.C. AND VISSCHER, M., "Sequential Location among Firms with Perfect Foresight." *Bell Journal of Economics,* Vol. 8 (1977), pp. 378–393.

ROSEN, J.B. "Existence and Uniqueness of Equilibrium Points for Concave n-Person Games." *Econometrica,* Vol. 33 (1965), pp. 520–534.

SELTEN, R. "Reexamination of the Perfectness Concept for Equilibrium Points in Extensive Games." *International Journal of Game Theory,* Vol. 4 (1975), pp. 25–55.

SPENCE, A.M. "Entry, Capacity, Investment, and Oligopolistic Pricing." *Bell Journal of Economics,* Vol. 8 (1977), pp. 534–544.

SYLOS-LABINI, P. *Oligopoly and Technical Progress.* Cambridge: Harvard University Press, 1962.

WARE, R. "Sunk Costs and Strategic Commitment: A Proposed Three-Stage Equilibrium." *Economic Journal,* Vol. 94 (1984), pp. 370–378.

[9]

Uncertainty and the value of strategic commitment*
with Roger Ware**

1. Introduction

The idea is well established that a firm with a first mover advantage may strategically invest in order to raise its profits in a subsequent game with later movers.[1] It is also well understood, perhaps not as widely, that the same commitment which confers strategic advantage to the first mover can carry with it the risk of an inappropriate investment, given a degree of uncertainty at the time it was made. In a strategic context, this amounts to a *second mover advantage* – a firm that is willing to wait until more information is revealed can benefit from tailoring its investment more appropriately to actual conditions. Thus a tension is created between the strategic advantage of moving early vs the informational advantage of moving later.

This paper presents a simple model of the trade-off, under uncertainty, between the strategic advantage of early commitment and the costs of inappropriate investments. The model is one of two firms with guaranteed access to the market, making sequential 'positioning' investments where there is uncertainty about demand. We show that as the magnitude of the uncertainty increases, the strategic advantage of the first mover diminishes, and can vanish altogether.

Some efforts have been made to consider the effects of uncertainty on the strategic commitment model. Perrakis and Warskett (1983) introduced demand uncertainty in a fairly general way into a two firm entry game similar to that of Spulber (1981). However, they do not explore what seems to us to be the central issue – the effect of uncertainty on the strategic value of incumbency, and on first mover advantages in general. In Perrakis and Warskett (1983), the authors suggest that uncertainty may create an advantage for the first mover, or at least induce him to behave more aggressively in deterring entry, because of the great undesirability of having to share the market in low states of demand. They do not indicate, however, whether the incumbent is made better or worse off as a result of the uncertainty.

The paper proceeds as follows: Section 2 describes a simple model that illustrates the trade-off between commitment and flexibility; and Section 3 discusses the results, suggests some extensions, and draws implications for models of market structure in industrial organization.

2. The model

The model has two periods. Firm One can produce in either period at a constant marginal cost. Firm Two can produce only in the second period, when sales take place. The model is thus one of strategic commitment to *inventory* by Firm One.[2]

* This paper was written in 1988.
** Department of Economics, Queen's University, Canada.

Without uncertainty, the game theoretic structure of the model is identical to that of Dixit (1980), except that both firms are assumed to be committed to production, so that there is no entry game, but a game of strategic precommitment or 'positioning' only.

Both firms are assumed to be risk-neutral. For simplicity, the uncertainty is assumed to affect only demand and to be discrete, such that in period 2, realized demand is either 'high' (H) or 'low' (L). Inverse demand is assumed to be linear, given by:

$$P = \begin{cases} \alpha_1 - x_1 - x_2 \text{ in the high demand state} \\ \alpha_2 - x_1 - x_2 \text{ in the low demand state} \end{cases}$$

where $\alpha_1 > \alpha_2$, and the high and low state occur with probabilities p and $1 - p$. As usual in models of this type, we solve the model backward, first finding equilibrium choices of x_1 and x_2 in period 2, conditioned on first period production by Firm One. The final period game is Cournot or, more precisely, Cournot constrained by the presence of inventory produced by Firm One in the first period.

The range of possibilities for period 2 equilibria can be clarified by reference to Figure 1. Firm Two's second period reaction function is illustrated in the high and low states. Firm Two makes its production decision under *certainty* in this model, that is, after the uncertainty is resolved, so all period 2 equilibria must lie on either Firm Two's high or low reaction function.

The symmetric Cournot points for H and L states are labelled T_1 and T_2. If Firm One produces some quantity x_1 in period 1, it will all be sold in period 2, up to the point at which Firm One's marginal revenue falls to zero. Firm One will also produce in period 2 if, at the point on the relevant reaction function for Firm Two corresponding

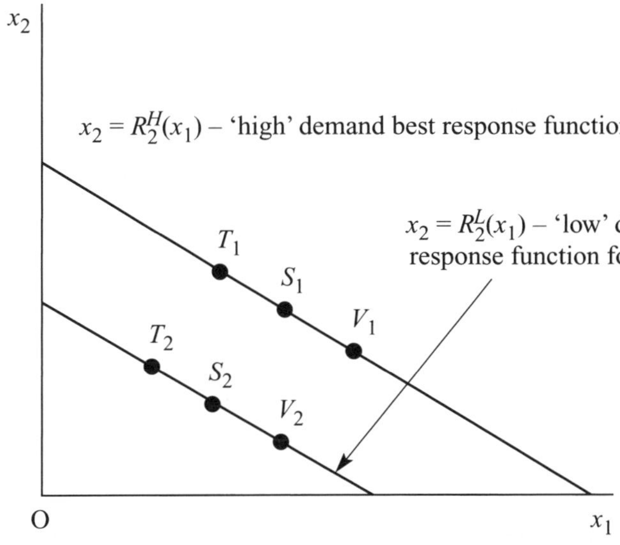

Figure 1. High and low demand reaction functions for Firm Two, and the relevant equilibrium points with uncertainty.

to Firm One's period 1 production, Firm One's marginal revenue exceeds marginal cost. In effect, this means that if Firm One chooses a point to the left of T_1, and the demand realization is H, T_1 will result. In all other cases, Firm One will stick with its first period production and not produce again in period 2.

Points V_1 and V_2 are the points on Firm Two's reaction functions at which Firm One's marginal revenue is zero. If Firm One commits to a larger quantity than either of these, the excess (that is, the quantity to the right of V_i) will not be put on the market and will be wasted. Finally, S_1 and S_2 indicate Stackelberg points, which, given a known certain realization of either H or L demand, are the best points for Firm One on the respective reaction functions. S_1 and S_2 may be to the right of the respective V_is and hence not be feasible, in which case the V_is are the best choices for Firm One under certainty.

Firm One's choice of production for inventory in period 1 may completely determine its own sales in period 2, and will certainly determine the expected profits of both firms in the period 2 equilibrium. By deriving the possible equilibria corresponding to different period 1 production choices for Firm One, we can trace out Firm One's best choice and hence the perfect equilibrium to the (sequential) game.

The key difference is whether Firm One produces to the left or right of T_1 in Figure 1. If the former, both firms will produce under the H state in period 2, and T_1 will result. Thus, Firm One is concerned only about maximizing L state profits as far as period 1 production is concerned. To the right of T_1, Firm One will not produce again in period 2, and Firm Two will produce at the point corresponding to x_1 on either its H or L reaction function. If the L state is realized, it is possible that Firm One may not sell all of its produced inventory, with a corresponding waste. Broadly speaking, if Firm One produces to the right of T_1 in period 1, it will be making a choice of an average Stackelberg point. To the left of T_1 only the L state is of concern, so that Firm One will choose the low Stackelberg point (labelled S_2 in Figure 1).[3]

For given values of α_1 and α_2 the perfect equilibrium can be derived, with some tedious computation, in the standard way. However, because we are interested particularly in the effect of uncertainty on *strategic* behaviour, we choose α_1 and α_2 so that uncertainty has *no effect* on firms' profits in either of two benchmark non-strategic cases: monopoly and non-strategic duopoly. Thus, let

$$\alpha_1 = (1+\beta)^{1/2} + c$$
$$\alpha_2 = (1-\beta)^{1/2} + c$$

where $\beta \in [0,1]$ now parameterizes the degree of uncertainty (the size of the fluctuations between H and L demand states) and c is marginal cost.

As regards the monopoly benchmark, it is easily verified that the expected profits of a monopolist are 1/4 for all permissible parameter combinations, and thus independent of the degree of uncertainty, β. In a non-strategic duopoly, neither firm is able to make a strategic commitment to inventory in period 1, and the outcome will simply be the Cournot equilibrium in whichever of the H or L states is realized. It is easily verified that the expected profits of either firm is 1/9 for all permissible parameter combinations, which is also independent of the degree of uncertainty.

In effect, by scaling α_1 and α_2 in the way that we have, demand shifts up and down from the mean in a fashion which exactly preserves non-strategic profits at the mean.

In this sense, variations in the parameter β amount to a mean-preserving spread in non-strategic profits. We investigate the effect of this mean-preserving spread on the strategic equilibrium.

3. Perfect equilibrium

Before reporting the complete solution to the model, it may be useful to summarize the solution where the uncertainty parameter β is zero, or $\alpha_1 = \alpha_2$. Since there is no uncertainty, Firm One has nothing to gain from producing in period 2, and we have an example of the model studied by Dixit (1980). If $c \geq 0.25$, then $S \leq V$, and Firm One will produce the Stackelberg quantity S in period 1. If $c < 0.25$, then $S > V$, and Firm One would be credibility constrained in period 2 at the Stackelberg quantity S and so produce only V in period 1. That is, Firm One exploits the strategic structure of the game to maximize its asymmetric advantage. Provided $c > 0.25$, Firm One's profits are exactly double those of Firm Two.

Given any values of β and c, expected profits for Firm One can be computed as a function of Firm One's period 1 production. The period 1 choice which maximizes Firm One's expected profits is the perfect equilibrium of the game. Figure 2 summarizes the resulting perfect equilibria in the space of the parameters β and c. The figure partitions the parameter space into different 'types' of equilibrium. The heavy line running east–west across the figure is the division, referred to above, between Firm One choosing a point to the left of T_1 (above the line, representing a higher level of uncertainty), and to the right of T_1 (below the line, representing a lower level of uncertainty). As we move across the line, for any value of c, the period 1 production of Firm One makes a discrete jump. More precisely, as the degree of uncertainty reaches a critical level, Firm One prefers to produce at the Stackelberg point (or

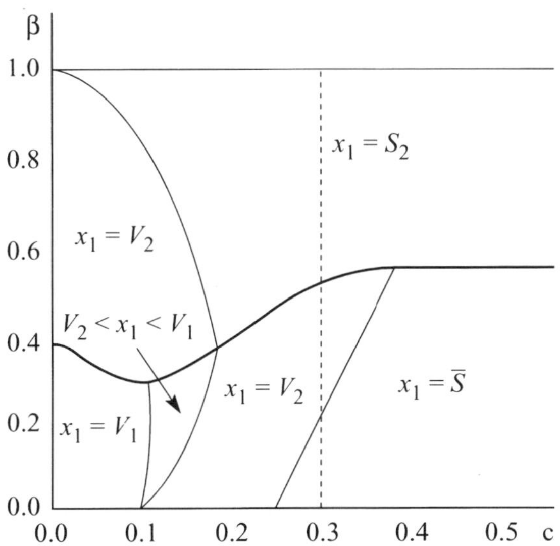

Figure 2. Perfect equilibria in the parameter space.

constrained Stackelberg point V_2) in the L state, and settle for symmetric Cournot profits if the H state should be realized, rather than produce more in period 1 and have to waste it if the L state should occur. In the south-west and north-west regions of the parameter space, Firm One is 'credibility constrained', in that an increase in production of one unit in period 1 would imply waste in the L state.

To clarify the analysis of these perfect equilibria, we can take a typical value of c, and explore the effect on the equilibrium of increasing uncertainty, starting at zero. Suppose $c = 0.3$. With zero uncertainty, the equilibrium is pure Stackelberg. As β becomes positive, Firm One chooses the mean of the two Stackelberg points S_1 and S_2. Firm One does not produce in period 2, as its mean Stackelberg output exceeds its output at T_1. At a value of β equal to 0.2, Firm One becomes credibility constrained in the L state, that is, if it continued to produce the mean Stackelberg quantity in period 1, some product would be wasted in the L state. Thus, for $0.2 < \beta < 0.53$ Firm One produces at V_2 in period 1. Since $V_2 > T_1$, Firm One still does not produce in period 2, in either state. When β reaches 0.53 the magnitude of the uncertainty is sufficiently large that Firm One is no longer gaining enough in the H state to justify its inefficiently large production in the L state, and Firm One switches, discretely, to producing S_2, and settling for symmetric Cournot profits in the H state.

Our main purpose is not the computation of these perfect equilibria *per se*, but to study the effect of uncertainty on the value of strategic commitment. To this end, we have computed the ratio of expected profits of Firm One to those of Firm Two, for $c = 0.3$, as a function of β. The comparison thus further tracks the qualitative description of the equilibria given above. Figure 3 illustrates the profits ratio. Starting from the certainty case where Firm One earns (Stackelberg) profits exactly double

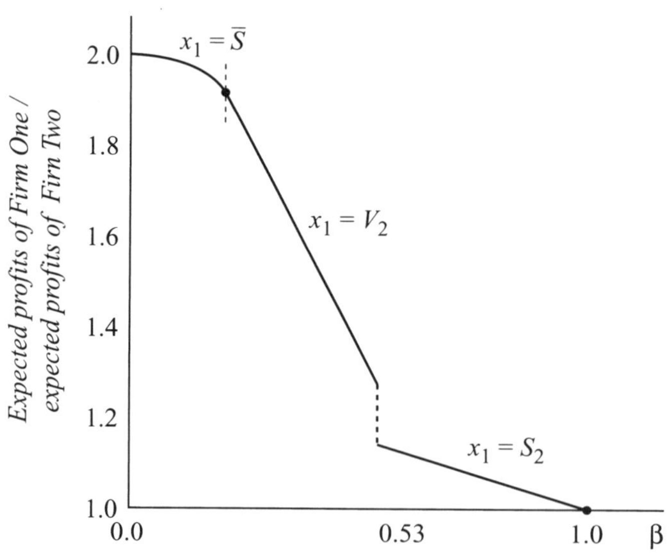

Figure 3. The ratio of expected profits of Firm One to the expected profits of Firm Two as a function of the uncertainty parameter.

those of Firm Two, the ratio of expected profits declines monotonically with β until, when β = 1, the ratio reaches unity. The latter result may seem surprising, because even with high values of β Firm One retains a strategic advantage in the L state by producing at the point S_2 in period 1. The explanation is that when β = 1, price falls to marginal cost in the L state, and so the *value* of Firm One's strategic advantage is zero (profits are zero for both firms). Recall that at high value of β, Firm One has conceded its strategic advantage in the H state, in favour of symmetric profits.

Figure 3 has three 'regimes', which have been described above. Note that the ratio of expected profits declines at a different rate in the different regimes. The ratio falls discontinuously at β = 0.53 because Firm One's discrete reduction in its period 1 production at this point leads to a corresponding discrete increase in Firm Two's expected profits. The decline in the ratio in the third segment, for large values of β, is due to the declining relative value of the L state, in which Firm One still has a strategic advantage.

The results provide striking confirmation of our initial conjecture: that the value of strategic commitment declines as uncertainty increases: alternatively, the strategic advantage has to be set against the potential costs of an inappropriate *ex post* choice of investment.

Many extensions to this basic model might be considered. An obvious one would be to extend the analysis to an entry game, in which the incumbent has the possibility of driving an entrant's profits negative. Although we have not investigated this case, since the rewards for successful deterrence are even greater than those of a strategic positioning investment, we conjecture that this would tilt the advantage more in favour of strategic over-investment, and less towards the caution induced by uncertainty.

Notes

1. Important early papers were Eaton and Lipsey (1979) and Dixit (1980). The structure of the model is extended to a sequential entry game with an endogenous number of firms in Eaton and Ware (1987).
2. The inventory model is perhaps the purest version of the strategic commitment paradigm. Examples are Ware (1985) and Arvan (1985).
3. This dichotomy needs to be qualified by credibility constraints. Any attempt to increase profits by choosing x_1 to the right of V_2 is expensive for Firm One, because some product is lost in the L state. This leads to a kink in Firm One's profit function, but does not contradict the basic dichotomy set out in the text.

References

Arvan, L. (1985), 'Some Examples of Dynamic Cournot Duopoly with Inventory', *Rand Journal of Economics*, **16**, pp. 569–78.

Dixit, A. (1980), 'The Role of Investment in Entry Deterrence', *Economic Journal*, **90**, pp. 95–106.

Eaton, B.C. and R.G. Lipsey (1979), 'The Theory of Market Preemption: The Persistence and Excess Capacity and Monopoly in Growing Spatial Markets', *Economica*, **46**, pp. 149–58.

Eaton, B.C. and R. Ware (1987), 'A Theory of Market Structure with Sequential Entry', *Rand Journal of Economics*, **18**, pp. 1–16.

Perrakis, S. and G. Warskett (1983), 'Capacity and Entry under Demand Uncertainty', *Review of Economic Studies*, **L**, pp. 495–511.

Spulber, D.F. (1981), 'Capacity, Output and Sequential Entry', *American Economic Review*, **68**, pp. 468–73.

Ware, R. (1985), 'Inventory Holding as a Strategic Weapon to Deter Entry', *Economica*, **52**, pp. 93–102.

[10]

Noncooperative equilibria in one-shot games: a synthesis*

with Mukesh Eswaran**

1. Introduction

A vast number of gaming situations that economists, political scientists, and evolutionary biologists consider have the distinct flavour of the prisoners' dilemma game. A cardinal feature of the equilibrium in such situations is that the outcome is individually rational (in the sense that no individual by herself has an incentive to do anything different from what she is doing in equilibrium), but is collectively irrational (in the sense that coordinated behaviour could make all players better off). Examples of such situations are the exploitation of commonly owned resources, investment in R&D by firms when there are spillovers in knowledge, choice of subsidies given by countries to domestic firms in competition with foreign rivals, the amount spent by neighbouring cities to control crime, competitive advertising by firms producing differentiated products, the amounts of time students spend studying for an examination when it is marked 'on the curve', the amount of money people spend on clothes when their preferences are such that they care about how well dressed they are relative to their friends, output or price choices of firms in an oligopoly – the list is virtually endless. In some of these situations, the collectively rational (i.e. Pareto efficient) outcome calls for higher levels of individual activity than the Nash equilibrium levels. In others, Pareto efficiency calls for lower levels of individual activity than in the Nash equilibrium. What essential aspect of the situation determines whether there is too much or too little of the activity, relative to the efficient outcome? To answer this question we set out a simple, yet powerful and surprisingly general framework, which we successively adapt to games of higher levels of sophistication. The answer to the question turns on the substitutability or complementarity of the actions of the players. Our analysis is carried out entirely in the context of symmetric, two-person games in which the strategies available to the players are continuous variables, and the equilibrium is interior.

We begin our analysis with the simplest scenario: a symmetric game involving two persons, called One and Two, and a single stage in which the players move simultaneously. The actions of the players are defined to be *plain substitutes* (respectively *plain complements*) if an increase in the level of one player's activity *decreases* (respectively *increases*) the other's payoff. We demonstrate that the Nash equilibrium choices of One and Two are higher than or lower than the corresponding choices in the symmetric Pareto-efficient outcome as their actions are plain substitutes or plain complements.

* The first draft of this paper was produced in 1991, and it was revised in December 2000.
** University of British Columbia, Canada.

The validity of this claim is verified and illustrated in the equilibria of seven gaming situations involving rent seeking, the use of performance-enhancing drugs by competing athletes, oligopolistic quantity setting, bribe taking in less developed countries, team-production, so-called Veblen effects, and the private provision of public goods.

We next consider a variant of the basic scenario by assuming that the moves are sequential. We allow One to be the first mover, thus conferring on One the privilege of Stackelberg leadership. We then ask how the levels of activities and the payoffs of One and Two in the equilibrium of the sequential move game compare to those in the equilibrium of the simultaneous move game. To answer this we need to invoke the notions of strategic substitutability and complementarity.[1] The actions of the players are *strategic substitutes* (respectively *strategic complements*) if an increase in the level of one player's activity lowers (respectively raises) the *marginal payoff* of the other. As one might expect, One is always better off in the equilibrium of the sequential move game. Two, it turns out, is better off or worse off in the equilibrium of the sequential move game as the actions are strategic complements or strategic substitutes. Thus in the case of strategic complementarity, a sequencing of the moves can result in a Pareto improvement over the Nash equilibrium with simultaneous moves. Once again we illustrate these results in the specific context of some examples; we revisit the duopoly problem introduced earlier and we examine the problem of double marginalization that arises when a monopolistic manufacturer sells its product to a monopolistic retailer.

We next move on to a consideration of two-stage games with simultaneous moves by both players in both stages. By interpreting the moves of the first stage as *commitments* which cannot be undone in the second stage, we are able to considerably enhance the scope of the problems we can capture in generic form. By invoking the assumption of foresighted behaviour, whereby players embody in their current decisions the future equilibrium consequences of their actions, we obtain a 'reduced form' game in commitments. In terms of the non-optimality of the equilibria of these two-stage games, precisely the same considerations that were important for one-stage games now become relevant for the reduced-form game. The difference is that it is now the substitutability or complementarity of the commitments of the players that becomes important. Thus parallel inferences can be drawn for two-stage games. We illustrate the usefulness of this approach by presenting two examples. The first looks at the strategic subsidization by countries of their own firms which are competing in oligopolistic international markets against foreign firms. The other example examines the strategic investment in cost-reducing R&D activities by a duopoly when there are spillovers in the knowledge generated.

Finally, we consider two-stage games in which the moves in the first stage (i.e. the commitments) are sequential. This construction enables us to examine in generic form situations where *incumbency* is important. A first-mover advantage given to One confers on her Stackelberg leadership in commitments. This introduces an asymmetry in an otherwise symmetric situation, and the reduced-form game has implications that parallel those of an earlier section. But the results here are of greater relevance because a first-mover advantage really is of consequence only when there are commitments available. The inferences drawn from this model are illustrated by two examples. The first examines strategic investment in cost-reducing R&D (without spillovers) in a duopoly where the incumbent has a first-mover advantage. This example serves to illustrate many features of the asymmetric equilibria that typically emerge in games where incumbency is of the essence. The second example looks at a duopoly producing differentiated products, in which the first mover invokes the so-called 'most favoured customer clause', as an expedient for promoting collusion. This example illustrates why it may be in the interest of players to contrive vehicles of commitment in situations where none may be apparent.

In this paper we do not consider games involving more than two stages. This is because the manner in which commitments influence the equilibria in many economic games can be adequately captured in games with only two stages. Also, we abstract from scenarios in which players repeatedly interact with each other. Repeated interaction, as is well known, affords the players an avenue to wholly or partly repair the inefficiency in the equilibria of one-shot games. This paper is devoted to an examination of the non-optimality of the equilibria of one-shot games – which is what gives repeated interaction its importance in the first place.

The emphasis in this paper is on providing a synthesis, that is, a general framework which captures the essential features of a large class of games. We do not seek to generate new results. In fact, most of the examples we provide have numerous antecedents in the economics literature. The examples chosen are such that, for the most part, they are interesting in themselves and illustrate important economic principles. They have also been chosen as simple representatives of important classes of phenomena in order to illustrate the scope of the synthesis we offer.

2. One-stage games with simultaneous moves

We begin our analysis with a simple game, which we subsequently embellish in following sections. The basic game comprises two players, One and Two, who each have one strategy available to them. We denote these strategies by x and y, and assume that they are both continuous variables drawn from the interval $[a, b]$, with $-\infty \leq a < b \leq +\infty$. We denote by the functions $U(x, y)$ and $V(x, y)$ the payoffs (or utilities) of One and Two, respectively. We assume that these payoff functions are strictly concave and twice continuously differentiable in their arguments. Strict concavity ensures that the upper level sets, or indifference curves, are strictly convex. We also assume that the payoff functions are symmetric, that is, $U(x, y) = V(y, x)$ for all $x, y \in [a, b]$.

When $U_2(x, y) < 0$ and $V_1(x, y) < 0$, if either player increases her strategy, the other's payoff decreases, and we have the case in which strategies are *plain substitutes*. (Here and throughout the paper, we use the convention that subscript i denotes the partial derivative with respect to the ith argument.) Conversely, when $U_2(x, y) > 0$ and $V_1(x, y) > 0$, if either player increases her strategy, the other's payoff increases, and we have the case in which strategies are *plain complements*.

The players choose their strategies simultaneously, under Nash conjectures. Thus if she expects Two's choice to be y, One will solve the following problem:

$$\max_{x} U(x, y). \tag{1}$$

Then One's best response to her conjecture of Two's choice will be the value of x that solves the following first-order condition:

$$U_1(x, y) = 0. \tag{2}$$

We assume that for each value of y, there is a unique solution to equation (2), denoted by $r(y)$. The function $r(y)$ is One's *best response* or *reaction function*. Similarly, if she expects One's choice of strategy to be x, Two's will solve

$$\max_{y} V(x, y) \tag{3}$$

and her best response is the value of y that solves the following first-order condition:

$$V_2(x, y) = 0. \tag{4}$$

Since the payoff functions are symmetric, $r(x)$ is Two's best response or reaction function.

To see how One's best response will change when y is increased slightly, we totally differentiate (2), to obtain

$$U_{11}(x, y)\, \mathrm{d}x + U_{12}(x, y)\, \mathrm{d}y = 0. \tag{5}$$

Since $U_{11}(x, y) < 0$ by strict concavity in x, it follows that if $\mathrm{d}y$ is positive, $\mathrm{d}x$ must be negative if $U_{12}(x, y) < 0$ and positive if $U_{12}(x, y) > 0$. In other words, if an increase in the value of Two's choice variable decreases the *marginal worth* to One of her own choice variable [if $U_{12}(x, y) < 0$], an increase in y will elicit a lower response from One ($\mathrm{d}x < 0$). We shall refer to x and y as *strategic substitutes* in this case. On the other hand, if an increase in the value of Two's choice variable increases the marginal worth to One of her own choice variable [if $U_{12}(x, y) > 0$], an increase in y will elicit a higher response from One ($\mathrm{d}x > 0$). In this case, we shall refer to x and y as *strategic complements*.

It follows from what has been said above that the reaction function, $r(\cdot)$, is a declining function of its argument when the choice variables are strategic substitutes; the reaction functions of One and Two for this case are represented by AB and CD, respectively, in Figure 1. When the choice variables are strategic complements, the reaction functions of One and Two are increasing in their arguments, and are represented by AB and CD, respectively, in Figure 2.

A strategy pair $(\hat{x}, \hat{y})$ is a Nash equilibrium if each strategy is a best response to the other, that is, if

$$\hat{x} = r(\hat{y}) \tag{6.1}$$

and

$$\hat{y} = r(\hat{x}). \tag{6.2}$$

In other words, $(\hat{x}, \hat{y})$ is an equilibrium in the sense that if One chooses her strategy expecting Two to choose $\hat{y}$ and Two chooses hers expecting One to choose $\hat{x}$, then both players' expectations are realized and neither player regrets her choice of strategy. Geometrically, the Nash equilibrium is obtained as the intersection of the reaction functions of the players, and is represented by point *N* in Figures 1 and 2. We shall assume, in what follows, that there exists one and only one Nash equilibrium.[2]

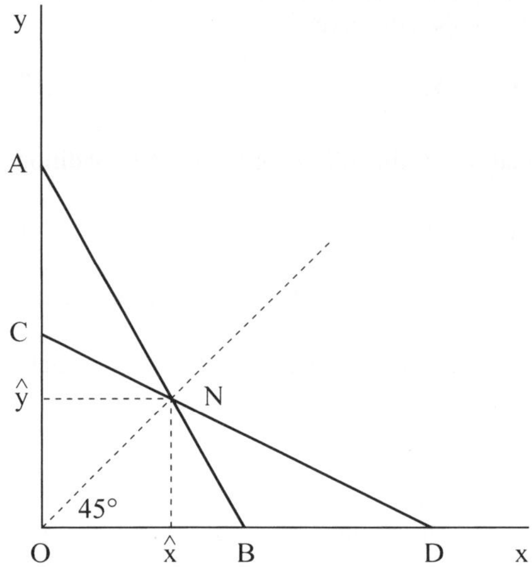

Figure 1. Reaction curves and the Nash equilibrium when the strategies are strategic substitutes.

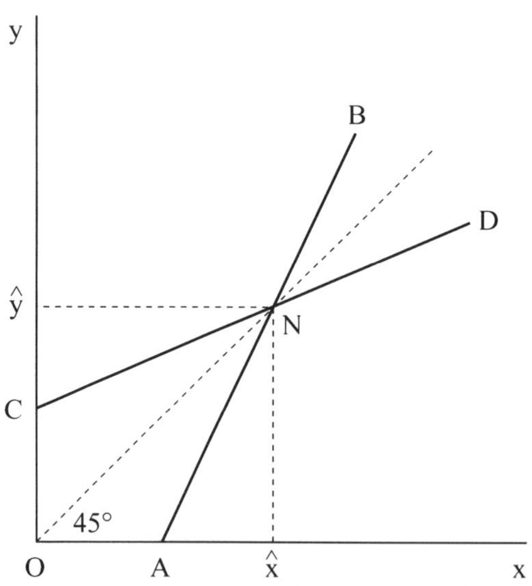

Figure 2. Reaction curves and the Nash equilibrium when the strategies are strategic complements.

Note that, given Two's choice, One's best response puts her on the highest possible indifference curve – by the definition of best response. Thus at every point on One's reaction function, her indifference curves will have zero slope. To see this, think of One as choosing x to maximize $U(x, y)$, subject to the constraint that Two's strategy is fixed at y. In the solution to this constrained maximization problem, One's indifference curve through the solution will be tangent to the constraint, which is simply a horizontal line. Thus the slope of One's indifference curve at the solution is zero. By similar reasoning, it follows that at every point on Two's reaction function, her indifference curves must be vertical.

Now let us consider what sort of strategy pairs (x, y) are Pareto efficient. By definition, such a pair will make One as well off as possible for a given level of Two's utility. Let us fix Two's utility at $\bar{V}$. Then for this $\bar{V}$ the Pareto-efficient strategy pair $(\bar{x}, \bar{y})$ is that point on Two's indifference curve (corresponding to utility level $\bar{V}$) which puts One on her highest possible indifference curve. This occurs at a point of tangency, Q, as shown in Figure 3, and the slopes of the two indifference curves are identical at this point. (Figure 3 is drawn on the presumption that the strategies are plain substitutes.) This point Q is, of course, conditional on the level $\bar{V}$ at which Two's utility was fixed. As we vary $\bar{V}$, the point Q will trace a locus $P'P''$, which will represent the entire set of Pareto-efficient strategy pairs. Since One and Two have symmetric utility functions, the Pareto-efficient strategy pair that generates the same utilities for the two players will be given by the intersection of $P'P''$ with the 45 degree line in Figure 3. This is denoted by point P, which has coordinates (x^*, y^*), with $y^* = x^*$.

We are now ready to see how the symmetric Pareto-efficient strategy pair (x^*, y^*) compares with the (symmetric) Nash equilibrium pair $(\hat{x}, \hat{y})$. Figures 4 and 5 illustrate this comparison. Since One's indifference curves have zero slope on her reaction

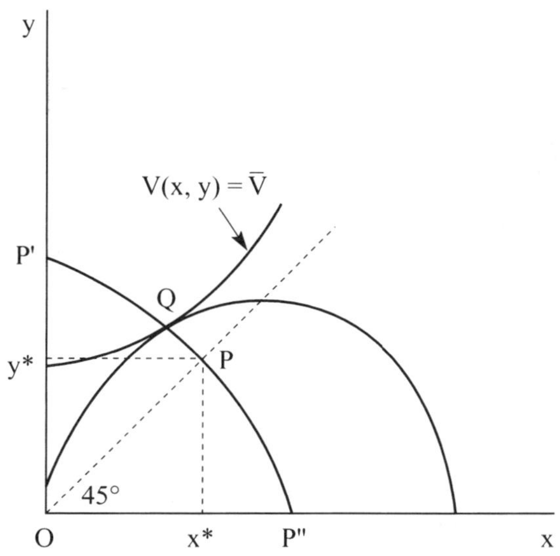

Figure 3. Construction of the Pareto-efficient frontier (for the case of plain substitutes).

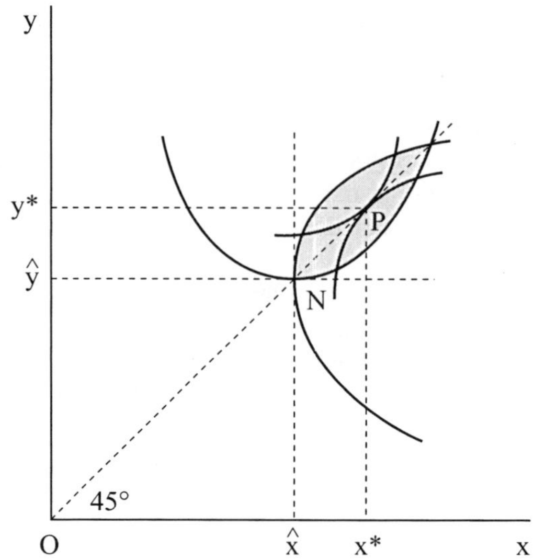

Figure 4. *The symmetric Pareto-efficient choices exceed the Nash equilibrium choices when the strategies are plain complements.*

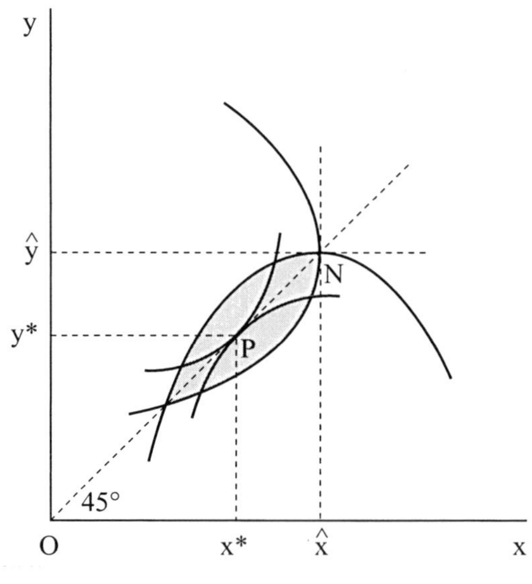

Figure 5. *The symmetric Pareto-efficient choices are less than the Nash choices when the strategies are plain substitutes.*

function, while Two's indifference curves have infinite slope on hers, One's and Two's indifference curves intersect at right angles at the Nash equilibrium point *N*. At the symmetric Pareto-efficient point P, however, One's and Two's indifference curves are tangential. Thus, it follows that, in general, the Nash equilibrium is *not* Pareto efficient – starting from the Nash equilibrium N, there is scope for both One and Two to be made better off.

Do One's and Two's Nash equilibrium choices exceed or fall short of their respective Pareto-efficient levels? The answer depends on whether x and y are plain substitutes or plain complements. We have seen that, at the Nash equilibrium, One's and Two's indifference curves intersect at right angles. This means that there is necessarily a lens-shaped area in which both One and Two are better off than at the Nash equilibrium. Since the utility functions of One and Two are symmetric, this lens-shaped area must be symmetrical about the 45 degree line, with the Nash equilibrium point at one end. Clearly, the symmetric Pareto-efficient point must lie in this region. If this region lies between the origin and the Nash equilibrium point, the Pareto-efficient choices will be smaller than the Nash equilibrium choices. If this region lies away from the Nash equilibrium point, the reverse will be true. As we shall see below, the former case obtains when One's and Two's strategies are plain substitutes and the latter when they are plain complements.

To arrive at the above inference we only need to ascertain the shapes of the players' indifference curves. Totally differentiating the expression $U(x, y) = \text{constant}$, which is the equation to an indifference curve of One, we have

$$U_1(x, y)\,\mathrm{d}x + U_2(x, y)\,\mathrm{d}y = 0$$

from which we obtain

$$\mathrm{d}y/\mathrm{d}x = -U_1(x, y)/U_2(x, y) \tag{7}$$

as the slope of an indifference curve of One at (x, y). Now by the definition of One's best response function, we know that $U_1(x, y) = 0$ at $x = r(y)$. By the strict concavity of $U(x, y)$ in x, it follows that $U_1(x, y) > 0$ for $x < r(y)$ and $U_1(x, y) < 0$ for $x > r(y)$.

When x and y are plain complements, $U_2(x, y) > 0$, and from equation (7) we have

$$\mathrm{d}y/\mathrm{d}x < 0 \text{ if } x < r(y) \quad \text{and} \quad \mathrm{d}y/\mathrm{d}x > 0 \text{ if } x > r(y).$$

So, in the case of plain complements, One's indifference curves have a negative slope to the left of her reaction function, and a positive slope to the right, as illustrated in Figure 4. Likewise, those of Two are as shown in the figure. It follows that when One's and Two's actions are plain complements, the efficient choices exceed the Nash choices. The intuition for this is simple: in Nash behaviour each player ignores the beneficial effect an increase in her choice variable has on the other's utility. So, from a welfare point of view, they both choose too low a value for their strategy variable. If it were possible for them to coordinate their strategies, One and Two could both make themselves better off by choosing higher values for x and y, respectively.

When x and y are plain substitutes, $U_2(x, y) < 0$, and from equation (7) we have

$$\mathrm{d}y/\mathrm{d}x > 0 \text{ if } x < r(y) \text{ and } \mathrm{d}y/\mathrm{d}x < 0 \text{ if } x > r(y).$$

So, in the case of plain substitutes, One's indifference curves have a positive slope to the left of her reaction function, and a negative slope to the right, as illustrated in Figure 5. Two's indifference curves are also shown in the figure. In this case, we see that One's and Two's Nash equilibrium choices exceed their efficient levels. This is because each player, in choosing her Nash strategy, ignores the deleterious effect it has on the other, and so in the equilibrium sets a value for her choice variable that is too large from a welfare point of view. If it were possible for One and Two to coordinate their strategies, they could both make themselves better off by choosing lower values for x and y, respectively.

To put things in perspective, it is helpful to consider two conditions that are necessary for the Nash equilibrium to be Pareto inefficient. First, it must be the case that either $U_2(x, y)$ or $V_1(x, y)$, or both $U_2(x, y)$ and $V_1(x, y)$, are non-zero – that is, One's strategy must impinge on Two's payoff, and vice versa. When this condition is not satisfied, there is no meaningful interaction among the players – there is no interesting sense in which the players are involved in a game. Notice that this condition is not satisfied in the perfectly competitive models of intermediate economic theory, where equilibrium is often Pareto efficient. Second, it must not be the case that $U(x, y) = V(x, y)$ for all x, y – that is, One's and Two's utility functions must not be identical. If they were, then in choosing x to maximize her own utility, One would also be maximizing Two's. Similarly, Two's optimal choice of y would also maximize One's utility. Clearly, the Nash equilibrium outcome will be Pareto efficient in this case. This second necessary condition is interesting from an institutional standpoint. Two rival firms in a duopoly, for example, can make their objective functions identical by means of an equity swap, thereby rendering the Nash equilibrium in the output market Pareto efficient.

3. Some illustrative examples

To show just how widely applicable this framework is, in this section we examine a number of games that fit the mould developed in Section 2.

3.1. Example 1: rent seeking

In situations where rent or pure profit exists but property rights are incomplete or non-existent, there is an incentive for parties to spend real resources in an effort to appropriate some or all of the rent. When these resources affect only the allocation of the rent and not its magnitude, the activity is called *rent seeking*. The net effect, of course, is that some portion of the rent is dissipated in the competitive rush to appropriate it. Rent seeking takes myriad forms in the real world. The classic examples concern the exploitation of resources when there is common access: when competing firms exploit the same reservoir of oil, thereby reducing the total quantity of oil that can be recovered from the reservoir; when competing fishers exploit the same stock of fish, thereby reducing the stock below its optimal level and possibly fishing it to extinction; and when villagers who privately own their own livestock dissipate the value of their common pasture land by overgrazing it. In addition there are many other examples: when competing interest groups spend real resources to affect their government's allocation of tax revenue, or when a firm engages in premature entry in order to pre-empt a market that promises future profit.[3]

The essence of rent-seeking activities is captured in a simple model developed by Tullock (1980). Imagine a winner-take-all game in which there is a money prize of magnitude Z, and two players, One and Two. The eventual winner is determined by a random process, but each player can influence her probability of winning by devoting resources to bias the allocation process. Let x and y denote the *resources* devoted by One and Two, respectively, to increasing their probabilities of success. Suppose that One's probability of winning is given by $x/(x+y)$, and that Two's probability is given by $y/(x+y)$. Then, the expected net winnings or payoffs of One and Two are given, respectively, by

$$U(x, y) = (Zx)/(x+y) - x \tag{8.1}$$

and

$$V(x, y) = (Zy)/(x+y) - y. \tag{8.2}$$

Maximizing $U(x, y)$ with respect to x and $V(x, y)$ with respect to y, under Nash conjectures, yields the following first-order conditions:

$$Z/(x+y) - (Zx)/(x+y)^2 - 1 = 0 \tag{9.1}$$

and

$$Z/(x+y) - (Zy)/(x+y)^2 - 1 = 0. \tag{9.2}$$

Solving these equations for x and y yields the Nash equilibrium values:

$$\hat{x} = \hat{y} = Z/4. \tag{10}$$

Equilibrium payoffs are

$$U(\hat{x}, \hat{y}) = V(\hat{x}, \hat{y}) = Z/4. \tag{11}$$

Notice that, in this equilibrium, each player has a probability $1/2$ of winning, and in aggregate they dissipate, through their rent-seeking activities, half the value of the prize. This is clearly not Pareto optimal. If they could agree, One and Two could both make themselves better off by, say, deciding the winner by the toss of a fair coin. The efficient levels of expenditures are clearly $x^* = y^* = 0$.

Building on what we learned in Section 2, the conclusion that the Nash equilibrium expenditures exceed their efficient levels could have been immediately inferred by recognizing that $U_2(x, y) < 0$ and $V_1(x, y) < 0$, that is, by recognizing that the rent-seeking expenditures of One and Two are plain substitutes. Given this recognition, we see immediately that the relationship of the equilibrium to the optimum is illustrated by Figure 5.

This rent dissipation game is ripe for laboratory experimentation. Just imagine a lottery with fixed prize Z, and tickets that can be purchased for a dollar each. Letting

x and y denote the number of tickets bought by One and Two, it is immediately clear that if the players are risk neutral, the payoff functions for this lottery are those written down in equations (8).

3.2. Example 2: athletes and performance-enhancing drugs

This example is a variation on the theme of example 1. Suppose One and Two are the only relevant rivals in an Olympic event. Both of them can take performance-enhancing drugs – for example, anabolic steroids. Let x and y denote the *amounts spent on these drugs* by One and Two, respectively. Denote by $p(x, y)$ the probability that One will win the event. It is natural to assume that $p_1(x, y) > 0$ (One's probability of winning increases as she spends more on performance-enhancing drugs), and that $p_2(x, y) < 0$ (One's probability of winning decreases as her opponent spends more on performance-enhancing drugs). Of course, if $p(x, y)$ is the probability that One wins, then $1 - p(x, y)$ is the probability that Two wins. Denote by W and L the athlete's utility of winning and losing, and suppose that $W > L$ (winning is better than losing). Then the expected utilities of One and Two are given, respectively, by

$$U(x, y) = p(x, y)W + [1 - p(x, y)]L - x \tag{12.1}$$

and

$$V(x, y) = [1 - p(x, y)]W + p(x, y)L - y. \tag{12.2}$$

Notice that $U_2(x, y) = p_2(x, y)(W - L) < 0$, and that $V_1(x, y) = p_1(x, y)(L - W) < 0$, indicating that this is another game in which the players' strategies are plain substitutes. It follows then that the essence of this game is captured in Figure 5 and hence that the Nash equilibrium levels of anabolic steroids are excessive, relative to the Pareto-efficient levels.

3.3. Example 3: a duopoly

In this example we assume that One and Two are firms producing differentiated products. Let x and y denote the *outputs* produced by One and Two, and assume that the prices $P^1(x, y)$ and $P^2(x, y)$ commanded by the products of One and Two are given, respectively, by

$$P^1(x, y) = \alpha - \beta x - \gamma y \tag{13.1}$$

and

$$P^2(x, y) = \alpha - \beta y - \gamma x \tag{13.2}$$

with $\alpha > 0$, $\beta > 0$ and $|\gamma| < \beta$. Notice that the products themselves are substitutes if $\gamma > 0$ (the more one firm sells, the lower is the price at which the other firm can sell its product) and complements if $\gamma < 0$ (the more one firm sells, the higher is the price at which the other firm can sell its product). For simplicity, assume that the costs of production are zero.

Given these assumptions, the profit functions are

$$U(x, y) = x(\alpha - \beta x - \gamma y) \tag{14.1}$$

and

$$V(x, y) = y(\alpha - \beta y - \gamma x). \tag{14.2}$$

Notice that the goods produced by One and Two are plain substitutes or plain complements as γ is positive or negative [since $U_2(x, y)$ and $V_1(x, y)$ are negative or positive as γ is positive or negative].

Under Cournot–Nash conjectures, the first-order conditions for One's and Two's maximization problems are given, respectively, by $\alpha - 2\beta x - \gamma y = 0$ and $\alpha - 2\beta y - \gamma x = 0$. These conditions yield the following reaction functions for One and Two, respectively:

$$r(y) = (\alpha - \gamma y)/2\beta \tag{15.1}$$

and

$$r(x) = (\alpha - \gamma x)/2\beta. \tag{15.2}$$

Note that these reaction functions are upward sloping in (x, y) space if γ is negative, indicating that the goods produced by One and Two are strategic complements. Conversely, these reaction functions are downward sloping in (x, y) space if γ is positive, indicating that the goods produced by One and Two are strategic substitutes.

In this duopoly example there is a nice link with demand theory: if the goods produced by the firms are substitutes (respectively, complements), then from a game theoretic perspective they are both plain substitutes (respectively, complements) and strategic substitutes (respectively, complements).

The unique and symmetric Cournot–Nash equilibrium outputs are easily computed to be

$$\hat{x} = \hat{y} = \alpha/(2\beta + \gamma) \tag{16}$$

and the associated equilibrium profits of One and Two are given by

$$U(\hat{x}, \hat{y}) = V(\hat{x}, \hat{y}) = \alpha^2\beta/(2\beta + \gamma)^2. \tag{17}$$

The symmetric outcome that is Pareto efficient from the point of view of One and Two is the one that maximizes their joint profit [that is, the sum of $U(x, y)$ and $V(x, y)$]. The output levels, x^* and y^*, that maximize joint profit are readily computed to be

$$x^* = y^* = \alpha/(2\beta + 2\gamma) \tag{18}$$

and the Pareto-efficient profit levels of One and Two are given by

$$U(x^*, y^*) = V(x^*, y^*) = \alpha^2/(4\beta + 4\gamma). \tag{19}$$

Comparing equations (16) and (18) we see that the Cournot–Nash equilibrium output levels are less than (respectively, greater than) the symmetric Pareto-efficient levels if the goods are plain complements (respectively, plain substitutes). Of course, this result was at our finger tips when, following equation (14), we observed that $U_2(x, y)$ and $V_1(x, y)$ are negative or positive as γ is positive or negative.

3.4. *Example 4: efficient bribe taking*

In many less-developed countries that espouse state intervention in order to promote economic development, the economies often end up becoming over-regulated. In consequence, the government officials involved in the regulatory process inevitably have the opportunity to solicit bribes in exchange for bending the rules. Often an entrepreneur who is subject to regulation has to get permission from officials at 10 or 15 different official levels. As she moves up the hierarchy of officials, the entrepreneur has to offer a bribe at each level. While bribe taking is not necessarily inefficient, it can become so if the government officials at various levels do not coordinate their demands. As a consequence, the aggregate bribe required of an entrepreneur can become inefficiently high – so high that entrepreneurs, government officials and the public at large could all be rendered better off if government officials coordinated their bribe demands. This insight, which essentially is due to Tullock (1980), can be formalized and couched in terms that fit the mould set out in Section 2.[4]

Suppose that, in order to engage in some legitimate entrepreneurial activity, entrepreneurs need permission from a two-level hierarchy of government officials, One and Two. The number of entrepreneurs, Q, who choose to engage in the said economic activity is a declining function of the total bribe needed to obtain permission.

$$Q = \alpha - \beta(x + y), \alpha > 0, \beta > 0 \tag{20}$$

where x and y are the *bribes* demanded by officials One and Two, respectively. The rents garnered by officials One and Two are just Qx and Qy, or, using equation (20),

$$U(x, y) = (\alpha - \beta x - \beta y)\, x \tag{21.1}$$

and

$$V(x, y) = (\alpha - \beta x - \beta y)\, y. \tag{21.2}$$

Comparing equation (21) with equation (14), we see that the present problem of bribe taking is isomorphic to the problem confronting duopolists producing differentiated products, with $\gamma = \beta$ in equation (14). Then, from equation (16) we see that Nash equilibrium bribes demanded by officials One and Two are

$$\hat{x} = \hat{y} = \alpha/3\beta \tag{22}$$

and from equation (18) we see that the efficient bribe for each to charge is

$$x^* = y^* = \alpha/4\beta \tag{23}$$

which is lower than the Nash equilibrium level. Thus if the government officials coordinated their bribe-taking activities, not only they themselves, but entrepreneurs also, would be better off. If needless regulations and the attendant bribe taking cannot be eliminated because of the strong vested interests of government officials, there might still be scope for minimizing the damage by encouraging efficiency in bribe taking. Notice that we could have arrived at this conclusion the minute we wrote down the two payoff functions in equation (21), since $U_2(x, y)$ and $V_1(x, y)$ are both negative, indicating that the bribes of the officials are plain substitutes and that Figure 5 captures essential features of this game.

3.5. Example 5: team production

Imagine a team, comprising individuals One and Two, that is engaged in a productive activity that requires effort from both team members. Let x and y denote the *effort levels* of One and Two, respectively, and let $q(x, y)$ be an index of the team's output. The index could be the volume of the output produced by the team or it could be a measure of the quality of the output. A joint term paper fits this situation exactly: two students work together to write a paper, x and y represent their respective effort levels in writing the joint paper, and $q(x, y)$ represents the grade they get on the paper.

We would expect that $q_1(x, y) > 0$ and $q_2(x, y) > 0$: output increases as the effort level of either team member increases. Suppose that both individuals have identical preferences defined over q and their own effort level e, and let $W(q, e)$ denote the utility function. It is natural to suppose that $W_1(q, e) > 0$ and $W_2(q, e) < 0$; in other words, that output is a good and effort is a bad. Given these assumptions, the utilities of One and Two as functions of effort levels x and y are given, respectively, by

$$U(x, y) = W[q(x, y), x] \tag{24.1}$$

and

$$V(x, y) = W[q(x, y), y]. \tag{24.2}$$

Notice that $U_2(x, y) = W_1[q(x, y), x]\, q_2(x, y)$ and that $V_1(x, y) = W_1[q(x, y), y]\, q_1(x, y)$. Both expressions are positive since utility increases as q increases [$W_1(q, 2) > 0$], and $q(x, y)$ increases as the other team members' effort increases [both $q_1(x, y) > 0$ and $q_2(x, y) > 0$]. We see then that the effort levels of the team members are plain complements, that Figure 4 is applicable, and that the Nash equilibrium effort levels of One and Two will fall short of the efficient levels. This is a standard result, which we may attribute to the moral hazard of players operating in teams.[5]

3.6. Example 6: Veblen effects

In *The Theory of the Leisure Class* (Veblen, 1899), Thorstein Veblen argued that, in much of what we humans do, we are motivated by a desire to be seen as more affluent than those with whom we associate, and that in the attempt to achieve the desired end, we focus our spending on *conspicuous consumption* – that is, on items of consumption that others can readily observe. Clearly, clothing is one such item, and in this example we see how a desire to be more well dressed than our friends leads all of us to spend more than we should on clothing.

Let x and y denote amounts spent respectively by One and Two on clothing (more generally, on conspicuous consumption). Suppose that both individuals care only about how much they spend on their own clothing (a good), how much the other person spends on her clothing (a bad), and how much they spend on all other goods (a good). Suppose too that they have the same income ($1, for convenience), and that their preferences are symmetric.

Denote by $W(x, y, z)$ One's utility function, where z is the amount One spends on items other than clothing. Clearly, $W_1(x, y, z) > 0$ (the more One spends on her own clothing, the better off she is), $W_2(x, y, z) < 0$ (the more Two spends on her clothing, the worse off is One, capturing Veblen's hypothesis), and $W_3(x, y, z) > 0$ (the more One spends on all items other than clothing, the better off she is). One's maximization problem can then be written as

$$\max_{x, z} W(x, y, z) \quad \text{subject to} \quad x + z = 1. \tag{25}$$

By symmetry, Two's preferences are captured by $W(y, x, v)$, where v is the amount Two spends on items other than clothing. Her maximization problem can then be written as

$$\max_{y, v} W(y, x, v) \quad \text{subject to} \quad y + v = 1. \tag{26}$$

Using One's budget constraint to eliminate z as a choice variable, and Two's budget constraint to eliminate v as a choice variable, the maximization problems can be rewritten as

$$\max_{x} U(x, y) \equiv W(x, y, 1 - x) \tag{27}$$

and

$$\max_{y} V(x, y) \equiv W(y, x, 1 - y). \tag{28}$$

Now observe that $U_2(x, y) = W_2(x, y, 1 - x) < 0$ and that $V_1(x, y) = W_2(y, x, 1 - y) < 0$. Hence, this is a game in which x and y are plain substitutes, the essence of which is captured in Figure 5. We conclude immediately that, relative to the symmetric Pareto-optimal expenditures on clothing, in the Nash equilibrium of this game, these individuals spend too much on clothing.

3.7. Example 7: the private provision of quasi-public goods

A good supplied by one individual is a quasi-public good if other individuals also benefit from the good. It is, of course, elementary that when individuals privately choose the amounts they spend on quasi-public goods, the goods are under-supplied relative to the Pareto optimum. We can readily adapt the Veblen effects model to show that this result – that quasi-public goods are under-supplied – arises from the fact that quantities of quasi-public goods supplied by different individuals are plain complements.

For concreteness, let us focus on two neighbours, each of whom spends money tending their private gardens. If each enjoys the other's garden, their gardens are quasi-public goods. Suppose then that One cares only about the amount she spends on her garden, x, the amount her neighbour spends on her garden, y, and the amount she spends on all goods other than her garden, z. Let $W(x, y, z)$ be her utility function and suppose that $W_1(x, y, z) > 0$, $W_2(x, y, z) > 0$, and $W_3(x, y, z) > 0$ – in other words, suppose that x, y and z are all goods. Supposing, for convenience, that her income is \$1, then One's maximization problem is the one written down in equation (25), and it can be rewritten as equation (27). Supposing that Two's preferences are symmetric to One's and that she too has just \$1 to spend; her maximization problem is the one written down in equation (26), which can be rewritten as equation (28). Then, since each enjoys the other's garden, $U_2(x, y) = W_2(x, y, 1-x) > 0$ and $V_1(x, y) = W_2(y, x, 1-y) > 0$, and we see that x and y are plain complements. Figure 4 is then seen to be applicable, and we conclude that, relative to the symmetric Pareto optimum, these neighbours spend too little on their gardens.

Notice that in equations (25)–(28) we have a quite general, two-person model of symmetric consumption externalities. If the consumption externalities are negative, the goods are plain substitutes, and if the externalities are positive, the goods are plain complements.

4. One-stage games with sequential moves

In the previous two sections we assumed that the players One and Two chose their strategies simultaneously. In many situations it is often the case that one player has the so-called *first-mover advantage*, that is, one player gets to choose her strategy first. In this section we briefly consider such games when each player has only one decision to make. We will focus attention on whether Two is necessarily worse off as a second mover than she is when both players move simultaneously. The answer, we shall see, depends on whether the actions of the players are strategic complements or strategic substitutes.

Suppose One is the first mover and chooses her strategy x before Two chooses y. The sequential nature of the moves introduces an asymmetry between One and Two even if they have symmetric payoff functions.[6] If One has made her choice, Two has no option but to take One's choice, x, as given and maximize her own payoff by choosing y to be her best response, $r(x)$. Recognizing the response of Two to her actions, One will see herself as a Stackelberg leader – she will choose x in order to maximize her own payoff, recognizing that Two will respond to her choice of x with $r(x)$. In other words, One will solve the following constrained maximization problem:

$$\max_{x} U(x, y) \text{ subject to } y = r(x). \tag{29}$$

The constraint in equation (29) merely says that for any value of One's choice, Two's choice will be such as to put her on her own reaction function. In solving this problem, One will choose the point on Two's reaction function which puts One on her highest indifference curve.

The Nash and Stackelberg equilibria are compared in Figure 6 for the case when x and y are plain and strategic complements. At the Nash equilibrium point, N, One's indifference curve has zero slope. Then, since Two's reaction function is positively sloped, the Stackelberg equilibrium point necessarily lies to the north-east of the Nash equilibrium point. Let $\tilde{x}$ and $\tilde{y}$ denote One's and Two's choices, respectively, in the Stackelberg equilibrium. It follows that, when the actions of One and Two are plain and strategic complements, their Stackelberg choices exceed their Nash choices, that is, $\tilde{x} > \hat{x}$ and $\tilde{y} > \hat{y}$. Furthermore, both One and Two are better off in the Stackelberg equilibrium relative to the Nash equilibrium.

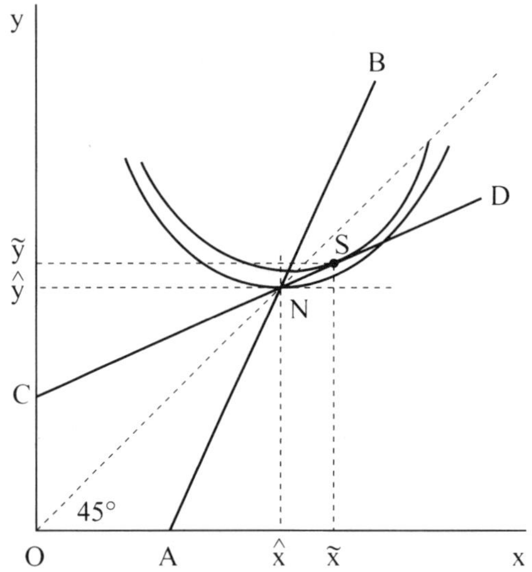

Figure 6. Comparison of Nash and Stackelberg equilibria when the strategies are plain and strategic complements.

The following argument explains why Stackelberg leadership leads to a Pareto improvement over the Nash outcome in the case of strategic complementarity.[7] At the Nash equilibrium, One takes Two's choice as given at $\hat{y}$ and sets her own choice so that the marginal payoff to her from a further small increase in x is zero, thus producing the Nash equilibrium point, $(\hat{x}, \hat{y})$. As a Stackelberg leader, however, One will not take Two's choice as given. Instead, One will recognize that when she increases x beyond $\hat{x}$, given strategic complementarity, Two's marginal payoff increases and that two will respond by increasing her own choice. This, in turn, will increase One's marginal payoff. Thus at $(\hat{x}, \hat{y})$, One's marginal payoff when she is a Stackelberg leader is strictly positive and so she will be induced to set x at a higher level than $\hat{x}$. Two will respond by also choosing a higher level than $\hat{y}$ for her decision variable. Given the strategic complementarity of x and y, both One and Two are thus better off at the Stackelberg equilibrium than they are at the Nash equilibrium. So, in this case, the introduction of an asymmetry by a sequencing of moves in an otherwise symmetrical situation renders both individuals better off.

When the actions of One and Two are plain and strategic substitutes, the relevant situation is depicted in Figure 7. One is again the leader and Two the follower. Here, the Stackelberg leader's choice exceeds her Nash equilibrium choice, while the reverse is true for the follower. Furthermore, One is better off in the Stackelberg equilibrium than in the Nash equilibrium, while the reverse is true of Two. Intuition for this outcome can be obtained by mimicking the logic of the previous paragraph. (It hinges on the fact that, due to strategic substitutability, an increase in One's choice lowers the marginal payoff to Two.) Thus, in this instance, the introduction of an asymmetry by a sequencing of moves in an otherwise symmetrical situation makes the first mover better off at the expense of the second mover.[8]

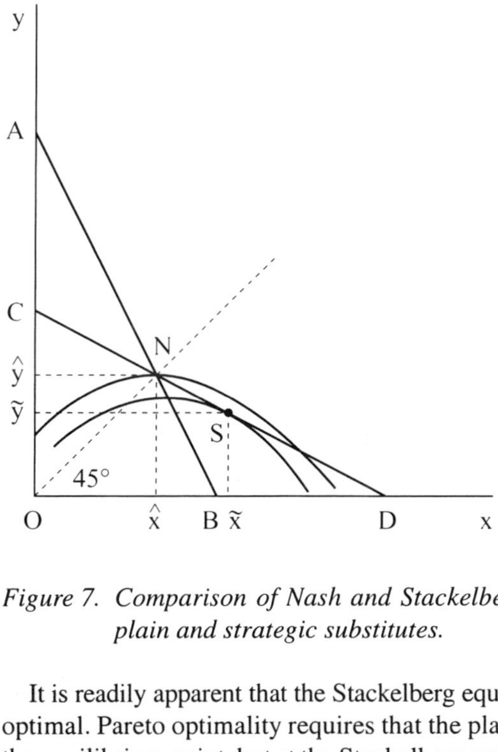

Figure 7. Comparison of Nash and Stackelberg equilibria when the strategies are plain and strategic substitutes.

It is readily apparent that the Stackelberg equilibria in Figures 6 and 7 are not Pareto optimal. Pareto optimality requires that the players' indifference curves be tangent at the equilibrium point, but at the Stackelberg point, One's indifference curve is tangent to Two's reaction and Two's indifference curve is vertical. In Figure 6 (respectively, Figure 7), points to the north-east (respectively, south-west) of the Stackelberg point Pareto dominate it. Qualitatively then, the distortions in these Stackelberg games are the same as the distortions in the corresponding simultaneous move games. In both cases, when strategies are plain complements (respectively, plain substitutes), equilibrium strategy values are too small (respectively, too large) from a welfare perspective.

5. Some examples of one-stage games with sequential moves

In this section we elaborate on example 3 and add an additional example of some interest.

5.1. Example 8: Stackelberg duopoly

Although the general model presented in example 3 is somewhat messy when decisions are sequential, by picking specific parameter values it is easy to generate clean illustrations of the points made in Section 4. Here we focus on the case in which the strategies of One and Two are both plain and strategic complements.

If we set $\alpha = 1$, $\beta = 2$, and $\gamma = -1$ in equations (14), we get the following payoff functions for firms One and Two:

$$U(x, y) = x(1 - 2x + y) \tag{30.1}$$

and

$$V(x, y) = y(1 - 2y + x). \tag{30.2}$$

Since $U_2(x, y)$ and $V_1(x, y)$ are both positive, strategies are plain complements for these particular parameter values. Substituting these parameter values into equations (15), we get the two reaction functions:

$$r(y) = (1 + y)/4 \tag{31.1}$$

and

$$r(x) = (1 + x)/4. \tag{31.2}$$

Since the reaction functions are positively sloped, this is a case of strategic complements as well. It is readily verified that the Nash equilibrium values of x and y are

$$\hat{x} = \hat{y} = 1/3 \tag{32}$$

and that the Nash equilibrium payoffs are

$$U(\hat{x}, \hat{y}) = V(\hat{x}, \hat{y}) = 2/9. \tag{33}$$

If we substitute Two's reaction function for y in One's objective function, we see that One's problem is:

$$\max_{x} U[x, r(x)] = x(5 - 7x)/4. \tag{34}$$

The first-order condition for this problem is $5 - 14x = 0$. Using this first-order condition and Two's reaction function we get the Stackelberg equilibrium values:

$$\tilde{x} = 5/14 > 1/3 = \hat{x} \tag{35.1}$$

and

$$\tilde{y} = 19/56 > 1/3 = \hat{y}. \tag{35.2}$$

Payoffs in the Stackelberg equilibrium are then

$$U(\tilde{x}, \tilde{y}) = 25/112 > 2/9 = U(\hat{x}, \hat{y}) \quad (36.1)$$

and

$$V(\tilde{x}, \tilde{y}) = 361/1568 > 2/9 = V(\hat{x}, \hat{y}). \quad (36.2)$$

These results are consistent with the general results for strategic complements from the previous section. When moves are sequential, both the leader and the follower are better off, and both produce more, relative to the Nash equilibrium with simultaneous choice.

5.2. Example 9: double marginalization

Suppose firms with market power are in a vertical relationship (i.e. the output of one firm is an input for another) and that each firm exercises its market power to maximize its profit. Then, as a result of *double marginalization*, the outcome may be inefficient from the point of view of the firms.[9] Stackelberg leadership helps by partially internalizing the externality responsible for the inefficient outcome, but it cannot altogether do away with the inefficiency. As we will see, by increasing the number of instruments available to the leader, however, it may be possible to generate Pareto efficiency.

Suppose One is a monopolist producing, at zero cost, a product that is used as an input by Two, a firm downstream. Two, the only buyer of One's output, uses the latter's output as the sole input in a production process that generates a final product, which Two sells as a monopolist to consumers. If we denote by x the *price* that One charges for her product and by y the *mark-up* that Two adds to One's price, we see that the total price consumers pay for the final product is $x + y$. By assumption, quantity Q is the following linear function of the total price paid by consumers:

$$Q = \alpha - \beta(x + y) \quad \alpha > 0 \quad \beta > 0.$$

Then payoff functions for One and Two are, respectively,

$$U(x, y) = x[\alpha - \beta(x + y)] \quad (37.1)$$

and

$$V(x, y) = y[\alpha - \beta(x + y)]. \quad (37.2)$$

Since both $U_2(x, y)$ and $V_1(x, y)$ are negative, this is a case of plain substitutes. As is easily verified, the reaction functions are

$$r(y) = (\alpha - \beta y)/(2\beta) \quad \text{and} \quad r(x) = (\alpha - \beta x)/(2\beta) \quad (38)$$

Since these are downward sloping, this is a case of strategic substitutes as well.

The Nash equilibrium values of x and y in the simultaneous move game and the equilibrium payoffs are readily computed as

$$\hat{x} = \hat{y} = \alpha/(3\beta) \tag{39}$$

and

$$U(x, y) = V(x, y) = (\alpha^2)/(9\beta). \tag{40}$$

In this game One is, in effect, a natural Stackelberg leader, and her maximization problem is to choose x and y to maximize $U(x, y)$ subject to the constraint that $y = r(x)$. Substituting the constraint into the objective function, One's problem is

$$\max_{x} U[x, r(x)] = x(\alpha - \beta x)/2. \tag{41}$$

The first-order condition for this problem is $\alpha - 2\beta x = 0$. Using this condition and $r(x)$ we get the following Stackelberg equilibrium values:

$$\tilde{x} = \alpha/2\beta > \alpha/3\beta = \hat{x} \tag{42.1}$$

and

$$\tilde{y} = \alpha/4\beta < \alpha/3\beta = \hat{y}. \tag{42.2}$$

The associated Stackelberg equilibrium payoffs are

$$U(\tilde{x}, \tilde{y}) = \alpha^2/(8\beta) > \alpha^2/(9\beta) = U(\hat{x}, \hat{y}) \tag{43.1}$$

and

$$V(\tilde{x}, \tilde{y}) = \alpha^2/(16\beta) < \alpha^2/(9\beta) = V(\hat{x}, \hat{y}). \tag{43.2}$$

These results are consistent with the general results from the previous section for the case in which the firm's strategies are both plain and strategic substitutes. When moves are sequential, the leader is better off and the follower worse off, and the leader chooses a larger value of her strategy and the follower a smaller value, relative to the Nash equilibrium with simultaneous choice.

The Stackelberg outcome computed above is not Pareto efficient. We can immediately infer this by recognizing that $U_2(x, y) < 0$ and $V_1(x, y) < 0$, or that x and y are plain substitutes. The intuitive reason for the inefficiency in this case is revealing. As follower, Two takes the input price as given and chooses her output price so as to set her marginal profits to zero. This generates a derived demand for One's output as a function of the price she charges Two, and One chooses her price by setting her marginal profits to zero. This 'double marginalization' results in a final price for consumers that is excessively high – in the sense that One and Two could both be potentially better off by a reduction in the final price.

Pareto efficiency can be restored in the present scenario by expanding the set of strategies available to One. We have assumed above that the only strategy variable at One's disposal is the price she charges Two for every unit of her output transacted. Suppose we now allow One to also charge Two a fixed fee, F, independent of the quantity transacted. For an arbitrary combination of x, y and F, the joint profit, $W(x, y)$, of One and Two is given by adding $U(x, y)$ and $V(x, y)$ in equations (37) to get

$$W(x, y) = (x + y)\,[\alpha - \beta(x + y)]. \tag{44}$$

Since a feasible fixed fee does not impinge on Two's marginal incentives, her reaction function remains $r(x)$ in equations (38). Substituting $r(x)$ for y in equation (43) we obtain One's and Two's joint profit as a function of x alone:

$$W[x, r(x)] = (\alpha^2 - \beta^2 x^2)/4\beta. \tag{45}$$

The optimal value of x is clearly zero (which is One's marginal cost of producing her output), and the maximized industry profit is $\alpha^2/4\beta$, which exceeds the industry profits of $3\alpha^2/16\beta$ in the Stackelberg equilibrium. The fixed fee, F, can now be used to effect a Pareto improvement over the Stackelberg equilibrium. With $x = 0$, any value of F in the range $\alpha^2/8\beta < F < 3\alpha^2/16\beta$ will yield a Pareto improvement. Thus, the expedient of a fixed fee solves the double marginalization problem. This example brings home the point that efficiency or inefficiency of an equilibrium depends non-trivially on the strategies available to the players.

6. Two-stage games with simultaneous moves

The results pertaining to the non-optimality of Nash and Stackelberg equilibria can be extended to games that entail decision-making at more than one stage. In what follows, in the interest of simplicity we restrict ourselves to two-stage games. This is adequate to cover a wide variety of games that are of interest to economists; generalization to games involving more than two stages is conceptually easy, although it may introduce technical difficulties. We shall focus attention on games in which decisions made in the first stage impinge non-trivially on choices in the second stage. (If first-stage choices could be costlessly reversed in the subsequent stage, or if they had no effect on second-stage choices, generalization from one-stage to two-stage games would be redundant.) So we assume that in the first stage players One and Two simultaneously make irreversible choices (i.e. commitments) denoted by X and Y, respectively. We assume that X and Y can be represented by continuous variables drawn from the interval $[A, B]$ with $-\infty \leq A < B \leq +\infty$. In the second stage, they simultaneously choose their strategies x and y, respectively, as before, and the game ends. We denote the payoffs to One and Two, obtained only after the second-stage choices are made, by $\tilde{U}(X, Y, x, y)$ and $\tilde{V}(X, Y, x, y)$, respectively. If we invoke symmetry, we shall have $\tilde{V}(Y, X, y, x) = \tilde{U}(X, Y, x, y)$.

We shall assume that One and Two entertain Nash conjectures in choosing X and Y, and also in choosing x and y, respectively. At what levels will One and Two set their choice variables? Since x and y are chosen in the second stage, when X and Y have been irreversibly set, One will choose x to maximize $\tilde{U}(X, Y, x, y)$ and Two will choose y to maximize $\tilde{V}(X, Y, x, y)$. The associated first-order conditions are

$$\tilde{U}_3(X, Y, x, y) = 0 \tag{46.1}$$

and

$$\tilde{V}_4(X, Y, x, y) = 0. \tag{46.2}$$

We shall assume that for every pair (X, Y) there is a unique Nash equilibrium in x and y, which solves these first-order conditions. This equilibrium will depend non-trivially on the (X, Y) pair that has been committed to in the first stage. We denote the Nash equilibrium pair by $[\hat{x}(X, Y), \hat{y}(X, Y)]$. For given commitments (X, Y), One's payoff is thus given by

$$U(X, Y) \equiv \tilde{U}[X, Y, \hat{x}(X, Y), \hat{y}(X, Y)] \tag{47}$$

and Two's by

$$V(X, Y) \equiv \tilde{V}[X, Y, \hat{x}(X, Y), \hat{y}(X, Y)]. \tag{48}$$

The 'reduced form' payoffs $U(X, Y)$ and $V(X, Y)$ given above – usually referred to as 'value functions' – embody the Nash equilibrium outcome in the second stage, for given X and Y.

Now we come to the question of how One and Two will choose their commitments X and Y, respectively. As rational individuals, they will both recognize that these choices, made in the first stage of the game, will influence the Nash equilibrium in the next (and final) stage and, hence, their payoffs. Thus, in her choice of X, One will seek to ascertain how a particular value of X will impinge on her utility through the Nash equilibrium of the second stage. This utility is precisely what is captured by the reduced form function $U(X, Y)$. Thus, under Nash conjectures, One will choose X to maximize $U(X, Y)$ and Two will choose Y to maximize $V(X, Y)$. The associated first-order conditions are

$$U_1(X, Y) = 0 \tag{49.1}$$

and

$$V_2(X, Y) = 0. \tag{49.2}$$

We assume that for every Y there is a unique value, $R(Y)$, that solves One's first-order condition; $R(Y)$ is, of course, One's reaction function. Symmetry implies that $R(X)$ is Two's reaction function.

We assume that there exists a unique Nash equilibrium pair, denoted by $(\hat{X}, \hat{Y})$, which solves the first-order conditions in equation (49). Given symmetry, we must have $\hat{X} = \hat{Y}$. Let (X^*, Y^*), with $X^* = Y^*$, denote the commitment pair that yields the (symmetric) Pareto-efficient outcome, given that the second-stage outcome is resolved under Nash conjectures. Since the second-stage choices $\hat{x}$ and $\hat{y}$ are not efficient, we can interpret (X^*, Y^*) as a *second-best* Pareto optimum in commitments.

We are now ready to compare the commitment levels in the Nash equilibrium with those in the symmetric, second-best Pareto optimum. In particular, we can ask whether there is 'over-commitment' or 'under-commitment' in the equilibrium, relative to the optimum. We can readily answer this question because the reduced-form game in commitments is identical in structure to the one-stage game considered in Section 2. If the commitments X and Y are plain complements [that is, if $U_2(X, Y) > 0$ and $V_1(X, Y) > 0$], in the Nash equilibrium there will be under-commitment (that is, $\hat{X} < X^*$). If X and Y are plain substitutes [that is, if $U_2(X, Y) < 0$ and $V_1(X, Y) < 0$], there will be over-commitment (that is, $\hat{X} > X^*$).

7. Some examples of two-stage games involving simultaneous moves

7.1. Example 10: strategic trade subsidies

An interesting strategic problem faces the governments of countries whose firms compete in oligopolistic international markets. If these governments can credibly commit to subsidizing the firms of their own country, the firms' reaction functions are altered in a manner that could potentially rig the ensuing Nash equilibrium in international markets in their own favour. Further, the gains to a country's firms can more than compensate for the cost of the subsidies: the net benefits can come at the expense of the firms of other countries. This prospect makes it individually rational, but collectively irrational, for governments to engage in subsidization activities.[10]

To formalize this problem, assume there are two countries One and Two, each of which has a single firm producing a homogeneous product. The two firms have no consumers of their product in countries One and Two, and they both sell their outputs in a common third market in country Three. The inverse demand curve from Three for this product is given by

$$P = \alpha - \beta Q \quad \alpha > 0, \beta > 0$$

where Q and P denote aggregate consumption and price in country Three.

The game comprises two stages, with simultaneous moves in each stage. In the first stage, the (governments of) countries One and Two announce *excise subsidies* of X and Y per unit of output, respectively. We shall assume that these announcements cannot be rescinded, so that they represent commitments. In the second stage, the firms of One and Two take the subsidies as given and produce *outputs* of amount x and y, respectively, at zero cost. We assume that each country's objective is to maximize its own firm's contribution to GNP, net of subsidy costs. Thus in terms of X, Y, x and y the payoff functions of countries One and Two, respectively, are

$$\tilde{U}(X, Y, x, y) = \tilde{u}(X, x, y) - Xx \tag{50.1}$$

and

$$\tilde{V}(X, Y, x, y) = \tilde{v}(Y, x, y) - Yy \tag{50.2}$$

where $\tilde{u}(X, x, y)$ and $\tilde{v}(Y, x, y)$ denote, respectively, the private profits of firms One and Two, and are given by

$$\tilde{u}(X, x, y) = [\alpha + X - \beta(x + y)]x \tag{51.1}$$

and

$$\tilde{v}(Y, x, y) = [\alpha + Y - \beta(x + y)]y. \tag{51.2}$$

Since countries One and Two will first examine how the Cournot–Nash equilibrium in the second stage will be influenced by their subsidies, we need to work out this equilibrium first. Maximizing the private profit of firms One and Two under Nash conjectures, we obtain the following Nash equilibrium quantities, given arbitrary subsidy levels X and Y:

$$\hat{x}(X, Y) = (\alpha + 2X - Y)/(3\beta) \tag{52.1}$$

and

$$\hat{y}(X, Y) = (\alpha + 2Y - X)/(3\beta). \tag{52.2}$$

Substituting the above expressions into equations (51) to obtain the firms' profits and these, in turn, into equations (50), we obtain the following expressions for $U(X, Y)$ and $V(X, Y)$, the reduced-form payoffs for countries One and Two, respectively.

$$U(X, Y) = (\alpha - X - Y)(\alpha + 2X - Y)/(9\beta) \tag{53.1}$$

and

$$V(X, Y) = (\alpha - X - Y)(\alpha + 2Y - X)/(9\beta). \tag{53.2}$$

For given (X, Y) the above reduced-form payoff functions for One and Two embody the Nash equilibrium outcome in the second stage of the game. To find equilibrium subsidy levels observe that, under Nash conjectures, One will choose X to maximize $U(X, Y)$ and Two will choose Y to maximize $V(X, Y)$. Since $U_2(X, Y) < 0$ and $V_1(X, Y) < 0$, this is a case in which the commitments are plain substitutes, and it follows immediately that the Nash equilibrium subsidies $\hat{X}$ and $\hat{Y}$ exceed the Pareto-efficient level.

Solving for the Nash equilibrium subsidy levels, we get

$$\hat{X} = \hat{Y} = \alpha/5. \tag{54}$$

To get the symmetric Pareto-optimal subsidy levels, we must choose X and Y to maximize the sum of $U(X, Y)$ and $V(X, Y)$. The optimal values are

$$X^* = Y^* = -\alpha/4. \tag{55}$$

In other words, optimality requires a tax, or *negative subsidy*, equal to $-\alpha/4$.

From equations (52), we see that the optimal subsidy induces each firm to produce quantity $\alpha/4$, so that their combined output is $\alpha/2$, the output that would be produced if a monopolist served this market. So, the optimal tax induces firms to restrict output just enough so that their combined output is identical to the monopoly output.

The crux of the problem here is illustrated in Figure 8. In (x, y) space, AB and CD represent the reaction functions of firms One and Two when the subsidy levels are zero, and the corresponding Nash equilibrium in outputs is represented by point N. Now observe from equations (50) and (51) that, for arbitrary x and y, the payoffs to countries One and Two are independent of X and Y. Hence, the iso-payoff curves of countries One and Two are identical to the iso-profit contours in (x, y) space of their respective firms. When the subsidy levels are increased to their Nash equilibrium levels $\hat{X} = \hat{Y} = \alpha/5$, the reaction functions of the two firms shift out to $A'B'$ and $C'D'$, respectively, and the new Nash equilibrium in outputs is at point N'. Since the indifference maps of One and Two do not change when the subsidy levels change, it is clear from the figure that both countries are worse off at N' than at N. Under the optimal subsidy levels, the reaction functions would intersect at the Pareto-efficient point P in the figure.

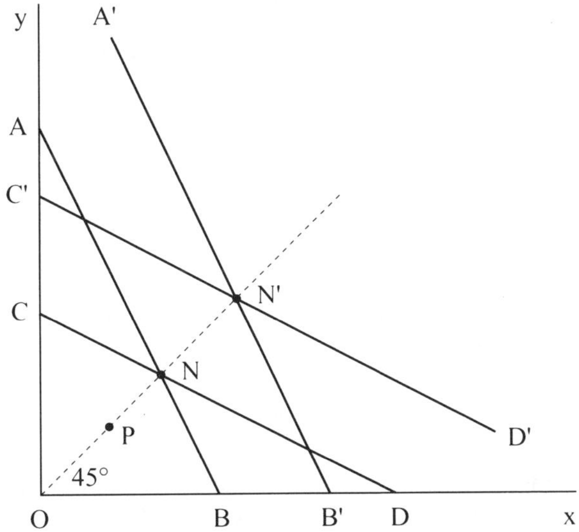

Figure 8. Illustrates why the Nash equilibrium with subsidies is inferior to that without.

This example illustrates the proposition that the introduction of a vehicle of commitment does not necessarily make a player better off. Here, both countries would have been better off had their governments been unable to commit themselves to subsidies. When the commitments are plain substitutes, their introduction into the game makes a bad situation (the Nash equilibrium in outputs at N^0 in Figure 8) worse by compounding the prisoners' dilemma problem.

7.2. Example 11: strategic R&D in presence of spillovers

An important aspect of commercial research and development activities by private firms has to do with the appropriability of the knowledge generated. It is often the case that the technical information generated by one firm's R&D expenditures can be accessed partially or fully by other firms in the industry. Patents usually provide only weak protection because they can be invented around. In fact, the very act of getting a technology patented may itself reveal information that rival firms can utilize to improve their performance. In this example, we wish to investigate how spillovers of technical knowledge between firms impinge on their R&D activities when the firms compete in an oligopolistic product market.

Consider an industry comprising two firms, One and Two, which produce a homogeneous product and undertake R&D expenditures X and Y, respectively. The R&D is for process innovation: it lowers the cost of producing the existing product. We assume that production proceeds at constant marginal cost, and that the *level* of this marginal cost can be lowered through R&D activity. For simplicity, we assume that all the information generated by a firm becomes common knowledge within the industry. Thus the marginal cost of production, $C(X+Y)$, will be the same for both firms and will be a declining function of their aggregate R&D expenditures. We assume that the firms commit their R&D expenditures simultaneously, and that this constitutes the first stage of the game. In the second stage, the firms compete in Cournot–Nash fashion in the output market, using the technology generated in the first stage. The inverse demand curve facing the industry is taken to be

$$P = \alpha - \beta(x + y)$$

where x and y denote One's and Two's outputs, respectively, and P denotes price. The payoff functions of One and Two are given, respectively, by

$$\tilde{U}(X, Y, x, y) = [\alpha - C(X+Y) - \beta(x+y)]x - X \tag{56.1}$$

and

$$\tilde{V}(X, Y, x, y) = [\alpha - C(X+Y) - \beta(x+y)]y - Y. \tag{56.2}$$

Solving for the Cournot–Nash equilibrium in the second stage for given R&D expenditures, and substituting the equilibrium outputs into equations (56), we obtain the reduced-form payoffs for firms One and Two:

$$U(X, Y) = [\alpha - C(X+Y)]^2/9\beta - X \tag{57.1}$$

and

$$V(X, Y) = [\alpha - C(X+Y)]^2/9\beta - Y. \tag{57.2}$$

Observe that $U_2(X, Y) = V_1(X, Y) > 0$, since $C(X+Y)$ is declining in its argument. Hence, the R&D expenditures of the firms are plain complements, and we see immediately that amounts spent on R&D in the first stage will be inefficiently low.

The result that firms undertake less than the optimal amount of R&D when the returns to their efforts are not fully appropriable should not be altogether surprising. There is a further point, however, which is more significant. Despite the fact that *all* the technical information generated by a firm becomes freely available to its rival, the Nash equilibrium R&D expenditure of a firm, generally, will be positive, even if suboptimal. That a firm engages in R&D at all stems from the fact that it has market power in the output market. This enables it to reap some returns to its R&D efforts. Increasing the extent of the competition in the output market would dilute the R&D incentives of the firms even more. This is at the heart of Schumpeter's (1942) powerful critique of perfect competition. While perfect competition may maximize society's welfare in a static world, in a dynamic context it loses this virtue. When knowledge is inherently inappropriable, market concentration in this second-best world is a good thing.

8. Two-stage games with sequential moves

This is the last class of games we shall consider in this paper, and it represents a fairly important class as a large number of strategic situations fall within its scope. We could assume that the moves in each of the stages are sequential, but we shall pursue the more realistic case where *only* the commitments are chosen sequentially. In other words, we look at the case where, say, One is able to commit X first and is then followed by Two with her commitment Y in the first stage. In the second stage, One and Two simultaneously choose x and y, respectively. The assumption that the second-stage choices are made simultaneously is particularly appropriate if x and y, by their very nature, cannot be commitments, that is, do not represent irrevocable choices.

When the second-stage game is resolved under Nash conjectures, the reduced-form payoffs to One and Two are the payoffs we denoted in Section 6 by $U(X, Y)$ and $V(X, Y)$, respectively. The reaction function representing Two's best commitment response to One's choice of X, we denoted by $R(X)$. Since One commits prior to Two, the former will take the latter's response into account in choosing X. In other words, a first-mover advantage in commitments makes One a Stackelberg leader. One will then choose X and Y to maximize $U(X, Y)$ subject to the constraint that $Y = R(X)$. Substituting the constraint into One's objective function, we see that One's problem is

$$\max_{X} U[X, R(X)]. \tag{58}$$

Let $(\tilde{X}, \tilde{Y})$ denote the solution to this problem.

We may now carry over the analysis of Section 4 without much ado. If X and Y are plain and strategic complements, their Stackelberg levels will exceed their Nash equilibrium levels: $\tilde{X} > \hat{X}$ and $\tilde{Y} > \hat{Y}$. Also, both One and Two will be better off at the Stackelberg point than at the Nash equilibrium. If X and Y are plain and strategic substitutes, One's Stackelberg commitment will exceed her Nash commitment and the reverse will be true of Two: $\tilde{X} > \hat{X}$ and $\tilde{Y} < \hat{Y}$. Also, One will be better off at the Stackelberg equilibrium relative to the Nash equilibrium, and the reverse would be true for Two.

We see from the above that, in the type of games we are considering here, the first mover in commitments is unambiguously better off relative to the outcome in which the commitments are chosen simultaneously. (The fate of the second mover in this respect is determined by whether the commitments are strategic substitutes or strategic complements.) It is from *this* effect that commitments derive their importance. Commitments lend strategic value to first movers by introducing an asymmetry where otherwise there would have been none. The opportunity to move first would be of little value in the absence of an appropriate vehicle of commitment.

9. Examples of two-stage games with sequential moves

9.1. Example 12: strategic R&D in the absence of spillovers

In this example, we reconsider example 11 in which private firms undertook cost-reducing R&D activities, but we introduce two variations that completely change the nature of the strategic interaction. First, we assume that the fruits of R&D are completely private – there are no spillovers whatsoever. If a firm expends an amount K on R&D, its constant marginal cost of production is given by $C(K)$, which is a declining function of its argument. Second, we assume that firm One has the first-mover advantage in committing to R&D expenditures. As before, X and Y denote One's and Two's respective R&D expenditures, while x and y denote their respective *outputs* in the second stage.

The payoff functions of firms One and Two are given, respectively, by

$$U(X, Y, x, y) = [\alpha - C(X) - \beta(x + y)]x - X \tag{59.1}$$

and

$$V(X, Y, x, y) = [\alpha - C(Y) - \beta(x + y)]y - Y. \tag{59.2}$$

The Cournot–Nash outputs of One and Two in the second-stage game are readily computed to be

$$\hat{x}(X, Y) = [\alpha - 2C(X) + C(Y)]/3\beta \tag{60.1}$$

and

$$\hat{y}(X, Y) = [\alpha - 2C(Y) + C(X)]/3\beta. \tag{60.2}$$

Observe from equations (60) that when a firm's marginal cost decreases, its own Cournot–Nash equilibrium output increases, while that of its rival decreases. Substituting these expressions into equations (59) we obtain the following reduced-form payoffs of One and Two, respectively:

$$U(X, Y) = [\alpha - 2C(X) + C(Y)]^2/9\beta - X \tag{61.1}$$

and

$$V(X, Y) = [\alpha - 2C(Y) + C(X)]^2/9\beta - Y. \tag{61.2}$$

Differentiating the above expressions we see that $U_2(X, Y) < 0$, $V_1(X, Y) < 0$ and that $U_{12}(X, Y) = V_{21}(X, Y) < 0$, so in this case the R&D expenditures of One and Two are plain and strategic substitutes. Thus it follows from the analysis of Section 8 that if One has the first-mover advantage, its R&D expenditure will exceed its Nash equilibrium level, while the opposite will be true of Two's R&D expenditures. And from equations (60) we see that One's market share will be higher than Two's in the second-stage output game. Here, R&D expenditure is of value not merely because it increases profits for a given market share by lowering costs, but also because it facilitates an increase in One's market share. It is only because the moves are sequential and there is a strategically substitutable vehicle of commitment at hand that the latter advantage is realized by One. Since R&D expenditures do double duty here – by directly lowering production costs and indirectly increasing revenues by altering market shares – we obtain what is a standard result in such models: costs are not minimized.[11] In other words, the Cournot–Nash equilibrium outputs of each of the two firms could be produced at lower total costs (aggregate of R&D and production costs).

9.2. Example 13: the most favoured customer clause

One of the difficulties with prices as strategies in one-shot games is that they do not represent commitments; they can be changed almost costlessly. As a result, an oligopoly in which firms interact just once (or a finite number of times) cannot enforce a collusive equilibrium which generates higher profits than the Bertrand equilibrium. The most favoured customer clause (MFCC) is an ingenious device which deliberately introduces a significant cost to changing prices, so prices become commitments. We present the gist of the mechanism below.[12]

One and Two are firms in a two-period duopoly producing differentiated products at zero cost. The *prices* charged by One (respectively, Two) in the two periods are denoted by X and x (respectively, Y and y). The demand curves facing the two firms are static. In the first period, the quantities demanded of One and Two are given by

$$Q^1(X, Y) = \alpha - \beta X - \gamma Y \tag{62.1}$$

and

$$Q^2(X, Y) = \alpha - \beta Y - \gamma X \tag{62.2}$$

where $-\beta < \gamma < 0$. The second-period demands are obtained by replacing prices X and Y by x and y, respectively. The two-period payoffs of One and Two, assuming no discounting, are given respectively by

$$\tilde{U}(X, Y, x, y) = (\alpha - \beta X - \gamma Y)X + (\alpha - \beta x - \gamma y)x \tag{63.1}$$

and

$$\tilde{V}(X, Y, x, y) = (\alpha - \beta Y - \chi X)Y + (\alpha - \beta y - \varphi x)y. \tag{63.2}$$

Consistent with our assumption in the previous section, suppose One is the first mover in the first period, while One and Two simultaneously choose prices in the second period. Yet the privilege of Stackelberg leadership, we have seen, is of no advantage to One if prices do not represent commitments. However, by invoking the MFCC, One can give credibility to its announcements of prices in excess of the Nash equilibrium level. In the first period, One announces to its buyers that they are its 'most favoured customers', meaning that if it charges a lower price in the next period, it will refund to each of them the difference between its prices in the two periods. By means of this expedient, One has made it costly – perhaps prohibitively so – to lower price in the next period.

Since $\gamma < 0$, in each period One's and Two's prices are plain and strategic complements. Thus in each period their reaction curves are upward sloping in price space. The Nash equilibrium prices in the absence of the MFCC are obviously the same for both firms in both periods; in fact, $\hat{X} = \hat{Y} = \hat{x} = \hat{y} = \alpha/(2\beta + \gamma)$. Also, in the absence of the MFCC, the reaction functions, $r(\cdot)$, are identical across the two periods.

With the invocation of the MFCC, if a price $\bar{X}$ greater than the Nash equilibrium price is a credible announcement by One, Two will respond by setting a price $\bar{Y} = r(\bar{X})$, which will also exceed the Nash equilibrium price. Notice too that the $(\bar{X}, \bar{Y})$ price combination can be credibly sustained in both periods. Since the prices in this differentiated duopoly are complements, both firms are made better off when one of them invokes the MFCC.

One point that emerges from this final example is that if a player's strategies do not represent commitments, it may pay her to contrive commitments that would constrain her strategy space. As Schelling (1956) has emphasized, in gaming situations more flexibility is not necessarily better.

Notes

1. The notion of strategic substitutes and complements was first introduced by Bulow *et al.* (1985).
2. The relative slopes of the reaction curves in Figures 1 and 2 are drawn under the presumption that the Nash equilibrium is stable.
3. Standard references to these phenomena are Gordon (1954) for common-property exploitation, Gilbert and Newberry (1982) for pre-emptive R&D, and Eaton and Lipsey (1979) and Schmalensee (1978) for market pre-emption.
4. The following model is formally identical to an unpublished model set out by David Donaldson to explain why traffic down the Rhine was eliminated by the Nash behaviour of toll booth operators who owned successive segments of the river.
5. The classic references for this problem are Alchian and Demsetz (1972) and Holmstrom (1982).
6. This argument is more compelling when the strategies are commitments, as in Section 6 to follow.
7. The argument to follow draws from Eswaran and Kotwal (1996).
8. To avoid a tedious taxonomy we do not explicitly consider the logically possible but unrealistic cases where the strategies are plain substitutes but strategic complements, and vice versa.
9. The problem of double marginalization was first considered by Spengler (1950) in relation to the incentives firms have for integrating vertically.
10. This problem was first considered by Brander and Spencer (1985). The model below is closest to that of Eaton and Grossman (1986).
11. See, for example, Eaton and Lipsey (1981).
12. The formal analysis of this problem, upon which the following discussion is based, is found in Cooper (1986). A lucid exposition may also be found in Chapter 8 of Tirole (1988).

References

Alchian, A. and H. Demsetz (1972), 'Production, Information Costs and Economic Organization', *American Economic Review*, **62**, pp. 777–95.

Brander, J. and B. Spencer (1985), 'Export Subsidies and International Market Share Rivalry', *Journal of International Economics*, **18**, pp. 83–100.

Bulow, J., J. Geanakoplos and P. Klemperer (1985), 'Multimarket Oligopoly: Strategic Substitutes and Complements', *Journal of Political Economy*, **93**, pp. 488–511.
Cooper, T. (1986), 'The Most-Favoured Customer Pricing and Tacit Collusion', *Rand Journal of Economics*, **17**, pp. 377–88.
Eaton, B. and R. Lipsey (1979), 'The Theory of Market Pre-emption: Persistence of Excess Capacity and Monopoly in Growing Spatial Markets', *Economica*, **47**, pp. 149–58.
Eaton, B. and R. Lipsey (1981), 'Capital, Commitment and Entry Equilibrium', *Bell Journal of Economics*, **12**, pp. 593–604.
Eaton, J. and G. Grossman (1986), 'Optimal Trade and Industrial Policy Under Oligopoly', *Quarterly Journal of Economics*, May, pp. 383–406.
Eswaran, M. and A. Kotwal (1996), 'Demand Externality as an Impediment to Industrial Growth', *Journal of International Trade and Economic Development*, March, pp. 1–22.
Gilbert, R. and D. Newberry (1982), 'Pre-emptive Patenting and the Persistence of Monopoly', *American Economic Review*, **72**, pp. 514–26.
Gordon, H. (1954), 'Economic Theory of the Common Property Resource: The Fishery', *Journal of Political Economy*, **62**, pp. 514–26.
Holmstrom, B. (1982), 'Moral Hazard in Teams', *Bell Journal of Economics*, **13**, pp. 324–40.
Schelling, T. (1956), 'An Essay on Bargaining', *American Economic Review*, **46**, pp. 557–83.
Schmalensee, R. (1978), 'Entry Deterrence in the Ready-to-Eat Breakfast Cereal Industry', *Bell Journal of Economics*, **9**, pp. 305–27.
Schumpeter, J. (1942), *Capitalism, Socialism and Democracy*, Harper & Brothers, New York.
Spengler, J. (1950), 'Vertical Integration and Antitrust Policy', *Journal of Political Economy*, **68**, pp. 347–52.
Tirole, J. (1988), *The Theory of Industrial Organization*, MIT Press, Cambridge, Massachusetts.
Tullock, G. (1980), 'Efficient Rent Seeking', Chapter 6 of J.M. Buchanan, R.D. Tollison and G. Tullock (eds), *Toward a Theory of the Rent Seeking Society*, Texas A&M University Press, College Station, Texas.
Veblen, T. (1899), *The Theory of the Leisure Class*, Unwin, London.

[11]

Flexible Manufacturing and Market Structure

By B. CURTIS EATON AND NICOLAS SCHMITT*

In this paper we investigate the implications of flexible manufacturing for market structure. In the received theory of market structure, based largely on inflexible techniques of production, a number of well-known forces work to limit concentration. In our model none of these forces exists. Hence, we conclude that flexible manufacturing promotes concentration through preemption and mergers, or equivalently through cartels. Interestingly, the concentrated market structures associated with flexibility may or may not be welfare-dominated by a regime in which monopolization is not allowed. (*JEL* D42, D43, L11, L12, L13)

This paper is motivated by two observations: (i) aside from the literature on contestable markets, economies of scope play no role in standard theories of market structure; (ii) increasingly, manufacturing firms produce an impressive array of differentiated products, using flexible techniques that exhibit economies of scope. This paper begins the development of the theory of market structure for such industries. In our model, flexibility promotes concentration through preemption and mergers, or the functional equivalent through cartels.

Although there exists no widely accepted definition of flexible manufacturing, there is agreement regarding certain features of it. Richard B. Chase and Nicholas J. Aquilano (1985) and Paul Milgrom and John Roberts (1990) focus on the ability to produce a variety of similar products, in random order and in small batches. Similarly, for Nigel R. Greenwood (1988 p. 7), the principal advantage of flexible manufacturing is that "[i]t makes possible the manufacture of the same basic product ... with a certain degree of customer-selectable variation." The following examples illustrate these features: Peerless Saw Company in Groveport, Ohio, whose computerized laser cutter is able to deliver customized sawblades (Jack R. Meredith, 1987); Toyota's car production system, described by its inventor as being "born of the need to make many types of automobiles, in small quantities with the same manufacturing process" (quoted by George Stalk, Jr. [1988 p. 44]); and Benetton, the Italian fashion company, whose information and production systems allow immediate response to hot-selling items and colors (Kim B. Clark, 1989). *Recent Trends in Flexible Manufacturing* (United Nations, 1986) documents the spread of such techniques on a country-by-country basis.

These few examples suggest that the essence of flexible manufacturing is *economies of scope* in the production of *differentiated goods*, and this is the approach we adopt. To incorporate product differentiation in our model, we adapt the familiar Hotelling model.[1] We introduce economies of scope by the device of a *basic product*. By incurring a sunk cost of product development, firms develop the ability to produce a basic product, described by a point in Hotelling's attribute space, at a constant marginal cost. A basic product can be modified to produce any other variant in the attribute space, but such modification in-

*Department of Economics, Simon Fraser University, Burnaby, BC V5A 1S6, Canada. We thank two anonymous referees for helpful comments. Financial support from the Social Sciences and Humanities Research Council of Canada (grant 410-92-0880) is gratefully acknowledged.

[1] Equally, we could have used some version of the J. Jaskold Gabszewicz and Jacques-François Thisse (1980) model of vertical differentiation (see Section IV).

volves additional costs; the *cost of switching* the production process from one variant to another, and a per-unit *cost of modification* that is proportional to the difference (in the attribute space) between the basic product and the variant. The model has three parameters related to economies of scope which we believe capture fundamental aspects of flexible manufacturing: the cost of developing the basic product, the cost of switching the production process from one variant to another, and a parameter that governs the rate at which the cost of modification increases with the extent of modification. Our model is essentially the same as that of W. Bentley MacLeod et al. (1988), but applied to different economic issues.

Lars-Hendrik Röller and Mihkel M. Tombak (1990) also model flexibility in terms of economies of scope but focus on different issues. They look at the choice of technology in a framework where there are two products, two firms, and three technologies: two are inflexible one-product technologies, and the third is a flexible two-product technology. Milgrom and Roberts (1990) and Milgrom et al. (1991) formulate a wide-ranging theory of the firm in which firms exercise flexibility in a number of dimensions, including inventory policy, product market strategy, and the internal organization of the firm, as well as the number and attributes of products. Our model captures only some of these concerns, but it does allow us to explore in some detail the implications of flexibility for market structure.[2]

In our model, provided that the technology is sufficiently flexible, firms choose to produce a continuum of goods. We develop five results concerning market structure for this case: (i) the ownership structure of basic products has no bearing on the expected profitability of an entrant; (ii) the possibility of entry has no bearing on the incentives of incumbent firms to merge or form a cartel; (iii) an entrant can never induce an incumbent to abandon one of its basic products; (iv) the firms involved in a merger (cartel) capture all the added profit created by their activity; and (v) in a game of sequential entry, monopoly preemption is the inevitable outcome. When manufacturing is inflexible, none of these results is true in general. Hence, we are led to the conclusion that flexibility, as we have modeled it, promotes concentration. Interestingly, the normative implications of flexibility in our model are ambiguous. Although flexibility leads to more concentrated market structures, the resulting equilibrium is not always welfare-dominated by the equilibrium in which firms are not allowed to merge, form cartels, or engage in market preemption.

I. The Model

We cast our analysis in an address model, similar in most respects to Harold Hotelling's (1929) model. In such models, each good is described by a point x in some continuum of product attributes. We choose to work in a one-dimensional attribute space with support [0,1].

A. *Preferences*

We begin with a standard, though quite restrictive representation of preferences, which we relax somewhat in Section III. From a consumer's perspective, any good is completely described by its address x in the attribute space and by its price, $p(x)$. Faced with the possibility of buying a number of goods, we suppose that any consumer buys exactly one unit of (at most) one good that he/she cannot customize. The utility from buying one unit of good x at price $p(x)$ is

$$(1)\quad U(x,p(x)) = V - p(x) - t|x - x^*|$$

where x^* in [0,1] describes the consumer's most preferred good (or the consumer's address), and V is the consumer's reservation price for that good. Given a choice among many goods, the consumer buys one unit of the good for which $U(x,p(x))$ is a maximum, provided that the maximum is positive. If the maximum is negative, the con-

[2]There is a well-known literature, initiated by George J. Stigler (1939), that focuses on an entirely different sort of flexibility, the trade-off between the curvature of the average cost function and its level.

sumer buys none of these goods. The distance from x to the consumer's most preferred good is $|x - x^*|$; hence t is the marginal disutility of distance in the attribute space. We assume that the parameters t and V are identical for all consumers, but that x^* varies from one consumer to another. Specifically, we suppose that x^* is uniformly distributed on $[0,1]$ with unit density. We have then a continuum of consumers (each one characterized by its most preferred good) that is coincident with the continuum of possible goods. Notice that equation (1) implies that a consumer may choose not to consume the product with most preferred characteristic x^* even if it is available. Whether the consumer chooses to do so or not will depend on the prices and addresses of all the available products.

B. *Flexibility*

In most models of product differentiation the costs of producing a particular good are composed of a sunk product development cost and a constant marginal cost of production. Regardless of how many goods a firm is currently producing, if it wants to produce another, the firm must incur the product development cost for that good. In this sense, the technology is perfectly inflexible, and there are no economies of scope. We introduce flexibility into this model by supposing that firms first develop one or more *basic products*, and then produce variations on those basic products.

We denote the location in the attribute space of basic product i by X_i, and the location of variant j by x_j. Letting q_j denote the quantity of variant j, we can describe a production plan by

$$(2)\quad (\mathbf{x},\mathbf{q}) = [(x_1,q_1),(x_2,q_2),\ldots,(x_m,q_m)]$$

where m is the total number of variants in the production plan. The *span of a production plan* is defined to be the maximal value of x_j minus its minimal value, and it is a measure of the diversity of goods included in the production plan.

The cost of producing $(\mathbf{x},\mathbf{q})$, using basic product X_i as an anchor, is given by the following expression:

$$(3)\quad C((\mathbf{x},\mathbf{q});X_i) = K + (m-1)s + \sum_{j=1}^{m} [q_j(c + r|x_j - X_i|)].$$

The parameters K, s, c, and r are nonnegative. K is the cost of developing basic product X_i, s is the cost of switching from one variant to another, and $c + r|x_j - X_i|$ is the marginal cost of producing a unit of variant x_j. We assume that the product development cost K is sunk and attribute-specific, which allows firms to commit to their basic products.[3] Interpret c as the marginal cost of producing a unit of the basic product, and $r|x_j - X_i|$ as the incremental cost of modification; the further variant x_j is from basic product X_i, the larger is the cost of modification.

We will say that there are *strong economies of scope* for a production plan $(\mathbf{x},\mathbf{q})$ if the least costly way to produce it involves just one basic product, and *weak economies of scope* if the least costly method of production involves fewer basic products than the number of goods in the production plan. Clearly, this technology exhibits strong economies of scope for some production plans. Consider, for example, the following plan: $[(0.25,100),(0.75,100)]$. The least-cost method of producing this plan involves either one basic product located in the interval $[0.25,0.75]$ or two basic products, one at 0.25 and the other at 0.75. The cost of the first method is $K + s + 200c + 50r$, and the cost of the second is $2K + 200c$. The first method is therefore cheaper, and the technology exhibits strong economies of scope for this production plan, if K exceeds $(s + 50r)$.

[3]It is customary to interpret the development cost K as a flow associated with a stock of expenditures on product development. If I is spent on product development and if i is a time-invariant interest rate, then K is equal to iI.

A necessary condition for economies of scope, weak or strong, is that K exceeds s. Beyond that, we have the following straightforward results. Assuming that K exceeds s, the technology exhibits strong economies of scope for any production plan $(\mathbf{x},\mathbf{q})$ if the following conditions hold:

(i) r is sufficiently small;
(ii) $(K-s)$ is sufficiently large;
(iii) the span of $(\mathbf{x},\mathbf{q})$ is sufficiently small.

It exhibits weak economies of scope if the number of variants in the production plan is sufficiently large (holding $\Sigma_{j=1}^{m} q_j$ constant).

To generate an extreme case of flexibility, we assume that the switching cost s is equal to zero and that the development cost K is strictly positive.[4] In addition, and with no further loss of generality, we assume that c is zero. Thus we use the following cost function:

$$C((\mathbf{x},\mathbf{q});X_i)=K+\sum_{j=1}^{m} q_j(r|x_j-X_i|). \tag{4}$$

Let $\mathrm{MC}_i(x)$ denote the marginal cost of good x using basic product X_i. Thus,

$$\mathrm{MC}_i(x)=r|x-X_i|. \tag{5}$$

As the reader familiar with Hotelling's (1929) classic model will recognize, there is just one major difference between his model and ours. In our model, once a firm has developed a basic product it can produce any good in the [0,1] attribute space, whereas in Hotelling's model, firms have no such flexibility. Note however that our model encompasses Hotelling's since as r approaches infinity, we obtain Hotelling's perfectly inflexible technology. Note also that, like Hotelling's model, ours can be interpreted in two ways. We have explicitly cast the model as one of differentiation in an attribute space, but it can also be interpreted as a model of spatial competition; the parameters r and t then represent the firm's and the consumer's costs of transportation, respectively.

C. *Price Equilibrium*

Now suppose that a number of different basic products, say l, have been developed by a number of different firms, say n, and let X_i denote the address of the ith basic product.[5] Taking these basic products and their ownership as given, four types of Nash price equilibrium are possible, depending upon the relative magnitudes of the parameters t and r. Here we discuss only two of these; a complete discussion of the price equilibria in these types of models can be found in Eaton and Schmitt (1992, 1993). One price equilibrium is familiar: when r is very large relative to t, only basic products are produced, and the price equilibrium is identical to the one in which the technology is completely inflexible.

In this article we focus on the price equilibrium for the case in which $r<t$. Since each firm can produce each good in the [0,1] continuum, a price equilibrium involves a complete price schedule for each firm. To find the equilibrium price schedules when r is less than t, think of a series of Bertrand price games involving all n firms, one game for every good x in [0,1]. Supposing for the moment that the parameter V is arbitrarily large, Bertrand competition will drive the price for good x down to the marginal cost of the second most efficient firm. For this to be an equilibrium, the most efficient firm must make the sale of

[4]This assumption not only simplifies the analysis, but as will become clear, it also brings significant insights into flexible manufacturing. Nonetheless relaxing this assumption is an important item on our research agenda.

[5]We assume that all basic products are unique, thus ignoring the possibility that two firms choose to develop the same basic product. This assumption has no bearing on our results, but it does allow us to ignore a number of uninteresting special cases.

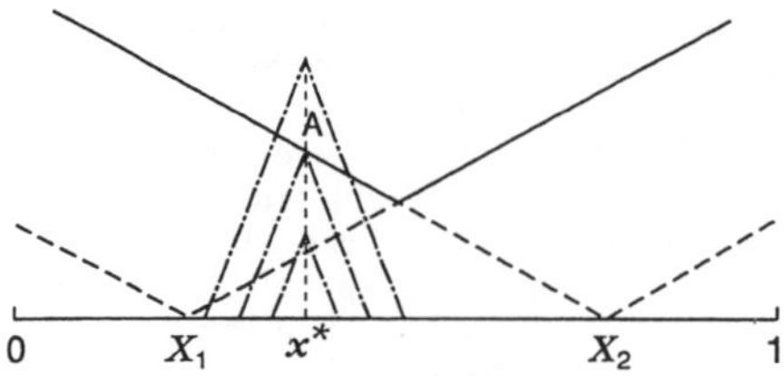

FIGURE 1. CONSUMER CHOICE GIVEN EQUILIBRIUM PRICES

good x.[6] We have then one set of equilibrium price schedules: for every good x, each firm's equilibrium price is the marginal cost of the second most efficient firm. For the 3rd, 4th, ..., and nth most efficient firms at attribute x, any higher price is also an equilibrium price.

Since t exceeds r, the consumer will always choose to buy her most preferred good in such a price equilibrium even though she is free to buy any good in the entire spectrum. This point is illustrated in Figure 1. In this figure, there are two basic products, located at X_1 and X_2, owned by different firms. The dashed lines represent marginal costs of production for any good in the attribute space, using X_1 and X_2 as bases, and the solid line represents the equilibrium price schedule. The slopes of these schedules are, in absolute value, equal to r. The dot-dashed lines represent the indirect indifference curves of the consumer whose most preferred good is x^*, and the slopes of the indifference curves are, in absolute value, equal to t. Consumer x^* buys good x^* since, of all the points on the equilibrium price schedule, point A is on the lowest, and therefore most preferred, indirect indifference curve. Hence, in this price equilibrium, the entire continuum of goods is produced, and each consumer buys her most preferred product.

Two refinements are necessary when we drop the assumption that V is arbitrarily large. Let $\mathrm{MC}^1(x)$ denote the smallest, and $\mathrm{MC}^2(x)$ the second smallest, marginal cost of producing good x among all the firms.[7] First, if V is less than $\mathrm{MC}^1(x)$, then the equilibrium price for x is any price greater than V; for concreteness, it is $\mathrm{MC}^1(x)$. Second, if V lies between $\mathrm{MC}^1(x)$ and $\mathrm{MC}^2(x)$, then the equilibrium price is V. The following is then a Nash equilibrium price schedule for all firms when t exceeds r:

$$(6)\quad p^*(x) = \begin{cases} \mathrm{MC}^1(x) & \text{if } V < \mathrm{MC}^1(x) \\ V & \text{if } \mathrm{MC}^1(x) \leq V \\ & \quad \leq MC^2(x) \\ \mathrm{MC}^2(x) & \text{if } \mathrm{MC}^2(x) < V. \end{cases}$$

In equilibrium, the two lowest-cost firms necessarily announce price $p^*(x)$, but any price greater than or equal to $p^*(x)$ is an equilibrium price for higher-cost firms. The equilibrium market segment captured by basic product i, $\mathcal{M}_i^*$, is

$$(7)\quad \mathcal{M}_i^* = \{x : \mathrm{MC}_i(x) \leq \min[\mathrm{MC}_j(x), V] \text{ for } j \neq i\}.$$

In the case where individual demand is not perfectly inelastic, simply interpret V as the monopoly price for the individual demand function. This price equilibrium is, in effect, the familiar discriminating-price equilibrium of spatial competition, originally identified by Edgar M. Hoover (1937) and reconsidered by Eaton and Richard G. Lipsey (1979), Philip J. Lederer and Arthur P. Hurter (1986), and MacLeod et al. (1988), among others.

[6] If the most efficient firm did not make the sale, it would have an incentive to shave price. Hence, if it does not make the sale, we have not found the equilibrium. But there can be no equilibrium in which the most efficient firm's price is less than the marginal cost of the second most efficient firm, since at any such price, the most efficient firm has an incentive to raise its price.

[7] A firm's marginal cost is the minimum of $\mathrm{MC}_i(x)$ over all basic products i owned by that firm.

II. Contrasting Implications of Flexible Manufacturing

In this section we establish four implications of flexibility for market structure, contrasting each with corresponding results for inflexible manufacturing. By flexibility, we mean both $s = 0$ and $r < t$. We show that certain forces that tend to limit concentration in other models are inoperative in ours.

We begin with a lemma concerning the link between a firm's equilibrium profit and the ownership structure for established basic products owned by other firms. An ownership structure for a set of basic products specifies the firm that owns each basic product.

LEMMA 1: *Given a fixed set of basic products owned by firm A, $\mathcal{S}_a$, and a fixed set of basic products owned by firms other than A, $\mathcal{S}_0$, the equilibrium profit of firm A is independent of the ownership structure of $\mathcal{S}_0$.*

PROOF:

Consider the case in which firm A owns just one basic product with address X_a and associated market segment $\mathcal{M}_a^*$. Firm A's profit is

$$(8) \quad \pi_a^* = \int_{x \in \mathcal{M}_a^*} [p^*(x) - \mathrm{MC}_a(x)]\, dx - K.$$

From (6) and the definitions of $\mathrm{MC}^1(x)$ and $\mathrm{MC}^2(x)$, we see that the equilibrium price schedule $p^*(x)$ depends on the parameters V and r and on the addresses of basic products, but not on the ownership structure of basic products in S_0. Similarly, from (7), we see that firm A's market segment, $\mathcal{M}_a^*$, is determined by the same list of arguments. Hence, π_a^* does not depend on the ownership structure of existing basic products. This argument clearly generalizes to the case in which firm A has many basic products.

The following special case helps to provide an intuitive understanding of Lemma 1 and a link to MacLeod et al. (1988). Suppose that the reservation price V is arbitrarily large so that all goods in the attribute space are produced. Then, from (6) we see that the equilibrium price for any variant x in $\mathcal{M}_a^*$ is equal to the marginal cost of the second most efficient firm for that variant, $p^*(x) = \mathrm{MC}^2(x)$. Of course, in the absence of firm A, variant x in $\mathcal{M}_a^*$ would be produced at cost $\mathrm{MC}^2(x)$. From (8) it is then clear that firm A's profit is equal to the cost savings attributable to its basic product. This cost savings is independent of ownership structure since, in equilibrium, goods are produced by the most efficient firm. The result that a firm's profit is equal to the cost savings attributable to that firm is, for a general attribute space, lemma 1 in MacLeod et al. (1988). In this sense, our Lemma 1 is a corollary of their lemma 1.

If in Lemma 1 we interpret firm A as an entrant and $\mathcal{S}_0$ as the set of basic products owned by established firms, we get our first proposition.

PROPOSITION 1: *The profitability of entry does not depend on the ownership structure of existing basic products.*

In other words, if entry is deterred for one structure of ownership, say, the case in which each basic product is owned by a separate firm, it is also deterred for any other structure, including the one in which all basic products are owned by just one firm. Figure 2 illustrates the point. In Figure 2A, basic products X_i and X_j are owned by separate firms, and in Figure 2B they are owned by the same firm; in both, X_h is the entrant's basic product. In both Figure 2A and Figure 2B, the dashed lines represent the marginal-cost schedules, the solid line is the equilibrium price schedule, and the shaded area is the entrant's profit. The entrant's profit is, of course, identical in Figure 2A and 2B.

By way of contrast, in any address model of which we are aware, Proposition 1 does not hold in the absence of flexible production; roughly, the more concentrated is ownership, the more attractive is entry. The same conclusion holds for nonaddress models as well. James A. Brander and Jonathan

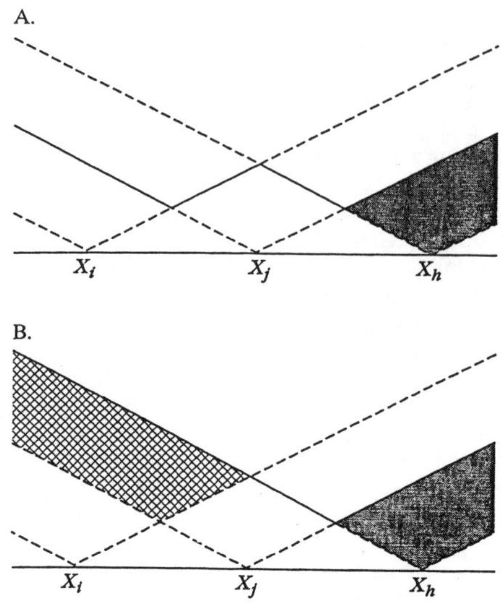

FIGURE 2. OWNERSHIP STRUCTURE, MERGERS, AND PROFIT: A) BASIC PRODUCTS OWNED BY SEPARATE FIRMS; B) TWO BASIC PRODUCTS OWNED BY THE SAME FIRM

Eaton (1984) is particularly instructive in this regard.

Proposition 1 has an obvious, though we think important, corollary:

PROPOSITION 2: *Mergers among incumbent firms (or cartelization) cannot induce entry.*

To put the point differently, since the configuration of basic products, not their ownership structure, determines the profitability of entry, the threat of this sort of entry is not a barrier to merger in our model. Like Proposition 1, Proposition 2 clearly does not hold with inflexible manufacturing.

If now we interpret firm A in Lemma 1 as being an established firm not participating in a merger (or a cartel), we have our third proposition.

PROPOSITION 3: *Mergers (or cartels) confer no profit externalities on firms not involved in the merger (cartel).*

Figure 2 also illustrates Proposition 3. In Figure 2A, there are initially three independent firms, and each firm owns one basic product; in Figure 2B the firms that initially owned basic product X_i and X_j have merged. The crosshatched area in Figure 2B represents the added profit created by the merger, all of which is captured by the merging firms.

There is a long literature, going back at least to Stigler (1950), in which it is shown that mergers and cartels may not be profitable, because the involved firms cannot capture all the profit created by their cooperative efforts. In this literature, if a merger does not involve all relevant firms, there is a positive profit externality conferred on non-involved firms and, hence, an incentive for each firm to free-ride on the cooperative efforts of others. Proposition 3 shows that this possibility does not exist with flexible manufacturing.

In Propositions 1 and 2 we considered what might be called *augmenting entry*, entry which simply augments the capacity devoted to the market. Kenneth L. Judd (1985) shows that with inflexible manufacturing, the possibility of *predatory entry* sometimes limits the ability to monopolize a market via preemption.[8] Consider, for example, a market for two close substitutes, say widgets and gadgets, and suppose that costs for each product are composed of a sunk product development cost and a constant marginal cost. Now imagine that firm A attempts to preempt by incurring the sunk costs for both products. Clearly, the preemption strategy would work if firm A were committed to produce both goods, since if firm B also produced one of the goods, say gadgets, the equilibrium price of gadgets would be equal to its marginal cost, and there would be no quasi-profit to cover B's product development cost. Unless there are significant exit costs, however, A is not committed to

[8]There is a third type of entry that is potentially important, entry for buyout, which we ignore; see Eric Rasmusen (1988).

producing gadgets since, given competition in gadgets from B, A's profit would increase if it exited from the gadget market. In effect, by ceasing to produce gadgets, A loses nothing in the gadget market and gains something in the widget market, since the price of gadgets increases, which tends to increase A's profit from the sale of widgets. Thus, when exit costs are insignificant, A cannot preempt both markets; if it tried to, B could, and would, drive A from one market.

That is, when technology is inflexible, the possibility of predatory entry implies that preemption is not always possible. In Judd's (1985) story, a necessary condition for predatory entry is that there exist circumstances such that a firm's profit increases when it abandons capacity. In Proposition 4 we show that such circumstances do not exist in our model. Hence, given the preferences and technology of Section I, and the dynamic structure of Judd's model, predatory entry is not possible.

PROPOSITION 4: *Given the set of basic products owned by other firms and the ownership structure for those basic products, a firm's equilibrium profit cannot increase if it abandons one or more of its basic products.*

PROOF:

Notice that the costs associated with product development are sunk and thus have no bearing on the exit decision, and also note that the equilibrium price for any good that a firm sells is never less than its marginal cost for that good. Suppose then that there exists at least one basic product owned by a firm other than A and that firm A has a number of basic products and abandons one of them. There are two sorts of effect on A's profit. First, its market gets smaller, an effect that can decrease but cannot increase its profit. Second, for any x that remains in firm A's market after abandonment, A's marginal cost may increase, but its price does not change; as a result, its profit from any such point may decrease but cannot increase. This argument clearly generalizes to the case in which firm A abandons any number of basic products.

A common theme runs through all four of these propositions: mergers, cartels, and preemption are all easier to pursue or are more attractive where technology is flexible than where it is inflexible. Accordingly, in the next section, we consider some positive and normative implications of preemption in a game of sequential entry.

III. Sequential Entry and Flexible Manufacturing

To determine the limits of concentration, the modern literature on market structure in differentiated product industries has focused on games of sequential entry. The early literature seemed to point to monopolistic preemption by means of product proliferation (see e.g., Edward C. Prescott and Michael Visscher, 1977). The currently accepted wisdom is somewhat different. Since the ownership structure of existing products affects the profitability of entry (as in Brander and Eaton [1984]), the first mover will sometimes allow entry of one or more additional firms because, relative to oligopolistic entry deterrence, monopolistic entry deterrence requires too many products and is therefore too costly. In addition, as Judd (1985) shows, preemption through product proliferation is not always credible because the would-be preemptor is sometimes vulnerable to predatory entry. Neither of these concentration-limiting forces exists in our model, and accordingly sequential entry necessarily generates monopoly preemption.[9] In this section, we examine some positive and normative implications generated by monopolistic preemption in two versions of our model: when individual demand is inelastic and when it is elastic.

[9]It is sometimes argued that there is a public-good aspect to entry deterrence which constitutes in itself a limit to monopolization (see e.g., Richard Gilbert and Xavier Vives, 1986). An obvious corollary of Proposition 3 is that such an externality does not exist in our model.

A. *Entry with Perfectly Inelastic Demand*

The first result that we establish is that the first mover preempts the market by establishing the configuration of basic products that maximizes profit, ignoring the possibility of subsequent entry. In other words, the first mover is unconstrained by the threat of subsequent entry. To show this, we use an argument by contradiction. Assume that (i) the first mover has chosen its basic products to maximize profit unconstrained by the possibility of entry, and (ii) given the first mover's choice, entry is profitable.

Let $\mathcal{S}$ denote the segment of the entrant's market that would have been served by the first mover had entry not occurred, and let $\mathcal{U}$ denote the segment of the entrant's market that would not have been served had entry not occurred.[10] Assumption (ii) can then be expressed by the following inequality:

$$(9)\quad [R_e(\mathcal{U}) - VC_e(\mathcal{U})] + [R_e(\mathcal{S}) - VC_e(\mathcal{S})] - n_e K > 0$$

where n_e denotes the number of basic products established by the entrant, $R_e(\mathcal{U})$ and $R_e(\mathcal{S})$ denote the entrant's revenues from the two segments of its market, and $VC_e(\mathcal{U})$ and $VC_e(\mathcal{S})$ denote the entrant's variable costs from the two segments. Observe now that, given the post-entry price equilibrium and price inelastic demand, the entrant's total revenue from segment $\mathcal{S}$ is equal to the variable costs the first mover would incur if it served segment $\mathcal{S}$. In other words, $R_e(\mathcal{S}) = VC_m(\mathcal{S})$, where $VC_m(\mathcal{S})$ denotes the first mover's variable costs when it serves segment $\mathcal{S}$. Hence,

$$(10)\quad [R_e(\mathcal{U}) - VC_e(\mathcal{U})] + [VC_m(\mathcal{S}) - VC_e(\mathcal{S})] - n_e K > 0.$$

[10]Although we would often expect the market to be covered ($\mathcal{U} = 0$), our argument does not depend on this assumption.

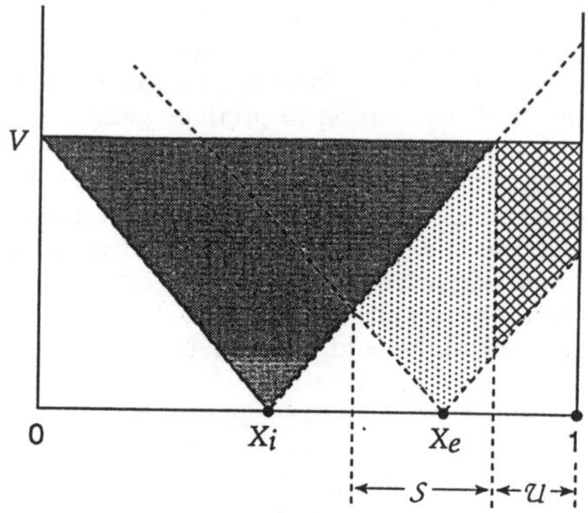

FIGURE 3. MONOPOLY PREEMPTION WITH INELASTIC DEMAND

But this inequality contradicts assumption (i)—that the first mover chose its basic products to maximize profit unconstrained by the possibility of entry—because it implies that the first mover's profit would have been larger had it established the n_e additional basic products. Supposing that the first mover did establish these additional basic products, the first term in square brackets of (10) represents the net revenue the first mover would earn from segment $\mathcal{U}$, the second term in square brackets is the reduction in costs the first mover would enjoy from serving segment $\mathcal{S}$, and the last term represents the development costs of the additional basic products. Since from (10) the first mover's profit from serving segments $\mathcal{S}$ and $\mathcal{U}$ is positive, and since these additional basic products could not possibly decrease the first mover's profit from the rest of the market, the first mover is not initially maximizing profit. That is, assumption (ii) contradicts assumption (i).

Figure 3 illustrates the argument. Assume (i) that the first mover maximizes profit (unconstrained by entry) by establishing basic product X_i and (ii) that the entrant gets a positive profit by establishing the additional basic product X_e. From (ii) we infer that, with reference to Figure 3,

$$\text{cross-hatched area} + \text{dotted area} - K > 0.$$

Given X_i and no entry, the first mover's profit is the shaded area in Figure 3, less K. If it had also established basic product X_e its profit would have been equal to

$$\text{shaded area} + \text{cross-hatched area} + \text{dotted area} - 2K.$$

The incremental profit associated with basic product X_e is then equal to

$$\text{cross-hatched area} + \text{dotted area} - K$$

which, given (ii), is positive. Hence (ii) contradicts (i).

Proposition 5 then follows.

PROPOSITION 5: *When individual demand is perfectly price-inelastic, the first mover will choose the configuration of basic products that maximizes total profit, and no other firms will enter the market.*

Given this sort of monopoly preemption, all the customers who are served pay their reservation price V for the product they buy. Hence, the preemptor captures the entire surplus that is created. Since it also bears all the costs, the monopoly preemption equilibrium is cost–benefit optimal.

PROPOSITION 6: *When demand is perfectly price inelastic, monopoly preemption is cost–benefit optimal.*

B. *Entry with Responsive Demand*

In this subsection we consider an example in which individual demand is responsive to price. In this example, the first mover cannot in general ignore the possibility of subsequent entry, nor is monopoly preemption necessarily cost–benefit optimal. To generate exact results we would have to consider two types of basic product: peripheral products (the first and last products in the attribute space) and interior products. Instead we generate approximate results by focusing exclusively on interior products. One can provide an exact justification of this simplification by supposing that the attribute space is the circumference of a circle, or by supposing that it is unbounded. In addition, we suppose that the number of basic products is a real number. We use the following individual demand function:

$$(11)\quad q(x) = \begin{cases} \dfrac{1}{p(x)} & \text{if } p(x) \le V \\ 0 & \text{if } p(x) > V. \end{cases}$$

Notice that price equal to V is the monopoly price for this demand function.

We start by solving the first mover's problem, ignoring the possibility of entry and assuming that parameter values are such that the market is viable and covered.[11] Since $p(x)$ equal to V maximizes revenue in (11), the first mover sells each good in $[0,1]$ at V, producing $1/V$ units of each. Its total revenue is then equal to 1. The cost of producing $1/V$ units of each good using n evenly spaced basic products is

$$(12)\quad \mathrm{TC}(n) = n\left[K + \frac{2}{V}\int_0^{1/2n} (rx)\,dx\right].$$

The cost-minimizing number of basic products, n^*, is then

$$(13)\qquad n^* = \frac{1}{2}\left(\frac{r}{VK}\right)^{1/2}$$

and minimized costs are

$$(14)\qquad \mathrm{TC}(n^*) = \left(\frac{rK}{V}\right)^{1/2}.$$

Hence, unconstrained by entry, a first mover would establish n^* evenly spaced products if $\mathrm{TC}(n^*)$ is less than 1, and none if $\mathrm{TC}(n^*)$ exceeds 1.

To discover when the entry constraint is binding, we compute the expected profit of an entrant given n basic products evenly spaced. The entrant can do no better than

[11] A sufficient condition for the market to be covered is that $V > r/2$.

to enter at the middle of the segment between two of the first mover's basic products, where its profit is

$$(15)\quad \pi_e(n) = 2\int_0^{1/4n}\{[p(x) - rx]q(x)\}\,dx - K$$

or

$$(16)\qquad \pi_e(n) = \frac{a}{n} - K$$

where

$$(17)\qquad a = 1 - \ln(2).$$

Hence the no-entry condition is

$$(18)\qquad n \geq \frac{a}{K}.$$

Surprisingly, although there are three parameters in this model (r, K, and V), its behavior is dependent on just one (composite) parameter, defined as

$$(19)\qquad Z = \frac{V}{rK}.$$

As the reader can easily verify by comparing (13) and (18), the first mover is constrained or unconstrained by entry as Z is greater than or less than $1/(4a^2)$.

Combining results, the solution to the first mover's problem is: (i) establish no basic products if $Z < 1$; (ii) establish n^* basic products if $1 \leq Z \leq 1/4a^2$; or (iii) establish a/K basic products if $1/4a^2 \leq Z$.

Given any set of basic products, cost–benefit optimality requires that all goods be priced at marginal cost. Trivially, the market structure generated by sequential entry is thus not cost–benefit optimal when individual demand is responsive to price.

It is perhaps more instructive to make welfare comparisons between the monopoly preemption equilibrium and the equilibrium that emerges when each firm is constrained to establish no more than one basic product. The results in Prescott and Visscher (1977) suggest that, in the one-firm/one-basic-product equilibrium, the number of basic products will be the smallest number consistent with no entry. The appropriate no-entry condition is, of course, given by inequality (18). Hence, there will be a/K evenly spaced basic products when firms are constrained to have no more than one basic product.

We have computed the standard cost–benefit welfare index (profit plus consumer's surplus) for these two cases, and we find that when Z is small, monopoly preemption is welfare-dominant, but when Z is large the one-firm/one-product solution is clearly preferable. When Z is small, more competitive market structures do not substantially decrease the deadweight losses associated with monopoly pricing, and it involves too many basic products relative to the preemption solution. When Z is large, the one-firm/one-product market structure is more desirable since not only does price competition offset to a significant degree the deadweight loss associated with monopolistic pricing, but preemption entails far too many products. Proposition 7 summarizes the results.

PROPOSITION 7: *When demand is not perfectly price inelastic, monopoly preemption is not cost–benefit optimal, and it may or may not be welfare-dominated by the equilibrium in which firms are constrained to have no more than one basic product.*

IV. Conclusions

We chose to use the Hotelling model as the kernel of ours because it is the most familiar address model of product differentiation. As regards address models, it is clear from MacLeod et al. (1988) that our results are quite general. And the following discussion indicates that the address framework itself is not necessary.

To see this, consider a less specific model with many goods and many technologies.

Assume the following:

(i) Firms choose prices noncooperatively.
(ii) Each technology is flexible in that it permits the production of all the goods.
(iii) For each technology, the cost of producing any mix of goods is a linear function of quantities produced; that is, there are no fixed costs, and the marginal costs of the different goods are all constant.
(iv) Each consumer consumes at most one unit of one good.

To identify each consumer's most preferred good, imagine that each good is priced at its smallest marginal cost over all technologies. A consumer's most preferred good is the one she would choose at these prices. Now, given any set of technologies and any ownership structure, suppose that all firms price all goods at the marginal cost of the second most efficient firm. Then assume:

(v) given these prices, all consumers buy their most preferred product.

Given the five assumptions above, for all goods, price equal to marginal cost of the second most efficient firm is an equilibrium. The most efficient firm for any good, say, good i, clearly will not raise the price of good i since by doing so it would lose all its sales and hence profit from good i, without affecting its sales and profit from other goods. Nor will it lower price: a price reduction will not attract new customers since all customers are initially buying their most preferred goods, nor will a price reduction increase sales to existing customers, since demand is unresponsive to price. In addition, none of the other firms has an incentive to change the price it charges for good i: a reduction in price entails sales at less than marginal cost in the market for good i and has no implications for sales of other goods; an increase in price leaves the firm's profit unchanged since it initially sells nothing, and no consumer responds to its price increase.

Lemma 1 states that the equilibrium profit of an arbitrary firm A is independent of the ownership structure of the existing technologies owned by other firms. The equilibrium prices of the goods produced by firm A are clearly independent of ownership structure of the technologies owned by other firms, and since in equilibrium consumers buy their most preferred product, so too are quantities demanded of firm A's products. Hence, assumptions (i)–(v) imply Lemma 1 and the three propositions that follow from it: 1) the profitability of entry is independent of ownership structure of existing technologies; 2) mergers among incumbent firms cannot induce entry; and 3) a merger confers no profit externalities on firms not involved in the merger.

Proposition 4, that multiproduct firms are not vulnerable to predatory entry, also follows from these assumptions. If a firm abandons a technology, neither the equilibrium prices nor quantities of the goods it produces subsequent to abandonment will change, and hence its profit cannot increase as a result of abandoning a technology.

Finally, make the following additional assumptions:

(vi) All firms have access to all technologies.
(vii) There is a positive sunk cost associated with each technology.

Then, the solution to the game of sequential entry in which no technologies have yet been created involves monopoly preemption by the first mover, and the monopoly-preemption equilibrium is cost–benefit optimal. (The argument presented in Subsection III-A is directly applicable.)

Assumption (v) merits some elaboration. It requires that customers have access to a less efficient customizing technology than do firms, as argued by MacLeod et al. (1988). If this were not the case, consumers might choose to buy only basic products as inputs into their own customization process. In addition, as we have stressed in this paper, when goods are priced at the marginal cost of the second most efficient firm, the money equivalent of the utility loss a consumer incurs by consuming a good other than her most preferred good must be larger than the price/marginal-cost differential between the two goods. Otherwise, all goods may not be produced in equilibrium, and equilibrium prices for the goods that are produced will be less than the marginal cost of the second most efficient producer as firms reduce price to draw customers away from their rivals.

The contribution of our version of the Hotelling model is to provide one set of circumstances in which these more general assumptions hold. Fairly clearly, any of a variety of familiar address models of competition could be adapted to serve the same purpose.

We are led then to two main conclusions. First, many of the forces that tend to limit concentration in standard theories of market structure are completely suppressed when these assumptions are satisfied. Second, the associated high level of market concentration may not reflect inefficiency —it all depends on the elasticity of individual demand. Hence, given the central role that flexibility plays in our results, and given the growing importance of flexible manufacturing techniques, a rethinking of competition policy in the context of flexible manufacturing seems called for.

REFERENCES

Brander, James A. and Eaton, Jonathan. "Product Line Rivalry." *American Economic Review*, June 1984, *74*(3), pp. 323–34.

Chase, Richard B. and Aquilano, Nicholas J. *Production and operations management: A life cycle approach*, 4th Ed. Homewood, IL: Irwin, 1985.

Clark, Kim B. "What Strategy Can Do for Technology." *Harvard Business Review*, November-December 1989, *89*(6), pp. 94–98.

Eaton, B. Curtis and Lipsey, Richard G. "A Comment on Location and Industrial Efficiency with Free Entry." *Quarterly Journal of Economics*, August 1979, *93*(3), pp. 447–50.

Eaton, B. Curtis and Schmitt, Nicolas. "Endogenous Pricing Modes in a Model of Spatial Competition." Mimeo, Simon Fraser University, 1992.

______. "Endogenous Pricing Modes in Markets for Inputs," in Hioshi Ohta and Jacques-François Thisse, eds., *Does economic space matter?* London: Macmillan, 1993, pp. 352–73.

Gabszewicz, J. Jaskold and Thisse, Jacques-François. "Entry (and Exit) in a Differentiated Industry." *Journal of Economic Theory*, April 1980, *22*(2), pp. 327–38.

Gilbert, Richard and Vives, Xavier. "Entry Deterrence and the Free Rider Problem." *Review of Economic Studies*, January 1986, *53*(1), pp. 71–83.

Greenwood, Nigel R. *Implementing flexible manufacturing systems*. London: Macmillan, 1988.

Hoover, Edgar M. "Spatial Price Discrimination." *Review of Economic Studies*, June 1937, *4*(3), pp. 182–91.

Hotelling, Harold. "Stability in Competition." *Economic Journal*, March 1929, *39*(153), pp. 41–57.

Judd, Kenneth L. "Credible Spatial Preemption." *Rand Journal of Economics*, Summer 1985, *16*(2), pp. 153–66.

Lederer, Phillip J. and Hurter, Arthur P. "Competition of Firms: Discriminatory Pricing and Location." *Econometrica*, May 1986, *54*(3), pp. 623–40.

MacLeod, W. Bentley; Norman, George and Thisse, Jacques-François. "Price Discrimination and Equilibrium in Monopolistic Competition." *International Journal of Industrial Organization*, December 1988, *6*(4), pp. 429–46.

Meredith, Jack R. *The management of operations*, 3rd Ed. New York: Wiley, 1987.

Milgrom, Paul; Qian, Yingyi and Roberts, John. "Complementarities, Momentum, and the Evolution of Modern Manufacturing." *American Economic Review*, May 1991 (*Papers and Proceedings*), *81*(2), pp. 84–88.

Milgrom, Paul and Roberts, John. "The Economics of Modern Manufacturing: Technology, Strategy, and Organization." *American Economic Review*, June 1990, *80*(3), pp. 511–28.

Prescott, Edward C. and Visscher, Michael. "Sequential Location among Firms with Foresight." *Bell Journal of Economics*, Autumn 1977, *8*(2), pp. 378–93.

Rasmusen, Eric. "Entry for Buyout." *Journal of Industrial Economics*, March 1988, *36*(3), pp. 281–99.

Röller, Lars-Hendrik and Tombak, Mihkel M. "Strategic Choice of Flexible Production Technologies and Welfare Implications." *Journal of Industrial Economics*, June 1990, *38*(4), pp. 417–31.

Stalk, George Jr. "Time: The Next Source of Competitive Advantage." *Harvard Business Review*, July-August 1988, *88*(4), pp. 41–51.

Stigler, George J. "Production and Distribution in the Short Run." *Journal of Political Economy*, June 1939, *47*(3), pp. 305–27.

______. "Monopoly and Oligopoly by Merger." *American Economic Review*, May 1950 (*Papers and Proceedings*), *40*(2), pp. 23–34.

United Nations. *Recent trends in flexible manufacturing*. New York: Economic Commission for Europe, 1986.

[12]

Supporting collusion by choice of inferior technologies

B. Curtis Eaton and Mukesh Eswaran*

1. INTRODUCTION

This chapter investigates tacit collusions by firms in the adoption of convex technologies that are ranked in terms of efficiency. We demonstrate that firms will not necessarily adopt the most efficient technology that is available. We find this result somewhat surprising because in the polar extremes of natural or protected monopoly and perfect competition if firms were given the choice among a set of ranked technologies, they would always choose the lowest-cost technology. More importantly, this chapter provides a lead into the general question of what cartels would find in their interests to agree on. It suggests that a choice of the technology to be adopted would be an important dimension in cartel agreements.

In the next section of this chapter, we focus on the choice between two convex technologies in a fixed-number oligopoly producing a homogeneous product. The technologies can be ranked since, for all positive quantities, costs are lower for one technology than they are for the other. We find, among other things, that the inferior technology is more likely to be adopted the larger is the number of firms.[1]

Hence, as we illustrate, it is entirely possible that an exogenous increase in concentration can be welfare improving because it may knock the oligopoly out of an equilibrium in which the inferior technology is chosen. Indeed it is not difficult to find circumstances in which an exogenous increase in concentration increases both consumers' and producers' surplus.

The collusive choice of an inefficient technology arises from the relative effects the two technologies have on the possibilities for collusion between firms. Consider an oligopoly in which firms collude in a supergame and support their collusion by reversion to the Cournot equilibrium in the event of defection, as in Friedman (1971). If the fully collusive (that is, monopoly) outcome associated with the efficient technology can be supported by this trigger strategy, then that technology will surely be chosen. But the cost conditions associated with one or both of the technologies may be such that they encourage defection at the fully collusive output level. If they do, the oligopolists will implement a partially collusive outcome in which each firm's output is less than the Cournot output but greater than the fully collusive output associated with that technology. Then, in choosing between the two technologies, the oligopolists will compare the *highest feasible* profit for the two technologies. If the efficient technology has a drastically lower marginal cost at higher levels of output – which makes defection with this technology relatively more attractive – the highest feasible profit may be larger for the inferior technology. If this is so, the industry will choose the inferior technology.

In Section 3 of this chapter we come at the choice of an inferior technology from another angle. We think of the oligopolists as collusively choosing both capacity (or capital stock) and output in a supergame in which, again, collusion is supported by Cournot reversion. The underlying production function exhibits constant returns to scale in two inputs, capital and a composite input, which are not perfectly complementary. An increase in the capital stock shifts the short-run (or restricted) marginal cost function down for all positive levels of output. In the equilibrium of this game it is easy to find circumstances in which the equilibrium capital stock of a firm is smaller than the cost-minimizing capital stock for the equilibrium output. Thus we have an *insufficient capacity* result for this model. Furthermore, an increase in the number of firms can be shown to decrease consumer surplus.

One way to understand the results in both models is to recognize that there are two effects associated with a downward shift in the cost function, which we dub the *cost* and *strategic effects*. The former refers to the usual effect that a decline in marginal cost at all levels of output increases profits, *ceteris paribus*. A change in the cost function also affects the incremental cost to a firm of raising its output to the optimal defection level. The strategic effect refers to the fact that a reduction in the incremental cost of defection makes defection more attractive, thus tending to reduce the maximum profit that can be supported by a trigger strategy. In Section 2, if the strategic effect associated with a shift from the inefficient to the efficient technology overwhelms the cost effect, the inefficient technology is chosen. In Section 3, the capital stock is chosen so that the cost reduction associated with a small increase in capacity is just balanced by the strategic effect that arises from the fact that increasing capacity shifts the marginal cost function down.

In both models the strategic effect tends to increase as the number of firms increases. In Section 2, this means that the larger is the number of firms the more likely it is that the industry will choose the inefficient technology. In Section 3, it means that the divergence from cost minimization increases as the number of firms increases. Hence in both models it is possible that an increase in concentration can increase aggregate welfare, despite the fact that the technologies available are strictly convex.

2. CHOICE BETWEEN DISCRETE TECHNOLOGIES

In this section we consider an oligopoly's choice between two off-the-shelf technologies, characterized by their cost functions $C_L(q)$ (L for low cost) and $C_H(q)$ (H for high cost), where q is output. The technologies are strictly convex and in addition, they are efficiency ranked; that is, for any positive q, $C_L(q)$ is strictly less than $C_H(q)$. The oligopoly's choice of technology is (tacitly) collusive, and is supported as a Nash equilibrium by a trigger strategy.

As we show, it is quite easy to find circumstances in which the industry rejects the low-cost technology in favour of the high-cost one. Moreover, this possibility is more likely when the industry is less concentrated. In fact, in circumstances where the high-cost technology is chosen, an exogenous increase in concentration that leads to the adoption of the low-cost technology can sometimes also lead to a decrease in equilibrium price, so that consumers benefit from the increase in concentration. Then, since increased concentration also leads to larger aggregate profit, in these circumstances an increase in concentration is unambiguously welfare improving.

Demand and Cost Conditions

We consider a fixed numbers oligopoly with an infinite number of periods. There are N firms, each producing a homogeneous product, and the inverse demand function is linear in aggregate output, Q:

$$P = \alpha - \gamma Q; \quad \alpha > 0, \quad \gamma > 0, \tag{13.1}$$

where P denotes price, α and γ are demand parameters. Each firm has free access to either of two technologies, characterized by the following cost functions. Technology H.

$$C_H(q) = a_H q + b_H q^2. \tag{13.2a}$$

Technology L:

$$C_L(q) = a_L q + b_L q^2 \tag{13.2b}$$

where q is output and a_H, a_L, b_H, and b_L are cost parameters. We assume that

$$0 \le a_L \le a_H \text{ and } 0 \le b_L \le b_H, \tag{13.2c}$$

and that

$$\text{either } a_L < a_H \text{ and/or } b_L < b_H. \tag{13.2d}$$

Thus, $C_L(q)$ is strictly less than $C_H(q)$ for all positive q. We will refer to Technology L as 'low-cost', and to Technology H as 'high cost'.

In our model, technology adoption is both *time intensive* and *observable.* Specifically, we suppose that there is a lag of T periods from the time a firm begins to implement a technology to the time when the technology becomes operational, and that any firm's current technology, and its efforts to implement a different technology, are observed by all other firms. Initial technology choices by all firms are made in period $-T$, so that production actually begins in period 0.

The Tacit Collusive Agreements

We consider two types of symmetric, tacit collusive agreements, supported by trigger strategies. The first is standard.

- *Type L agreement* Along the equilibrium path, firms use the low-cost technology and collude in the choice of output. In the event of defection, the trigger strategy dictates that all firms revert to Cournot behaviour in all subsequent periods.

With a Type L agreement, the high-cost technology is irrelevant since no firm would ever choose to implement the high-cost technology, given that the tacit agreement calls for all its competitors to use the low-cost technology. The second type of agreement is more complex.

- *Type H agreement* Along the equilibrium path, firms use the high-cost technology and collude in the choice of output. If a firm chooses to defect in any period, its defection strategy is double-barrelled: in the defection period, it both produces a non-collusive output, and begins to implement the low-cost technology. The trigger strategy is also double-barrelled: in the event of defection, all firms revert to Cournot behaviour in all subsequent periods, and, in addition, all other firms begin, in the first period subsequent to defection, to implement the low-cost technology.

Given the adoption lag, the low-cost technology becomes available to the defector T periods after defection, and to all other firms $T + 1$ periods after defection.[2]

We compute and compare the *maximum sustainable profits* for each of these tacit agreements. We suppose that the agreement which provides the larger profit is the one that the oligopoly chooses. We are particularly interested in finding conditions such that the maximum sustainable profit is larger with the Type H agreement (in which all firms use the high-cost technology) than with the Type L agreement (where all firms choose the low-cost technology). To compute the maximum sustainable profits, we need the incentive compatibility or no-defection constraints associated with these agreements.

No-defection Constraints

To articulate the no-defection constraints we need some additional notation, which we introduce below.

q_i: output of firm i.
Q_{-i}: aggregate output of all firms other than i.
$\Pi_i^k(q_i, Q_{-i})$: profit of firm i when it adopts technology k, $k \in \{L, H\}$, as a function of q_i and Q_{-i}
$R_i^k(Q_{-i})$: the best response function of firm i when it adopts technology k, $k \in \{L, H\}$.
Γ^k: the Cournot equilibrium profit of a firm, when all firms are using technology k, $k \in \{L, H\}$.
Φ^{LH}: the Cournot equilibrium profit of a firm using the low-cost technology when all other firms are using the high-cost technology.
δ: the discount factor, common to all firms.

Under the Type L agreement, where all firms use the low-cost technology, the no-defection constraint (NDC_i^L) for firm i, $i = 1,2,\ldots,N$, is

$$\Pi_i^L(q_i, Q_{-i})/(1-\delta) \geq \Pi_i^L(R_i^L(Q_{-i}), Q_{-i}) + [\delta/(1-\delta)]\Gamma^L. \qquad (13.3)$$

In (13.3), Q_{-i} is the aggregate agreed-upon output of all firms other than i. The left-hand side of (13.3) is the present value of firm i's profit under the collusive agreement that it produce q_i in each period, and the right side is the maximal present value of profit for a defector. If firm i defects, it will get $\Pi_i^L(R_i^L(Q_{-i})Q_{-i})$ in the period it defects and the Cournot profit Γ^L in every period thereafter, since all firms are initially using the low-cost technology and since the trigger strategy calls for Cournot reversion.

Under the Type H agreement, where all firms initially use the high-cost technology, the incentive compatibility constraint is more complex since both the defection and trigger strategies are double-barrelled. If firm i defects, it will choose a non-cooperative output for the defection period, and it will begin to implement the low-cost technology, which will come on-line T periods subsequent to defection. Similarly, the trigger strategy involves both Cournot reversion and the adoption by all other firms of the low-cost technology. For these firms, the low-cost technology will come on-line $T + 1$ periods subsequent to the defection. Thus the no-defection constraint (NDC_i^H) for firm i, $i = 1,2,\ldots,N$, is

$$\Pi_i^H(q_i, Q_{-i})/(1-\delta) \geq \Pi_i^H(R_i^H(Q_{-i}), Q_{-i})$$

$$+[\delta+\delta^2+\ldots+\delta^{T-1}]\Gamma^H+\delta^T\Phi^{LH}+[\delta^{T+1}+\delta^{T+2}+\ldots]\Gamma^L. \quad (13.4a)$$

The left-hand side of (13.4a) is the present value of profit in the collusive agreement to firm i when it produces an output q_i and all other firms produce Q_{-i} in aggregate in all periods using the high-cost technology. The right side is the maximized present value of firm i's profit if it defects, given Q_{-i}, and given the trigger strategy. In the defection period its maximized profit is $\Pi_i^H(R_i^H(Q_{-i})Q_{-i})$; in each of the next $T - 1$ periods its Cournot equilibrium profit is Γ^H; in period T its profit is Φ^{LH}, since in this period firm i has the low-cost technology and all other firms still have the high-cost technology; in period $T + 1$ and all subsequent periods, its Cournot equilibrium profit is Γ^L, since all firms then have the low-cost technology.

Inequality (13.4a) is the no-defection constraint for firm i from period 0 onwards. There are separate no-defection constraints for periods $-T$ to -1. We do not spell out these latter no-defection constraints because defection in the choice of technology prior to beginning production is a somewhat uninteresting possibility: the defector does not get to capture the benefits of free-riding from the output restriction of other firms. The only advantage to cheating in periods $-T$ to -1 is the one-period advantage of higher Cournot profit, arising from having a more efficient technology than one's rival.

Rewriting (13.4a), we have

$$\Pi_i^H(q_i, Q_{-i})/(1-\delta) \geq \Pi_i^H(R_i^H(Q_{-i}), Q_{-i})+[(\delta-\delta^T)/(1-\delta)]\Gamma^H$$

$$+\delta^T\Phi^{LH}+[\delta^{T+1}/(1-\delta)]\Gamma^L. \quad (13.4)$$

If the implementation lag T is large, some of the terms on the right-hand side of (13.4) will be insignificant. In that case, we could use the following approximation of the no-defection constraint for firm i ($i = 1,2,\ldots,N$) under a Type H agreement:

$$\Pi_i^H(q_i, Q_{-i})/(1-\delta) \geq \Pi_i^H(R_i^H(Q_{-i}), Q_{-i}) + [\delta/(1-\delta)]\Gamma^H. \qquad (13.4b)$$

Notice that, with this simplification, the incentive compatibility constraints for both types of agreement, inequalities (13.3) and (13.4b), have the same form. (In the numerical results we present in this section, we have chosen a lag of $T = 10$, which implies that for all practical purposes (13.4b) is the relevant constraint for these results.)

Maximum Sustainable Profits

To proceed we need to use the demand and cost functions specified in equations (13.1) and (13.2), respectively. We restrict attention to the reasonable case where the tacitly agreed-upon output of all firms is the same in a collusive agreement, and we denote this output by q. In the appendix we derive the following, straightforward expressions:

$$\Pi_i^k(q,(N-1)q) = (\alpha - a_k)q - (\gamma N + b_k)q^2, \qquad (13.5a)$$

$$\Pi_i^k(R_i^k((N-1)q),(N-1)q)$$

$$= [\alpha - a_k - \gamma(N-1)q]^2/[4(\gamma + b_k)], \qquad (13.5b)$$

$$\Gamma^k = (\gamma + b_k)(\alpha - a_k)^2/[\gamma(N+1) + 2b_k]^2, \qquad (13.5c)$$

where $i = 1,2,\ldots,N$, and $k \in \{L, H\}$.

When all firms use technology k and produce q units of output each, expression (13.5a) gives the profit (per period) of one firm, expression (13.5b) the maximum profit for a defector in the defection period, and (13.5c) the Cournot equilibrium profit (per period) of one firm. The expression for the one-period Cournot profit, Φ^{LH}, of a firm using the low-cost technology when all other firms are using the high-cost technology can be found in the appendix. Then, for technology k, the maximum sustainable profit is the solution to the following problem:

$$\max_q \Pi_i^k[q,(N-1)q] \qquad (P1)$$

$$\text{s.t.} \quad NDC_i^k, \quad k \in \{L, H\}$$

where, NDC_i^L is given by (13.3) and NDC_i^H by (13.4).

In Figure 13.1 we illustrate the solution when the no-defection constraint is binding. Collusive profit (on the left-hand side of the constraint in (P1)) initially increases and then decreases as q increases, and is represented by 0ABC in the figure. Defection profit (on the right-hand side of the constraint in (P1)) is represented by DBE. If defection was not a problem, the oligopoly would choose output q^* per firm, and each firm's profit would be given by 0F in the figure. But, when output per firm is q^*, the defection profit exceeds collusive profit, and the no-defection constraint is not satisfied. The maximum sustainable profit is distance 0G, less than 0F, and each firm produces $\hat{q}$ units in the constrained solution.

Now consider the comparative statics of the solution in Figure 13.1 with respect to the cost parameter b_k, $k \in \{L, H\}$. As b_k increases, the collusive profit and the defection profit both shift downwards since, for given q, an increase in b_k means an increase in cost. Notice that if the shift in defection profit to (D′B′E′) is large relative to the shift in collusive profit to (0A′B′C′), the maximum sustainable profit will increase from 0G to 0H, as illustrated in Figure 13.1. This is a schematic illustration of one of the outcomes we emphasized above, namely, it is possible for the maximum sustainable profit in the Type H collusive agreement to exceed the maximum sustainable profit

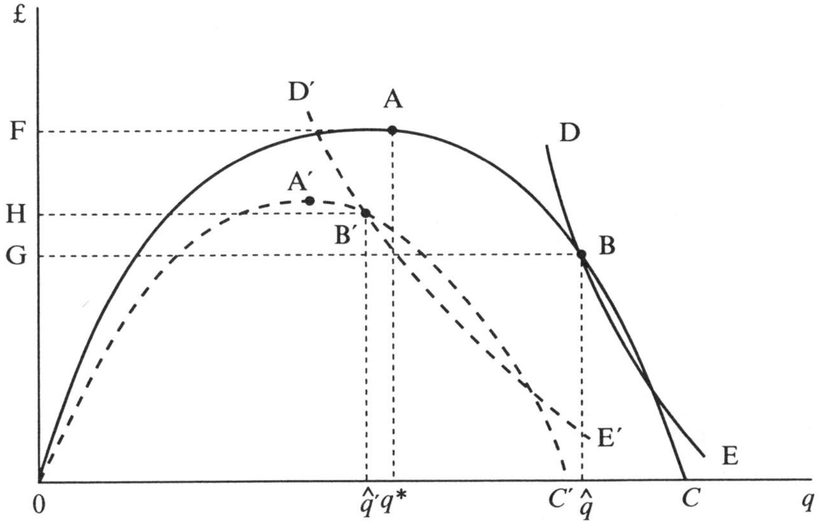

Figure 13.1 Illustration of how the maximum sustainable profits can increase when costs increase

in the Type L agreement. That this possibility is not vacuous will become clear from the results reported below.

When the no-defection constraint binds, a change in b_k has two distinct effects, which we earlier referred to as the cost effect and the strategic effect. By the former we mean the obvious effect that, *ceteris paribus*, as b_k increases costs increase and hence profits fall. The strategic effect is driven by the impact of b_k on the no-defection constraint; *ceteris paribus*, as b_k increases, defection profits decrease – which permits a decrease in the collusive output per firm and a corresponding increase in profits (when the no-defection constraint is binding). When the strategic effect dominates the cost effect, as in the illustration of Figure 13.1, an increase in b_k results in an increase in the maximum sustainable profit.[3]

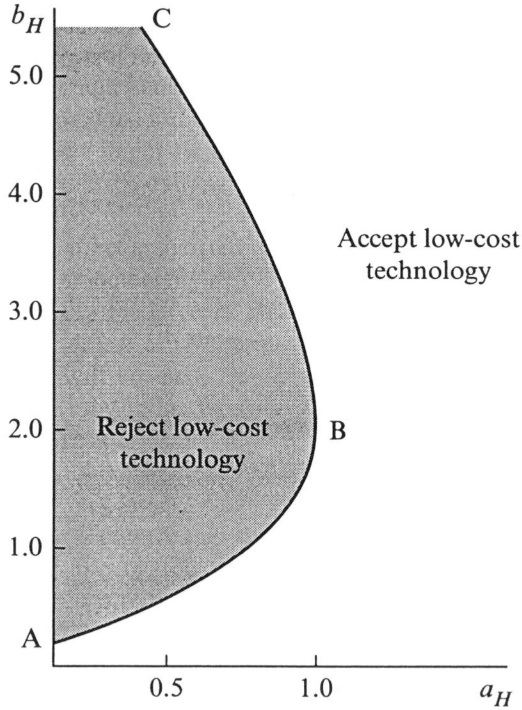

Note: Parameter values: $N = 10$, $T = 10$, $\alpha = 10$, $\gamma = 1$, $\delta = 0.2$, $a_L = 0.126$, $b_L = 0.2$.

Figure 13.2 Partition of (a_H, b_H) *parameter space into regions where the low-cost technology is rejected and accepted, respectively*

In Figure 13.2 we illustrate the partition of the (a_H, b_H) parameter space into one region where the Type H agreement is preferred and another where the Type L agreement is preferred (holding all other parameters fixed at the values indicated at the bottom of the figure). The two regions are separated by the locus of indifference ABC along which both types of agreement generate the same maximum sustainable profit. In the shaded area the Type H agreement (in which firms use the high-cost technology) generates the larger maximum sustainable profit. Segment AB of the locus of indifference is upward sloping because in this part of the (a_H, b_H) parameter space the strategic effect overwhelms the cost effect. Thus, starting from any point on segment AB, an increase in b_H increases the maximum sustainable profit for the Type H agreement, rendering it strictly more profitable than the Type L agreement; accordingly, to maintain indifference, the increase in b_H must be coupled with a simultaneous increase in a_H. (Note that an increase in the parameter a_H of the cost function is equivalent to decreasing the intercept, α, of the demand curve.) Along segment BC of the locus of indifference, the cost effect dominates the strategic effect; so starting at any point on segment

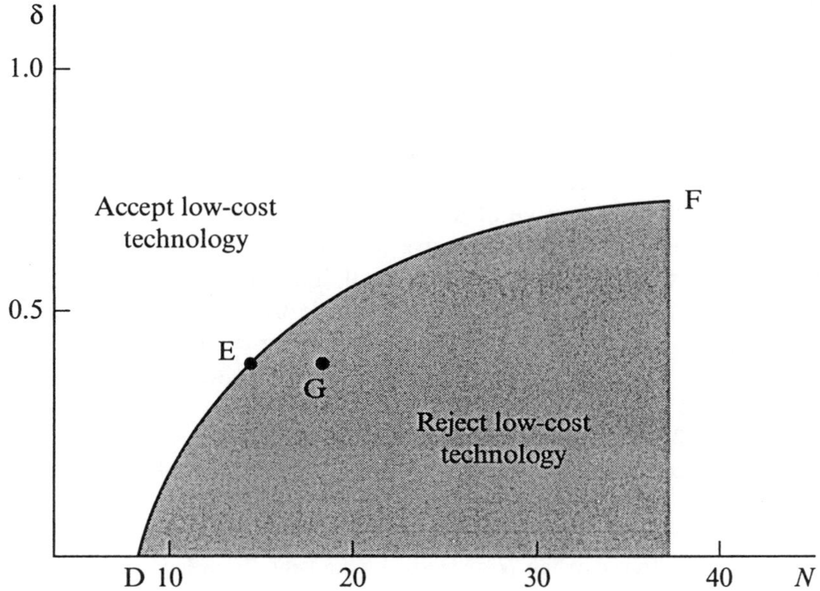

Note: Parameter values: $T = 10$, $\alpha = 10$, $\gamma = 1$, $\delta = 0.2$, $a_H = 1.0$, $b_H = 2.0$, $a_L = 0.126$, $b_L = 0.2$.

Figure 13.3 Partition of (N, δ) space into regions where the low-cost technology is rejected and accepted, respectively

BC, an increase in b_H must be coupled with a decrease in a_H to maintain indifference.

In Figure 13.3 we illustrate the partition of the (δ, N) parameter space into one region where the Type H agreement is preferred and another where the Type L agreement is preferred (holding all other parameters fixed at the values indicated at the bottom of the figure). The two regions are separated by the upward-sloping locus of indifference DEF, and in the shaded area below DEF the Type H agreement generates the larger maximum sustainable profit. As N increases, preventing defection is increasingly difficult, which makes the high-cost technology relatively more attractive. So, beginning at a point on DEF, an increase in N leads the oligopoly to reject the low-cost technology. As δ increases, preventing defection is increasingly easier, which makes the low-cost technology relatively more attractive. So, beginning at a point on DEF, an increase in δ leads the oligopoly to choose the low-cost technology. These effects imply that DEF is upward sloping.

The above illustration of the rejection of the low-cost technology when the number of firms is large is particularly interesting since it goes counter to the presumption that the smaller the market share of a firm, the more atomistically it would tend to behave. In this instance, firms in a relatively unconcentrated market might be expected to adopt the more efficient technology as the individually rational choice. What the above demonstrates is that, when the number of firms is large, the strategic effect can oppose and overwhelm the cost effect associated with the adoption of the efficient technology. However, this monotonicity result is an artefact of the model and must not be taken too literally for large N. Recall that we have ignored the possibility that firms may defect at the initial stage of technology adoption. This is a possibility that will become increasingly attractive to firms as N becomes very large. When the collusive profit to each firm is small, it may be overwhelmed by the one-period gain in Cournot profit made possible by its use of the superior technology when all other firms are using the inferior technology. Thus, as N gets very large, firms could be expected to choose the efficient technology if this effect were incorporated.

In Figure 13.4 we display various aspects of industry performance as functions of the number of firms in the industry, holding all other parameters fixed at the values indicated in the figure. The two types of agreement generate the same maximum sustainable profit when N equals 10, while the Type H agreement is preferred when N exceeds 10, and the Type L when N is less than 10. As expected, industry profit is a smoothly decreasing function of N. Similarly, within either regime, consumer surplus smoothly increases as the number of firms increases. However, there is a discrete drop in consumer surplus, and hence in total surplus as well, associated with the shift from the Type L agreement to the Type H agreement. Beginning with 10 firms, an

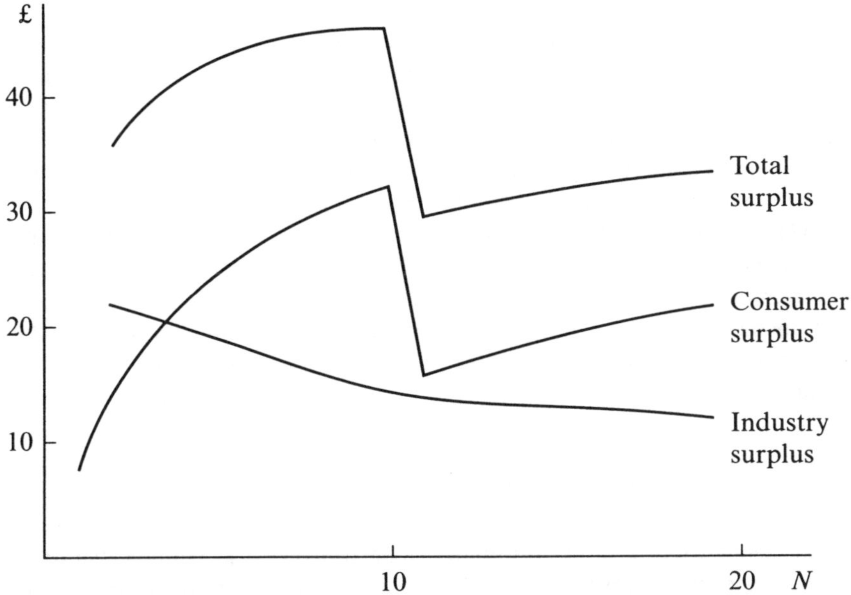

Note: Parameter values: $T = 10$, $\alpha = 10$, $\gamma = 1$, $\delta = 0.2$, $a_H = 1.0$, $b_H = 2.0$, $a_L = 0.126$, $b_L = 0.2$.

Figure 13.4 Displays the consumer, producer and total surplus generated by the industry as a function of the number of firms

increase in N results in a switch from the low-cost technology to the high-cost technology, inducing a drastic increase in equilibrium price and a corresponding drastic decrease in consumer surplus. As Figure 13.4 illustrates, consumer (and total) surplus does not recover the value achieved at N equal to 10 even after the number of firms has doubled.

To put the same point differently, an increase in concentration that results in a switch from the high-cost technology to the low-cost one can result in an increase in both industry profit and consumer surplus. This apparent anomaly arises because firms in our model are interested in maximizing profit, not total surplus, subject to no-defection constraints. When an increase in concentration facilitates the adoption of the low-cost technology by relaxing the no-defection constraints, the decline in price associated with lower costs can more than compensate for the tendency of increased concentration to push prices up.

It is well known that there are circumstances in which higher concentration is associated with higher social welfare. An obvious case arises when there are significant non-convexities in the firm's technology. For example, if there are large fixed costs associated with product development, fewer firms would mean fewer resources devoted to product development – raising the clear possibility of a direct relationship between social welfare and concentration. Consumers, however, are unlikely to benefit from higher concentration in this case. And in a dynamic framework, if higher concentration means more innovation, it can – through the well-known process of 'creative destruction' – result in higher social welfare for the reasons first enunciated by Schumpeter (1942). In contrast to these scenarios, in our model the higher welfare of both producers and consumers associated with higher concentration requires neither non-convexities nor innovation, since the technology set is both convex and unchanging. Our results provide yet another case against a fundamental presumption of antitrust law, namely, that concentration of market power is socially detrimental.

3. CHOOSING CAPACITY

In this section we develop a different perspective on the possibility that firms may choose an inferior technology by looking at the firm's choice of capacity or capital stock. We maintain the demand conditions specified above, but suppose that goods are produced using the following Cobb–Douglas production function.

$$q = l^{1/2}k^{1/2}, \tag{13.6}$$

where k is quantity of product specific, infinitely durable, capital and l is a composite of all other inputs. We will refer to k as the firm's capital stock or as its capacity.

To maintain obvious parallels with our earlier model, we suppose that capital creation entails a lag of T periods, and that all costs associated with capital creation are incurred in the very last period. The T period lag is then a (costless) planning or ordering lag.

Given k, the total cost, $C(q,k)$, of producing q units of output in any period is given by

$$C(q,k) = rk + wq^2 / k, \tag{13.7}$$

where r and w are exogenously given input prices of capital and the composite input, respectively.

We consider a tacit collusive agreement analogous to the Type H agreement of the previous section.

Collusive Agreement

Along the equilibrium path firms (collusively) choose capital stock k per firm and output q per firm. If a firm chooses to defect in any period t, its defection strategy is double-barrelled: in the defection period, it both produces the optimal non-collusive output, and begins to implement the Nash equilibrium capacity choice for all periods subsequent to $t + T - 1$. The trigger strategy is also double-barrelled: in the event of defection, all firms revert to Cournot behaviour in all subsequent periods, and, in addition, all other firms begin to implement Nash equilibrium choices of capacity for all periods subsequent to $t + T$.

Given that all firms have capacity k and produce output q, the profit of a firm i, $i = 1,2,\ldots,N$, is

$$\Pi_i(q,k) = (\alpha - \gamma Nq)q - rk - wq^2 / k. \tag{13.8}$$

Given that all firms have capital stock k and that all other firms produce output q, a firm's maximal defection profit is readily seen to be

$$\Pi_i^d(q,k) = [\alpha - \gamma(N-1)q]^2 /[4(\gamma + w/k)] - rk. \tag{13.9}$$

The profit, Γ, in the Cournot equilibrium, given that all firms have capital stock k, is given by

$$\Gamma = (\gamma + w/k)\alpha^2 /[\gamma(N+1) + 2w/k]^2 - rk. \tag{13.10}$$

We will assume that the time lag T is large. In fact, it is convenient (but not essential) to assume that, once installed, capacity takes arbitrarily long to change. The no-defection constraint will then approach the constraint in the following collusive choice problem, and (P2) below will then approximate the problem confronting the oligopoly.

$$\max_{k,q} \Pi_i(q,k)/(1-\delta) \tag{P2}$$

$$\text{s.t.} \quad \Pi_i(q,k)/(1-\delta) \geq \Pi_i^d(q,k) + [\delta/(1-\delta)]\Gamma.$$

Figure 13.5 illustrates the solution to this problem in (q,k) space. The oval-shaped curves represent a firm's isoprofit contours and U denotes the unconstrained maximum. At any given level of the capital stock, there are two output levels at which the no-defection constraint is satisfied with equality: the Cournot equilibrium output associated with that capital stock, and an

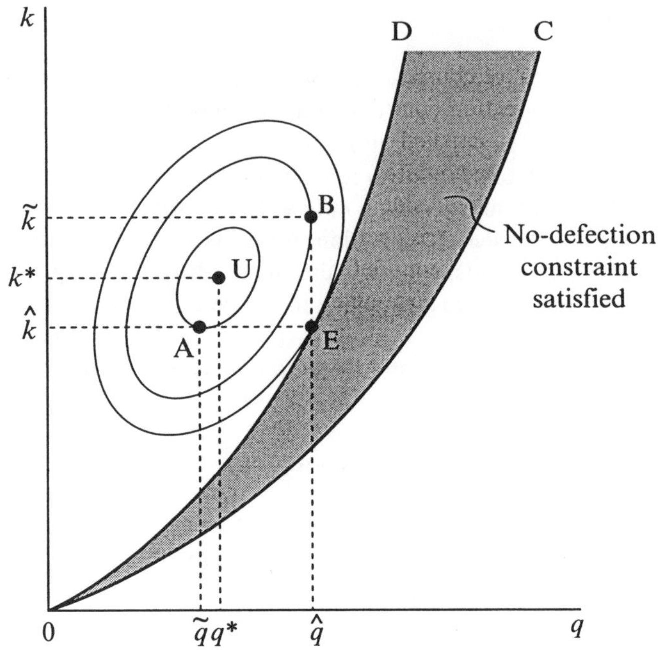

Figure 13.5 Illustration of a constrained equilibrium in (q,k) *space when firms collusively choose capacity*

output level that is smaller than the Cournot output. As the capital stock is varied, these two output levels trace out the loci 0C and 0D, respectively, shown in the figure. The shaded area represents the combinations of (q,k) for which the no-defection constraint is satisfied for each firm. The constrained, collusive equilibrium, $(\hat{q},\hat{k})$ is at point E where the locus 0D is tangential to an isoprofit contour. Given capital stock $\hat{k}$ profit is maximized when output is $\tilde{q}$. Hence, in this solution, each firm produces more than the profit-maximizing quantity (given $\hat{k}$). Similarly, given output $\hat{q}$ per firm, profit is maximized when capital stock is $\tilde{k}$; hence in this solution, firms choose a capital stock that is smaller than the cost-minimizing capital stock (given $\hat{q}$). To prevent defection, profit is dissipated both by producing excessive output and by using too little capital. Since defection constrains the equilibrium and since firms have two instruments to control defection, they use them both.

The fact that firms can dissipate profit by using insufficient capacity and excessive output reflects an interesting trade-off that can occur in the no-defection constraint between output and capital stock (in the neighbourhood of the solution at E). Starting at a point where the no-defection constraint is satisfied with equality, an increase in q decreases the right-hand side of the no-defection constraint by more than it decreases the left-hand side. That is, in the neighbourhood of an equilibrium, an increase in q creates slack in the no-defection constraint. This, of course, is standard in this sort of supergame equilibrium when the no-defection constraint is binding. Starting again at a point where the constraint is satisfied with equality, a decrease in k can decrease the left-hand side of the no-defection constraint because it increases costs, and it decreases the right-hand side because, costs having risen, defection is less attractive. On balance, the decrease in k could result in a larger decrease in the right-hand side of the no-defection constraint than in the left-hand side. Then, a decrease in k, like an increase in q, would create slack in the constraint. The no-defection constraint, in this case, is upward sloping – the slack created by an increase in q can be taken up by an increase in k.[4] The constrained equilibrium that obtains is of the sort pictured in Figure 13.5. This, indeed, is the scenario that occurs in the results reported below.

In Table 13.1 we illustrate various features of the solutions that emerge as the number of firms varies. In the second column we record the ratio of the per firm capacity, $\hat{k}$, that is the solution to (P2) to the capacity, $\tilde{k}$ that minimizes the cost of producing the equilibrium output, $\hat{q}$. In the third column (labelled $\hat{C}/\tilde{C}$) we record the ratio of the cost ($\hat{C}$) of producing the equilibrium output to the minimum cost ($\tilde{C}$) of producing that output, while in the fourth, fifth and sixth columns we record producer, consumer and total surplus, respectively. From the second column we see that as N increases, the capacity of a firm in the supergame equilibrium monotonically declines as a proportion of the capacity that would minimize the cost of producing the firm's equilibrium output. As indicated by the third column, surplus dissipation through insufficient capacity increases as the number of firms increases. Producer surplus (*PS*) naturally declines as N increases, while both consumer surplus (*CS*) and total surplus (*TS*) initially increase and subsequently de-

Table 13.1 Supergame equilibria

N	$\hat{k}/\tilde{k}$	$\hat{C}/\tilde{C}$	*PS*	*CS*	*TS*
1	1.00	1.00	16.00	8.00	24.00
2	0.87	1.01	15.77	9.57	25.34
4	0.76	1.04	15.20	10.84	26.05
8	0.65	1.10	14.60	11.06	25.65
16	0.59	1.14	14.19	10.99	25.18
32	0.56	1.17	13.97	10.88	24.85
64	0.55	1.18	13.85	10.84	24.69

Note: Parameter values $\alpha = 10, \gamma = 1, \delta = 0.3, w = 1, r = 1$.

crease as N increases. These results are consistent with similar results from the preceding section. In particular, cost minimization is not a property of these supergame equilibria, and an increase in concentration may increase both producer and consumer surplus.

The non-monotonic behaviour of the consumer (and total) surplus as a function of the number of firms again arises from the strategic effect. As N increases, *ceteris paribus*, defection becomes more of a problem and so aggregate equilibrium output would tend to increase on this count. But firms can respond to the problem of increased defection incentives by curtailing the installed capacity. (In fact, the aggregate industry capacity can even decline as N increases.) If the aggregate capital stock is sufficiently curtailed, the equilibrium output of the industry can decline as N increases. Since the latter possibility is more likely especially for large N – which is when the consequences of defection are particularly deleterious – the equilibrium price first decreases and then increases with N.

The nature of the capacity distortion that arises in this model is quite different from the distortion that arises in models where capacity choice in the supergame equilibrium is non-cooperative. In the latter kind of models there is a tendency for excess capacity to emerge in equilibrium because a firm's capacity affects both its costs and its market share: at the cost-minimizing capacity, any firm has an incentive to add capacity because added capacity means added market share.[5] As our results illustrate, when capacity choice in the supergame equilibrium is collusive, there is a tendency for insufficient capacity to arise in equilibrium.

CONCLUSIONS

In Section 2 of this chapter we showed that a collusive oligopoly can reject a convex technology in favour of another that is inferior (and also convex), and in Section 3 that a collusive oligopoly can underinvest in capacity. In both cases the apparently perverse choice arises because it facilitates collusion by making defection less attractive. Significantly, in both scenarios an increase in concentration can lead to an increase in both consumer and producer surplus.

These findings have potentially serious implications for antitrust law and practice, where a fundamental presumption has been that an increase in market concentration is inimical to the public interest.[6] Important exceptions to this presumption are recognized in situations where innovation is important and where technologies exhibit significant non-convexities. To our knowledge, this chapter is the first to suggest that exceptions may be justified even when the technology is unchanging and convex. As long as firms have at least some flexibility in the determination of their marginal variable costs (whether by choice among technologies or by choice of capacity or by the commitment to any input in the production process), the case against market concentration is suspect.

When the technology is convex, our assumption of fixed numbers may be unreasonable; in the long run, if entry is free, it will render the industry perfectly competitive. We see at least two responses to this argument. First, in many industries there exist artificial barriers to entry that are sanctioned by the state, so that our analysis is directly applicable. We discuss this briefly below. Second, the results of this chapter are often reinforced by the introduction of non-convexities. Consider, for example, the non-convexity implied by a setup cost, associated with learning about a convex technology. Given such a setup cost, the industry can accommodate only a finite number of firms. A marginal increase in the setup cost which reduces the number of firms in the industry could clearly be welfare improving since it could both make the surviving firms more profitable, and reduce aggregate setup costs. This, of course, is just a variation on a familiar story. What we have added to it is the possibility that a decline in the number of firms occasioned by the increase in the setup cost may also lead to a price reduction, thereby making consumers better off.

The professions provide good examples of industries where the fixed-numbers assumption of our models is particularly appropriate, since the state often gives professional associations the right to determine the number of professionals who can operate in an industry. As Evans (1980) has argued, the limited time available to individual professionals acts as a natural constraint that enables them to earn rents even when each individual perceives him/herself as operating in a competitive environment. The mere fact that any one professional has a limited amount of time that can be devoted to work means that the professional firm's marginal cost function is steeply upward sloping in the neighbourhood of capacity, which facilitates collusion by making defection relatively unattractive. This is reinforced by the fact that the medical associations often disallow doctors from working as employees in private firms, thereby preventing private medical firms from lowering their marginal cost schedules. We may also argue that any attempt by a regulatory agency to reduce the scope of the work actually done by professionals will be met with stiff opposition by the professional association because the move would undermine the support for collusive agreements among its members.

Finally, we note a possible bias in the incentives to innovate implied by our analysis. Clearly, an innovator's incentives are determined in part by his/her perceptions regarding possible adoption of any technology which might be developed. Our analysis suggests the possibility of a bias in the innovator's choice towards innovations that facilitate collusion.

NOTES

* We are particularly indebted to Ralph Winter for extensive suggestions and comments on an earlier draft. We would also like to thank Nancy Gallini, Ken Hendricks, Nick Schmitt and the seminar participants at the University of Tasmania for their comments. All remaining errors or shortcomings are our own.

1. If technology is broadly interpreted as anything that may affect cost curves, the point that cartels may prefer inferior technologies is often recognized informally. For example, Maloney, McCormick and Tollison (1979) argue that cartels may force their marginal cost curves to be more vertical by signing union contracts that require double wages for overtime work (cited in Carleton and Perloff 1990, p. 226).
2. It is logically possible that the defecting firm might choose to stick with the high-cost technology. However, given defection, and given the trigger strategy, any firm would always switch to the low-cost technology at the earliest possible point in time. It can be verified that, in our model, the Cournot profits to a firm which is the sole user of the high-cost technology is lower than its Cournot profits if it, too, adopted the low-cost technology.
3. The opposite effect can occur if only the firms punishing a defector are faced with higher costs while increasing output. An extreme form of this occurs when foreign firms, which are colluding with domestic firms, are up against quotas imposed by the home country. Rotemberg and Saloner (1989) show that since quotas limit the punishment that can be inflicted on a domestic firm that cheats, the level of collusion sustained will be lower with quotas than with tariffs.
4. Even in this simple model, it turns out that we cannot analytically rule out downward-sloping segments in 0D, though such a possibility is unlikely. Thus, we do not claim that the deficient capacity outcome considered here is a general result, although in our numerical simulations deficient capacity seems to be the invariable outcome.
5. See Tirole (1988, Chapter 8) for an analysis of models where overinvestment in capacity obtains when capacity is chosen non-cooperatively.
6. Scherer (1980, Chapter 20) gives an overview of the traditional antitrust case against market concentration.

REFERENCES

Carleton, D.W. and J.M Perloff (1990), *Modern Industrial Organization*, New York: Harper Collins.

Evans, R.G. (1980), 'Professionals and the Production Function: Can Competition Policy Improve Efficiency in the Licensed Professions?', in S. Rottenberg (ed.), *Occupational Licensure and Regulation*, Washington, DC: American Enterprise Institute for Policy Research.

Friedman, J. (1971), 'A Noncooperative Equilibrium for Supergames', *Review of Economic Studies*, **28**, 1–12.

Maloney, M.T., R.E. McCormick and R.D. Tollison (1979), 'Achieving Cartel Profits Through Unionization', *Southern Economic Journal*, **46**, 628–34.

Rotemberg, J.J. and G. Saloner (1989), 'Tariffs vs Quotas with Implicit Collusion', *Canadian Journal of Economics*, **22**, 237–44.

Scherer, F.M. (1980), *Industrial Market Structure and Economic Performance*, 2nd edn, Chicago: Rand-McNally.

Schumpeter, J.A. (1942), *Capitalism, Socialism and Democracy*, London: Unwin University Books.

Tirole, J. (1988), *The Theory of Industrial Organization*, Cambridge, MA: MIT Press.

APPENDIX 13A

In this appendix we derive expressions (13.5a) to (13.5c).

Using (13.1) and (13.2), we have, for $k \in \{L, H\}$,

$$\Pi_i^k(q_i, Q_{-i}) = [\alpha - \gamma(q_i + Q_{-i})]q_i - a_k q_i - b_k q_i^2. \quad (13A.1)$$

When the outputs of all firms are identical and equal to q, (13A.1) trivially yields (13.5a).

Given Q_{-i}, the optimal output of firm i is given by the solution to the first-order condition associated with the maximization of (13A.1):

$$(\alpha - a_k) - 2(\gamma + b_k)q_i - \gamma Q_{-i} = 0. \quad (13A.2)$$

Solving (13A.2) we get firm i's best response function:

$$R_i^k(Q_{-i}) = [(\alpha - a_k) - \gamma Q_{-i}]/[2(\gamma + b_k)]. \quad (13A.3)$$

Setting $q_i = R_i^k(Q_{-i})$ and $Q_{-i} = (N - 1)q$ in (13A.1), we get

$$\Pi_i^k(R_i^k((N-1)q), (N-1)q)$$

$$= [\alpha - a_k - \gamma(N-1)q]^2 / [4(\gamma + b_k)], \quad (13A.4)$$

which is expression (13.5b) in the text. This represents the optimal defection profit of firm i when all firms agree to produce an amount q each. To obtain the Cournot output, q_c^k, of each firm, we invoke symmetry and set $q_j = q_c^k$ for $j = 1,\ldots,N$, in (13A.2). Solving, we get

$$q_c^k = (\alpha - a_k)/[\gamma(N+1) + 2b_k]. \quad (13A.5)$$

Setting $q_i = q_c^k$ and $Q_{-i} = (N - 1)q_c^k$ in (13A.1) we get each firm's Cournot profits, Γ^k:

$$\Gamma^k = (\gamma + b_k)(\alpha - a_k)^2 / [\gamma(N+1) + 2b_k]^2, \quad (13A.6)$$

which is expression (13.5c) in the text. It remains to derive an expression for Φ^{LH}, which denotes the Cournot profit of a firm using the low-cost technology when all other firms are using the high-cost technology. Let q_c^L and q_c^H denote the outputs of the low-cost firm and of a typical high-cost firm, respectively, in the Cournot equilibrium. Evaluating the first-order condition

(13A.2) for the low and high-cost firms, respectively, at the Cournot equilibrium outputs, we obtain

$$(\alpha - a_L) - 2(\gamma + b_L)q_c^L - \gamma(N-1)q_c^H = 0, \tag{13A.7a}$$

$$(\alpha - a_H) - 2(\gamma + b_H)q_c^H - \gamma(N-2)q_c^H + q_c^L = 0. \tag{13A.7b}$$

Solving (13A.7a) and (13A.7b) we obtain the Cournot outputs

$$q_c^L = [\gamma(N-1)(\alpha - a_H) - (\gamma N + 2b_H)(\alpha - a_L)] / \Delta \tag{13A.8a}$$

$$q_c^H = [\gamma(\alpha - a_L) - 2(\gamma + b_L)(\alpha - a_H)] / \Delta, \tag{13A.8b}$$

where

$$\Delta \equiv \gamma^2(N-1) - 2(\gamma + b_L)(\gamma N + 2b_H). \tag{13A.8c}$$

Setting $q_i = q_c^L$ and $Q_{-i} = (N-1)q_c^H$ in (13A.1), we obtain

$$\begin{aligned} \Phi^{LH} &\equiv \Pi_i^L(q_c^L, (N-1)q_c^H) \\ &= (\alpha - a_L)q_c^L - \gamma(q_c^L + (N-1)q_c^H)q_c^L - b_L(q_c^L)^2. \end{aligned} \tag{13A.9}$$

PART II

EFFICIENCY WAGES

Economic Inquiry
Vol. XX, July 1982

AGENT COMPENSATION AND THE LIMITS OF BONDING

B. CURTIS EATON* and WILLIAM D. WHITE**

Agents in positions of trust may engage in malfeasance which is difficult to detect. This paper develops a model in which employers seek to control malfeasance by paying wages contingent on imperfect monitoring and agents may be required to pay entry fees or post bonds. We conclude that entry fees which exceed agents' assets are ineffective in controlling malfeasance. As a result, conditions exist in which it is optimal to pay agents more than their opportunity cost. Such conditions lead to an excess supply of applicants and allow employers to engage in discrimination at zero cost to themselves.

I. INTRODUCTION

Why do individuals of similar abilities and tastes receive different wages in different occupations? Adam Smith suggested four reasons in the *Wealth of Nations*. Firstly, some occupations are inherently more disagreeable than others. Secondly, some occupations are more risky. Thirdly, some occupations have higher entry costs. The first two reasons have been developed into the modern theory of equalizing wage differentials, the third into human capital theory. In all three, wage differentials across occupations are compensating differentials — in equilibrium, the occupational wage structure will be such that individuals with identical tastes and abilities will be indifferent between occupations.

Smith's fourth reason relates to trust occupations, occupations where employees act as agents for and make decisions on behalf of their employers and are in positions to engage in theft or other forms of direct or indirect malfeasance. This fourth reason has been the object of formal analysis in recent models of agent behavior.[1] These models treat trust wage differentials as another form of compensating differential. In some models, trust wage differentials directly compensate employees for the onus of responsibility and are interpreted as a special case of Smith's first reason. In others, trust wage differentials arise from contingent contracts designed to control malfeasance.

Economic models of agent behavior based on contingent contracts can be divided into two types — models in which compensation is contingent on observed productivity and models in which compensation is contingent

*The authors are respectively Professor of Economics, University of Toronto and **Assistant Professor of Economics, University of Illinois at Chicago Circle. We are grateful to Thomas E. Borcherding and an anonymous referee for helpful comments.

1. See Holmstrom (1979) or Ross (1973) for a general statement of the agent-principal problem. See Wood (1978) for a discussion of the historical development of the concept of trust wages.

on the results of monitoring for evidence of malfeasance. Piece rates and profit sharing plans are examples of first approach. (See Jensen and Meckling 1976, and Stiglitz 1975).

In the second type of model, compensation is contingent on evidence of violation of trust, such as theft or failure to work at some minimum level of effort. Possible arrangements include bonding, fines, or deferred compensation with entry fees. For instance, Jensen and Meckling (1976) suggest that employers may try to alter agents' incentives and control malfeasance by asking agents to post bonds which are forfeit if they are found engaging in violation of trust. The same sort of model can be developed for fines.[2] Even in the absence of formal contracts, implicit bonding may occur directly through investment in entry requirements which cannot be recovered if workers are fired. For example, foregone earnings (see Lazear 1979) or investments in training which workers cannot use elsewhere (see White 1980) may serve the function of a bond. These models imply that wage rates will just compensate workers for meeting the costs of formal bonds or other entry requirements and that in equilibrium workers will be indifferent between trust and non-trust jobs.

Becker and Stigler (1974) offer an alternative model. They argue that one way to deal with the agency problem is for employers to allow violations of trust and then deduct a compensating differential from workers' wages equal to the value of workers' gains if they engage in the maximum violation of trust. However, if losses to employers are greater than gains to workers, this differential will not cover the full cost of violation of trust. They suggest that in this case, employers may prefer to monitor workers and offer them a positive wage differential such that workers' expected income in trust jobs will be greater if they remain honest than if they cheat and run the risk of being fired and losing the opportunity to earn premium wages.

If employers simply elect to pay agents this type of wage premium, it will create a non-compensating differential; workers will prefer trust jobs over other types of employment. But Becker and Stigler argue that employers can recapture any non-compensating differentials by charging entry fees for trust jobs. They conclude that with entry fees, their model is equivalent to bonding and that in equilibrium workers will be indifferent between trust and non-trust jobs.

Klein and Leffler (1981) draw on the literature on fraud and self-enforcing contracts (see Darby and Karni 1973, and Telser 1980) to develop a similar model of consumer purchases. In this model, consumers cannot determine immediately if they have been cheated, but they can boycott firms (or agents) later. Klein and Leffler show that the repeat purchase mechanism can lead to conditions in which price premiums (prices which exceed the competitive price) can be used to create incentives for firms to maintain quality. Such premiums represent non-

2. See Goldberg (1977) for some interesting empirical evidence on fines and monitoring.

compensating differentials. But Klein and Leffler argue that in a competitive market, these premiums will be dissipated through investments in non-salvagable assets which will indirectly serve the function of bonds (e.g., investments in advertising to establish a reputation).

However, what if the investments necessary to dissipate wage or price premiums exceed agents' assets? Neither Becker and Stigler (1974) nor Klein and Leffler (1981) nor other researchers in the area examine the limitations of bonding, fines or entry fees. These issues are raised at a more general level in the literature on the use of collateral in enforcing contracts (see Benjamin 1978) and the literature on the economics of crime and optimal fines (see Polinsky and Shavell 1979). This literature suggests that the effectiveness of bonds and fines in controlling malfeasance is not independent of agents' assets.

In section II of this paper, we explore these issues in a one-period model of agent compensation. Employers charge agents entry fees, which are functionally equivalent to bonds, and compensation is contingent on the results of monitoring for violation of trust. We use this model to examine the incentives which an employer has to use entry fees and/or non-compensating differentials to control malfeasance, and to explore the effectiveness of entry fees which exceed agents' assets. We conclude that it will be optimal for employers to recapture wage premiums when the entry fee involved is less than or equal to agents' assets. However, entry fees (or bonds) which exceed agents' assets will be ineffective as a means of controlling malfeasance. As a result, there exist conditions in which it will be in the interest of employers to offer agents non-compensating wage differentials in connection with entry fees (or bonds) equal to the agents' assets.

In this regard, it is interesting to note that wage premiums appear common for workers in positions of trust and responsibility. Responsibility for equipment, materials, products, and the safety of others are important categories in job evaluation schemes in many industries. For example, two of the best known job evaluation plans, those of the National Metal Trades Association and the National Electrical Manufactures Association, both give overall relative weights of 20% for responsibility for non-supervisory workers in hourly rated jobs (Pigors and Myer 1977). In the specific category covering damage to materials or products in these plans, workers in a position to do over \$500 damage per incident may receive as much as five times as many "points" for this type of responsibility as workers in a position to do less than \$10 damage (Kress 1950).

In section III, we discern some implications of non-compensating differentials for labor market organization. We argue that the use of non-compensating differentials leads to the non-market allocation of trust jobs and creates situations in which employers may discriminate against applicants for these jobs on the basis of non-economic characteristics at zero cost to themselves. We also note that if workers differ with respect to assets, employers may prefer workers with greater assets. Moreover, we argue that intangible assets such as social position and esteem may serve the function of bonds as well as financial assets. Section IV presents our conclusions.

II. THE MODEL

The firm demands an entry fee, e, of an agent when he accepts a position of trust and pays the agent compensation, w, on completion of the assignment. This compensation is contingent on not apprehending the agent in violation of trust. Thus, if the agent is apprehended in violation of trust he forfeits w. The agent's gains from trust violation are either consumed during the period or effectively concealed, in a numbered account in a Swiss bank, for example. Given w and e, the agent chooses the level of trust violation, v, to maximize expected net worth. Recognizing the dependence of v on w and e, the firm chooses w and e to maximize expected profits.[3]

We distinguish two cases, defined by the magnitude of e relative to the agent's financial assets, E. Initially we arbitrarily impose the constraint that $e \leq E$ and show that there exist circumstances in which the firm will elect to pay agents more than their opportunity cost. We then go on to show that when $e > E$ there exist no feasible solutions which dominate the profit maximizing solution with $e \leq E$. Thus entry fees which exceed agent's assets serve no economic purpose.

A. *Entry Fee Constrained By Assets: $e \leq E$.*

Let $\gamma(v)$ represent the value to the agent of v units of trust violation. We measure v as the proportion of agent's working time, assumed to be constant, devoted to trust violation, and thus: $0 \leq v \leq 1$. We assume that $\gamma(v)$ is continuously twice differentiable and

$$(1) \qquad \gamma(0) = 0, \quad \gamma'(v) > 0, \quad \gamma''(v) < 0.$$

Let $\alpha(v)$ represent the probability that the agent is not apprehended in violation of trust. We assume that $\alpha(v)$ is continuously twice differentiable and

$$(2) \qquad \alpha(0) = 1, \quad \alpha(1) = 0, \quad \alpha'(v) < 0, \quad \alpha''(v) < 0.$$

With $e \leq E$ the agent can pay the entry fee either by liquidating assets or by using assets as collateral to borrow the entry fee. The discounted present value of expected earnings in the position of trust is then

$$(3) \qquad \omega(v; w, e) = -e + R[\alpha(v)w + \gamma(v)],$$

3. We assume firms never fire agents unless they are actually detected in violation of trust. This rules out the possibility that workers are fired because of monitoring errors or that firms engage in malfeasance. The possibility of malfeasance by firms raises a variety of interesting issues. For example, it may create incentives for agents to monitor their employers. However, we make no attempt to deal formally with these issues here.

where R is the reciprocal of one plus the appropriate interest rate. We assume that agents are risk neutral. Given w and e, the agent will choose v to maximize $\omega(v; w, e)$.

ω is a strictly concave function of v. Three possibilities for the agent's choice of v^*, the optimal level of v, require attention. These are illustrated in figure 1. If w is small enough $(w \leq w_1)$, the agent has so little to lose if apprehended in violation of trust that he devotes all his time to malfeasance $(v^* = 1)$, and collects only his ill-gotten gains. At the other extreme, if w is large enough $(w \geq w_2)$, the agent has so much to lose that $v^* = 0$. When $w_1 < w < w_2$ the agent equates the marginal gain from trust violation with the expected marginal loss (if detected), and $0 < v^* < 1$. In this case, dv^*/dw is negative since the expected marginal loss from trust violation increases with w. In addition, dv^*/de is zero since, having paid e, marginal gains and losses from trust violation are independent of e.[4]

However, while the magnitude of e will not affect the agent's behavior on the job, it will affect his decision to accept (or reject) the trust job. Define

$$\tilde{\omega}(w, e) \equiv \omega(v^*; w, e). \tag{4}$$

FIGURE 1

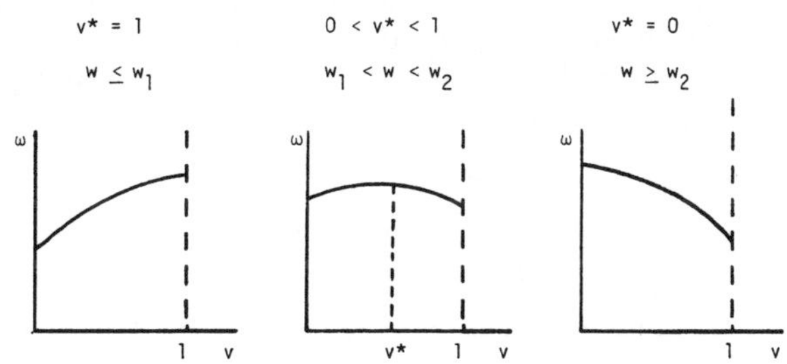

4. Differentiating (3),

$$\omega_1(v; w, e) = R[\alpha'(v)w + \gamma'(v)],$$

$$\omega_{11}(v; w, e) = R[\alpha''(v)w + \gamma''(v)] < 0.$$

The inequality follows from the restrictions in (1) and (2). If $\omega_1(1; w, e) \geq 0$, $v^* = 1$. This will occur if $w \leq w_1$, where $w_1 = -\gamma'(1)/\alpha'(1)$. If $\omega_1(0; w, e) \leq 0$, $v^* = 0$. This will occur if $w \geq w_2$, where $w_2 = -\gamma'(0)/\alpha'(0)$. If $w_1 < w < w_2$, $0 < v^* < 1$, and v^* will satisfy

$$\alpha'(v^*)w + \gamma'(v^*) = 0, \quad w_1 < w < w_2.$$

Differentiating, we have

$$\frac{dv^*}{dw} = \frac{-\alpha'(v^*)}{\alpha''(v^*)w + \gamma''(v^*)} < 0, \quad w_1 < w < w_2,$$

and

$$\frac{dv^*}{de} = 0.$$

Then the labour supply constraint is

$$\tilde{\omega}(w, e) = w_a,$$

where w_a is the discounted present value of earnings in the best alternative.

Let $\beta(v)$ represent the revenues which accrue to the firm from employing an agent. We assume that $\beta(v)$ is continuously twice differentiable and that

(5) $$\beta(1) = 0, \quad \beta'(v) < 0, \quad \beta''(v) < 0.$$

We assume perfect capital markets, so that the agent and the firm have the same discount rate, and that the firm is risk-neutral. The discounted present value of expected profits is then

(6) $$\Pi(w, e) = e + R[\beta(v^*) - w\alpha(v^*)].$$

The firm's problem is then to maximize $\Pi(w, e)$ subject to $\tilde{\omega}(w, e) \geq w_a$ and to $e \leq E$ (which we have arbitrarily imposed).

Note first of all that if gains to the worker from trust violation are symmetric with losses to the firm, violation of trust is not an economic problem. That is, if $-\beta'(v) = \gamma'(v)$, there is some level surface of $\Pi(w, e)$ which is coincident with the labor supply constraint.[5] Along the labor

5. Definition (4), and equation (3) imply:

$$\tilde{\omega}(w, e) \equiv \omega(v^*; w, e) = \begin{cases} -e + R\gamma(1) & , w \leq w_1 \\ -e + R[\alpha(v^*)w + \gamma(v^*)], & w_1 < w < w_2 \\ -e + Rw & , w \geq w_2 \end{cases}$$

Differentiating, and using the first order condition for v^* (when $0 < v^* < 1$), we have

$$\left.\frac{de}{dw}\right|_{\tilde{\omega}(w, e) = w_a} = \begin{cases} 0 & , w \leq w_1 \\ R\alpha(v^*) & , w_1 < w < w_2 \\ R & , w \geq w_2 \end{cases}$$

We can write $\Pi(w, e)$ as

$$\Pi(w, e) = \begin{cases} e + R\beta(1) & , w \leq w_1 \\ e + R[\beta(v^*) - w\alpha(v^*)] & , w_1 < w < w_2 \\ e + R[\beta(0) - w] & , w \geq w_2 \end{cases}$$

Differentiating and again using the first order condition for v^* (when $0 < v^* < 1$) we have

$$\left.\frac{de}{dw}\right|_{\Pi(w, e) = \overline{\Pi}} = \begin{cases} 0 & , w \leq w_1 \\ R[\alpha(v^*) - \frac{dv^*}{dw}(\beta'(v^*) + \gamma'(v^*))] & , w_1 < w < w_2 \\ R & , w \geq w_2 \end{cases}$$

It is then evident that some level surface of $\Pi(w, e)$ is coincident with the labor supply constraint when $-\beta'(v) = \gamma'(v)$.

supply constraint the expected present value of earnings is equal to w_a and, since what the firm loses from trust violation just equals what the agent gains, the expected value of profits is also constant on the constraint. The firm would prefer combinations of w and e above the constraint since $\Pi(w, e)$ is strictly increasing in e. The agent would prefer combinations of w and e below the constraint since $\tilde{\omega}(w, e)$ is strictly decreasing in e. Thus any point on the constraint solves the firm's problem, and both the agent and the firm are indifferent to the magnitude of trust violation.

Accordingly, we assume that losses to the firm from trust violation exceed gains to the agent ($|\beta'(v)| > \gamma'(v)$ for all v). Two cases require our attention. First, suppose that E is so large that the labour supply constraint intersects the line $e = E$ to the right of $w = w_2$. This case is pictured in figure 2. Points on or below the constraint are feasible and since profits are increasing in e the profit maximizing solution will lie on the constraint in this case. Consider now combinations of w and e on the labor supply constraint as w increases. For $w \leq w_1$, profits are constant. Since $v^* = 1$, wages are never paid, the agent receives only his ill-gotten gains, and the firm receives only the agent's entry fee. For $w_1 < w < w_2$ profits are increasing as we move along the constraint from left to right. To see this consider moving rightward from point A in figure 2. As illustrated, the slope of the level surface of $\Pi(w, e)$ at A is less than the slope of the constraint. Since $\Pi(w, e)$ is increasing in e, it follows that profits are increasing as we move rightward from point A. Intuitively, the firm moves along the constraint increasing w and e. The increase in w induces the agent to reduce v^* while the increase in e has no effect on v^*. Since the firm's losses from trust violation exceed the agent's gains, combinations of w and e which leave the agent on his constraint and decrease v^* must increase the firm's profits. When $w \geq w_2$, profits are constant as we move along the constraint. Since $v^* = 0$ the trust problem has been resolved and only the time profile of agent's remuneration and firm's profits is

FIGURE 2

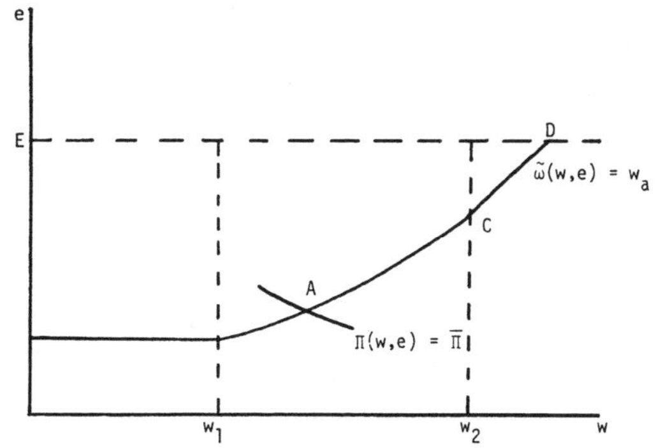

changing. Thus any point on CD in figure 2 solves the firm's maximization problem. (To verify these results see footnote 5).

Turning to the second case, suppose that E is small enough so that the labor supply constraint intersects the line $e = E$ to the left of $w = w_2$. This case is illustrated in figure 3. The argument of the previous paragraph implies that, *on the labor supply constraint*, profits are maximized at point $F(w = w_F, e = E)$. Given the constraint that $e \leq E$, and noting that $\Pi(w, e)$ increases with e, any solution to the firm's maximization problem which is not on the labor supply constraint could only be at some point like G in figure 3 $(w = w_G > w_F, e = E)$. To see that such a solution is possible, consider starting at point F, holding $e = E$ and increasing w. As long as $w < w_2$, increases in w induce the agent to reduce v^*. If the reduction in trust violation is sufficiently valuable to the employer this will be a profitable course of action. Indeed, if the firm's losses from trust violation are sufficiently large (i.e., if $\beta'(0)$ is sufficiently large) the profit maximizing solution is $e^* = E$ and $w^* = w_2$ so that $v^* = 0$. This need not be the case, and it is clearly possible to have solutions where $v^* > 0$.[6]

In this case the firm chooses to pay the agent more than his opportunity cost in order to reduce or eliminate malfeasance. Before dropping the apparently arbitrary constraint that $e < E$, it is instructive to consider some of the factors which can lead the firm to pay this type of non-compensating differential.[7] Asymmetry is necessary for this result and the greater the asymmetry between the agent's gains and the firm's losses from trust violation, the more likely is a non-compensating differential. In addition, the smaller is E, the more likely is a non-compensating differential. Indeed when $E = 0$ this will necessarily be the case.

FIGURE 3

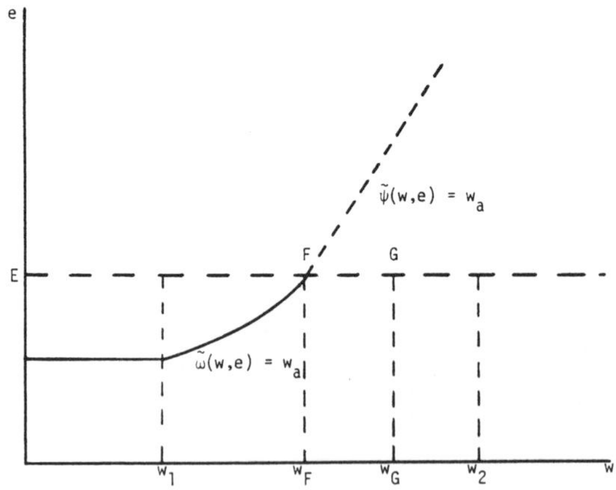

B. The Limits of Bonding: Relaxing the Constraint on e

Since the constraint that $e \leq E$ binds only in the case pictured in figure 3, we limit our discussion here to this case. Suppose the firm sets $e > E$. The agent will then be forced to (attempt to) borrow $e - E$, offering as security his expected future earnings in the position of trust. Let s denote the total dollar amount, including interest and any risk premium, which the agent must agree to repay in order to obtain a loan of $e - E$ dollars. Then the discounted present value of expected earnings in the position of trust will be

$$(7) \qquad \psi(v; w, e) = -E + R[\alpha(v)(w-s) + \gamma(v)].$$

The agent pays E of his own funds, borrows $e - E$ and pays this to the employer, incurring an obligation to repay s dollars. Note that we assume here that in the event of an apprehended violation of trust the ill-gotten gains (which the agent has consumed or concealed) will not be used for loan repayment, and the agent will instead default on the loan.

Consider the case where $0 < v^* < 1$ (which is the only case we need to examine for our purpose). v^* will then satisfy the first order condition for maximization of $\psi(v; w, e)$ by choice of v:

$$(8) \qquad \alpha'(v^*)(w - s) + \gamma'(v^*) = 0.$$

Assuming that the loan market is risk neutral, competitive and informed with respect to the probability of default, s will satisfy

$$(9) \qquad s = \frac{e - E}{R\alpha(v^*)}.$$

It should be obvious that there exist circumstances in which an informed market would not make the loan of $e - E$ on any terms. In general, if $\alpha(v^*)w < s$ the loan will never be made. See Benjamin (1978) for a discussion of this problem. However, we need not explore this issue here.

6. Differentiating $\Pi(w, e)$ with respect to w,

$$\Pi_1(w, e) = R[-\alpha(v^*) + \frac{dv^*}{dw}(\beta'(v^*) - w\alpha'(v^*))], \quad w_1 < w < w_2.$$

Using the first order condition which defines v^* this can be written as

$$\Pi_1(w, e) = R[-\alpha(v^*) + \frac{dv^*}{dw}(\beta'(v^*) + \gamma'(v^*))], \quad w_1 < w < w_2.$$

If $\beta'(v)$ is large enough it is clear that $\Pi_1(w_F, E) > 0$.

7. Here we assume that the level of monitoring is constant. Elsewhere we show that when the level of monitoring can be varied at a cost, this can, by itself, lead to non-compensating differentials. Eaton and White (1981).

Assume that the agent can borrow the required sum. Then combining (8) and (9), v^* will satisfy

$$\alpha'(v^*)[w - \frac{(e-E)}{R\alpha(v^*)}] + \gamma'(v^*) = 0. \tag{10}$$

Recall that when $e \leq E$, $dv^*/de = 0$. From (10) it is clear that when $e > E$, $dv^*/de > 0$. Intuitively, as e increases the loss to the agent when he is apprehended in violation of trust, $w - s$, decreases since s increases with e. Accordingly, dv^*/de is positive. In addition, it is clear from (10) that dv^*/dw is again negative.

Differentiating (10) we can characterize iso-violation contours, loci of w and e along which $v^* = \bar{v}$, a constant.

$$\left.\frac{de}{dw}\right|_{v^* = \bar{v}} = R\alpha(\bar{v}). \tag{11}$$

Given (9), it is evident that $w - s$ is constant along the iso-violation contours when $e > E$.

Define $\tilde{\psi}(w, e) \equiv \psi(v^*; w, e)$. Then we have

$$\tilde{\psi}(w, e) = -E + R[\alpha(v^*)[w - \frac{(e-E)}{R\alpha(v^*)}] + \gamma(v^*)]. \tag{12}$$

Differentiating (12), and using (10), we can characterize the level of surfaces of $\tilde{\psi}(w, e)$:

$$\left.\frac{de}{dw}\right|_{\tilde{\psi}(w, e) = \bar{\psi}} = R\alpha(v^*). \tag{13}$$

Comparing (11) and (13) we conclude that the level surfacẽs of $\tilde{\psi}(w, e)$ are coincident with the iso-violation contours when $e > E$. It follows immediately that the level surfaces of profits are also coincident with the iso-violation contours. Along a level surface of $\tilde{\psi}(w, e)$ the agent's compensation is constant, as is v^*; hence profits are also constant.

In figure 3 the line $\tilde{\psi}(w, e) = w_a$ represents the labor supply constraint. It follows from the argument in the previous paragraph that the firm's profits are constant along $\tilde{\psi}(w, e) = w_a$. Hence, on the constraint, the firm can do no better than point F. Assuming that G is more profitable than F, then G is preferred to any point on the constraint. Moreover, since the level surfaces of profits and $\tilde{\psi}(w, e)$, and the iso-violation contours are coincident (when $e > E$) there is no feasible solution which cannot be replicated on the line $e = E$. If the firm finds it profitable to pay agents more than their opportunity cost when we impose $e < E$, it will find it profitable to do so when this constraint is removed.

It is evident that setting $e > E$ serves no economic purpose. The intuition of this result is simple. When $e \leq E$, the agent stands to lose w if apprehended in violation of trust. Thus increasing w and e, holding $\tilde{\omega}(w, e)$ constant reduces $v^*(dv^*/dw < 0, dv^*/de = 0)$. The asymmetry of gains and losses from trust violation imply that this is a profitable strategy. When $e > E$, the agent stands to lose $w - s$ if apprehended in violation of trust. Increasing w and e, holding $\tilde{\psi}(w, e)$ constant, leaves v^* unchanged since $w - s$ remains constant — the increase in w is just offset by the increase in s. Since v^* remains constant this strategy cannot increase profits.

C. A Market With No Function.

In order to demonstrate that the effectiveness of entry-fees and/or bonds in controlling trust violation is constrained by the assets of the agent we have entertained the notion of an "informed" loan market — a competitive market where agents can borrow funds to pay entry fees in excess of their assets which is perfectly informed with respect to the probability of default. This, of course, is a rather curious financial market and one could argue that the information necessary to evaluate the probability of default is so inaccessible that such a market is not feasible.

Our purpose in entertaining the possible existence of the "informed" loan market is to demonstrate that even in the most favorable circumstances the agent's asset position is a *tight* constraint on the efficiency of entry-fees and/or bonding in controlling trust violation. In general the firm's problem is to maximize profits subject to the constraint that the agent's expected compensation be at least as great as his opportunity cost. There are no solutions to this problem which dominate the solution to the same profit maximizing problem with the added constraint that the entry fee be less than or equal to the agent's assets. Thus the "informed" loan market is a market which serves no socially useful purpose and, if there are any costs of forming such a market or transacting in it, it will not exist.

III. LABOR MARKET ORGANIZATION

If employers pay agents non-compensating differentials, the labor market will not clear for trust jobs. Instead, there will be an excess supply of workers willing to accept these jobs at the market wage. Under these conditions, the allocation of jobs will be problematic. It is clear, however, that it will not be in the interests of employers to permit the development of secondary markets for entry rights into trust jobs, since this would reduce the assets workers have available for bonding and therefore reduce the employer's ability to control violation of trust. In order for non-compensating differentials to be effective, jobs must be allocated independently of any kind of market or quasi-market system; once employers opt for non-compensating differentials to resolve problems of malfeasance, they must also opt for a non-market system for allocating trust jobs in order to preserve these differentials.[8]

If there are no differences in the tastes, abilities, or assets of workers and employers are indifferent between workers on non-economic grounds, then it would seem optimal for employers simply to select workers at random from the available labor pool. However, if it is difficult to identify qualified workers because of differences in abilities or tastes, then it is possible that it is in the interests of employers to engage in screening practices, which may involve queues. But it will not be in the interests of employers to allow queues to form purely in response to non-compensating differentials: if agents spend time waiting in queues when they could be employed, this will dissipate assets which could be used for bonding.

The non-market allocation of trust jobs may allow employers to discriminate at zero cost. Suppose that workers differ with respect to some non-economic characteristic. If there is an excess supply of qualified workers willing to accept trust jobs because of non-compensating differentials, employers will be able to discriminate between workers without affecting profits. For example, suppose employers prefer white workers over black workers. If there is an excess supply of white workers willing to accept trust jobs, then employers can discriminate against black workers at no cost to themselves.

Our model also suggests that if workers differ with respect to assets, employers will discriminate on the basis of wealth. For example, suppose that the bond necessary to prevent malfeasance exceeds the assets of at least part of the labor force. In this case, the costs of controlling malfeasance will be higher for poor workers than for rich workers, since rich workers can post larger bonds. As a result, profits will be higher if employers use rich workers.

We have limited our analysis of bonding to financial assets. However, it is clear that intangible assets such as social position and esteem may serve the function of a bond. Employers may therefore discriminate on the ground of social position when hiring agents. This obviously creates incentives for potential agents to seek such intangible assets through the

8. An example worth considering is where agents who are not observed in violation of trust have the right to sell access to the job. Suppose that P is the market value of access, and let $e^* = E$ for convenience. Then, if optimal v does not change, the loss consequent on being observed in violation of trust will be

$$w + P - \frac{P}{R\alpha(v^*)} < w.$$

The second term on the left is the value of the right to resell access and the third term the repayment on the loan of P necessary to initially obtain the job. The inequality implies that the loss consequent on being observed in violation of trust is smaller when agents sell access to the job and thus v^* will increase, which is costly to the employer. As a result it will be in the employer's interest to prevent this type of secondary market. Alternatively, if the agent pays for the job out of his assets, this depletes assets available for bonding, which reduces the employer's ability to control malfeasance.

cultivation of social connections. Church membership, positions of civic responsibility and visible involvement in charitable undertakings are possible examples. If such behaviour is distasteful, such activities dissipate potential rents to agents.[9] Conversely, employers of agents may find it advantageous to encourage social relations centered on the work place. For example, in many Japanese firms, employee's life-styles are centered on the firm and being fired involves a devastating loss of face as well as pecuniary loss.[10]

IV. CONCLUSIONS

The discussion in the previous sections suggests four principal conclusions. Firstly, entry fees or bonds which exceed agents' assets are ineffective as controls on malfeasance. As a result, conditions exist in which it will be in the interest of employers to pay agents non-compensating wage differentials in connection with entry fees or bonds in order to control malfeasance. In general our results suggest that non-compensating differentials are more likely to occur the greater the asymmetry between gains to agents and losses to employers from violation of trust and the smaller agents' assets. Secondly, if non-compensating differentials actually occur, this will create a labor market situation in which trust jobs will be preferred to other types of employment and there will be an excess supply of workers willing to accept these jobs in equilibrium. In order to preserve trust wage differentials, employers will be forced to adopt non-market systems for allocating jobs. Thirdly, the existence of an excess supply of workers willing to accept jobs with non-compensating differentials allows employers to discriminate between applicants for trust jobs on non-economic grounds at zero cost to themselves. Finally, if workers differ in respect to assets, employing richer workers may be more profitable.

Throughout we have ignored the possibility that employers may engage in malfeasance — firing workers when they have not violated trust. This possibility may explain why bonding and/or entry fees appear to be rare. It also suggests that non-compensating differentials may be an important tool for controlling malfeasance — if employer malfeasance is an important problem, workers will not pay entry fees. These are mere speculations which require further study. When we entertain the notion that employers may engage in malfeasance we have a problem in which both employees and employers are agents and principals. A marriage of the analysis in this paper and the analysis of Klein and Leffler, which focuses on the repeat purchase mechanism, is one way to approach this dual agency problem.

9. Recall Mark Twain's definition of hell — "sitting in church for eternity."

10. In addition, sociologists have suggested that employers, occupational groups, or society at large may seek to encourage the development of values like honesty and loyalty to prevent malfeasance. See Kahn and Katz (1966) for a general discussion of issues in the motivation of workers, and Parsons (1968) or Moore (1970) for discussions of professionalism.

REFERENCES

Becker, G., and Stigler, G., "Law Enforcement, Malfeasance, and Compensation of Enforcers," *Journal of Legal Studies*, January 1974, *3*, 1-18.

Benjamin, D. K., "The Use of Collateral to Enforce Debt Contracts," *Economic Inquiry*, July 1978, *16*, 333-359.

Darby, M. R., and Karni, E., "Free Competition and the Optimal Amount of Fraud," *Journal of Law and Economics*, April 1973, *16*, 67-88.

Eaton, B. C., and White, W. D., "The Economy of High Wages: An Agency Problem," (mimeo), August 1981.

Goldberg, I., "Enforcement of Work Discipline: An Economic Analysis," unpublished paper, 1977 (mimeographed).

Holmstrom, B., "Moral Hazard and Observability," *The Bell Journal of Economics*, Spring 1979, *10*, 74-91.

Jensen, M., and Meckling, W., "The Theory of the Firm: Managerial Behavior, Agency Costs and Ownership Structure," *Journal of Financial Economics*, October 1976, *3*, 305-360.

Kahn, L. R., and Katz, P., *The Social Psychology of Organization*, Wiley, New York, 1966.

Klein, B., and Leffler, K. B., "The Role of Market Forces in Assuring Contractual Performance," *Journal of Political Economy*, August 1981, *89*, 615-641.

Kress, A., "Sound Wage Payment Policies," in M. J. Dooher and V. Marquis (eds.) *The American Management Association Handbook of Wage and Salary Administration*, American Management Association, New York, 1950.

Lazear, E., "Why is There Mandatory Retirement?" *Journal of Political Economy*, December 1979, *87*, 1261-1284.

Moore, W. E., *The Professions: Rules and Roles*, Russell Sage, New York, 1970.

Parsons, T., "Professions," *International Encyclopedia of the Social Sciences*, ed., D. L. Sills, New York, MacMillan Co., 1968, *12*, 536-47.

Pigors, P., and Myer, C., *Personnel Administration: A Point of View and a Method*, 8th edition, McGraw-Hill, New York, 1977.

Polinsky, A.M., and Shavell, S., "The Optimal Tradeoff Between the Probability and Magnitude of Fines," *American Economic Review*, December 1979, *69*, 880-891.

Ross, S. A., "The Economic Theory of Agency: The Principal's Problem," *American Economic Review*, May 1973, *63*, 134-139.

Smith, A., *An Inquiry into the Nature and Causes of the Wealth of Nations*, Modern Library, New York, 1937.

Stiglitz, J., "Incentives, Risk, and Information: Notes Towards a Theory of Hierarchy," *Bell Journal of Economics*, Autumn 1975, *6*, 552-579.

Telser, L. G., "A Theory of Self-Enforcing Agreements," *Journal of Business*, 1980, *53*, 27-44.

White, W. D., "On-the-Job Screening and Investments in General and Specific Training," *Southern Economic Journal*, July 1980, *47*, 14-20.

Wood, A., *A Theory of Pay*, Cambridge University Press, Cambridge, U.K., 1978.

Economica, **50**, 175–181

The Economy of High Wages: an Agency Problem

By Curtis Eaton and William D. White

University of Toronto and University of Illinois

Introduction

The textbook treatment of the labour input implicitly assumes that employees have no choice with respect to the level of effort they supply or, alternatively, that either effort or output can be costlessly observed: *a unit of an employee's time is a unit of labour.* In most situations employees have some latitude with respect to the effort they supply, and monitoring of effort and output is costly. In this paper we examine the agency problem that arises in these circumstances.

The agent (employee) is assumed to maximize expected utility, which depends on wages and effort (a "bad"). We assume that output is a deterministic function of effort, that either effort or output can be accurately monitored, and that monitoring is costly. The firm's problem is to select a level of monitoring and a compensation package that will minimize the cost of obtaining a desired level of effort, given the cost of monitoring, the agent's preferences and the agent's opportunity cost of accepting employment with the firm (his labour supply constraint).

The firm chooses a compensation scheme from the set in which compensation is contingent on effort if the agent is monitored, and is equal to a standard wage otherwise. Our reason for choosing this particular set of compensation schemes is that, both by custom and law, the burden of proof in labour contracts is on the firm to demonstrate that the agent has not fulfilled his contract. Thus workers receive the standard wage unless there is evidence that they have not supplied the agreed-upon level of effort.

There is an extensive literature on the use of monitoring and contingent contracts to influence agent behaviour (see for example Harris and Raviv, 1978; Holmstrom, 1979; and Mirrlees, 1976). In this literature, issues of risk-sharing and supervision are intermixed. In this paper we develop a framework in which there is no risk of any kind to be shared. Thus our focus here is exclusively on the issue of supervision.

We discover that some non-zero level of monitoring is necessary to induce agents to supply non-zero effort, from which we infer that costly monitoring, in the absence of any risk, gives rise to a quite basic agency problem. Perhaps more surprisingly, we encounter situations in which it is cost-minimizing for the firm to offer compensation schemes with a higher utility payoff than the agent could obtain in his best alternative activity (thus our title—"The Economy of High Wages"). In the concluding section we relate this and other results of our analysis to the literature on agency problems, and speculate on the possible significance of our results.

I. The Model

To emphasize the existence of a non-trivial—indeed, we believe fundamental—agency problem associated only with the fact that monitoring (information) is costly, we assume that output is a deterministic function of effort, that the price of output is known with certainty, and that output or effort can be accurately observed at some positive cost. Whether the firm chooses to observe output or effort will, of course, be determined by relative costs. For simplicity we focus on monitoring effort.

We examine the following problem. The firm wants to induce an agent to supply a fixed level of effort, $\bar{e}$, at minimum cost to the firm. The agent maximizes expected utility, and his utility is decreasing in effort, e, and increasing in income, y:

$$(1) \qquad u = U(e, y), \qquad U_1(e, y) < 0, \qquad U_2(e, y) > 0.$$

Further $U(e, y)$ is differentiable and quasi-concave. The agent's best alternative offers utility level $\bar{u}$. The firm chooses a probability of monitoring the agent's effort, p, and a compensation scheme.

The compensation scheme is characterized by a "standard wage", $w \geq 0$, and a function of observed effort, $v(e)$. The domain of $v(e)$ is the non-negative real numbers excluding $\bar{e}$, and its range is the non-negative real numbers. If the agent is monitored, and if $e \neq \bar{e}$, the agent receives $v(e)$. If the agent is not monitored, or if he is monitored and $e = \bar{e}$, his compensation is w.[1]

Suppose the agent does supply $\bar{e}$, the desired level of effort. His utility would then be $U(\bar{e}, w)$, since he would be paid w with certainty. Define the agent's maximum utility over $e \neq \bar{e}$ as

$$(2) \qquad G\{v(e), p, w\} = \max_{e \neq \bar{e}} [pU\{e, v(e)\} + (1-p)U(e, w)].$$

A necessary condition for the agent to choose to supply $\bar{e}$ is then

$$(3) \qquad U(\bar{e}, w) \geq G\{v(e), p, w\}$$

since the agent chooses e to maximize expected utility. We assume that when (3) holds with equality the agent prefers to supply $\bar{e}$; other things equal, the agent prefers to fulfill his contract. Inequality (3) is a *performance constraint*—it must be satisfied if the agent is to supply $\bar{e}$. given p and the compensation scheme. In addition we have the standard labour supply constraint:

$$(4) \qquad U(\bar{e}, w) \geq \bar{u}.$$

Let m be the expected costs of monitoring effort. We assume that these costs are an increasing and convex function of p: $m = M(p)$. The firm's problem is then to choose p, w and the function $v(e)$ to minimize

$$(5) \qquad C(p, w) = w + M(p)$$

subject to the performance constraint (inequality (3)) and the labour supply constraint (inequality (4)). The new wrinkle here is clearly the performance constraint, which we examine and simplify in the next section.

II. The Performance Constraint

Observe that

$$(6) \qquad \min_{v(e)} G\{v(e), p, w\} = \max_{e \neq \bar{e}} \{pU(e, 0) + (1-p)U(e, w)\}$$

since $v(e) \geq 0$ by assumption and $U(e, y)$ is increasing in y. That is, $v(e) = 0$ (for all e in the domain of v) minimizes $G\{v(e), p, w\}$. Moreover, the maximization on the right in (6) is easily solved since $U(e, w)$ is decreasing in e. Thus

$$(7) \qquad \min_{v(e)} G\{v(e), p, w\} = pU(0, 0) + (1-p)U(0, w).$$

Now reconsider the firm's minimization problem. The function $v(e)$ occurs only in the performance constraint, inequality (3). Note that, by minimizing $G\{v(e), p, w\}$ with respect to $v(e)$, we maximize the set of p and w that satisfies the performance constraint. Thus $v(e) = 0$ is a solution to the firm's cost minimization problem with respect to $v(e)$. Note, however, that this solution is not unique. For example, $v(e) = 0$ for $e < \bar{e}$ and $v(e) = w$ for $e > \bar{e}$ is also a solution.

Choosing $v(e) = 0$, we can then simplify the performance constraint to

$$(8) \qquad U(\bar{e}, w) \geq pU(0, 0) + (1-p)U(0, w).$$

The firm's problem has been correspondingly simplified: choose p and w to minimize $C(p, w)$ subject to (4) and (8).

III. Results

Given that monitoring costs are increasing and convex in p, $C(p, w)$ is quasi-convex: that is, the level surfaces of $C(p, w)$ are concave to the origin, as illustrated in Figure 1. The properties of the performance constraint are more complex, and perhaps more interesting.

Note first that, for all $\bar{e} > 0$, there exists an $\varepsilon > 0$ such that the performance constraint cannot be satisfied for $p < \varepsilon$. To see this simply observe that when $p = 0$ the right-hand side of (8) is strictly greater than the left. Thus we have

Proposition. A strictly positive probability of monitoring is necessary to induce agents to supply positive effort (when the cat's away, with certainty, the mice will play).

It is then obvious that costly monitoring alone implies the existence of a non-trivial agency problem. This we take to be the essence of "supervision". It is perhaps interesting, if mildly disturbing, to observe that this type of supervision represents a deadweight loss: if we could devise "better contracts" we could eliminate supervision and obtain the same effort with fewer resources.

We can show that, in some neighborhood of $p = 1$, the slope of the performance constraint is negative ($dp/dw < 0$) and there exists some segment of the constraint over which it is convex to the origin as well.[2] In Figure 2 we illustrate three possible curves of the performance constraint. On and to the right of the constraint the agent supplies $\bar{e}$ units of effort, while he supplies zero to the left of the constraint. The performance constraint may be convex to the origin throughout, as illustrated in curve 3. For example, if

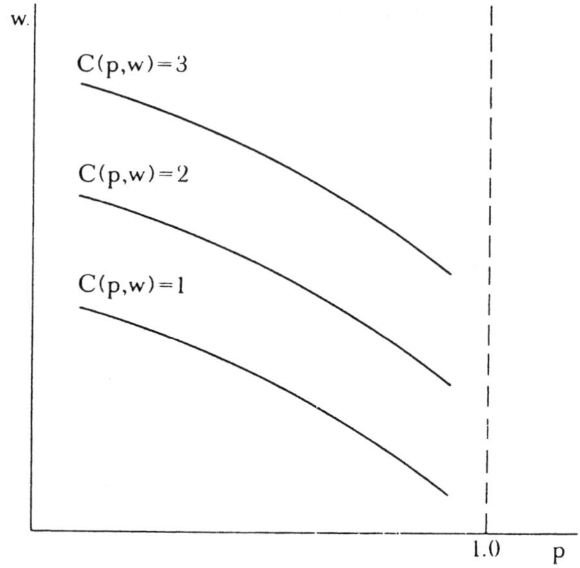

FIGURE 1

$U(e, w) = (E - e) + (E - e)w + w$, where $E > 0$, the constraint is convex throughout. Alternatively, it may be negatively sloped but concave over part of its range (as in curve 2), and it may even become positively sloped over the upper part of its range (as in curve 1).

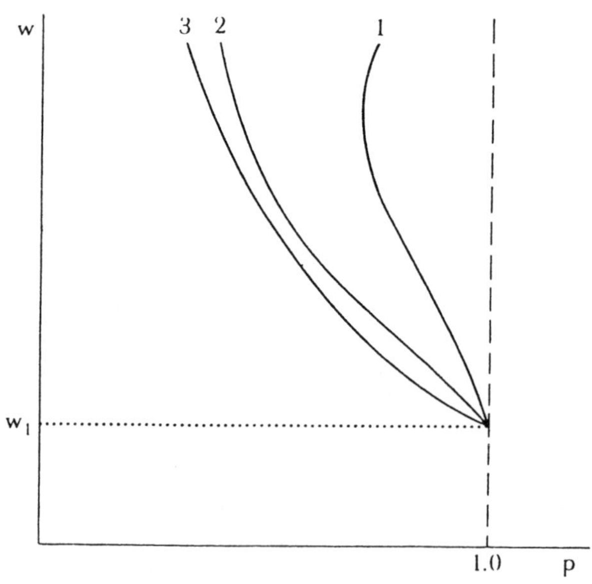

FIGURE 2

It is now quite easy to characterize solutions to the firm's cost-minimization problem. Let $\hat{p}$ and $\hat{w}$ minimize $C(p, w)$ subject only to the performance constraint.[3] The point $(\hat{p}, \hat{w})$ will obviously lie on the convex portion of the performance constraint, if $\hat{p} < 1$.

Define

$$\tilde{w} = \{w \mid U(\bar{e}, w) = \bar{u}\} \tag{9}$$

and

$$\tilde{p} = \{p \mid U(\bar{e}, \tilde{w}) = pU(0, 0) + (1-p)U(0, \tilde{w})\}. \tag{10}$$

Denote the solution to the firm's problem by p^* and w^*. Then

$$\left.\begin{array}{l} p^* = \hat{p} \\ w^* = \hat{w} \end{array}\right\} \quad \text{if } \hat{w} > \tilde{w} \tag{11}$$

and

$$\left.\begin{array}{l} p^* = \tilde{p} \\ w^* = \tilde{w} \end{array}\right\} \quad \text{if } \tilde{w} \geq \hat{w}. \tag{12}$$

We have illustrated the first possibility in Figure 3. In this case the firm chooses to offer the agent a compensation package which is strictly preferred to his best alternative: $U(\bar{e}, w^*) > U(\bar{e}, \tilde{w}) = \bar{u}$. The reason is simple. At wage $\tilde{w}$, the firm must choose $p = \tilde{p}$ to induce the agent to perform (to supply $\bar{e}$). But monitoring is costly, and since the performance constraint is negatively sloped at $(\tilde{p}, \tilde{w})$, the firm has the option of decreasing p and increasing w along the performance constraint. If monitoring is costly enough (as it is in

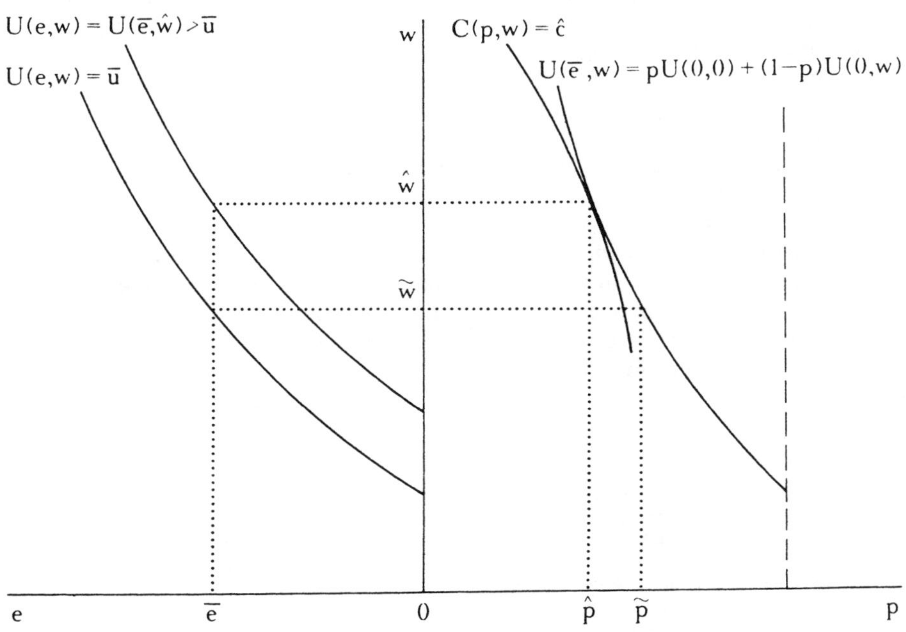

FIGURE 3

Figure 3), this option will decrease the firm's costs. This is the "economy of high wages" alluded to in our title—in this case, "high wages" are a substitute for costly monitoring.

Our analysis to this point has assumed that the firm desired a fixed level of effort from an agent. A further problem concerns the least-cost way of obtaining effort *per se*—that is, the least-cost way of obtaining effort when the firm is indifferent to the level of effort supplied by an individual agent. This problem is easily managed using the apparatus developed here, and the salient results of our analysis survive—the "economy of high wages" is a possibility and some supervision is necessary to extract effort.

IV. Conclusions

One solution to agency problems discussed by Becker and Stigler (1974), Jensen and Meckling (1976) and others is implicit or explicit bonding through the use of bonds, fines, entry fees or investments in entry requirements which agents cannot recover if they are found in violation of contract. Such solutions to the agency problem do not involve the "economy of high wages". Consider the economy of high wages case in our model. The firm could set $w^* = \hat{w}$ and $p^* = \hat{p}$ *and require the agent to pay an entry fee equal to* $\hat{w} - \tilde{w}$. Alternatively, if we relaxed the restriction that $v(e)$ be non-negative, $v(e) = \tilde{w} - \hat{w}$ (for all e in the domain of v) would accomplish the same result. Either scheme would leave the agent on his labour supply constraint and would satisfy the performance constraint. Both schemes, of course, ignore the possibility that firms themselves will violate the contract—firing the agent when he actually supplies $\bar{e}$. Apparently, bonding raises yet another agency problem—the employer as an agent for his bonded employees. This observation may explain why we do not widely observe bonding.

Further, as Eaton and White (1982) demonstrate, the effectiveness of bonding is limited by an agent's assets if there are bankruptcy constraints. In the current model, restrict $v(e)$ to be greater than or equal to $-A$, where A is the value of the agent's assets. It is obvious that the "economy of high wages" case survives.

In this case the labour market will not clear, which gives rise to a variety of problems associated with the non-market allocation of jobs. These problems are discussed at length in Eaton and White (1982). Here we may mention the possibility that employers can indulge their own prejudices at no economic cost to themselves, and we may have an important insight into the phenomenon of discrimination in labour markets.

NOTES

[1] An equivalent representation of this compensation scheme is that the firm chooses a function $v(e)$ with domain $e \geq 0$, and pays $v(e)$ with probability p and $v(\bar{e})$ with probability $(1-p)$. In this case $v(\bar{e})$ is the "standard" wage. Although this notation is more compact, the former is more convenient.

[2] Solving the performance constraint for p, we have

$$p = \frac{U(\bar{e}, w) - U(0, w)}{U(0, 0) - U(0, w)}.$$

Differentiating, we have

$$\frac{dp}{dw}=\frac{U_2(0,w)\{U(\bar{e},w)-U(0,0)\}+U_2(\bar{e},w)\{U(0,0)-U(0,w)\}}{\{U(0,0)-U(0,w)\}^2}.$$

Observe that when $p=1$, $U(\bar{e},w)=U(0,0)$ is on the constraint. In addition, $U(0,w)>U(0,0)$ for $w>0$ (which is necessary to satisfy the constraint). Thus dp/dw is negative in some neighbourhood of $p=1$. The constraint is undefined in some neighbourhood of $p=0$ and it is defined for all $w\geq w_1=\{w|U(\bar{e},w)=U(0,0)\}$. This information, together with the differentiability of the constraint, implies that its curve must have a segment over which both $dp/dw<0$ and the curve is convex to the origin.

[3] There are two cases to consider. If $M'(1)$ (the marginal cost of monitoring when $p=1$) is small enough, $\hat{p}=1$ and $\hat{w}=w_1$, where $w_1=\{w|U(\bar{e},w)=U(0,0)\}$. If $M'(1)$ is large enough, then $(\hat{p},\hat{w})$ lies on the convex portion of the performance constraint and $\hat{p}<1$, $\hat{w}>w_1$. Notice that if the performance constraint is convex throughout, then $\hat{w}$ is not bounded above: given any $w\geq w_1$, there exists an $M(\hat{p})$ that makes that $w=\hat{w}$.

REFERENCES

Becker, G. and Stigler, G. (1974). Law enforcement, malfeasance, and compensation of Enforcers. *Journal of Legal Studies*, **3**, 1–18.

Eaton, B. C. and White, W. (1982). Agent compensation and the limits of bonding. *Economic Inquiry*, **20**, 330–343.

Harris, M. and Raviv, A. (1978). Some results on incentive contracts with applications to education and employment, health insurance, and law enforcement. *American Economic Review*, **68**, 20–30.

Holmstrom, B. (1979). Moral hazard and observability. *Bell Journal of Economics*, **10**, 74–91.

Jensen, M. and Meckling, W. (1976). The theory of the firm: managerial behaviour, agency costs and ownership structure. *Journal of Financial Economics*, **3**, 305–360.

Mirrlees, J. (1976). The optimal structure of incentives and authority within an organization. *Bell Journal of Economics*, **7**, 105–131.

[15]

Wealth: the support of institutions and the limits of control[*]

with William D. White[**]

Abstract

This paper focuses on the roles of society's wealth and its distribution in systems of economic control. The analysis focuses on some simple models of crime and punishment. We show that the wealthier an individual is the less costly it is to devise a control mechanism which induces the individual to obey the law. We discover situations in which redistribution of income is Pareto-improving because the redistribution reduces the cost of inducing all individuals to respect the rights of property, allowing individuals to conduct their private affairs more efficiently.

1. Introduction

One of the fundamental insights of economics is that institutions, properly conceived, can create wealth. Institutions of private property are the obvious example. Such institutions, defining property rights and establishing a framework for their transfer, play a key role in facilitating trade and production, enabling individuals to appropriate the fruits of their labours and creating incentives accordingly.

More precisely, we should say that institutions have the potential to create wealth. The extent to which they actually perform this function depends on their costs of operation. Ironically, a major determinant of these costs is society's wealth and its distribution.

Fundamentally, institutions are systems of control. Their purpose is to alter individual incentives – for instance, to induce some individuals to choose action A in preference to B when, in the absence of institutional intervention, B would be preferred. Ultimately, the effectiveness of such systems of control rests on the cooperation of the individuals subject to them – on the institutionally constrained choices of individuals. Cooperation may be induced by threat of loss. For example, property rights may be enforced through sanctions for theft or fraud. Monitoring will, of course, be necessary to make these sanctions effective. Beyond this, the effectiveness of sanctions will be limited by the extent that individuals can be placed at risk; a person who has nothing to lose has no reason to cooperate.

Accordingly, the effectiveness of economic sanctions will be limited by wealth. The greater an individual's wealth, the greater the potential social bond and hence the greater the opportunities for inducing cooperation. Indeed, it may be optimal to combine the carrot with the stick and transfer wealth to individuals in order to extend the basis for control.

---

[*] Working Papers in Economics, Hoover Institution, E-86-26.

[**] University of Illinois, USA.

Both bonds and wealth transfers have been discussed extensively in the efficiency wage literature (see Stiglitz, 1984; Yellen, 1984) and also in the agency literature (see Sappington, 1979). The focus, however, has been on the implications for labour market organization and unemployment. There has been relatively little analysis of the role of wealth in defining or extending the limits of control.

How robust, for instance, are standard results regarding the role of wealth in the face of changes in the character of monitoring or the control system? Beyond this, Marxian economists criticize standard models of control, which Bowles (1985) dubs 'neo-Hobbsian', for ignoring the division between labour and capital. Whether or not one accepts this critique, it is symptomatic of a more general feature of control models: with a few exceptions, such as Eswaran and Kotwal (1984, 1985), they do not consider issues of distribution at all.

Using some very simple models of crime and punishment, we explore the role of wealth in this paper at two levels. First, we explore the role that an individual's wealth plays in the effort to control that individual's behaviour. Second, we explore the role which the distribution of wealth plays in a simple control system.

Concerns about the organization of firms have motivated much of the control literature. We make no attempt to consider questions of production or exchange here. Our focus is exclusively on issues of control. This is not accidental. The basic control problem is distinct in its own right. Much may be learned from studying it in its pure form, while attempting to examine it in the context of the firm may obscure important issues.

The starting point for our analysis is a standard problem in the economics of control: how may an individual's wealth serve as a bond, either explicitly or implicitly, when society can monitor behaviour and impose sanctions? Using an agency framework, we find in Section 2 that, where monitoring costs are non-negligible, the agent's wealth directly defines the limits of control. As is well known, the optimal sanction will be equal to the agent's total wealth which, implicitly, serves as a bond. In Section 3 we demonstrate that it may be efficient to extend the limits of control through conditional wealth transfers to the agent (the standard efficiency wage result).

In Sections 4 and 5 we explore the robustness of these results. We discover that the optimal sanction may be less than the agent's wealth when, for example, there is a significant possibility that agents may be misapprehended or there is a desperate option available, such as flight. The basic efficiency wage result is, however, robust. Conditional wealth transfers may still increase efficiency even when opportunities for bonding have not been exhausted.

In Section 6 we extend our analysis to consider issues of distribution using a simple two-person, two-period model. We discover that the limits of control systems may be defined not only by the absolute levels of wealth of the individuals who are subject to them, but by the distribution of wealth as well. Moreover, wealth transfers may be mutually beneficial and increase the efficiency of the control system. We conclude with a discussion of the possible implications of our findings.

2. A standard problem

To set the stage we consider a standard problem in the economics of control. We imagine that some individual, whom we will call the 'agent', is faced with the temptation to commit some anti-social act. By saying that the act is *anti-social* we mean that if society (the principal) could induce the agent to resist temptation at no cost to anyone it would choose to do so. It is convenient to think of this anti-social act as an illegal act.

We focus on two questions. First, what can we do to induce the agent to resist temptation, that is, to comply with the law? In other words, given the controls we have on the agent's behaviour (policing and fines, for example), we ask what values of the control parameters will induce the agent to resist temptation. Second, what can we say about the optimal social policy? What are the best values of the control parameters?

For simplicity, we suppose that the temptation facing the agent is the opportunity to steal T dollars. Initially we confine our attention to two control parameters: p, the probability that the agent will be apprehended if he/she does succumb to temptation; and s, a monetary sanction or fine which will be imposed in the event that the agent is apprehended. The analysis extends in a straightforward way to non-monetary temptations and penalties.

If the agent resists temptation, his/her utility will be $U(W)$ with probability 1, where $U(\cdot)$ is a Neumann–Morgenstern utility function and W is the agent's initial wealth. If he/she does not, with probability p his/her utility will be $U(W-s)$ and with probability $(1-p)$ it will be $U(W+T)$. Here we suppose that full restitution occurs if the agent is apprehended. Assuming that the agent understands the choice problem which temptation presents and that he/she knows the relevant parameter values, the agent will resist temptation if and only if

$$U(W) \geq pU(W-s) + (1-p)\, U(W+T). \tag{1}$$

We may think of this inequality as a *compliance constraint* – when it is satisfied, the agent complies with the law. As a convenience, we suppose that when equation (1) holds with equality, the agent resists temptation.

We assume that $U'(\cdot)$ is positive – more wealth is preferred to less – and that $U''(\cdot)$ is negative – the agent is risk averse. Further we interpret initial wealth, W, in the broadest possible sense. It includes, for example, human capital as well as financial wealth. Given this interpretation, it is clear that W is an upper bound on the effective sanction which can be imposed on the agent.

We then have an answer to our first question, which we illustrate in Figure 1. Any point in the shaded area will induce the agent to resist temptation. We have plotted combinations of p and s such that the compliance constraint, inequality (1), holds with equality. Observe that this line intersects the p axis where p is equal to 1 – if the fine is zero the compliance constraint demands that the probability of apprehension be one. Observe also that this line lies everywhere above the s axis – if the probability of apprehension is zero, it is impossible to satisfy inequality (1) even if W, and hence the maximum effective sanction, is arbitrarily large. This, of course, means that $\overline{p}$ in Figure 1 is necessarily positive – $\overline{p}$ is implicitly defined by

$$U(W) = \overline{p}U(0) + (1-\overline{p})\, U(W+T). \tag{2}$$

Finally, observe that the compliance constraint is downward sloping. Consider, for example, point A in Figure 1. If we increase the sanction by Δs, the right side of equation (1) decreases since the agent has more to lose in the event that he/she is apprehended. We can therefore decrease p, which increases the right side of equation (1), while still satisfying the constraint. The economic interpretation of the fact that the compliance constraint is negatively sloped is that p and s are substitutes in the effort to control the agent's behaviour. Beginning at any point on the constraint where s is less than W, if we increase either s or p we can decrease the other without violating the constraint. A sufficient condition for p and s to be substitutes is that $U(\cdot)$ is increasing in its argument. Once s is equal to or exceeds W, they are no longer substitutes. Increasing s, which we can regard as the nominal sanction, no longer increases the effective sanction.

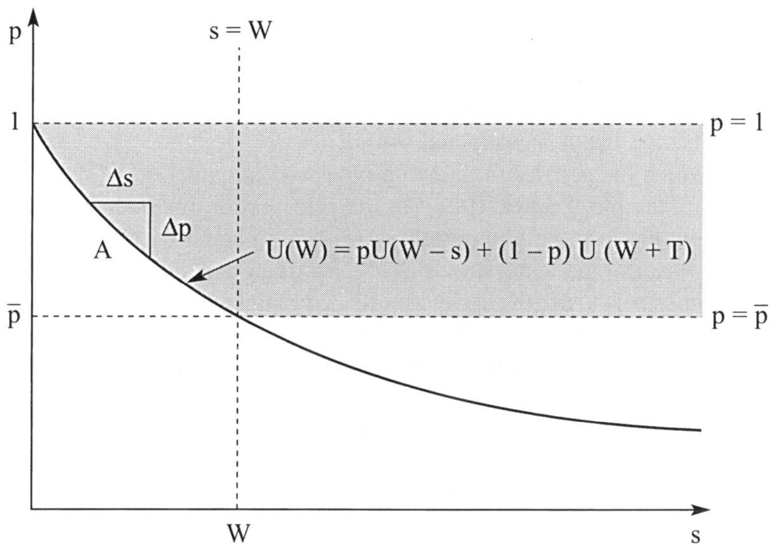

Figure 1

What can we say about the best policy in this problem? We obviously need to know something more about the social objective function – so far we know only that if we could deter the act at no cost we would choose to do so. We also need to know something about the costs of running systems of control. Both operating the monitoring system which produces p and imposing the sanction s may be costly. For example, operating a police department may involve substantial real resources. We consider only monitoring costs since sanctions are never imposed in our model if the control problem is optimally solved.[1] Denote the costs of monitoring by $M(p)$ and assume that $M(p)$ is positive for any positive p – no free policing – and that $M'(p)$ is also positive – the marginal cost of p is positive. Assume also that, *other things equal*, our social objective is to minimize the cost of policing. Two propositions about the best policy follow from these assumptions.

First, the best policy may be to choose p equal to zero, inducing or allowing non-compliance. In order to achieve compliance, we require that p be no smaller than $\bar{p}$

and hence to achieve compliance is costly. If $M(\overline{p})$ is large enough, the cost of achieving compliance may dominate the social cost of the act itself. In this case p equal to zero is the best policy.

Second, if we choose to induce compliance, then the best policy is to choose $\overline{p}$ and a sanction greater than or equal to W. That is,

$$p^* = \overline{p} \tag{3.1}$$

$$s^* \geq W. \tag{3.2}$$

Two observations lead to this conclusion. First, given that we want to induce compliance, the best solution will lie on the lower boundary of the shaded area in Figure 1 since the marginal cost of p is positive. Second, given that we achieve compliance, the magnitude of s itself is of no concern to anyone since the agent resists temptation and the fine is never paid nor received. The sanction is, however, a substitute for policing. As long as s is less than W, by substituting s for p along the constraint in Figure 1, we reduce costs since p is costly and s is not.

This solution, in which the penalty for non-compliance is maximal, is, of course, well known (see, for example, Posner, 1977). In the next section we maintain this basic model and show that in some circumstances we can do better by choosing to augment the agent's wealth (and again imposing the maximal penalty). That is, we show that it is sometimes best to use the carrot as well as the stick. Here we are simply adapting arguments from the 'efficiency wage' literature (see, for example, Eaton and White, 1983; Shapiro and Stiglitz, 1984). In subsequent sections we alter the basic model, showing that the maximal penalty result is not robust and that the carrot continues to be an attractive control in some cases.

3. Wealth transfer as an additional control

Totally differentiating equation (2) with respect to $\overline{p}$ and W, we have

$$d\overline{p}/dW = [(1 - \overline{p})\, U'(W + T) - U'(W)] \,/\, [U(W + T) - U(0)]$$

which is negative since $U'(\cdot)$ is positive and $U''(\cdot)$ is negative. That is, added wealth reduces the minimum probability of apprehension necessary to induce compliance. An implication of this is that additional wealth in the agent's pocket has value to society over and above the value of the additional wealth to the agent. This suggests that society might find it useful to augment the agent's wealth simply because added wealth reduces the cost of controlling his/her behaviour.

Letting t denote the magnitude of wealth transferred to the agent, the compliance constraint can be written as

$$U(W + t) \geq pU(W - s + t) + (1 - p)\, U(W + T + t). \tag{4}$$

We now have three controls on the agent's behaviour – p, s and t. The question we wish to ask is whether it ever makes sense to choose a positive value of t for the sole purpose of controlling the agent's behaviour. (There may, of course, be other reasons for transferring wealth to the agent but they are not a matter of concern here.)

Obviously we would choose t greater than zero only in the case where we intended to induce compliance. As above, since s will never be paid nor received in this case, its magnitude is of no direct concern to anyone. That is, it is not an argument of the social objective function. However, since the sanction is again a substitute for policing, which is costly, its value will be chosen to achieve the maximum effective sanction:

$$s^* \geq W + t. \tag{5}$$

Using this result we can rewrite the compliance constraint:

$$U(W + t) \geq pU(0) + (1 - p)\, U(W + T + t). \tag{6}$$

In Figure 2 we plot the compliance constraint for this problem. It is satisfied for any combination of t and p in the shaded area. Since the marginal cost of p is positive, the best policy will obviously lie on the lower boundary of this area. Let us focus on the lower boundary. It is downward sloping and, hence, given that we always choose the maximal penalty, t is a substitute for p in this problem. A sufficient condition for this result is that the agent be risk averse. The result that t is a substitute for p is intuitive. Choosing the maximal penalty means that the wealth transfer is effectively a conditional transfer – from equation (6) we see that the agent will realize the transfer if he/she resists temptation or if he/she succumbs and is not apprehended, but he/she will not realize it if he/she succumbs and is apprehended. Risk aversion implies that $U'(W + t)$ exceeds $U'(W + T + t)$, and hence any wealth transfer increases the utility associated with compliance by more than it increases the utility associated with non-compliance, even if p is arbitrarily small. Thus if the constraint is initially satisfied

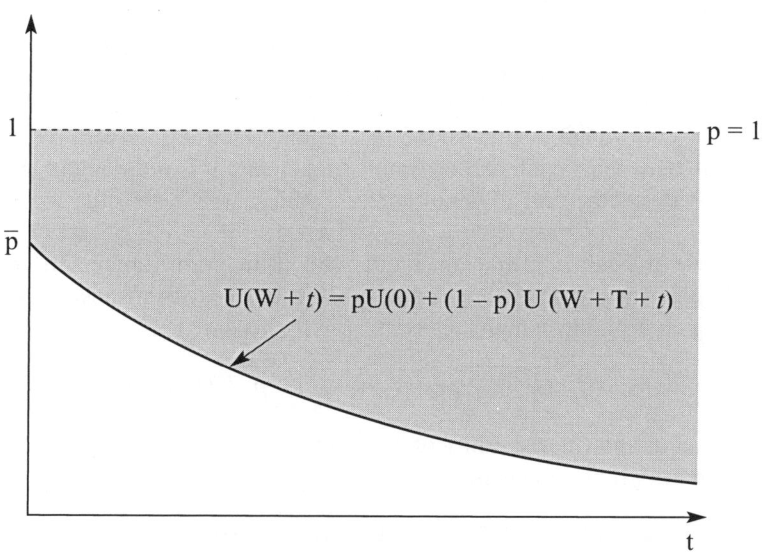

Figure 2

with equality and we increase t, compliance is then strictly preferred to non-compliance, which allows us to decrease p without violating the constraint. That is, as controls on the agent's behaviour, t and p are substitutes.

Thus we can substitute t for p. Whether we would choose to do so depends upon the relative costs of the two controls and upon how t enters our objective function. It is, however, clear that there exist circumstances in which we would choose a positive t. Suppose, for the purpose of developing an example, that the over-riding social objective is to induce the agent to comply, and that the social objective function gives zero weight to the agent him-/herself. Then the social control problem reduces to the following: choose p and t to minimize $M(p) + t$, subject to the compliance constraint [inequality (6)]. That is, minimize the aggregate cost of achieving compliance. The optimal transfer, t^*, will be positive if for small t the reduction in $M(p)$ (as we move down the compliance constraint in Figure 1) is sufficiently large.

We have discovered two propositions: (i) *ceterus paribus*, the larger an agent's wealth, the less costly it is to control his/her behaviour for the simple reason that the wealthier he or she is the more he or she has to lose if he or she does not comply, always supposing that we choose the maximum effective sanction; (ii) this effect may be strong enough that it is sensible to augment the agent's wealth, even when we completely discount the value of the transfer to the agent. In the balance of the paper we examine the robustness of these results.

4. Apprehension and misapprehension

In the preceding sections we assumed that the policing mechanism was imperfect in only one respect – given non-compliance, the agent would not be apprehended with probability $1 - p$. An equally important imperfection is the possibility that, given compliance, the policing mechanism infers non-compliance, and inappropriately imposes the sanction, s. The possibility of *misapprehension* is important in this paper for the following reason. We have shown that when we choose the largest possible effective sanction, additional wealth in the agent's pocket makes it easier or less costly to control his/her behaviour. If, however, the probability of misapprehension is significant, we may choose not to impose the maximum effective sanction. In this case, the direct link between wealth and control is broken and it is not obvious that added wealth still reduces the cost of control. This is the issue we consider in this section.

Let q denote the probability that an agent who is in compliance will be misapprehended. Ignoring for the moment the possibility of wealth transfer as a means of extending control, the compliance constraint in this case is

$$qU(W - s) + (1 - q)\, U(W) \geq pU(W - s) + (1 - p)\, U(W + T). \tag{7}$$

As is evident from equation (7), the utility of an agent subject to the control system will be reduced if misapprehension is possible:

$$qU(W - s) + (1 - q)\, U(W) < U(W) \quad \text{for} \quad q > 0, s > 0.$$

We assume here for simplicity that exit from the control system is not an option. (We will discuss 'desperate' options such as flight in the next section.)

A necessary, though not sufficient, condition for equation (7) to hold is that the probability of apprehension (p) exceeds the probability of misapprehension (q).[2] Therefore, assuming that we want to induce compliance, we know that p^* will exceed q^*. Can we say more about the best policy? Let $M(p, q)$ be the costs associated with the policing mechanism. Assume that $M_1(p, q)$ is positive – the marginal cost of p is positive – and that $M_2(p, q)$ is negative – it is costly to reduce the probability of misapprehension. Given our purpose, we have no need to say more about the properties of $M(p, q)$.

In this circumstance, the best policy may involve a positive probability of misapprehension – $q^* > 0$. Indeed it may be impossible to eliminate misapprehension while also inducing compliance. If q^* is positive, we may well choose a sanction less than the maximum possible sanction – $s^* < W$.

Suppose then that q^* exceeds zero and s^* is less than W when the set of controls includes only q, s and p. Again assuming that, *ceterus paribus*, the social objective is to minimize the cost of compliance, the compliance constraint will hold with equality:

$$q^*U(W - s^*) + (1 - q^*)\,U(W) = p^*U(W - s^*) + (1 - p^*)\,U(W + T). \qquad (8.1)$$

Further,

$$q^* < p^* \qquad (8.2)$$

$$s^* < W. \qquad (8.3)$$

Now consider a *conditional* transfer of wealth, $t > 0$, to the agent, a transfer which he/she will realize with probability $1 - q^*$, given compliance, or with probability $1 - p^*$, given non-compliance. Equivalently, consider an unconditional transfer combined with an increase of the same magnitude in s. Risk aversion and the fact that q^* is less than p^* imply that compliance is now strictly preferred:

$$q^*U(W - s^*) + (1 - q^*)\,U(W + t) > p^*U(W - s^*) + (1 - p^*)\,U(W + T + t). \qquad (9)$$

Further, the agent is strictly better off:

$$q^*U(W - s^*) + (1 - q^*)\,U(W + t) > q^*U(W - s^*) + (1 - q^*)\,U(W). \qquad (10)$$

Thus, positive t creates slack in the compliance constraint.

We can use the slack created by the transfer to reduce p, which reduces policing costs and leaves the agent strictly better off. If our only option, relative to (p^*, q^*, s^*), were to choose positive t and reduce p, we would choose it if the reduction in policing costs was large enough – we certainly would if the reduction in costs exceeded t since everyone would benefit. Alternatively, we could use the slack to increase q, a strategy which would leave the agent just as well off as he/she was prior to the transfer and which would decrease policing costs. As above, if our only option were to choose positive t and then use the slack to increase q, we would choose to do so if the cost reduction was large enough. In other words, in this problem we can substitute a conditional wealth transfer for a reduction in p, or for an increase in q (or some combination of the two), while both satisfying the compliance constraint and leaving the agent no worse off than he/she would be in the absence of the transfer. In addition, such a transfer may be socially desirable, even ignoring the value of the transfer to the agent.

As in the previous section, a conditional wealth transfer is then a potentially attractive control on agent behaviour. It follows that an exogenous increase in the agent's wealth potentially reduces the social burden of control. These results follow even when we choose not to impose the maximum effective sanction.

5. Desperation and credibility

Let us return to the basic model of Sections 1 and 2. In formulating that model we assumed that in the event of apprehended non-compliance two things would automatically happen: the agent would be forced to pay restitution, and he/she would be forced to pay the effective fine – s, or W if s exceeds W. These consequences are, of course, not automatic. Whether they do follow apprehended non-compliance may depend upon the agent's own decisions, and the decisions of other parties who are involved in the policing mechanism. In this section we introduce these possibilities into our model.

5.1. Desperation

There are many actions which the agent may be able to choose which will affect his/her availability for social sanctions – 'bribe the cop', 'shoot the witness', 'fly the coop' and so on. Here we assume that, apprehension having occurred, the agent has the opportunity to decide to either make him-/herself available or to take up some such option. We refer to this option as the *desperate option* or as *desperation*. We are thus assuming that availability is completely at the agent's discretion.

To model this decision we suppose that the agent has some well-defined utility function, $\tilde{U}(\cdot)$, in the desperate option whose single argument is wealth, and that it is increasing in its argument and concave – $\tilde{U}'(\cdot) > 0$ and $\tilde{U}''(\cdot) < 0$. For a common value of their arguments, say, W, we assume that $\tilde{U}(W) < U(W)$: other things equal, the agent would prefer not to take up the desperate option.

The compliance constraint is then

$$U(W) \geq p \max [\tilde{U}(W+T), U(W-s)] + (1-p)\, U(W+T). \tag{11}$$

Here we imagine that the agent has the foresight to ask what the utility maximizing choice is, given apprehended non-compliance.

Define $\bar{s}$ to be the value of s such that $U(W+T)$ is equal to $U(W-s)$. That is, $\bar{s}$ satisfies

$$\tilde{U}(W+T) = U(W-\bar{s}).$$

Assume that $\bar{s}$ is less than W. (If it exceeds W, then the analysis of Sections 1 and 2 does not require amendment since $\bar{s}$ could never be an effective sanction.) Given $\bar{s}$ and apprehended non-compliance, the agent is indifferent between desperation and making him-/herself available for social sanctions. We can then rewrite the compliance constraint as

$$U(W) \geq \begin{cases} pU(W-s) + (1-p)\,U(W+T), & \text{if } s \leq \overline{s} \\ p\tilde{U}(W+T) + (1-p)\,U(W+T), & \text{if } s > \overline{s} \end{cases} \tag{12}$$

illustrated in Figure 3. Again, values of p and s in the shaded region induce compliance. Values of p and s in the cross-hatched area induce non-compliance and, in the event of apprehension, they induce the agent to take up the desperate option. Values in the unshaded area also induce non-compliance, but in the event of apprehension the agent chooses to incur the social sanction (pay s and return T) in preference to desperation.

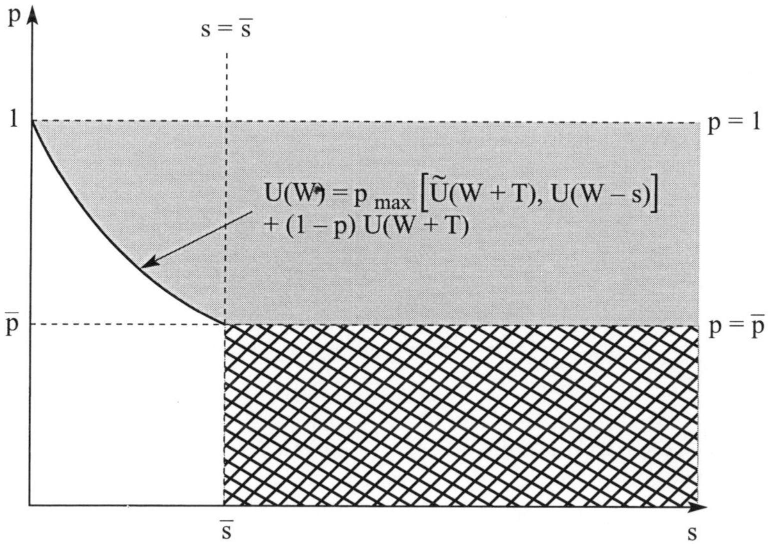

Figure 3

In contrast to Section 1, here the maximum effective sanction, $\overline{s}$, is determined not by W, but by the condition that it not be so large as to render the desperate option preferred to staying and accepting society's sanctions. Assuming that we want to induce compliance, the best solution is $\overline{s}$ and $\overline{p}$ (implicitly defined in Figure 3). In this case, wealth transfer is an effective control if $\tilde{U}'(W+T)$ is less than $U'(W-s)$. If it is, then wealth transfer increases the maximum effective sanction, and therefore is a substitute for p. Further, any other policy which increases the agent's utility within society, but not outside it, serves as a substitute for p.

5.2. *Credibility*

Let us return to the issue of credibility. Credibility is concerned with the incentives of other individuals involved in the policing mechanism. Given non-compliance and apprehension, is it in their self-interest to set (or keep) the policing mechanism in motion? For example, cooperation of witnesses imposes costs on them – a day in court, if nothing else. If these costs are sufficiently large, witnesses may not cooperate.

If the agent foresees this possibility, then the sanction is not credible. The maximum effective sanction may then be zero.

Given the focus of this paper, we are particularly concerned with the possibility that the magnitude of s may itself affect the credibility of s. If it does, then credibility may provide the upper bound on the effective sanction. To illustrate, suppose that some individual, a witness or a law enforcement officer for example, empathizes with the agent. If the potential sanction is large enough, he/she may be led to refuse to testify or to arrest the agent, given non-compliance. The story is by now familiar. If the agent anticipates these possibilities, credibility provides an upper bound on the effective sanction. If this is the binding constraint on the effective sanction, added wealth in the agent's pocket has no obvious bearing on the control problem.

Suppose that credibility does provide the binding constraint and let $\hat{s}$ denote the maximum credible sanction. Then, in Figure 4, the compliance constraint is satisfied only in the shaded area. In contrast to previous cases, there is an obvious problem associated with 'excessive' sanctions – they induce non-compliance.

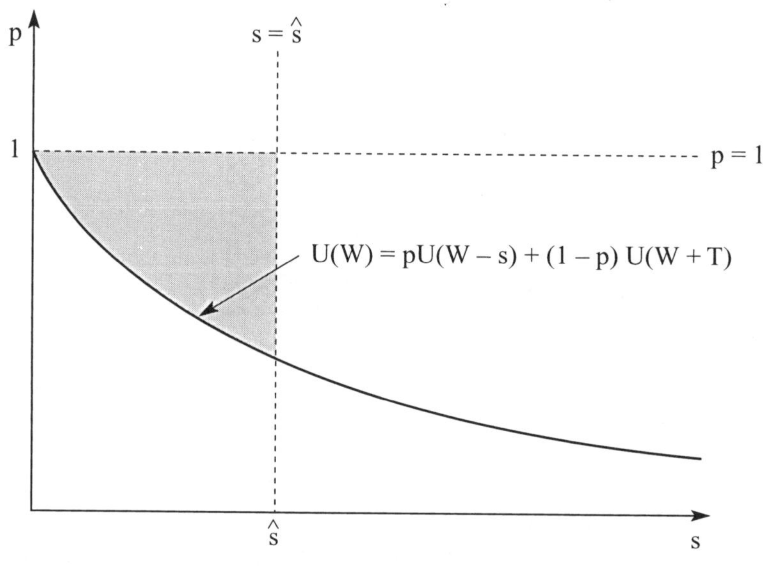

Figure 4

6. Distribution of wealth

In the previous sections, we have focused exclusively on the behaviour of a single agent. Using a partial equilibrium framework, we have considered the best means of controlling this agent. We have not, however, explicitly identified either the temptations the agent is subject to or the motivation of other parties to control the agent's behaviour. It is readily apparent that responses to control systems are jointly determined by the agent's own wealth and the wealth of others. Thus an agent's decision to engage in anti-social behaviour – for example theft – will depend not only on the agent's own wealth (what the agent has to lose), and the type of sanctions he or she faces, but also on what there is to gain from such behaviour, a function of the wealth of others.

In this section we extend our analysis to consider issues of distribution using a simple two-person, two-period model. Assume that each individual is endowed with a fixed quantity of wealth and that, except for differences in wealth, these individuals are otherwise identical. Ignoring for the moment the possibility of theft, the economic problem which the individual faces is the allocation of wealth to consumption over the two periods. Each individual solves

$$\max_{x_i, y_i} U(x_i) + U(y_i) \quad s \cdot t \cdot \quad x_i + y_i = W_i$$

where x_i is the ith individual's consumption in period 1 and y_i his/her consumption in period 2. We assume that $U(\cdot)$ is increasing in its argument and concave [$U'(\cdot) > 0$, $U''(\cdot) < 0$] and, without further loss of generality, that $U(0)$ is 0. The solution to this problem is for each individual to allocate half of his/her wealth to consumption in each period and the utility associated with this solution is

$$2U(W_i/2).$$

That is, the individual chooses a balanced consumption profile.

We suppose that each individual has the opportunity to steal a portion b, $0 < b < 1$, of the other's (remaining) wealth at the end of the first period. We imagine also that there is in place a policing mechanism characterized by a probability of apprehension, p, $0 < p < 1$, and a *maximum* feasible sanction. That is, if an individual is apprehended, he/she pays full restitution and forfeits his/her remaining wealth.

We first ask when the policing mechanism will support the private utility maximizing solution we identified above. There are two compliance constraints which must be satisfied if the private solution is to be supported:

$$2U(W_i/2) \geq \max_{x_i} [U(x_i) + (1-p)\, U(W_i - x_i + bW_j/2)], \quad i = 1, 2; \; j \neq i. \tag{13}$$

The expression on the right is maximized utility of individual i (if the individual chooses to steal), given that the other individual consumes $W_j/2$ in period 1, and therefore has $W_j/2$ in wealth at the beginning of period 2.

Ignoring the possibility of a corner solution, the value of x_i which solves this utility maximizing problem, $\hat{x}_i$, will satisfy

$$U'(\hat{x}_i) - (1-p)\, U'(W_i - \hat{x}_i + bW_j/2) = 0. \tag{14}$$

Since $U''(\cdot)$ is negative we infer that

$$\hat{x}_i > W_i - \hat{x}_i + bW_j/2$$

or equivalently that

$$\hat{x}_i > W_i/2 + bW_j/4. \tag{15}$$

Using this notation we can rewrite the compliance constraints in equation (13):

$$2U(W_i/2) \geq U(\hat{x}_i) + (1-p)\,U(W_i - \hat{x}_i + bW_j/2). \tag{16}$$

The derivative of the left side of this constraint with respect to W_i is $U'(W_i/2)$. Using equation (14) we see that the derivative of the right side with respect to W_i is $(1-p)\,U'(W_i - \hat{x}_i + bW_j/2)$, which is, using equation (14) again, equal to $U'(\hat{x}_i)$. From equation (15) and the fact that $U''(\cdot)$ is negative, we infer that

$$U'(W_i/2) > U'(\hat{x}_i).$$

That is, the derivative of the left side of equation (16) with respect to W_i exceeds the derivative of the right with respect to W_i.

From this exercise, we see that if the compliance constraint is satisfied for the less wealthy individual, it is also satisfied for the more wealthy individual. Further, observe that it is impossible to satisfy equation (16) when W_i is 0 – in this case i's only access to wealth is through theft and he/she has nothing to lose if apprehended.

To focus on distribution, we fix aggregate wealth. For convenience, let

$$W_1 + W_2 = 1,$$

and suppose that

$$W_2 \leq W_1.$$

Suppose that p is large enough so that equation (16) is satisfied when W_1 is equal to W_2. That is, suppose that the policing mechanism will support the private utility maximizing solution when the two individuals are equally wealthy.

As we decrease W_2, correspondingly increasing W_1, we must eventually encounter a (positive) value of W_2, call it $\bar{W}_2$, such that the compliance constraint for the second individual is satisfied with equality. For smaller W_2 individual Two will not satisfy equation (16). This follows from the observations we made concerning the derivatives of the right and left sides of equation (16) with respect to wealth and from the observation that it is impossible to satisfy equation (16) when W_2 is 0.

Thus, the ability of a given policing mechanism to support the private utility maximizing consumption pattern depends upon the distribution of wealth. In our model, the more unequal the distribution of wealth, the larger p must be to support the private solution. Further, for any p less than 1, if the distribution is sufficiently unequal, then the policing mechanism will not support the private utility maximizing consumption pattern.

Let us now suppose that W_2 is less than $\bar{W}_2$ and ask what will happen in this circumstance. Individual One will, of course, not be tempted to steal from Two, but must be concerned with the possibility that Two will steal from him/her. Assuming that One understands Two's behaviour, and ignoring the possibility of wealth transfer, One has two options in this model. One option is to constrain period 2 consumption to a level which is low enough so that individual Two will not, in fact, steal from One.

A second option is to maintain consumption above this level in period 2 and absorb losses resulting from theft.

Turning to the first option, the price which individual One pays, relative to the individually maximizing solution, is an unbalanced consumption profile – to ensure that Two will not steal when W_2 is less than $\bar{W}_2$, One must consume less in period 2 than in period 1. The degree to which One's consumption profile is unbalanced in this option depends upon the magnitude of W_2 – the smaller W_2 is, the more unbalanced will One's consumption profile be – the higher the utility price which One must pay to induce Two not to steal. Under this option, One's utility, which we denote by $\tilde{U}_1(W_2)$, is

$$\tilde{U}_1(W_2) = U(1 - W_2 - \tilde{y}_1) + U(\tilde{y}_1)$$

where $\tilde{y}_1$ is defined by

$$2U(W_2/2) = \max_{x_2} [U(x_2) + (1-p)\, U(W_2 - x_2 + b\tilde{y}_1)].$$

Here we use the fact that W_1 is just $1 - W_2$. As the reader can verify, $\tilde{y}_1$ is less than $W_1/2$ (when $W_2 < \bar{W}_2$) and further $\tilde{y}_1$ decreases as W_2 decreases.

Observe,

$$\tilde{U}_1(\bar{W}_2) = 2U[(1 - W_2)/2] \tag{17}$$

and

$$\tilde{U}_1(W_2) < 2U[(1 - W_2)/2] \quad \text{when } W_2 < \bar{W}_2. \tag{18}$$

The first of these observations follows from the fact that One's balanced consumption profile does not induce Two to steal when W_2 is equal to $\bar{W}_2$ and the second is obvious.

The second option which One faces is to allow Two to appropriate $b(W_1 - x_1)$ of One's (remaining) wealth in period 2. In this case, One will solve the following problem:

$$\max_{x_1} [U(x_1) - pU(W_1 - x_1) + (1-p)\, U[(1-b)(W_1 - x_1)]].$$

The formulation of this objective function presumes that if Two is apprehended, restitution occurs. Thus with probability p, y_1 will be $W_1 - x_1$, and with probability $(1-p)$, y_1 will be $(1-b)(W_1 - x_1)$. Denote One's utility under this option by $\hat{U}_1(W_2)$. It is obvious that

$$\hat{U}_1(W_2) < 2U[(1 - W_2)/2] \tag{19}$$

for all W_2 less than or equal to $\bar{W}_2$. Further, $\hat{U}_1(\cdot)$ is strictly decreasing in W_2.

From equations (17) and (19) we can infer that the first option will dominate the second in some (left-hand) neighbourhood of $\bar{W}_2$. It is, of course, possible that the second dominates the first for sufficiently small values of W_2. If, for example, $U'(0)$ is infinite the second necessarily dominates the first in some (right-hand) neighbourhood of W_2 equal to zero. To see this observe that $\tilde{y}_1$ is zero when W_2 is zero. When $U'(0)$ is infinite, rather than consume zero in period 2, One will incur the risk of theft in period 2.

We illustrate one interesting possibility in Figure 5. The qualitative features illustrated in the figure arise, for example, when the utility function is consumption raised to the power 0.25, p is 0.2 and b is 0.7. When W_2 exceeds $\bar{W}_2$, the private solution is supportable. When W_2 exceeds $\dot{W}_2$ and is less than $\bar{W}_2$, One constrains period 2 consumption to the level which just induces Two not to steal. One's utility is $\tilde{U}_1(W_2)$ and Two's utility is $2U(W_2/2)$. Relative to the private solution, the utility cost to One of inducing Two not to steal is the distance from $\tilde{U}_1(W_2)$ to the dashed line in the top portion of the figure. Notice that there is no compensating utility gain for Two – this loss is a 'dead weight loss'. When W_2 is less than $\dot{W}_2$, One 'allows' Two to steal – One's utility is $\hat{U}_1(W_2)$ and Two's is $\hat{U}_2(W_2)$. In this case, there is a redistribution of wealth from One to Two, and Two's utility is larger than it would be in the private solution.

Individual One has, of course, another control on Two's behaviour. One could, in period 1, voluntarily transfer wealth to Two. In the case illustrated, One would choose to do so whenever W_2 is less than $\check{W}_2$, ignoring any other controls which One might devise. The perhaps surprising feature of the illustration which is necessary for this result is that $\tilde{U}_1(W_2)$ is increasing in W_2 over some range – One's utility increases as One transfers wealth to Two. To see the forces at work here, we write $\tilde{U}_1(W_2)$ as

$$\tilde{U}_1(W_2) = U(1 - W_2 - \tilde{y}_1) + U(\tilde{y}_1).$$

Differentiating the right hand side with respect to W_2, we have

$$(d\tilde{y}_1/dW_2)\,[U'(\tilde{y}_1) - U'(1 - W_2 - \tilde{y}_1)] - U'(1 - W_2 - \tilde{y}_1).$$

The first term is positive – $\tilde{y}_1$ increases as W_2 increases, which tends to increase One's utility since the marginal utility of consumption in period 2 exceeds marginal utility in period 1 when One's consumption is unbalanced. The second term, which is negative, reflects the obvious – One's aggregate command over consumption decreases as One transfers wealth to Two. If the first term dominates the second (as it does to the left of $\check{W}_2$ in the figure), One may choose to transfer wealth to Two for purely selfish reasons. We have then the possibility of Pareto-optimal redistribution even in the absence of benevolent motives.

This is not an inevitable feature of this model. It is possible that $\tilde{U}_1(W_2)$ intersects $\hat{U}_1(W_2)$ at a point where $\tilde{U}_1(W_2)$ is decreasing in W_2. This is the case, for example, when the utility function is consumption raised to the power 0.8, p is 0.4 and b is 0.3.

This analysis may be extended to production by considering the case in which individuals differ in respect to their productivity (for instance their human capital), rather than their monetary wealth. For example, suppose that individuals can produce in the first period and consume in both. The possibility of theft may then lead to a reduction in the level of wealth produced. Again, wealth transfers may increase the welfare of both parties.

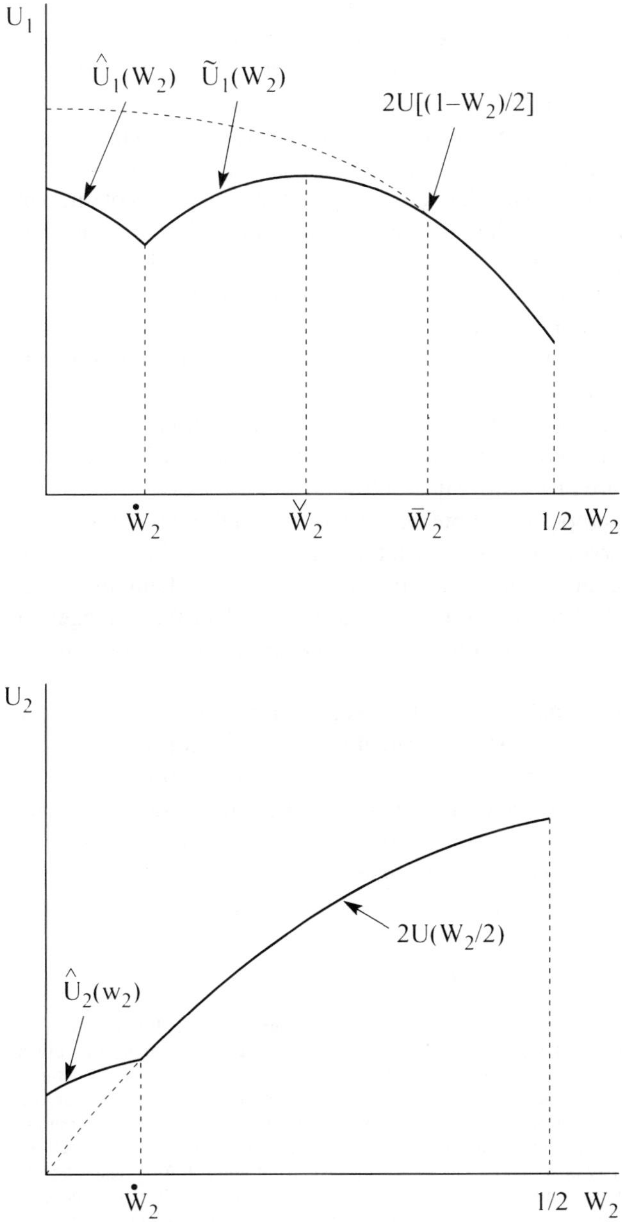

Figure 5

7. Discussion

We began by noting that institutions, properly conceived, have the potential to create wealth. The extent to which they do so depends on the costs of making them function.

Ironically, as we have seen, an important determinant of these costs is wealth itself. The wealthier an individual agent is, the less costly it will be to create an effective institutional structure to control that agent's behaviour because the individual's wealth can be used as a social bond. Moreover, the limits of control may be extended by augmenting the individual's wealth through conditional transfers. This result holds even when the optimal social bond is less than the agent's wealth, for instance in the case where the agent has a desperate option available such as flight.

The decision to engage in anti-social behaviour will, of course, depend not only on the individual agent's own wealth and the sanctions the agent faces, but also on what the agent stands to gain, a function of the wealth of others. In turn, the wealth of others will determine the extent to which they are willing (and able) to offer the agent conditional transfers to alter his or her behaviour.

We are struck here by a simultaneity. The overall effectiveness of the institutional structure of society depends on society's wealth and its distribution. Yet, at the same time, society's wealth depends on the effectiveness of these institutions. As Bowles (1985) notes, the traditional dichotomy in welfare economics between efficiency and equity collapses when there are problems with control.

As we have seen in the example in the previous section, conditions may exist in which redistribution is in everyone's self-interest. Eswaran and Kotwal (1984) make a similar point in a different context when they consider the impact of land reform on efficiency in underdeveloped countries. In both cases, it is evident that changes in distribution may affect the efficiency of control, while changes in control may affect distribution.

An obvious extension of this analysis is to the theory of the firm. It seems likely that the conditions which determine why coordinating the allocation of resources through command systems is preferred to the market will, with wealth, play a key role in determining the organization and efficiency of control institutions. Beyond this, an interesting issue is the choice between private and social systems of control. For example, why in the production process are some actions, such as embezzlement, subject to public as well as private sanctions, while others, such as shirking, at least at this point in history, are not?

Notes

1. For a general discussion of the costs associated with sanctions see Posner (1977). As Posner notes, the issue of optimal sanctions becomes considerably more complex where a system of sanctions is involved (as opposed to the case being considered here where there is only a single crime and a single sanction). For example, perverse effects may arise from applying the same sanction for crimes with varying social costs; if the penalty for unarmed robbery is the same as for armed robbery, this may encourage the latter. Note also that we implicitly rule out any problems with moral hazard in imposing sanctions in our analysis. Moral hazard may be a major issue in private systems of control. As a result, agents may refuse to post any bonds. If no bonding is feasible, we move directly to the analysis in Section 3.
2. This can be easily seen by considering the case in which $q = p$, in which case the left side of equation (7) will always be less than the right and the inequality will not hold. Nor will equation (7) hold for values of $q > p$, as any increase in q will reduce the value of the left side of the inequality.

References

Bowles, S. (1985), 'The Production Process in a Competitive Economy', *American Economic Review*, **75**, pp. 16–36.

Eaton, B.C. and W.D. White (1983), 'The Economy of High Wages: An Agency Problem', *Economica*, **50**, pp. 175–81.

Eswaran, M. and A. Kotwal (1984), 'Access to Capital as a Determinant of the Organization of Production and Resource Allocation in an Agrarian Economy', University of British Columbia.
Eswaran, M. and A. Kotwal (1985), 'A Theory of Two-Tier Labor Markets in Agrarian Economies', *American Economic Review*, **75**, pp. 162–77.
Posner, R. (1977), *Economic Analysis of Law*, Little Brown, Boston, Massachusetts.
Sappington, D. (1979), 'Limited Liability Contracts Between Principal and Agent', *Journal of Economic Theory*, **10**, pp. 55–73.
Shapiro, C. and J. Stiglitz (1984), 'Equilibrium Unemployment as a Worker Discipline Device', *American Economic Review*, **74**, pp. 433–44.
Stiglitz, J.E. (1984), 'Theories of Wage Rigidity', National Bureau of Economic Research Working Paper no. 1442.
Yellen, J. (1984), 'Efficiency Wage Models of Unemployment', *American Economic Review Proceedings*, **74**, pp. 200–205.

[16]

THE DISTRIBUTION OF WEALTH AND THE EFFICIENCY OF INSTITUTIONS

B. CURTIS EATON and WILLIAM D. WHITE*

This paper explores the effect on economic efficiency of the distribution of wealth and systems for enforcing property rights. We construct a two-person, two-period economy in which each person can consume, plant, transfer or steal corn. We find circumstances in which redistribution of wealth is Pareto optimal and in which increasing sanctions against theft to their maximum level is not. These results suggest that it is not only important to consider distribution in the design of property institutions, but also that redistribution itself may serve to increase the efficiency of systems of property rights.

I. INTRODUCTION

A fundamental insight of economics is that property rights may foster creation of wealth. Nevertheless, property rights which can be freely violated serve no function, so that to be meaningful, they must be enforceable. Effective enforcement requires the existence of enforcement systems to monitor violations, impose sanctions and provide for restitution of stolen property.

An effective enforcement system produces obvious desirable effects. By deterring theft and providing for restitution, it assures that individuals will appropriate the fruits of their labors, and hence enforcement serves to increase efficiency. It is a standard observation in the literature on crime and punishment that the possibility of crime may lead potential victims to alter their behavior in efficiency-reducing ways. The possibility of street crime may, for example, empty the streets [Neher 1978]. Conversely, the establishment of an effective enforcement system can return people to the streets both by deterring theft, or reducing the probability that it will occur, and by providing for restitution in the event theft occurs and the thief is apprehended. We refer to these efficiency-enhancing effects of enforcement as *deterrence* and *restitution effects.*

However, the benefits of operating an enforcement system must be weighed against its costs. Such a system may be resource using, and may yield undesirable as well as desirable effects. Thus, maintaining a criminal justice system entails direct costs—resources to operate a police force, courts and prisons—and indirect costs in that potential criminals may modify their behavior to adjust to the prospect of sanctions in efficiency-reducing ways (see Becker 1968, Usher 1986). A criminal may, for instance, dissipate resources in the face of expected sanctions, or otherwise deploy them in an inefficient fashion to escape appropriation. Hence, the tendency of criminals to exhibit apparently high discount rates observed by Wilson and Herrnstein [1985] may reflect the prospect of sanction rather than indicate a strong preference for immediate gratification, as they suggest. Likewise, the reduced risk of appropriation may explain the willingness of criminals to pay large transactions costs to maintain secrecy in Swiss bank accounts. We refer to these

* Simon Fraser University and the University of Illinois at Chicago. We would like to thank the participants of more than a dozen workshops, two anonymous referees, and Tom Borcherding for valuable suggestions.

Economic Inquiry
Vol. XXIX, April 1991, 336–350

efficiency-reducing effects of enforcement systems as *sanction effects*.

Cheung [1970] and others have observed that the costs of enforcing property rights may depend on their distribution.[1] Ehrlich's [1973] finding that there is a positive relation between the level of crime and the degree of income inequality is supportive of this view. Beyond this, it has frequently been suggested that redistribution may increase respect for property rights along with monitoring and sanctions. The notion that giving people more to lose can render them more law abiding is central to liberal theories of rehabilitation. It is also embedded in efficiency wage models, where high wages are shown to be economical to the extent they increase the efficacy of sanctions and extend an employer's basis for control. (See for example Eaton and White [1983], Yellen [1984]).

Any wealth transfers to individuals must, of course, come from other individuals. Redistribution may serve to control behavior not only because it gives those who potentially may violate property rights more to lose, but also because it reduces what is left for them to steal. For instance, Johnson [1986] draws on this notion to explore the role of ritual gift giving to guests during potlach ceremonies among the Kwakiutl Indians. He argues that in the Pacific Coast salmon fisheries, where yearly harvests were highly variable, gifts from tribal groups who had experienced a good year (typically potlach hosts) to those who had experienced a lean one (typically guests) served, through the resulting redistribution of wealth, to deter theft in both ways.

In this paper we focus on the role of wealth distribution in a very simple general equilibrium model in which deterrence, restitution, and sanction effects are possible. Our model is a two-person, two-period, corn economy. Both individuals in our model have the option of consuming initial endowments of corn in the first period or planting them for harvest in the second period. The yield in the second period exceeds the amount planted. But whereas property rights are assumed inviolate in the first period, they are not in the second; corn is safe in hand, but not on the stalk. Attempts to enforce property rights may entail deterrence and restitution effects—individuals plant corn they otherwise would have consumed because they feared theft. However, enforcement may also entail sanction effects—those intending to steal anyway may consume corn instead of planting it since they anticipate its confiscation through sanctions.

The enforcement mechanisms we consider involve a probability of apprehension and wealth-constrained sanctions. We discover that whether a particular mechanism produces an efficient or an inefficient outcome is very much dependent on the distribution of the economy's initial endowment of corn. Indeed, when the mechanism produces an inefficient equilibrium, Pareto-optimal redistribution is a distinct possibility.

Our model captures the externalities which are associated with theft and with attempts to control it. Since theft uses resources, it raises other economic issues which we have ignored. Benoit and Osborne [1987] examine the role of distribution in a model where the only economic problem raised by the possibility of theft is that it is resource using. Hence their analysis is complementary to ours, as are their results. They too discover that distribution plays a central role in determining the efficiency of any system of property rights.

The balance of this paper is organized as follows. In section II we present our model. In sections III and IV, we explore

1. See also Bush's [1972] discussion of the formation of property right systems and Umbeck [1981] on the development of early property right systems in the California gold fields.

equilibria of the model. In section V we examine comparative statics with respect to the distribution of wealth. In section VI we close with a brief discussion of our results.

II. A TWO-PERSON, TWO-PERIOD CORN ECONOMY

We begin our examination of the role which the distribution of wealth plays in supporting property institutions by developing a primitive two-person, two-period, corn economy. The preferences of the two individuals, *One* and *Two*, are captured in the following linear utility functions:

(1) $$U_i(x_i,y_i) = x_i + y_i\,, \quad i = 1,2,$$

where x_i is corn consumed in period 1 and y_i is corn consumed in period 2.[2] The aggregate initial endowment of corn is W units, and W_i denotes i's initial endowment. Thus

(2) $$W_1 + W_2 = W.$$

We assume throughout that $W_1 \geq W_2$. A unit of corn planted in period 1 yields $G > 1$ units in period 2. Since utilities are linear in aggregate corn consumption and G exceeds unity, efficiency or Pareto-optimality requires that all the corn be planted in period 1 and the harvest consumed in period 2.

The Problem

We assume that either individual can eat some or all of his endowment in period 1, where there is an inviolate property right in corn for one period. However, once corn is planted and ready for harvest a question arises. How much of the total harvest will *One* appropriate and how much will *Two* appropriate? To answer this question, we need an assumption regarding the technology of corn harvesting. It seems natural to assume that each individual will harvest half of the corn in the field. That is, in the absence of an institution of property, corn in the field is common property.

The equilibrium of the common property model depends on the magnitude of G. Let z_i denote the quantity of corn planted by individual i. Thus

(3) $$z_i = W_i - x_i, \quad i = 1,2,$$

that is, the individual plants what he does not consume in period 1. Objective functions, $V_i(z)$, can then be written as

(4) $$V_i(z) = (W_i - z_i) + G(z_1 + z_2)/2\,,$$

where $z = (z_1, z_2)$. The first term is x_i, equal to $W_i - z_i$, and the second is y_i, equal to one-half the total harvest.

The partial derivative of $V_i(z)$ with respect to z_i is $-1 + G/2$. This derivative is positive if and only if G exceeds two. Hence in a Nash equilibrium, each individual will plant all of his initial endowment if G exceeds two, and none of it if G is less than two. In the former case there is no interesting economic problem since the economy is on its utility possibilities frontier. Thus we assume that G is less than two. For simplicity, we let

(5) $$G = 3/2$$

In this case the sum of utilities in the common property equilibrium is W, which is less than the maximum potential utility, $3W/2$.

2. One might object that if x_i were zero, the individual would starve. To blunt this objection we could assume that there are many goods in the economy (berries, nuts and game as well as corn), but that corn is the only *scarce* good.

Now we have a problem—the economy is inside its utility possibilities frontier—that an institution of property rights might solve. Before we proceed, we should be clear about the nature of the economic problem our model captures. Given an institution of property, harvesting the other person's corn is theft. As noted above, there are two distinct economic problems associated with theft: it wastes resources, and it creates an externality. We are ignoring the first of these—theft is not resource using in our model. It does however create a negative externality—theft reduces the private return to planting corn and hence may induce either or both individuals to plant no corn, forcing the economy inside its utility possibilities frontier.

This externality is quite similar to the externality associated with common property. If, for example, we were to simply promulgate property rights by announcing that "in period 2, Gz_i is the property of individual i," but provided no enforcement mechanism, then each (amoral) individual would steal half of the other's harvest. Consequently, neither would capture all the returns to the corn he plants. Anticipating this externality, neither would plant any corn, and the economy would be inside its utility possibilities frontier just as it was when corn in the field was common property.

An enforcement mechanism that uses sanctions to deter theft and pays restitution to victims of theft may solve this problem. However, it may also create a negative externality borne by the thief. Suppose, for example, that the enforcement mechanism does not fully deter theft, so that one individual steals from the other in equilibrium. Sanctions then imply that the thief cannot capture all the returns to the corn he plants; that is, there are sanction effects. In our model, the sanction effect sometimes leads the thief to plant none of his corn. This in turn implies that maximal sanctions are not necessarily optimal.

These two externalities, the first associated with theft, and borne by the victim of theft, and the second associated with the attempt to control theft, and borne by the thief, imply that the design of efficient property institutions is a delicate matter. Increasing the effective sanction for theft mitigates the externality which the potential victim of theft bears, but it increases the externality which the potential thief bears.

Institutions of Property

There are many possible systems of property rights. To produce a tractable model, we choose to examine a system which can be characterized by two parameters. Each individual is endowed with a nominal property right to the corn he plants—if individual i plants z_i, then Gz_i is nominally i's property in period 2. An enforcement mechanism exists, characterized by the parameters P and λ: $0 \leq P \leq 1$, $0 \leq \lambda \leq 1$. P is a probability of apprehension and l characterizes the sanction imposed on the (apprehended) thief. The enforcer is an external policeman—not *One* or *Two*—who is presumed to be incorruptible.

If individual i steals from j, he will be apprehended with probability P. In the event that he is apprehended, i is forced to return all of the stolen corn to j and, in addition, is forced to pay a sanction to j. The sanction paid to j is λGz_i; that is, the thief pays a proportion λ of his corn harvest to the victim.[3]

If both individuals steal, the situation is more complex. A thief may choose not to

3. We have analyzed the model with a more conventional variant of the property institution in which the sanction paid by the thief is some absolute amount S if $Gz_i > S$, and Gz_i otherwise. That is, the sanction for theft is a fixed, corn-constrained, sanction. This version of the model is considerably more complex, but produces the same general insights. For this reason we consider here the less conventional but more tractable proportional sanction.

report the theft of his own corn if by doing so he increases the probability that his own transgression will be discovered. Hence the enforcement mechanism may or may not come into play. And if it does come into play, the probability that either thief is caught will be less than P, given a fixed effort from the enforcer. For these reasons it is not clear what we ought to assume regarding the probability of apprehension in this case. Guided again by tractability, we assume that when both individuals steal, the probability of apprehension is zero.

Note that while the magnitude of sanctions is here bounded by the thief's tangible wealth, it is straightforward to extend our analysis to consider other sorts of sanctions: for example, sanctions involving loss of life or liberty. It is sufficient for our purposes that the utility cost of sanctions be finite. In this regard, observe that even the death penalty has not always proved adequate to deter theft. In any case, society routinely sets limits on the magnitude of sanctions—the U. S. Constitution, for instance, prohibits cruel and unusual punishments. Such limitations may reflect humanitarian considerations or concerns about misapprehension, the perverse incentives that can be created when multiple types of offenses are involved (see Stigler [1970] on this sanction effect), or other sanction effects.

Equilibrium

The structure of the game we analyze is this: at the beginning of period 1 both individuals simultaneously choose x_i (or z_i); at the beginning of period 2 both individuals simultaneously choose how much corn, if any, to steal from the other; decisions with respect to theft having been made, thieves are instantaneously apprehended, and restitution and sanctions instantaneously paid.

Rational choice with respect to x_i (or z_i) in period 1 requires individual i to anticipate his own choices and j's choices in period 2. Hence the appropriate equilibrium concept is perfect Nash equilibrium, which ensures that individuals correctly anticipate both their own and each others actions in period 2. That is, perfect Nash equilibrium ensures that decisions are perfectly informed and individually utility maximizing. The common property equilibrium we found above is a perfect Nash equilibrium since, when making his own planting decision in period 1, each individual correctly anticipated that he would appropriate half of the total harvest in period 2.

In the common property equilibrium, both individuals plant all of their corn when $G > 2$ and none of it when $G < 2$. These corner solutions are obviously driven by the linearity of the basic model—utility is linear in x_i and y_i, and corn harvested is linear in corn planted. Not surprisingly, this linearity, in conjunction with the linearity of the property institution, produces corner solutions in the property rights model as well—in any pure strategy equilibrium each individual plants all of his corn or none of it. Hence we can greatly simplify the analysis by restricting individual strategies to these extreme cases. That is, we assume that z_i (or x_i) is either zero or W_i. A version of the paper in which we do not use this simplifying assumption is available from the authors.[4]

III. PERIOD 2 EQUILIBRIA

Our assumption of a perfect Nash equilibrium requires that we begin the analysis by characterizing the equilibrium of the period 2 game of theft, taking period 1

4. Without this restriction on strategies, there are cases in which the model has no equilibrium in pure strategies. In these cases, the equilibrium of the simplified model is different from the equilibrium of the unrestricted model.

planting decisions as given. Since there are four possible combinations of planting decisions in period 1, we must consider four possible subgames in period 2: Subgame I, in which $z = (0,0)$; Subgame II, in which $z = (W_1, 0)$; Subgame III, in which $z = (0, W_2)$; Subgame IV, in which $z = (W_1, W_2)$. In Subgame I, there is no corn to steal and hence no theft. In Subgame II, *Two* will steal half of *One's* corn since *Two* has no corn of his own and hence nothing to lose in the event that he is apprehended. Similarly, in Subgame III, *One* will steal half of *Two's* corn.

All of the interesting possibilities arise in Subgame IV where each individual is both a potential thief and a potential victim of theft. If i chooses to steal from j, he will steal as much as possible, half of j's harvest, since both the probability of apprehension and the sanction are independent of the amount of corn stolen. The payoffs in this game of theft are presented in Table I. An S denotes the strategy "steal" and a D the strategy "don't steal," and the first entry in each strategy combination is *One's* strategy and the second *Two's*.

With strategy combination (D,D) each individual consumes his own harvest, $(3/2)W_1$, and with combination (S,S) each individual eats half of his own harvest and half of the other's. With strategy combination (D,S), *Two* steals and *One* does not. In this case realized payoffs depend on whether *Two* is apprehended. If he is, *One*'s consumption is $(3/2)(W_1 + \lambda W_2)$ and *Two*'s is $(3/2)(1-\lambda)W_2$ since there is full restitution and *Two* pays sanction $(3/2)\lambda W_2$ to *One*. If *Two* is not caught, *One's* consumption is just $(3/2)W_1/2$ and *Two*'s is $(3/2)[W_2+W_1/2]$ since *Two* has successfully stolen half of *One*'s corn. The payoffs associated with strategy combination (D,S) are obviously symmetric to those associated with (S,D).

The equilibrium of this two by two matrix game depends upon the nature of the enforcement mechanism, on (P,λ). The circumstances in which both property rights are honored—(D,D) is an equilibrium—are of central interest. Given strategy D for *Two*, *One* will prefer strategy D if

$$(6.1) \qquad (3/2)W_1 \geq (3/2)[P(1-\lambda)W_1 + (1-P)(W_1+W_2/2)]$$

and, given strategy D for *One*, *Two* will prefer D if

$$(6.2) \qquad (3/2W_2 \geq (3/2)[P(1-\lambda)W_2 + (1-P)(W_2+W_1/2)]$$

When both of these inequalities are satisfied, (D,D) is an equilibrium strategy combination in Subgame IV.

These inequalities can be written in a more compact way.

$$(7.1) \qquad P \geq R/(R+2\lambda),$$

$$(7.2) \qquad P \geq 1/(1+2\lambda R),$$

where R is defined to be W_2/W_1. R parameterizes *relative wealth* and is bounded by zero and one since, by assumption, $W_1 \geq W_2$. Notice that if (7.2) is satisfied, then so is (7.1), since $R \leq 1$. Hence (D,D) is the equilibrium strategy combination whenever (7.2) is satisfied. From (7.2) we see that large values of P, λ and R tend to produce the equilibrium in which property rights are respected in Subgame IV.

Strategy combinations (D,S) and (S,S) are also equilibria of Subgame IV for certain values of the parameters P, λ and R. However, strategy combination (S,D) is never an equilibrium combination—that is, in Subgame IV if just one individual steals in equilibrium, the poorer individual is the thief. We record results for

TABLE I
Payoffs in Subgame IV

Strategy Combination	One's Payoff	Two's Payoff
(D,D)	$(3/2)W_1$	$(3/2)W_2$
(D,S)	$(3/2)[P(W_1+\lambda W_2) + (1-P)W_1/2]$	$(3/2)[P(1-\lambda)W_2 + (1-P)(W_2+W_1/2)]$
(S,D)	$(3/2)[P(1-\lambda)W_1 + (1-P)(W_1 + W_2/2)]$	$(3/2)[P(W_2 + \lambda W_1) + (1-P)W_2/2]$
(S,S)	$(3/2)[W_1/2+W_2/2]$	$(3/2)[W_1/2+W_2/2]$

Subgame IV in proposition 1. In each of the three cases the first inequality pertains to *One*'s choice and the second to *Two*'s. Binding inequalities are indicated by asterisks.

PROPOSITION 1: *Equilibria of Subgame IV*

A. (D,D) is an equilibrium if

$P \geq R/(R+2\lambda)$,

$*P \geq 1/(1+2\lambda R)$.

B. (D,S) is an equilibrium if

$*P \geq R/(1+2\lambda R)$,

$*P \leq 1/(1+2\lambda R)$.

C. (S,S) is an equilibrium if

$*P \leq R/(1+2\lambda R)$,

$P \leq 1/(R+2\lambda)$.

These results are illustrated in Figure 1. In the upper-right portion of the figure neither individual steals, in the middle of the figure, *Two* steals but *One* does not, and in the lower-left portion, both of them steal. The dashed lines indicate how the partition of the parameter space responds to an increase in R—that is, a reduction in inequality.

IV. PERFECT EQUILIBRIA

The fact that Subgame IV, in which both individuals planted their corn in period 1, has three types of equilibrium in period 2 means that we must consider three different games in period 1. The first game we consider is the one in which there would be no theft if both *One* and *Two* planted their corn, which requires that the institution, (P, λ), be in the upper-right portion of Figure 1. This game seems to be the most interesting of the three, and consequently we discuss it at some length. We simply present results for the other two with minimal commentary.

Game One: $P \geq 1/(1+2\lambda R)$

In period 1 an individual's strategy is either to plant *all* his corn, denoted by A, or *none* of it, denoted by N. Observe that in Game One, P is always greater than 1/3. In Table II we present the payoffs or utilities associated with the four possible strategy combinations. The payoffs associated with strategy combinations (A,A) and (N,N) are straightforward. With strategy combination (A,N), in the first period *One*

FIGURE 1

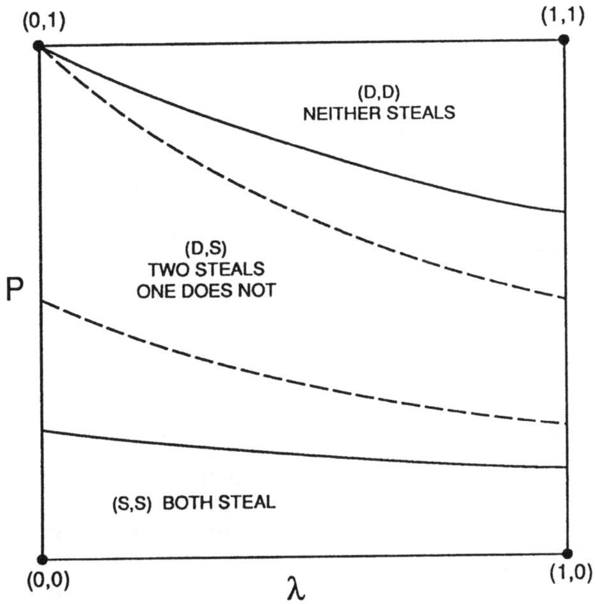

plants his corn and *Two* eats his, and in the next period, *Two* steals from *One*. Hence *Two's* expected consumption is W_2, what he eats in the first period, plus the expected value of his theft in the second period, $(1-P)(3/2)(W_1/2)$. *One's* consumption is $(3/2)W_1$ if *Two* is caught and $(3/2)W_1/2$ if he is not, and his expected consumption is therefore $(3/2)W_1[P+(1-P)/2]$. The payoffs associated with (N,A) are, of course, symmetric to those associated with (A,N).

The first thing to note about Game One is that (N,N) is never an equilibrium—at least one individual will plant his corn. Suppose, for example, that *Two* chose N. *One* would then anticipate that *Two* would steal from him in period 2 if he chose A. Whether *One* then chooses A or N depends upon the probability of apprehension, or more insightfully, the *probability of restitution*, since *Two* will pay full restitution if he's caught. As you can easily verify, when P exceeds 1/3, which is always the case in Game One, the *restitution effect* is strong enough to induce one individual to choose A if the other chooses N. Hence, (N,N) is never an equilibrium when $P > 1/3$. (On the other hand, (N,N) is always an equilibrium when $P < 1/3$.)

Now suppose that i does plant his corn, and consider j's strategy choice. If j also chooses A, he will anticipate that there will be no theft in period 2 and his utility will therefore be $(3/2)W_j$. If j chooses N—to eat his corn in period 1—he will anticipate successfully stealing (1/2) of i's harvest with probability $1-P$, and his expected utility will therefore be $W_j + (1-P)(3/4)W_i$. Hence i choosing A and j choosing

TABLE II
Payoffs for Game One

Strategy Combination	One's Payoff	Two's Payoff
(A,A)	$(3/2)W_1$	$(3/2)W_2$
(A,N)	$(3/2)W_1[P+(1-P)/2]$	$W_2+(1-P)(3/2)(W_1/2)$
(N,A)	$W_1+(1-P)(3/2)(W_2/2)$	$(3/2)W_2[P+(1-P)/2]$
(N,N)	W_1	W_2

N is a subgame perfect equilibrium if

$$(8.1) \quad W_j + (1-P)(3/4)W_i \geq (3/2)W_j,$$

or if

$$(8.2) \quad (3/2)(1-P) \geq W_j/W_i.$$

Because $P \geq 1/3$ in Game One, it's clear that if someone does choose N it won't be the richer individual since (8.2) can never hold when $W_j > W_i$. That is, *One* will never choose N in Game One.

Letting $i = 1$ and $j = 2$, condition (8.2) can be written as

$$(8.3) \quad 3 \geq 3P + 2R.$$

If this inequality is satisfied then (A,N) is the subgame perfect equilibrium, and if it is not satisfied (A,A) is the equilibrium. (Both are equilibria if (8.3) holds with equality.) Note that large values of P and significant equality in the distribution of wealth (large values of R) work to produce the efficient equilibrium in which all the corn is planted. In particular, the inefficient equilibrium in which *Two* does not plant his corn is impossible if the distribution of wealth is equal (if $R = 1$), or if $P = 1$.

It makes sense that it will be the poorer individual who inefficiently eats his corn in the first period and steals in the second. Suppose that i does plant his corn. Then for individual j, the opportunity cost of not planting the corn is the increased quantity of corn that is foregone, equal to $(1/2)W_j$, and the inducement is the corn that would be stolen in period 2, equal to $(3/4)W_i\,(1-P)$. Thus the opportunity cost is proportional to one's own wealth, and the inducement is proportional to the other individual's wealth.

We record our results in proposition 2 and illustrate them in Figure 2. The first restriction in each case pertains to *One*'s choice and the second to *Two*'s. The restrictions pertaining to *One*'s choice are always satisfied in Game One, and hence those pertaining to *Two*'s choice are binding, and therefore marked by an asterisk.

PROPOSITION 2: *Perfect Equilibria of Game One*

Game One Restriction: $P \geq 1/(1+2\lambda R)$

A. (A,A) is an equilibrium if

$3PR + 2 \geq 3R,$

$*3P + 2R \geq 3.$

No theft in period 2.

FIGURE 2

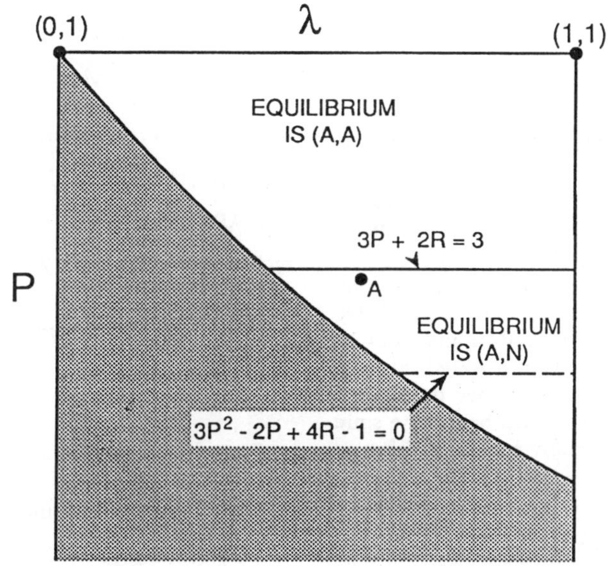

B. (A,N) is an equilibrium if

$$3P \geq 1,$$

$$*3P + 2R \leq 3.$$

Two steals in period 2.

When (8.3) holds with equality, *Two* is indifferent between strategies A and N. If *Two* chooses A, the economy is on its utility possibility frontier, and if he chooses N, the economy is inside the frontier. Since *Two* is indifferent between these options, we see that *One* bears the full utility cost, equal to $W_2/2$, if *Two* chooses strategy N instead of strategy A. This result implies that Pareto-optimal redistribution of wealth prior to planting decisions in period 1 is a possibility in Game One. Given the initial distribution of wealth, if (P,λ) is at a point like A in Figure 2, then there is a redistribution of wealth from *One* to *Two* which transforms the inefficient (A,N) equilibrium into an efficient (A,A) equilibrium in which both individuals are better off.

Two is, of course, always better off if *One* redistributes wealth to him. Hence to discover the conditions under which Pareto-optimal redistribution is possible, we can focus on One's utility. Suppose that the initial distribution, $R^0 = W_2^0/W_1^0$, is such that (8.3) holds with strict inequality, so that the equilibrium without redistribution is (A,N). Then *One*'s utility is $(3/2)W_1^0\ [P+(1-P)/2]$. Now consider the subsequent distribution, $R^1 = W_2^1/W_1^1$, such that (8.3) holds with equality. R^1 is the most unequal distribution which produces an efficient equilibrium. Given R^1, *One*'s utility in the efficient equilibrium is $(3/2)W_1^1$. Pareto-optimal redistribution is possible when

$$(9.1)\quad (3/2)W_1^1 \geq (3/2)W_1^0\,[P+(1-P)/2]$$

Using the (implicit) definition of R^1 and the identity $W = W_1^i + W_2^i$, condition (9.1) can be reduced to

$$(9.2) \qquad 3P^2 - 2P + 4R^0 - 1 \geq 0.$$

For any (P,λ) in Game One, if $R^0 \geq 1/4$, then (9.2) is satisfied. Hence, if the equilibrium of Game One without redistribution is (A,N) and if $W_1^0 \leq 4W_2^0$, then it is always Pareto-optimal for *One* to redistribute just enough corn to *Two* so that the equilibrium with redistribution is (A,A). If $R^0 < 1/4$, then redistribution may or may not be Pareto-optimal. We've illustrated this case in Figure 2. If (P,λ) lies above the dashed line $(3P^2-2P+4R-1=0)$ and below the solid line $(3P+2R=3)$, then redistribution is Pareto-optimal.

Game Two: $1/(1+2\lambda R) \geq P \geq R/(1+2\lambda R)$

In Game Two if both individuals plant their corn in period 1, the equilibrium in period 2 is (D,S)—*One* respects *Two*'s property right, but *Two* does not respect *One*'s. Hence payoffs in Game *Two* will differ from those in Game One (presented above in Table II) for strategy combination (A,A). One's payoff is $(3/2)[P(W_1+\lambda W_2) + (1-P)W_1/2]$, since *One* eats all of his own corn and a proportion λ of *Two*'s when *Two* is caught, and eats just half of his own corn when *Two* is not caught. *Two*'s payoff is $(3/2)[P(1-\lambda)W_2 + (1-P)(W_2+W_1/2)]$, since *Two* eats a proportion $1-\lambda$ of his own corn if he is caught, and all of his own corn and half of *One*'s if he is not.

In Game Two anything is possible in the sense that there are permissible parameter values such that any of the four possible strategy combinations is a perfect equilibrium. The possibilities are summarized in proposition 3, and illustrated in Figure 3. Asterisks again indicate binding restrictions, and the first restriction is applicable to *One* and the second to *Two*.

PROPOSITION 3: *Perfect Equilibria of Game Two*

Game Two restrictions:

$1/(1+2\lambda R) \geq P \geq R/(1+2\lambda R)$

A. (A,A) is an equilibrium if

*$3P[1+(1+2\lambda)R] \geq 1+3R$,

*$3\lambda P \leq 1$.

Two steals in period 2.

B. (A,N) is an equilibrium if

$3P \geq 1$,

*$3\lambda P \geq 1$.

Two steals in period 2.

C. (N,A) is an equilibrium if

*$3P[1+(1+2\lambda)R] \leq 1+3R$,

*$3P \geq 1$.

One steals in period 2.

D. (N,N) is an equilibrium if

*$3P \leq 1$,

*$3P \leq 1$.

Two points are worth making: the first concerns sanction effects and the second concerns the possibility of Pareto-optimal redistribution from *Two*, the poorer individual, to *One*. If the institution is described by point V in Figure 3, then a small increase in P or λ transforms the efficient equilibrium, in which both individuals plant their corn and *Two* steals from *One* in period 2, into the inefficient equilibrium in which *Two* does not plant his corn and continues to steal from *One*. This result illustrates how the property institution can seriously distort the thief's incentives. At V the thief plants his corn just as efficiency demands, but a small increase

FIGURE 3

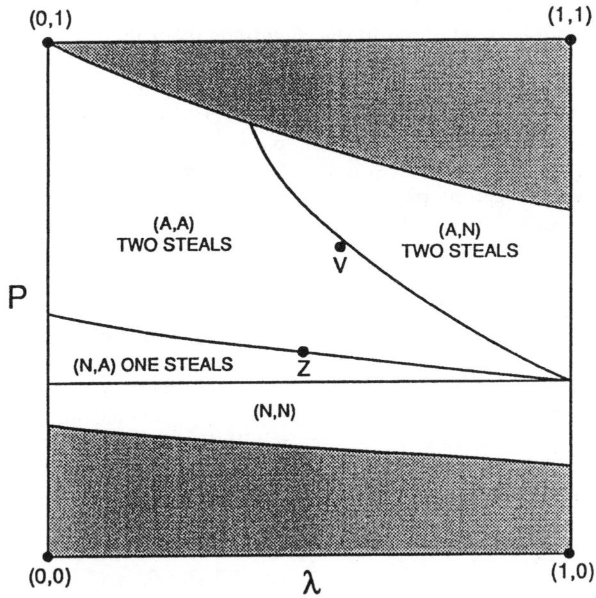

in P or λ induces him to eat his corn in period 1 so that he can avoid the sanction in the event that he's caught in period 2. Interestingly, it is *One* who bears the burden of inefficiency. On the boundary separating these two types of equilibria, *Two* is indifferent between strategies *A* and *N*. If he chooses *N* instead of *A*, total utility is smaller by $W_2/2$, which is identical to the (expected) sanction which *Two* pays to *One* if he chooses *A*. Hence *One* bears the entire burden of foregone utility if *Two* chooses *N*.

Now consider point Z in Figure 3. At Z, *One* is indifferent between *A* and *N*. If *One* chooses *N*, the economy is inside its utility possibility frontier, and if he chooses *A*, the economy is on the frontier. Since *One* is indifferent, *Two* bears the entire burden of the inefficiency. Because the boundary separating these two regions shifts downward as the distribution of wealth becomes more unequal, it's now possible that redistribution from *Two* to *One* is Pareto-optimal. That is, if the property institution is in region (*N*,*A*) but close enough to the boundary with region (*A*,*A*), *Two* will transfer just enough wealth to *One* to transform the inefficient (*N*,*A*) equilibrium into an efficient (*A*,*A*) equilibrium.

Game Three: $P \leq R/(1+2\lambda R)$

In Game Three if both individuals plant their corn in period 1, the equilibrium in period 2 is (*S*,*S*)—property rights are not respected. For both individuals, the payoffs in Game Three associated with strategy combination (*A*,*A*) are then $3(W_1+W_2)/4$ since total utility is $3(W_1+W_2)/2$ and each gets half the total. (The payoffs for the other strategy combinations are those presented in Table II above.)

In Game Three there are three possible equilibria, (N,N), (N,A), and (A,A). The possibilities are summarized in proposition 4. The first inequality pertains to *One*'s choice and the second to *Two*'s, and an asterisk indicates a binding restriction. The equilibria in parts B and C entail a third restriction on R. If this restriction is not satisfied, then the set of parameter values that satisfy all relevant restrictions is empty.

PROPOSITION 4: *Perfect Equilibria of Game Three*

Game Three restriction:

$$P \leq R/(1+2\lambda R)$$

A. (N,N) is an equilibrium if

$$*P \leq 1/3,$$

$$*P \leq 1/3.$$

B. (N,A) is an equilibrium if

$$*P \leq 1/3R,$$

$$P \geq 1/3,$$

$$*R \geq 1/3.$$

C. (A,A) is an equilibrium if

$$*P \geq 1/3R,$$

$$P \geq R/3,$$

$$R* \geq 1/\sqrt{3}.$$

As in Game Two, Pareto-optimal redistribution from *Two* to *One* is again a possibility.

V. DISTRIBUTION AND EFFICIENCY

We have already seen that the distribution of wealth plays a crucial role in determining the equilibrium of our model and that Pareto-optimal redistribution is a possibility. This, of course, means that distribution and efficiency cannot be disentangled—efficiency demands that both individuals plant their corn, but whether any property institution induces them to do so depends on the distribution of wealth. In this section we briefly present some comparative static results that illustrate just how central the role of distribution is in this model.

When P is less than ⅓, neither individual ever plants his corn and distribution is therefore irrelevant. Hence we ignore this portion of the parameter space in Figure 4. (The last panel in the figure depicts the portion of the parameter space on which we focus.) The shaded areas in each of the first eleven panels indicate the institutions which produce inefficient results. In the upper-right shaded area, *Two* fails to plant his corn, and in the lower-left shaded area *One* fails to plant his. *One* has the entire initial endowment of corn in panel 1 ($R = 0$), and distribution gets progressively more equal in panels 2 through 11. As the distribution gets more equal, the upper-right shaded area gets progressively smaller, while the lower-left shaded area initially increases and subsequently decreases. Interestingly, when the initial endowment is equally distributed, inefficiency is never a possibility, and when it is unequally distributed, there are institutions which induce either individual to behave inefficiently.

VII. DISCUSSION

As we observed in the introduction, it is evident that the allocation of property rights can affect their efficiency. Who has what *can* make a difference. It is also evident that when there are externalities associated with both theft and the use of sanctions, the effects of changes in distribution on efficiency cannot be predicted a priori. Society is faced with a balancing act between deterrence and restitution effects on the one hand, and sanction effects on the other. Because the relative importance

FIGURE 4

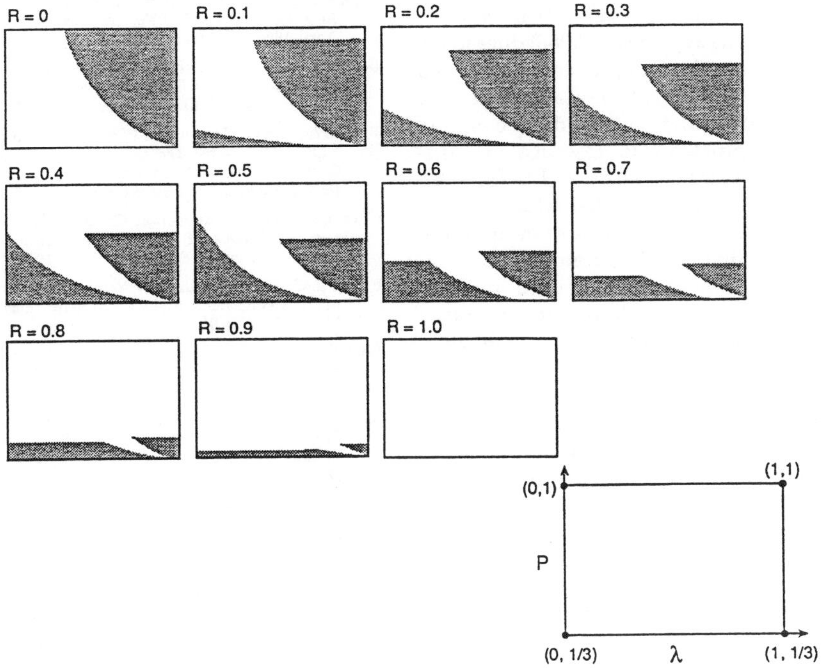

of the two types of externalities, as well as the direct costs of operating enforcement systems, may vary, they must be evaluated on a case by case basis.

From a policy perspective, our analysis suggests two broad conclusions. First, it is important to consider the underlying distribution of wealth in designing enforcement systems. For example, we discover circumstances in which increasing the magnitude of sanctions and/or the probability of apprehension may reduce the efficiency of property institutions so that output falls. Second, it is evident from our analysis that redistribution itself may increase efficiency. That is, holding sanctions and the probability of apprehension fixed, circumstances exist in which it is optimal to redistribute wealth.

A key empirical question is whether in practice the magnitude of distribution effects is large enough to merit attention. That is, *does* (or could) distribution really matter in determining the costs and benefits of operating enforcement systems? We offered a number of empirical examples to motivate the discussion in our introduction. But we view these as suggestive, rather than conclusive, and see a challenging research agenda emerging out of the analysis presented here.

One promising area for research is the impact of changes in the distribution of wealth on economic efficiency when the structure of enforcement systems remains fixed. Extending the type of analysis performed by Ehrlich [1973] to consider changes in wealth distribution over time is one possibility. Another promising area for research is to explore the use of redistribution as a control variable in enforcement systems as Johnson [1986] does in his analysis of potlatching. There have been a number of studies of the development of systems of regulation to address common property problems in resource management, for example in oil fields [Libecap and Wiggins 1985] or fisheries [Karpoff 1987]. A common observation in these studies is that small operators receive favorable treatment. The standard interpretation is that favorable treatment reflects equity concerns and political lobbying. While not ruling out this possibility, we note a second possible explanation, namely that enforcement costs may be lower when small operators are given more to lose.

REFERENCES

Becker, Gary S. "Crime and Punishment: An Economic Approach." *Journal of Political Economy*, March-April 1968, 169–217.

Benoit, J. P. and M. J. Osborne. "Crime and the Redistribution of Wealth." Working paper, Department of Economics, Columbia University, 1987.

Bush, Winston C. "Individual Welfare in Anarchy," in *Explorations in the Theory of Anarchy*, edited by Gorden Tullock. Blacksburg, VA: Virginia Polytechnic Institute and State University, 1972, 5–18.

Cheung, Steven. "Transaction Costs, Risk Aversion, and the Choice of Contractual Arrangement." *Journal of Law and Economics*, April 1970, 23–42.

Eaton, B. Curtis and William D. White. "The Economy of High Wages: An Agency Problem." *Economica*, May 1983, 175–81.

Ehrlich, Isaac. "Participation in Illegitimate Activities: A Theoretical and Empirical Investigation." *Journal of Political Economy 81*(3), 1973, 521–65.

Johnsen, D. Bruce. "The Formation and Protection of Property Rights Among the Southern Kwakiutl Indians." *Journal of Legal Studies 15*(1), 1986, 41–68.

Karpoff, Jonathan M. "Suboptimal Controls in Common Resource Management: The Case of the Fishery." *Journal of Political Economy, 95*(1), 1987, 179–94.

Libecap, Gary D. and Steven N. Wiggins. "The Influence of Private Contractual Failure on Regulation: The Case of Oil Field Unitization." *Journal of Political Economy, 93*(4), 1985, 690–714.

Neher, Philip A. "The Pure Theory of the Muggery." *American Economic Review 68*(3), 1978, 437–45.

Stigler, George. "The Optimal Enforcement of Laws." *Journal of Political Economy, 78*(3), 1970, 526–36.

Umbeck, John. *A Theory of Property Rights with Application to the California Gold Rush*. Ames, Iowa: Iowa State University Press, 1981.

Usher, Dan. "Police, Punishment, and Public Goods." *Public Finance 41*(1), 1986, 96–115.

Wilson, James Q. and Richard J. Herrnstein. *Crime and Human Nature*. New York: Simon and Schuster, 1985.

Yellen, Janet T. "Efficiency Wage Models of Unemployment." *American Economic Review, 74*(2), 1984, 200–205.

PART III

APPLIED PRICE THEORY

[17]

Unemployment, Underemployment, and Optimal Job Search

B. Curtis Eaton and Philip A. Neher

University of British Columbia

A three-sector general equilibrium model is employed to analyze the consequences of changes in aggregate demand, union power, workers' time horizons, and labor force size on "unionized" industries, industries with competitive labor markets, and unemployment. Workers are "voluntarily" unemployed while searching for jobs, attempting to arbitrage a wage gap created by partial "unionization." Many reduced-form elasticities are ambiguous in algebraic sign. For example, decreased aggregate demand may increase employment in industries with competitive labor markets. However, a larger and younger work force with enhanced aspirations for higher-paying jobs will have unambiguously higher unemployment.

> In all those occupations which the dismissed workers take up, their productivity is less than in the occupations they have left. For if it were not so, they would have engaged in them already. [JOAN ROBINSON, 1936]
>
> I'm really a university professor. Recently, I've been stringing beads for a living. [ANONYMOUS, 1974]

I. Introduction

Neoclassical economics teaches that factors of production will search out and find occupations of highest reward. Yet we observe people in occupations of last resort "selling match boxes in the Strand, cutting brushwood in the jungles, digging potatoes on allotments" (Robinson 1936, p. 226). Failing to find jobs for which they are suited by training

We are indebted to members of the University of British Columbia Labour Workshop for valuable comments. In addition, we owe a great debt to an anonymous referee who has twice offered invaluable comments which have led us to a final product that is very much better than, and substantially different from, our original effort.

[*Journal of Political Economy*, 1975, vol. 83, no. 2]

and temperament, they disappear into the statistical never-never land of underemployment where rewards are meager but available. University graduates selling underground newspapers on campuses, flowers on street corners, narcotics on city streets, or encyclopedias from door to door illustrate underemployment of the young and educated. Even the "hard-core" employed are affected. The laid-off tool and die maker reappears pumping gasoline or sharpening knives from door to door. The marine architect returns to the family farm and feeds the chickens.

Underemployment has hardly been ignored in the literature. But since the classic articles of the 1930s, it has been chiefly studied in the context of underdeveloped or semideveloped economies (Rosenstein-Rodan 1943; Lewis 1955; Fei and Ranis 1964; Todaro 1969; Harris and Todaro 1970). Yet, if the Great Depression gave birth to the concept in the framework of an industrialized society, our current circumstances require that we return for another look.

Recently, H. G. Johnson and P. Mieszkowski and E. Diewert showed that a properly constrained general equilibrium model can be used to investigate the consequences of successful unionization of part of the labor force (Johnson and Mieszkowski 1970; Diewert 1972). Union labor works in the relatively high-paid "general run of industries," while, in our interpretation, the rest of the labor force is "underemployed." But a wage gap is an invitation for the underpaid to seek out high-paid job opportunities as they become available due to natural turnover.

In this view, unemployment and underemployment are *concomitant* consequences of "union power." Union power gives rise to underemployment and wage dispersion. Wage dispersion gives rise to unemployment as workers try to arbitrage the wage gap. If people must quit low-paid work to search for high-paid work, it is natural to turn to a job search model in the tradition of M. P. Todaro (1969), C. C. Holt (1970), D. T. Mortensen (1970), and A. C. Harberger (1971) to explain unemployment.

Our contribution is twofold. First, we refine the usual job search model by articulating an explicit aggregation procedure to derive an unemployment function. Second, the unemployment function is embedded in a general equilibrium framework.

The concept of equilibrium in an economy with institutionally generated wage differentials requires careful interpretation. Differentials may reflect real differences in skill, training, cost of living, and so on. In this case, the institution (union) simply validates a free-market solution. We have in mind a true "contrived scarcity" created by people banding together to create a monopoly in the sale of their labor. Our "equilibrium" recognizes that such monopolies can be successful over the period of time relevant to the analysis. If pressed to justify our assumption of effective institutional power, we should probably proceed along lines suggested by C. C. von Weizsäcker in his Wicksell Lectures (Weizsäcker 1972). We do not pursue the point here. We simply assume that institutionally generated wage differentials can persist.

But institutions are sluggish in response to changing circumstances. Three-year union-management contracts, for example, are not uncommon in Canada. Hence, our idea of equilibrium includes the concept of an institutional *rigidity* which is effective over the relevant period of analysis. In short, we assume that institutional (union) power to create wage differentials exists but that it can be temporarily diluted from time to time because of a sluggish response to unexpected changes in the economy at large.

We shall first set out a short-run, general equilibrium, comparative statics model which allows for unemployed labor searching for high-wage jobs. The model is then solved for the reduced-form elasticities of chief concern. We use these results to assess demand management policies and to trace out the consequences of changes in demographic variables, social attitudes, and the degree of union power. We conclude with conclusions.

II. The Model

There are three sectors: the X industry (characterized by labor market rigidities), the Y sector (marked by flexible wages and ease of entry), and an unemployment sector.

A. The X Industry

We include here all activities where access to jobs is limited (in the sense that an applicant cannot enhance his employment prospects by offering his services at a wage lower than the prevailing one) due to institutional constraints. We have in mind Harberger's "protected industries" or Robinson's "general run of industries" (Robinson 1936; Harberger 1971).

The short-run production function is conditioned by the quantity of nonhuman resources already committed to that sector, so that output (X) depends on the labor input (L_X):

$$X = F(L_X), \qquad F' > 0, F'' < 0. \tag{1}$$

Labor is paid the value of its marginal product:

$$w_X = F'p, \tag{2}$$

where p is the price of X.

Institutional rigidities are embodied in the supply of labor function. We characterize these rigidities as two polar cases. First, a rigid supply of labor is maintained by restricting entry through unions, professional associations, and the like:

$$L_X = \bar{L}_X. \tag{3a}$$

We take it that $\bar{L}_X$ is set to obtain a wage in excess of the free-market wage. Alternatively, a rigid wage is set above the free-market wage so that the supply of labor is perfectly elastic over the relevant range of employment:

$$w_X = \bar{w}_X. \tag{3b}$$

The quantity of X demanded is a function of relative prices and real income. Money income (equals aggregate demand, D) is, for simplicity, assumed proportional (by V) to the exogenous nominal money supply ($\bar{M}$), $D = V\bar{M}$. For notational convenience, we shall simply let aggregate demand be exogenous ($D = \bar{D}$). Then, normalizing on the price of $Y(q)$, X demanded depends on its relative price (p/q) and on real income, or real aggregate demand, ($\bar{D}/q$):

$$X = X(p/q, \bar{D}/q), \qquad X_1 < 0, X_2 > 0. \tag{4}$$

B. The Y Industry

The short-run production function for Y is

$$Y = G(L_Y), \qquad G' > 0, G'' < 0. \tag{5}$$

The wage in Y is the value of L_Y's marginal product:

$$w_Y = G'q, \tag{6}$$

where q is the price of Y. Labor supplied to Y is the residual of all labor ($\bar{L}$) which is not employed in X (L_X) or unemployed (L_U):

$$L_Y = \bar{L} - L_X - L_U. \tag{7}$$

The quantity of Y demanded is given by the budget constraint $\bar{D} = Xp + Yq$, or

$$Y = \frac{\bar{D}}{q} - \frac{Xp}{q}. \tag{8}$$

Note that (8) can be written $Y = Y(p/q, \bar{D}/q)$. We assume that $Y_1 > 0$.

C. The Unemployment Sector

Employment in the high-wage industry is preferred to unemployment and to employment in the low-wage industry (underemployment). We assume that in order to obtain a job in the X industry, an individual must specialize in information generation; he must be unemployed in search of a job in X. (The weaker assumption that the probability of obtaining a job in the X industry is greater for the unemployed than for the underemployed would not change the qualitative nature of our results.)

Given a turnover rate, t, in industry X, which is demographically determined by retirements and deaths, the number of job vacancies in industry X is tL_X per period. Assuming a random process of matching between unemployed persons and job vacancies, the probability that an unemployed person will find a job in X in one period is tL_X/L_U. This implies that an individual must expect to experience approximately $L_U/(tL_X)$ periods of unemployment before obtaining a job in industry X. Since entry into the underemployed (Y) sector is assumed to be free, the expected value of earnings foregone in search of a job in X is

$$w_Y \int_0^u e^{-rt}\, dt,$$

where u, the expected duration of unemployment, is $L_U/(tL_X)$ and r is the individual's rate of discount.

On the other hand, if the individual expects the wage differential to persist indefinitely, he will expect to gain

$$(w_X - w_Y) \int_u^K e^{-rt}\, dt$$

from a decision to be unemployed in search of a job in X, where K is the number of periods left in the individual's working life. Thus, the individual will choose to be unemployed (underemployed) if

$$(w_X - w_Y) \int_u^K e^{-rt}\, dt \; (\gtrless) \; w_Y \int_0^u e^{-rt}\, dt.$$

Evaluating the integrals and rearranging this decision rule can be written as

$$e^{-ru} \; (\gtrless) \; \frac{[w_X e^{-rK} - w_Y(1 - e^{-rK})]}{w_X}.$$

Taking logs and rearranging, we have

$$L_U \; (\gtrless) \; \frac{tL_X}{r} \{\log w_X - \log [w_X e^{-rK} + w_Y(1 - e^{-rK})]\}.$$

Up to this point, our model of the individual's unemployment-underemployment decision is substantially the same as that developed by Todaro for analysis of the rural-urban migration decision (Todaro 1969). His rural sector is our Y industry, his urban sector our X industry. Todaro postulates dependence of the rate of growth of the urban labor force on the difference in discounted-income prospects between the two regions.[1] Todaro's formulation, which assumes that the planning horizon, the cost of migration, and the rate of discount are the same for all rural workers, shares a problem common to most migration and job search models: it implies that all (or none) of the rural labor force ought to migrate. The introduction of individual differences with respect to discount rates and age, as is done in this paper, or the introduction of some random selection procedure enables one to skirt this problem.[2] There remain the problems (which are also common to most migration and job search models) of stability of the job search function over time and of aggregation.

In any disequilibrium situation which is working itself out, one is aggregating some decision rule over a changing population. This immediately implies that *one ought not to expect such relationships to be stable over time.* We turn first to the problem of aggregating the decision rule at a point in time. For an infinite horizon (letting $K \to \infty$) the individual decision rule reduces to

$$L_U \ (\gtrless) \ \frac{tL_X}{v} \log\left(\frac{w_X}{w_Y}\right),$$

where v is the discount rate appropriate to an infinite horizon. In the aggregation procedure and subsequent analysis, this inequality is easier to work with; however, it apparently eliminates individual differences with respect to the working horizon, and we are interested in analyzing the comparative statics with respect to changing time horizons (Sec. IV*C*). If we can somehow incorporate both the individual's discount rate and his time horizon in a pseudo discount rate over an infinite horizon, we can make use of the simplifications offered by the infinite horizon while retaining the ability to analyze the implications of changing time horizons. Letting v be the pseudo discount rate over an infinite horizon, we require that v be a function of the individual's discount rate, r, and his time horizon, K. This we obtain by equating the right-hand side of the two previous expressions and solving for v:

$$v = r\left\{\frac{\log w_X - \log w_Y}{\log w_X - \log\left[w_Y + e^{-rK}(w_X - w_Y)\right]}\right\}.$$

Note that $\partial v/\partial r > 0$ and $\partial v/\partial K < 0$.

[1] Zarembka rightly notes that Todaro's model is more suited to the analysis of changes in the rural labor force (migration from rural to urban) than to the direct analysis of changes in the urban labor force (Zarembka 1970).

[2] Mortensen, for example, introduces randomness in the frequency with which employees consider the search decision (Mortensen 1970).

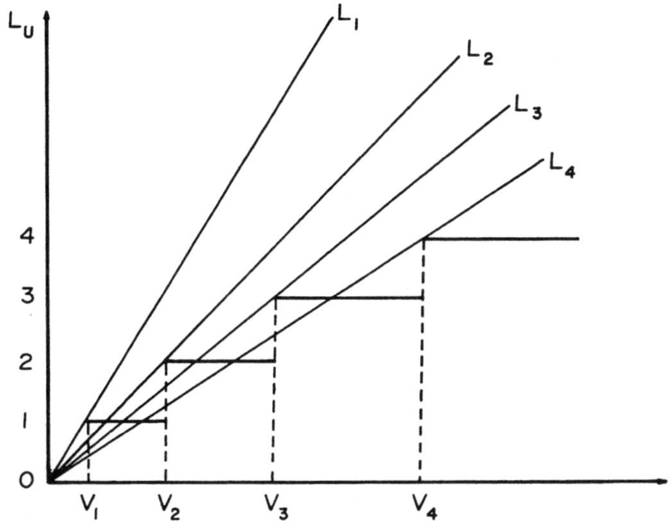

FIG. 1

For the jth individual, consider the locus of points

$$L_U = \frac{tL_X}{v_j} \log\left(\frac{w_X}{w_Y}\right) = JC_j,$$

where $C_j = 1/v_j$ and $J = tL_X \log (w_X/w_Y)$. Plot this locus in the (J, L_U) space. Our decision rule tells us that, for points below and to the right of the line, the jth individual will choose to be unemployed. For points above and to the left, he will choose to be underemployed. Several such loci are plotted in figure 1. Individual 1 in the figure is the least averse to unemployment. For J in the interval $[0, V_1]$, he will choose to be employed in industry Y. But in the interval $[V_1, V_2]$, he will choose to be unemployed while individuals 2, 3, and 4 will not. Accordingly, the aggregate unemployment function is 0 in the interval $[0, V_1]$, 1 in the interval $[V_1, V_2]$, 2 in the interval $[V_2, V_3]$, etc. Or, helping ourselves to a continuous approximation,

$$L_U = U(J), \qquad U' > 0, U'' < 0. \tag{9}$$

It is clear from the aggregation procedure that the second derivative of L_U with respect to J must be negative. This reflects the fact that the individuals who are least averse to unemployment are the first to become unemployed.

In each period, tL_X job vacancies occur in X, and, accordingly, tL_X of the unemployed obtain employment in X. And in each period all individuals in the Y and U sectors grow older, some die, and others retire. If the unemployment function is to be stable over time, in each period enough new individuals must enter the labor force to offset those who have taken employment in X plus those individuals in U and Y who have died or retired. Further, the entry of new individuals plus the aging of individuals in the U and Y sectors must be such as to maintain the distribution of the C_j's.

This completes the specification of the model. There are nine equations and nine unknowns (w_X, w_Y, p, q, L_X, L_Y, X, Y, L_U), with exogenous variables $\bar{w}_X$ or $\bar{L}_X$, $\bar{D}$, and $\bar{L}$. The reduced-form (partial) elasticities are derived in the next section.

III. General Equilibrium

We wish to know how each of the endogenous variables, particularly unemployment, respond when an arbitrary change in one of the exogenous variables is imposed. Total (logarithmic) differentiation of equations (1)–(9) expresses the structural equations in terms of proportional changes. Cramér's rule could then be employed to render the system in the desired reduced form. Instead, it is more instructive to "solve" the model by combining equations market by market until only one endogenous variable appears in each equation. Our strategy is first to combine equations relating to the product markets (parameterizing momentarily on labor market variables), then to combine equations relating to the labor markets (parameterizing momentarily on product market variables), and finally to bring together the results of the first two steps.

Letting the asterisk denote a proportional change, the system of structural equations is:

$$X^* = aL_X^*, \qquad (1')$$

where a = the elasticity of X output with respect to labor input or labor's imputed share;

$$w_X^* = -gL_X^* + p^*, \qquad (2')$$

where g = the (inverse Marshallian) elasticity of labor demand, equal to capital's imputed share $(1 - a)$ divided by the elasticity of substitution (σ_X);

$$L_X^* = \bar{L}_X^* \qquad (3a')$$

or

$$w_X^* = \bar{w}_X^*; \qquad (3b')$$

$$X^* = -e_1 p^* + e_2 q^* + e_3 \bar{D}^*, \qquad (4')$$

where e_1 = the "own price" elasticity of demand for X, e_2 = the "cross price" elasticity of demand for X, and e_3 = the income elasticity of demand for X;

$$Y^* = bL_Y^*, \tag{5'}$$

where b = analogue of a;

$$w_Y^* = -hL_Y^* + q^*, \tag{6'}$$

where h = analogue of g;

$$L_Y^* = \frac{L}{L_Y} L^* - \frac{L_X}{L_Y} L_X^* - \frac{L_U}{L_Y} L_U^*; \tag{7'}$$

$$Y^* = -e_4 q^* + e_5 p^* + e_6 \bar{D}^*, \tag{8'}$$

where e_4 = analogue of e_1, e_5 = analogue of e_2, and e_6 = analogue of e_3. Equation (8′) is the budget constraint combined with the demand for X function (4). The elasticities (e's) are related as follows: From (4),

$$X^* = -\varepsilon(p^* - q^*) + \eta(\bar{D}^* - q^*),$$

where ε = the "primitive" elasticity of demand for X with respect to relative prices and η = the "primitive" elasticity of demand for X with respect to real income. Then

$$e_1 = \varepsilon, \qquad e_2 = \varepsilon - \eta, \qquad e_3 = \eta,$$

$$e_4 = 1 + \frac{A}{1 - A}(\varepsilon - \eta), \qquad e_5 = \frac{A}{1 - A}(\varepsilon - 1), \qquad e_6 = \frac{1}{1 - A}(1 - \eta A),$$

where $A = Xp/\bar{D}$. Note that $e_1 - e_2 = e_3$ and $e_4 - e_5 = e_6$ and that

$$(e_1e_4 - e_2e_5) = (e_1e_6 + e_3e_5) = (e_2e_6 + e_3e_4) = \frac{\varepsilon - \eta A}{1 - A},$$

$$e_1 = 1 \Leftrightarrow e_5 = 0, \qquad e_2 = 0 \Leftrightarrow e_4 = 1, \qquad e_3 = 1 \Leftrightarrow e_6 = 1.$$

Finally, we have

$$L_U^* = EW(w_X^* - w_Y^*) + EL_X^*, \tag{9'}$$

where E = the elasticity of the unemployment function with respect to its argument and $W = 1/\log(w_X/w_Y)$.

While we have given explicitly neoclassical interpretations to the elasticities, we need not have done so, and the skeptical reader is welcome to furnish his own. For example, one could disbelieve that labor is paid the value of its marginal product and still accept (2) and (6) on the grounds that demand curves for labor exist, and slope downward, but for other reasons. We believe that the model is quite general in that it bears a wide variety of interpretations.

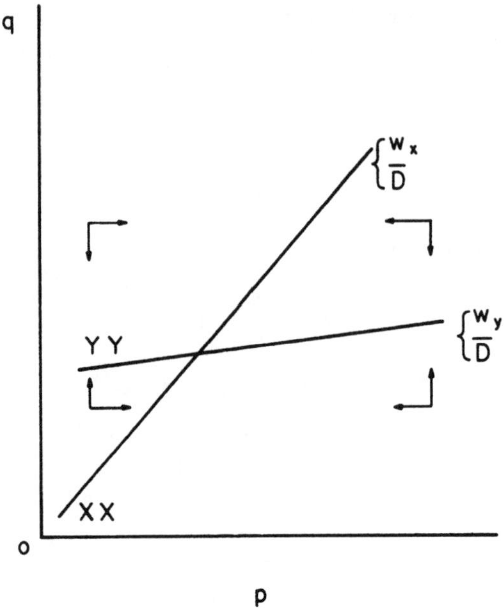

Fig. 2

We first investigate the "product side" of the model. Combining (1′) and (2′) gives a supply of X function with the wage as a parameter. Taken along with the demand for X function, equation (4′), we have, following Hicks, combinations of prices which clear the X market, with the X-sector wage and aggregate demand as parameters (Hicks 1946, chap. 5):

$$p^* \left(\frac{a}{g} + e_1\right) = e_2 q^* + \frac{a}{g} \cdot w_X{}^* + e_3 \bar{D}^*. \tag{10}$$

Likewise, equations (5′), (6′), and (8′) yield equilibrium price combinations which clear the Y market:

$$q^* \left(\frac{b}{h} + e_4\right) = e_5 p^* + \frac{b}{h} \cdot w_Y{}^* + e_6 \bar{D}^*. \tag{11}$$

Equations (10) and (11) are depicted in figure 2. The XX curve illustrates (10) and the YY curve (11) on the assumption that XX is more steeply upward sloping. A sufficient condition for this is that $e_1 e_4$ exceed $e_2 e_5$; the product of the "own price" elasticities must exceed the product of the "cross price" elasticities; or, from above,

$$\frac{\varepsilon - \eta A}{1 - A} > 0. \tag{12}$$

We shall regard this as the "normal" case, for if prices rise in response to excess demand, the product markets would be stable. The reader can confirm that if YY is steeper than XX, the equilibrium, if it exists, is unstable.

Solving for p^* and q^* in (10) and (11) gives us

$$p^* = \frac{a(b/h + e_4)}{g\Delta_1} w_X^* + \frac{e_2 b}{h\Delta_1} w_Y^* + \frac{e_2 e_6 + e_3(b/h + e_4)}{\Delta_1} \bar{D}^*, \tag{13}$$

$$q^* = \frac{b(a/g + e_1)}{h\Delta_1} w_Y^* + \frac{e_5 a}{g\Delta_1} w_X^* + \frac{e_3 e_5 + e_6(a/g + e_1)}{\Delta_1} \bar{D}^*, \tag{14}$$

$$\Delta_1 = e + \frac{e_4 a}{g} + \frac{e_1 b}{h} + \frac{ab}{gh}, \qquad e = (e_1 e_4 - e_2 e_5) > 0.$$

Note that these equations express precisely the consequences of "wage push" (w_Y^*, $w_Y^* > 0$) and "demand pull" ($\bar{D}^* > 0$).

Turning now to the "labor side," we seek combinations of wages which "clear" the respective labor markets. Demand for L_X is given by (1′), (2′), and (4′), with supply of L_X determined by (3a′) or (3b′). Equilibrium combinations of w_X and w_Y are given by

$$w_X^* = \frac{e_2}{e_1} q^* + \frac{e_3}{e_1} \bar{D}^* - \frac{e_1 g + a}{e_1} L_X^*, \tag{15}$$

with either w_X^* or L_X^* given exogenously.

Similarly, for the L_Y market, demand for L_Y is derived from (5′), (6′), and (8′). However, the supply of L_Y must take into account alternate employment in X and unemployment. Taking (7′) and (9′) along with demand, we have

$$\begin{aligned} w_Y^* &= \frac{e_5}{e_4} \cdot \frac{1}{\Delta_2} p^* + \frac{e_6}{e_4} \cdot \frac{1}{\Delta_2} \bar{D}^* \\ &+ \frac{e_4 h + b}{e_4} \cdot \frac{L_U}{L_Y} \cdot \frac{EW}{\Delta_2} \cdot w_X^* \\ &+ \frac{e_4 h + b}{e_4} \left(\frac{L_X}{L_Y} + E \cdot \frac{L_U}{L_Y} \right) \cdot \frac{1}{\Delta_2} L_X^* \\ &- \frac{e_4 h + b}{e_4} \cdot \frac{L}{L_Y} \cdot \frac{1}{\Delta_2} L^*, \end{aligned} \tag{16}$$

$$\Delta_2 = 1 + \frac{e_4 h + b}{e_4} E \cdot \frac{L_U}{L_Y} \cdot W,$$

with either w_X^* or L_X^* given exogenously.

Equations (15) and (16) are plotted in figure 3. The *xx* curve illustrates (15) and the *yy* curve (16). The *xx* curve is vertical, reflecting the common

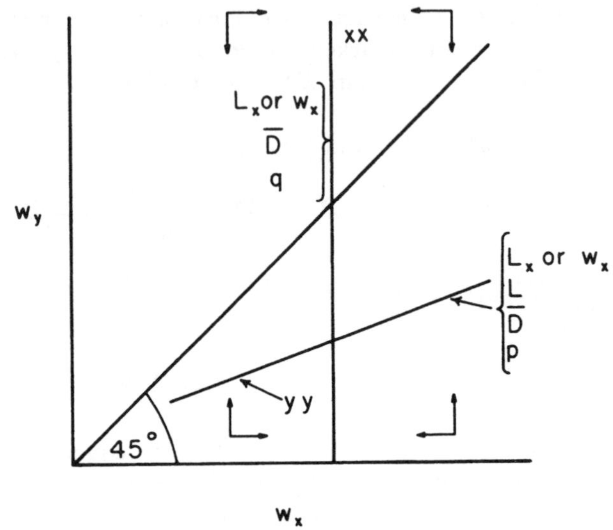

FIG. 3

observation that a wage policy ($w_X{}^* = \bar{w}_X{}^*$) or an employment policy ($L_X{}^* = \bar{L}_X{}^*$) of labor unions can give rise to equivalent labor market "equilibria." The *yy* slopes upward because higher wages in X increase the payoff from being unemployed in search of those wages. Workers in Y are thus induced to down tools and become unemployed while searching for employment in X. Wages rise in Y as workers depart.

Wages are assumed to fall in response to excess supply, and the labor markets are stable. Note, however, that a special interpretation of "disequilibrium" is required in the market for X labor. We take either $L_X = \bar{L}_X$ or $w_X = \bar{w}_X$ to be the short-run "equilibrium" supply curves. "Disequilibrium" adjustments are relative to those curves.

The original system of nine structural equations has now been reduced to (13), (14), (15), and (16); unknowns are p^*, q^*, $w_X{}^*$ or $L_X{}^*$, and $w_Y{}^*$; exogenous variables are $\bar{D}^*$, $\bar{L}_X{}^*$ or $\bar{w}_X{}^*$, and $\bar{L}^*$. Further details of the solution are omitted to save space. The results are set out in table 1. It reports the algebraic sign of the reduced-form (partial) elasticities where the institutional rigidity is a fixed supply, $L_X = \bar{L}_X$. These link proportional changes in exogenous variables with proportional changes in the endogenous ones of chief concern.

As can be seen from the last column of table 1, the comparative static results with respect to $\bar{L}_X{}^*$ are in most cases ambiguous. An increase in $\bar{L}_X$ ensures that production of X will increase and that the wage differential will become smaller. The other results are ambiguous, depending on the sign of some very complicated terms. (Three of these conditions appear in table 1.) The comparative statics with respect to $\bar{D}^*$ and $\bar{L}^*$ are discussed in Section IV below.

TABLE 1

$L_X^* = \bar{L}_X^*$

Endogenous	Exogenous: $\bar{D}^*$	$\bar{L}^*$	$\bar{L}_X^*$
w_X^*	+	−	? sign C_1
w_Y^*	+	−	? sign C_2
$w_X^* - w_Y^*$	0	+	−
p^*	+	−	?
q^*	+	−	?
L_X^*	0	0	+
X^*	0	0	+
L_Y^*	0	+	?
Y^*	0	+	?
L_U^*	0	+	? sign C_3

$$C_1 = -\left[ge + \frac{e_4 a}{g} + gh\Delta_1 \cdot E \cdot \frac{L_U}{L_Y} W - e_2 \left(\frac{L_X}{L_Y} + E \cdot \frac{L_U}{L_Y}\right)\right]$$

$$C_2 = \left[(he + e_1 b)\left(\frac{L_X}{L_Y} + E \cdot \frac{L_U}{L_Y}\right) - gh\Delta_1 \cdot E \cdot \frac{L_U}{L_Y} \cdot W - e_5 a\right]$$

$$C_3 = -\left[W\left(he + e_3 b \cdot \frac{L_X}{L_Y} + ge + e_6 a\right) - e\right] \cdot E$$

When we consider the comparative statics when the wage rate is fixed, the results are similar. Almost none of the comparative statics results is determinate with respect to sign. In fact, if we apply Cramér's rule, the determinant of the matrix in the denominator is unsigned. Further, the "economic sense" of conditions which would guarantee a determinate result is not obvious.

The indeterminacy of these results is itself interesting. However, in order to derive results which are more readily amenable to interpretation but which reflect essential features of the model, we impose additional restrictions. We specify that in the neighborhood of equilibrium: (1) the "primitive" elasticity of demand for X with respect to relative prices (ε) is unity; (2) the "primitive" elasticity of demand for X with respect to real income (η) is unity; and (3) the elasticities of substitution in both production sectors (σ_X and σ_Y) are unity. Both demand relations are thus "Graham type" (constant expenditure) functions, and the production functions are "Cobb-Douglas." For convenience, we shall refer to this simple version as the "log-linear model."

The structural equations relating proportional changes are now

$$w_X^* = -(1 - a)L_X^* + p^*, \qquad (2'')$$

$$X^* = -p^* + \bar{D}^*, \qquad (4'')$$

$$w_Y^* = -(1 - b)L_Y^* + q^*, \qquad (6'')$$

$$Y^* = -q^* + \bar{D}^*. \qquad (8'')$$

Equations (1′), (3a′) or (3b′), (5′), (7′), and (9′) complete the model.

TABLE 2

	Exogenous			
	$L_X^* = \bar{L}_X^*$	$w_X^* = \bar{w}_X^*$		
Endogenous	$\bar{L}_X^*$	$\bar{D}^*$	$\bar{L}^*$	$\bar{w}_X^*$
w_X^*	—	0	0	+
w_Y^*	sign $-d_1$	+	—	sign $+d_1$
p^*	—	+	0	+
q^*	sign $-d_1$	+	—	sign $+d_1$
L_X^*	+	+	0	—
L_Y^*	sign $+d_1$	sign $+d_1$	+	sign $-d_1$
X^*	+	+	0	—
Y^*	sign $+d_1$	sign $+d_1$	+	sign $-d_1$
L_U^*	sign $+d_2$	sign $+d_2$	+	sign $-d_2$

$$d_1 = U' - 1/\left\{t\left[1 - \log\left(\frac{\bar{w}_X}{w_Y}\right)\right]\right\}$$

$$d_2 = \log\left(\frac{\bar{w}_X}{w_Y}\right) - 1 - \frac{L_X}{L_Y}$$

Again, solving market by market, we obtain four equations corresponding to (13), (14), (15), and (16) but which are far simpler and tractable:

$$p^* = aw_X^* + g\bar{D}^*, \tag{13''}$$

$$q^* = bw_Y^* + h\bar{D}^*, \tag{14''}$$

$$w_X^* = -L_X^* + \bar{D}^*, \tag{15''}$$

$$w_Y^* = \frac{\bar{D}^*}{\Delta_2} + \frac{L_U}{L_Y} \cdot \frac{E}{\Delta_2} \cdot W \cdot w_X^* + \frac{1}{\Delta_2}\left(\frac{L_X}{L_Y} + \frac{L_U}{L_Y} E\right) \cdot L_X^* - \frac{\bar{L}}{L_Y} \cdot \frac{1}{\Delta_2} \bar{L}^*, \tag{16''}$$

$$\Delta_2 = 1 + \frac{L_U}{L_Y} \cdot E \cdot W.$$

These structural equations give rise to the reduced-form elasticities. The algebraic signs of these elasticities are recorded in table 2 for future reference.

IV. Applications

A. Demand Management

1) $L_X = \bar{L}_X$. If the institutional rigidity is a restriction of labor supply to the X sector, then, even in the general case, *all real variables are homogeneous of degree zero in aggregate demand*, with prices bearing the whole of the

required adjustment. In this case, even the short-run Phillips curve is vertical (see the first column of table 1).

This is a trivial result in one-sector neo-Keynesian models of the post-war period.[3] If aggregate employment is fixed, so is output, and prices alone absorb demand changes. Simple enough. Not so in our two-sector model, however. Here, the Y sector can respond to demand pressures. Suppose the income elasticity for Y is high relative to that for X. Then an increase in $\bar{D}$ will be channeled mainly into the Y sector, raising the derived demand for Y labor relative to X labor and raising Y wages relative to X wages. The narrowing of the wage differential reduces the profitability of being unemployed, and some of the unemployed give up looking for X-sector employment and enter Y-sector jobs, expanding the output of Y while the output of X remains fixed.

The fact that this cannot occur strikes us as a rather surprising implication of our assumptions. The clue lies in the demand functions which are homogeneous of degree zero in relative prices and real income. The demand relations are satisfied if $\bar{D}$, p, and q rise by equal percentage amounts, with the output of X and Y unchanged. Now, suppose L_X and L_Y are unchanged. Then X and Y are constant, and equal percentage rises in p and q will be reflected in equal percentage rises of w_X and w_Y. With $\bar{L}_X$ unchanged, there is no reason for L_U, and thus L_Y, to change.

2) $w_X = \bar{w}_X$. We must turn to the log-linear model for interpretable results in this case. See the second column of table 2. An increase in aggregate demand induces an increase in X-sector employment and output, and both prices and the Y-sector wage increase. However, the change in unemployment and the changes in Y-sector employment and output are ambiguous. The change in unemployment depends on the sign of

$$\log\left(\frac{\bar{w}_X}{w_Y}\right) - 1 - \frac{L_X}{L_Y}.$$

Although the sign is ambiguous, we expect it to be negative. The single positive term, $\log(\bar{w}_X/w_Y)$, will be less than 1 if $\bar{w}_X/w_Y$ is less than $e \simeq 2.72$. Then $\bar{w}_X/w_Y$ less than 2.72 is a sufficient condition to ensure that $dL_U{}^*/d\bar{D}^*$ be negative. Accordingly, we assume that unemployment decreases in response to increased demand.

The Y-sector ambiguities turn on the sign of

$$U' - \frac{1}{\{t[1 - \log(\bar{w}_X/w_Y)]\}}.$$

[3] For example, see Tobin (1955), who assumes $w_X = \bar{w}_X$. But, according to Tobin, if $L_X = \bar{L}_X$, then the elasticity of aggregate supply is zero.

We interpret this condition below, while noting here that the Y sector will behave as a "countercyclical" sector of "last resort" employment if unemployment is relatively unresponsive to the arguments which determine it: the wage spread and X-sector employment.

To see this, let $\bar{w}_X{}^* = 0$ in equations (13″)–(16″) and let $\bar{D}^* > 0$. Equation (15″) reveals that L_X increases concomitantly, but (16″) tells us that w_Y increases as well. Increases in L_X increase the incentive to become unemployed, while increases in w_Y tend to reduce unemployment by narrowing the wage spread. Unless the wage spread is quite large ($\bar{w}_X$ greater than $2.72w_Y$), the latter effect dominates the former so that $\bar{D}^* > 0$ implies $L_U{}^* < 0$.

But $\bar{D}^* > 0$ may not have the effect of increasing employment in the Y sector. Recall that $L_Y = \bar{L} - L_X - L_U$. With L_X rising and L_U falling as $\bar{D}$ increases, L_Y can go either way. If the "unemployment effect" ($L_U{}^* < 0$) dominates the "employment effect" ($L_X{}^* > 0$), then L_Y increases. This will occur if the "unemployment effect" is sufficiently large.[4] Unemployment is determined by

$$U\left[tL_X \log\left(\frac{\bar{w}_X}{w_Y}\right)\right].$$

Since the argument of the U function is proportional to t, the magnitude of the unemployment effect is directly related to the exogenous turnover rate and, of course, to the slope of the unemployment function. For a given value of L_X, t determines the number of job openings per period, and hence it directly affects the desirability of unemployment.

If we once again consider the aggregation procedure used to derive the unemployment function, we can say a bit more about the ambiguous comparative statics. In figure 1 the change in J associated with a change from any integer value of L_U to the next is given by the slope of the ray of indifference of the last individual to become unemployed. This implies

[4] There is some evidence that perverse or countercyclical employment trends in the Y sector have occurred in both the pre- and postwar periods in the United States. During the Great Depression, the farm sector exhibited some of the characteristics of our underemployed sector. Theodore Shultz observed that in 1932, when urban wages were still considerably higher and falling less rapidly than rural wages, there was a definite reversal of the historical flow of workers from the farm to the city. In fact, 1932 witnessed a net urban-to-rural migration (Schultz 1945). In discussing regulatory problems in the motor-carrier industry during the 1930s, Kahn notes that "with the sharp reductions in industrial employment, large numbers of workers moved into the owner-operation of service stations, farms, trucks, and small grocery stores, so that the supply of labor in these industries actually expanded in the face of declining remuneration" (Kahn 1971, p. 181). Economic conditions have not recently been so severe as to make the identification of occupations of last resort an easy chore. For intuitive support, we can point to the reemergence of street vendors in large numbers; to the countercyclical variations of employment in taxicabs, despite the regulated nature of the industry (Bureau of Labor Statistics, various issues); and to the plight of Vancouver barbers, who complain of continued entry in the face of sharply reduced demand and earnings in the industry.

that the slope of unemployment function at any point is approximated by the slope of the ray of indifference of the last individual to become unemployed. For the *j*th individual this slope is, from Section II*C* above, $C_j = 1/v_j$. Since $\partial v_j/\partial r_j > 0$, $\partial C_j/\partial r_j < 0$. Higher individual rates of discount then decrease the responsiveness of unemployment to J. This then implies that imperfect capital markets tend to contribute to "perverse" results in industry Y because, for any value of J, they reduce the sensitivity of unemployment to changes in J.

The slope of the unemployment function will also be quite sensitive to the demographic composition of the labor force. Since $\partial v_j/\partial K_j < 0$, $\partial C_j/\partial K_j > 0$. Assuming that younger people have longer planning horizons, the younger the labor force, the steeper will be the unemployment function for any value of the argument J. We comment on this and related points below.

Before departing our discussion of demand management, a general observation on the effectiveness of demand management in reducing unemployment is in order. The effectiveness of changes in $\bar{D}$ in reducing unemployment are dependent on the slope of the aggregated unemployment function. Other things equal, the greater is U', the more effective is demand management in reducing unemployment. Given the aggregation procedure, the value of U' is dependent on the arrays of individual rates of discount and time horizons. Thus, the effectiveness of changes in $\bar{D}$ as a control on unemployment is sensitive to the demographic composition of the labor force, the degree of imperfection in capital markets, and, as we shall see below, the progress of disadvantaged groups in removing discriminatory barriers to employment. There have been significant changes in at least two of these factors in recent years.

B. Union Power

Referring once again to table 2, an increase in union power ($\bar{L}_X^* < 0$ or $\bar{w}_X^* > 0$) will decrease employment and output in the X industry. The price of X will rise. Unemployment rises provide, once again, that the wage spread is not too large. But variables which describe the Y-sector response (w_Y, L_Y, Y, q) can move in either direction. Again, the outcome turns on the sign of $U' - 1/\{t[1 - \log (\bar{w}_X/w_Y)]\}$. Only if unemployment is sufficiently insensitive to the arguments which determine it do we predict a rise in Y-sector output and employment and a fall in the Y-sector wage and price.

We focus on the matter of Y-sector employment (L_Y). A rise in X-sector wages (or additional restrictions on labor input) thrusts workers onto the streets ($L_U^* > 0$) or into jobs of last resort ($L_Y^* > 0$). Unemployment rises. If the increase of unemployment is sufficiently small, Y-sector employment will increase. The magnitude of the unemployment response is conditioned by two (possibly) conflicting forces. On the one hand, the reduction of X-sector employment reduces the incentive to become unemployed because fewer new jobs become available for any given turnover rate. On the other hand, the wage differential widens, increasing the incentive to become unemployed. The latter effect dominates so that unemployment increases, but the increase could be small if unemployment is relatively insensitive. If so, then some of the newly unemployed become underemployed in the Y sector.

C. Changing Time Horizons

Substantial demographic changes have occurred and continue to occur in the North American labor force. The impact of these changes in the labor market, and particularly the relationship which these changes bear to the problem of price inflation, has begun to receive attention (Perry 1970; Schultze 1971). Although this is not the place to explore these problems in depth, we can indicate the role that these changes play in our model.

As more women begin seriously to pursue careers, it will pay them to invest in more thorough search activity, that is, in more unemployment in the context of our model. This, of course, implies an upward shift of the aggregate unemployment function. And it also has implications for the structure of unemployment. It implies that for a given level of unemployment a larger proportion of the unemployed will be women, or that the unemployment among women will increase relative to the rate among men.

The relative increase in the unemployment rate of women can be most readily understood in terms of figure 1. The lengthening of women's career horizons would result in more steeply inclined loci of indifference between unemployment and underemployment for women. Recall that $\partial v_j/\partial K_j < 0$, and hence $\partial C_j/\partial K_j > 0$. This implies that at any given level of unemployment the proportion of the unemployed who are women will increase as a result of changing career horizons. If we put this implication slightly differently, the model suggests that a result of increasing aspirations of women is an increase in the unemployment rate of women relative to that of men (see n. 5 below).

The effects of the removal or lessening of racial discrimination are analogous. If "equal opportunity" is interpreted in our model as increasing the probability that members of minority groups can obtain employment in the high-wage sector, then this results in an increased slope of the loci of indifference between unemployment and underemployment for members of minority groups. As with the women's liberation effect, the "equal-opportunity effect" implies an increase in the unemployment rates of minority groups relative to nonminority groups.

In terms of our model, we can think of the postwar baby boom as having essentially two implications. The baby boom obviously represents an increase in the labor force. In tables 1 and 2, the comparative statics are unambiguous. An increase in the labor force has no effect on the X sector and the increase in the labor force is split between increases in unemployment and increases in Y-sector employment. Production of Y increases as a result of the increased supply of labor, and both the wage rate and the price in the Y sector fall.

There is, however, another implication of the baby boom in our model, for it means that the age composition of the labor force has changed. The baby boom means that the proportion of young people in the labor force has increased. Presuming that young people have longer planning horizons, the implication of the increased proportion of young people in the labor force is to increase the slope of the aggregated unemployment function for any given value of the argument J. This is, of course, the same effect which the changing pattern of women's participation in the labor force and the lessening of discriminatory barriers had on the unemployment function. As with the other two effects, the increased proportion of young people in the labor force implies that unemployment among young workers ought to increase relative to the rate among older workers.[5]

V. Conclusions

A feature of our model is that it cannot be used to analyze involuntary unemployment in the usual sense. There is no person in our model economy who cannot find a job *at some wage*. The unemployed have "only themselves to blame," so to speak, in the sense that they have made a rational calculation to improve their economic position. They are *voluntarily* unemployed. Put another way, we have excluded consideration of those persons who do not have, and cannot invent, an occupation of last resort. It is impossible to know whether this group is empirically important, since one cannot measure the bounds of human inventiveness. But if it is true that this excluded group is small, then we must argue that a large measure of observed unemployment is strictly voluntary.

But if unemployment is voluntary in our model, the occupational mix, including job search, is not. Ours might be called a theory of involuntary dislocation. The unemployed (L_U) and the underemployed (L_Y) are pre-

[5] It is perhaps interesting to note that there is evidence which suggests that the implied effect has occurred in all three situations. The unemployment rate among nonwhites relative to whites seems to have increased sharply in the mid-1950s and the ratio of female to male unemployment rates seems to have increased over the decade of the 1960s. Finally, the unemployment rate among young males relative to that among males age 35–44 increased sharply in the late 1960s. The unemployment rates referred to are those from the Bureau of Labor Statistics Household Survey (Bureau of Labor Statistics, various issues).

pared to work in the X sector at the going wage, but they cannot readily find employment there. The trouble, of course, lies in the failure of prices and employment to adjust to their competitive levels in the X industry. If they did, we could drop equations (3). Then, if we add the equilibrium condition that $w_X = w_Y$, dislocation (including unemployment) wipes out. Our definition of involuntary dislocation is: *People are involuntarily dislocated if, at current wage rates, they must wait to find a job in their best alternative occupation.*

The consequences for overall economic efficiency of institutional constraints, and resulting involuntary dislocation, are twofold in our model. Resulting price distortions emphasized by Johnson and Mieszkowski and by Diewert occur here as well (Johnson and Mieszkowski 1970; Diewert 1972). But, in addition, there is a dead-weight loss as people become unemployed in an effort to arbitrage the wage gap. Not only are tangency conditions along the production possibilities curve being violated, but equilibrium occurs at an interior point in the production possibilities set which corresponds to full employment of labor.

There is a further loss which is difficult to document but which may be more important: the frustration and sense of injustice felt by those left out of the X industry. In Weizsäcker's pressure group society, these are the citizens who do not know how to organize and/or cannot finance "profitable" pressure groups (Weizsäcker 1972). Those who can, organize; those who can't, protest!

References

Bureau of Labor Statistics. *U.S. Employment and Earnings Statistics.* Washington: Government Printing Office, various issues.

Diewert, E. *The Effects of Unionization on Wages and Employment: A General Equilibrium Analysis.* Ottawa: Dept. Manpower and Immigration, 1972.

Fei, John C. H., and Ranis, Gustav. *Development of the Labour Surplus Economy: Theory and Policy.* Homewood, Ill.: Irwin, 1964.

Harberger, A. C. "On Measuring the Social Opportunity Cost of Labour." *Internat. Labour Rev.* 103 (June 1971): 559–79.

Harris, John R., and Todaro, Michael P. "Migration, Unemployment, and Development: A Two-Sector Analysis." *A.E.R.* 60 (March 1970): 126–43.

Hicks, J. *Value and Capital.* 2d ed. Oxford: Clarendon, 1946.

Holt, C. C. "Job Search, Phillips Wage Relation, and Union Influence: Theory and Evidence." In *Microeconomic Foundations of Employment and Inflation Theory,* edited by E. S. Phelps et al. New York: Norton, 1970.

Johnson, H. G., and Mieszkowski, P. "The Effects of Unionization on the Distribution of Income: A General Equilibrium Approach." *Q.J.E.* 84 (November 1970): 539–61.

Kahn, Alfred E. *The Economics of Regulation.* Vol. 2. New York: Wiley, 1971.

Lewis, W. Arthur. *Theory of Economic Growth.* London: Allen & Unwin, 1955.

Mortensen, D. T. "A Theory of Wage and Employment Dynamics." In *Microeconomic Foundations of Employment and Inflation Theory,* edited by E. S. Phelps et al. New York: Norton, 1970.

Perry, George L. "Changing Labour Markets and Inflation." *Brookings Papers Econ. Activity* 1, no. 3 (1970): 411–41.

Robinson, J. "Disguised Unemployment." *Econ. J.* 46 (June 1936): 225–37.

Rosenstein-Rodan, Paul N. "Problems of Industrialization of Eastern and Southeastern Europe." *Econ. J.* 53 (September 1943): 202–11.

Schultz, T. W. *Agriculture in an Unstable Economy.* New York: McGraw-Hill, 1945.

Schultze, Charles L. "Has the Phillips Curve Shifted? Some Additional Evidence." *Brookings Papers Econ. Activity* 2(1971): 452–67.

Tobin, J. "A Dynamic Aggregative Model." *J.P.E.* 63 (April 1955): 103–15.

Todaro, Michael P. "A Model of Migration and Urban Unemployment in Less Developed Countries." *A.E.R.* 59 (March 1969): 138–48.

Weizsäcker, C. C. von. *The Political Economy of Stability in Western Countries.* Stockholm: Almquist & Wicksell, 1972.

Zarembka, Paul. "Labour Migration and Urban Unemployment: Comment." *A.E.R.* 60 (March 1970): 184–86.

Firm-specific human capital: a shared investment or optimal entrapment?

DAVID DONALDSON, B. CURTIS EATON / University of British Columbia

Firm-specific human capital: a shared investment or optimal entrapment? This paper argues that the accepted analysis of firm-specific human capital as a shared investment is erroneous. In the accepted analysis the employer shares the investment in specific capital with employees in order to reduce turnover. The analysis yields an increasing wage profile, which inhibits quits of trained workers. This paper argues that the employer can inhibit quits simply by offering an increasing wage profile while maintaining a constant present value of earnings. The paper demonstrates that the employer also has an incentive to minimize layoffs, and this can be achieved by adopting a decreasing wage profile.

Le capital humain spécifique à la firme: co-investissement ou piège optimal? L'analyse conventionnelle du capital humain spécifique à une firme suggère que les coûts d'investissement dans ce type de capital humain sont partagés par l'employeur et l'employé. Dans cette analyse, l'employé investit durant la période de son apprentissage en acceptant un salaire moins élevé que ce qu'il pourrait obtenir ailleurs et il reçoit un rendement sur cet investissement dans les périodes subséquentes quand son salaire en vient à excéder les salaires alternatifs. Pour sa part l'employeur investit durant la période d'apprentissage en payant un salaire qui est plus grand que le produit marginal de l'employé et il reçoit un rendement dans les périodes subséquentes quand la productivité marginale de l'employé excède son salaire.

Ce profil de salaire implique que le taux de roulement du personnel va être réduit. De fait cette stabilité plus grande de sa main d'œuvre est l'un des facteurs qui incitent l'employeur à partager les frais de l'investissement spécifiquement utile à la firme.

Le présent mémoire suggère que l'employeur n'a pas à assumer une portion de l'investissement pour obtenir cette stabilité. Il peut arriver au même résultat en manipulant le profil de salaire tout en maintenant constante la valeur présente des gains totaux de l'employé. En effet l'employeur a avantage à réduire le taux de roulement de sa main d'œuvre causé par les départs volontaires ou les mises à pied. Si l'instabilité est causée par des départs volontaires, l'employeur devrait adopter un profil croissant de salaire avec le temps. Si l'instabilité vient du fait que les variations stochastiques dans les prix futurs peuvent engendrer des mises à pied, l'employeur devrait adopter un profil décroissant de salaire avec le temps.

The authors wish to acknowledge the helpful comments and criticism of G. C. Archibald, R. G. Evans, C. K. Harley, the members of the Labour Workshop at the University of British Columbia, and the editorial staff of this JOURNAL.

Canadian Journal of Economics/Revue canadienne d'Economique, IX, no. 3
August/août 1976. Printed in Canada/Imprimé au Canada.

THE PROBLEM

Certain skills or knowledge which an employee may acquire while working for a particular firm are of no value to other firms, even though such skills contribute to the productivity of the employee in that particular firm. Since these 'firm-specific' skills are of no value to other firms they will not be priced in any market, and the employee has little or no incentive to acquire them. The employer, on the other hand, has a definite incentive to create these skills through on-the-job training programs. The accepted analysis of the firm's decision to invest in specific human capital is that the firm is led to share the investment with its employees.[1]

In the accepted view, the worker 'invests' during training by accepting a wage rate lower than the alternative market wage and receives a return on his investment in subsequent periods in the form of a wage higher than the alternative. The firm 'invests' in specific capital during the training period through direct outlays on training and/or through paying a wage in excess of the marginal product of the trainee, and it receives a return on the investment in subsequent periods when it pays a wage rate less than the marginal product of the trained worker.

The sharing is thought to reduce labour turnover. Because the worker has 'invested' in specific capital, his wage rate is higher than the wage rate he could obtain in alternative employment, and this reduces the probability that the worker will quit. The firm too has 'invested' in specific capital, and consequently is receiving a marginal product which is higher than the wage it pays. It is therefore less likely to lay off a specifically trained worker if product demand declines. Thus the relationship, the shared investment, is seen to be mutually beneficial: both parties receive a return on their investment, and the investment, by reducing turnover probabilities, increases the security of both parties. It is the possibility of reducing voluntary turnover which leads the firm to share the valuable opportunity for investment in human capital:

> Firms paying for specific training might take account of turnover merely by obtaining a sufficiently large return from those remaining to counterbalance the loss from those leaving. (The return on 'successes' – those remaining – would, of course, overestimate the average return on all training expenditures.) Firms could do even better, however, by recognizing that the likelihood of a quit is not fixed but depends on wages. Instead of merely recouping on successes what is lost on failures, they might reduce the likelihood of failure itself by offering higher wages after training than could be received elsewhere. In effect, they would offer employees some of the return from training. Matters would be improved in some respects but worsened in others, for the higher wage would make the supply of trainees greater than the

1 The interpretation is usually attributed to Becker (1964, 18–28). It is implicit in Mincer's (1962) estimates of on-the-job training and Oi's (1962) analysis of labour as a quasi-fixed factor of production. See also Bodenhöfer (1967) and Telser (1972). The most ambitious and most recent pursuit of this interpretation is Parsons (1972). A recent textbook reproduces the Becker interpretation without change (Rees, 1973).

demand, and rationing would be required. The final step would be to shift some training costs as well as returns to employees, thereby bringing supply more in line with demand. When the final step is completed, firms no longer pay all training costs nor do they collect all the return but they share both with employees. (Becker, 1964, 22).

The wage profile over the investment and payout period is of particular interest. While the worker is investing in specific human capital he receives a relatively low wage rate; during the payout period he receives a relatively high wage rate. This wage profile seems to be consistent with observed age-earnings profiles of some workers.

It is our contention that this age-earnings profile may be evidence of firm-specific human capital, but it is *not* (necessarily) evidence of a shared investment. It is our interpretation that this wage profile may be evidence of deliberate entrapment of workers by firms. Becker, of course, acknowledges the incentive which firm-specific capital gives the employer to entrap his employees (see, for example, his discussion of incompletely vested pensions: Becker, 1964, 26–7). Indeed Becker's reasoning, reproduced above, indicates that the employer's willingness to share the opportunity to invest in firm-specific human capital arises out of the desire to minimize or reduce turnover. What we hope to show is simply that the employer need not share the investment opportunity to reduce turnover; rather he can achieve this end merely by manipulating the wage profile.

How one evaluates some public policies depends critically on which interpretation one accepts. For example, with Becker's interpretation one might be willing to support publically funded on-the-job training schemes which create firm-specific human capital. However, given our interpretation, the primary benefits of such schemes are likely to accrue to employers. Further, one's attitude toward any entrapment device will be different, depending on which interpretation is accepted.

We use the simplest (competitive) models which allow us to develop our alternative interpretation. More elaborate and more realistic models could be developed, but we do not think that the elaborations (at least those which seem obvious to us) would significantly alter our interpretation.

The following labour market assumptions are incorporated in the three models we develop below: 1/ workers are risk neutral; 2/ both the capital and labour markets are perfect; 3/ when a worker quits or is laid off at the end of any period he endures one period of unemployment.

We adopt the following general criterion as evidence that the investment in specific human capital is shared: an investment in specific human capital is shared if, and only if, the worker is made better off. Given our labour market assumptions, perfect labour and capital markets and risk neutrality, a worker is made better off by accepting employment in a firm in which an investment in specific capital is undertaken only if the expected discounted present value of earnings in that firm (PVE_F) exceeds the expected discounted present value of earnings in alternative employment (PVE_A) where no investment in specific human capital is undertaken.

We present two-period models in which the firm maximizes the expected present value of discounted profits and all factors of production other than labour and human capital are fixed. In period one the firm hires untrained labour, creates firm-specific human capital through on-the-job training, and produces good X according to the production function

$$X_1 = f^1(L_1, \lambda), \qquad 0 \leqslant \lambda \leqslant 1. \tag{1}$$

L_1 is the amount of labour hired in period one, and λ is the proportion of each worker's time in period one which is devoted to training. We assume a fixed work week for convenience, and hence L_1 and the number of employees are proportional.

Then $f_1{}^1(= \partial f^1/\partial L_1)$ is positive and $f_2{}^1(= \partial f^1/\partial\lambda)$ is negative. For convenience we assume that there are no money costs of the training program and hence costs of training will show up as forgone output. The introduction of money costs of the training program would not significantly alter anything that follows.

In period two the firm hires no new untrained labour, engages in no further training, and produces with some or all of the employees hired in period one according to the production function

$$X_2 = f^2(L_2, \lambda); \qquad f_1{}^2 > 0, \qquad f_2{}^2 > 0. \tag{2}$$

We assume that for any specific value of the arguments, $\bar{L} = L_1 = L_2$,

$$f_1{}^1(\bar{L}, \lambda) < f_1{}^2(\bar{L}, \lambda), \tag{3}$$

if λ is greater than zero, or if there exists learning by doing.[2] Assumption (3) indicates that the "trained" labour of period two is more productive than the 'untrained' labour of period one. This assumption reflects either the acquisition of specific human capital in period one (when $\lambda > 0$) or simply learning by doing. The subsequent analysis applies to both.

We focus on two questions. First, will a profit-maximizing employer be led to share the investment in specific human capital with his employees; that is, will profit maximization lead the employer to offer a wage profile such that $\text{PVE}_F > \text{PVE}_A$? Second, we explore the implications of firm-specific capital for the wage profile. We distinguish three cases.

THE SIMPLEST CASE

Two features characterize this case. 1/ The firm knows with certainty the price at which it can sell its product in each of the two periods. For simplicity

2 (3) embodies the conventional assumption that firm-specific human capital can be captured by conditions on marginal products. Although (3) is sufficient for a positive return on investment, it is not necessary. Marginal product may fall for some values of $\bar{L} = L_1 = L_2$ and λ while average product rises.

we let the price be common to both periods and denote the common price as $\bar{p}$. 2/ The firm anticipates and experiences no voluntary quits at the end of period one.

Let $\bar{w}$ represent the alternative wage rate, w_1 and w_2 the firm's two-period wage profile, and r the discount rate. The firm may lay off workers at the beginning of period two, but each worker is able to anticipate correctly the probability that he will be laid off. Then, letting $v(v \leqslant 1)$ represent the proportion of workers retained in period two, the firm's wage profile must satisfy

$$\bar{w} + \bar{w}/(1 + r) \leqslant w_1 + vw_2/(1 + r). \tag{4}$$

That is, the firm must offer a wage profile such that PVE_F is greater than or equal to PVE_A if it is to attract any employees. If PVE_F is less than PVE_A, the firm can attract no labour, and if (4) is satisfied the firm can, in a perfect labour market along with a perfect capital market, attract all the labour it wants. Profit maximization ensures that (4) will hold with equality. It is then immediately obvious that there will be no shared investment in this case. It is, nevertheless, instructive to consider the wage profile.

The present value of the firm's profits is

$$\text{PV}_\pi = \bar{p}X_1 - w_1L_1 - F + (1/(1 + r))(\bar{p}X_2 - w_2L_2 - F), \tag{5}$$

where F is fixed costs. Using the equality in (4) and the fact that $L_2 = vL_1$ we can rewrite equation (5) as

$$\text{PV}_\pi = \bar{p}X_1 + \bar{p}X_2/(1 + r) - (w_1 + vw_2/(1 + r))L_1 - (1 + 1/(1 + r))F, \tag{6}$$

or

$$\text{PV}_\pi = \bar{p}X_1 + \bar{p}X_2/(1 + r) - (\bar{w} + \bar{w}/(1 + r))L_1 - (1 + 1/(1 + r))F. \tag{7}$$

Since costs are independent of v and revenue is increasing in v, v will be chosen at 1 and the firm will not reduce its work force in period two. With no layoffs or quits $L_1 = L_2 = \bar{L}$. Since PV_π is independent of the wage profile, the firm (and its employees) is indifferent to the wage profile as long as (4) holds with equality.

First-order conditions for maximizing PV_π imply that the present value of the marginal products $[\bar{p}(f_1^1 + f_1^2/(1 + r))]$ equals the present value of wage rates $[\bar{w} + \bar{w}/(1 + r) = w_1 + vw_2/(1 + r)]$, provided of course that L^*, the optimal employment level, is greater than zero. Further, the first-order condition with respect to λ implies that the marginal cost of training $(-\bar{p}f_2^1)$ equals the marginal return from training $[\bar{p}f_2^2/(1 + r)]$, provided that λ is not zero or one.

No determinate wage profile exists in this case, and the period-two wage rate is independent of the increase in productivity associated with the existence of human capital or learning by doing. In fact, on a period-by-period basis, the wage rate is, in general, independent of the marginal product of labour. Since there is no shared investment in this case, a wage profile with w_2 greater than w_1 is not evidence of a shared investment. In the human capital case, the firm invests and the firm receives a return on its investment. In the learning by doing case, no investment as such occurs, and the firm receives the rents to learning by doing.

It is, however, the possibility of labour turnover which is thought to lead to the shared investment. We therefore turn to a consideration of the implications of, first, the possibility that the firm will want to discharge workers and, second, the possibility that workers will voluntarily leave the firm.

STOCHASTIC DEMAND AND LAYOFFS

Assumption A: The firm knows with certainty the price in period one, $\bar{p}_1$, but knows the price in period two only stochastically. That is, the firm knows the probability density of period-two prices, $g(p_2)$.
Assumption B: As in case one, the firm anticipates (and experiences) no voluntary turnover after period one.

Assumption A introduces the possibility that, at the beginning of period two (when p_2 is revealed), the firm may wish to reduce its labour force through layoffs. We assume that the firm is not free to change w_2 in period two. To allow the firm to violate this implicit wage agreement is not consistent with the spirit of specific human capital models. If the firm were free to promise one wage rate in period two and to deliver another, it would always choose to pay the lowest possible wage in period two. Obviously this chicanery will succeed only once.

The firm's objective is to maximize the expected present value of profits $E(\mathrm{PV}_\pi)$, or to maximize

$$E(\mathrm{PV}_\pi) = \bar{p}_1 X_1 - w_1 L_1 - F + 1(/1 + r) \times \left[\int_0^\infty g(p_2)(p_2 X_2 - w_2 L_2)dp_2 - F\right], \quad (8)$$

subject to the constraint that $L_2 \leqslant L_1$.

We are interested in the effect of the possibility of layoff on the wage profile and the implications of the wage profile for the interpretation of specific human capital as a shared investment. The firm's maximization problem is now a two-stage maximization. The decision variables are L_1, L_2, λ, w_1, and w_2. L_2 will not be chosen until period two, when the period-two price is known with certainty. Because of this sequential nature of the firm's decision process, we first ask how L_2 is chosen, given L_1, λ, w_1, w_2, and p_2. Then we comment on the choice of a wage profile.

If, when the period-two price is realized, the marginal revenue product at $L_2 = L_1$ is less than the predetermined wage rate w_2, the firm will reduce its labour force until the marginal revenue product is equal to the wage rate. The firm's layoff rule then dictates that we write L_2 as

$$L_2 = R(p_2, w_2), \qquad R_1 \geqslant 0, \qquad R_2 < 0. \tag{9}$$

We again assume that workers' anticipations with respect to the probability of layoff are correct. When laid off, the worker, by assumption, remains unemployed for one period. The firm's wage profile will then satisfy

$$\bar{w} + \bar{R}\bar{w}/(1 + r) = w_1 + w_2(E(L_2)/L_1)/(1 + r), \tag{10}$$

where $\bar{R}$ is the probability of not being laid off in the competitive sector and $E(L_2)/L_1$ is the expected value of the probability of not being discharged in period two. Again, PVE_F is equal to PVE_A, and there is no shared investment. Solving (10) for w_1 we can rewrite the firm's objective function as·

$$E(\text{PV}_\pi) = \bar{p}_1 X_1 - [\bar{w} + \bar{R}\bar{w}/(1 + r) - w_2 E(L_2)/((1 + r)L_1)]L_1 - F$$
$$+ 1/(1 + r)\left[\int_0^\infty g(p_2)(p_2 X_2 - w_2 L_2)dp_2 - F\right]. \tag{11}$$

But $E(L_2)$ is $\int_0^\infty g(p_2)L_2 dp_2$, which allows us to simplify (11) to

$$E(\text{PV}_\pi) = \bar{p}_1 X_1 - [\bar{w} + \bar{R}\bar{w}/(1 + r)]L_1 - F + 1/(1 + r)$$
$$\times \left[\int_0^\infty g(p_2)p_2 X_2 dp_2 - F\right]. \tag{12}$$

The partial derivative with respect to w_2 is

$$\partial E(\text{PV}_\pi)/\partial w_2 = \int_0^\infty g(p_2)p_2 f_1{}^2 R_2 dp_2, \tag{13}$$

which is negative. This implies that the firm will want to reduce its period-two wage rate to the lowest possible level.

The sense of this result can be understood by considering (10). The firm must offer a wage profile which satisfies (10), and because workers are correctly able to anticipate the probability of being laid off, the firm's expected wage costs for any value of L_1 are independent of its wage profile. But its expected revenues are not independent of the wage profile, because period two revenues, given the firm's layoff rule, are inversely related to w_2.

If employees did not experience unemployment when laid off, the period-two wage rate would be $\bar{w}$; if employees do experience one period of unemployment, the lowest possible wage might be the minimum wage. The significant point is that the stochastic demand which gives rise to layoffs leads the firm to offer a declining wage profile.

QUITS AND ENTRAPMENT

Assumption A′: As in the second section, the firm is assumed to know with certainty the common price which will prevail in both periods, $\bar{p}$.

Assumption B′: We introduce, however, the possibility of labour turnover at the end of the training period. We assume that the proportion of the labour force which the firm can retain in period two, s, is a concave function of w_2,

$$s = s(w_2). \tag{14}$$

A simple interpretation of $s(w_2)$ is that workers, for reasons other than the wage decision of the firm, may want to quit in period two. Since, as in the preceding section, we assume that a worker who quits is unemployed for one period, w_2 is then the opportunity cost of quitting. For the same reasons considered in the second section the firm will not wish to lay off workers in period two.

In this case the firm's objective function is given in equation (5). Equation (14) implies that L_2 is a function of L_1 and w_2, since

$$L_2 = s(w_2)L_1. \tag{15}$$

The firm's wage profile must satisfy the condition that

$$\bar{w} + \bar{s}\bar{w}/(1 + r) = w_1 + s(w_2)w_2/(1 + r), \tag{16}$$

where $\bar{s}$ is the probability of retention from one period to the next in the competitive sector. (It is not necessarily true that $\bar{s} = s(\bar{w})$; the individual's turnover behaviour need not be the same in all firms.) Equations (15) and (16) allow us to write the firm's objective function as

$$\begin{aligned}\text{PV}_\pi = \bar{p}X_1 - (\bar{w} + \bar{s}\bar{w}/(1 + r) - s(w_2)w_2/(1 + r))L_1 - F \\ + 1/(1 + r)[\bar{p}X_2 - w_2 s(w_2)L_1 - F].\end{aligned} \tag{17}$$

The first-order condition with respect to w_2 is

$$\begin{aligned}\partial\text{PV}_\pi/\partial w_2 = L_1/(1+r)[s(w_2) + w_2 s'(w_2)] + L_1/(1 + r)[\bar{p}f_1{}^2 s'(w_2) \\ - s(w_2) - w_2 s'(w_2)] \geqslant 0,\end{aligned} \tag{18}$$

with equality if the optimal value of s is less than 1.

The first-order condition in (18) reduces to

$$f_1{}^2 s'(w_2) \geqslant 0. \tag{19}$$

$f_1{}^2$ cannot be zero since, from equation (3), $f_1{}^2(\bar{L}, \lambda) > f_1{}^1(\bar{L}, \lambda)$, $L_2 \leqslant L_1$, and we assume diminishing marginal products.

Thus $s'(w_2{}^*)$ must equal zero or s must equal 1, where $w_2{}^*$ is the optimal value of w_2. The optimal policy is to maximize the rate of retention. The firm does this by increasing w_2 (and simultaneously reducing w_1 in the manner implied by equation 16) until the retention rate is maximized. That is, maximal entrapment is optimal.[3] When capital markets are not perfect, there will be a cost associated with entrapment, and maximal entrapment will not necessarily be optimal.

3 The turnover relationship in (14) is a determinate, not a stochastic, relationship. However, the major result of this section, that maximal entrapment is optimal, is unchanged if the turnover relationship is truly stochastic.

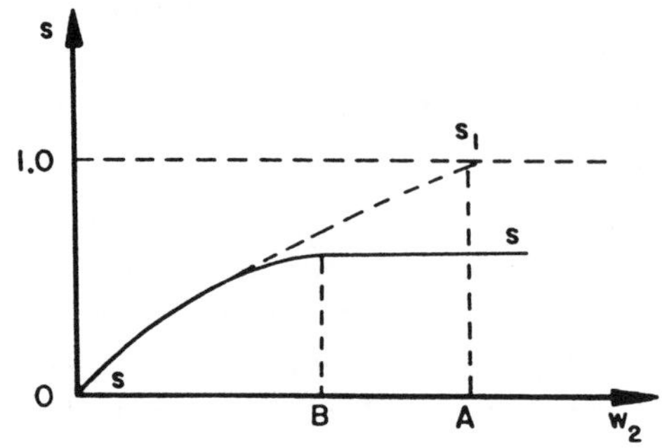

FIGURE 1

In Figure 1, if the retention function is SS, the firm will pay a period-two wage rate of at least OB. If the retention function is SS_1, the firm will pay a period-two wage rate of at least OA. The wage profile will have $w_2 > w_1$, provided that $s(w_2^*) > \bar{s}$.[4]

The sense of this result also revolves around the labour supply constraint, equation (16). Since workers correctly anticipate the possibility of turnover the firm's expected wage costs over the two periods are independent of the wage profile, but expected revenues increase with w_2 as long as increases in w_2 enable the firm to retain more of the trained workers in period two.

The positive wage profile which results in this case is not the result of the worker investing in period one and receiving a return on that investment in period two, but merely reflects the employer's attempt to reduce turnover in period two so that he can realize the maximum return on his investment in specific human capital. As in the two previous models, the wage rate, period by period, is independent of the marginal product of labour (in this firm) period by period.

CONCLUSIONS

In the three models we have examined we have shown that a profit-maximizing firm will offer a wage profile to its employees such that PVE_F, the expected present value of earnings in the firm, is precisely equal to PVE_A, the expected

4 From (16) the wage profile must satisfy

$$\bar{w} + \bar{s}\bar{w}/(1 + r) = w_1 + w_2E(L_2)/((1 + r)L_1). \qquad \text{(i)}$$

And $E(L_2) = s(w_2)L_1$, so that

$$\bar{w} + \bar{s}\bar{w}/(1 + r) = w_1 + w_2s(w_2)/(1 + r). \qquad \text{(ii)}$$

Solving explicitly for w_1,

$$w_1 = 1/(1 + r)(\bar{w}(1 + r + \bar{s}) - w_2s(w_2)). \qquad \text{(iii)}$$

Since $s(w_2)$ is a non-decreasing function of w_2, w_1 and w_2 are inversely related. Letting $w_1 = w_2 = w'$ we obtain

$$w' = \bar{w}(1 + r + s)/(1 + r + s(w')). \qquad \text{(iv)}$$

This implies that for w_1^* to equal w_2^*, $\bar{s}$ must equal $s(w_2^*)$, otherwise (ii) is not satisfied. Returning to (iii), we see that if $s(w_2^*)$ is greater than $\bar{s}$, w_1^* must be less than w_2^*.

present value of earnings in alternative employment. We therefore conclude that the employer has no incentive to share the investment in specific capital. However, the employer does have an incentive to manipulate the wage profile. Two opposing forces are at work. On the one hand, stochastic variation in future product prices produces an incentive for the employer to minimize the second-period wage rate. Given the optimal layoff rule, this strategy enables the employer to retain the largest number of trained employees in the second period. On the other hand, the possibility of voluntary quits produces an incentive for the employer to manipulate the wage profile (decrease w_1 and increase w_2) so as to minimize voluntary quits. In both cases the employer is attempting to maximize the rate of retention of the more productive period-two employees.

Our models are based on the assumptions that both the capital and labour markets are perfect. These assumptions are not necessary for our conclusion that the employer has no incentive to share the investment in specific capital. Assume first that the capital market open to workers is imperfect. In order to attract an employee the firm still must offer a wage profile such that PVE_F is greater than or equal to PVE_A, where PVE_F and PVE_A are based on the discount rate facing the worker in the imperfect capital market. There is clearly no incentive for the employer to offer anything other than PVE_A to the worker. To make a more generous offer would be folly in a world of profit maximization, and suicide in a world of free entry. Second, assume that the employer has some monopsony power; the supply of workers available to the firm in the initial period is an increasing function of PVE_F. For the marginal worker the firm will offer a wage profile such that the worker is just indifferent between joining the firm and pursuing alternative employment. All intramarginal employees will, of course find employment in the firm more attractive than alternative employment, and we might conclude that the employer has 'shared' the investment in specific capital with these intramarginal employees. But the fact that such employees find employment with the firm more attractive than alternative employment simply reflects the employer's monopsony power and is unrelated to the opportunity to invest in specific capital.

With respect to rising wage profiles we must conclude that they are not evidence of a shared investment but that they may be evidence of the employer's attempt to entrap his employees. In this connection it is interesting to note that the rising wage profile peaks for many groups of workers in the middle forties – just at the time when most workers are quite immobile and the necessity to entrap is the least.

Becker implies that, in light of his analysis, economists should rethink their position on compensation devices which tend to inhibit labour turnover. He saw such devices as increasing the security of both parties in the 'shared investment' (Becker, 1964, 27). If our interpretation is correct, then Becker's position is not justified. Devices such as non-vested pensions, deferred stock options, paid vacations which increase with an employee's tenure in a firm, the allocation of the most desired office space by seniority, and even the perquisite of a key to the executive washroom are, in our interpretation, simply devices employed by the firm to maximize the return from its investment in firm-specific human capital. The recent outcry of the business community in Manitoba to the Manitoba government's proposed legislation which would require that all pensions be portable is not inconsistent with our interpretation that non-vested pensions simply serve to entrap.

Our interpretation of job-specific human capital also calls for some scepticism towards publicly financed on-the-job training programs which are now quite common in the United States and the United Kingdom. Such programs are presumably intended to provide workers with general skills. But, to the extent that they create firm-specific skills, the public is subsidizing an investment on which the employer alone will realize a return. This perhaps explains employers' willingness to participate in such schemes.

Our interpretation also has implications for the system of permanent employment which has emerged in Japan in the twentieth century. The system involves a steeply inclined seniority-earnings profile, which may be interpreted as a device for entrapment. It also involves an implicit promise not to discharge workers and an implicit non-raiding agreement between employers (see Shinohora, 1970, 312–20; Rosovsky, 1961). This may be seen as a scheme to capture the returns to what would otherwise be general human capital. It would be presumptuous for us to suggest this as a definitive interpretation – we simply offer it as a hypothesis.

REFERENCES

Becker, Gary (1964) *Human Capital* (New York: NBER)

Bodenhöfer, Hans-Joachim (1967) 'The mobility of labour and the theory of human capital.' *Journal of Human Resources* 2, 431–48.

Mincer, Job (1962) 'On-the-job training: cost, returns, and some implications.' *Journal of Political Economy* 70, 50–79

Oi, Walter (1962) 'Labor as a quasi-fixed factor.' *Journal of Political Economy* 70, 538–55

Parsons, Donald O. (1972) 'Specific human capital: an application to quit rates and layoff rates.' *Journal of Political Economy* 80, 1120–43

Rees, Albert (1973) *The Economics of Work and Pay* (New York: Harper and Row)

Rosovsky, Henry (1961) *Capital Formation in Japan – 1868–1940* (Glencoe, Illinois: The Free Press)

Shinohora, Miyohei (1970) *Structural Changes in Japan's Economic Development* (Tokyo: Kinokuniyo)

Telser, Lester (1972) *Competition and Collusion* (Chicago: Aldine)

[19]

Patience, more than its own reward: a note on price discrimination

DAVID DONALDSON and B. CURTIS EATON /
University of British Columbia

Abstract. Suppose that a monopolist's customers can be divided into two groups – the *impatient*, who place a relatively high value on their time, and the *long-suffering*, who place a relatively low value on their time. In this circumstance the monopolist can separate the two submarkets, even when he cannot identify any individual's group membership, by offering his product under two options which involve different combinations of money and time prices. In this paper we examine the conditions under which this strategy is profitable. We discover that a relatively high demand elasticity for the long-suffering and a relatively high value of time for the impatient contribute to the profitability of this type of price discrimination. Further, we demonstrate that this strategy can be profitable even where arbitrage is possible, provided that it is costly. We argue that the model explains a wide range of observed behaviour, much of which is not ordinarily recognized as price discrimination.

La patience est bien plus que sa propre récompense: une note sur la discrimination par les prix. Supposons que les clients d'un monopoleur puissent être départagés en deux groupes: les *impatients* qui donnent une valeur relativement élevée au temps libre et *ceux-qui-prennent-leur-mal-en-patience* qui attachent une valeur relativement moindre à leur temps libéré. On assume que le monopoleur peut séparer les deux marchés en offrant au public son produit selon deux modes plus ou moins chronophages avec des prix monétaires explicites moins et plus élevés respectivement et ce même s'il ne peut pas identifier l'appartenance d'une individu en particulier à l'un ou l'autre groupe.

Dans ce mémoire, les auteurs examine les conditions qui rendent profitable une telle stratégie de discrimination. Ils ont découvert que la profitabilité d'une telle stratégie repose sur une élasticité de demande relativement élevée de la part de ceux qui prennent leur mal en patience et sur une valeur relativement élevée pour leur temps libéré chez les impatients. De plus ils démontrent que cette stratégie de discrimination est profitable même si l'arbitrage est possible à condition que l'arbitrage soit coûteux. Les auteurs suggèrent que ce modèle explique un éventail de comportements observés qui ne sont pas d'habitude considérés comme des cas de discrimination par les prix.

For the practice of ordinary third-degree price discrimination, two conditions are necessary:

We are grateful to Robert Evans, Leslie Robb, and an anonymous referee for helpful comments and to the Social Sciences and Humanities Research Council for research support.

Canadian Journal of Economics/Révue canadienne d'Economique, XIV, No. 1
February/février 1981. Printed in Canada

0008-4085 / 81 / 0000–0093 $01.50

1. the monopolist must be able to identify buyers or groups of buyers with different demand elasticities;
2. arbitrage must be physically impossible (as in the provision of personal services such as body rubs) or rendered unprofitable by institutional barriers (e.g., tariffs).

In this note we discuss another sort of third-degree price discrimination – 'queue discrimination' – that requires the fulfilment of neither of these conditions.[1] In this model, the monopolist offers the same good at different combinations of money and time prices. Thus the full price to the consumer is the money price plus the value of his time. We show that, if the money and time prices are set correctly by the monopolist, consumers will voluntarily separate themselves into submarkets, and that, if certain conditions are fulfilled, this strategy of market separation will be profitable. Further, we show that these results carry over to the case in which arbitrage is possible, but time consuming. We refer to this phenomenon as queue discrimination for convenience, but the time price need not arise from a queueing process. In the concluding section we discuss different ways in which the monopolist can manipulate time prices.

The acquisition of most products requires an expenditure of time, which must be accounted in full price. Furthermore, there are often other 'psychic costs' – 'muzak' or the crush of the crowd on 'dollar days.' Although we focus on money and time costs only, the propositions we generate clearly generalize to other elements of full price. Our model can be interpreted as a formalization of some aspects of Machlup's intuitive ideas with respect to 'product discrimination.' 'Product discrimination does not depend upon a separation of buyers in such a way that they cannot evade the demarcation lines, but upon a differentiation of products in such a way that the buyers will separate themselves and buy at discriminating prices. A seller may do this by differentiating his products as to design, label, quality, time of sale, or distribution channel having a different appeal to different customers – or by offering different products' (1955, 418).

Formally this paper draws on the ideas on self-selection developed by Spence (1973) and Stiglitz (1975), among others. In our model a monopolist plays on divergent valuations of time among his customers in order to devise a structure of full prices which will cause his customers voluntarily to reveal their group membership. It is also related to two recent papers which examine the use of self-selection mechanisms for price discrimination. Salop (1977) builds on the observation that if consumers, faced with price dispersion, have different costs of search or different search strategies, they will have different reservation prices. Thus, the monopolist can separate markets and engage in price discrimination by creating price dispersion. Stokey (1979) examines a

1 Third-degree price discrimination involves charging different prices in separated markets. The original formulation of the model is due to Pigou (1962, 275–89).

form of intertemporal price discrimination for new products. If consumers value 'newness' of products differently, then a monopolist can induce self-selection and engage in price discrimination by announcing a declining intertemporal price schedule.

In the first section we develop the basic model of queue discrimination when the nature of the good dictates that arbitrage is impossible. In the second section we explore the possibilities for queue discrimination when arbitrage is possible. In these sections we assume that prices are simply announced in terms of a money price and a time price. In the third section we consider alternative ways in which the monopolist can control time prices, and we argue that the model explains a wide range of observed pricing behaviour, much of which is not ordinarily recognized as price discrimination.

A MODEL OF QUEUE DISCRIMINATION

A monopolist produces a product (X) which he markets under two options (we assume two options for simplicity of presentation). With Option 1, a unit of X can be purchased at a money price of p_1 and a time price of q so that the full price of the product to a consumer whose money valuation of his time is w is

$$r_1 = p_1 + qw. \quad (1)$$

Under Option 2, a unit of X can be purchased at a money price of p_2 and a time price of zero so that the full price is simply the money price. We assume initially that arbitrage of X is impossible.

First, consider the consumer's choice problem when he faces these options for the purchase of X. Let $U(x, y, l)$ be the image of the (continuously differentiable, strictly quasi-concave) utility function, where x is quantity of X consumed per day, y is income spent per day on a Hicksian composite good, and l is leisure measured in hours per day. For simplicity we assume that no time is required for acquisition of the composite good and that consumption of goods requires no time. With these simplifications, the twenty-four hours of the day will be devoted to work, to leisure and possibly to the acquisition of good X. The consumer's maximization problem is then to choose x_1, x_2, y and l to maximize $U(x, y, l)$ subject to

$$p_1x_1 + p_2x_2 + y \leqslant I + w(24 - l - qx_1), \quad (2)$$

where x_1 is quantity of X purchased under Option 1, x_2 is quantity of X purchased under Option 2, $x = x_1 + x_2$, and I is non-wage income.

Denoting the optimal bundle as (x^*, y^*, l^*), the first order conditions require $U_x(x^*, y^*, l^*) \leqslant \lambda(p_1 + wq)$, with equality if $x_1^* > 0$, and $U_x(x^*, y^*, l^*) \leqslant \lambda p_2$, with equality if $x_2^* > 0$. λ is a Lagrange multiplier. There are two interesting cases. If $wq < p_2 - p_1$, then $x_1^* \geqslant 0$ and $x_2^* = 0$. In other words, if the consumer's money valuation of the time cost in Option 1 (wq) is less than the money price differential ($p_2 - p_1$), the consumer will prefer Option 1.

Conversely, if $wq > p_2 - p_1$ then $x_1^* = 0$ and $x_2^* \geqslant 0$. These results are independent of the utility function.

It is then clear that the monopolist can effectively separate submarkets if its customers value their time differently. We wish to explore the conditions which render this strategy of market separation profitable, and we focus on the simplest possible case. We assume that the monopolist's customers can be divided into two mutually exclusive and exhaustive subgroups: the 'patient' or 'long-suffering' with wage rate w_1, and the 'impatient' with wage rate w_2, $w_1 < w_2$. The 'long-suffering' and 'impatient' submarkets are effectively separated when

$$p_1 + w_1 q \leqslant p_2 \leqslant p_1 + w_2 q, \quad q \geqslant 0. \tag{3}$$

If $p_2 > p_1 + w_2 q$, both groups prefer Option 1, if $p_2 < p_1 + w_1 q$, both groups prefer Option 2, and if (3) holds, the long-suffering prefer Option 1 and the impatient Option 2. The firm need never choose $p_2 < p_1 + w_1 q$, since this is equivalent to setting $p_2 = p_1$ and $q = 0$, satisfying (3). Similarly, the firm will not choose $p_2 > p_1 + w_2 q$ with $q > 0$. In that case $q > 0$ serves no useful purpose, since both groups prefer Option 1 and profit maximization requires $q = 0$.

Given (3), the full price to the patient is $r_1 = p_1 + qw_1$, and hence $p_1 = r_1 - qw_1$. Inequalities (3) can be rewritten as

$$r_1 \leqslant p_2 \leqslant r_1 + q(w_2 - w_1), \quad q \geqslant 0. \tag{4}$$

The firm's problem is to choose p_1, p_2, and q, satisfying (3), or alternatively r_1, p_2, and q, satisfying (4). The monopolist's profit can thus be written as

$$\Pi(r_1, p_2, q) = p_2 f(p_2) + (r_1 - qw_1)g(r_1) - C[f(p_2) + g(r_1)], \tag{5}$$

where f and g are demand functions for the impatient and long-suffering respectively and C is the firm's cost function. We assume that f, g and C are continuously twice-differentiable, that f and g are decreasing in their arguments, and that C is non-decreasing in its argument. Now

$$\frac{\partial \Pi(r_1, p_2, q)}{\partial q} = -w_1 g(r_1) < 0. \tag{6}$$

Given r_1 and p_2, profits are decreasing in q and q will be chosen as small as possible consistent with (4). Thus

$$\hat{q} = \frac{p_2 - r_1}{w_2 - w_1}. \tag{7}$$

The intuition of this result is straightforward. The demand for X under Option 1 depends on r_1. Holding r_1 and p_2 (and hence quantity demanded under both options) constant, the monopolist's revenues increase as q is decreased while costs remain constant. Hence,the monopolist will set q at its minimum value consistent with maintaining separation of the two submarkets, that is, consistent with inequality (4).

Notice that when $q = \hat{q}$ the long-suffering strictly prefer Option 1, while the impatient are indifferent between the two options, and the submarkets are not strictly separated. We impose strict separation by assuming that the impatient choose Option 2 when $q = \hat{q}$ and our rationale is the standard one: the impatient would strictly prefer Option 2 for any $q > \hat{q}$. If the time price arises from a queueing process, the equilibrium is self-enforcing, since switching by any of the impatient will increase the time price under Option 1, thus making Option 2 strictly preferred.

With $q = \hat{q}$, the firm's profit can be written as

$$\hat{\Pi}(r_1, p_2) = \Pi(r_1, p_2, \hat{q}) = p_2 f(p_2) + \frac{w_2 r_1 - w_1 p_2}{w_2 - w_1} g(r_1) - C[f(p_2) + g(r_1)], \quad (8)$$

since

$$\hat{p}_1 = r_1 - \hat{q} w_1 = \frac{w_2 r_1 - w_1 p_2}{w_2 - w_1}. \quad (9)$$

The monopolist's problem is, then, to choose r_1 and p_2 to maximize $\hat{\Pi}$, subject to $r_1 \leqslant p_2$.

First-order conditions for a maximum of profits are

$$p_2^* f'(p_2^*) + f(p_2^*) - \left(\frac{w_1}{w_2 - w_1}\right) g(r_1^*) - C'[f(p_2^*) + g(r_1^*)] f'(p_2^*) + \mu = 0, \quad (10.1)$$

$$\left(\frac{w_2 r_1^* - w_1 p_2^*}{w_2 - w_1}\right) g'(r_1^*) + \left(\frac{w_2}{w_2 - w_1}\right) g(r_1^*) - C'[f(p_1^*) + g(r_1^*)] g'(r_1^*) - \mu = 0, \quad (10.2)$$

$$p_2^* - r_1^* \geqslant 0, \quad (10.3)$$

and

$$\mu(p_2^* - r_1^*) = 0, \quad (10.4)$$

where μ is a Lagrange multiplier and asterisks denote optimal values of the variables.

There are two cases of interest. In the first, $p_2^* = r_1^*$ and $\mu \geqslant 0$. Then from (7), $\hat{q} = 0$. Combining (10.1) and (10.2) to eliminate μ, and letting $p_2^* = r_1^* = p^*$, we obtain

$$f(p^*) + g(p^*) + p^*(f'(p^*) + g'(p^*)) - C'[f(p^*) + g(p^*)][f'(p^*) + g'(p^*)] = 0. \quad (11)$$

This is simply the first-order condition for non-discriminatory profit maximization; the first-order condition for maximization of $p[f(p) + g(p)] - C[f(p) + g(p)]$ is equation (11). In the second case $p_2^* > r_1^*$ and $\mu = 0$. This is the queue discrimination case. In this case equations (10.1) and (10.2) can be written as

$$p_2^* + \frac{f(p_2^*)}{f'(p_2^*)} - \left(\frac{w_1}{w_2 - w_1}\right)\frac{g(r_1^*)}{f'(p_2^*)} = \text{MC}, \tag{12.1}$$

$$\frac{w_2 r_1^* - w_1 p_2^*}{w_2 - w_1} + \left(\frac{w_2}{w_2 - w_1}\right)\frac{g(r_1^*)}{g'(r_1^*)} = \text{MC}, \tag{12.2}$$

where MC is marginal cost of production evaluated at $f(p_2^*) + g(r_1^*)$. The left side of (12.1) is the derivative of the firm's total revenue with respect to $x_2(= f(p_2))$ evaluated at p_2^*. The first term is marginal revenue in the impatient submarket. The second term is the revenue reponse in the long-suffering submarket to changes in x_2. The left hand side of (12.2) is, from (7) and (9), $p_1^* + g(r_1^*)/[\partial g(r_1^*)/\partial p_1]$, or marginal revenue in the patient submarket.

In order to determine the conditions under which queue discrimination is profitable we focus on the non-discriminatory profit maximizing solution, characterized by (11), and then ask if $\hat{\Pi}$ will increase when r^* is decreased or p_2 increased. To do this, we assume that $\tilde{\Pi}(p) \equiv \hat{\Pi}(p, p)$ is strictly pseudo-concave in p. Strict pseudo-concavity of $\tilde{\Pi}(p)$ means that whenever $d\tilde{\Pi}(p)/dp = 0$, $\tilde{\Pi}$ is locally strictly concave. This implies that p^*, given by (11), represents a maximum of $\tilde{\Pi}$, and that it is unique.[2]

The usual assumption of monopoly theory is that profit is 'strongly concave' in quantity sold at a single price. (A function of one variable is strongly concave if its second derivative is everywhere negative.) This assumption implies strict pseudo-concavity of $\tilde{\Pi}(p)$. To see this write

$$\tilde{\Pi}(p) \equiv \hat{\Pi}(p, p) = R(x) - C(x),$$

where $x = f(p) + g(p)$ and $R(x) = px$. Then

$$\frac{d\tilde{\Pi}(p^*)}{dp} = [R'(x^*) - C'(x^*)]\frac{dx}{dp} = 0 \tag{13}$$

for a maximum at $p = p^*$, and

$$\frac{d^2\tilde{\Pi}(p)}{dp^2} = [R'(x) - C'(x)]\frac{d^2x}{dp^2} + [R''(x) - C''(x)]\left(\frac{dx}{dp}\right)^2 \tag{14}$$

Combining (13) and (14):

2 A directionally differentiable function $h: R^n \rightarrow R$ is strictly pseudo-concave if, at any point where a directional derivative vanishes, the function is locally strictly concave in that direction. If there is a point where $\nabla h(x) = 0$, then that point is the unique global maximum. Strict pseudo-concavity implies strict quasi-concavity but is slightly stronger, ruling out points where $\nabla h(x) = 0$ that are not the maximum. See Diewert, Avriel, and Zang (1979) for a discussion.

$$\frac{d^2\tilde{\Pi}(p^*)}{dp^2} = [R''(x^*) - C''(x^*)]\left(\frac{dx}{dp}\right)^2. \tag{15}$$

Hence $\tilde{\Pi}$ is strictly pseudo-concave in p if profit is strongly concave in x,

Ignoring the case where unconstrained maximization of $\hat{\Pi}$ and non-discriminatory profit maximization give rise to the same solution, there are two cases of interest, illustrated in figures 1a and 1b. The non-discriminatory profit maximizing solution is at (p^*, p^*) where the line $p_2 = r_1$ is tangent to the iso-profit line $\hat{\Pi}(r_1, p_2) = \hat{\Pi}(p^*, p^*)$, labeled *CD* in figures 1a and 1b. In figure 1a there exists an unconstrained maximum of $\hat{\Pi}$ in the region where $p_2 > r_1$ and queue discrimination is profitable. Since $\tilde{\Pi}(p) = \hat{\Pi}(p, p)$ is strictly pseudo-concave, the iso-profit line $\hat{\Pi}(r_1, p_1) = \hat{\Pi}(p^*, p^*)$ has only one point in common with the line $p_2 = r_1$. In figure 1b there exists an unconstrained maximum of $\hat{\Pi}$ in the region where $p_2 < r_1$, but this maximum is unattainable, since it violates the constraint that $r_1 \leqslant p_2$. We want to discover the condition for the case illustrated in figure 1a.

At the point (p^*, p^*) the derivatives $\partial\hat{\Pi}/\partial p_2$ and $\partial\hat{\Pi}/\partial r_1$ are

$$\frac{\partial\hat{\Pi}(p^*, p^*)}{\partial p_2} = p^*f'(p^*) + f(p^*) - \left(\frac{w_1}{w_2 - w_1}\right)g(p^*) - \text{MC}f'(p^*), \tag{16.1}$$

$$\frac{\partial\hat{\Pi}(p^*, p^*)}{\partial r_1} = p^*g'(p^*) + \left(\frac{w_2}{w_2 - w_1}\right)g(p^*) - \text{MC}g'(p^*), \tag{16.2}$$

and from equation (11) we know that p^* must satisfy

$$p^*f'(p^*) + f(p^*) - \text{MC}\,f'(p^*) = -[g(p^*) + p^*g'(p^*) - \text{MC}\,g'(p^*)]. \tag{17}$$

Using (17) it is easy to show that

$$\frac{\partial\hat{\Pi}(p^*, p^*)}{\partial r_1} \lesseqgtr 0 \leftrightarrow \frac{\partial\hat{\Pi}(p^*, p^*)}{\partial p_2} \gtreqless 0. \tag{18}$$

This occurs because at (p^*, p^*) the line $p_2 = r_1$ is tangent to an iso-profit line.

Now suppose that $\partial\hat{\Pi}(p^*, p^*)/\partial r_1 < 0$. In that case, we must have the situation shown in figure 1a, since profits are locally decreasing in r_1 and increasing in p_2. So $\partial\hat{\Pi}(p^*, p^*)/\partial r_1 < 0$ represents a sufficient condition for the profitability of queue discrimination but not a necessary condition. If $\hat{\Pi}$ is pseudo-concave, then it is a necessary condition as well. Using (16.2), and remembering that $g'(p^*) < 0$, this condition can be written

$$p^* + \left(\frac{w_2}{w_2 - w_1}\right)\frac{g(p^*)}{g'(p^*)} > \text{MC}. \tag{19}$$

From (17) we have

$$\text{MC} = p^* + \frac{f(p^*) + g(p^*)}{f'(p^*) + g'(p^*)}. \tag{20}$$

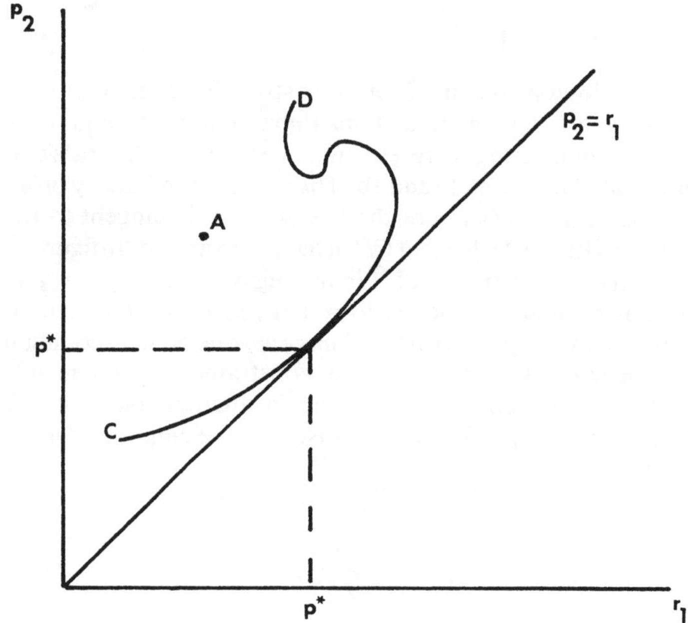

FIGURE 1a

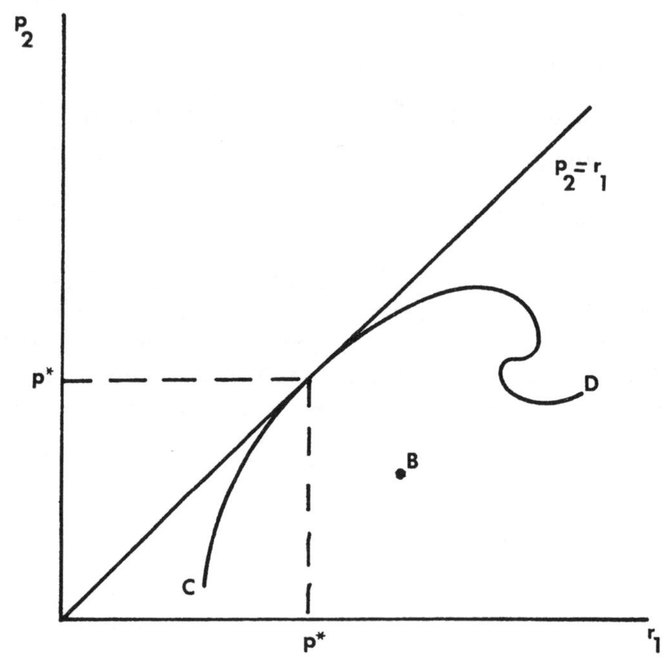

FIGURE 1b

Combining (19) and (20), we get

$$\left(\frac{w_2}{w_2 - w_1}\right)\frac{g(p^*)}{g'(p^*)} > \frac{f(p^*) + g(p^*)}{f'(p^*) + g'(p^*)}, \tag{21}$$

or, with a little manipulation,

$$\frac{f(p^*)}{f'(p^*)} - \left(\frac{w_1}{w_2 - w_1}\right)\frac{g(p^*)}{f'(p^*)} < \left(\frac{w_2}{w_2 - w_1}\right)\frac{g(p^*)}{g'(p^*)}. \tag{22}$$

Inequality (22) together with (20) implies (19), so (22) is sufficient for queue discrimination to be profitable. Letting η_1 and η_2 be the price elasticities of demand of the patient and impatient respectively, evaluated at (p^*, p^*), and noting that $f(p^*)/f'(p^*) = -p^*/\eta_2$, and that $g(p^*)/g'(p^*) = -p^*/\eta_1$, inequality (22) can be reduced to

$$\frac{\eta_2}{\eta_1} + \frac{w_1}{w_2}\left(1 + \frac{g(p^*)}{f(p^*)}\right) < 1. \tag{23}$$

Inequality (23) indicates that three factors contribute to the profitability of queue discrimination: a high demand elasticity of the long-suffering relative to that of the impatient, a low value of time for the long-suffering relative to the impatient, a small quantity demanded by the long-suffering relative to the impatient.

The condition with respect to demand elasticities is readily understood. An inescapable feature of the queue discrimination problem is that if the markets are to be separated, the long-suffering must face the lower money price. Beginning at the point (p^*, p^*) it follows that profits will increase as p_2 is increased and p_1 is decreased only if the demand elasticity of the long-suffering exceeds that of the impatient.

To see the role played by relative valuations on time let w_1 equal zero, the case of complete patience by the long-suffering. In this case queue discrimination will be profitable whenever η_2 is less than η_1 since the monopolist can separate markets at no cost to himself; he can select the profit-maximizing money prices as if the markets were separated and then choose q large enough to insure their separation, since the time cost paid by the long-suffering will have no effect on profits. Profits in this case will be identical with those which could be earned if the markets were actually separate. As w_1 rises above zero, the profits which can be earned through queue discrimination fall, relative to the profits which could be earned if the markets were actually separate, since, as w_1 increases, revenues forgone in the process of separating the submarkets increase.

The reason the relative smallness of the long-suffering submarket contributes to the profitability of queue discrimination is closely related to the above; revenues forgone in the process of separating the submarkets are smaller the smaller the long-suffering submarket is. The forgone revenue is

$qw_1g(r_1)$. In a more realistic model with a distribution of wage rates, the size of the two submarkets would obviously be endogenously determined.

QUEUE DISCRIMINATION AND ARBITRAGE

To this point we have simply assumed that arbitrage was not a physical possibility (because our monopolist is in the body rub business, say). We now wish to consider the possibility of queue discrimination when arbitrage is not ruled out by the nature of the product.

If a consumer's wage rate is w and the activity of arbitrage is costless, the return from arbitrage is $(p_2 - p_1 - wq)$ per unit arbitraged, where q is again the time price of buying a unit of the product at money price p_1. Note that the time price of buying the product at money price p_1 is paid on each unit. Thus, if the time price arises from a queueing process the added restriction that the consumer can buy only one unit when he gets to the head of the queue is required. If the return to arbitrage is positive, the consumer will prefer to 'work' at arbitrage rather than for wages. In our model it is obviously the patient who would first find arbitrage profitable as the price differential increased, and in order to rule out arbitrage we then require that $p_2 - p_1 - w_1q \leqslant 0$, or $q \geqslant (p_2 - p_1)/w_1$. If the two submarkets are to be separated, we again require that inequality (3) be satisfied, and $q = (p_2 - p_1)/w_1$ is the only possible value of q. At this value of q the impatient strictly prefer Option 2, the long-suffering are indifferent between the two options for their own consumption needs, and they are also indifferent between working at wage w_1 and working at arbitrage. Ordinarily we can break such 'ties' in any way we please, and the usual justification (used in the previous section of this paper) is that an infinitesimal movement in the variable will produce the desired outcome. Thus with $q = (p_2 - p_1)/w_1$, we might assume that for their own consumption needs the patient choose Option 1 and that they choose not to engage in arbitrage. However, if q is decreased a bit, the patient all choose Option 1 for their consumption needs and all engage in arbitrage, and if q is increased a bit, the patient all choose Option 2 for their consumption needs and all reject arbitrage as an occupation. The usual justification obviously does not work, and thus $q = (p_2 - p_1)/w_1$ must be regarded as a degenerate case of our model.

Suppose, however, that arbitrage is costly: let s be the time costs incurred in reselling a unit of X, and assume for simplicity that money costs of arbitrage are zero. Then returns to the patient from arbitraging a unit of X are $(p_2 - p_1 - w_1q - w_1s)$, and arbitrage will be unprofitable if $q \geqslant (p_2 - p_1)/w_1 - s$.

Combining this result with inequality (3) we obtain

$$p_1 + w_1q \leqslant p_2 \leqslant \min\{p_1 + w_2q, p_1 + w_1(q + s)\} \tag{24}$$

as the conditions which are necessary and sufficient to separate submarkets and prevent arbitrage. Following the argument of the previous section

$$q^* = \max\left(\frac{p_2 - p_1}{w_2}, \frac{p_2 - p_1}{w_1} - s\right), \tag{25}$$

and the model of queue discrimination when arbitrage is not physically ruled out is a straightforward generalization of the previous model.

It is possible, of course, that the costs of arbitrage are not exogenous but can be directly controlled by the monopolist. For example, in a spatial model the monopolist could choose the location of his Option 1 outlet relative to the location of the Option 2 outlet so as to control costs of arbitrage. Or in a less subtle fashion, the monopolist could effectively control arbitrage by directly limiting quantity sold to any individual in any period ('no more than one to a customer').

CONCLUSION

To this point, we have not considered how the monopolist controls time prices. Following Barzel (1974), the monopolist could use a scheme of rationing-by-waiting. Imagine that the impatient and long-suffering arrive at the monopolist's outlet uniformly over time and that the monopolist chooses p_1, p_2, x_1, x_2 so that $x_2 = f(p_2)$ and $x_1 < g(p_1)$. If a queue is allowed to form (and if each customer can buy only one unit of X at the head of the queue), and if $r_1 = g^{-1}(x_1)$ is the long-suffering's demand price, they will be willing to spend up to $q = (r_1 - p_1)/w_1$ in the queue. If only the long-suffering enter the queue, this will be the equilibrium that emerges. The impatient will use Option 2 as long as $p_2 \leqslant p_1 + w_2 q$, which is the second half of (3). Thus, the monopolist may set quantities and prices only, knowing that, with $q = (r_1 - p_1)/w_1$ satisfaction of (3) results in separation of markets in a queueing equilibrium.

Many illustrations of the use of queues to separate markets spring to mind. Most obvious are discount days by large retailers (or 'children's days' at large fall fairs). Customers buy the same items on discount and non-discount days, lower prices are accompanied by queues, and the discounted market is a fairly small part of the total. Many of the discriminatory schemes employed by airlines, particularly stand-by fares, seem to fit our model of queue discrimination.

However, the monopolist has other, less transparent options available for controlling time prices. For example, he could locate a low price outlet inconveniently so that the time price is paid in travel time. This would seem to fit the operation of 'warehouse stores' by large department stores. Alternatively, he could impose a time price by making it difficult to obtain information about when and where the low price option will be available and the time price is paid in gathering information. Or the firm can offer less service at the lower price and the time price is paid as a transaction cost. Bargain basements seem to fit this case. If less service is less costly this option renders queue discrimination even more attractive.

Governments also engage in queue discrimination.[3] We observe, for example, public tennis courts and public hospital beds (in the U.K.) rationed by queuing, with privately provided services available at a higher price, without waiting. Presumably, governments that engage in this sort of behaviour are maximizing some social objective function rather than profits. However, without access to lump-sum taxes and transfers, this rationing behaviour may be rational. Minimizing the length of the queue subject to keeping the markets separated becomes an efficiency condition rather than a necessary condition for a profit maximum since a longer queue induces people to substitute waiting for work without any other behavioural change. Given that, the analysis proceeds as above.

The model presented above provides a framework for a general model of queue discrimination. Each consumer may be treated as a submarket, with a separate price and queuing time. In the optimal strategy for the firm many, perhaps all, of these queuing times will be the same. Thus the theory provides a rationale for the number of submarkets as well as a strategy for servicing them. Further, given that the firm picks the queuing times and prices correctly, it need not police the markets at all. Consumers will separate themselves into submarkets according to their marginal valuations of their time. Lovell (1978) has analysed the problem of the optimal number of markets in a more traditional context and his ideas would be useful in developing a general model of queue discrimination.

We hope that our model will serve to explain an interesting phenomenon that has received little attention to date. It does not explain the general behaviour of firms in fixing queuing times and other unpleasantries of the market place. In our model queuing serves only to separate markets and is itself unproductive, but this is quite clearly not always so. For example, where demand is stochastic, queuing may serve a productive function as well, since it allows the firm to economize on fixed inputs (e.g., stand-by air fares and the utilization of airplanes). Other marketing schemes which demand time inputs from the consumer do not involve queuing at all but rather the transfer of productive activities from the firm to the consumer. Food co-ops, and some discount supermarkets clearly must be viewed in this light. These examples suggest that a number of approaches are necessary for a general understanding of queuing and related phenomena. Our model contributes one motive and strategy to that understanding.

3 See Nichols, Smolensky, and Tideman (1971) for a discussion of the possible use of queues to separate markets for 'merit' goods. Although it is seminal, there are serious problems with their analysis. In particular they confuse the use of queues to separate markets, which represents a dead weight loss, with the apparently similar, but conceptually distinct phenomenon of firms shifting some productive activity out of the firm and onto the consumer. The confusion is most apparent in their discussion of the *FF* frontier in their figure 1. When queuing is used to separate markets, the *FF* frontier is *endogenous*. When consumer time inputs reflect the portion of productive activity carried by the consumer relative to the firm, the *FF* frontier is exogenous and determined by technology.

REFERENCES

Barzel, Y. (1974) 'A theory of rationing by waiting,' *Journal of Law and Economics* 17, 73–95

Diewert, W.E., M. Avriel, and I. Zang (1979) 'Nine kinds of quasi-Concavity and Concavity.' Discussion Paper 79-29. Department of Economics, University of British Columbia (forthcoming in *Journal of Economic Theory*)

Machlup, F. (1955) 'Characteristics and types of price discrimination.' In *Business Concentration and Price Policy.* National Bureau of Economic Research (Princeton: Princeton University Press), 397–435

Nichols, D., E. Smolensky, and T. Tideman (1971) 'Discrimination by waiting time in merit goods.' *American Economic Review* 61, 312–23

Pigou, A.C. (1962) *The Economics of Welfare* (London: MacMillan)

Salop, S. (1977) 'The noisy monopolist: imperfect information, price dispersion and price discrimination.' *Review of Economic Studies* 44, 393–406

Spence, M. (1973) 'Job market signalling.' *Quarterly Journal of Economics* 87, 321–44

Stokey, N. (1979) 'Intertemporal price discrimination.' *Quarterly Journal of Economics* 93, 355–72

Stiglitz, J. (1975) 'The theory of "screening," education, and the distribution of income.' *American Economic Review* 65, 283–300

[20]

Person-specific costs of production: hours of work, rates of pay, labour contracts

DAVID DONALDSON AND B. CURTIS EATON/
University of British Columbia

Abstract. This note focuses on some implications of person-specific costs of production, costs of production which are proportional to the number of persons employed. Costs of providing office space, lockers, written instructions, specialized clothing, and on-the-job training are examples of person-specific costs of production. Such costs imply that aggregate production costs are dependent upon both hours utilized and on the number of employees. In order to economize on such costs the employer will induce employees, through premium wage rates, salaries, or other contractual arrangements, to work longer hours than they normally would.

Les coûts de production reliés à la main d'oeuvre: heures de travail, taux de rémunération, contrats de travail. Cette note examine les impacts de certains coûts de production reliés à la main d'oeuvre: les coûts de production qui sont proportionnels au nombre de personnes employées. Des exemples de ces types de coûts pourraient être le coût des bureaux qu'on doit leur fournir, des armoires pour leurs choses, des livrets d'instructions qu'il faut leur fournir, des uniformes et de la formation sur le tas. Ces coûts impliquent que les coûts de production au total dépendent à la fois du nombre des employés et du nombre d'heures de travail. Afin de rentabiliser ces investissements, l'employeur va être amené à inciter ses employés à travailler durant des heures plus longues qu'ils ne le feraient normalement par des indemnités ou autres arrangements contractuels ou salariaux.

The concept of firm-specific human capital (SHC) has proved to be fruitful in understanding the cyclical variation of employment, in interpreting age-earnings profiles and in understanding many industrial relations problems (see Oi, 1962; Becker, 1964; Parsons, 1972; Clark, 1973; Donaldson and Eaton, 1976). In all these applications the key insight is that the wage rate of the worker with SHC lies above wage rates available to him elsewhere and below his marginal product. This result arises because the employer increases the wage rate of workers as SHC is embodied in order to reduce labour turnover and thereby economize on SHC. That is, in an uncertain environment where the quit rate responds to the wage rate the employer can economize on SHC by manipulating the wage profile. One theme of the current paper is that there is another, in a sense logically prior, way of economizing on SHC – since

We are indebted to G.C. Archibald, Charles Blackorby, J.S. Flemming, and William Schworm for helpful comments and criticisms. The support of the Social Science and Humanities Research Council is gratefully acknowledged.

Canadian Journal of Economics / Revue canadienne d'Economique, XVII, No. 3
August / août 1984. Printed in Canada / Imprimé au Canada

0008-4085 / 84 / 441–449 $1.50

SHC is embodied in specific employees, the employer can economize on SHC by inducing employees with SHC to work longer hours than they normally would.

A second theme of this paper is that SHC is one example, of obvious importance, of a wider category of *person-specific costs of production* (PSCP), all of which have important implications in common. This concept is introduced, but not carefully analysed, by Doeringer and Piore (1971) and by Lucas and Thurow (1972). The existence of PSCP implies that aggregate costs of production are dependent upon both the number of man hours utilized and *upon the number of employees*, and this again creates an incentive for the employer to economize on PSCP by inducing his employees to work long hours. An increased wage rate is the necessary inducement.

We distinguish three types of PSCP. The first is *person-specific physical capital costs*, costs associated with physical capital that are proportional to the number of employees (not to man hours of labour). The phenomenon is perhaps most easily recognized in its extreme manifestations: on the trans-Alaska pipeline the employer housed and transported to and from the work site a very large portion of its work-force. The housing modules and vehicles used by Alyeska are items of physical capital that are proportional to the number of persons employed rather than the number of man-hours of labour employed. It seems to us that such costs occur in almost all production; office space, bathrooms, lockers, showers, elevators, pens and pencils, written instructions, and specialized clothing all are items of capital equipment that are related to the number of employees and not necessarily to man-hours of labour.

Payroll costs are perhaps the most important example of our second category of person-specific costs of production: *person-specific ongoing costs*. These costs are ongoing or recurring non-capital costs of production that are dependent upon the number of employees. The third category of person-specific costs of production is, of course, *firm-specific human capital costs*, costs arising from capital that is firm-specific and embodied in persons.

We develop a simple model that illustrates the incentive created by PSCP for employers to induce their employees, through increased incomes, to work longer hours. The analysis generates insights into the form of labour contracts, it sheds new light on the labour-hoarding phenomenon, and suggests that the ordinary characterization of a competitive labour market conceals some important phenomena.

THE MODEL

We assume that a firm produces one good, in quantity x, with r categories of labour indexed by $i = 1, \dots, r$ according to the continuously twice-differentiable production function F, whose image is

$$x = F(h_1, \dots, h_r; n_1, \dots, n_r) = F(h, n), \tag{1}$$

where n_i is the number of workers in category i, and h_i is the number of hours (per time period) that each of them works. For simplicity, we assume that each n_i is a continuous variable and that non-labour factors of production are fixed.

This formulation is identical to that of Feldstein (1967). However, there is no reason to believe that F is a concave function of its arguments. For example, if $x = l^{3/4}$ where l is a single labour input and $l = hn$, then $x = h^{3/4}n^{3/4}$. Thus strict concavity of the conventional production function is compatible with a non-concave F. We assume, however, the existence of labour aggregates $l = (l_1, \dots, l_r)$, where

$$l_i = \tilde{A}_i(h_i, n_i), \ i = 1, \dots, r, \tag{2}$$

$$x = F(h, n) = G(l) \tag{3}$$

for all h, n in the domain of F. This imposes some (weak) separability on the function F (see Blackorby, Primont and Russell, 1978). We assume that G is strongly concave in l (though not, of course, in (h, n)).[1] A reasonable restriction on each $\tilde{A}_i$ is that it be homogeneous of degree one in n_i (doubling the number of people doubles the labour input, ceteris paribus), so that we can write

$$l_i = \tilde{A}_i(h_i, 1)n_i = : A_i(h_i)n_i.^2 \tag{4}$$

A reasonable restriction on A_i is that it be concave. Thus it is possible that $l_i = h_i n_i$ *or* that two workers at four-hour days are more productive than one worker at eight-hour days.

We assume that all workers within each job category have an identical ordinal utility function of "income" (a Hicksian composite good) and leisure. Further, we assume that they have the opportunity to work elsewhere and, if they do, they are on an indifference curve indexed by $\bar{u}_i (i = 1, \dots, r)$. Thus the firm can attract all the labour in category i that it requires by offering a combination of hours of work and income which provides utility level $\bar{u}_i$. If y_i is the income of workers in category i, the labour supply constraint is

$$U_i(y_i, T - h_i) \geq \bar{u}_i, \tag{5}$$

where T is number of hours in the time period. Assuming U_i to be strongly quasi-concave,[3] (5) may be rewritten as

$$y_i \geq Y_i(h_i), \tag{6}$$

where Y_i is strongly convex. Thus we assume Y_i to be continuously twice differentiable with $Y_i''(h_i) > 0$ for all $h_i \geq 0$ and $Y_i(h_i) > 0$ for all $h_i > 0$. Profit maximization will ensure that (6) holds with equality.

Letting the (parametric) price of output be p, the firm's (gross) profits are

$$\Pi(p, c, h, n) = pG[A_1(h_1)n_1, \dots, A_r(h_r)n_r] - \sum_{i=1}^{r} [c_i + Y_i(h_i)]n_i, \tag{7}$$

1 A twice-differentiable function is strongly concave if and only if its Hessian matrix is negative definite at each point in its domain. Strong concavity thus implies strict concavity but is not implied by it. See Diewert, Avriel, and Zang (1981). We also assume, of course, that G and each $\tilde{A}_i$ are continuously twice-differentiable, that $\tilde{A}_i(0, n_i) = 0$ and that $\tilde{A}_i(h_i, n_i) > 0$ for all $h_i, n_i > 0$.

2 $a = : b$ means that b is defined by a.

3 See Diewert, Avriel, and Zang (1981, corollary 12.1).

where $c = (c_1, \ldots, c_r)$ is the vector of person specific costs of production, and labour costs in the ith category are $[c_i + Y_i(h_i)]$ per worker. The firm will choose h and n to maximize profits. However, since F is not necessarily concave in (h, n), neither is Π, and the maximization is not straightforward.

Suppose, however, that we fix l at $\bar{l}$, an arbitrary vector. Then a necessary condition for profit maximization is that the second term in (7) be minimized subject to $A_i(h_i)n_i = \bar{l}_i$, $i = 1, \ldots, r$. We therefore require that h_i and n_i be chosen to minimize

$$[c_i + Y_i(h_i)]n_i \tag{8}$$

subject to

$$A_i(h_i)n_i = \bar{l}_i \tag{9}$$

$i = 1, \ldots, r$. But this is equivalent to choosing h_i to minimize

$$B_i(h_i) = [c_i + Y_i(h_i)]/[A_i(h_i)] \tag{10}$$

and then choosing n_i to satisfy (9). B_i is not necessarily strictly convex, but it is *strictly pseudo-convex*. (See Diewert, Avriel and Zang, 1981, 408; or Mangasarian, 1969, 141–5.) B_i is strictly pseudo-convex if and only if $B_i'(\bar{h}_i) = 0$ implies that B_i is locally strictly convex at $\bar{h}_i > 0$. If $B_i'(\bar{h}_i) = 0$ then

$$B_i''(\bar{h}_i) = \{A_i(\bar{h}_i)Y_i''(\bar{h}_i) - [c_i + Y_i(\bar{h}_i)]A_i''(\bar{h}_i)\}/[A_i(\bar{h}_i)]^2, \tag{11}$$

which is positive, since $Y_i''(\bar{h}_i) > 0$ and $A_i''(h_i) \leq 0$. Thus B_i is strictly pseudo-convex. Strictly pseudo-convex functions are also strictly quasi-convex (in addition, inflection points with horizontal tangents are ruled out) and thus $B_i'(\hat{h}_i) = 0$ is sufficient for $\hat{h}_i > 0$ to be a global minimizer of B_i (we ignore the possibility of corner solutions). Differentiating (10) we obtain the first-order condition for minimization of B_i at $\hat{h}_i$,

$$A_i(\hat{h}_i)Y_i'(\hat{h}_i) - [c_i + Y_i(\hat{h}_i)]A_i'(\hat{h}_i) = 0. \tag{12}$$

Solving for $\hat{h}_i$, we may write

$$\hat{h}_i = : H_i(c_i). \tag{13}$$

Thus $\hat{h}_i$ is independent of p, $\bar{l}$ and c_j, $j \neq i$. Therefore $\hat{h}_i$ is the profit maximizing value of h_i. From (9) we know that $\hat{n}_i$ will satisfy

$$\hat{n}_i = \bar{l}_i/A_i(\hat{h}_i) = \bar{l}_i/H_i(c_i) = : \hat{N}_i(\bar{l}_i, c_i). \tag{14}$$

Using (12), the implicit wage rate for workers in category i, $Y_i(\hat{h}_i)/\hat{h}_i$, can be written as

$$w_i = [A_i(\hat{h}_i)/\hat{h}_i]\,[Y'(\hat{h}_i)/A_i'(\hat{h}_i)] - c_i/\hat{h}_i = : W_i(c_i). \tag{15}$$

Again using (12) the minimized cost per unit of type i labour, $[c_i + Y_i(\hat{h}_i)]/A_i(\hat{h}_i)$, can be written as

$$q_i = Y_i'(\hat{h}_i)/A_i'(\hat{h}_i) = : Q_i(c_i). \tag{16}$$

Given that $h_i = \hat{h}_i = H_i(c_i)$ and $n_i = \hat{n}_i = \hat{N}_i(\bar{l}_i, c_i)$, profit maximization requires that l be chosen to maximize

$$\Pi(p, c, \hat{h}, \hat{n}) = pG(l) - \sum_{i=1}^{r} q_i l_i. \tag{17}$$

Since G is strongly concave, the optimal solution, $l = l^*$, is unique and we have

$$pG_i(l^*) - q_i = 0, \; i = 1, \dots, r, \tag{18}$$

and therefore

$$l_i^* = : \tilde{L}_i(p, q) = : L_i(p, c), \; i = 1, \dots, r, \tag{19}$$

(since $q_i = Q_i(c_i)$). It follows that

$$h_i^* = H_i(c_i) \tag{20}$$

and

$$n_i^* = \hat{N}_i(l_i^*, c_i) = : N_i(p, c), \; i = 1, \dots, r. \tag{21}$$

Comparative static results are presented in

THEOREM 1. *For each $i = 1, \dots, r$,*
i) $dh_i^*/dc_i = H_i'(c_i) > 0$,
ii) $\partial l_i^*/\partial c_i = \partial L_i(p, c)/\partial c_i < 0$,
iii) $\partial n_i^*/\partial c_i = \partial N_i(p, c)/\partial c_i < 0$.

Proof.
i) From (12),

$$dh_i^*/dc_i = H_i'(c_i) = 1/\{A_i(h_i^*)Y_i''(h_i^*) - [c_i + Y_i(h_i^*)]A_i''(h_i^*)\} > 0, \tag{22}$$

since $A_i(h_i^*) > 0$, $Y_i(h_i^*) > 0$, $A_i''(h_i^*) \leq 0$, and $Y_i''(h_i^*) > 0$.
ii) Combining (18) and (16), we have

$$pG_i(l^*) - Q_i(c_i) = 0, \; i = 1, \dots, r. \tag{23}$$

Differentiating, we obtain (setting $p = 1$ for convenience)

$$\begin{bmatrix} G_{11} & \cdots & G_{1r} \\ \vdots & & \vdots \\ G_{r1} & \cdots & G_{rr} \end{bmatrix} \begin{bmatrix} \partial l_1^*/\partial c_i \\ \vdots \\ \partial l_i^*/\partial c_i \\ \vdots \\ \partial l_r^*/\partial c_i \end{bmatrix} = \begin{bmatrix} 0 \\ \vdots \\ Q_i'(c_i) \\ \vdots \\ 0 \end{bmatrix} \tag{24}$$

Since $Q_i(c_i) = Y_i'(h_i^*)/A_i'(h_i^*)$ (equation (16)),

$$Q_i'(c_i) = \{[Y_i''(h_i^*)A_i'(h_i^*) - Y_i'(h_i^*)A_i''(h_i^*)]/[A_i'(h_i^*)]^2\}H_i'(c_i) > 0. \tag{25}$$

Since the Hessian matrix of G is negative definite, $\partial l_i^*/\partial c_i < 0$.

iii) Since $n_i^* = l_i/A_i(h_i^*)$, result (iii) is an immediate consequence of (i) and (ii). □

Result (i) can be explained by a simple intuition. Rewriting $B_i(h_i)$ as

$$B_i(h_i) = [Y_i(h_i)/A_i(h_i)] + [c_i/A_i(h_i)], \tag{26}$$

$B_i(h_i)$ can be interpreted as the average full cost of a unit of labour from one worker, and it has two components. The term $Y_i(h_i)/A_i(h_i)$ is 'average direct labour cost'; the term $c_i/A_i(h_i)$ can be thought of as 'average fixed cost' per worker. The relationship between the two is analogous to that between (textbook) 'average variable cost' and 'average fixed cost.' It follows that the value of h_i that minimizes average full cost is greater than the value of h_i that minimizes average direct cost. Further, the value of h_i which minimizes average full cost increases with c_i.

(ii) is proved by noticing that q_j, the minimized full cost of a unit of type j labour, is independent of c_i if $j \neq i$, and an increasing function of c_i if $j = i$. Result (ii) then follows from the usual comparative static result in the theory of the firm that derived demand curves for factors of production slope downwards (see Bear, 1965).

There are, we believe, some interesting implications of these results for the nature of labour contracts. To develop these implications it is convenient to consider two special cases. Assume first that $l_i = n_ih_i$ so that labour services from a worker are identical to hours worked, and rewrite (15) to obtain

$$W_i(c_i) = Y'(h_i^*) - c_i/h_i^*. \tag{27}$$

When $c_i = 0$, the firm will choose h_i so that the implicit wage rate, $W_i(c_i)$, is equal to the worker's marginal rate of substitution of income for leisure, MRS $= Y'(h_i^*)$, and the optimal solution will be at point A in figure 1. Since the implicit wage rate is equal to the worker's MRS, the firm could simply offer jobs at this wage rate, allowing each worker to choose hours of work freely. However, when $c_i > 0$ the optimal solution will be at a point like B in figure 1, where the worker's MRS exceeds the implicit wage rate. If the firm offered jobs at wage rate $W_i(c_i)$ and allowed workers freely to choose hours of work, an issue of incentive compatibility would immediately arise, since workers would choose to work fewer than h_i^* hours. If the employer chose to characterize jobs in terms of an explicit wage rate, $W_i(c_i)$, *and* hours of work, h_i^*, an implicit issue of incentive compatibility remains. At this wage rate workers would prefer to work fewer than h_i^* hours, and one would anticipate absenteeism as workers attempt to establish equality of the wage rate and their MRS (and hence achieve a higher level of utility). Non-linear wage rates can eliminate the problem and would therefore seem to be a preferred form of labour contract (when $c_i > 0$). For example, the wage schedule in figure 1 denoted by OCB would enable the employer to attain point B while eliminating the divergence between the wage rate and the workers' MRS. The wage schedule denoted by OCB in the figure obviously carries with it a guarantee

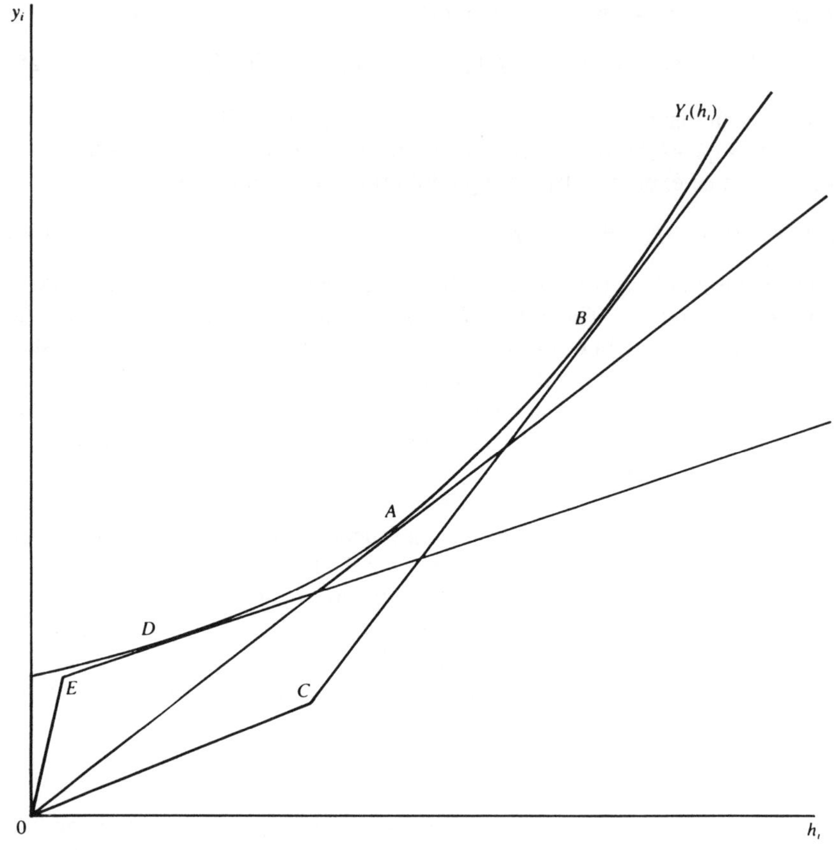

FIGURE 1

that 'overtime work' will be available, and we do not ordinarily regard overtime work as guaranteed. However, it would appear that there is an implicit guarantee in many manufacturing industries where overtime work is the rule and not the exception (see *Hours and Earnings*, United States Bureau of Labor Statistics).

Now assume that A_i is strictly concave and that $c_i = 0$, and rewrite (15) to obtain

$$W_i(0) = [A_i(h_i^*)/h_i^* A_i'(h_i^*)]\, Y_i'(h_i^*) > Y_i'(h_i^*), \tag{28}$$

since strict concavity of A_i and $A_i(0) = 0$ implies that $A_i(h_i)/h_i A_i'(h_i) > 1$ when $h_i > 0$. In this case the optimal wage rate exceeds the worker's MRS, and the optimal solution will be at a point like D in figure 1. In this case, at wage rate $W_i(0)$, workers prefer to work more than h_i^* hours, and, to the extent that workers can control their hours of work, there is again an incentive-compatibility problem. A non-linear contract, such as OED in figure 1, would eliminate the problem. An appropriately chosen piece rate would also eliminate it, since it arises from concavity of labour in hours worked.

This model makes an interesting prediction for length of the work week over the business cycle. Since h_i^* is independent of p, changes in output price have, ceteris paribus, no effect on the work week. Further, if we derive the demand functions by quantity-constraining the firm, equation (12) again results. Thus, changes in output have no effect, by themselves, on the work week. However, in times of unemployment, some person-specific factors (such as offices) will have a reduced or zero opportunity cost. The short-run effect will be to reduce some or all the c_is. Thus, the firm will reduce h_i^* in those cases. Consequently, when the firm wishes to reduce the ith labour input, it will do so by reducing (at least initially) the work week, engaging in 'labour-hoarding' over the cycle. This is consistent with the labour-hoarding hypothesis of Oi (1962), although it arises for a different reason.

CONCLUSIONS

In partial-equilibrium analysis we ordinarily characterize a competitive labour market by assuming that firms face a perfectly elastic supply of labour at some market determined wage rate. In this note we characterize a competitive labour market by assuming that firms face a perfectly elastic supply of employees at some market determined level of utility. This leaves firms to choose the optimal combination of hours of work and income (or a wage rate) along the market determined iso-utility constraint. Our analysis implies that the two characterizations are equivalent if and only if there are no person-specific costs of production and if the labour input from an employee is proportional to hours of work.

When there exist PSCP and / or when labour is strictly concave in hours of work the ordinary characterization conceals some interesting phenomena. The firm must choose hours of work and the wage rate or salary in addition to quantity of labour. Further, the firm must concern itself with issues of incentive compatibility and the form of the labour contract. Of course, under these conditions, observed incomes or wage rates are not indices of workers' utility.

REFERENCES

Bear, D.V.T. (1965) 'Inferior inputs and the theory of the firm.' *Journal of Political Economy* 73, 287–89

Becker, G. (1964) *Human Capital* (New York: NBER

Blackorby, C., D. Primont, and R. Russell (1978) *Duality, Separability, and Functional Structure: Theory and Economic Applications* (New York: North-Holland)

Clark, C.S. (1973) 'Labour hoarding in durable goods industries.' *American Economic Review* 63, 811–24

Diewert, W.E., M. Avriel, and I. Zang (1981) 'Nine kinds of quasi concavity and concavity.' *Journal of Economic Theory* 25, 397–420

Donaldson, D. and B.C. Eaton (1976) 'Firm specific human capital: a shared investment or optimal entrapment?' This JOURNAL 462–72

Doeringer, P. and M. Piore (1971) *Internal Labour Markets and Manpower Analysis* (Lexington, MA: D.C. Heath)

Ehrenberg, R.G. (1971) *Fringe Benefits and Overtime Behaviour* (Lexington, MA: Lexington Books)

Feldstein, M.S. (1967) 'Specification of the labour input in the aggregate production function.' *Review of Economic Studies* 34, 375–6

Lucas, R. and L. Thurow (1972) *The American Distribution of Income: A Structural Problem*, Joint Economic Committee Print (Washington: U.S. Government Printing Office)

Mangasarian, O.L. (1969) Nonlinear Programming (New York: McGraw-Hill)

Oi, W. (1962) 'Labour as a quasi-fixed factor.' *Journal of Political Economy* 70, 538–55

Parsons, D.O. (1972) 'Specific human capital: an application to quit rates and layoff rates.' *Journal of Political Economy* 80, 1120–43

[21]

Sweezy's kink: the original consistent-conjectural equilibrium?*

with Jeremiah M. Allen**

Abstract

An approach to oligopoly, or duopoly, equilibria, known as 'consistent-conjectural' variations, has recently attracted some attention. We show here that, while previously unacknowledged, Paul Sweezy's well-known kinky demand curve is a consistent-conjectural equilibrium. We believe Sweezy's to be the first such equilibrium in the economics literature.

1. Introduction

In 1980 the *Quarterly Journal of Economics* published an article which introduced the concept of 'consistent', or 'rational', conjectures, and applied it to duopoly or oligopoly equilibria (Laitner, 1980). This article was quickly followed by a number of others.[1] It is well known that Paul Sweezy's model of oligopolistic price rigidity, published in 1939, is based on conjectured reactions of rival firms, but the recent work on conjectural variations has, without exception, failed to cite Sweezy or to note that his kinky demand curve solution is a consistent-conjectural equilibrium. We show here that the Sweezy kink is a consistent-conjectural equilibrium – the original one, we believe.[2]

2. Definitions

Oligopoly firms must consider the actions of rival firms in their own pricing decisions; the profit maximizing price for one firm depends on the prices set by its rivals. The relationship between a firm's profit maximizing price and rival firm's price is the firm's *reaction function*. The slope of a firm's reaction function is the change in that firm's profit maximizing price, given a change in a rival's price. Knowing that it has a reaction function, it is reasonable that a firm believes its rivals also to have reaction functions. The rivals' reaction functions are not known to the firm, but the firm may have *conjectures* about these functions. The slopes of the conjectured functions are called *conjectural variations*. A *constant* conjectural variation means the conjectured reaction function is linear; two interesting special cases are the *zero* conjectural variation – a firm conjectures that a rival firm will ignore a price change (the Bertrand conjecture) – and the *unity* conjectural variation – a firm conjectures that a rival firm will match any price change. A conjectural variation is *consistent* if it is the rival firm's true reaction function, that is, if the conjectured behaviour is the rival firm's actual profit maximizing behaviour.[3]

---

* This paper was written in 1985.
** Department of Economics, University of Lethbridge.

Both static and dynamic models have been developed, generating two types of conjectural equilibria. A *static* conjectural equilibrium is determined by assuming that an industry exists in the form of an industry demand curve, with no output; each firm in the industry, in complete isolation from the others, determines its price (output) from its own reaction function and its conjectural variations. A *dynamic* conjectural equilibrium is determined when no firm, given its own reaction function and its conjectural variations, can increase its profit by altering its price (output). Either is a *consistent-conjectural* equilibrium if the firms' conjectural variations are consistent.

The familiar Sweezy kink is clearly a conjectural equilibrium. Firms conjecture that all other firms will match a price decrease – an M (match) reaction, or the unity conjectural variation – and will ignore a price increase – an O (ignore) reaction, or the zero conjectural variation. (Note that the Sweezy conjectural variations are neither continuous nor symmetric.) When the marginal cost curve of each firm intersects its Sweezy-conjectured marginal revenue function in the gap, the industry is in a dynamic conjectural equilibrium. We show below that the Sweezy conjectures are consistent, and that Sweezy kinky equilibria are dynamic consistent-conjectural equilibria.

3. Proof

We demonstrate the consistency of the Sweezy conjectures, and of the kinky equilibria, for a duopoly; extension to a small number of additional firms is self-evident. We employ the usual assumptions:

$$\Pi_1(p_1, p_2) = S(p_1, p_2), \text{ and } \Pi_2(p_1, p_2) = S(p_2, p_1)$$

denote the profits of Firms One and Two respectively, where p_1 and p_2 are the prices of firms One and Two; the function $S(\cdot, \cdot)$ is symmetric and strictly concave in its arguments; the goods produced by the duopolists are substitutes, so the partial derivative of $S(\cdot, \cdot)$ is negative with respect to its first argument, and positive with respect to its second; the marginal costs for both firms are constant or increasing; and both firms attempt to maximize profit.

3.1. Nash and cooperative equilibria

The Nash and cooperative equilibria are shown in Figure 1. In that figure, $R_1(0)$ is Firm One's profit maximizing price, *holding p_2 constant*, and $R_2(0)$ is Firm Two's profit maximizing price, *holding p_1 constant*. Firm One's profit increases as p_1 moves horizontally toward R_1 from either direction, and Firm Two's profit increases as p_2 moves vertically toward R_2 from either direction. $R_1(0)$ and $R_2(0)$ are also the reaction functions of Firms One and Two respectively, beginning from points on $R_1(0)$ or $R_2(0)$ and given zero conjectural variations.

There exists a unique and stable Nash equilibrium, (p_1^n, p_2^n), shown as N in Figure 1. The Nash equilibrium is the intersection of the R functions, and is the conjectural equilibrium given that both firms hold conjectural variations equal to zero – each firm believes the other will ignore a price change. The Nash equilibrium is also the familiar Bertrand equilibrium, and at (p_1^n, p_2^n):

$$MC_1 = MR_1 \mid O_1 \text{ and } MC_2 = MR_2 \mid O_2.$$

(At the Nash equilibrium the marginal cost curve of each firm intersects its Sweezy-conjectured marginal revenue function at the *top* of the gap.)

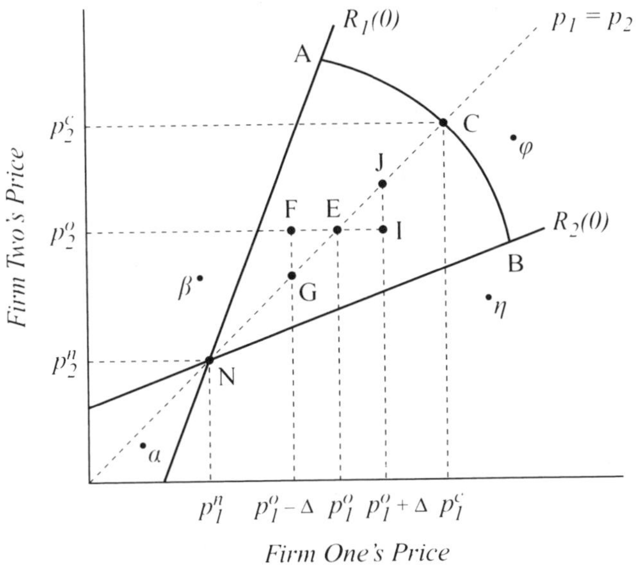

Figure 1

There also exists a common cooperative, or collusive, equilibrium, (p_1^c, p_2^c), shown as C in Figure 1. The common cooperative equilibrium maximizes the profit of each firm subject to the constraint that $p_1 = p_2$, and is the conjectural equilibrium given that both firms hold conjectural variations equal to one – each firm believes the other will match a price change. The profits of both firms increase as they move from N toward C along the line $p_2 = p_1$, and decrease as they move beyond C.

With no constraint to a common price for both firms, there exists a set of cooperative, or collusive, equilibria, shown as line segment ACB in Figure 1. Each cooperative equilibrium maximizes joint profits and is a conjectural equilibrium given that both firms hold conjectural variations equal to one. The profits of both firms decrease as they move away from ACB along a 45 degree line, and, at any point on ACB:

$$MC_1 = MR_1 \mid M_1 \text{ and } MC_2 = MR_2 \mid M_2.$$

(At any cooperative equilibrium, the marginal cost curve of each firm intersects its Sweezy-conjectured marginal revenue function at the *bottom* of the gap.)

3.2. Sweezy non-equilibria

The set of Sweezy equilibria is the area NAB in Figures 1 and 2. Points outside NAB cannot be Sweezy equilibria; at these points, Sweezy conjectures would cause one or both firms to change price. Consider a point in the triangle below N, point α in Figure 1, for example. Both firms Sweezy-conjecture that price increases will be ignored.

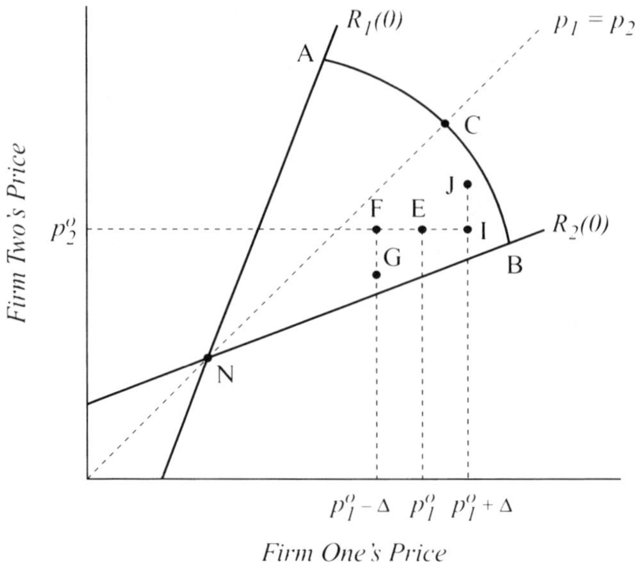

Figure 2

Since α is to the left of R_1 and below R_2, each firm anticipates higher profit from an unmatched price increase, so both would increase their prices until they equal p^n. Any point inside the triangle below N cannot be a Sweezy equilibrium. (At any point inside the triangle below N, the marginal cost curve of each firm intersects its Sweezy-conjectured marginal revenue function *above* the gap.)

Now consider points to the left of the R_1 function, or below the R_2 function, points β and η in Figure 1, for example. Firm One (Two) Sweezy-conjectures that a price increase will be ignored. Since β (η) is to the left of R_1 (below R_2), Firm One (Two) anticipates higher profit from an unmatched price increase, so it would increase its price until it reaches R_1 (R_2). Any point to the left of R_1, or below R_2, cannot be a Sweezy equilibrium. [At any point to the left of R_1 (below R_2), the marginal cost curve of Firm One (Two) intersects its Sweezy-conjectured marginal revenue function *above* the gap.]

Finally, consider a point above the line segment ACB, ψ in Figure 1, for example. Both firms Sweezy-conjecture that price decreases will be matched. Since ψ is above ACB, each firm anticipates higher profit from a matched price decrease, so both firms would decrease their prices until they reach ACB. Any point above ACB cannot be a Sweezy equilibrium. (At any point above ACB, the marginal cost curve of each firm intersects its Sweezy-conjectured marginal revenue function *below* the gap.) Points outside the area NAB of Figures 1 and 2 are not Sweezy equilibria.

3.3. Sweezy equilibria

Sweezy equilibria must lie inside NAB of Figures 1 and 2. Points E, in Figures 1 and 2, are Sweezy equilibria, the first with a common price, the second with differing prices for each firm. At those points, Firm One's price is p_1^o and Firm Two's price is p_2^o.

To demonstrate equilibrium, suppose that, from point E, Firm One considers decreasing its price; its Sweezy conjecture is that Firm Two's reaction would be to match the price decrease. For that conjecture to be consistent, matching must be Firm Two's profit maximizing reaction to a price decrease, with reactions restricted to matching or ignoring. Were Firm One to decrease its price by Δ, to $p_1^o - \Delta$, Firm Two could choose between points G (match) or F (ignore). Since G is closer to R_2 than is F, Firm Two's profit at G exceeds its profit at F; Firm Two would choose G. Firm Two's profit maximizing Sweezy-reaction would be to match the price decrease – Firm One's Sweezy conjecture is consistent.

Now suppose that, from point E, Firm One considers increasing its price; its Sweezy conjecture is that Firm Two's reaction would be to ignore the price increase and hold its price constant. For this conjecture to be consistent, holding price constant must be Firm Two's profit maximizing reaction to a price increase, with reactions restricted to matching or ignoring. Were Firm One to increase its price by Δ, to $p^o + \Delta$, Firm Two could choose between J (match) or I (ignore). Since I is closer to R_2 than is J, Firm Two's profit at I exceeds its profit at J; Firm Two would choose I. Firm Two's profit maximizing Sweezy-reaction would be to ignore the price increase – Firm One's Sweezy conjecture is consistent.

Holding Sweezy conjectures, then, Firm One can choose among points E, I or G. E is closer to line segment ACB than is G, so Firm One's profit is higher at E than at G. E is closer to R_1 along a horizontal line than is I, so Firm One's profit is higher at E than at I. Of the three, a profit maximizing Firm One will choose E; given Sweezy conjectures, E is an equilibrium for Firm One.

The argument above can be reversed in an obvious way to show that, with its conjectural variations restricted to the Sweezy conjectures, Firm Two's conjectures about Firm One's reactions are also consistent, and point E is also an equilibrium for Firm Two. If conjectural variations are restricted to the Sweezy conjectures, E is a consistent-conjectural equilibrium. The argument for point E can be applied to any point in the area NAB, and, if conjectural variations are restricted to the Sweezy conjectures, any of those points could be a consistent-conjectural equilibrium. Therefore the Sweezy kink is a dynamic consistent-conjectural equilibrium.

4. Conclusion

We have shown that, if conjectural variations are restricted to matching or ignoring rivals' price changes, the Sweezy conjectures are consistent and the Sweezy kink is a dynamic consistent-conjectural equilibrium. We believe the Sweezy kink to be the first consistent-conjectural equilibrium, and we note that it pre-dated the recent 'discovery' of this approach by 40 years. We reiterate that we are not trying to rehabilitate Sweezy – this note can be considered simply as the demonstration of a historical curiosity.

There may, however, be some lessons here. For instance, rewriting Sweezy with more modern tools illustrates more clearly some of the well-known weaknesses of the kinky equilibrium: it imposes a static model on dynamic behavioural assumptions; its restriction of conjectural variations to two – zero and unity – is unnecessarily, and not usefully, limiting; it characterizes a very large number of equilibria, ranging from the Nash to the collusive; and it says nothing about how any possible equilibrium is reached.

On the other side, we note that the recent work on consistent-conjectural variations failed to rediscover Sweezy. That failure was almost certainly due to the recent literature's reliance on mathematical models applying calculus. The Sweezy conjectural variations are asymmetric and discontinuous, and are therefore not amenable to easy manipulation with calculus. In addition, attention was focused on static equilibria, while the Sweezy kink is (implicitly) dynamic.[4]

We further note that the recent flurry of interest in consistent-conjectural variations seems to be fading, with the approach having added little to our understanding of duopoly, or oligopoly, equilibria. This may be related to the failure to rediscover Sweezy. Understanding that Sweezy's kink is a consistent-conjectural equilibrium suggests that the recent work, with its emphasis on static analysis and continuous reaction functions, failed to explore an entire class of consistent-conjectural variations: those with asymmetric reaction functions. If oligopoly behaviour is indeed asymmetric – if, in circumstances one could plausibly assume to exist, a consistent reaction to a rival's decrease in price is even a little different from the consistent reaction to an increase – an appreciation of Sweezy's insight might have proved useful to the recent development of consistent-conjectural variations models of that behaviour.

Notes

1. A current comprehensive bibliography would include at least 15 published articles and another eight to 10 unpublished discussion papers, all of them written between 1980 and 1986, most of them written between 1980 and 1983. See Perry (1982), Kamien and Schwartz (1983) and the references below.
2. It seems clear to us, but comments suggest we should make explicit, that we are *not* presenting Sweezy's kink as a valid or useful description of an oligopoly equilibrium. All we intend to show is that the Sweezy conjectures are consistent and the Sweezy kink is a consistent-conjectural equilibrium. We believe that the Sweezy kink is the first consistent-conjectural equilibrium to be found in the economics literature.
3. The concept of conjectural variations pre-dates modern economics; it is first found in Cournot (1838). What's new in the work beginning with Laitner (1980) is the concept of 'consistency' or 'rationality'. Although Perry (1982) notes that the idea of 'consistency' can be found earlier in other literatures, most notably in the literature on rational expectations, he fails to note that Sweezy's conjectures are consistent.
4. Of the papers cited in the references below, only Laitner (1980) uses a dynamic model.

References

Boyer, M. and M. Moreaux (1983), 'Consistent Versus Non-Consistent Conjectures in Duopoly Theory: Some Examples', *Journal of Industrial Economics*, **32**, pp. 97–110.

Bresnahan, T. (1981), 'Duopoly Models with Consistent Conjectures', *American Economic Review*, **71**, pp. 934–5.

Bresnahan, T. (1983), 'Existence of Consistent Conjectures: Reply', *American Economic Review*, **73**, pp. 457–8.

Cournot, A.A. (1838), *Recherches sur les principles mathematiques de la theorie des richesses*, Hachette, Paris.

Holt, C. A. (1985), 'An Experimental Test of the Consistent-Conjectures Hypothesis', *American Economic Review*, **75**, pp. 314–25.

Kamien, M.I. and N.L. Schwartz (1983), 'Conjectural Variations', *Canadian Journal of Economics*, **16**, pp. 191–211.

Kolstad, C.D. and F.A. Wolak (1986), 'Conjectural Variation and the Indeterminacy of Duopolistic Equilibria', *Canadian Journal of Economics*, **19**, pp. 656–77.

Laitner, J. (1980), 'Rational Duopoly Equilibria', *Quarterly Journal of Economics*, **95**, pp. 641–62.

Perry, M.K. (1982), 'Oligopoly and Consistent Conjectural Variations', *Bell Journal of Economics*, **13**, pp. 197–205.

Robson, A.J. (1983), 'Existence of Consistent Conjectures: Comment', *American Economic Review*, **73**, pp. 454–6.

Sweezy, P.M. (1939), 'Demand under Conditions of Oligopoly', *Journal of Political Economy*, **47**, pp. 568–73.

Trujillo, J. (1985), 'Rational Responses and Rational Conjectures', *Journal of Economic Theory*, **36**, pp. 277–8.

Ulph, D. (1983), 'Rational Conjectures in the Theory of Oligopoly', *International Journal of Industrial Organization*, **1**, pp. 131–54.

[22]

The Geometry of Supply, Demand, and Competitive Market Structure with Economies of Scope

By B. CURTIS EATON AND S. Q. LEMCHE*

The geometry of a two-good partial-equilibrium model with economies of scope is presented. There are three types of firms: diversified firms that produce both goods and two types of specialized firms. Thus, there are five possible industry market structures: one involving all three types of firms, three involving two types of firms, and one involving only diversified firms. We show that the equilibrium market structure is jointly determined by supply (cost) and demand conditions and that any market structure involving more types of firms than goods is an unlikely occurrence. (JEL L11)

From their inception, it has been clear that economies of scope nicely account for the existence of multiproduct firms (see William J. Baumol et al., 1982). As our title emphasizes, they also provide a theory of competitive market structure. Moreover, our analysis shows that certain easily recognizable market structures are inconsistent with this theory, providing at least a crude test of it.

We analyze a very simple partial-equilibrium model with economies of scope in which there are two goods which can be produced either by diversified firms, which realize economies of scope by producing both goods, or by single-product specialized firms. In a recent paper, Glenn M. MacDonald and Alan Slivinski (1987) analyze a similar model. Our assumptions with respect to technologies are quite unrestrictive; in contrast, theirs are quite restrictive, relying heavily on fixed costs. Hence our model can be seen as a significant generalization of theirs. By using profit functions, which allow us to operate in price space, we generate quite general results with respect to market structure in a simple intuitive manner. In addition, we develop demand and supply diagrams to illustrate the salient features of competitive equilibrium with economies of scope.

I. The Model

We focus on the case in which there are two goods, X_1 and X_2, and three technologies, two pertaining to specialized production of X_1 or X_2 and the third to joint production of X_1 and X_2. We write demand functions as $D^i(p_1, p_2)$ for $i = 1,2$ and assume that they are continuous and that quantity demanded of X_i is inversely related to its price, p_i. The two goods may be complements, substitutes, or unrelated in consumption.

We characterize technologies by cost functions and write the specialized cost functions as $C^i(x_i)$, for $i = 1,2$, and the joint cost function as $C(x_1, x_2)$. We assume that the cost functions are continuous and strictly increasing in their arguments and that it costs nothing to produce nothing: $C^i(0) = 0$ for $i = 1,2$, and $C(0,0) = 0$. We assume that the average cost functions for the specialized technologies and the ray average cost function for the joint technology all have a strictly positive minimum efficient scale and a finite maximum efficient scale.[1] These av-

*Department of Economics, Simon Fraser University, Burnaby, BC V5A 1S6, Canada. We have benefited from comments from the participants in seminars at S.F.U. during January 1989 and at the Carleton University Annual Conference in Industrial Organization in July 1990. The computer graphing was done very ably by Larry Boland.

[1]Ray average cost can be defined as follows. For a given $\alpha \geq 0$, let the ray defined by α be $r_\alpha =$

erage cost functions are then U-shaped, perhaps with a flat bottom, or W-shaped with one or two flat bottoms, and so on. (These assumptions are stronger than we need; weaker assumptions are discussed below.)

We sometimes use the following joint cost function for purposes of illustration:

$$(1)\quad C(x_1,x_2) = \begin{cases} F + \sum_{i=1}^{2}(a_i x_i + b_i x_i^2) + c x_1 x_2 & \text{if } x_i > 0\ (i=1 \text{ or } i=2) \\ 0 & \text{otherwise} \end{cases}$$

where the parameters a_i, b_i, and F are assumed to be positive. The sign of c is unrestricted, but we require that $c^2 < 4b_1b_2$. There are two parameters relating to economies of scope in this cost function: the setup cost (F) and c. A negative c reflects complementarity in production, and a positive c reflects substitutability.

Now consider the three profit functions, defined by the following maximization problems:

$$(2)\quad \Pi^i(p_i) = \max_{x_i}\{p_i x_i - C^i(x_i)\} \quad \text{for } i=1,2$$

$$(3)\quad \Pi(p_1,p_2) = \max_{x_1,x_2}\{p_1x_1 + p_2x_2 - C(x_1,x_2)\}.$$

Note that these functions give *maximized* profit for given prices. Given our cost assumptions, these profit functions are well defined. $\Pi^i(p_i)$ is nondecreasing in p_i and strictly increasing in p_i if the profit-maximizing quantity of X_i is positive. Hence, there is a maximum value of p_i, say $\mathring{p}_i$, such that $\Pi^i(p_i)$ is zero. Since $C^i(0)=0$, then $\Pi^i(p_i)=0$ for $p_i \le \mathring{p}_i$; and if $p_i < \mathring{p}_i$, then the profit-maximizing quantity of x_i is zero. On the other hand, when $p_i = \mathring{p}_i$, there is at least one positive output at which profit is zero. Obviously, $\mathring{p}_i$ is the minimum value of average cost for a type-i firm, and hence we call the vector $\mathring{\mathbf{p}} = (\mathring{p}_1, \mathring{p}_2)$ the *minimum-average-cost vector* for the specialized technologies.

Free entry of specialized firms implies that the *competitive equilibrium price* for X_i, p_i^e, is less than or equal to $\mathring{p}_i$.

No-Entry Condition 1: $p_i^e \le \mathring{p}_i$, for $i=1,2$.

Free entry and exit of specialized firms imply that if specialized firms of type-i exist in equilibrium, then the equilibrium price for X_i is equal to $\mathring{p}_i$.

Equilibrium Price Condition 1: If type-i firms exist in equilibrium, then $p_i^e = \mathring{p}_i$.

The profit function associated with the joint technology, $\Pi(p_1,p_2)$, is (i) nondecreasing in p_i and strictly increasing in p_i if the profit-maximizing quantity of X_i is positive and (ii) convex in $\mathbf{p}=(p_1,p_2)$.[2] The upper boundary of the set of prices such that maximized profit is zero plays a crucial role in determining competitive equilibrium, just as it does in the case of specialized firms. Let Z denote the set of prices such that $\Pi(p_1,p_2)$ is equal to zero, and call the upper boundary of Z the P locus. Both Z and the P locus are illustrated in Figure 1. Below the P locus the firm produces nothing, and maximum profit is zero. On the P locus there is a profit-maximizing supply bundle, $\mathbf{x}^* = (x_1^*, x_2^*)$, in which at least one quantity is positive, and another in which

---

$\{(x_1,x_2)|x_2 = \alpha x_1\}$. For $(x_1,x_2)\in r_\alpha$, the ray average cost at (x_1,x_2) is defined as $\text{RAC}_\alpha(x_1,x_2) = C(x_1,x_2)\cdot(x_1^2+x_2^2)^{-1/2}$. The minimum r_α-ray average cost is the minimum of $\text{RAC}_\alpha(x_1,x_2)$ along the r_α-ray.

[2]The profit function $\Pi(\mathbf{p})$ is convex in $\mathbf{p}$ if, given any two price pairs $\bar{\mathbf{p}}$ and $\hat{\mathbf{p}}$ and any convex combination of them, $\mathring{\mathbf{p}} = \lambda\bar{\mathbf{p}} + (1-\lambda)\hat{\mathbf{p}}$ for $0 \le \lambda \le 1$, $\Pi(\mathring{\mathbf{p}}) \le \lambda\Pi(\bar{\mathbf{p}}) + (1-\lambda)\Pi(\hat{\mathbf{p}})$. Now, $\Pi(\mathring{\mathbf{p}}) = \mathring{\mathbf{p}}\mathring{\mathbf{x}} - C(\mathring{\mathbf{x}})$, where $\mathring{\mathbf{x}}$ are the profit-maximizing quantities associated with prices $\mathring{\mathbf{p}}$. Using the fact that $\mathring{\mathbf{p}}$ is a convex combination of $\bar{\mathbf{p}}$ and $\hat{\mathbf{p}}$, we have $\Pi(\mathring{\mathbf{p}}) = \lambda(\bar{\mathbf{p}}\mathring{\mathbf{x}} - C(\mathring{\mathbf{x}})) + (1-\lambda)(\hat{\mathbf{p}}\mathring{\mathbf{x}} - C(\mathring{\mathbf{x}}))$. However, $\bar{\mathbf{p}}\mathring{\mathbf{x}} - C(\mathring{\mathbf{x}}) \le \Pi(\bar{\mathbf{p}})$ and $\hat{\mathbf{p}}\mathring{\mathbf{x}} - C(\mathring{\mathbf{x}}) \le \Pi(\hat{\mathbf{p}})$. Hence, $\Pi(\mathring{\mathbf{p}}) \le \lambda\Pi(\bar{\mathbf{p}}) + (1-\lambda)\Pi(\hat{\mathbf{p}})$.

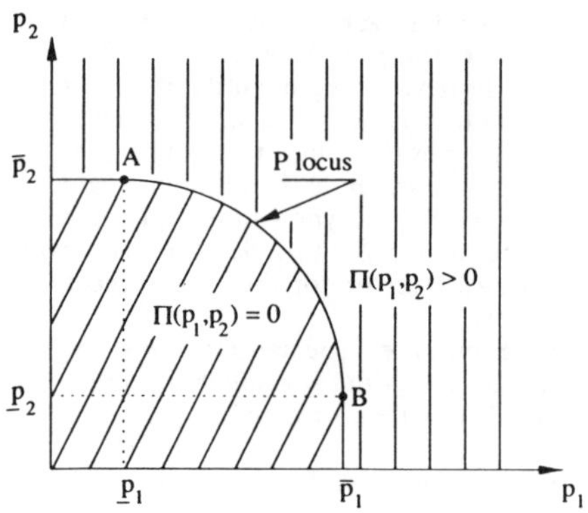

FIGURE 1. THE P LOCUS

both quantities are zero. Where the locus is horizontal (segment $\bar{p}_2$A), x_2^* is positive and x_1^* is zero; and where it is vertical (segment $\bar{p}_1$B), x_1^* is positive and x_2^* is zero. Otherwise, both quantities are positive. Note that $\bar{p}_i$ is the diversified firm's minimum average cost when it produces only X_i. The convexity and nondecreasingness of $\Pi(p_1, p_2)$ imply that the P locus is (weakly) concave to the origin and that it cannot be upward-sloping. If (p_1, p_2) is above the P locus, then $\Pi(p_1, p_2)$ is strictly positive.[3]

The P locus associated with our illustrative cost function is

$$\text{(4a)} \quad b_2\omega_1^2/\Delta - F = 0 \quad \text{if } 2b_1\omega_2 - c\omega_1 \leq 0$$

$$\text{(4b)} \quad b_1\omega_2^2/\Delta - F = 0 \quad \text{if } 2b_2\omega_1 - c\omega_2 \leq 0$$

$$\text{(4c)} \quad \left(b_2\omega_1^2 + b_1\omega_2^2 - c\omega_1\omega_2\right)/\Delta - F = 0 \quad \text{otherwise}$$

where $\omega_i \equiv p_i - a_i$ and $\Delta \equiv 4b_1b_2 - c^2$. Equation (4a) defines the vertical segment of the P locus along which $x_2^* = 0$, (4b) defines the horizontal segment along which $x_1^* = 0$, and (4c) defines a segment that is strictly concave to the origin. The P locus in Figures 1–7 is the special case in which $b_1 = b_2 = 1$ and $c = 0$. Notice that if c is negative, so that X_1 and X_2 are complementary in production, then the vertical and horizontal segments of the P locus may or may not exist.

Free entry of diversified firms implies that the equilibrium price vector, $\mathbf{p}^e = (p_1^e, p_2^e)$, is in the set such that maximized profit for a diversified firm is zero.

No-Entry Condition 2: $\mathbf{p}^e$ is in Z.

Free entry and exit of diversified firms imply that, if diversified firms exist in equilibrium, then equilibrium prices are on the P locus.

Equilibrium Price Condition 2: If diversified firms exist in equilibrium, then $\mathbf{p}^e$ is on the P locus.

II. Equilibrium Prices and Market Structure

In this section, we develop the implications of the no-entry and equilibrium price conditions for prices and market structure. The no-entry conditions for all three firm types and the equilibrium price conditions for the firm types that exist in equilibrium must be satisfied in competitive equilibrium. If the equilibrium price condition for some firm type is satisfied, then so too is the no-entry condition for that firm type. To eliminate some uninteresting cases, we assume that there is sufficient demand so that equilibrium quantities are positive. In addition, we suppose that the competitive equilibrium exists. In essence then, this section explores the implications of the cost side of our model for equilibrium prices and market structure.

Feasible market structures and associated equilibrium prices are determined by the location of the minimum-average-cost vector, $\mathring{\mathbf{p}}$, relative to the P locus. To facilitate discussion of the various possibilities, we have partitioned the price space in Figure 2 into eight parts: region I below the P locus, regions II–VII above the P locus, and the P locus itself.

[3] If $C(x_1, x_2)$ is additive, then the P locus has only a horizontal and a vertical segment. This, of course, is the uninteresting case in which the joint technology does not exhibit economies of scope.

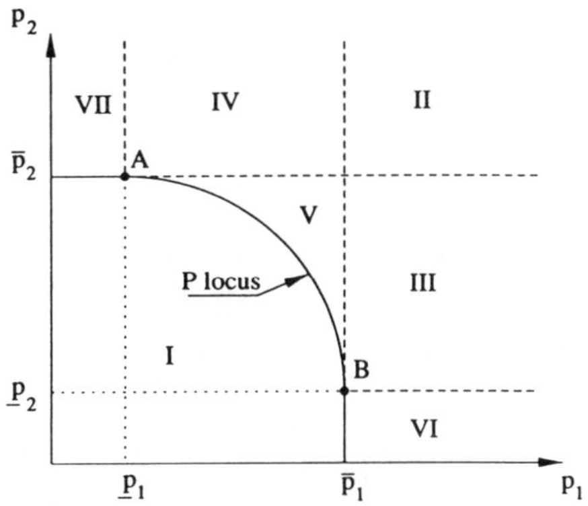

FIGURE 2. EQUILIBRIUM MARKET STRUCTURES, CASE 1

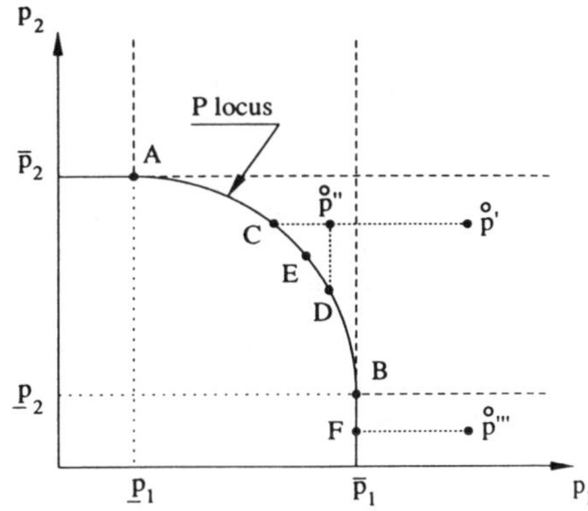

FIGURE 3. EQUILIBRIUM MARKET STRUCTURES, CASE 2

I.—If $\mathring{\mathbf{p}}$ lies below the P locus in region I, the equilibrium price vector is equal to the minimum-average-cost vector, $\mathbf{p}^e = \mathring{\mathbf{p}}$. Equilibrium price condition 1 is then satisfied for both types of specialized firms, while for diversified firms no-entry condition 2 is satisfied and equilibrium price condition 2 is not. To produce the positive equilibrium quantities, both types of specialized firms must exist, since diversified firms cannot. This is the familiar textbook partial-equilibrium model in which equilibrium prices are completely determined by costs. That is, when $\mathring{\mathbf{p}}$ is in region I, the joint technology is irrelevant.

If $\mathring{\mathbf{p}}$ lies above the P locus, then $\mathbf{p}^e$ is necessarily on the P locus. Since no-entry condition 2 is not satisfied for price vectors above the P locus, equilibrium price vectors lie on or below the P locus. Further, since none of the three firm types supplies a positive quantity at price vectors below the P locus, and since equilibrium quantities are positive, the equilibrium price vector must lie on the P locus. In addition, equilibrium price condition 2 is always satisfied so that diversified firms are always possible when $\mathring{\mathbf{p}}$ lies above the P locus. To say more we need to consider $\mathring{\mathbf{p}}$ in each of the six regions above the P locus.

II.—If $\mathring{\mathbf{p}}$ is in region II (where $p_1 > \bar{p}_1$ and $p_2 > \bar{p}_2$), then equilibrium price condition 1 is violated for both types of specialized firms since $p_i^e < \mathring{p}_i$ for $i = 1,2$. Hence, neither type of specialized firm can exist in equilibrium, and diversified firms must exist to supply the demand for both goods. Any price vector on segment AB of the P locus is a feasible equilibrium price vector, but price vectors on the vertical and horizontal segments are not, because diversified firms supply only X_1 on the vertical segment and only X_2 on the horizontal segment. This case contrasts nicely with the first one: if $\mathring{\mathbf{p}}$ is in region I, the joint technology is irrelevant; if $\mathring{\mathbf{p}}$ is in region II, the specialized technologies are irrelevant.

III.—If $\mathring{\mathbf{p}}$ is in region III of Figure 2 (where $\mathring{p}_1 > \bar{p}_1$ and $\bar{p}_2 \geq \mathring{p}_2 \geq \underline{p}_2$), the possibilities are richer. The minimum-average-cost vector $\mathring{\mathbf{p}}'$ in Figure 3 illustrates this possibility. Since $\mathring{p}_1' > \bar{p}_1$, type-1 specialized firms cannot exist. Thus, diversified firms must exist to satisfy demand for X_1. No-entry condition 1 for type-2 specialized firms dictates that $p_2^e \leq \mathring{p}_2'$ or that $\mathbf{p}^e$ is at or to the right of point C on the P locus. Note also that $\mathbf{p}^e$ cannot be on the vertical segment of the P locus, (e.g., at point F in Fig. 3), because at such a price vector no firm of any type supplies X_2. Hence, $\mathbf{p}^e$ is on segment CB of the P locus. If $\mathbf{p}^e$ is coincident with point C, specialized firms of type-2 may exist, and they will not exist if $\mathbf{p}^e$ is to the right of C.

IV.—If $\mathring{\mathbf{p}}$ is in region IV of Figure 2 (where $\bar{p}_1 \geq \mathring{p}_1 \geq \underline{p}_1$ and $\mathring{p}_2 > \bar{p}_2$), analogous possibilities arise. Feasible equilibrium prices are on the segment of the P locus where $\underline{p}_1 \leq p_1 \leq \mathring{p}_1$. Diversified firms will exist in equilibrium, and type-2 specialized firms will not. If $p_1^e = \mathring{p}_1$, then type-1 specialized firms may exist; otherwise, they will not.

V.—If $\mathring{\mathbf{p}}$ is in region V (above the P locus, with $p_i \leq \bar{p}_i$ for $i = 1,2$), then on the basis of cost considerations alone it is not possible to exclude any type of firm from the equilibrium market structure. We can, however, exclude both the possibility that all three types of firms coexist and the possibility that only specialized firms exist. This case is illustrated by the minimum-average-cost vector $\mathring{\mathbf{p}}''$ in Figure 3, where segment CD of the P locus is the set of feasible equilibrium price vectors. At C, $p_2 = \mathring{p}_2$, and at D, $p_1 = \mathring{p}_1$. If $\mathbf{p}^e$ is in the interior of segment CD, only diversified firms will exist. If $\mathbf{p}^e$ is coincident with either C or D, then the equilibrium market structure may entail one type of specialized firm but not the other, and it will entail diversified firms. Suppose, for example, that $\mathbf{p}^e$ is coincident with C. Then, type-1 specialized firms will not exist, type-2 specialized firms may exist, and diversified firms must exist to satisfy demand for X_1.

VI.—If $\mathring{\mathbf{p}}$ is in region VI of Figure 2 (where $\mathring{p}_1 > \bar{p}_1$ and $\mathring{p}_2 < \underline{p}_2$), then equilibrium prices and the equilibrium market structure are uniquely determined.[4] Minimum-average-cost vector $\mathring{\mathbf{p}}'''$ in Figure 3 illustrates this case. The no-entry condition for type-2 specialized firms dictates that $\mathbf{p}^e$ be on segment $\underline{p}_1$F of the P locus. However, since diversified firms produce only X_1 on the vertical segment of the P locus, type-2 specialized firms must exist to meet the demand for X_2, which requires that $p_2^e = \mathring{p}_2$, or that $\mathbf{p}^e$ be coincident with F. The equilibrium market structure then entails diversified and type-2 specialized firms, but no type-1 specialized firms.

VII.—Similarly, if $\mathring{\mathbf{p}}$ is in region VII of Figure 2, $\mathbf{p}^e$ is the point on the horizontal segment of the P locus where $p_1 = \mathring{p}_1$, and the equilibrium market structure involves diversified and type-1 specialized firms, but not type-2 specialized firms.

Notice that the equilibrium market structures associated with $\mathring{\mathbf{p}}$ in regions VI and VII are observationally indistinguishable from the equilibrium market structure associated with $\mathring{\mathbf{p}}$ in region I. Since the diversified firms that exist in the first two market structures produce only one good, in all three cases the market structure involves one type of firm producing just X_1 and another producing just X_2.

VIII.—Up to now, we have looked at the cases in which $\mathring{\mathbf{p}}$ was either below or above, but not on the P locus, and all the feasible market structures have involved at most two of the three firm types. If $\mathring{\mathbf{p}}$ lies on the P locus, then the equilibrium price conditions for all three firm types are satisfied, and it is therefore possible, though by no means necessary, for all three firm types to exist in equilibrium.[5] If $\mathring{\mathbf{p}}$ lies on the vertical or the horizontal segment of the P locus, and if all three firm types exist in equilibrium, then the diversified firms that necessarily produce just one good are observationally indistinguishable from the specialized firms producing the same good.

We summarize our results regarding feasible market structures in the following proposition.

[4] Regions VI and VII may or may not exist, since the P locus may or may not have vertical and horizontal segments.

[5] This is what MacDonald and Slivinski call the "knife edge" case. Using the tools developed in this section, it is easy to show that when $\mathring{\mathbf{p}}$ is on the P locus there is always an equilibrium with specialized firms of one type together with diversified firms, another with only specialized firms, and a third with all three types of firms. In addition, it is possible, though not likely, that there is an equilibrium with only diversified firms.

PROPOSITION 1: *If a competitive equilibrium exists, and if the equilibrium quantities of both goods are positive, then there are five feasible equilibrium market structures, and corresponding to each there are necessary cost and equilibrium price implications.*

1. *Diversified firms*:
   $\mathring{\mathbf{p}}$ *is on or above the* P *locus*;
   $\mathbf{p}^e$ *is on the* P *locus and* $\mathbf{p}^e \le \mathring{\mathbf{p}}$.
2. *Both types of specialized firms*:
   $\mathring{\mathbf{p}}$ *is on or below the* P *locus*;
   $\mathbf{p}^e = \mathring{\mathbf{p}}$.

3,4. *Diversified and type-i specialized firms* $(i = 1,2)$:
   $\mathring{\mathbf{p}}$ *is on or above the* P *locus*;
   $p_i^e = \mathring{p}_i$ *and* $p_j^e \le \mathring{p}_j$ $(i, j = 1,2$ *and* $i \ne j)$.

5. *All three types of firms*:
   $\mathring{\mathbf{p}}$ *is on the* P *locus*;
   $\mathbf{p}^e = \mathring{\mathbf{p}}$.

If we imagine that the three cost functions that drive this analysis are randomly selected from the population of cost functions that satisfy our cost assumptions, then the probability that $\mathring{\mathbf{p}}$ lies on the P locus is zero, and hence the probability of an equilibrium market structure with all three firm types is also zero. In this sense, the possibility in part 5 of the proposition is inconsistent with this theory of market structure, thus providing a possible test of the theory.

At this point it is useful to consider briefly the two cost assumptions that are necessary for this proposition. (i) Both the P locus and the minimum average cost vector $\mathring{\mathbf{p}}$ must be well defined. (ii) In addition, there must be a strictly positive minimum-efficient scale of production for all firms so that a finite number of firms can supply equilibrium quantities. That is, average cost, including ray average cost for the joint technology, must attain a minimum value at some positive quantity.

In the standard partial-equilibrium model with no joint production, prices are completely cost-determined. In our model, although costs restrict the range of equilibrium prices and market structures, in general they do not completely determine either equilibrium prices or market structure. In the next section, we introduce demand considerations and develop what amount to demand and supply diagrams for our model. Although we confine our attention to the case in which $\mathring{\mathbf{p}}$ lies in region V of Figure 2, the analytical apparatus is easily adapted to the remaining cases.

III. Supply and Demand for Joint Production

To avoid the usual nonexistence problem associated with integer numbers of firms, we assume that numbers of firms of each type (N_1, N_2, and N_3) are (nonnegative) real numbers. Let $S_1(p)$ and $S_2(p)$ denote the supply functions of a diversified firm. Hotelling's lemma tells us that $S_i(p)$ is the partial derivative of $\Pi(p)$ with respect to p_i, which implies that the slope of the P locus at the point p is $-S_1(p)/S_2(p)$. In Figure 4 we use this result to construct a diagram in which we map potential equilibrium price vectors on the segment CD of the P locus into rays of aggregate supply.

We have plotted the P locus in the first quadrant, and the line $x_2 = 1$ is plotted in the third quadrant. Since the absolute value of the slope of the P locus is $S_1(p)/S_2(p)$, for $x_2 = 1$, this slope becomes the supply of X_1 per unit supply of X_2. Since each p_1 in the relevant range corresponds to only one point on segment CD of the P locus, we can plot in the fourth quadrant the relationship between p_1 and the relative supply of X_1, given $x_2 = 1$. Now, pick a price vector $\mathbf{p}$ at, say E, and by projection into the fourth quadrant establish the *aggregate supply ray*, OE′. The ray OE′ is the aggregate supply ray for diversified firms given prices at E because any output vector on OE′ can be supplied at zero maximum profit by an appropriate (real) number of diversified firms. Supply rays OD′ and OC′ are associated with the endpoints of segment CD.

For price vectors in the interior of segment CD of the P locus, only diversified firms exist in equilibrium, and hence equilibrium quantities must lie on the associated aggregate supply rays. For the points C and D, aggregate supply is more complex. Any supply vector on or below supply-ray OD′ is possible at prices D. Consider supply vector

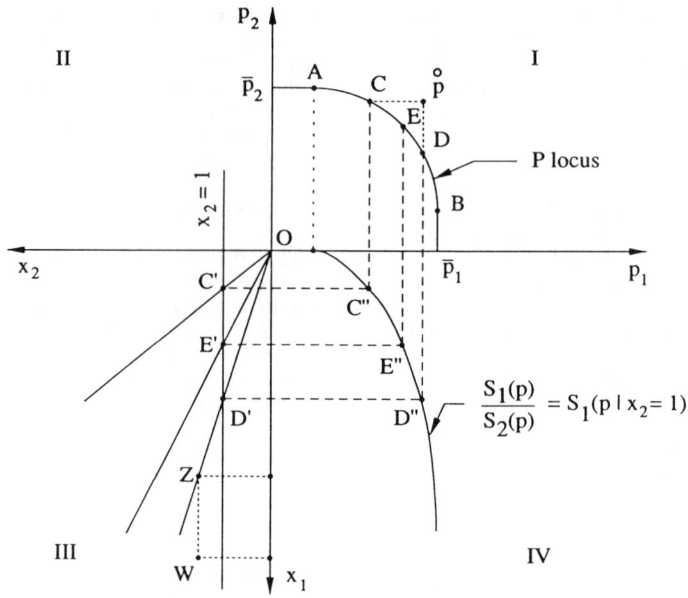

FIGURE 4. SUPPLY

W for example. At prices D, diversified firms must supply all of X_2, and hence will supply vector **Z** on supply ray OD′, while type-1 specialized firms will supply the residual of X_1, equal to the vertical distance from **Z** to **W**. Similarly, any quantity vector on or above supply ray OC′ is possible at prices C. In this case, diversified firms supply all of the X_1 and some of the X_2, while type-2 specialized firms supply the residual of X_2.

In Figure 5, we use a four-quadrant diagram to create a map from possible equilibrium-price vectors on the P locus in the first quadrant to vectors of aggregate demand in the third quadrant. In the fourth quadrant, we have constructed the graph of $D^1(p_1, p_2)$ as $\mathbf{p} = (p_1, p_2)$ varies along the P locus. Similarly, in the second quadrant we have constructed the graph of $D^2(p_1, p_2)$, evaluating the demand function at alternative price vectors on the P locus. It is important to note that the demand curves plotted in the second and fourth quadrants fully reflect all price interdependencies between the demands for the two products. Hence, they are ordinary demand functions only if the demand for each good is independent of the other good's price. Moreover, these graphs will be downward-sloping, as we have drawn them, if the ordinary demand curve for X_i is downward-sloping and good X_i is either independent, a substitute, or weakly complementary to the other product. It is now easy to construct, in the third quadrant, the locus of pairs of quantities demanded as a function of the pairs of potential equilibrium prices on segment CD of the P locus. In Figure 5, this locus is labeled C″D″, and we call it the D locus. A vector on the D locus is a *vector of aggregate demands*. Observe that the D locus is continuous, since the demand functions are continuous.

In Figure 6, we overlay the demand and supply diagrams to illustrate the determination of competitive equilibria. There are two possible sorts of equilibrium. First, if the D locus lies entirely between rays OC′ and OD′ or intersects either ray, then the

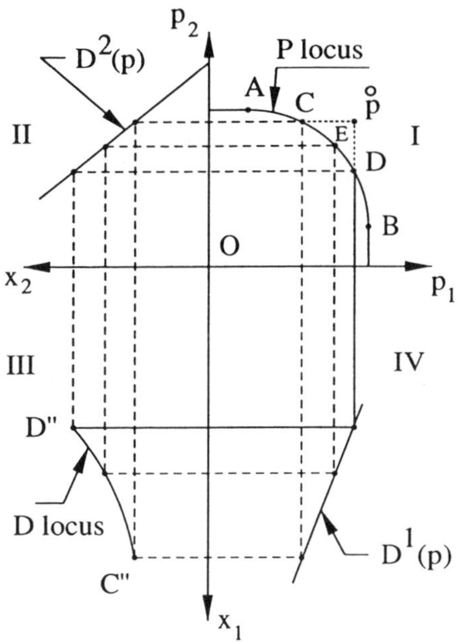

FIGURE 5. DEMAND

competitive equilibrium prices are in the interior of segment CD of the P locus, and only diversified firms exist in equilibria. Point E illustrates such a price equilibrium, with corresponding equilibrium quantities, E″. As the diagram shows, with prices at E the aggregate demand bundle is at E″, a bundle which is on the aggregate supply ray OE′ associated with prices E. Hence, prices E and quantities E″ are equilibrium prices and quantities. Moving left from E along the P locus causes the associated supply ray to move leftward toward ray OC′ and causes the demand bundle to move rightward along the D locus toward C″. Hence, for prices on the P locus to the left of E, there will be excess supply of X_2 relative to X_1. Similarly, for prices on the P locus to the right of E, there will be excess supply of X_1 relative to X_2.

On the other hand, if the D locus lies entirely above ray OC′, then equilibrium prices are at C, and in addition to diversified firms there will be specialized firms of type 2. The line D‴C‴ in Figure 6 illustrates such a D locus. The equilibrium price vector is C, and C‴ is the equilibrium quantity vector. Diversified firms collectively supply bundle H, and type-2 specialized firms supply the residual amount of X_2 equal to the horizontal distance C‴H in the figure. Any price vector on the P locus below and to the right of C cannot be an equilibrium-price vector. For any such price vector, only diversified firms could exist. However, there is then no aggregate supply ray that intersects the D locus and, hence, no equilibrium. A similar argument shows that, if the D locus is below the supply ray OD′, then the equilibrium price vector is at D, and the market supply is produced by diversified firms together with specialized type-1 firms.

The comparative statics of demand shifts are now quite easy to work out. In Figure 7, the initial equilibrium prices and quantities are at E and E″. A reduction in demand for X_1, illustrated by the shift of the demand function to $\tilde{D}^1(p)$, will shift the D locus to $\tilde{D}''\tilde{C}''$. At the initial equilibrium prices, the new demand is the bundle $\tilde{E}''$. This bundle lies above the supply ray associated with the initial prices, ray OE″, and hence prices will have to change. To restore equilibrium, prices must move leftward from E along the P locus, which shifts the supply ray leftward and shifts the bundle demanded rightward along the new D locus. The new equilibrium is at prices E* and quantities $\tilde{D}^*$.

It is interesting to note the peculiar comparative statics that result from economies of scope. In the above exercise we observe that a reduction in the demand for X_1 leads to a fall in both the equilibrium price and quantity of X_1, as expected. However, the decrease in demand for X_1 [upward shift of $D^1(p)$ in Fig. 7] also produces a rise in the equilibrium price and a fall in the equilibrium quantity of X_2. The inverse relationship between the equilibrium prices is a consequence of the restriction of these prices to the P locus, which, of course, is a characteristic of economies of scope. The observed response of equilibrium p_2 to a decrease in demand for X_1 will occur whether X_1 and X_2 are substitutes, independent, or complements in terms of con-

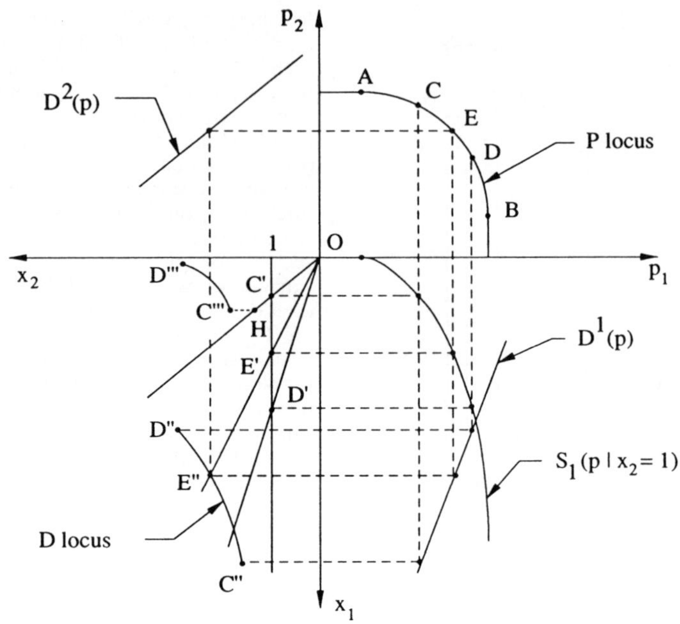

FIGURE 6. SUPPLY AND DEMAND

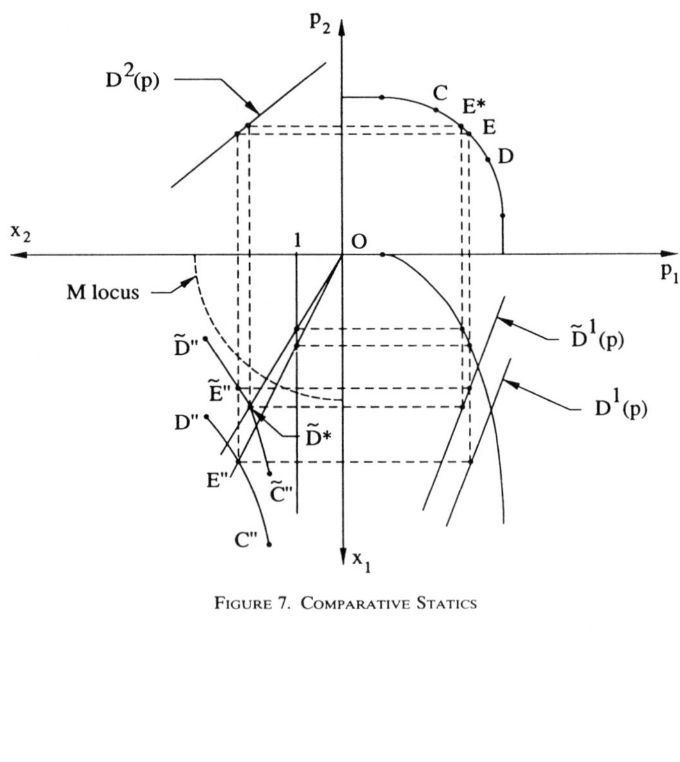

FIGURE 7. COMPARATIVE STATICS

sumption.[6] The change of equilibrium p_2 and x_2 in opposite directions is the kind of response typically associated with moves along a downward-sloping demand curve due to shifts in market supply. Yet in the above case, the initial shift is in the demand for X_1, and moreover, the observed change in equilibrium x_2 may be reversed if the goods are complements in consumption.

Two points are now obvious. First, given any bundle of goods, there is some price vector on CD such that the bundle can be supplied. Hence, having assumed that N_1, N_2, and N_3 are real numbers, it is clear that equilibrium always exists in our model. (Recall that the D locus is continuous in our model, since the demand functions are continuous.) In other words, joint production does not give rise to any new sources of nonexistence of equilibrium. Second, if the D locus is downward-sloping, then equilibrium is unique. Of course, it is possible, though unlikely, that the D locus is not everywhere uniformly either downward- or upward-sloping, which raises the possibility of multiple equilibria and associated bizarre comparative statics with respect to demand shifts.

To determine the equilibrium number and size of firms, we need additional assumptions. For specialized firms of type i, we need the assumption that the supply function has a unique positive value for price $\mathring{\mathbf{p}}_i$ (or equivalently that the specialized average cost functions have unique minima). The size and number of specialized firms are then determined in the obvious way. For diversified firms, we need the analogous assumption that both of the diversified firm's supply functions have unique positive values for any price vector on segment CD of the P locus. This in turn implies that the ray average cost functions for the diversified firms have unique minima. Baumol et al. (1982 p. 58) call the locus of points in (x_1, x_2) space through these minima the "M locus." For our illustrative technology (see Section II), the M locus is

$$(5) \qquad b_1 x_1^2 + b_2 x_2^2 + c x_1 x_2 - F = 0.$$

In Figure 7, the dashed line in the lower left quadrant illustrates the M locus for the case in which $b_1 = b_2 = 1$ and $c = 0$. For diversified firms, the equilibrium firm size is determined by the intersection of the equilibrium supply ray with the M locus, and the number of firms is then determined in the obvious way. If these additional assumptions are not satisfied, then neither the size of firms nor their number is uniquely determined in competitive equilibrium.

IV. Concluding Remarks

Our model is, in effect, a theory of competitive market structure driven by economies of scope. Seeing it in this way, we are led to ask what market structures the theory rules out. Strictly speaking, none of the possible market structures is inconsistent with the theory, but the one with all three firm types is highly unlikely. If two types of firms exist, then equilibrium prices are uniquely determined by the zero-profit conditions for these two firm types. Hence, if we imagine parameters of the three cost functions being drawn from some joint probability density function with no mass points, the probability that the third type of firm will earn zero profit at the equilibrium prices is zero. In this sense, the market structure with three firm types is a zero-probability event.

This way of looking at the likelihood of different market structures extends to more elaborate cases than the one considered in this paper. Suppose, for example, that there are three goods and seven technologies: three specialized technologies, three technologies in which the firm produces two goods, and one three-good technology. The kind of reasoning outlined above reveals that any market structure with more than three firm types is unlikely. If four firm types exist in equilibrium, there is always a subset of three types that, in combination, produces all three goods. The zero-profit conditions for these three firm types then uniquely determine the three equilibrium

[6] For this to be true, it is sufficient that the demands for both goods are positive at $(\mathring{p}_1, 0)$ and $(0, \mathring{p}_2)$.

prices. Hence, a fourth firm type must earn precisely zero profit at these prices if it is to exist in equilibrium, an unlikely event.

This view of market structure leads to the following crude test. Suppose that we observe a group of firms and count both the number of different products that they produce and the number of firm types. Then, the theory suggests that the number of firm types should be less than or equal to the number of products.

REFERENCES

Baumol, William J., Panzar, John and Willig, Robert D, *Contestable Markets and the Theory of Industry Structure*, New York: Harcourt Brace Jovanovich, 1982.

MacDonald, Glenn M. and Slivinski, Alan, "The Simple Analytics of Competitive Equilibrium with Multiproduct Firms," *American Economic Review*, December 1987, 77, 941–53.

[23]

Price versus quantity competition in the Gabszewicz–Thisse model of vertical differentiation*

B. Curtis Eaton and Paul Harrald

12.1 Introduction

Since Bertrand's review of Cournot's book it has been painfully clear that the properties of oligopoly equilibria are quite sensitive to the mode of competition. Consider, for example, Cournot's model of oligopoly competition in mineral water, where demand is linear in total quantity and there are no costs of production. If the duopolists compete non-cooperatively in quantities, as Cournot assumed, equilibrium price exceeds zero (the marginal cost of production), decreases as the number of oligopolists increases, and approaches zero as the number of firms gets large. On the other hand, if the firms compete non-cooperatively in prices, as Bertrand assumed, equilibrium price is equal to zero when there are at least two oligopolists.

When these two modes of competition are embedded in otherwise identical sequential games of entry, the resulting theories of market structure are quite different. For example, suppose we introduce a small sunk cost of entry, e, into the mineral springs model. If oligopolists compete in prices, there will be no entry wherever the number of firms is at least one, since a second firm could not recover the sunk cost of entry. Hence Bertrand's model, embedded in a sequential entry game, implies a monopoly market structure.

In contrast, if oligopolists compete in quantities, the no-entry condition takes the following form: $n \geq N(\mathbf{x}, e)$, where n is the number of firms, $\mathbf{x}$ is a vector of demand parameters, and e is the sunk cost of entry. The function N is obviously decreasing in e, and its response to demand parameters is also intuitive – roughly speaking, $N(\mathbf{x}, e)$ increases as the size of the market increases. Hence Cournot's model, embedded in a sequential entry game,

* Richard Lipsey is in part responsible for many of the ideas articulated in this paper. Indeed the conjectures which inspired this paper are contained in Eaton and Lipsey (1987).

yields a theory of market structure which covers the whole spectrum. If the market is small relative to the entry cost, a small number of firms will serve it, and if it is large, a large number will serve it.

These observations raise some obvious and embarrassing questions. Since these modes of competition produce quite different results, we cannot thoughtlessly choose one or the other as convenience dictates. Instead, we must somehow try to choose between them, or to identify the circumstances in which one or the other is appropriate. Two recent theoretical approaches seem to us to suggest that in many circumstances competition in quantities is a more appropriate assumption than competition in prices.

Kreps and Scheinkman (1983) (see Chapter 13) observe that oligopolists can often be thought of as playing a sequential game in which they produce goods (or acquire capacity) in one period, and market them in a subsequent period. To analyse this situation, which we call the *production to inventory* model, they characterize the subgame perfect equilibrium of a two-stage game in which duopolists choose quantities in Stage One and prices in Stage Two. They show that the equilibrium of this two-stage game is identical to the equilibrium of the corresponding one-stage game in which the duopolists choose quantities. Their analysis clearly suggests that in situations where firms produce to inventory it is sometimes appropriate to think of them as playing a one-stage game in which they compete in quantities. Their result is, however, sensitive to the rationing rule which allocates demand to firms in Stage Two, and hence one must be cautious in declaring victory for Cournot in the production to inventory model.

If one cannot unambiguously declare victory for Cournot, the structure of the production to inventory model strongly suggests that one can declare defeat for Bertrand. To see the nature of the argument, suppose that there is a constant marginal cost, c, and denote the demand function by $D(p)$ and its inverse by $H(\mathbf{x})$. Then the equilibria of the one-stage price game can be described as follows:

$$(p_1^*, p_2^*) = (c, c)$$

$$(x_1^*, x_2^*) = (x_1, D(c) - x_1) \qquad 0 \leq x_1 \leq D(c)$$

Now consider any equilibrium quantity pair, (x_1^*, x_2^*), and ask first if (c, c) is the price equilibrium of the implied quantity constrained game. Edgeworth's analysis of capacity-constrained price games implies that it may not be. Indeed, if $D(p)$ is linear and c is small relative to the choke price, then there appears to be no rationing rule such that it is.

Suppose, however, that (c, c) is the price equilibrium of the Stage Two quantity constrained game in which the firms have produced (x_1^*, x_2^*) in Stage One. In addition, for ε positive but small, assume that $p_1 = p_2 = H(x_1^* + x_2^* - \varepsilon)$ is the equilibrium price in the quantity constrained game defined by $(x_1^*, x_2^* - \varepsilon)$. Then, in Stage One, x_2^* is not a best reply to x_1^*, since

$$(x_2^* - \varepsilon)[H(x_1^* + x_2^* - \varepsilon) - c] > 0$$

In other words, if (c, c) is a price equilibrium of the Stage Two quantity constrained game implied by (x_1^*, x_2^*), and if the rationing rule is such that the price equilibrium is locally continuous in the quantity constraint, then (x_1^*, x_2^*) is not an equilibrium in Stage One.

Singh and Vives (1985) approach the debate from another perspective. They too consider the subgame perfect equilibrium of a two-stage game involving two firms. In Stage One of their model the firms choose their mode of competition – price or quantity – and in Stage Two they compete using their predetermined modes. If both modes are 'quantity' ('price'), the Stage Two equilibrium is Cournot (Bertrand), and if one mode is price and the other quantity, the Stage Two equilibrium is a hybrid of the two. They show that the quantity mode is a dominant strategy in Stage One. That is, regardless of which mode a firm's competitor chooses, profit in the Stage Two equilibrium is higher if the firm chooses the quantity mode. Again one must be cautious in declaring victory for Cournot, primarily because it is not clear how a firm could commit itself to compete in one mode or the other.

Nevertheless, we are convinced by these arguments that in many situations, in particular those where firms produce to inventory, it is more appropriate to think of them as competing in quantities than it is to think of them as competing in prices. Interestingly, outside the Chamberlinian tradition, the vast bulk of the literature on product differentiation assumes that firms compete in prices. Salant (1986), which is largely concerned with existence problems in models of spatial competition, is a noteworthy exception. Since Edgeworth's analysis of capacity constrained price games it has been clear that pure strategy price equilibria often do not exist. As d'Aspremont, Gabszewicz and Thisse (1979) show, non-existence of price equilibrium is a generic problem in standard models of spatial competition. Salant argues, as we have, that quantity competition is often more realistic than price competition, and goes on to show that a pure strategy quantity equilibrium often exists when a price equilibrium does not.

In this chapter we continue the exploration begun by Salant of the implications of quantity competition in models of product differentiation. Specifically, we consider a well-known model of vertical differentiation in which goods are differentiated by quality. The model was invented by Gabszewicz and Thisse (1979), and various aspects of it have been explored in Gabszewicz and Thisse (1980), Gabszewicz *et al.* (1981) and Shaked and Sutton (1982, 1983).

Competition in prices is a universal feature of this literature on vertical differentiation. In this paper we begin the exploration of the behaviour of the Gabszewicz–Thisse model, hereafter called the GT model, when quantity competition is substituted for price competition. We focus here on a version of the model which does not exhibit the so-called natural oligopoly property.

12.2 The quality model

We develop a version of the GT model in which there are just two firms, which we call A and B. They produce goods which are differentiated by 'quality' – something of which more is better in the eyes of all consumers. Our notation is summarized in Table 12.1. The quality of A's good is a, its price is p, and its quantity is x. Similarly, the quality of B's good is b, its price is q, and its quantity is y.

Although consumers have identical preferences, they are differentiated by income, t, which is uniformly distributed on [0, 1] with density D. The triple (X, Y, T) denotes a consumption bundle, and $U(X, Y, T)$ the common utility function, where X is consumption of Firm A's good, Y is consumption of B's good, and T is quantity of a composite commodity. An individual consumes 0 or 1 unit of each good so that X and Y are either 0 or 1. Using the prices p and q, and supposing that the price of the composite commodity is unity, consumers' preferences take the following form:

$$U(0, 0, t) = t \quad \textbf{(12.1)}$$

$$U(1, 0, t - p) = a(t - p) \quad \textbf{(12.2)}$$

$$U(0, 1, t - q) = b(t - q) \quad \textbf{(12.3)}$$

$$U(1, 1, t - p - q) = \max(a, b)(t - p - q) \quad \textbf{(12.4)}$$

If the consumer buys neither good, expenditure on the composite commodity is t, which is equal to utility. If the consumer buys either good, utility is equal to the quality of the good, a or b, times expenditure on the composite commodity, $t - p$ or $t - q$. Finally, if the consumer were to buy back goods, utility would be the maximum of a or b times expenditure on the composite commodity, which, of course, implies that the consumer will not buy both goods (if prices are positive).

From Equations (12.1)–(12.4) we see that by purchasing one of the two goods, the consumer is, in effect, buying a marginal utility of income. In the absence of either good this marginal utility is one, and hence an obvious necessary condition for the consumer to buy A's goods (B's good) is $a > 1$ ($b > 1$). It also seems appropriate to assume that the marginal utility of income

Table 12.1 Summary of notation.

Firm	Quality	Price	Quantity
A	a	p	x
B	b	q	y

is bounded, which requires that quality be bounded. Accordingly we assume that a and b are contained in the closed interval $[1, 2]$. That is, the minimum possible quality for either good is 1, and the maximum possible quality is 2.

Notice that when $a > b$ and $p > q$ consumers with large incomes will prefer A's good to B's, and those with small incomes will prefer B's good to A's. The consumer with income

$$\bar{t} = (ap - bq)/(a - b) \tag{12.5}$$

will be indifferent between the two goods since $U(1, 0, \bar{t} - p) = U(0, 1, \bar{t} - q)$. Notice also that if both p and q exceed zero, consumers with very small incomes will buy neither good. The consumer with income:

$$\tilde{t} = bq/(b - 1) \tag{12.6}$$

will be indifferent between good B and buying neither good since $U(0, 1, \tilde{t} - q) = U(0, 0, \tilde{t})$. Similarly the consumer with income:

$$\hat{t} = ap/(a - 1) \tag{12.7}$$

will be indifferent between good A and buying neither good. These results, in combination with the assumptions that t is uniformly distributed on $[0, 1]$ and that consumers buy (at most) one unit of their most preferred good, allow us to derive demand functions.

$$\text{if} \quad bq + a - b \geq ap \geq bq(a - 1)/(b - 1) \quad \text{and } a \geq b \tag{12.8}$$
$$x(p, q, a, b) = (1 - \bar{t})D$$
$$y(p, q, a, b) = (\bar{t} - \tilde{t})D$$

$$\text{if} \quad ap < \min[a - 1, bq(a - 1)/(b - 1)] \quad \text{and } a \geq b \tag{12.9}$$
$$x(p, q, a, b) = (1 - \hat{t})D$$
$$y(p, q, a, b) = 0$$

$$\text{if} \quad bq < \min[b - 1, ap + b - a] \quad \text{and } a \geq b \tag{12.10}$$
$$x(p, q, a, b) = 0$$
$$y(p, q, a, b) = (1 - \tilde{t})D$$

$$\text{if} \quad ap > a - 1, bq > b - 1 \quad \text{and } a \geq b \tag{12.11}$$
$$x(p, q, a, b) = 0$$
$$y(p, q, a, b) = 0$$

When $b > a$, the demand functions are obviously symmetric to those in Equations (12.8)–(12.11). In addition, when $b = a$ and $p = q$ we assume that each firm captures half of the total market.

The GT model is ordinarily completed by specifying cost conditions which include a quality associated sunk cost of entry, and a marginal cost of production that is independent of quality. To highlight the differences between the price and quantity games we initially assume that there are no costs of production. Notice that this means that costs of production are independent of the quality of the good being produced – it costs no more to produce a high quality good than it does to produce a low quality good. This observation, combined with the observation that quality is valuable to consumers, suggests the following naive conjecture – firms will always choose to produce goods of maximal quality. Since more quality is valuable to consumers and costs the firm nothing, why would a firm choose less than maximal quality? As we will see, the maximal quality conjecture is correct if firms compete in quantities and incorrect if they compete in prices.

In Section 12.3 we compute the subgame perfect equilibria of two sequential games. The first is a two-stage game – in Stage One A and B simultaneously choose a and b, and in Stage Two they simultaneously choose p and q. The second is a three-stage game – in Stage One A chooses a, in Two B chooses b, and in Three the firms simultaneously choose p and q. We call these games the two-stage and three-stage 'price games' since, in the last stage of each, the equilibrium is a price equilibrium. In Section 12.4 we compute the equilibria of the corresponding two and three-stage 'quantity games', compare the equilibria of the price and quantity games, and attempt to understand why the equilibria are so different.

In Section 12.5 we introduce a sunk cost associated with product quality, and again compute and compare subgame perfect equilibria of the price and quantity games. Our objective in this section is to demonstrate that the insights developed in Sections 12.3 and 12.4 are robust with respect to costs associated with product quality.[1]

12.3 The price games

Given a and b, in the last stage of price games A chooses p to maximize its revenue, R_A, and B chooses q to maximize its revenue, R_B. When $a \geq b$, equilibrium prices, quantities and revenues are:

$$p^* = 2(a-1)(a-b)/[a(4a-b-3)] \qquad a \geq b \qquad \textbf{(12.12)}$$

$$q^* = (b-1)(a-b)/[b(4a-b-3)] \qquad a \geq b \qquad \textbf{(12.13)}$$

$$x^* = 2D(a-1)/[4a-b-3] \qquad a \geq b \qquad \textbf{(12.14)}$$

$$y^* = D(a-1)/[4a-b-3] \qquad a \geq b \qquad \textbf{(12.15)}$$

$$R_A^* = 4D(a-1)^2(a-b)/[a(4a-b-3)^2] \qquad a \geq b \qquad \textbf{(12.16)}$$

$$R_B^* = D(a-1)(b-1)(a-b)/[b(4a-b-3)^2] \qquad a \geq b \qquad \textbf{(12.17)}$$

Notice that x^* is twice as large as y^* and that p^* is more than twice as large as q^* (when $a > b$). Hence in the price equilibrium R_A^*/R_B^* exceeds 4. That is, the firm with the higher quality is more than four times as profitable as the firm with lower quality. Notice also that when $a = b$, $p^* = q^* = 0$. That is, we have Bertrand's model of price competition with an undifferentiated product in which equilibrium prices are equal to zero, the marginal cost of production.

When $b > a$, the equilibrium is obviously symmetric to the one described in Equations (12.12)–(12.17). It is nevertheless useful to record results.

$$p^* = 2(b-1)(b-a)/[a(4b-a-3)] \qquad b > a \qquad \textbf{(12.18)}$$

$$q^* = (a-1)(b-a)/[b(4b-a-3)] \qquad b > a \qquad \textbf{(12.19)}$$

$$x^* = 2D(b-1)/[4b-a-3] \qquad b > a \qquad \textbf{(12.20)}$$

$$y^* = D(b-1)/[4b-a-3] \qquad b > a \qquad \textbf{(12.21)}$$

$$R_A^* = 4D(b-1)^2(b-a)/[a(4b-a-3)^2] \qquad b > a \qquad \textbf{(12.22)}$$

$$R_B^* = D(b-1)(a-1)(b-a)/[b(4b-a-3)^2] \qquad b > a \qquad \textbf{(12.23)}$$

In Figure 12.1 we have graphed R_B^* as b varies over its domain, [1, 2], and holding a constant. R_B^* is equal to zero when $b = 1$, because no consumer will pay a positive price for a good which gives a marginal utility of income equal to one, and again when $b = a$, because the equilibrium price is equal to zero. When $b < a$, R_B^* attains a local maximum in the open interval $(0, a)$ at $\hat{b}$, where $\partial_B^*/\partial b = 0$. The value $\hat{b}$ is characterized by the following first-order condition:

$$0 = -\hat{b}^3 + 5\hat{b}^2 - 2\hat{b}^2 a - 3a\hat{b} + 4a^2 - 3a \qquad \textbf{(12.24)}$$

When $b > a$, R_B^* is increasing in b and hence attains a second local maximum on the boundary of its domain at $b = 2$. The value of B's revenue at the interior local maximum, $R_B^*(a, \hat{b})$, is increasing in a, and the value at the boundary local maximum, $R_B^*(a, 2)$, is decreasing in a, and the two values are equal when a is approximately 1.94. Hence the global maximum of R_B^* is at $b = 2$ when $a < 1.94$ and at $b = \hat{b}$ when $a > 1.94$.

We have then derived B's best response function, given a. When $a < 1.94$, the revenue maximizing value of b is 2, and when $a > 1.94$ it is the value $\hat{b}$ characterized in Equation (12.24). Given b, A's best response function is, of course, symmetric to B's. The two best response functions are graphed in Figure 12.2. The solid line is B's response function, and the dashed line is A's. The points labelled E are the pure-strategy perfect equilibria of the two-stage price game (in which a and b are chosen simultaneously in Stage One, and p and q in Stage Two). One firm chooses maximal quality, and the other chooses quality (approximately) equal to 1.48.

There is, of course, a serious coordination problem in this game. If both firms choose maximal quality, or if both choose 1.48, their profit is zero. This suggests that we should consider the more elaborate three-stage game in which A chooses a in Stage One, B chooses b in Stage Two, and A and B simultaneously choose p and q in Stage Three.

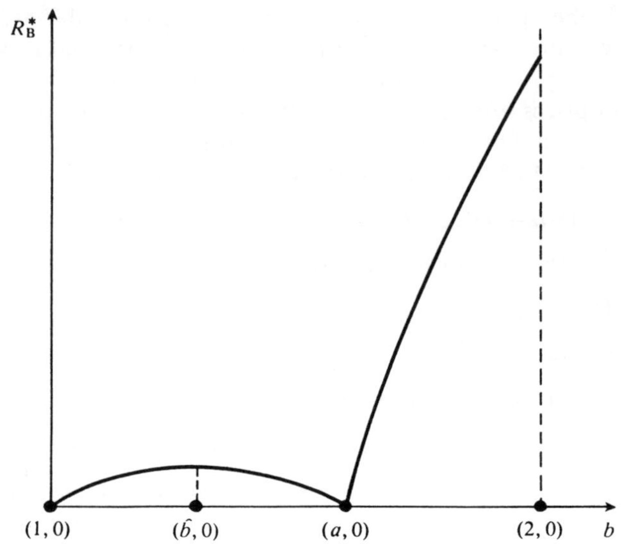

Figure 12.1 Revenue R_B as b varies over its domain [1, 2].

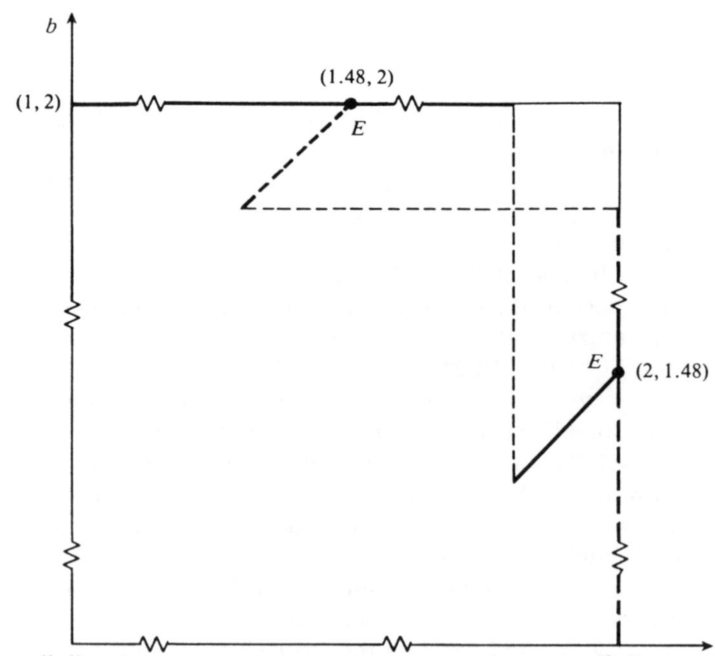

Figure 12.2 The response function for B.

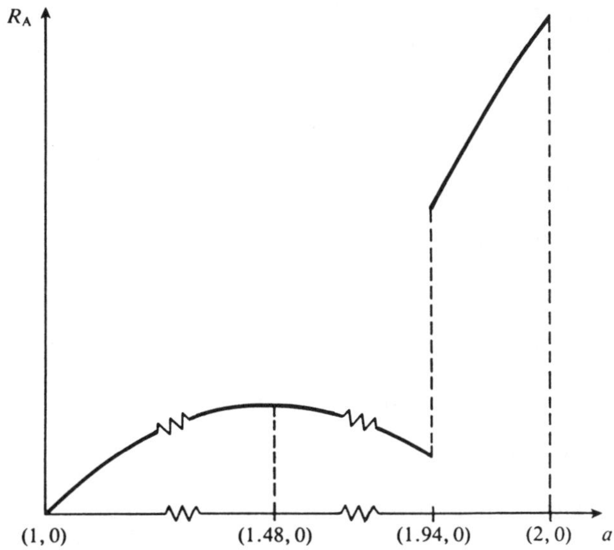

Figure 12.3 A's revenue given B's best response.

The graph of A's profit function, given B's best response to a, is presented in Figure 12.3. For a less than 1.94, B chooses maximal quality and A's good is the lower quality good. For a in this interval, [0, 1.94], A's revenue is relatively small, and attains a local maximum at a (approximately) equal to 1.48. For a greater than 1.94, B chooses to be the low quality firm, and in this interval, [1.94, 2], A's revenue is relatively large, and increasing in a. It is then apparent that in the subgame perfect equilibrium of this three-stage game, A chooses maximal quality, and B chooses a discretely lower quality, approximately 1.48, to differentiate its product from A's.

12.4 The quantity games

Inverting the demand system in (12.8) we have the following inverse demand functions:

$$p(x, y, a, b) = [D(a-1) - (a-1)x - (b-1)y] / [Da] \qquad a \geq b \qquad \textbf{(12.25)}$$

$$q(x, y, a, b) = [b-1]\,[D - x - y] / [Db] \qquad a \geq b \qquad \textbf{(12.26)}$$

Symmetric expressions apply when b exceeds a. (Since both firms produce positive quantities in equilibrium, we ignore the cases covered in Equations (12.9) to (12.11)).

Given a and b, in the last stage of both quantity games A chooses x to maximize its revenue, and B chooses y to maximize its revenue. When a exceeds b, equilibrium prices, quantities and revenues are:

$$\tilde{p} = (a-1)(2a-b-1)/[a(4a-b-3)] \qquad a \geq b \tag{12.27}$$

$$\tilde{q} = (b-1)(a-1)/[b(4a-b-3)] \qquad a \geq b \tag{12.28}$$

$$\tilde{x} = D(2a-b-1)/(4a-b-3) \qquad a \geq b \tag{12.29}$$

$$\tilde{y} = D(a-1)/(4a-b-3) \qquad a \geq b \tag{12.30}$$

$$\tilde{R}_A = D(a-1)(2a-b-1)^2/[a(4a-b-3)^2] \qquad a \geq b \tag{12.31}$$

$$\tilde{R}_B = D(b-1)(a-1)^2/[b(4a-b-3)^2] \qquad a \geq b \tag{12.32}$$

When b exceeds a we have:

$$\tilde{p} = (a-1)(b-1)/[a(4b-a-3)] \qquad b > a \tag{12.33}$$

$$\tilde{q} = (b-1)(2b-a-1)/[b(4b-a-3)] \qquad b > a \tag{12.34}$$

$$\tilde{x} = D(b-1)/(4b-a-3) \qquad b > a \tag{12.35}$$

$$\tilde{y} = D(2b-a-1)/(4b-a-3) \qquad b > a \tag{12.36}$$

$$\tilde{R}_A = D(a-1)(b-1)^2/[a(4b-a-3)^2] \qquad b > a \tag{12.37}$$

$$\tilde{R}_B = D(b-1)(2b-a-1)^2/[b(4b-a-3)^2] \qquad b > a \tag{12.38}$$

Figure 12.4 is the graph of $\tilde{R}_B$ as b varies over $[1, 2]$, holding a constant. Observe that B's revenue in the quantity equilibrium is strictly increasing in b, regardless of whether b is larger than or smaller than a. Hence, B's best response function is independent of a, and B always chooses maximal quality. Similarly, for any value of b, A's best response is to choose maximal quality.

Now consider the two sequential quantity games. In the two-stage game A and B simultaneously choose a and b in Stage One, and x and y in Stage Two. In the three-stage game A chooses a in Stage One, B chooses b in Stage Two, and A and B simultaneously choose x and y in Stage Three. Given the best response functions derived above, it is clear that in the subgame perfect equilibrium of both quantity games, both firms choose maximal quality and the model of vertical differentiation degenerates (endogenously) into the Cournot model for undifferentiated products.

To understand the differences in the equilibria of the price and quantity games, we focus on B's best response functions. Given a and b, B's revenue in the quantity or Cournot equilibrium can be written as

$$\tilde{R}_B(a, b) = \tilde{y}q(\tilde{x}, \tilde{y}, a, b) \tag{12.39}$$

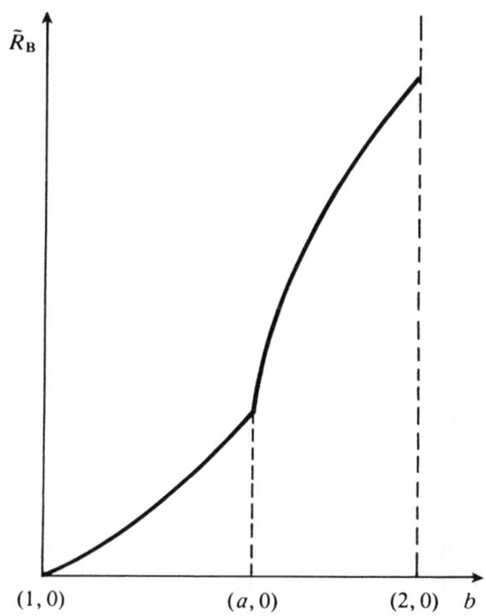

Figure 12.4 $\tilde{R}_B$ as b varies over $[1, 2]$.

Differentiating with respect to b, and using the fact that $\partial\tilde{R}_B/\partial y = 0$ in the quantity equilibrium we have

$$\partial\tilde{R}_B/\partial b = \tilde{y}[\underset{(-\text{ve})}{(\partial q/\partial x)}\underset{(-\text{ve})}{(\mathrm{d}\tilde{x}/\mathrm{d}b)} + \underset{(+\text{ve})}{\partial q/\partial b}] \quad \textbf{(12.40)}$$

Similarly, B's revenue in the price or Bertrand equilibrium can be written as

$$R^*_B(a, b) = q^* y(p^*, q^*, a, b) \quad \textbf{(12.41)}$$

and the derivative of equilibrium revenue with respect to b as

$$\partial R_B/\partial b = q^*[\underset{(+\text{ve})}{(\partial y/\partial p)} \quad \underset{\substack{(-\text{ve if } b < a)\\(+\text{ve if } b > a)}}{(\mathrm{d}p^*/\mathrm{d}b)} \quad + \underset{(+\text{ve})}{\partial y/\partial b}] \quad \textbf{(12.42)}$$

An understanding of the differences between the two games can be developed from Equations (12.40) and (12.42).

The two games share the same demand system, which means that what we might call the 'structural' or 'non-game theoretic' derivatives in (12.40) and (12.42) are determined by common forces. In particular, since the two goods are substitutes, $\partial q/\partial x$ in (12.40) is negative and $\partial y/\partial p$ in (12.42) is positive. And, since quality is something of which 'more is better', $\partial q/\partial b$ in (12.40) and $\partial y/\partial b$ in (12.42) are both positive.

The game theoretic derivatives provide the key to understanding the divergent results. In (12.40), $d\tilde{x}/db$ is always negative. This reflects the fact that as the quality of B's good increases, B's demand function shifts to the right and A's to the left, and in the quantity equilibrium A's output decreases. Hence $\partial\tilde{R}_B/\partial b$ is always positive and B's best response is to choose maximal quality. In (12.42) if $b < a$, dp^*/db is negative, implying that the first term in the square brackets in (12.42) is negative and the second positive. In some (right-hand) neighbourhood of $b = 1$, the second term dominates and R_B^* is increasing in b, and in some (left-hand) neighbourhood of $b = a$, the first dominates and R_B^* is increasing in b. Hence R_B^* attains a local maximum for some value of b in the open interval $(0, a)$. When $b > a$, dp^*/db is positive so that R_B^* is increasing in b, implying that R_B^* attains a second local maximum at $b = 2$ (supposing, of course, that $a < 2$). When a is small (less than 1.94), the second local maximum dominates the first and when a is large the first dominates the second.

The differences in the price and quantity games are then attributable to a qualitative difference in the game theoretic derivatives. In the quantity game absolutes matter. As the quality of one good increases, equilibrium output of the other good always decreases. Hence, in equilibrium both firms choose maximal quality. In the price game it is the degree of differentiation that matters. As the degree of differentiation diminishes – as b approaches a from above or from below – A's equilibrium price continues to decrease until, when $b = a$, A's (and B's) price (and revenue) is driven to zero. Hence in the price game the two goods are always differentiated.[2]

12.5 Quality associated costs

In this section we explore some of the implications of sunk costs associated with product quality. Our objective is not an exhaustive analysis but rather to show that the insights generated from the no-cost case can be generalized. We consider two cases, costs associated with *product adulteration* and costs associated with *quality enhancement*.

12.5.1 *Product adulteration*

To motivate the product adulteration case, consider again the mineral springs model. As we observed in the introduction, if there is a small sunk cost of entry, if competition is in prices, and if the products of the duopolists are undifferentiated, then the market structure associated with foresighted entry is monopoly. Since the equilibrium price is equal to marginal cost when two firms produce an undifferentiated product, the second firm could not cover the sunk cost of entry. Of course, the second may have the option of producing a differentiated product. In particular, it has the option of polluting its own mineral springs – of adulterating its product. In this case it is sensible to assume that the sunk cost of entry is inversely related to product quality. For convenience we assume that the sunk cost associated with maximal quality is zero.

The general implications of such costs in the GT demand system are obvious. In the quantity games, there are none since neither firm would ever choose to adulterate its product. Adulteration is costly and, if firms compete in quantities, it also reduces the firm's revenue in equilibrium. Once again the model degenerates into the Cournot model with undifferentiated products.

In the price games, there are two possibilities. If product adulteration is costly enough, the equilibrium market structure is monopoly. However, if the costs associated with adulteration are not too large, the equilibrium market structure will be duopoly, one firm will produce an unadulterated product, and the other will choose to pollute its mineral springs. If one firm produces an unadulterated product of maximal quality, the other must adulterate its product since its revenue in the price equilibrium would be zero if it did not.

The general tenor of these results is quite similar to our earlier results. The GT model of vertical differentiation does not in fact produce differentiation when competition is in quantities, and it does when competition is in prices (and when the equilibrium market structure is not monopoly).

12.5.2 *Quality enhancement*

In the quality enhancement case, we denote the sunk cost of quality by $F(v)$, and assume that $F(v)$ is twice differentiable, increasing in v, and convex. To ensure that the equilibrium market structure is duopoly, we assume that $F(1) = 0$ and that $F'(1) = 0$. Given these assumptions, it is easy to show that both firms enter in all of the sequential games we have considered.

Given a particular cost function, $F(v)$, the equilibria of the price and quantity games are, in important respects, quite similar when D is small, and, as in the previous cases, quite different when D is large. To illustrate the similarities when D is small, assume that $F(v) = 3(v - 1)^2$, and that D is equal to 12. The best response functions relevant to the price games are pictured in Figure 12.5, and those relevant to the quantity games in Figure 12.6. In both figures the solid line is B's best response function and the dashed line is A's. In each figure, the points labelled E_2 are equilibria of the two-stage game, and the point labelled E_3 is the equilibrium of the three-stage game. To understand these results, we need to understand why the best response functions in the quantity games have the same sort of discontinuities as do those for the price games.

In the price games the best response functions are discontinuous because of the extreme non-concavity of the revenue functions in own quality (see Figure

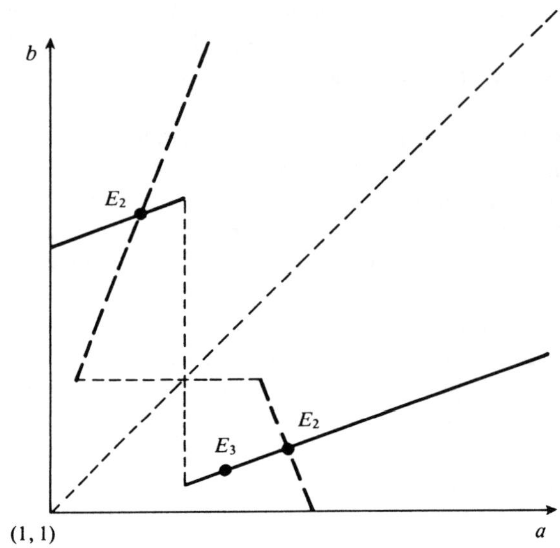

Figure 12.5 Price competition.

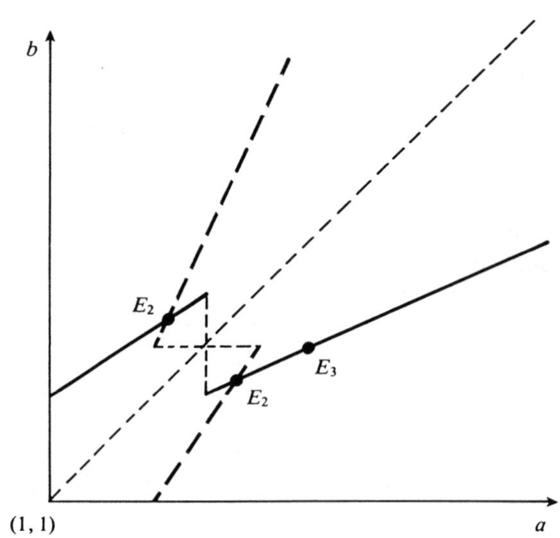

Figure 12.6 Quantity competition.

12.1). Revenues are zero when qualities are identical, and there are two local maxima of the revenue functions. Hence the best response functions are necessarily discontinuous.

In the quantity games the revenue functions are also non-concave and kinked (see Figure 12.3). In particular, the derivative of $\tilde{R}_B$ with respect to b is discontinuous at $b = a$, and is larger as b approaches a from above than it is as a approaches b from below. Profit functions obviously inherit these properties. When there are no costs of production they are irrelevant since revenue is strictly increasing in own quality, and consequently maximal quality is the universal best response. When quality associated costs enter the model, it is no longer necessarily the case that profit is always increasing in own quality, and when it is not the non-concavity results in a discontinuity in the best response function just as it does in the price games. Given a particular cost function, the profit function will not be increasing in quality over the entire quality domain if D is small. Hence when D is small, the equilibria of the price and quantity games are similar.

Notice that in the quantity games, the rate at which revenue increases as own quality increases is proportional to D. Hence, given any $F(v)$, if D is sufficiently large the profit functions are strictly increasing in own quality, and maximal quality is again the universal best response. In the price games, for a given $F(v)$, as D increases without bound quality associated costs become essentially irrelevant, and the best response functions approach those pictured in Figure 12.2. Thus, when D is large the equilibria of the quantity and price games are again quite different.

12.6 Conclusions

In what circumstances is the GT model an adequate explanation of observed product differentiation? Theory alone can provide no definitive answer to this question, but it does shed some light on it. In the version of the GT model which we examined, when firms compete in prices, products are always differentiated. If firms did produce undifferentiated products, revenues in the price equilibrium would be zero – hence firms always find a way to differentiate their product, even if one of them must adulterate its product to achieve differentiation. When firms compete in quantities, the model often produces no differentiation – in effect, the model degenerates into Cournot's model for an undifferentiated product. Hence the attractiveness of the GT model as an explanation for observed product differentiation depends in part on where one stands in the Cournot versus Bertrand debate. There are, we think, compelling reasons to prefer Cournot's version of oligopoly competition to Bertrand's in the situation where firms produce to inventory. It is, of course, entirely possible that neither of these simple models is in fact appropriate, but as regards the choice between them, it seems to us that Cournot is the clear winner. Hence we are sceptical about the power of the GT model as an explanation for real product differentiation.

Notes

1. All of the qualitative results in this chapter generalize quite easily to the following situation. Consumer incomes are uniformly distributed on $[t, u]$, the domain of possible qualities is $[v, w]$, and there is a constant marginal cost of production, c. We require that $c \geq t$ and that $w > 1$. For obvious reasons we choose not to include these five additional parameters.
2. We have also examined the Singh and Vives (1985) game for the GT model with no costs of production. In Stage One each firm chooses its mode of competition and in Stage Two, given predetermined modes, the Nash equilibrium is realized. As in Singh and Vives, the quantity mode is a dominant strategy.

References

Eaton, B. Curtis and Richard G. Lipsey (1987), Product differentiation, in R. Schmalensee and R. Willig (eds), *Handbook of Industrial Organization*, North-Holland, Amsterdam.

Gabszewicz, Jean J. and Jacques-François Thisse (1979), Price competition, quality and income disparities, *Journal of Economic Theory*, vol. 20, pp. 340–59.

Gabszewicz, Jean J. and Jacques-François Thisse (1980), Entry (and exit) in a differentiated industry, *Journal of Economic Theory*, vol. 22, pp. 327–38.

Gabszewicz, Jean J., A. Shaked, J. Sutton and Jacques-Francois Thisse (1981), Price Competition Among Differentiated Products: A Detailed Study of a Nash Equilibrium. ICERD working paper no. 37, London School of Economics.

Kreps, David M. and José A. Scheinkman (1983), Quantity precommitment and Bertrand competition yield Cournot outcomes, *Bell Journal of Economics*, vol. 14(2), pp. 326–37. See Chapter 13.

Salant, D.J. (1986), Equilibrium in a spatial model of imperfect competition with sequential choice of locations and quantities, *Canadian Journal of Economics*, vol. 19, pp. 685–715.

Shaked, A. and J. Sutton (1982), Relaxing price competition through product differentiation, *Review of Economic Studies*, vol. 49(1), pp. 3–13.

Shaked, A. and J. Sutton (1983), Natural oligopolies, *Econometrica*, vol. 51(5), pp. 1469–83.

Singh, N. and Xavier Vives (1985), Price and quantity competition in a differentiated duopoly, *Rand Journal of Economics*, vol..15, pp. 546–54.

[24]

Endogenous Pricing Modes in Markets for Inputs*

B. Curtis Eaton and Nicolas Schmitt

18.1 INTRODUCTION

Today in North America commercial dairies typically transport raw milk from the dairy farmers to their processing plants, while fifty years ago it was the dairy farmers who transported the raw milk. In the salmon fishery in the Pacific north-west, fishers sometimes transport their catch to the fish processor, and processors sometimes buy the fish on the fishing grounds, transporting the catch to their own processing plants. On the Canadian prairies, wheat farmers usually transport the wheat they grow to the grain elevator. In most labour markets, the seller accepts responsibility for getting to work, but this is not universally the case; harvest labour, for example, is often transported to the work site by the buyer. And in some labour markets the responsibility is shared – the company provides the car and the petrol, and the employee the time needed to get to and from work.

The price theory applicable to each of these modes is, of course, quite different. Consider the two most familiar modes. When the buyers do the transporting, the appropriate model is one of discriminating oligopsony in which buyers choose price schedules that specify the prices they are prepared to offer at each point in their potential basins of supply. In contrast, when the sellers do the transporting, the appropriate model is one of non-discriminating oligopsony in which each buyer chooses the one price it is prepared to pay for a unit of the input delivered to its plant. Clearly, whether buyers or sellers transport inputs is not exogenous, as is assumed in these models, and it is

* We thank Jacques Thisse for useful comments and the Social Sciences and Humanities Research Council of Canada (Grant 410–92–880) for financial support.

the purpose of this chapter to offer a model in which choice of mode is endogenous.

It might be thought that any sensible theory of modal choice will conclude that the agent that is more efficient in transporting the input will in fact transport it. Surprisingly, this conclusion is not true in our model; there exist equilibria in which buyers behave as discriminating oligopsonists, even though they are less efficient at transporting the input than their suppliers.

In most respects, ours is a standard model of duopsony. There are two buyers located at the ends of a linear supply area over which suppliers are uniformly dispersed. Either buyers or sellers can transport the input, but their unit costs of transport differ. Buyers announce price schedules for the entire market. Given buyers' announced price schedules, each seller chooses the point at which it will sell its supply of the input and the buyer to whom it will sell, in order to maximize price received from the buyer less transport costs incurred by the seller. The buyers may, and for certain parameter values do, choose price schedules such that all transactions occur at the buyers' plant, generating a non-discriminating duopsony equilibrium. In this case, the price schedules are degenerate – prices for all locations other than the buyer's location are, in effect, zero. Notice that the model permits an infinity of other possibilities. For example, price schedules in which transactions occur at any subset of points in the supply area are permitted in the model. We discover three sorts of Nash equilibria, two of which are familiar and one of which is novel, and a case in which there appears to be no equilibrium in pure price strategies. Two of the equilibria are discriminatory (all transactions occur at suppliers' locations) and the third is non-discriminatory (all transactions occur at buyers' locations).

The importance of endogenous transport modes was first discussed by Beckmann (1976) and later analyzed by Gronberg and Meyer (1981). Using a standard spatial model where firms sell consumer goods, Gronberg and Meyer discover that in some circumstances firms may choose to transport products even though it would be more efficient to let sellers do the transporting. This result is analogous to the corresponding inefficiency result in our model. However, their conclusion is based on a pairwise comparison of profits under different pricing modes given symmetric equilibria, fixed market areas, and a large number of firms. In contrast, our analysis uses game-theoretic tools with a small number of firms. While firms in the Gronberg and Meyer model are restricted to using the same pricing mode, our firms are free to adopt any pricing mode. Thus the equilibria we find are robust to the possibility that a firm might choose to adopt a pricing mode different to its rival's mode. Interestingly, it is this freedom of modal choice that gives rise to non-existence of equilibrium in our model.

The chapter is organized as follows. In Section 18.2 the model is presented, and in Section 18.3 sellers' behaviour is analyzed. In Section 18.4, the main section of the chapter, we examine in great detail the mill price equilibrium of our model. Building on this analysis, the other possible cases are presented in Sections 18.5 to 18.7. Section 18.8 offers some concluding remarks.

18.2 THE MODEL

We cast our analysis in an address model similar in most respects to Hotelling's (1929) model. There are two buyers and a continuum of sellers located on the interval [0, 1]. We denote the locations of sellers or input owners by z, and assume that z is uniformly distributed on [0, 1] with density equal to 1, and that each owner is endowed with one unit of a perishable input in each period. Each owner's reservation selling price is assumed to be zero; specifically, we assume that the owner will sell if and only if the highest price offered, less any transport costs incurred by the seller, *exceeds* zero. There are two firms buying this input, one called A, with a plant located at $x^A = 0$, and the other, called B, with a plant located at $x^B = 1$. Both firms use the input to produce a final good and the production function which describes this transformation is such that one unit of input generates one unit of output. Firms sell their final product at an exogenous price q and the unit of account is chosen such that $q = 2$. Buyers, like sellers, can transport the input. We assume that the transport cost for a seller is equal to 1 per unit of distance, while it is equal to t for a buyer. We assume that t exceeds 0; thus sellers are more efficient in transporting inputs than buyers when t exceeds 1, and less efficient when t is less than 1.

The timing of events in our model is the following: in each period buyers act first by choosing price schedules; sellers then choose the buyer to whom they will sell their input and the point in the market at which they will sell it. We call this point the *seller's supply point.* Sellers maximize price net of any transportation costs they incur, and buyers maximize profit.

A firm's *buying price schedule* specifies the price the firm will pay for one unit of the input at any location x in [0, 1]. Buying price schedules are given by the functions

$$p_i(x), \quad i = A, B \tag{18.1}$$

With no loss of generality we suppose that these prices are non-negative. Thus, firm i's strategy space is the set of price schedules such that $p_i(x) \geq 0$ for all x in [0, 1].

Although there is an infinity of possible buying price schedules, we identify two subclasses of special interest. A *mill price schedule* is one in which, given the other firm's price schedule, the firm actually buys inputs only at its mill. In contrast, a *discriminating price schedule* is one in which, given the other firm's price schedule, the firm actually buys inputs only at corresponding sellers' locations. A mill price schedule then corresponds to one in which the buyer lets the sellers do all the transporting, whereas with a discriminating price schedule, the buyer does all the transporting. Firms are, of course, free to choose price schedules that are neither mill price schedules nor discriminating price schedules.

We suppose that this is a game of perfect information, and look for subgame-perfect Nash equilibria in pure price strategies. A pair of price schedules, $p_A(x)$ and $p_B(x)$, constitute Nash equilibrium price schedules if (i) $p_A(x)$ maximizes A's profit, given $p_B(x)$, and (ii) $p_B(x)$ maximizes B's profit, given $p_A(x)$.

18.3 SELLER'S BEHAVIOUR

Since this is a game of perfect information, we must first characterize the behaviour of all sellers for any pair of price schedules the buyers might offer, and then use this characterization to compute equilibrium price schedules for the two buyers. Consider then the seller at an arbitrary location z in [0, 1]. By assumption, it has full information about $p_i(x)$ ($i = A, B$), and it can transport its input from z to any point x at cost $|z - x|$. Hence, define the following maximum value function:

$$D_i(z) = \max_x \{p_i(x) - |x - z|\}, \quad i = A, B \tag{18.2}$$

This function gives us the *maximum price* over all x, net of own transport cost, that the seller at z can extract from firm i. Further, denote by

$$X_i[p_i(x), z], \tag{18.3}$$

the value of x that solves the maximization problem.

These two functions characterize the seller's behaviour: the seller at z chooses to sell to the buyer for which $D_i(z)$ is larger, and the seller's supply point is the corresponding value of $X_i[p_i(x), z]$. As always in this sort of model, we must make assumptions about a seller's behaviour when the seller is indifferent between two or more options. If the seller is indifferent between offers made by two different buyers, we assume that the seller chooses to sell to the buyer that places the highest value on the input.[1] If the buyers place the same value on the input, then we assume the seller chooses buyer A. Similarly, if a seller is indifferent between several offers from the same buyer, we arbitrarily assume that the seller chooses as its supply point the point that is closer to the buyer. Given these assumptions, the seller's optimizing behaviour is uniquely determined.

To illustrate the seller's behaviour, consider a simple example with a single buyer (firm A). Suppose that firm A proposes the following buying price schedule:

$$p_A(x) = \begin{cases} \frac{1}{2} & \text{for } x = \frac{1}{8} \text{ and } x = \frac{5}{8} \\ \frac{1}{16} & \text{for } x = \frac{1}{2} \text{ and } x = 1 \\ 0 & \text{for all other } x \in [0, 1] \end{cases} \tag{18.4}$$

Faced with this buying price schedule, what will the input owners dispersed on [0, 1] do?

Given any pair $(x, p_A(x))$ on the buyer's price schedule, the price to the seller at z, net of the seller's transport cost, is $p_A(x) - |x - z|$. The function $D_A(z)$ selects for us the best net price for the seller located at z. For this example, $D_A(z)$ is simply

$$D_A(z) = \begin{cases} \frac{1}{2} - |\frac{1}{8} - z| & \text{for } 0 \leq z \leq \frac{3}{8} \\ \frac{1}{2} - |\frac{5}{8} - z| & \text{for } \frac{3}{8} < z \leq 1 \end{cases} \tag{18.5}$$

Figure 18.1 illustrates both $D_A(z)$ and $p_A(x)$ for this example.

Further, for this example the function $X_A[p_A(x), z]$ is the following:

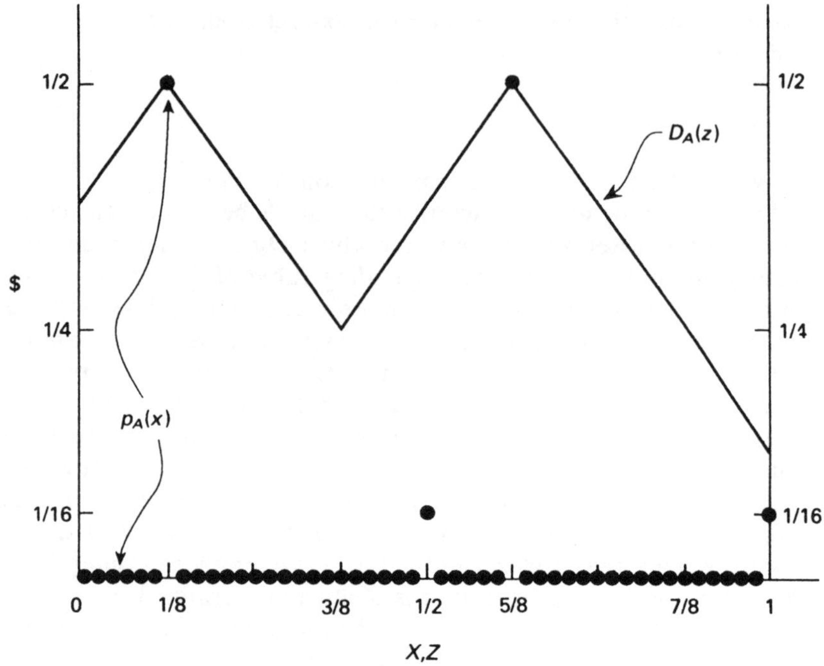

Figure 18.1 $p_A(x)$ and the associated $D_A(z)$

$$X_A[p_A(x), z] = \begin{cases} \frac{1}{8} & \text{for } 0 \leq z \leq \frac{3}{8} \\ \frac{5}{8} & \text{for } \frac{3}{8} < z \leq 1 \end{cases} \tag{18.6}$$

Notice that in this example, sales are made at precisely two locations in the [0, 1] interval: $\frac{1}{8}$, and $\frac{5}{8}$. Notice also that the functions $p_A(x)$ and $D_A(z)$ have just two points in common in this example: $\left(\frac{1}{8}, \frac{1}{2}\right)$, and $\left(\frac{5}{8}, \frac{1}{2}\right)$.

Knowing how to capture the seller's behaviour given arbitrary buying price schedules, we can turn to the determination of equilibrium price schedules when the two buyers compete for the inputs.

18.4 MILL PRICE EQUILIBRIUM

We begin by computing the standard mill price equilibrium in which, by assumption, firms do not transport the input. Given prices, $p_A \geq 0$

at $x^A = 0$ for firm A and $p_B \geq 0$ at $x^B = 1$ for firm B, the total volume of inputs bought by firm A (V_A) is

$$V_A = \begin{cases} \frac{(p_A - p_B + 1)}{2} & \text{if } p_A - 1 \leq p_B \text{ and } p_B - 1 \leq p_A \\ 1 & \text{if } p_A - 1 > p_B \\ 0 & \text{if } p_B - 1 > p_A \end{cases} \tag{18.7}$$

Recalling that the exogenous price of the final good produced by firms A and B is 2, and that one unit of input is needed to produce one unit of the product, A's profit as a function of p_A and p_B, is

$$\pi_A = \begin{cases} \{2 - p_A\}\left(\frac{p_A - p_B + 1}{2}\right) & \text{if } p_A - 1 \leq p_B \text{ and } p_B - 1 \leq p_A \\ 2 - p_A & \text{if } p_A - 1 > p_B \\ 0 & \text{if } p_B - 1 > p_A \end{cases} \tag{18.8}$$

Given the symmetry of the problem and the concavity of this profit function, it is routine to show that the mill price equilibrium is

$$p_A^* = p_B^* = 1 \tag{18.9}$$

Since our interest is in the equilibrium choice of complete buying price schedules where firms can transport inputs if they choose to do so, we want to rewrite the mill price equilibrium in terms of complete buying price schedules. The mill price schedules for firms A and B corresponding to (18.9) are respectively,

$$\begin{aligned} p_A^*(0) &= 1 \\ p_A^*(x) &= 0 \quad \text{for} \quad 0 < x \leq 1 \\ p_B^*(x) &= 0 \quad \text{for} \quad 0 \leq x < 1 \\ p_B^*(1) &= 1 \end{aligned} \tag{18.10}$$

A zero price for all locations other than the location of the buyer's mill is our way of saying that the firm refuses to buy inputs at those locations. Recall that a seller's reservation price is zero: it will sell at a net price greater than zero, but will not sell at a net price equal to zero. Thus transactions cannot occur at a zero price in our model.[2] Notice also that, if for zero we substitute any positive price that is sufficiently low that no seller chooses to sell at that price given the two mill prices of 1, we get equivalent price schedules. In this sense, the equilibrium mill price schedules are not unique.

We will prove the following propositions:

PROPOSITION 18.1 *The mill price schedules $p^*_A(x)$ and $p^*_B(x)$ for $0 \leq x \leq 1$ constitute a Nash price equilibrium when $t > 3$.*

Accordingly, we assume throughout this section that $t > 3$.

Note that firm A's profit, given price schedules $p^*_A(x)$ and $p^*_B(x)$, is equal to $\frac{1}{2}$ since its market extends from 0 to $\frac{1}{2}$, and it therefore buys $\frac{1}{2}$ units of the input at unit price 1 and produces $\frac{1}{2}$ units of output which it sells at unit price 2. Similarly for firm B. Thus,

$$\pi_A[p^*_A(x), p^*_B(x)] = \pi_B[p^*_A(x), p^*_B(x)] = \frac{1}{2} \tag{18.11}$$

Given the symmetry of the problem, to prove Proposition 18.1 it is sufficient to show that $p^*_A(x)$ is a best response to $p^*_B(x)$. Since the proof is somewhat intricate it is useful to outline our approach. Starting with the complete set of possible price schedules for firm A, we first show that there is a best response to $p^*_B(x)$ in the set of price schedules such that $p_A(x) \leq (2 - tx)$. This result allows us to focus our search for a best response on this restricted set of price schedules. We then show that any price schedule for firm A that could be a best response to $p^*_B(x)$ can be characterized by two parameters: a location in [0, 1] called w, and a buying price at w, called v. Finally, we choose w and v to maximize profit, generating $p^*_A(x)$ as a best response to $p^*_B(x)$ when $t > 3$.

We begin by arguing that, in the search for a best response to $p^*_B(x)$, we can ignore price schedules in which $p_A(x) > (2 - tx)$. Notice that $(2 - tx)$ is firm A's reservation price for inputs bought at point x; if it paid this price for a unit of input at point x, its profit would be zero since it would sell the resulting output at price 2 and must incur a transport cost equal to tx to get the input to its plant. So, suppose that $p_A(x_i) > (2 - tx_i)$ for some point $x_i \in [0, 1]$. There are two possibilities: first, if firm A actually buys inputs at price $p_A(x_i)$, its profit must clearly increase if $p_A(x_i)$ is replaced by an arbitrary price less than or equal to $(2 - tx_i)$ since only sellers for whom x_i at price $p_A(x_i)$ is the best deal could change their behaviour as a result of the price decrease, and since A makes a loss on inputs that it buys at $p_A(x_i) > (2 - tx_i)$. Second, if no sales are made at price $p_A(x_i)$, firm A's profit does not change if $p_A(x_i)$ is replaced by an arbitrary price less than or equal to $(2 - tx_i)$. If $p_A(x) > (2 - tx)$ for many points x in [0, 1], then A's profit increases when all such prices are replaced by arbitrary prices less than or equal to $2 - tx$. Hence, for any schedule in which $p_A(x) > (2 - tx)$ for some $x \in [0, 1]$, there exists another schedule, say $p'_A(x)$, such that $p'_A(x) \leq (2 - tx)$ for all $x \in [0, 1]$, and, in addition,

$$\pi_A[p'_A(x), p^*_B(x)] \geq \pi_A[p_A(x), p^*_B(x)] \tag{18.12}$$

Thus, although we cannot rule out the possibility that $p_A(x)$ may be a best response to $p^*_B(x)$, in the case that it is, so also is $p'_A(x)$. So, if there is a best response to $p^*_B(x)$, there is one in the set of price schedules such that $p_A(x) \leq (2 - tx)$ for all x in [0, 1]. In what follows we confine our search to this set.

Now, we proceed to show that any price schedule $p_A(x)$ that is a best response to $p^*_B(x)$ can be described by two parameters. Consider first the maximum net price that sellers can get when they deal with firm B; given $p^*_B(x)$, the associated $D^*_B(z)$ is defined by

$$D^*_B = \max_x\{p^*_B(x) - |x - z|\} \tag{18.13}$$

Since $p^*_B = 0$ for all $x \neq 1$, $X_B[p^*_B(x), z] = 1$ solves this maximization problem. In other words, if the input-owner chooses to sell to firm B, he/she will transport the input to B's plant. Thus,

$$\begin{aligned} D^*_B(z) &= p^*_B(1) - |1 - z| \\ &= z \end{aligned} \tag{18.14}$$

That is, the maximum price net of own transport cost that the seller at z can extract from firm B is z. $D^*_B(z)$ is illustrated in Figure 18.2(a).

Consider now any price schedule $p_A(x)$ such that $p_A(x) \leq (2 - tx)$ for all x in [0, 1], and the associated $D_A(z)$. There are two possibilities for $D_A(z)$. It will be a line of slope -1 throughout, just as $D^*_B(z)$ is a line of slope 1 throughout, if A chooses to offer a mill price schedule, leaving it to sellers to transport the good. Consider, for example, $p^*_A(x)$; the corresponding $D_A(z)$ is $D^*_A(z) = 1 - z$. In all the other cases, $D_A(z)$ will be composed of linear connected segments with slopes that alternate between 1 and -1 as in the case illustrated by the broken line *ABDFGH* in Figure 18.2(a). Notice that if the first kink in $D_A(z)$ lies below $D_B^*(z)$, then $D_A(z)$ lies everywhere below $D_B^*(z)$. In this case, firm A buys no inputs, generating no profit. Clearly, the associated price schedule is not a best response to $p_B^*(x)$. For this reason, we confine our attention to price schedules $p_A(x)$ such that the first kink in $D_A(z)$ lies on or above $D_B^*(z)$. Several points regarding the relationship between $p_A(x)$ and $D_A(z)$ deserve attention. First, points like B, D, and F in Figure 18.2(a), where $D_A(z)$ attains a local maximum, are necessarily on $p_A(x)$. Second, other points on $D_A(z)$ to the left of G may or may not be on $p_A(x)$. Third, no points above $D_A(z)$ are on $p_A(x)$. Finally, no points on segment GH of $D_A(z)$ are on $p_A(x)$ since, by assumption, $p_A(x) > (2 - tx)$.

Suppose now that, given $D_A(z)$ as illustrated $ABDFGH$, points B, D, and F are the only points on both $D_A(z)$ and $p_A(x)$; denote these points by (x_1, p_1), (x_2, p_2) and (x_3, p_3). All other points on $p_A(x)$ are necessarily below $D_A(z)$; for concreteness, we suppose that all such prices are equal to zero as illustrated in Figure 18.2(a). Given this price schedule, firm A will buy quantity z' at price p_1, quantity $z'' - z'$ at price p_2, and quantity $z''' - z''$ at price p_3. Profit per unit on the z' (respectively $z'' - z'$ and $z''' - z''$) units bought at price p_1 is $2 - tx_1 - p_1$ (respectively, $2 - tx_2 - p_2$ and $2 - tx_3 - p_3$). The total profit generated by this price schedule is then equal to the shaded area.

We now want to find a price schedule, $p_A'(x)$, that generates the maximum possible profit given $D_A(z)$ as illustrated in Figure 18.2(a). Consider first a point x in interval $[0, x_1)$. By choosing $p_A'(x) = p_1 - (x_1 - x)$, that is the price corresponding to x on AB in Figure 18.2(a), firm A induces the seller at $z = x$ to accept the lower price, while increasing its net output price from $(2 - tx_1)$ to $(2 - tx)$. Hence, for all x in $[0, x_1)$, to maximize profit, set $p_A'(x) = p_1 - (x_1 - x)$.

Now consider a point x in $(x_1, z']$. Initially, the supply point for the input owner at $z = x$ is x_1, and the firm's net profit is $[(2 - tx_1) - p_1]$. While the firm could induce this seller to accept the lower price $[p_1 - (x - x_1)]$, the buyer's profit would fall since the decrease in input costs, $x - x_1$, is smaller than the decrease in output price, net of transport costs, $t(x - x_1)$, when $t > 1$. Hence, to maximize profit, set $p_A'(x) < p_1 - (x - x_1)$ for all x in $(x_1, z']$. For concreteness, we choose $p_A'(x) = 0$ for all x in $(x_1, z']$.

Generalizing these results to the entire market, we conclude that the following price schedule maximizes A's profit given the $D_A(z)$ as illustrated in Figure 18.2(a):

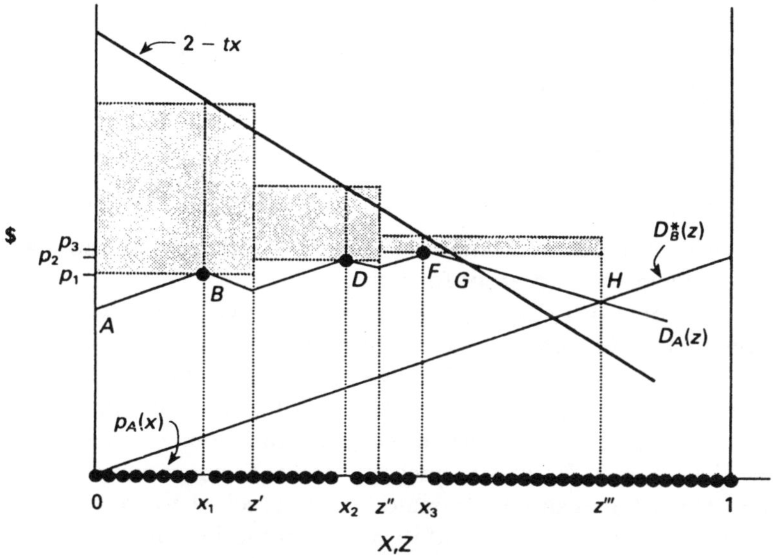

Figure 18.2(a) *A*'s profit given $p_A(x)$

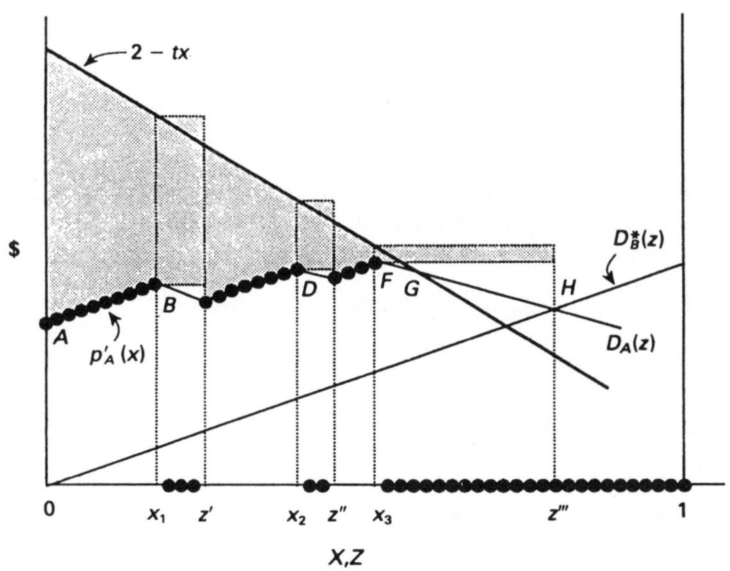

Figure 18.2(b) *A*'s maximum profit given $D_A(z)$

$$p'_A(x) = \begin{cases} p_1 - (x_1 - x) & \text{for } 0 \leq x \leq x_1 \\ 0 & \text{for } x_1 < x < z' \\ p_2 - (x_2 - x) & \text{for } z' \leq x \leq x_2 \\ 0 & \text{for } x_2 < x < z'' \\ p_3 - (x_3 - x) & \text{for } z'' \leq x \leq x_3 \\ 0 & \text{for } x_3 < x \leq 1 \end{cases} \tag{18.15}$$

This price schedule is illustrated in Figure 18.2(b), where the shaded area is the associated profit for firm A.

Next, supposing that $D_A(z)$ has at least two kinks, we want to show that profit increases either when we eliminate the first kink by choosing $p_1 = p_2 + (x_2 - x_1)$, or when we eliminate the second kink by choosing $p_1 = p_2 - (x_2 - x_1)$. Using the example illustrated in Figure 18.2(b), we could write the profit function corresponding to the shaded area. However, since our aim is to show that the first or the second kink can be eliminated, it is sufficient to work with the profit generated from segment $[0, x_2]$. Considering only this segment of its market, firm A's profit as a function of p_1, p_2, x_1, and x_2 is

$$\begin{aligned} & x_1(2 - tx_1 - p_1) + \frac{x_1^2}{2}(1 + t) \\ & + (z' - x_1)(2 - tx_1 - p_1) \\ & + (x_2 - z')(2 - tx_2 - p_2) + \frac{(x_2 - z')^2}{2}(1 + t) \end{aligned} \tag{18.16}$$

The first line of this expression is the area of the shaded trapezoid above $(0, x_1)$ in Figure 18.2(b), the second is the rectangular shaded area above (x_1, z'), and the third is the trapezoidal shaded area above (z', x_2). Using the fact that z' is equal to $\left(\frac{p_1 - p_2 + x_1 + x_2}{2}\right)$ we have

$$\begin{aligned} & \frac{1}{2}(x_2 - x_1)[4 - (p_1 + p_2) + t(p_1 - p_2 - x_1 - x_2)] - \frac{1}{2}(p_1 - p_2)^2 \\ & + x_1(2 - tx_1 - p_1) + \frac{1}{2}(1 + t)x_1^2 \\ & + \frac{1}{8}(x_2 - x_1 + p_2 - p_1)^2(1 + t) \end{aligned} \tag{18.17}$$

Note that the second derivative of this expression with respect to p_1 is $\frac{1}{4}(t-3)$, which is positive when $t > 3$. Hence, the function is at a maximum with respect to p_1 at either the lower or the upper bound on p_1. The restrictions on p_1 implicit in Figure 18.2(b) are

$$p_2 + (x_2 - x_1) > p_1 > p_2 - (x_2 - x_1) \tag{18.18}$$

Notice that when $p_1 = p_2 - (x_2 - x_1)$, the first kink in $D_A(z)$ vanishes, and when $p_1 = p_2 + (x_2 - x_1)$, the second kink vanishes.

This result places further strong restrictions on price schedules that are potential best responses to $p^*_B(x)$. Given a price schedule that is a best response to $p^*_B(x)$, the corresponding $D_A(z)$ can have at most one kink; if it had more than one, the result in the previous paragraph implies that profit increases when the first or the second kink is eliminated.

In other words, any price schedule that is a best response to $p^*_B(x)$ can be characterized by two parameters: w, the location of the single kink, and v, the delivered price at the kink. The associated price schedule, $p_A(x; w, v)$, is the following:

$$p_A(x; w, v) = \begin{cases} v - (w - x) & \text{for } 0 \leq x \leq w \\ 0 & \text{for } w < x \leq 1 \end{cases} \tag{18.19}$$

The optimal pair (v^*, w^*) must lie within triangle ABC in Figure 18.3 since v cannot exceed $(2 - tx)$ and firm A would have no market if v was below $D^*_B(z)$. The implied restrictions on (v, w) are $0 \leq w \leq \frac{2}{1+t}$ and $w \leq v \leq 2 - tw$. To prove Proposition 18.1, all we need to show is that $w^* = 0$ and $v^* = 1$.

Consider the point (v, w) as illustrated in Figure 18.3 and the price schedule given by (18.19); the shaded area is the figure is the associated profit. Algebraically, it is given by the following expression:

$$\pi_A(w, v) = \frac{1}{2}[w^2(1 + t) + (v + w)(2 - tw - v)] \tag{18.20}$$

Differentiating (18.20) with respect to v, we get

$$\frac{\partial \pi_A(w, v)}{\partial v} = -2v - w(1 + t) + 2 \tag{18.21}$$

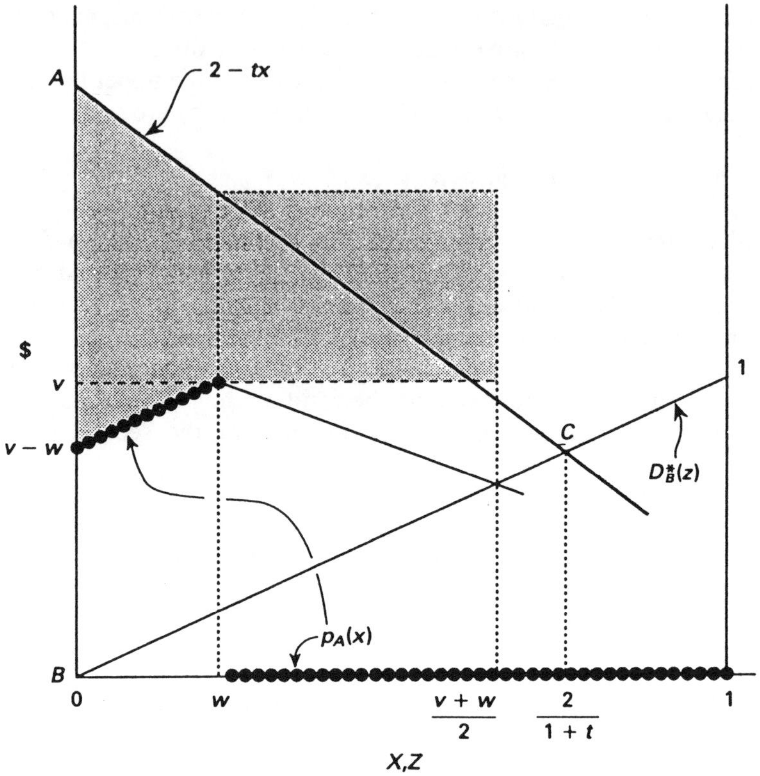

Figure 18.3 Optimal choice of v and w for $t > 3$

Clearly, firm A's profit is a concave function of v. Given w, we get an interior maximum in which $\partial\pi_A/\partial v = 0$ if $w \leq 2/(3 + t)$ and a boundary maximum in which $v = w = D_B^*$ otherwise. Hence, given w, the optimal price v^* is

$$v^* = \begin{cases} \frac{1}{2}[2 - w(1 + t)] & \text{if } 0 \leq w \leq \frac{2}{3+t} \\ w & \text{if } \frac{2}{3+t} \leq w \leq \frac{2}{1+t} \end{cases} \tag{18.22}$$

and firm A's corresponding profit, as a function of w, is

$$\pi_A(w, v^*) = \begin{cases} \frac{(1+t)w^2}{2} + \frac{1}{8}[2 + w(1 - t)]^2 & \text{if } 0 \leq w \leq \frac{2}{3+t} \\ 2w - \left[\frac{1+t}{2}\right]w^2 & \text{if } \frac{2}{3+t} \leq w \leq \frac{2}{1+t} \end{cases} \tag{18.23}$$

Consider now the choice of w; (18.23) attains its maximum at a boundary since $\partial\pi_A(w, v^*)/\partial w < 0$ when $0 \leq w \leq 2/(3 + t)$ and $\partial\pi_A(w, v^*)/\partial w > 0$ when $2/(t + 3) \leq w \leq 2/(1 + t)$. At the lower bound $w = 0$, $v^* = 1$ and $\pi_A = \frac{1}{2}$. This solution implies that firm A proposes the mill price schedule $p^*_A(x)$ of Proposition 18.1. At the upper boundary $w = 2/(1 + t)$, $v^* = 2t/(t + 1)$ and $\pi_A = 2/(1 + t)$. In this case, firm A proposes a discriminating price schedule coincident with BC, capturing the triangle ABC as its profit. Comparing profit levels,

$$\pi_A(w = 0, v^* = 1) = \frac{1}{2} > \pi_A\left(w = \frac{2}{1 + t}, v^* = \frac{2t}{1 + t}\right) = \frac{2}{1 + t}$$

when $t > 3$. Hence, firm A's best response is $w^* = 0$ and $v^* = 1$, generating $p^*_A(x)$ as a best response to $p^*_B(x)$, thus proving Proposition 18.1.

Notice also that we have shown that there is no mill price equilibrium when $t < 3$. Both mill prices must be equal to 1 in any such equilibrium, but as just shown, the best response to a mill price of 1 is a discriminating price schedule when $t < 3$.

Finally, A's best response to $p^*_B(x)$ when $t < 3$ points to the possibility of a new sort of discriminating price schedule, one that can be called a *constrained discriminating price schedule*, since prices are determined, not by the other firm's cost of transport, but jointly by a price of the other firm and the possibility that sellers might accept that price, transporting the good themselves. We explore this sort of equilibrium in the next section.

18.5 CONSTRAINED DISCRIMINATING PRICE EQUILIBRIUM

In this section, we focus on the following input buying price schedules for A and B:

$$p^*_A(x) = \frac{3 - t}{2} + x \qquad \text{for } 0 \leq x \leq \frac{1}{2}$$

$$p^*_A(x) = 0 \qquad \text{for } \frac{1}{2} < x \leq 1 \qquad (18.24)$$

and

$$p^*_B(x) = \frac{3-t}{2} + (1-x) \quad \text{for } \frac{1}{2} \leq x \leq 1$$
$$p^*_B(x) = 0 \quad \text{for } 0 \leq x < \frac{1}{2} \tag{18.25}$$

Given these price schedules, firm A buys and transports inputs from all sellers in $[0, \frac{1}{2}]$ at a price which makes the sellers just indifferent to selling their input to A at their doorstep, and selling to firm B at its buying price at $x = \frac{1}{2}$, and transporting the input from their doorstep to $\frac{1}{2}$. The constraint on A's buying price at any point x in $[0, \frac{1}{2}]$ is then determined by B's buying price at $\frac{1}{2}$ in combination with the seller's cost of transporting the good from x to $\frac{1}{2}$. Symmetrically, B's buying price at any point in its market is jointly determined by A's buying price at $x = \frac{1}{2}$ and the seller's transport cost.

We will prove the following proposition:

PROPOSITION 18.2 *Price schedules $p^*_A(x)$ and $p^*_B(x)$ for $0 \leq x \leq 1$ constitute a Nash price equilibrium when $1 < t < 5/3$.*

In this case,

$$D^*_B(z) = \frac{3-t}{2} + z \quad \text{for } 0 \leq z \leq \frac{1}{2}$$
$$D^*_B(z) = \frac{3-t}{2} + (1-z) \quad \text{for } \frac{1}{2} \leq z \leq 1 \tag{18.26}$$

$D^*_B(z)$ is then the tent-shaped function drawn in Figure 18.4. It is coincident with $p^*_B(x)$ for z in $[\frac{1}{2}, 1]$, and for z in $[0, \frac{1}{2}]$, it is B's buying price at $x = \frac{1}{2}$ minus the seller's transport cost between z and $\frac{1}{2}$.

Some important results from Section 18.4 are also applicable here. First, firm A's best response can be characterized by just two parameters (w, v). Second, since $t > 1$, for customers to the left of w, A will transport the input, and for customers to the right of w, the customers themselves will transport the input to w. Third, (w, v) will lie on or below the line $(2 - tx)$, and on or above $D^*_B(z)$; that is

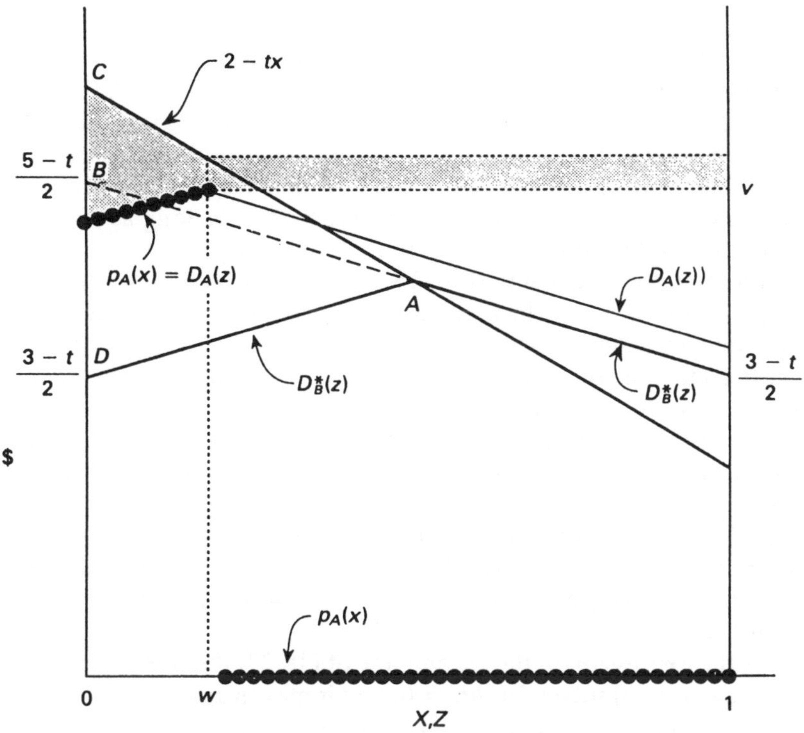

Figure 18.4 Optimal choice of v and w for $1 < t < 5/3$

(w, v) will lie in triangle DAC of Figure 18.4. So, to find A's best response to $p^*_B(x)$, all we need to do is to solve a maximization problem similar to the one solved in the previous section. In contrast to Section 18.4 however, there is now a discontinuity in A's profit function. If (w, v) lies in triangle BAC in Figure 18.4, firm A captures the whole market. If, on the other hand, it lies in triangle DAB, it captures only part of the market. There is thus a discontinuity in A's profit function along the line BA. Algebraically, A's profit function for these two cases is given by the following:

$$\pi_A(w, v) = \begin{cases} 2 - tw - v + \left(\frac{1+t}{2}\right)w^2 & \text{for } \frac{5-t}{2} - w \le v \le 2 - tw \\ \frac{1}{4}(2 - v - tw)(t - 3 + 2w + 2v) + \left(\frac{1+t}{2}\right)w^2 & \text{for } \frac{3-t}{2} + w \le v \le \frac{5-t}{2} - w \end{cases} \tag{18.27}$$

In order to find the optimal choice (v^*, w^*), we proceed as follows. We first ask what firm A's choice of v and w would be if it was restricted to maximize profit as given by the first part of (18.27). We discover that $\hat{v} = 2 - t/2$ and $\hat{w} = 1/2$ is the solution to this problem provided that $t < 5/3$. Next, we ask the same question with respect to the second part of (18.27). We again find that $\hat{v}$ and $\hat{w}$ are firm A's choices when $t < 3$. We conclude therefore that, as long as $t < 5/3$, the optimal solution is $w^* = 1/2$ and $v^* = 2 - t/2$.

Differentiating the first part of (18.27) with respect to v, we see that $\partial\pi_A(v; w)/\partial v = -1$. Thus, given w, firm A selects the lowest price consistent with the restrictions for this case. This is $\hat{v} = (5 - t)/2 - w$. Substituting $\hat{v}$ in the profit function, and observing that its second derivative with respect to w is positive (that is, $\partial^2\pi_A(w; \hat{v})/\partial w^2 > 0$), we see that the optimal solution for w lies on a boundary. One possible solution is $w = 0$; in this case, $\hat{v} = (5 - t)/2$ generating profit equal to $(t - 1)/2$. The other boundary solution is at $w = 1/2$; in this case, $\hat{v} = (2 - t)/2$, which generates profit equal to $(1 + t)/8$. Comparing profit levels, firm A selects $w = 1/2$ and corresponding $\hat{v}$ when $\pi_A(w = 1/2, \hat{v}) = (1 + t)/8 > \pi_A(w = 0, \hat{v}) = (t - 1)/2$, or when $t < 5/3$.

For the expression in the second line of (18.27) the price $\tilde{v} = 1/4[7 - t - 2w(1 + t)]$ solves $\partial\pi_A/\partial v = 0$, and it maximizes A's profit given w as long as $w \leq (1 + t)/2(3 + t)$. Over the range $(1 + t)/2(3 + t) \leq w \leq 1/2$, to maximize profit given w, A chooses a price on line DA. That is, it chooses $\tilde{v} = (3 - t)/2 + w$. Substituting these prices $\tilde{v}$ into firm A's profit function and differentiating, we discover that $\partial^2\pi_A(w; \tilde{v})/\partial w^2 > 0$, indicating another boundary maximum. We find that $\pi_A(w = 1/2, \tilde{v}) = (1 + t)/8 > \pi_A(w = 0, \tilde{v}) = (1 + t)^2/32$ whenever $t < 3$.

It follows from these results that the price schedule $p_A^*(x) = (3 - t)/2 + x$ for $0 \leq x \leq 1/2$ and $p_A^* = 0$ for $1/2 < x \leq 1$ is a best response to $p_B^*(x)$ provided that $t < 5/3$, establishing Proposition 18.2.

Interestingly, although input-owners are more efficient at transporting goods in this case, firms do the transporting in equilibrium. Hence, the solution is not cost–benefit optimal.

18.6 NO EQUILIBRIUM

Although we have not proved it, it seems that there is no price equilibrium when $5/3 < t < 3$. In Section 18.4, we saw that there is no mill price equilibrium for t in this range, and in Section 18.5, we

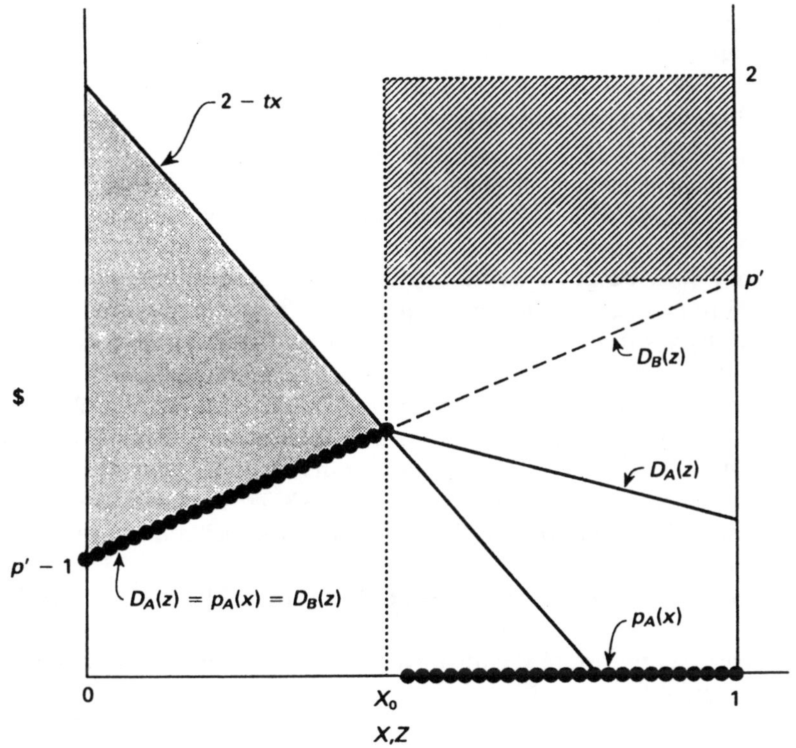

Figure 18.5 No mixed mode equilibria

found that there is no constrained discriminating price equilibrium.

Further, mixed mode equilibria in which one firm offers a single mill price and the other offers a discriminating price schedule are not possible. In Figure 18.5, firm *B* is mill pricing with price p' and, given p', firm *A* has responded with the best possible discriminating price schedule $(p' - 1 + x)$ for $0 \leq x \leq x_0$ and 0 otherwise. *B*'s profit is the cross-hatched area and *A*'s is the shaded area. Clearly, this cannot be an equilibrium since firm *B* can easily capture *A*'s entire market and increase its profit by offering a mill price slightly above p' rising $D_B(z)$ above $D_A(z)$ for all $z \in [0, 1]$. This is true for any $p' < 2$. Further, $p' = 2$ cannot be a best response to the optimal discriminating price schedule for *A* induced by $p' = 2$ since *B*'s profit is then zero. Hence, there is no mixed mode equilibrium in which one firm proposes a mill price schedule and the other a discriminating price schedule.

Whether there exist other exotic pure strategy equilibria we cannot say, but we strongly suspect not.

18.7 DISCRIMINATING PRICE EQUILIBRIUM

When $t < 1$, we get a discriminating price equilibrium in which the equilibrium price at any point in a buyer's market is equal to the other buyer's reservation price at that point. Given that A transports the input from $x > 0$ to its plant at $x^A = 0$, its reservation price, or the maximum price it would ever pay for the input at x is $2 - tx$. Similarly, B's reservation price for the input at x is $2 - t(1 - x)$, so if firm A (alternatively, B) buys the inputs from $[0, \frac{1}{2}]$ (respectively, $[\frac{1}{2}, 1]$) at firm B's (respectively, firm A's) reservation price, the corresponding equilibrium discriminating price schedules are

$$p_A^*(x) = p_B^*(x) = \min[2 - tx, 2 - t(1 - x)] \tag{18.28}$$

This price equilibrium is equivalent to Hoover's (1937) discriminating price equilibrium.

PROPOSITION 18.3 *Price schedules $p_A^*(x)$ and $p_B^*(x)$ for $0 \leq x \leq 1$ constitute a Nash price equilibrium when $t < 1$.*

In this case, $D_B^*(z)$ is coincident with $p_B^*(x)$ (for $x = z$) as illustrated in Figure 18.6. Now pick an arbitrary price schedule for firm A, $p_A(x)$, such that $p_A(x) \leq (2 - tx)$ for all x, and assume that $D_A(z)$ has at least one kink above $D_B^*(z)$, as illustrated in Figure 18.6. Points B, D and F are clearly on $p_A(x)$. When $t < 1$, the price schedule $p_A'(x)$ that is profit-maximizing, given that points B, D and F are also on p_A', is coincident with $ABCDEFG$. That is, to maximize profit when the buyer's transport cost is smaller than the seller's, the firm will offer a discriminating price schedule. This contrasts with the corresponding result in Sections 18.4 and 18.5 where the firm chose to offer discriminating pricing only on the upward-sloping portions of $D_A(z)$. Clearly, to maximize profit given $p_B^*(x)$, firm A will push the entire discriminating price schedule down to $p_B^*(x)$ for x in $[0, \frac{1}{2}]$. For $\frac{1}{2} < x \leq 1$, any $p_A(x) \leq p_B^*(x)$ is profit-maximizing. In particular, $p_A(x) = p_B^*(x)$ is profit-maximizing, establishing Proposition 18.3.

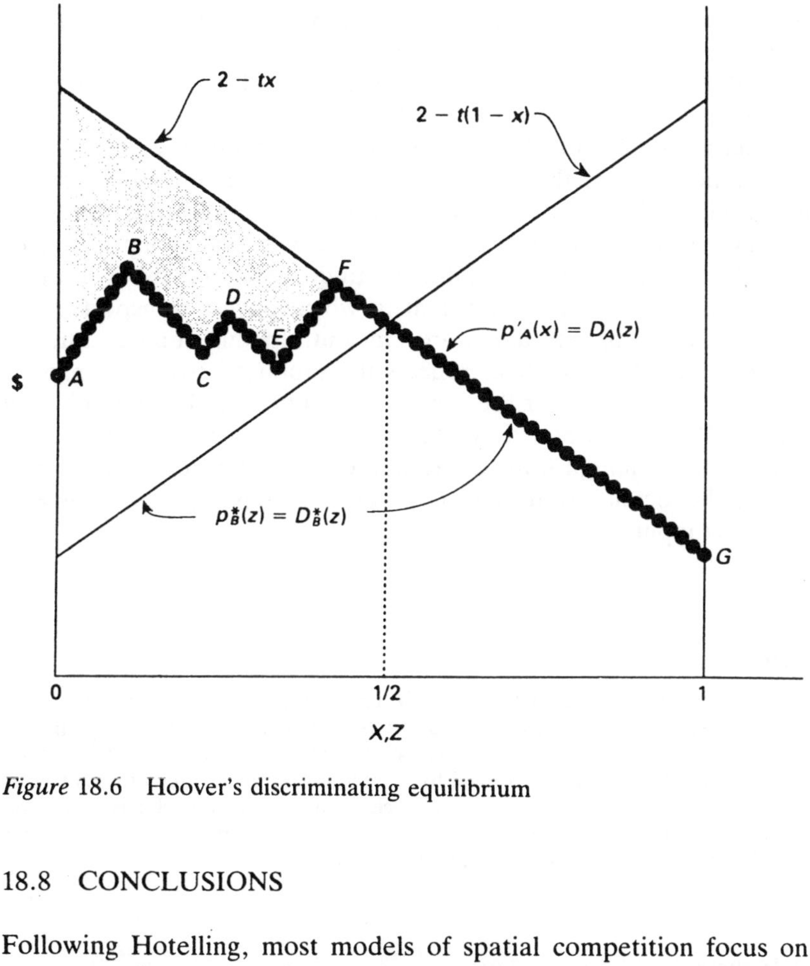

Figure 18.6 Hoover's discriminating equilibrium

18.8 CONCLUSIONS

Following Hotelling, most models of spatial competition focus on output markets rather than on input markets. This imbalance does not reflect the relative importance of transportation in the two sorts of markets. The value of resources devoted to transportation of inputs is surely at least as large as the value of resources devoted to transportation of final goods. Compare, for example, the resources devoted to commuting to and from work with the resources devoted to transporting final goods from retailers to consumers' homes. It is partially to redress this imbalance that we have focused on input markets in this chapter.

Another undesirable feature of standard models of spatial competition is that the transportation mode is, in most cases, exogenously determined. In models like Hotelling's, which focus on spatial oligopoly, either firms or their customers are arbitrarily assigned the task of transporting goods. And in models of spatial oligopsony, either buyers or sellers are arbitrarily assigned the task of transporting inputs. In our model, who does the transporting is endogenously determined. We are then not only able to show that the more efficient agents do not invariably do the transporting in equilibrium, but that, depending on transport cost parameters, only one group of agents does the transporting in equilibrium. In doing so, we discover a new sort of discriminating equilibrium in which buyers transport goods even though suppliers are more efficient. In this equilibrium, the slope of the price schedules reflects the suppliers' cost of transport, and is a consequence of the suppliers' ability to pick their points of supply. This ability constrains the buyers' ability to extract location rents; thus, although firms discriminate, they capture a smaller portion of the location rent than they would if suppliers were unable to transport inputs.

Notes

1. Thus, if it happens that $D_A(z) = D_B(z)$, our assumption implies that the seller located at z sells its input to firm B (that is, selects x_B) if $2 - p_B(X_B) - t(1 - X_B) > 2 - p_A(X_A) - tX_A$, and to firm A otherwise.
2. We could have denoted refusal to buy by a separate strategy instead of by an offer to purchase at a zero price. Indeed, we could have allowed negative prices and denoted refusal to buy by a price equal to minus infinity. The choice is a matter of no consequence.

References

Beckmann, Martin (1976) 'Spatial Price Policies Revisited', *Bell Journal of Economics*, vol. 7, no. 2, pp. 619–29.

Gronberg, Timothy and Jack Meyer (1981) 'Transport Inefficiency and the Choice of Spatial Pricing Model', *Journal of Regional Science*, vol. 21, no. 4, pp. 541–49.

Hoover, Edgar (1937) 'Spatial Price Discrimination', *Review of Economic Studies*, vol. 4, pp. 182–91.

Hotelling, Harold (1929) 'Stability in Competition', *Economic Journal* vol. 39, pp. 41–57.

[25]

An Address Model of Patent Breadth with Two Countries

Drawing on Hotelling's model of spatial competition, we develop an address model in which normative and positive aspects of the choice of patent breadth in an international setting can be examined. In each of two countries a number of different entrepreneurs face the following sort of opportunity: by investing a sum c in product research and development the entrepreneur makes possible the production of an entire spectrum of products. Any entrepreneur's incentive to do so is determined jointly by patent breadths in the two countries where the spectrum of products will be sold. As before, patent breadth is measured by the portion of the product spectrum over which the patentholder exercises monopoly power. In each country there is a population of entrepreneurs, each of whom can develop a different product spectrum; entrepreneurs differ with regard to the magnitude of the development cost c that must be incurred to create the spectrum of products.

Even in a one-country setting this poses a difficult and typical policy problem because there are many incentive problems to be solved, one for each entrepreneur, while there are two policy instruments, patent breadths in the two countries. To complicate matters, if we assume that in making decisions with regard to patent breadth, each country has regard only to the welfare of its own citizens, significant international externalities distort the policy-setting game.

Given patent breadths in the two countries, only those entrepreneurs who (correctly) anticipate that they can cover their development costs do, in fact, develop (and, of course, patent) their separate product spectrums. Knowing the distribution of opportunities and associated development costs in the two countries, and knowing how entrepreneurs will respond to the incentives created by patent breadth, each country non-cooperatively chooses its own patent breadth to maximize a weighted sum of profit and consumers' surplus earned by the country's citizens.

We establish the following results. First, when countries place equal weight on profit and consumers' surplus of their own citizens, relative to the social optimum, patent breadths are too narrow. This result reflects the existence of a positive externality flowing from each country's patent breadth to the profit and consumers' surplus enjoyed by citizens of the other country. Second, the first result generalizes to other facets of intellectual property rights. Intellectual property rights tend to be too weak if countries non-cooperatively choose them to maximize total surplus of their own citizens. Third, to the extent that profit is weighted more heavily than consumers' surplus in political objective functions, the tendency for property rights to be too weak in equilibrium is offset. Indeed, if the weight given to profit in the political objective function is large enough, property rights will be too strong in equilibrium. The final result is that, except in very special circumstances, equilibrium patent breadths are not identical in the two countries, and in all cases there is a continuum of optimal mixes of patent breadth, only one of which is symmetric. Further, if equilibrium patent breadths are sufficiently asymmetric, there is no symmetric patent policy that Pareto-dominates the original equilibrium.

This chapter is structured as follows. Section 7.1 discusses the literature that is related to the questions posed here. The core model with one country is presented in section 7.2. Section 7.3 examines the entry game, i.e., the stage where firms make decisions on their innovations. The stage where two countries choose their patent policies interdependently is studied in section 7.4. Some concluding remarks and possible applications are discussed in the final section 7.5.

7.1 Related Literature

Chapter 2 has already discussed the theoretical patent models from the Industrial Organization literature. All these models (for example, Nordhaus 1969, Klemperer 1990, Scotchmer and Green 1990), essentially analyse a trade-off between innovation incentive and monopolistic welfare loss. In an international context, this trade-off between R&D incentives and deadweight losses occurs at the level of global welfare, but is complicated by the distribution of benefits and costs over individual countries. Extending Nordhaus (1969), Berkowitz and Kotowitz (1982) have examined the optimal patent length for a small country. The size of process innovation is a function of patent lengths in a small country and in the rest of the world. The small country assumption ensures that no retaliation of other countries is to be expected if the country shortens the national patent life. Whether a single country should set long or short patent lifetimes depends on the industrial organization of the domestic invention market. Berkowitz and Kotowitz conclude that a competitive invention industry calls for short-lived patents and a concentrated invention industry for long-lived patents.

Inspired by the contentious discussion on intellectual property rights in the Uruguay Round, Chin and Grossman (1990), Diwan and Rodrik (1991) and Deardorff (1992) have developed models which analyse patent protection in north-south trade relations. Many southern countries do not provide patent protection; they either have no patent system or do not enforce it effectively. Their claim is that southern welfare only decreases if patent protection is provided for northern innovations that will be generated anyway. Northern countries, particularly those representing northern firms, want protection against imitation in the south in order to be able to recoup their R&D investments.

In the present chapter patent protection is defined within a model of horizontal product differentiation similar to Klemperer's (1990) model. Both types of welfare loss in his analysis, i.e., substitution to less preferred varieties and to not buying, can potentially arise in our model. Unlike Berkowitz and Kotowitz (1982) we do not use a small country assumption. Hence, the strategic interactions between two countries which determine their patent breadths are taken fully into account. For certain parameter configurations, for example, when demand in one country is very weak, our model comes close to the setting studied by Berkowitz and Kotowitz. Our model can also be used to investigate the optimal protection levels for the north and the south. Unlike previous studies in that area, we do not assume beforehand that only the north has potential innovators. This situation occurs in our model as a special case, more precisely when the innovation density in the south is zero, as will become clear below.

7.2 The Core Model

In this section we focus on just one country as we develop the core of our model. In passing, we comment briefly on the choice of patent breadth in a one-country setting. By spending c on product development the entrepreneur can create an entire spectrum of products. An individual product is described by its address w in the product spectrum, which extends from $-\sigma$ to $+\sigma$, where parameter $\sigma > 0$.

If the product is developed, we assume that any firm is technically able to produce any product in the spectrum at a marginal cost, which we set equal to 0 for convenience. Hence, in the absence of some form of property right, the entrepreneur has no incentive to develop the spectrum: with no property right to any portion of the product spectrum, the equilibrium price for all products in the spectrum is 0. Similar to the analysis in chapter 4, we suppose such property rights take the form of a monopoly right granted to the developer to produce products in interval $[-b/2, b/2]$, where $0 < b < \sigma$. Thus, subsequent to development, the entrepreneur has the right to monopolistically exploit a market of length b.

As in Hotelling's (1929) model, there is a continuum of consumers. Each consumer has a most preferred product in each spectrum, which we denote by w^*. The demand side of the model is created by positing a continuum of consumers with a uniform distribution of w^* on $[-\sigma, \sigma]$. We set the density of this distribution equal to 1. Denote the price of product with address w, or more simply product w, by p(w) (for w in $[-\sigma, \sigma]$). Given prices, the consumer first chooses which product to buy, and then chooses how much to buy of the product chosen in stage one. Consumer w^* buys the good w for which

$$p_d(w, w^*) = p(w) + t|w - w^*| \tag{7.1}$$

is smallest. The parameter t is analogous to the cost of transport in familiar models of spatial competition; here, of course, it is a utility penalty associated with consuming a product that differs from the consumer's most preferred product. And the function $p_d(w, w^*)$ is analogous to a delivery price schedule.

If for two goods, w^1 and w^2,

$$p(w^1) + t|w^1 - w^*| = p(w^2) + t|w^2 - w^*| \tag{7.2}$$

we assume that consumer w^* prefers the good that is nearer to his most preferred good, while if they are equidistant from w^* the consumer randomly picks one of them.

The demand function for the consumer's *chosen* product is the following linear function of p_d:

$$x(p_d) = (a - p_d)/F(n) \tag{7.3}$$

Parameter a is the intercept of the inverse demand function and F(n) is its slope. The slope of the inverse demand function, F(n), is an increasing function of n, the number of developed spectra:

$$F(n) = \gamma n^\theta \qquad 0 < \theta < 1 \qquad \gamma > 0 \tag{7.4}$$

Notice that as the number of developed spectra increases, the consumer buys less of his chosen product in each spectrum. The larger parameter θ, the more pronounced this demand interdependence effect is. This inter-spectrum demand effect assures that the marginal benefit of an additional product spectrum decreases as the number of developed spectra increases.

Given patent breadth b, equilibrium prices are 0 in the two unprotected intervals of the product spectrum, intervals $[-\sigma, -b/2]$ and $[b/2, \sigma]$, since any firm can produce these goods at 0 marginal cost. In the protected interval the monopolist maximizes profit by providing all conceivable varieties and by choosing $p(w)$ equal to $a/2$ if the consumer with $w^* = w$ prefers buying the monopolist's good at this price rather than buying good $w = b/2$ (or good $w = -b/2$) at price 0. If, however, the monopolist is constrained by the possibility that the customer with $w^* = w$ would prefer the nearest competitively priced good to the monopolist's good at price $a/2$, to maximize profit the monopolist sets $p(w)$ equal to $t|w - b/2|$ (or $t|w + b/2|$). Thus, equilibrium prices in the monopolist's protected segment are

$$p(w) = \min [a/2, t|w - b/2|, t|w + b/2|] \tag{7.5}$$

The first term is the unconstrained monopoly price, and the second (respectively, third) is the highest price which will induce the consumer with address $w^* = w$ to choose the monopolist's good w in preference to good $b/2$ (respectively, $-b/2$), which is available at price 0). In this price equilibrium, each consumer buys her most preferred good. The price equilibrium is illustrated in figure 7.1.a, for the case in which $tb > a$, and in figure 7.1.b, for the case in which $tb < a$.

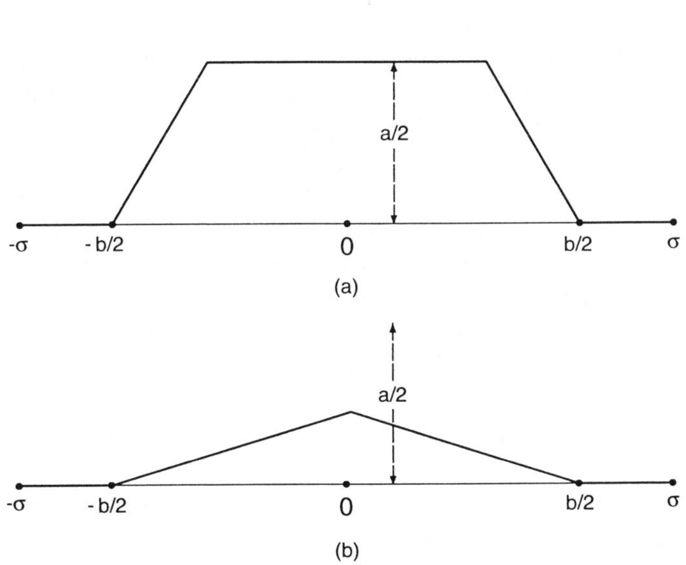

Figure 7.1 Equilibrium price schedules

At this point we have seven parameters: a, t, θ, b, γ, σ and c. The preference parameters θ and γ in equation (7.4) are common to both countries throughout the analysis, while, in the following sections of the chapter, the preference parameters a and σ and the policy variable b are country-specific. Experience with the model suggests that very little is lost if we choose parameter t to be infinite. In this case, the monopolist's profit-maximizing price is a/2 throughout the protected portion of the spectrum, which permits a significant simplification of the algebra in the balance of the analysis. Accordingly, we set t equal to infinity. Given this simplification, the developer's gross profit from a country with patent breadth b is just

$$\pi(b) = (a^2 b)/(4F(n)) \tag{7.6}$$

Consumers' surplus from the protected, monopoly portion of the spectrum is $(a^2 b)/(8F(n))$, and from the unprotected, competitive portion of the spectrum it is $(a^2(2\sigma - b))/(2F(n))$. Hence, the consumers' surplus from a product spectrum breadth b is

$$\phi(b) = (a^2/8F(n))(8\sigma - 3b) \tag{7.7}$$

Notice that total surplus (the sum of profit and consumers' surplus) and consumers' surplus are decreasing functions of b, while profit is an increasing function of b. Hence, if there was just one spectrum and one country, the optimal patent breadth would satisfy $\pi(b) = c$; that is, patent breadth would be just broad enough to allow the developer to recover his development costs. However, even in a one-country setting, when there is more than one spectrum to be developed, a difficult trade-off inevitably arises. Suppose the policy maker is considering patent breadth b′, and has identified all the spectra for which $\pi(b') - c > 0$. To induce an additional entrepreneur to develop his valuable spectrum, the policy maker will realize both that he must increase b and that any increase in b entails a reduction in total surplus from each spectrum that would be developed given b′. The cost-benefit optimal policy must balance these opposing effects. If it were possible to design spectrum-specific patent policies, this unfortunate trade-off would not arise.

Our focus in this chapter is on the externalities driven by patent breadth policy in a multi-country context. In section 7.3, we model entrepreneurial decisions given the opportunity to sell in different countries with (possibly) different patent policies. Following that, in section 7.4 we examine the two-country policy game in which countries choose patent policies.

7.3 The Entry Game

Here we suppose there are two countries, 1 and 2, and look at the game in which the number of spectra that entrepreneurs choose to develop in the two countries is determined. The two parameters in equation (7.4), θ and γ, are assumed to be common to the two countries, while the remaining parameters are country-specific: a_1 and a_2 are intercepts of the inverse demand functions; σ_1 and σ_2 are spectrum length parameters. In the entry game of this section, patent breadths in the two countries, b_1 and b_2, are exogenous. In the following section we build on the results of the entry game to determine equilibrium values of these policy parameters.

We assume that the developer of any spectrum will receive local patent protection in both countries. It is this assumption that drives the inter-country externalities in our model. An immediate consequence of the assumption is that any spectrum that is developed will be available in both countries. Hence, from equation (7.6), the developer's aggregate gross profit or inducement to innovate, which we denote by $V(b_1, b_2; n_1, n_2)$, is given by the following expression

$$V(b_1, b_2; n_1, n_2) = (b_1(a_1)^2 + b_2(a_2)^2)/(4F(n_1 + n_2)) \tag{7.8}$$

where n_i ($i = 1, 2$) is the number of spectra developed by citizens of country i.

To capture the notion of many development opportunities, we assume a uniform distribution of development costs c in the two countries, and denote the density of opportunities in country i by D_i ($i = 1, 2$). In the equilibrium of the entry game all spectra for which

$$V(b_1, b_2; n_1, n_2) \geq c$$

will be developed. Given the uniform distribution of c in country i, the number of spectra in country i that satisfy this inequality is just $D_iV(b_1, b_2; n_1, n_2)$ (when starting from 0). Hence, the equilibrium of the entry game is determined by the following two conditions:

$$n_i = V(b_1, b_2; n_1, n_2), \qquad i = 1, 2 \tag{7.9}$$

For simplicity we suppose that n_i is a real number, not an integer. Solving these entry equilibrium conditions, and letting N_i denote the equilibrium value of n_i, we get

$$N_i = (D_i(Z)^{1/(1+\theta)})/(D_1 + D_2)^{\theta/(1+\theta)}) \tag{7.10.a}$$

where

$$Z = (b_1(a_1)^2 + b_2(a_2)^2)/(4\gamma) \tag{7.10.b}$$

From (7.10) we get a number of useful comparative static results:

(i) N_i increases with both policy parameters, b_1 and b_2. Further, the rate at which N_i increases as b_k (k = 1, 2) increases is proportional to $(a_k)^2$; this reflects the facts that developers who reside in country i have access to patent protection in both countries, and that protection is more valuable as the individual consumers' demand for the productis higher. Conversely, N_i increases with a_k (k = 1, 2) and the rate of increase is proportional to b_k. Finally, N_i is concave in b_k (k = 1, 2).

(ii) Naturally, N_i increases as D_i increases. And N_i decreases as D_k (k not equal to i) increases. This latter result is driven by inter-spectrum demand dependence; as D_k increases, so does N_k, but a larger N_k shifts individual demand down in both countries, thereby decreasing N_i.

(iii) Given that b_k is less than $2\sigma_k$ (spectrum length), N_i is independent of σ_k. Given that the protected portion of the spectrum is smaller than the entire spectrum, the size of the spectrum has no bearing on profitability and hence no bearing on the number of developers that find it profitable to develop their spectra.

The inducement to enter evaluated at equilibrium values for N_1 and N_2, which we denote by $V^*(b_1, b_2)$, is

$$V^*(b_1, b_2) = (Z^{1/(1+\theta)})/(D_1 + D_2)^{\theta/(1+\theta)}) \tag{7.11}$$

This is the gross profit of each of the developed spectra in equilibrium. Of course, net profit differs from spectrum to spectrum due to differences in development costs. At one extreme, net profit is identical to $V^*(b_1, b_2)$, and at the other it is 0.

We can readily compute aggregate development costs in equilibrium for country i. They are equal to

$$C_i = (D_i(Z)^{2/(1+\theta)})/(2(D_1 + D_2)^{2\theta/(1+\theta)}) \tag{7.12}$$

The total net profit accruing to developers in country i, $\pi_i(b_1, b_2)$, is then $N_i^*(b_1, b_2) - C_i$, which reduces to

$$\pi_i = (D_i(Z)^{2/(1+\theta)})/(2(D_1 + D_2)^{2\theta/(1+\theta)}) \qquad (7.13)$$

The total net profit for country i inherits the comparative static properties of N_i: both N_i and π_i are increasing in b_i, a_i, and D_i, decreasing in D_k (k not equal to i), and independent of σ_i. Interestingly, despite the inter-spectrum demand dependence and the ever-increasing marginal cost of an additional developed spectrum, $\pi_i(b_1, b_2)$ is convex in b_k (k = 1, 2) (recall that $\theta < 1$). That is, aggregate profit of country i increases at an increasing rate as patent breadth in either country increases.

Finally, since all developed spectra are available in both countries, from (7.7) we see that aggregate consumers' surplus for country i is

$$\phi_i(b_1, b_2) = (N_1 + N_2)((a_i)^2/(8F(N_1 + N_2)))(8\sigma_i - 3b_i) \qquad (7.14)$$

Using previous results this can be rewritten as

$$\phi_i(b_1, b_2) = W(a_i)^2(Z(D_1 + D_2))^{(1-\theta)/(1+\theta)} \qquad (7.15.a)$$

where

$$W = (8\sigma_i - 3b_i)/8\gamma \qquad (7.15.b)$$

The consumers' surplus comparative statics are also interesting:

(i) Consumers' surplus of country i is increasing in b_k (k not equal to i). An increase in country k's patent breadth increases the number of developed spectra available in country i, while having no direct effect on consumers' surplus per spectrum in country i, thus increasing consumers' surplus in country i. (There is, of course, an indirect effect on consumer surplus per spectrum driven by the downward shift of the individual demand curve as the number of spectra increases, but the increase in consumers' surplus resulting from the increase in the number of developed spectra dominates this indirect effect.)

(ii) Provided that b_k is not too large, consumers' surplus in country i (i not equal to k) initially increases as b_i increases and subsequently decreases. Here there are two offsetting effects: consumers' surplus in country i tends to increase as b_i increases because the increase in patent breadth results in an increase in the number of developed spectra in country i; offsetting this effect is the fact that surplus per available spectrum in country i decreases as b_i increases. The second effect eventually dominates the first, and if b_k is sufficiently large, it dominates from the outset.

(iii) Naturally, consumers' surplus in country i increases as a_i increases. In addition, it increases as a_k (k not equal to i) increases. The causality runs through the effect of a_k on N_i (i = 1, 2): an increase in a_k results in an increase in the number of spectra developed in both countries, thereby increasing consumers' surplus in country i.

(iv) Understandably, consumers' surplus increases in country i increases as σ_i, the width of the product spectrum in country i, increases, and is independent of σ_k (k not equal to i).

In the next section we build on these results as we analyze the policy game in which patent breadths are determined.

7.4 The Policy Game

In this section we analyze the game in which patent breadths are chosen independently and non-cooperatively by the two countries to maximize a weighted sum of profit and consumers' surplus of the country's citizens. Letting λ_1 and λ_2 denote the weights given to profit in the political objective functions in the two countries, we get the following objective functions:

$$W_i(b_1, b_2) = \lambda_i\pi_i(b_1, b_2) + (1 - \lambda_i)\phi_i(b_1, b_2) \qquad i = 1, 2 \qquad (7.16)$$

For purposes of comparison we also need the total surplus functions for the two countries:

$$\omega_i(b_1, b_2) = \pi_i(b_1, b_2) + \phi_i(b_1, b_2) \qquad i = 1, 2 \qquad (7.17)$$

Of course, when equal weight is given to profit and consumers' surplus (when λ_i is equal to 1/2), the objective of the policy maker is the maximization of total welfare.

Profit and Consumers' Surplus Weighted Equally

We begin by looking at the case in which profit and consumers' surplus are weighted equally in the political objective functions. The important qualitative features of the equilibrium of this game are illustrated in figure 7.2. In this equilibrium, country 1 chooses b_1 = 8.9 and country 2 chooses b_2 = 5.2. Although the parameter values on which this diagram is based are reported in the figure,

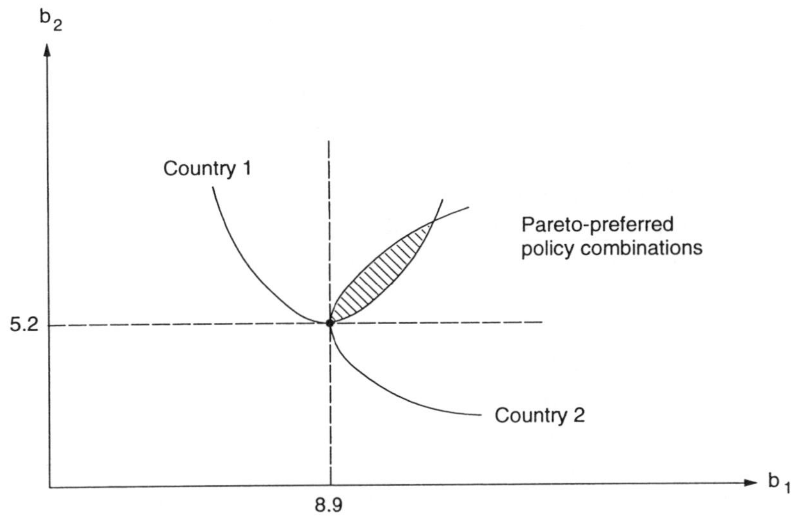

Figure 7.2 Asymmetric innovation densities ($\gamma = 10$; $\theta = 0.5$; $a_1 = a_2 = 10$; $\sigma_1 = \sigma_2 = 30$; $\lambda_1 = \lambda_2 = 0.5$; $D_1 = 1.5$; $D_2 = 1.0$)

we will not focus on them since, at this point, we are interested in the qualitative properties of equilibrium.

One useful way to regard this equilibrium is to think of each country as maximizing its own objective function, subject to the constraint that the other chooses its equilibrium value of b. Focusing for concreteness on country 1, it is then apparent that a level surface (or indifferent curve) of country 1's objective function is tangent to the constraint $b_2 = 5.2$ at the equilibrium. Importantly, the curvature of country 1's level surface in the neighbourhood of the equilibrium, and the set of policy combinations that are preferred by country 1 to the equilibrium policy combination, are determined by the sign of the partial derivative of $W_1(b_1, b_2)$ with respect to b_2. The sign of this derivative is, of course, positive since both profit and consumers' surplus for country 1 increases as b_2 increases. For country 1 then, the set of preferred policy combinations lies above 1's level surface through the equilibrium. Now, beginning at the equilibrium suppose we alter (increase or decrease) b_1 slightly: $W_1(b_1, b_2)$ necessarily decreases since, given $b_2 = 5.2$, $b_1 = 8.9$ maximizes $W_1(b_1, b_2)$; then, to get back to the original level surface, the positive sign of the partial derivative of $W_1(b_1, b_2)$

with respect to b_2 dictates that we must increase b_2; hence, the level surface of country 1's objective function through the equilibrium is U-shaped in the neighbourhood of the equilibrium. Similarly, the level surface of country 2's objective function through the equilibrium is tangent to $b_1 = 8.9$ at the equilibrium. The level surface through the equilibrium has the shape of a backwards C, and preferred policy combinations lie to the right of the level surface. It is then apparent that the equilibrium is not Pareto-optimal as regards the welfare of the two countries and that there is too little patent protection in the equilibrium - policy combinations in the cross-hatched, lens-shaped area of the figure Pareto-dominate the equilibrium policy combination.

These results are generic in games in which there are positive externalities. So there is a more general message in figure 7.2 regarding intellectual property rights in an international setting. Interpret b_1 and b_2 as any two intellectual property rights parameters in two countries. Given an interior equilibrium, smooth objective functions and a positive cross-first partial derivative, the qualitative features of figure 7.2 follow. Hence, any dimension of intellectual property rights that confers a positive externality on the welfare of other countries - length of patent, for example - will tend to be too weak in equilibrium, if countries choose such policies non-cooperatively to maximize aggregate welfare of their own citizens. As we argue below, this conclusion does not necessarily follow if profit is weighted more heavily than consumers' surplus in the political objective function.

The comparative statics of the policy equilibrium are also of some interest. Our approach in figures 7.3 through 7.6 is to use the equilibrium of what we call the baseline model as a point against which to compare the equilibria that emerge as we change various parameters of the model. Although we used numerical techniques to generate results, they are readily understood. In figure 7.3 we have drawn the best-response functions for the baseline model, the solid lines in the figure that generate the equilibrium E_0. We have also drawn the best-response functions that arise when we increase spectrum width in country 1, the dashed line for country 1 and again the solid line for country 2 that generate the equilibrium at E_1. An increase in spectrum width in country 1 leads to an increase in the equilibrium value of b_1 and a decrease in the equilibrium value of b_2.

The first thing to notice about figure 7.3 is that the best-response functions are downward sloping. This reflects the fact that an increase in one country's policy parameter not only increases welfare in the other country, but also decreases the rate at which the other country's welfare changes as it increases its own policy parameter. It is this second effect that results in downward-sloping best-response functions, and it is readily understood. Suppose we are initially on country 1's best-response functions, and consider a discrete increase in b_2, holding b_1 fixed. As we emphasized in the preceding section, this increase in b_2 results in an increase in the number of spectra developed in both countries and, of course, an increase in the number of spectra available to consumers in each country. In consequence, the demand for goods in each spectrum in country 1 shifts down (reflecting the inter-spectrum demand effect discussed above), reducing the consumers' surplus of the marginal spectrum. That is, as b_2 increases, the consumers' surplus associated with an additional developed spectrum decreases. Interestingly, despite this inter-spectrum demand effect and the fact that the marginal development cost of additional spectra is ever increasing, as b_2 increases, the partial derivative of $\pi_i(b_1, b_2)$ with respect to b_1 also increases, reflecting the strong positive externality that one country's patent policy has on profitability of spectra developed in the other country. However, the effect on consumers' surplus dominates the effect on profit with the net result that the marginal social value of an additional spectrum in country 1 diminishes as we increase b_2. Then, since the marginal social value was equal to 0 in the initial position on country 1's best response, country 1's best response to this exogenous increase in b_2 is to decrease b_1. That is, country 1's best-response function is downward sloping.

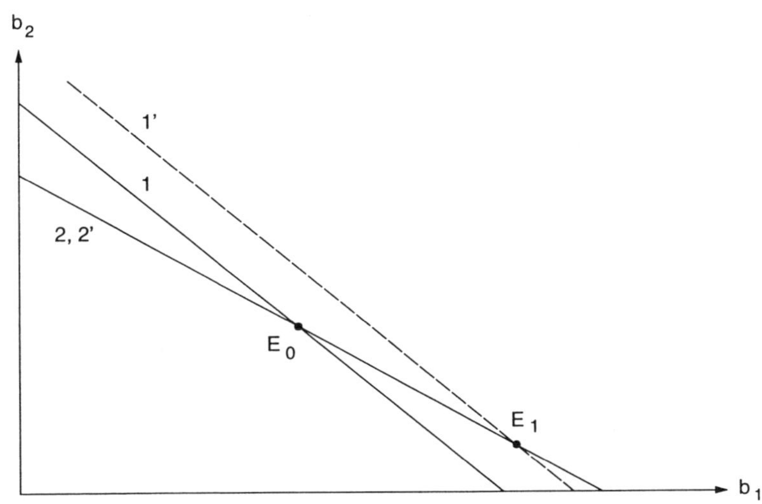

Figure 7.3 Asymmetric spectrum width ($\gamma = 10$; $\theta = 0.5$; $a_1 = a_2 = 10$; ; $\lambda_1 = \lambda_2 = 0.5$; $D_1 = D_2 = 1.0$; $\sigma_1 = \sigma_2 = 30$ (solid lines: baseline model); $\sigma_1 = 40$; $\sigma_2 = 30$ (dashed lines: asymmetric spectrum width)

From figure 7.3 we see that the increase in σ_1 shifts country 1's best-response function to the right, while having no effect on country 2's best-response function. The key to understanding these effects is that while σ_1 clearly increases consumers' surplus per spectrum in country 1, it has no effect on the inducement to entry (or gross profit) and therefore none on the number of developed spectra. The increase in consumers' surplus per spectrum in country 1 translates into an increase in the marginal social value of an additional spectrum in that country, and hence into a rightward shift in that country's best-response function since b_1 is the country's only control on development. Further, since all the externalities from one country to another are channelled through the number of developed spectra and since σ_1 has no effect on the number of developed spectra, country 2's objective function and therefore its best-response function are independent of σ_1.

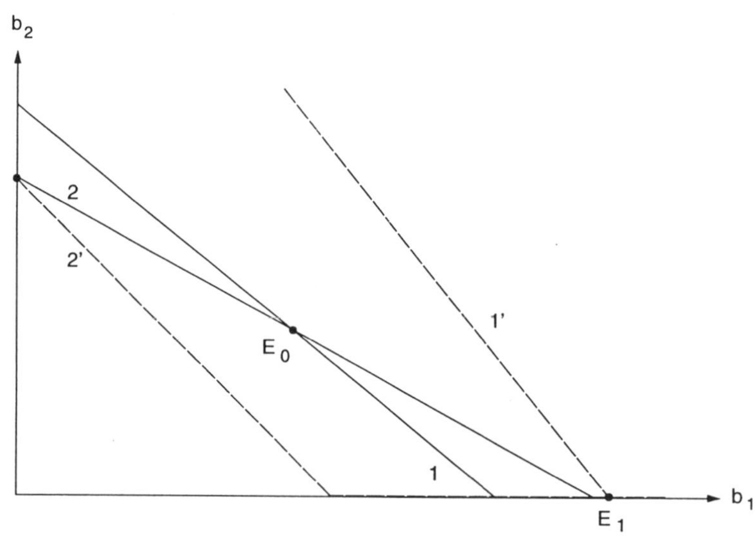

Figure 7.4 Asymmetric demand intercept ($a_1 = 15$; $a_2 = 10$)

In figure 7.4 the solid lines are the best-response functions for the baseline model and the dashed lines the best-response functions that arise when the intercept of the inverse demand function in country 1, a_1, increases. As we saw in the previous section, this increase in a_1 results in an increase in both N_1 and N_2

(given b_1 and b_2). In country 2 this results in a decrease in the social value of an additional spectrum, and country 2's best-response function shifts downward. In country 1, the increase in a_1 increases the social value of an additional spectrum and the best-response function shifts rightward. Both shifts work to produce an asymmetric equilibrium. In the case illustrated the asymmetry is extreme - b_2 is equal to zero.

As illustrated in figure 7.5, an increase in innovation density in country 1, D_1, has a similar effect on the equilibrium. Country 2's best-response function shifts downward and 1's shifts rightward producing an asymmetric equilibrium in which b_1 increases and b_2 decreases.

It is then apparent that, except when both countries are identical, the equilibrium of the policy game is asymmetric. Further, if the equilibrium is sufficiently asymmetric there will be no symmetric policy combination that Pareto-dominates the initial equilibrium. This suggests that it will be difficult and perhaps unwise to attempt to create uniform policies with respect to intellectual property rights across very different countries.

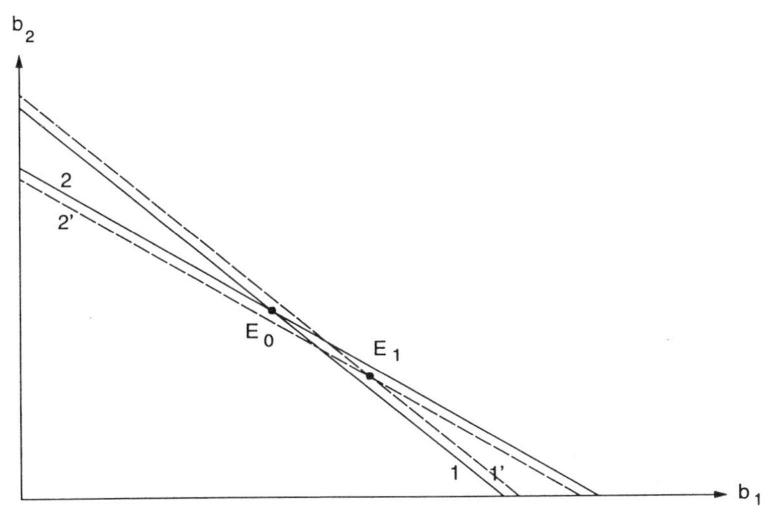

Figure 7.5 Asymmetric innovation densities (D_1 = 1.5; D_2 = 1.0)

Profits Weighted More Heavily Than Consumers' Surplus

One crude way to introduce the possibility that strongly focused interests receive more weight than diffuse interests in the political objective function is to suppose that countries choose policies to maximize a weighted sum of profit and consumers' surplus. In the current context it seems sensible to suppose that profit receives the larger weight; that is, that λ_i (i = 1, 2) exceeds 1/2. In this subsection we explore some implications of profit-biased weights in the political objective functions.

Notice first that $\pi_i(b_1, b_2)$ and $\phi_i(b_1, b_2)$ are independent of both profit weights (λ_1 and λ_2). Hence, changes in profit weights have no direct impact on the endogenous variables that are determined in the entry game analyzed in section 7.3. The real effects of changes in the weight given to profit in the political objective functions work entirely through their impact on equilibrium policy parameters.

Given b_k (k not equal to i), on country i's best-response function b_i is such that the partial derivative of $\pi_i(b_1, b_2)$ with respect to b_i, weighted by λ_i, is equal to the partial derivative of $\phi_i(b_1, b_2)$, weighted by $(1 - \lambda_i)$. Necessarily, then, on i's best-response function profit is increasing in b_i and consumers' surplus is decreasing in b_i. An increase in λ_i then necessitates that b_i be increased to maintain the equality. That is, an increase in λ_i shifts country i's best-response function up and to the right, and has no effect on the best-response function of country k.

Relative to the baseline model, the effect of a simultaneous and symmetric increase in the political weight given to profit in both countries is illustrated in figure 7.6. As the weight given to profit increases, both best response func tions shift up and to the right producing a new equilibrium in which both patent breadths are larger. Interestingly, this may result in a higher level of total surplus in both countries. That is, a bias toward profit in the political objective function can work to offset the free-rider problem that is inherent in this model. Of course, if the bias toward profit is too large, the result will be an equilibrium that lies above and to the right of the locus of Pareto-optimal policy combinations. The other side of this story is not so encouraging. If patent breadth is cooperatively chosen in an international forum, and if profit receives a larger weight than consumers' surplus in that forum, then the policy equilibrium will inevitably involve property rights that are too strong relative to the social optimum.

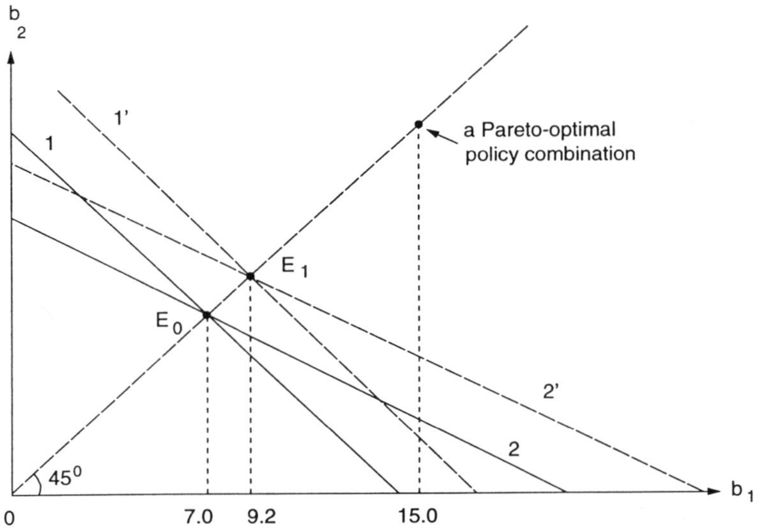

Figure 7.6 Profit weighted more heavily ($\lambda_1 = \lambda_2 = 2/3$)

This story would seem to apply more generally to many facets of intellectual property rights in an international setting. Strengthening intellectual property rights in one country often involves positive externalities on firms and consumers in other countries. Then, if each country chooses its intellectual property rights policy to maximize total welfare of its own citizens, the positive externalities imply that property rights will be too weak in equilibrium. However, to the extent that profit is weighted more heavily than consumers' surplus in the political objective function, the tendency for too weak property rights is offset. Indeed, if the weight given to profit is sufficiently large, property rights will be too strong in equilibrium.

7.5 Concluding Remarks

This chapter has developed an address model of product differentiation (à la Hotelling 1929) in which the normative and positive aspects of the patent breadth policies for two countries can be studied. We have established the following results. First, when countries place equal weight on profit and consumers' surplus of their own citizens, relative to the social optimum, patent breadths are too narrow. This result reflects the existence of a positive externality flowing from each country's patent breadth to the profit and consumers' surplus enjoyed by citizens of the other country. Second, to the extent that profit is weighted more heavily than consumers' surplus in political objective functions, the tendency for property rights to be too weak in equilibrium is offset. Third, except in very special circumstances, equilibrium patent breadths are not identical in the two countries, and in all cases there is a continuum of optimal mixes of patent breadth, only one of which is symmetric. Further, if equilibrium breadths are sufficiently asymmetric, there is no symmetric patent policy that Pareto-dominates the original equilibrium.

Especially this last result is an important one as it applies to recent developments in international patent policy. The first is the on-going harmonisation of national patent systems in Europe, as described in chapter 4. In the perspective of our results, this trend towards symmetric protection, starting from divergent breadths, is not necessarily to be applauded. The above analysis shows that a uniform European patent does not Pareto-improve the European welfare if national patents vary much. This conclusion is driven by the positive externalities that arise in non-cooperative policy games played by independent countries. In addition to the welfare loss due to harmonisation, another welfare loss may occur if the European Community acts as a forum for producers. Relative to the social optimum, too strong patent protection may emerge if profits are weighted more heavily than consumers' surplus in the total surplus functions.

For a different environment, however, chapter 4 has presented an opposite result. Given that European competition policy prevents price discrimination, chapter 4 showed that European welfare increases when patent breadth is uniform. The force driving the result was the unequal evolution of consumer surplus and profits in patent breadth. Different patent breadths in order to provide sufficient incentive to innovate are too costly in terms of welfare. By harmonisation of patent protection, the European Community can easily keep profits to the innovator the same while reducing the overall Community static welfare loss.

Another application of the model presented in this chapter concerns the discussion on intellectual property rights in the Uruguay Round, as briefly outlined in section 7.1. The two countries in our model can be interpreted as the northern and the southern region in the world. The north generates many innovations whereas the south generates only few. In terms of our model, one could say that the north has a high and the south has a low innovation density. The model predicts that asymmetric innovation densities lead to extensive patent protection in the innovation-intensive region and narrow protection in the weaker region. This situation can indeed be observed in the world (the north provides strong, the south weak protection) and has caused the contentious discussion in the GATT Round between north and south. The proposal of northern countries, however, to extend their standards of protection to the south does not Pareto-improve the global welfare if innovation densities are too different (as they seem to be). Moreover, if the strong industry lobby has the effect of weighting profits more heavily than consumers' surplus, the standard of protection will be too high, relative to the global optimum. In addition to the analysis presented here, the next chapter will concentrate completely on this north-south issue of intellectual property protection.

References

Berkowitz, M.K. and Y. Kotowitz. 1982. "Patent Policy in an Open Economy." *Canadian Journal of Economics* XV: 1–17.

Chin, J.C. and G.M. Grossman. 1990. "Intellectual Property Rights and North-South Trade." In R.W. Jones and A.O. Krueger (eds.), *The Political Economy of International Trade: Essays in Honor of Robert E. Baldwin*, Cambridge MA: Basil Blackwell.

Deardorff, A.V. 1992. "Welfare Effects of Global Patent Protection." *Economica* 59: 35–51.

Diwan, I. and D. Rodrik. 1991. "Patents, Appropriate Technology, and North-South Trade." *Journal of International Economics* 30: 27–47.

Hotelling, H. 1929. "Stability in Competition." *Economic Journal* 39: 41–57.

Klemperer, P. 1990. "How Broad should the Scope of Patent Protection Be?" *RAND Journal of Economics* 21: 113–130.

Nordhaus, W.D. 1969. *Invention, Growth, and Welfare. A Theoretical Treatment of Technological Change*. Cambridge MA: MIT Press.

Scotchmer, S. and J. Green. 1990. "Novelty and Disclosure in Patent Law", *RAND Journal of Economics* 21: 131–146.

Image advertising*
with William D. White**

Abstract
The heart of this paper is a model of social interaction in which players use costumes and other visible consumption goods as signals about the identity of other players. If these signals are informative enough, players use them to condition their social interaction. Importantly, accurate signals are mutually beneficial. This game is then wrapped in another in which players choose their costumes. There are many equilibria in this expanded game, some of which allow individuals to perfectly signal their type in all social interactions, and others of which do not. The perfect signalling equilibria Pareto dominate the others, but since there are many of them, the players face a difficult coordination problem. In this paper we explore the hypothesis that image advertising solves this coordination problem. Two implications of our theory are that image advertising campaigns are necessarily massive, and that the targeted audience for the advertising campaign is necessarily larger than the targeted group of buyers of the advertised product. We offer anecdotal evidence in support of both implications.

1. Introduction

For the most part, the economist's vision of the individual is founded on the notion of private consumption goods. For example, if asked to think about two women sitting down to have lunch together, most economists would think of the relationship between each woman and her food as a purely private one; in the economist's eye, what one woman has for lunch has no bearing on the other's well-being. Garlic aside, this is a sensible working hypothesis for many sorts of consumer choices.

There is, however, another sort of choice for which the fiction of private consumption goods is definitely not sensible. For example, when one of those curious fellows from the City of London puts on his bowler hat and grabs his black umbrella, he is at least as concerned about the image he is projecting to other people (i.e. what they make of him) as he is about keeping his head warm and dry. Similarly, when you look at yourself in the mirror – when buying a new suit or getting dressed for a job interview, for example – your behaviour reflects more a concern for the image you project than a purely private relationship between you and your clothes. Engagement and wedding rings provide more obvious examples of goods that are worn primarily for the image they project.

It is decisions about these sorts of goods, which we call *costumes*, that are the focus of this paper. We are concerned with the kinds of decisions that Harry Rosen, haberdasher for Toronto's male power elite, will advise you about in his recent

* This paper was written in 1995.
** Yale University, USA.

booklet – *Image: The Art of Dressing Well.* To quote the journalist Stephen Brunt, quoting Rosen: 'The passage that all but leaps off the page is about what it means to be inappropriately attired. "It's a no-possible-win situation that says you're either cheap, poor, without manners, illiterate, forgetful or uninvited. Any one of these could be enough to impede your march to the corner suite"' (*The Globe and Mail*, 6 September, 1990, p. 18).

We propose to take these sometimes amusing, but nevertheless interesting and perhaps important, decisions seriously. Our goal is to develop an economic theory of 'image building'. Our starting point is the observation that in a wide range of situations, from social gatherings to job interviews, the outcomes of personal interactions depend heavily on the appropriate matching of hard-to-observe individual characteristics. The novel twist is to apply signalling notions to explore how 'images' projected by choices of 'costumes' may help to solve these matching problems.

Several generic problems exist with any type of signalling (cf. Spence, 1974; Frank, 1988). One problem is that establishing a signalling equilibrium may involve complex coordination problems of its own. There is thus an issue of derivation; the process by which signals originate demands investigation. One central thrust of this paper is the argument that image advertising serves to solve this coordination problem.

A second problem is that hand in hand with mutually beneficial signalling can come opportunities for dissembling (i.e. fraud) which can lead a signalling equilibrium to unravel. In this paper we assume an environment in which there is no motive for fraud. Thus, while we recognize that issues of fraud are important in many circumstances (see for example Carr and Landa, 1983), these circumstances do not arise in our model.

An implication of our analysis is that when costumes serve as signals, consumers' choices of costumes are interdependent. The idea that consumption choices are sometimes interdependent is familiar. However, interdependence has typically been considered in a context of directly interdependent utility functions – the consumption bundle of one consumer enters the utility function of another, for example. The cases of altruism and conformity are examples (Wintrobe, 1983; Jones, 1984). In the absence of directly interdependent utility functions, standard models of consumer choice and advertising assume that behaviour is purely private. Consider for instance standard paradigms of advertising. At least three functions are identified: to directly inform consumers about product attributes (cf. Nelson, 1974); to serve an indirect informational function, where, for example, by investing in advertising, a firm may convey commitment to a product (Kihlstrom and Riordan, 1984; Klein and Leffler, 1981); and to enhance product attributes through a process of 'affect', for example serving to create pleasurable associations with the consumption of a product (Cafferata and Tybout, 1989).

In all of these cases, the contribution of advertising is private. Failure to reach a potential customer may lose a sale, but it has no impact on sales to others. In our analysis, utility functions are independent, but individuals interact in social situations. Information as to type is valuable in these social interactions, hence individuals attempt to signal their type by their choices of costumes. This, of course, generates interdependent demands for the costumes that are used as signals. We show that through image advertising firms often can and will engineer a signalling equilibrium. Interestingly, an image advertising campaign that does not reach most of the consumers in the relevant market will fail to create an accepted image, and hence will have minimal impact on demand for the advertised good.

In Section 2 we outline a two-stage game of social interaction: in stage 1, each player chooses a costume; subsequently, in stage 2, players meet in random, pairwise encounters in which they use costumes as clues about the underlying characteristics of other players. We close this section with a discussion of the nasty coordination problem that bedevils this game. In Section 3 we show how image advertising can solve this coordination problem. In Section 4 we close with a brief discussion of some of the stylized facts of image advertising in the context of our theory.

In common usage, the terms 'image' and 'image advertising' are slippery concepts, more easily illustrated than defined. In contrast, in our model they are perfectly well defined. Giving these slippery concepts precise meaning is, we believe, one contribution of this paper.

2. The game of dress-up

In this section we explore a two-stage game in which players choose costumes in the first stage, and engage in a series of random, pairwise, anonymous *encounters* in the second stage. Naturally, the costumes bought in the first stage may serve as type signals in the encounters that occur in the second stage. We begin by describing the encounter game. Then we find equilibrium actions for a typical encounter, taking the known frequency distribution of player types over costumes as given.

Building on these results, we step back to the first stage in which players choose costumes to find the equilibria of the entire two-stage game. There are three distinct sorts of equilibrium, and many equilibria of each sort – hence a difficult *coordination problem*. The heart of our paper is Section 3, where we examine the possibility that image advertising is successful because it helps to solve this coordination problem.

2.1. Payoffs for an encounter

For lack of a better term we call the players in an encounter *partners*. Since encounters are anonymous and arise through random matches of two players, in an encounter a player's partner may be any of T possible types. For a player of type i whose partner is a player of type j, there is a unique best action which we call the *appropriate action* and which we denote by A^i_j. For reasons that will become clear, we say that action A^i_j is *inappropriate* if the partner's type is $k \neq j$. The set $A^i = \{A^i_1, A^i_2, \ldots . A^i_T\}$ is called the set of *type-specific actions* for a player of type i.

In addition to these type-specific actions, there is a *neutral* action which we denote by N^i. The neutral action can be thought of as spending resources to directly determine the partner's type as opposed to attempting to infer her type from the costume she wears. In any encounter, the set of actions open to a player of type i is then $\{A^i_1, A^i_2, \ldots, A^i_T, N^i\}$.

Now consider an encounter between players of types i and j, and let a^i and a^j denote the players' respective actions. Player i's payoff is

$$\Pi^i(a^i, a^j) = x_{ij} + v + w \tag{1}$$

where

$v = y$ if a^i is appropriate $(a^i = A^i_j)$
$v = z$ if a^i is neutral $(a^i = N^i)$
$v = 0$ if a^i is inappropriate $(a^i = A^i_k,\ k \neq j)$
$w = g$ if a^j is appropriate $(a^j = A^j_i)$
$w = h$ if a^j is neutral $(a^j = N^j)$
$w = 0$ if a^j is inappropriate $(a^j = A^j_k,\ k \neq i)$.

The first element of player i's payoff, x_{ij}, can be thought of as the *baseline payoff* for a player of type i in an encounter with a player of type j. The second and third elements, v and w, capture the type communication aspects of the game that are the focus of this paper. Notice that player i's action determines v, while player j's action determines w. We assume that $y > z > 0$ and that $g > h > 0$. Then, as regards both her own action and the action of her partner, player i prefers an appropriate action to a neutral action, and a neutral action to an inappropriate action.

In Table 1 we illustrate the row player's payoff in an encounter in which the row player is type 2, the column player is type 3, and $T = 3$. The baseline payoff x_{23} has no behavioural significance since this payoff occurs in each cell of the payoff matrix. In other words, the communication aspects of the game determine payoffs that are incremental to x_{23}. Notice that for each player there are just three payoff-relevant actions since any action is either appropriate, inappropriate or neutral. The largest possible payoff occurs when both players choose the action that is appropriate, given their partner's type. And the lowest possible payoff occurs when both players choose an action that is inappropriate, given their partner's type. If both players choose neutral actions, they are both better off than if they both choose inappropriate actions (since $z + h > 0$), but they are worse off than if they choose appropriate actions (since $z + h < y + g$).

Table 1. Row player's payoffs; row player, type 2; column player, type 3

	$a^3 = A^3_1$ Inappropriate	$a^3 = A^3_2$ Appropriate	$a^3 = A^3_3$ Inappropriate	$a^3 = N^3$ Neutral
$a^2 = A^2_1$ Inappropriate	$x_{23} + 0 + 0$	$x_{23} + 0 + g$	$x_{23} + 0 + 0$	$x_{23} + 0 + h$
$a^2 = A^2_2$ Inappropriate	$x_{23} + 0 + 0$	$x_{23} + 0 + g$	$x_{23} + 0 + 0$	$x_{23} + 0 + h$
$a^2 = A^2_3$ Appropriate	$x_{23} + y + 0$	$x_{23} + y + g$	$x_{23} + y + 0$	$x_{23} + y + h$
$a^2 = N^2$ Neutral	$x_{23} + z + 0$	$x_{23} + z + g$	$x_{23} + z + 0$	$x_{23} + z + h$

It is useful to represent the payoff structure for an encounter more compactly by focusing on payoff-relevant actions, and by suppressing the baseline payoff. Table 2 gives the row player's payoff in terms of the three payoff-relevant actions for an encounter in which the player types are arbitrary. In each cell, the first payoff element is determined by the row player's action and the second by the column player's action.

Table 2. Row player's payoffs in terms of payoff-relevant actions

	Appropriate	Neutral	Inappropriate
Appropriate	$y + g$	$y + h$	$y + 0$
Neutral	$z + g$	$z + h$	$z + 0$
Inappropriate	$0 + g$	$0 + h$	$0 + 0$

2.2. Equilibrium strategies for an encounter

In an encounter both players observe their partner's costume before they choose an action, so it is possible for a player to use the partner's costume as a type signal. We want to know when a player will regard the partner's costume as a type signal. More precisely, we want to know when a player of type i will choose an action from the set A^i of type-specific actions in preference to the neutral action N^i.

Define $P(t, c)$ as the relative frequency (or proportion) of players wearing costume c who are type t, and suppose that all players know this frequency distribution. In choosing an action the player faces the following dilemma. Since encounters are anonymous, the partner's type is not directly observable, but the frequency distribution of costumes over types permits the player to form subjective probabilities regarding the partner's type. If the player chooses an action from the set of type-specific actions, the action may be appropriate or it may be inappropriate. Then, since the player prefers to take an appropriate action as opposed to a neutral action, and a neutral action as opposed to an inappropriate action, the player will choose a type-specific action only if the subjective probability that the chosen type-specific action is appropriate is sufficiently high.

Let $\Omega(c)$ denote the most frequent player type wearing costume c, and $\Phi(c)$ the relative frequency of player type $\Omega(c)$. Clearly,

$$\Phi(c) = P[\Omega(c), c]. \tag{2}$$

Then, if player i's partner is wearing costume c, the best action from the set A^i of type-specific actions is $A^i_{\Omega(c)}$. This action will be appropriate with probability $\Phi(c)$ and it will be inappropriate with probability $1 - \Phi(c)$. (Throughout the paper we assume, strictly for convenience, that players are atomless. The numbers of players of each type are then to be interpreted as real numbers, not as integers.) The other viable strategy for player i is to take action N^i. The expected payoff to action $A^i_{\Omega(c)}$ is no smaller than the expected payoff to action N^i if

$$\Phi(c)(y + u) + [1 - \Phi(c)](0 + u) \geq (z + u) \quad u \in \{g, h, 0\}.$$

Whether u is equal to g, h or 0 is determined by the partner's action: it is g if the partner's action is appropriate, h if it is neutral, and 0 if it is inappropriate. The inequality reduces to

$$\Phi(c) \geq z/y. \tag{3}$$

Hence, in any encounter, player i has a dominant strategy: (i) take action $A^i_{\Omega(c)}$ if $\Phi(c) \geq z/y$; (ii) otherwise take action N^i. Recall that both y and z are positive, and that y (the incremental payoff to player i if player i chooses the appropriate type-specific action) exceeds z (the incremental payoff to player i if player i chooses the neutral action). Hence, $0 < z/y < 1$.

The dominant strategy result is intuitive. Given that the partner wears costume c, if the subjective probability that the partner is of type $\Omega(c)$ is large enough, the player will choose action $A^i_{\Omega(c)}$, but if the subjective probability is too small, the player will choose the neutral action N^i.

2.3. The coordination problem

The fundamental coordination problem in dress-up arises from the fact that all players are better off if, in stage 1, they manage to coordinate their choices of costumes in such a way that each costume is worn only by players of the same type. When they achieve this sort of coordination – *perfect* coordination – costumes serve as perfect type signals, and all players get the maximum possible payoff in all encounters. The trouble is that there are as many ways of achieving perfect coordination as there are ways of assigning player types to costumes, and no director of costuming to prescribe a solution.

To be more precise, it is useful to look at the subgame perfect equilibria of the game in which players simultaneously choose their costumes in stage 1, and then engage in random pairwise encounters in stage 2, knowing the frequency distribution of costumes over types that is generated in stage 1. We assume that there are at least as many costumes as player types.

Corresponding to each possible frequency distribution generated in stage 1, there is a stage 2 subgame. From the above we know the equilibrium strategies for these subgames. Then, to identify the subgame perfect equilibria of the entire two-stage game, we need to identify the frequency distributions such that no player regrets her choice of costume in stage 1, given that players implement the associated equilibrium strategies in all stage 2 subgames.

At the one extreme are all the equilibria in which all players perfectly signal their type. Suppose in stage 1 that player choices of costumes are such that $\Phi(c) = 1$ for all costumes c that are purchased. Then in all stage 2 encounters, both players know with certainty the type of the other player, and choose the appropriate action for their partner's type. Since this generates the highest possible payoff in all encounters for all players, no player regrets her choice of costume in stage 1. There are, obviously, many perfect signalling equilibria.

In a perfect signalling equilibrium the costumes have a signalling value, in addition to any inherent use value (assumed to be identical for all costumes) they might have. Consider a player of type i. Relative to a costume for which $\Omega(c) \neq i$, any costume for which $\Omega(c) = i$ gives the player a payoff in each encounter that is larger by amount g, since the former costume elicits an inappropriate action in all encounters while the latter elicits an appropriate action. Notice too that player i does not capture all the gains that arise when she chooses a costume for which $\Omega(c) = i$ in preference to one for which $\Omega(c) \neq i$, since all the partners she encounters in stage 2 are better off by y.

At the other extreme are all the equilibria that involve no (effective) type signalling. Suppose in stage 1 that $\Phi(c) < z/y$ for all costumes. Then, in all stage 2 encounters both players will choose a neutral action. Further, although each player would have preferred in stage 1 to have chosen a costume that did serve as an accurate type signal, given the choices made by other players in stage 1, there are no such costumes. Hence, no player regrets her choice of costume in stage 1. There are, obviously, many non-signalling equilibria. In all these equilibria, all costumes are equally attractive to all players.

Clearly, mixed equilibria in which some players manage to signal their type and others do not are also possible. Suppose that player choices of costumes in stage 1 are such that, for some costumes, $\Phi(c) = 1$, and for others, $\Phi(c) < z/y$. Then players who chose the first sort of costume will be sending perfect signals regarding their type, and those who chose the second sort will be sending no effective signal. For this situation to constitute an equilibrium we must suppose, in addition, that players who could have chosen a costume in stage 1 that would have perfectly signalled their type in stage 2, did buy such a costume.

Holding the configuration of stage 2 encounters fixed, any perfect signalling equilibrium Pareto dominate any of the mixed equilibrium, and any mixed equilibrium Pareto dominate any of the non-signalling equilibria.

In the game as specified, the coordination problem is overwhelming. Except by chance, the players will not arrive at any equilibrium, let alone a perfect signalling equilibrium. In the next section we see how image advertising might achieve imperfect coordination in a suitably expanded game. In a closely related paper, Eaton and Arifovic (1998) use the genetic algorithm in a framework in which dress-up is played repeatedly to explore the possibility that learning may lead to a perfect signalling equilibrium.

3. Image advertising

In that it involves both senders and receivers, image building is like any other form of communication, and like other forms of communication, successful image building entails the solution to a coordination problem since the accurate projection of images requires both senders and receivers to have a common vocabulary of images. It is this need to establish a common vocabulary that distinguishes image advertising from other forms of advertising.

Fundamentally, an image advertising campaign attempts to associate an image with a product, to write a new entry in the dictionary of images: 'People who display product A are projecting image I.' More succinctly, 'Product A is associated with image I.' Like any other advertising campaign, the image campaign must communicate with potential buyers of the image product. That is, the image campaign must communicate the intended product/image association to *targeted buyers* – a group of people who want to project image I and will therefore buy product A, if they can be convinced that this association is accepted by their *targeted audience*. However, this means that the image campaign must also convince the targeted buyers that the targeted audience has also received and accepted the intended association. At a minimum, this would seem to require that the image advertising campaign actually communicates the intended product/image association to the targeted audience. That is, unlike other advertising campaigns, to be effective the image campaign must communicate with a group that is broader than the group of targeted buyers. As we see it, the need to communicate with both potential buyers and with the audience with whom these buyers want to communicate – that is, the need to establish a common vocabulary of images – is what distinguishes image advertising from other forms of advertising.

This feature of imaging advertising has two immediate implications. First, image advertising will be broadly pitched, to a group that includes both targeted buyers and their targeted audience. Second, given that a successful campaign must convince the targeted buyers that a substantial portion of the targeted audience has also received and accepted the intended product/image association, to be successful an image advertising campaign must also be massive. In other words, quantity demanded is a non-concave function of expenditure on image advertising. To be more precise, and to explore related aspects of image advertising, we extend the game of dress-up to include image advertising. It should be clear, however, that these two features of image advertising are quite general.

3.1. The image advertising model

We need a little more notation. Let $n_i (i = 1, T)$ denote the number of players of type i, $n (= \Sigma n_i)$ the total number of players, $p_i (= n_i/n)$ the proportion of all players who are type i, and M the total number of products. We assume that all players know $n_i (i = 1, T)$ and M. Since players are atomless, we can interpret n_i and n as real numbers. In contrast, M is an integer.

In the context of dress-up, the images to be associated with costumes are player types. We will think of the advertiser as trying to create the association of costume c and player type i by broadcasting the following *message*: 'All players of type i who receive this message will buy costume c, and all players of types other than i who receive this message will not buy costume c.'

Targeted buyers are the n_i players of type i, and the targeted audience is the entire group of n players, since players of type i interact with the whole population.

The technology of advertising is captured by the following function:

$$\Lambda_c^i = f(E_c^i) \tag{4}$$

where E_c^i is the amount spent to communicate the message and Λ_c^i is the proportion of the entire population of players that receives the message. We assume that $f(0) = 0$, and that $f(E_c^i)$ is increasing in its argument for all E_c^i such that $\Lambda_c^i < 1$.

We assume also that the technology of message sending is such that anyone who receives the message can infer Λ_c^i. This important assumption is not entirely unrealistic. Anyone who receives a message broadcast in conjunction with a telecast of the Super Bowl, for example, can be sure that something like 150 million other viewers also got the message. Similarly, elaborate and expensively produced TV ads assure the viewer that the advertiser intends to reach a large audience – the more elaborate and expensive the ad, the larger the intended audience. It is also possible for an individual to make inferences regarding the coverage of a campaign from the number of times the individual is exposed to a particular ad, or series of ads. What is crucial for our story is that people who receive image messages are able to make inferences regarding the number of other people who also received the message. It is, we believe, realistic to suppose that people can and do make such inferences. To facilitate analysis, we assume that these inferences are perfectly accurate, which is, of course, quite unrealistic.

It is convenient to assume that p_i is large relative to $1/M$ for all player types. Image advertising is definitely not attractive in our model unless this restriction is satisfied for at least one player type – to see this, notice that any costume that has managed to establish a universally accepted image of type i is trading a market share of $1/M$ for a market share of p_i. As a matter of convenience, we will assume that the restriction is satisfied for all player types. Specifically, we assume that $p_i > 1/(M - 1)$.

For simplicity we want to ensure that in their stage 2 encounters players respond to costumes that have not been advertised with a neutral action. A sufficient condition is that none of the relative player frequencies in the group of players for which there has been no attempt to establish an image costume be greater than z/y. This will be true if the number of advertised costumes is small and if, for all player types i, p_i is small enough relative to z/y.

Since we want to focus on image advertising, we suppose that the prices of all costumes are identical (and larger than marginal cost of producing a costume). In addition, we assume that each player will buy one costume for reasons that are unrelated to dress-up. A costume then has an *inherent value* to a player, and possibly a *value as a type signal*. The value as a type signal can be positive or negative, depending on whether the image associated with the costume is the player's own type or some other type. For each player, one costume, which we call the *inherently preferred costume*, has an inherent value that is marginally larger than the inherent value of all other costumes. The inherently preferred costumes of all player types are uniformly distributed over the M costumes. However, the margin of preference for the inherently preferred costume is so small that a player will always choose an inherently non-preferred costume that serves as an accurate type signal to an inherently preferred costume that does not, and will choose an inherently non-preferred costume that does not serve as a type signal to an inherently preferred costume that serves as an inaccurate type signal.

3.2. One image advertising campaign

Now let us look at the case in which there is just one image campaign. Specifically, suppose that, just before players buy their costumes in stage 1 of dress-up, the firm that produces costume c spends E_c^i to create an association of costume c with player type i.

The players who do not receive the advertiser's message are easy to model. Since they have no way of coordinating their actions, they will buy their inherently preferred costumes, their purchases will be uniformly distributed over the M available costumes, and they will choose the neutral action in all stage 2 encounters.

As regards the players who receive the advertiser's message, some additional terminology is useful. We will call these players *messaged* players, and we will speak of the messaged players as *accepting or rejecting* the advertiser's intended image in stage 1 of dress-up, and of *validating or failing to validate* the intended image in their stage 2 encounters. When we say that the messaged players *accept* the advertiser's intended image in stage 1, we mean that messaged players of type i buy costume c, that messaged players of types other than i whose inherently preferred costume is c

randomly choose among costumes other than c, and that all other messaged players buy their inherently preferred costume. When we say that the messaged players *reject* the advertiser's intended image in stage 1, we mean that they buy their inherently preferred costumes. When we say that the messaged players *validate* the intended image in their stage 2 encounters, we mean that if their partner in any encounter is wearing costume c they choose the type-specific action that is appropriate for a partner of type i, and when their partner is wearing a costume other than c they respond with a neutral action. When we say that the messaged players *fail to validate* the intended image in stage 2 encounters, we mean that they choose the neutral action in all encounters regardless of the costume worn by their partner.

We want to answer two closely related questions. In stage 1 of dress-up, will the messaged players accept the intended image? In stage 2 encounters, will the messaged players validate the intended image?

Notice first that, in stage 1, a messaged player will accept the intended image if it is anticipated that in stage 2 encounters messaged players will validate the image. To see this, suppose messaged players do anticipate validation. Then, by accepting the image in stage 1, a messaged player of type i elicits an appropriate (as opposed to a neutral) action in all encounters with other messaged players, and messaged players of types other than i elicit a neutral (as opposed to an inappropriate) action in their encounters with other messaged players.

So, to answer these two questions, we will suppose that the image is accepted in stage 1, and ask whether it will be validated in stage 2 encounters. Using the dominant strategy result from Section 2.2, we know that a messaged player's decision to validate the advertiser's intended image depends on the subjective probability that a player wearing costume c is of type i. Only if the subjective probability is large enough ($\geq z/y$) will the messaged player respond to costume c with a type-specific action appropriate for a player of type i. Given the assumptions we have made, we can calculate that probability. That is, supposing that the intended image is accepted in stage 1, we can determine the circumstances in which it will be validated in stage 2.

A messaged player who makes the provisional assumption that the intended image is accepted in stage 1 will reason as follows. Unmessaged players will choose their inherently preferred costumes in stage 1, and their choices will be uniformly distributed over the M available costumes. This is true even if they are sophisticated enough to infer that some firm has an incentive to try to establish an image for its costume. The expected number of unmessaged players is $(1 - \Lambda_c^i)n$. (It is here that we use the assumption that a messaged player can infer Λ_c^i.) The expected number of unmessaged players who buy costume c is $(1 - \Lambda_c^i)n/M$, and the expected number of unmessaged players of type i who buy costume c is $(1 - \Lambda_c^i)n_i/M$. The expected number of messaged players is $\Lambda_c^i n$, and given the provisional assumption that the image is accepted by these players, the expected number of players from this group who buy costume c is $\Lambda_c^i n_i$, and all of these players are type i. Hence, in the group of players wearing costume c, the expected relative frequency of type i players, Φ_c^i, is

$$\Phi_c^i = \frac{(1 - \Lambda_c^i)n_i/M + \Lambda_c^i n_i}{(1 - \Lambda_c^i)n/M + \Lambda_c^i n_i} \tag{5}$$

Naturally, when $\Lambda_c^i = 0$, $\Phi_c^i = n_i/n = p_i$, and when $\Lambda_c^i = 1$, $\Phi_c^i = 1$. Notice also that Φ_c^i is an increasing function of Λ_c^i.

Let $\bar{\Lambda}$ be the value of Λ_c^i such that $\Phi_c^i = z/y$, and implicitly define $\bar{E}$ by $\bar{\Lambda} = f(\bar{E})$. By assumption $p_i < z/y$, so $\bar{\Lambda} > 0$ and $\bar{E} > 0$. Hence, $\Phi_c^i \geq z/y$ only if $\Lambda_c^i \geq \bar{\Lambda} > 0$ (or $E_c^i \geq \bar{E} > 0$). So, if $\Lambda_c^i < \bar{\Lambda}$ (or $E_c^i < \bar{E}$), then $\Phi_c^i < z/y$, and messaged players will not validate the intended image in stage 2 encounters, even if the image is accepted by messaged players in stage 1. Yet there is then no reason for messaged players to accept the image in stage 1. We conclude that messaged players will reject the advertiser's intended image in stage 1 if $\Lambda_c^i < \bar{\Lambda}$ (or $E_c^i < \bar{E}$). In other words, there is threshold level for image advertising below which it has no effect on anyone's choice of costume.

Conversely, if $\Lambda_c^i \geq \bar{\Lambda}$ then $\Phi_c^i \geq z/y$, and messaged players will validate the intended image in stage 2 encounters, assuming that the image is accepted in stage 1. In this case there is good reason for messaged players to accept the intended image in stage 1: by accepting the image, messaged players of type i elicit an appropriate (as opposed to a neutral) response in their encounters with other messaged players and messaged players of types other than i elicit a neutral (as opposed to an inappropriate) action in their encounters with other messaged players. We conclude that messaged players will accept the advertiser's intended image if $\Lambda_c^i \geq \bar{\Lambda}$.

It is useful to express these results in terms of the self-confirming beliefs of messaged players that are implicit in what we have said. We will look first at the case in which image advertising is effective ($\Lambda_c^i \geq \bar{\Lambda}$). We propose the following self-confirming beliefs.

(B.1) When $\Lambda_c^i \geq \bar{\Lambda}$, all messaged players believe (i) that all other messaged players will accept the advertiser's intended image in stage 1 and (ii) that all other messaged players will validate the intended image in their stage 2 encounters.

Beliefs (B.1) lead the individual messaged player to adopt the following strategy: accept the proposed image in stage 1, and validate it in stage 2. In other words, these beliefs are self-confirming. It may be useful to articulate this crucial point more carefully. Given beliefs (B.1), the individual messaged player believes that all other messaged players of type i will buy costume c and that all other messaged players of types other than i will buy a costume other than c. These beliefs lead to a subjective probability $\Phi_c^i \geq z/y$ since $\Lambda_c^i \geq \bar{\Lambda}$. Hence these beliefs lead the individual messaged player to validate the intended image in stage 2 encounters – that is, to respond to costume c with an action appropriate for a player of type i and to other costumes with a neutral action – thus confirming part (ii) of (B.1).

Now consider the decision to buy a costume in stage 1. Consider first a messaged player of type i. She will anticipate an appropriate response in all encounters with other messaged players if she buys costume c and a neutral response if she buys any other costume. Since an appropriate response is preferred to a neutral, and since the choice of costume has no effect on the actions of unmessaged partners, beliefs (B.1) lead a messaged player of type i to buy costume c. Now consider a messaged player of type other than i. She will anticipate an inappropriate response in all encounters with other messaged players if she buys costume c and a neutral response if she buys any other costume. Since a neutral response is preferred to an inappropriate response, and since the choice of costume has no effect on the actions of unmessaged partners, beliefs (B.1) lead a messaged player of type other than i to buy a costume other than c. Thus part (i) of (B.1) is also confirmed.

The following beliefs are also self-confirming when $\Lambda_c^i \geq \bar{\Lambda}$.

(B.1)′ When $\Lambda_c^i \geq \bar{\Lambda}$, all messaged players believe (i) that other messaged players will reject the advertiser's intended image in stage 1 and (ii) that all other messaged players will fail to validate the intended image in their stage 2 encounters.

Clearly, all messaged players are worse off in the equilibrium associated with (B.1)′ than they are in the equilibrium associated with (B.1). Hence, beliefs (B.1) would seem to be salient.

Now let us look at the case in which $\Lambda_c^i < \bar{\Lambda}$. We propose the following self-confirming beliefs.

(B.2) When $\Lambda_c^i < \bar{\Lambda}$, all messaged players believe (i) that other messaged players will reject the advertiser's intended image in stage 1 and (ii) that all other messaged players will fail to validate the intended image in their stage 2 encounters.

We leave it to the reader to show that these beliefs are self-confirming. Given beliefs (B.2), image advertising is completely ineffective.

Given our proposed beliefs, (B.1) and (B.2), quantity demanded of costume c, $Q_c(E_c^i)$, is

$$\begin{aligned} Q_c(E_c^i) &= n/M \quad \text{if } E_c^i < \bar{E} \\ & f(E_c^i)n_i + [1 - f(E_c^i)]\,(n/M) \quad \text{if } E_c^i \geq \bar{E} \end{aligned} \tag{6}$$

Two features of this demand function are noteworthy. First is the non-concavity in quantity demanded as a function of expenditure on image advertising at $E_c^i = \bar{E}$. When $E_c^i = \bar{E}, f(E_c^i)n_i + [1 - f(E_c^i)]\,(n/M) > n/M$ when $p_i > 1/M$. Of course, if $p_i < 1/M$, image advertising is pointless since, if effective, it leads to a decrease in demand. It is for this reason that we assumed above that $p_i > 1/M$. Second, the larger p_i is, relative to 1/ M, the more attractive image advertising is since the probability that the firm sells its costume to an unmessaged player is $1/M$ and (given that $E_c^i \geq \bar{E}$) the probability it sells to a messaged player is p_i. Hence, other things being equal, if there is to be just one image costume, the image will be the most frequent player type.

3.3. The same image for two costumes

Now let's look at the possibility that two costumes establish the same image. We suppose that the firms producing costumes c and d have spent amounts E_c^i and E_d^i to establish an association between their product and player type i. The probability that any player receives message d (respectively c) is then $\Lambda_d^i = f(E_d^i)$ [respectively $\Lambda_c^i = f(E_c^i)$]. We want to partition the $(\Lambda_c^i, \Lambda_d^i)$ space into four regions: messaged players accept both images; messaged players accept neither image; messaged players accept image c but not image d; and messaged players accept image d but not image c. As above, an image will be accepted by messaged players only if they anticipate that the images will be validated in subsequent encounters.

First we must be more specific as regards the technology of advertising. We assume that the technology is *perfectly ordered.* A technology is perfectly ordered if the following conditions are satisfied: (i) when $E^i_c = E^i_d$, both messages are received by the same group of players; (ii) when $E^i_c < E^i_d$, all players who receive message *c* also receive message *d*. To get some feeling for the circumstances in which the assumption would be true, suppose that television is the medium for image messages, and that different players watch different numbers of programmes. The advertising technology will be perfectly ordered if the rank orderings of the available programmes for all players are identical. In this circumstance, if player *u* watches more programmes than player *v*, player *u* will receive all the messages received by player *v*.

The other salient assumption is that the technology of advertising is *random and independent*. A technology is random and independent if the probability that any player receives any message is dependent only on the amount spent to communicate the message, *E*. [The probability itself is $f(E)$.] Assume again that television is the image medium, and that different players watch different numbers of television programmes. If, from the set of available programmes, all players randomly choose without replacement the programmes they watch, the technology will be random and independent. It is not at all clear which of these extreme assumptions regarding the technology of messages is more realistic. We choose to work with a perfectly ordered technology because it is more tractable.

Figure 1 illustrates the proposed partition of the $(\Lambda^i_c, \Lambda^i_d)$ space. $\bar{\Lambda}$ and Λ' are implicitly defined by the following equations:

$$\frac{(1-\bar{\Lambda})N_i/M + \bar{\Lambda}N_i}{(1-\bar{\Lambda})N/M + \bar{\Lambda}N_i} = \frac{z}{y} \tag{7.1}$$

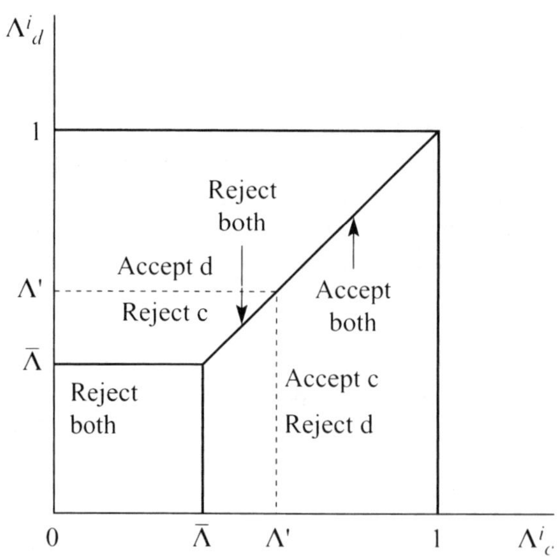

Figure 1

$$\frac{(1-\Lambda')N_i/M + \Lambda'(N_i/2)}{(1-\Lambda')N/M + \Lambda'(N_i/2)} = \frac{z}{y} \tag{7.2}$$

From equation (5) we see that $\bar{\Lambda}$ is the smallest value of Λ^i_c such that the image for costume *c* would be validated, if messaged players accepted the image for costume *c* and rejected the image for costume *d*. Alternatively, $\bar{\Lambda}$ is the smallest value of Λ^i_d, such that the image for costume *d* would be validated, if messaged players accepted the image for costume *d* and rejected the image for costume *c*.

If both Λ^i_c and Λ^i_d are less than $\bar{\Lambda}$, following results established in Section 3.1, it is natural to propose that neither image will be accepted. The supporting, self-confusing, beliefs are:

(B.3) When $\Lambda^i_c < \bar{\Lambda}$ and $\Lambda^i_d < \bar{\Lambda}$, all messaged players believe (i) that all other messaged players will reject the image messages they receive in stage 1 and (ii) that all other messaged players will fail to validate the intended images in their stage 2 encounters.

If $\Lambda^i_c > \max(\bar{\Lambda}, \Lambda^i_d)$, we propose that the intended image for costume *c* will be accepted and the intended image for costume *d* rejected. Given a perfectly ordered technology, all messaged players will receive message *c*. Further, since the technology is known to be perfectly ordered, messaged players can infer that the image message for costume *c* has deeper market penetration than the image message for any other good, regardless of whether they receive the other message or not. Hence, all messaged players of type *i* will buy costume *c* in preference to costume *d*; knowing this, all messaged players will accept the intended image for costume *c* and reject the intended image for costume *d*. The supporting beliefs are:

(B.4) When $\Lambda^i_c > \max(\bar{\Lambda}, \Lambda^i_d)$, all messaged players believe (i) that all other messaged players will accept the intended image for costume *c* and reject the intended image for costume *d* (if they also receive this message) in stage 1 and (ii) that all other messaged players will validate the intended image for costume *c* in their stage 2 encounters and will fail to validate the intended image for costume *d*.

The case in the upper/left portion of Figure 1, in which $\Lambda^i_d > \max(\bar{\Lambda}, \Lambda^i_c)$, is, of course, symmetric, so we propose that in this portion of the figure the image for costume *d* will be accepted and the image for costume *c* rejected.

Λ', implicitly defined by equation (7.2), is the smallest common value of $\Lambda^i_c = \Lambda^i_d$ such that if messaged players of type *i* chose costume *c* or costume *d* with probability 1/2, and other messaged players bought neither costume, the intended images of both costumes would be validated in subsequent encounters. Clearly, $\Lambda' > \bar{\Lambda}$. When $\Lambda^i_c = \Lambda^i_d \geq \Lambda'$ we propose that both images will be accepted. The equilibrium in which all messaged players accept one of the images and reject the other gives messaged players a larger expected payoff, but there is no way they can coordinate their choices. Hence, the equilibrium in which both images are accepted, which for messaged players Pareto dominates the equilibrium in which both images are rejected, seems salient. The supporting beliefs are easily constructed.

The only remaining case is the one in which $\bar{\Lambda} \leq \Lambda^i_c = \Lambda^i_d < \Lambda'$. In this case if both images were accepted in stage 1 they would not be validated in stage 2, so 'accept both images' is not an equilibrium. 'Accept one image but not the other' is an equilibrium, but there is no way for messaged players to coordinate their choices. We therefore propose the equilibrium in which neither image is accepted. Here too the supporting beliefs are easily constructed.

To explore the associated demand functions, let $\bar{E} = f(\bar{\Lambda})$ and $E' = f(\Lambda')$. We will focus on the demand for costume c. If $E_d^i < \bar{\Lambda}$, demand for costume c is given by equation (6) above. Assume then that $E_d^i \geq \bar{\Lambda}$. One important thing to notice is that there is then a non-concavity in $Q_c(E_c^i, E_d^i)$ at $E_c^i = E_d^i$. Regardless of the magnitude of E_c^i, costume c will get fraction $1/M$ of the custom of unmessaged players, so focus on the choices of messaged players. For $E_c^i < E_d^i$, costume c will get fraction $1/(M-1)$ of the custom of messaged players of types other than i, and for $E_c^i > E_d^i$, costume c will get all the custom of all messaged players of type i. Given the assumption that $p_i > 1(M-1)$, we see that demand for good c increases discretely as E_c^i passes through E_d^i: in other words, the limit of $Q_c(E_c^i, E_d^i)$ as E_c^i approaches E_d^i from above exceeds the limit of $Q_c(E_c^i, E_d^i)$ as E_c^i approaches E_d^i from below. What happens when $E_c^i = E_d^i$ depends on the value of E_d^i relative to Λ'. If it is less than Λ', neither image will be accepted and costume c will get the custom of fraction $1/M$ of all messaged players; if it is larger than Λ', costume c will get the custom of 1/2 of the messaged players of type i. In either case, the limit of $Q_c(E_c^i, E_d^i)$ as E_c^i approaches E_d^i from above exceeds $Q_c(E_c^i, E_d^i)$, evaluated at $E_c^i = E_d^i$. Another important thing to notice is that a little bit of image advertising does nothing. That is, $Q_c(E_c^i, E_d^i)$ is independent of E_c^i when $E_c^i < E_d^i$.

Let us turn briefly to the game in which competing firms choose the amount to spend on image advertising, assuming still that their costume prices are parametric and identical. An immediate implication of the non-concavity in the demand functions is that there is only one possible equilibrium in which two firms establish the same image for their goods – both firms must saturate the target market. There is absolutely no point in spending less than one's competitor on image advertising since it can have no effect on demand, and it cannot be an equilibrium to spend the same amount as one's competitor since an infinitesimal increase in expenditure will discretely increase demand. Unless, of course, $\Lambda_c^i = \Lambda_d^i = 1$; that is, unless both firms have saturated the target group.

The analysis of this section generalizes immediately to the case in which more than two firms try to establish the same image for their costumes. In particular, there is a non-concavity in own quantity demanded as a function of own amount spent on image advertising at the point where own amount is equal to the largest amount spent by one's competitors; own quantity demanded is independent of own amount spent when a firm spends less than the largest amount spent by its competitors; in the game where firms non-cooperatively choose expenditures on image advertising, the only possible equilibrium is the one in which all firms saturate the target group.

4. Discussion

As we see it, the following are the important features of our theory of image advertising. First, the target group for an image campaign is necessarily larger than the group of intended buyers of the good, for the target group includes as well the target audience of the intended buyers – the group of people with whom the buyers want to communicate through their purchase and use of the image good. Second, to be effective, an image campaign must convince some of the intended buyers that a substantial portion of their target audience have received and understood the good's intended image; hence, a little bit of image advertising is bound to be ineffective. Successful image campaigns are massive. Third, if two or more goods attempt to establish the same image, the advertising campaigns will achieve virtual saturation of the target group.

Consistent with all three features, image advertising campaigns are frequently associated with very wide coverage. Moreover, discussions with media practitioners suggest that firms are willing to pay a premium to ensure that image ads are coordinated and reach large groups of consumers simultaneously. Thus, they may be willing to pay high up-front rates for advance purchase of TV, air time, or print media to ensure that slots for image ads are locked in, even though rates for spot advertising based on current availability are significantly lower.

Saturation aspects of image advertising are also evident in the projection of images far beyond immediate purchasers of a good. One well-publicized example is the recent controversial 'Old Joe' campaign for Camel cigarettes launched in 1988, which critics claim was aimed at youths (Pierce *et al.*, 1991). In 1990 about 26% of the US population over 18 smoked. Reported use of cigarettes by youths aged 12–18 was about 12% (National Center for Health Statistics, 1992). Among smokers, Camel's market share has historically been modest, although growing recently (under 5% of smoking adults in 1986; 8.1% of teenage smokers in a 1989 survey; Centers for Disease Control, 1990, 1992). Nevertheless, a 1991 survey of high school students in selected states indicated that over 97% had seen 'Old Joe' and 93% knew the Camel brand. The analogous figures for adults were 72 and 57% (DiFranza *et al.*, 1991). Thus, although a minority of the population smoked at all and only a tiny fraction of the population smoked Camels, the 'Old Joe' campaign reached virtually all of the youths surveyed and a majority of adults. In this regard, the image campaigns associated with the introduction of the Lexus and Infinity automobiles are instructive. Both cars are intended for buyers with annual incomes in excess of $100,000, yet both campaigns were massive and broad-based. The North American advertising budget for each of the cars in the year in which it was launched was more than $125,000,000. To put this in perspective, the total North American advertising budget for The Honda Corporation in a typical year is only $125,000,000. TV ads for both cars were also broadcast in connection with a number of popular programmes, watched by a wide variety of viewers.

References

Cafferata, P. and A.M. Tybout (eds) (1989), *Cognitive and Affective Responses to Advertising*, D.C. Heath, Lexington, Massachusetts.

Carr, J.L. and J.T. Landa (1983), 'The Economics of Symbols, Clan Names, and Religion', *Journal of Legal Studies*, **22**, pp. 135–54.

Centers for Disease Control (1990), 'Cigarette Brand Use Among Adult Smokers – United States', *Morbidity and Mortality Weekly Report*, **76**, pp. 665–7.

Centers for Disease Control (1992), 'Comparison of the Cigarette Brand Preferences of Adult and Teenaged Smokers – United States, 1989, and 10 U.S. Communities, 1988 and 1990', *Morbidity and Mortality Weekly Report*, **41**, pp. 169–73.

DiFranza, J.R. *et al.* (1991), 'RJR Nabisco's Cartoon Camel Promotes Camel Cigarettes to Children', *Journal of the American Medical Association*, **266**, pp. 3149–53.

Eaton, B.C. and J. Arifovic (1998), 'The Evolution of Communication in a Sender/Receiver Game of Common Interest with Cheap Talk', *Journal of Economic Dynamics and Control*, **22**, August, pp. 1187–208.

Frank, R.H. (1988), *Passions Within Reason*, W.W. Norton, New York.
Jones, S.R.G. (1984), *The Economics of Conformism*, Basil Blackwell, Oxford.
Kihlstrom, R.E. and M.H. Riordan (1984), 'Advertising as a Signal', *Journal of Political Economy*, **92**, pp.427–50.
Klein, B. and K. Leffler (1981), 'The Role of Market Forces in Assuring Contractual Performance', *Journal of Political Economy*, **94**, pp. 615–41.
National Center for Health Statistics (1992), 'Health United States 1991', US Public Health Service.
Nelson, P. (1974), 'Advertising as Information', *Journal of Political Economy*, **82**, pp. 729–54.
Pierce, J.P. *et al.* (1991), 'Does Tobacco Advertising Target Young People to Start Smoking?', *Journal of the American Medical Association*, **266**, pp. 3154–8.
Spence, M.A. (1974), *Market Signaling: Informational Transfer in Hiring and Related Screening Processes*, Harvard University Press, Cambridge, Massachusetts.
Wintrobe, R. (1983), 'Taxing Altruism', *Economic Inquiry*, **21**, pp. 255–70.

RAND Journal of Economics
Vol. 28, No. 1, Spring 1997
pp. 135–149

Technology-trading coalitions in supergames

B. Curtis Eaton*

and

Mukesh Eswaran**

We attempt to explain the observation that rival firms often share their technologies. We show that the trading of technical information over the long haul can be sustained as an equilibrium in supergames. The strategy of ejection of a cheating firm from a technology-trading coalition, followed by the continuation of technology trading by the noncheating members, better facilitates trading than does a strategy in which cheating results in the dissolution of the coalition. Technology trading is often welfare improving, and firms may form small coalitions.

1. Introduction

■ Economists have usually characterized the search for technical knowledge by firms in decentralized economies as a competitive patent race in which the winner takes all. In this view, rival firms are deliberately excluded from access to the fruits of other firms' R&D activities, though these are essentially nonrivalrous in nature; any spillovers to other firms are unintended. This view is at odds with the stylized facts of many industries: firms within an industry are often observed to share their technological information with their rivals (von Hippel, 1988; Carter, 1989). This article attempts to make sense of this observation and builds on the contributions of von Hippel and Baumol (1993). We show that rival firms have an incentive to form technology-trading coalitions, and the stability of these coalitions is ensured over time by the fact that the trading relationships can potentially be ongoing ones. We propose that this phenomenon is best understood in terms of a supergame equilibrium that is different from the one traditionally used by practitioners.

The sharing of technological information by rivals seems to be a pervasive, if paradoxical, phenomenon. The existing empirical evidence on this phenomenon is reviewed in Baumol (1993). In his empirical study of the U.S. steel minimill industry, von Hippel (1988) found that rival firms routinely exchanged technical information. This often went so far as firms having their engineers set up plants for rival firms. Allen (1983), in his study of the evolution of the blast furnace between 1850 and 1875 in England, finds a similar phenomenon—which he dubs "collective invention." The

* Simon Fraser University; eaton@sfu.ca.

** University of British Columbia; eswaran@econ.ubc.ca.

We are indebted to Roger Ware and an anonymous referee for useful suggestions on an earlier version of this article. We alone are responsible for any remaining shortcomings.

considerable increase in fuel efficiency brought about by the increase in the height of the furnace and the temperature of operation was essentially made possible because firms passed on their technological information to rivals.

To understand the phenomenon of technology trading, it is natural to consider a framework in which the trading firms confront each other in a supergame. It is well known that adding a time dimension to static games facilitates the sustenance of equilibria that, in each stage game, yield outcomes that Pareto dominate those that obtain as equilibria in the stage games. In repeated games, the players have the latitude of conditioning their strategies on the past behavior of all players. Typically, this is implemented by means of trigger strategies: deviation by a player from the tacitly agreed-upon strategy triggers a switch to a punishment phase in which cooperation is abandoned by all players for a period of time (Friedman, 1971; Abreu, 1986).

The profitability of the equilibria sustained by trigger strategies depends directly on the severity of the punishment that can be inflicted on cheaters. More severe punishments are more efficacious in supporting equilibria. But more severe punishments are costlier to inflict, since in doing so the noncheaters have to forgo greater profits. Therefore, severe punishments may not be plausible. Thus there is usually a tension between what may be defined as the efficacy of the punishment strategies and their plausibility. An interesting feature of the phenomenon of technology trading is that no such tension exists: the most efficacious strategy for noncheaters to follow in the event of cheating is also the most plausible. That is, the trigger strategy that minimizes the incentive to cheat also maximizes the profit of the noncheaters subsequent to defection. In this observation, we are preceded by the illuminating, if informal, analysis of Baumol (1993).

In this article the firms of an industry form coalitions within which each firm freely trades its private technological information in exchange for technological information of others in the same coalition. The information given by each firm lowers the marginal production costs of others. Cheating occurs in this model when, for bonafide information received from other coalition members, a member offers vacuous information in exchange. The cheater gains in that period by having a lower marginal production cost than all other coalition members. In subsequent periods, the cheater is ejected from the coalition and is not accepted in any other coalition. The noncheating members of the original coalition continue trading technological information among themselves. We first consider the problem of technology sharing between firms within a coalition when, after the technological information for each period has been traded, firms collusively set prices. In this version of the model, the strategy of continued cooperation among noncheaters in the event of cheating does not impinge on the incentives to cheat. However, trigger strategies that eject a cheater from the technology-trading coalition, while maintaining cooperation among the noncheaters, are shown to generate more plausible subgame-perfect equilibria than those that obtain when the entire coalition is dissolved in the event of cheating.

We then consider a model in which firms, after engaging in technology sharing in each period, set quantities instead of prices. As in the above model, we show that trigger strategies that permanently eject a cheater from the technology-trading coalition, while maintaining technology trading among the noncheating members, can form a subgame-perfect equilibrium. More interestingly, such strategies generate equilibria that can sustain collusion at higher discount rates than is possible when the coalition is dissolved in the event of cheating. This arises from the fact that in the event of cheating, continued cooperation by the noncheating members imposes a greater cost on the cheater in the postdeviation phase than when technology trading is completely abandoned. Apart from inflicting greater costs on the cheater in the punishment phase, continued technology sharing by the noncheaters is also in their own self-interest, a point that

Baumol (1993) has made in his discussion of technology sharing. Further, we show with a simple numerical example that it is not necessarily the case that all the firms in the industry would want to form a single coalition; the industry may fragment itself into two or more stable, technology-sharing coalitions.

In a different context, Gallini (1984) has demonstrated that it may be in the interests of a firm to share its technology with a rival firm. The motivation there was to deter a rival from doing R&D that might later prove damaging to the former. The scenario considered there was one in which the sharing of technology is a one-shot possibility. In the scenario we consider here, firms trade technologies repeatedly over time. As a result, the motivation driving the sharing of technologies is quite different.

Although this article specifically addresses the phenomenon of technology trading, our approach is more generally applicable. Indeed, any nonrivalrous input that is relevant to firms in an industry generates a similar problem. The incentives of oligopolists to share private information about demand and/or cost parameters have been examined in a series of articles, including Fried (1984), Gal-Or (1985, 1986), Novshek and Sonnenschein (1982), Okuno-Fujiwara, Postlewaite, and Suzumura (1990), Shapiro (1986), and Vives (1984). In our model, if one firm shares its technology with another, the receiving firm's costs are reduced, while in the information-sharing literature just referred to, if one firm shares its private information with another, the receiving firm's perception of the competitive environment is sharpened. The basic problems are similar in that they involve the exchange of nonrivalrous information. The way the problems are addressed, however, is quite different. We address technology sharing in the context of a supergame, while the information-sharing problem is modelled as a one-shot game (with multiple stages). Given the similarity of the basic problems, a potentially interesting avenue for future research is to model this sort of information sharing as a supergame.

2. The model

■ Consider an industry comprising n firms. We assume that the demand curve facing the industry is given by $D(p)$, with $D'(p) < 0$, where p is the lowest price prevailing in the market. The inverse demand curve for the good is written as $P(Q)$, with $P'(Q) < 0$, where Q is the aggregate output.

In each period a firm, at no cost to itself, receives a production technology from nature. The technological information received by different firms is different but is such that the production costs of all the firms are identical if each firm keeps its information private. By sharing information, firms can reduce their costs of production; the larger the number of firms sharing their finds, the lower the marginal production cost of each firm that has access to the pooled information.

The firms confront each other in an infinite number of periods. In every period, each firm receives new technological information, and the knowledge acquired in previous periods is worthless. This rather stark characterization is expedient for our purposes, since it ensures that the one-period payoffs are stationary. Let C_1 denote the marginal cost of production, assumed independent of output, of a single firm that uses only the technological information that nature has revealed to it. Let $C(k)$ denote the (constant) marginal cost of each member of a k-firm coalition, with $C(1) = C_1$. We shall take it that $C(k) > 0$ for all coalition sizes and that $C'(k) < 0$.

Within a coalition, firms exchange information simultaneously in each period. This implies that, in any period, a firm in one such coalition could obtain access to the information of the other coalition members but give out vacuous information in exchange. This firm, by reneging on the coalition's implicit agreement to share information, will have a lower marginal cost than the other members in that period. It is assumed here that in the event of cheating by one of the coalition members, the cheating firm is ejected from the coalition from the next period on, and that the remaining members continue sharing information among themselves in subsequent periods. Information about the cheater is made public by the noncheaters in the coalition. It is assumed that no other coalition accepts a firm that has revealed itself to be a cheater; that is, the ejected firm operates outside all coalitions forever.[1]

The above idea may be formalized as follows. Consider a coalition that initially in period 0 starts out as coalition Z^0, and that evolves over time as Z^t, $t = 0, 1, 2 \ldots,$ as firms possibly cheat and get ejected from the coalition. Denote by s^t_{ij} the decision of firm i of the coalition with regard to sharing its technology with firm j of the same coalition in period t: s^t_{ij} is equal to one if firm i shares its technology with firm j in period t, and zero if it does not. The coalition Z^t comprises the members of the original coalition that have never cheated through period $t - 1$:

$$Z^t = \{i \in Z^0 \,|\, s^{t-1}_{ij} = 1 \ \forall\, j \in Z^{t-1}\},\ t = 1, 2 \ldots. \tag{1}$$

The kind of technology-sharing strategy s^t_{ij} that is being envisaged here for an arbitrary firm i in the industry in period t is

$$s^t_{ij} = \begin{cases} 1 & \text{if } i \in Z^t \text{ and } j \in Z^t \\ 0 & \text{otherwise.} \end{cases} \tag{2}$$

The above characterization says, in effect, that (i) Firm i shares its technology with the coalition members in period t only if it has itself never cheated in the past. (ii) If firm i has never cheated, in period t it will share its information with other firms of the initial coalition that have never cheated in the past.

To keep the analysis simple, we assume that the industry organizes itself into at most two nontrivial coalitions, denoted by K and M, that are mutually exclusive. Members of these coalitions trade technologies among themselves. There is a (possibly empty) set, denoted by S, comprising firms that operate by themselves ("independents"). That is, members of S are outsiders that do not trade technologies among themselves or with members of the two coalitions.

In what follows, the sizes of the coalitions defined above will be endogenously determined. One question to be addressed is whether the entire industry would necessarily end up within a single information-trading coalition. In particular, we wish to determine if there are forces that would prevent global information sharing, while encouraging sharing to some partial extent. This is considered below first in the context of price-setting firms and then in the context of quantity-setting ones.

□ **The Bertrand case.** With a homogeneous product and price-setting firms with constant marginal cost, coalitions that trade technologies but do not also attempt to fix prices are uninteresting, since price competition eliminates all profits. We thus assume that the members of a coalition set prices collusively after sharing their technological information, but they entertain Bertrand conjectures with respect to the collusive price set by the rival coalition. Assume that the number of members in K, M, and S is k, m, and s, respectively, with $k + m + s = n$. The marginal costs of members of K, M, and S are $C(k)$, $C(m)$, and $C(1)$, respectively. We take it that $k > m$, so that members of

[1] We assume here that the trading of technological information between coalition members is the only tacit agreement in place. Tacit agreements along other dimensions (such as price) can be accommodated in a straightforward manner.

coalition K have lower marginal cost than those of M.[2] If price collusion could be sustained in coalition K, the optimal price, $p^*(k, m)$, for this coalition is given by

$$p^*(k, m) = \min\{\hat{p}(k), C(m)\}, \tag{3}$$

where $\hat{p}(k)$ is the unconstrained monopoly price that could be set by coalition K; that is,

$$\hat{p}(k) = \underset{p}{\operatorname{argmax}}\, D(p)(p - C(k)). \tag{4}$$

Consider the optimal defection strategy of a firm in coalition K. A firm here has the option of cheating with respect to the sharing of technology and also of cheating by shaving its price below the tacitly agreed level. Prices are assumed to be set after technological information is revealed. Therefore, cheating in any period with regard to the sharing of information is revealed before firms set their prices. It is reasonable, then, to assume that in a defection period the noncheating members play Nash in prices even with respect to their own coalition members. This inflicts the maximal punishment on the cheater. This is also in the spirit of making the best of a bad situation. Given that a member has cheated with respect to technology sharing and expects to be ejected from the coalition from the next period on, the cheater can rationally be expected to play its one-period Nash strategy in price. The best response of the noncheating coalition members to this is also to play Nash in prices in the defection period—for, in any case, they will make zero profits in this period. In subsequent periods, the cheater is ejected from the coalition, as described above, and the noncheating members continue sharing technology and setting prices collusively.

This formulation is slightly more involved than the one we sketched out earlier to describe the evolution of coalitions. However, the principle is the same. There we had assumed that technology sharing was the only purpose of a coalition. Here we are assuming that coalitions also collusively set prices after the trading of technology.

If a member of coalition K witholds its technological information from other members of the coalition in any period, the price that will prevail in this defection period is $C(k - 1)$, since this is the marginal cost of all the noncheating members. In this case, the defector's profit in the defection period will be given by[3]

$$D[C(k - 1)][C(k - 1) - C(k)].$$

Alternatively, a firm contemplating cheating could share its technology, even in the defection period, but cheat by shaving the price. This would avoid the dissipative price competition with the noncheating coalition members in the defection period. In this case, the defection profit of a cheating firm in the defection period is given by

$$D[p^*(k, m)][p^*(k, m) - C(k)].$$

From the definition of $p^*(k, m)$ in (3) it follows that the latter defection strategy is at least as profitable to the cheating firm.

A firm that belongs to a technology-sharing coalition will opt not to cheat if its present-value profit from not defecting is at least as large as its present-value profit

[2] Coalition structures with $k = m$ are uninteresting, since Bertrand competition between the coalitions drives profits to zero.

[3] This presumes that it is optimal for the defector to limit price, that is, that the unconstrained monopoly price of the defector exceeds $C(k - 1)$.

from cheating. Thus, if $\delta(0 \leq \delta < 1)$ denotes the common discount factor for all firms, the incentive-compatibility constraint, ICC_k, that must be satisfied if the members of coalition K are not to cheat, is given by

$$\frac{1}{1-\delta}\frac{1}{k}D[p^*(k, m)][p^*(k, m) - C(k)] \geq D[p^*(k, m)][p^*(k, m) - C(k)], \quad (5)$$

which is satisfied if and only if

$$\delta \geq \delta_c(k) \equiv 1 - \frac{1}{k}. \quad (6)$$

Inequality (6) is also the necessary and sufficient condition for price collusion to be sustained by Nash-reversion trigger strategies between k identical firms with constant marginal cost. Under Bertrand behavior with respect to outsiders, ejection from the technology-sharing coalition automatically reduces the cheater's future profits to zero. Thus, continuation of technology sharing by the noncheating coalition members imposes no greater punishment on the cheater here than does a complete breakup of the coalition. Nevertheless, it is in the self-interest of the noncheating members to continue sharing their technological information.[4]

Since $\delta_c(k)$ is increasing in k, it follows that if ICC_k is satisfied, then so is ICC_j for $j < k$. Thus we have the following proposition.

Proposition 1. If $\delta \geq \delta_c(k)$, the trigger strategies entailing ejection of cheaters from a coalition, with continuation of technology sharing and price collusion among the noncheating members of coalition K, sustain technology sharing as a subgame-perfect Nash equilibrium. Compared to the strategy of Nash reversion in both technology sharing and price setting in the event of cheating, the above trigger strategy (i) is just as efficacious, and (ii) supports a more plausible equilibrium, since it offers higher profits to noncheaters.

From the above proposition it follows that if $k > m$ and $\delta \geq \delta_c(k)$, coalition K is stable with respect to an attenuation of the coalition size. We now turn to the question of whether the coalition is also stable against the possibility of an increase in size. It is possible that for a coalition K (which is larger than coalition M) the incentive-compatibility condition stated above is satisfied, but yet that the addition of another coalition member may make each member better off. (The outsider that joins will clearly be better off, since outside the dominant coalition all firms make zero profits in every period.) If this is so, coalition K would be robust against cheating but not robust with respect to the addition of a new member.

Suppose the profit per member of a technology-trading coalition is single peaked in the size of the coalition. Let $k_{max} \in \{1, 2, \ldots, n\}$ be the coalition size that maximizes the profit per member of coalition K, and $k_u(\delta) \in \{1, 2, \ldots, n\}$ be the largest coalition size that satisfies the incentive-compatibility condition for given δ. If $k_{max} \geq k_u(\delta)$, clearly there is only one stable coalition, and that is the coalition comprising $k_u(\delta)$ members. On the other hand, if $k_{max} < k_u(\delta)$, any coalition with cardinality $k \in [k_{max}, k_u(\delta)]$

[4] It is assumed that since information about cheating is made public, the other coalition (which is not producing since its costs are too high) does not accept the cheater. Since the cheater will subsequently be earning zero profit in every period anyway, what is to prevent it from from unilaterally disclosing its technological information to the other coalition? At no cost to itself, the ejected cheater can conceivably inflict a cost on coalition K for ejecting it. This possibility, however, can be eliminated by introducing a small cost to disclosing information.

will be stable, though it does not necessarily maximize each member's profit. A coalition with a size that falls in this range will persist over time because no coalition member has an incentive to cheat, and the addition of new members will not be deemed desirable by the existing coalition members because that can only reduce each member's profit. Thus we have the following proposition.

Proposition 2. If the dominant coalition's profit per firm is single peaked in the size of the coalition, (i) if $k_{max} \geq k_u(\delta)$, the only stable coalition is of size $k_u(\delta)$, and (ii) if $k_{max} < k_u(\delta)$, all coalitions of size $k \in [k_{max}, k_u(\delta)]$ are stable.

The welfare effects of technology trading are interesting to consider. One thing is clear: Relative to the scenario in which there is no technology trading and no price collusion, any equilibrium involving technology sharing within a coalition that is smaller than the entire industry is weakly Pareto superior. The reason is that in the former case, the price that would prevail in equilibrium is C_1. In the latter case, C_1 is an upper bound on the equilibrium price.

What are the welfare effects in this model of increasing the size of a coalition, say *K*? Even when firms attempt to set prices collusively (as is assumed here), larger coalitions are not necessarily welfare decreasing. An increase in the size of coalition *K* lowers the marginal cost of its members and, if the additional members come from coalition *M*, this raises the highest price that coalition *K* can charge. If the marginal cost of coalition *M*'s members was originally the limit price set by coalition *K*, the decrease in coalition *M*'s size could very well result in an increase in the equilibrium price. On the other hand, if the marginal cost of the members of coalition *M* was not binding on the price set by coalition *K*, it is entirely conceivable that an increase in the size of coalition *K* could lower its most profitable collusive price. By making consumers better off, this would bring about a Pareto improvement. Thus even when price collusion is present, the welfare effect of increases in coalition size is not unambiguously deleterious.

This completes our treatment of technology sharing under price setting. In this scenario, while continuation of technology sharing by the noncheating members of a coalition in the event of cheating is in their self-interest, relative to the dissolution of the entire coalition, no greater punishment is imposed on a cheater by such a strategy.[5] In the quantity-setting scenario considered next, even the punishment inflicted on the cheater is greater.

□ **The Cournot case.** We now consider the case where the firms in a coalition trade technological information and then set quantities. There is one difference from the price-setting model considered above. There, price setting by the dominant coalition reduced the profits of the smaller coalition to zero. There was no scope for the smaller coalition to free ride on the price-collusive activity of the larger coalition. With quantity setting, however, the situation is different. If one coalition restricts output, the other coalition benefits through the effect on price. We assume here that each firm plays Cournot-Nash with respect to all other firms in the industry—including those belonging to the same technology-sharing coalition. This enables us to abstract from the standard free-rider problem in cartel formation, which is well understood and so is not the focus of our interest. Thus, in the quantity-setting case, a firm's membership or nonmembership in a coalition impinges only on the firm's cost of production.

[5] It must be noted that in the model spelled out above, prices were set after the technologies were traded. If the order were reversed, by cheating a firm would inflict a loss in the defection period on the other coalition members but would not increase its own profits thereby. In other words, that formulation would do away with the possibility of cheating, and thus it would not be an appropriate vehicle for investigating the possibilities of interest here.

The one-period problem confronting a firm, say i, belonging to set I, I $\in$ {K, M, S}, is

$$\max_{q_i} [P(q_i + Q_{-i}) - C_i]q_i,$$

where q_i and Q_{-i} are the outputs of firm i and of all the other firms, respectively, and C_i is the marginal cost of firm i. Denote the Cournot-Nash equilibrium profit of members of K, M, and S by $\Pi_K(k, m)$, $\Pi_M(k, m)$, and $\Pi_S(k, m)$, respectively. It is assumed that all these profits are positive, i.e., that members of all the coalitions have strictly positive outputs in the Cournot-Nash equilibrium.

If a member of coalition K, say, decides to cheat, in the defection period this firm (denoted by c) will solve

$$\max_{q_c} [P(q_c + Q_{-c}) - C(k)]q_c,$$

while a noncheating member, say i, of this coalition will solve

$$\max_{q_i} [P(q_i + Q_{-i}) - C(k - 1)]q_i,$$

and a member, say j, of set I $\in$ {M, S} solves

$$\max_{q_j} [P(q_j + Q_{-j}) - C_j]q_j.$$

Denote by $\Omega_K(k, m)$ the Cournot-Nash profit of the defecting firm in the period of defection. It is assumed here that in the period of defection, the outputs of all other firms are strictly positive in the Cournot-Nash equilibrium.

The continuation game following an act of cheating by a member of coalition K entails the determination of the one-period Cournot-Nash equilibrium of a scenario in which there are three coalitions: K_{-1}, M, and S_{+1}, where S_{+1} is the set of $(s + 1)$ nontrading firms that now includes the cheater, and K_{-1} is the coalition that remains from K after the cheater has been ejected, assuming that the cheater belonged to K originally. The one-period Cournot-Nash profits of the members of coalitions K_{-1}, M, and S_{+1} are given by $\Pi_K(k - 1, m)$, $\Pi_M(k - 1, m)$, and $\Pi_S(k - 1, m)$, respectively. As before, the outputs of all firms are assumed to be strictly positive in the Cournot-Nash equilibrium.[6]

The incentive-compatibility constraint that must be satisfied for a member of coalition K, under the assumption that coalition M is stable, is given by

$$\frac{1}{1 - \delta} \Pi_K(k, m) \geq \Omega_K(k, m) + \frac{\delta}{1 - \delta} \Pi_S(k - 1, m). \tag{7}$$

The left-hand side of the above inequality represents the present-value profit of an honest firm in coalition K. The first term on the right-hand side is the one-period profit to a member of coalition K from cheating, while the second term is the present-value

[6] As assumed earlier, the cheater ejected from coalition K is not accepted by coalition M. In contrast to the scenario in the Bertrand case, here, even in the absence of disclosure costs, the cheater will be made strictly worse off by unilateral revelation of its technological information (since this makes its competitors more efficient).

profit to the firm from operating without the benefit of trading from the next period on in the presence of coalitions K_{-1} and M. The difference between this formulation and standard formulations of supergames is in the second term.

The standard assumption of the supergame literature of reversion to Nash behavior will be referred to as "Nash reversion." In the case of Nash reversion, a defection in coalition K results in the dissolution of the coalition, and all the k members operate as independents from the next period on. The incentive-compatibility condition for a member of coalition K in the case of Nash reversion is

$$\frac{1}{1-\delta}\Pi_K(k, m) \geq \Omega_K(k, m) + \frac{\delta}{1-\delta}\Pi_S(0, m). \tag{8}$$

The function $\Pi_S(0, m)$ represents the profit per period of an independent (a member of set S) when coalition K is dissolved and its original k members are all operating as independents in the presence of a single coalition M.

Let $\delta_K^S(k, m)$ and $\delta_K^N(k, m)$ denote the smallest values of the discount factors ("critical" discount factors) for which the incentive-compatibility conditions (7) and (8), respectively, for coalition K are satisfied. From inequalities (7) and (8), these critical discount factors are easily seen to be

$$\delta_K^S(k, m) = \frac{\Omega_K(k, m) - \Pi_K(k, m)}{\Omega_K(k, m) - \Pi_S(k-1, m)} \tag{9}$$

and

$$\delta_K^N(k, m) = \frac{\Omega_K(k, m) - \Pi_K(k, m)}{\Omega_K(k, m) - \Pi_S(0, m)}. \tag{10}$$

Now an independent's Cournot-Nash profit will be at least as large when coalition K is completely dissolved as when the noncheating members continue to trade technologies, that is, $\Pi_S(k-1, m) \leq \Pi_S(0, m)$. (This inequality is strict for $k > 2$, whereas it holds with equality for $k = 2$.) Thus it follows from (9) and (10) above that $\delta_K^S(k, m) \leq \delta_K^N(k, m)$, with the latter weak inequality holding with equality for $k = 2$ and holding strictly for $k > 2$. Thus we have the following proposition.

Proposition 3. If the incentive-compatibility condition for technology trading is satisfied when the coalition is dissolved in the event of cheating, it is necessarily satisfied when only the cheater is ejected from the coalition. The converse is not true.

Now, for the punishment mechanism in which only the cheater is ejected from coalition K to be credible, the coalition K_{-1} that remains must be robust against defection, too. A defection in K_{-1} will result in the ejection of the defector, leading to a coalition K_{-2}, etc. Thus, if coalition K is to be robust against cheating, a whole series of "stacked" incentive-compatibility conditions must be satisfied:

$$\frac{1}{1-\delta}\Pi_K(i, m) \geq \Omega_K(i, m) + \frac{\delta}{1-\delta}\Pi_S(i-1, m), \qquad i = 2, \ldots, k. \tag{11}$$

We shall refer to this type of reversion in the event of defection as "stacked reversion." If the above set of inequalities is satisfied, the stacked reversion strategies form a subgame-perfect equilibrium. In writing down the above set of conditions, we have assumed that coalition M is robust against cheating by its members. Conditions analogous to those stated above must clearly be satisfied for coalition M if it is to be stable.

It is relatively easy to obtain sufficient conditions for which stacked reversion strategies can sustain technology-trading coalitions as subgame-perfect equilibria. The essential feature of such equilibria is the requirement that every subcoalition of coalition K be robust against cheating if coalition K is to be robust. The argument leading to Proposition 3 above showed that the critical discount factor under Nash reversion is an upper bound on the critical discount factor for the scenario where only the cheater is ejected. Thus, if the incentive-compatibility condition under Nash reversion strategies is satisfied for K and every subcoalition of K, then so is it under stacked reversion. Thus we have the following proposition.

Proposition 4. If the technology-trading coalition K and all its subcoalitions can be supported as subgame-perfect equilibria by Nash reversion strategies, then coalition K is supportable as a subgame-perfect equilibrium under stacked reversion strategies.

At first glance, the sufficient condition invoked in the above proposition may appear to be eminently plausible. For example, in the Bertrand case considered in the previous subsection, it is readily seen from (6) that if coalition K is supportable under Nash reversion, then so is every subcoalition of K. In the case of Cournot being considered here, this sufficient condition is overly strong and is not always satisfied. To demonstrate, however, that in the Cournot case also the notion of equlibria involving stacked reversion is not vacuous, we now restrict ourselves to two specific cases that are analytically tractable.

We now assume for the rest of the article that the inverse demand curve facing the industry is linear:

$$P(Q) = \alpha - \beta Q, \qquad \alpha > 0, \beta > 0, \tag{12}$$

where Q denotes the industry output and P the marginal willingness to pay.

Case 1: Linear cost, with marginal cost of coalition members declining in coalition size. In this subsection we assume that the marginal cost of a member of a coalition with k members is independent of output, and is given by

$$C(k) = \max\{C_1 - (k - 1)\gamma, 0\}, \qquad \gamma > 0, \tag{13}$$

where, recall, C_1 is the marginal cost of a firm that has access only to its own technological information. The addition of another member to a coalition reduces each member's marginal cost by γ. We take it that γ is small enough that even if the entire industry forms a single coalition, the marginal cost of each firm after technology sharing remains strictly positive.

Proposition 3 above makes no reference to whether the satisfaction of coalition K's incentive-compatibility condition necessarily implies that that of K_{-1} is also satisfied. This question is addressed in the following lemma.[7]

Lemma 1. When the parameter $\gamma \ll C_1$, the critical discount factor under stacked reversion is given by

[7] The authors acknowledge the use of the software package *Mathematica,* Version 2, copyright Wolfram Research, Inc., for facilitating the derivation of the expressions for one-period profits in this specification and for the Taylor series reported below.

$$\delta_K^S(k, m) = \frac{1}{n} + \frac{1}{2n(\alpha - C_1)}[(n-1)k + 1]\gamma + O(\gamma^2),$$

where $O(\gamma^2)$ denotes terms that are second order or higher in γ.

From the above lemma it follows that when the marginal cost reduction of coalition members upon adding a new member is small, the critical discount factor under stacked reversion is increasing in the coalition size, when the size of the other trading coalition is held fixed. Thus, if the incentive-compatibility condition (11) is satisfied for coalition K, so is it for coalitions K_{-1}, K_{-2}, and so on. This leads to the following result.

Proposition 5. Suppose the demand curve facing the industry is linear, and the marginal cost of a coalition member is independent of output but declines linearly and gradually in the size of the coalition. Then if $\delta \geq \delta_K^S(k, m)$, the strategy of stacked reversion in the event of cheating supports technology trading in coalition K as a subgame-perfect equilibrium. The strategy of stacked reversion is more efficacious than Nash reversion, and it also supports a more plausible equilibrium.

Although the above result has been analytically demonstrated only when the cost parameter γ is small (relative to C_1), the result may be valid even for values of γ that are not small, as the numerical results presented below illustrate. The example below considers a case when there are only four firms in the industry. This ensures that we cannot have more than two nontrivial, technology-trading coalitions as a logical possibility. Much of what we have to say about stacked reversion can be said with $n = 4$, without engaging in the tedious taxonomy of cases that would warrant consideration when n is larger.

Tables 1 and 2 display numbers obtained from a straightforward computation pertaining to the feasibility of technology sharing in various coalitions. The parameter values used in these tables are $\alpha = 10$, $\beta = 1$, and $C_1 = 5$, with γ taking on two different values, .2 and .8, respectively.

Table 1 gives the smallest discount factor at which each of the feasible coalitions satisfies its incentive-compatibility conditions under Nash reversion and stacked reversion, respectively. Of course, the two types of reversion are different only when the number of members in a coalition is at least three. In the case of only one nontrivial coalition, the critical value of the discount factor, as seen from Table 1, is increasing in the size of this coalition under both types of reversion, for given γ. Notice, however, that for $k \geq 3$, the critical discount factor is considerably smaller under stacked reversion than under Nash reversion. This is because the ejection from the coalition of only the defecting firm inflicts a greater punishment on the cheater than does a dissolution

TABLE 1 **Critical Discount Factors Under Stacked and Nash Reversion for Various Coalitions**

	Critical Discount Factors			
	Stacked Reversion		Nash Reversion	
Coalition	$\gamma = .2$	$\gamma = .8$	$\gamma = .2$	$\gamma = .8$
One two-firm	.264	.296	.264	.296
One three-firm	.278	.341	.357	.405
One four-firm	.295	.430	.527	.581
Two two-firm	.265	.310	.265	.310

TABLE 2 **Profit per Firm Under Stacked Reversion for Various Coalitions**

	Single-Period Profit per Firm			
	$\gamma = .2$		$\gamma = .8$	
Coalition	Insider	Outsider	Insider	Outsider
All independents	1.000	1.000	1.000	1.000
One two-firm	1.254	.846	2.190	.462
One three-firm	1.346	.578	2.690	.002
One four-firm	1.254	—	2.190	—
Two two-firm	1.082	—	1.346	—

of the coalition. In addition, continuation of collaboration among the noncheaters is in their own interest. As Table 2 shows, when $\gamma = .2$, the per-period profit of a firm when all firms operate as independents is 1.000, which is always lower than the profit of an insider of a technology-trading coalition.

From Table 2 we see that from the point of view of the insiders of a coalition, it is not necessarily the most profitable outcome for all members of the industry to form a single large coalition. The per-period profit of an insider is seen to be highest when only three of the firms share their technologies. Inviting the outsider into the coalition would make that firm better off, but the insiders would become worse off. Thus, a three-firm coalition in this industry will not evolve voluntarily into a four-firm coalition even if the discount factor is large enough to ensure that the latter is viable. But if the industry began as a four-firm coalition, the coalition would remain stable. This implies that if a member of the four-firm coalition voluntarily leaves it for some extraneous reason, the three remaining members would not be willing to renegotiate the fourth firm's return. Thus, while both three-firm and four-firm coalitions are stable, the former are more stable, in some sense.

In contrast, if the discount factor is large enough to support a three-firm sharing arrangement, a two-firm coalition would not be stable. This is because the coalition would be willing to accept another member, and one of the outsiders would have an incentive to join. Thus, for the parameter values shown, both three-firm and four-firm coalitions are stable for sufficiently high discount factors.

The reason the firms may not opt to form just one technology-sharing coalition covering the entire industry is that the addition of a member impinges on the profit of an existing member in two opposing ways. On the one hand, the addition lowers the marginal cost of all the existing members of a coalition and will be desirable on that count. On the other hand, increasing the coalition size drastically lowers the marginal cost of a firm that is currently an outsider. Since all firms are taken to be Cournot players here, the lowering of a firm's marginal cost necessarily increases its output. The drastic increase in the new member's output has a deleterious effect on the profits of the existing coalition members. Thus, depending on the precise tradeoff between these two opposing effects, technology-sharing arrangements could stop short of including all members of the industry.

If two firms in the industry form a coalition and the discount factor is not high enough to sustain a three-firm coalition (e.g., it is less than .278 in the example considered in Table 1, when $\gamma = .2$), it is clearly in the interest of the two outside firms to form a separate coalition. This is feasible if the discount factor exceeds .265. It is also profitable for these outside firms to form a coalition, because (as seen from Table 2) their one-period profit increases from .846 to 1.082, while that of the members of the other coalition is reduced from 1.254 to 1.082. Indeed, if the discount factor lies in the range $.265 \leq \delta < .278$, the unique equilibrium outcome in the industry will be the formation of two two-firm technology-sharing coalitions. Thus it appears that the fragmentation of an industry into more than one coalition may be a natural outcome in the kind of scenario being considered here. This may be one rationale for the emergence of numerous R&D joint ventures now being observed in the U.S. computer industry.

The above discussion suggests that the process of technology-trading coalition formation is quite an intricate one. This is so even in the simple case in which there is initially only one trading coalition, say *K*, confronting a collection of some nontrading independents, *S*. In deciding whether to admit another member into the coalition, it is not enough for the existing members of *K* to ask if the incentive-compatibility constraint would be satisfied and if the profit per firm would increase. The coalition members would also have to consider the possibility that the outsiders may have incentives to form a trading coalition of their own, say *M*. The formation of such a coalition would lower the costs of production of the firms currently in *S*, and thus would be detrimental to the members of *K*. Determining whether a coalition is stable would necessarily entail a simultaneous consideration of the stability of all coalitions.

It is important to note that in the exercises conducted in this article, the number of firms in the industry is being taken as exogenously given. Were we to introduce a fixed entry cost and endogenize the number of firms, we could find that this number may be higher or lower with technology trading than without. On the one hand, since technology trading lowers the variable cost of production for each coalition member, an existing coalition might invite more firms to participate in the industry if initially there are very few. On the other hand, the existence of a coalition in the industry makes it more difficult for an outsider to operate profitably. Thus, the formation of a technology trading coalition might deter the entry of firms that might have been viable had the coalition not formed. In general, the welfare effects of technology trading when the number of firms is endogenous would be ambiguous.

Case 2: Quadratic costs, with coalition size affecting the slope of the marginal cost. In this subsection we assume that the production costs of a firm are quadratic in the output, and that the slope of the marginal cost function depends inversely on the size of the coalition of which the firm is a member. The total cost of producing output q to a firm that belongs to a coalition of size k is given by

$$\frac{1}{2}C(k)q^2,$$

where it is now assumed that $C(k) = C_1/k$. In this formulation, the addition of another member to an existing coalition has a powerful effect on the cost functions of the coalition members.

Figure 1 illustrates the results of a simulation exercise.[8] The demand parameters are set at $\alpha = 1$ and $\beta = 1$, the cost parameter at $C_1 = 1$, the total number of firms in the industry at $n = 10$, and the size of coalition M at $m = 3$. The figure displays the critical discount factors required to support technology trading in coalition K with Nash reversion and stacked reversion strategies, as the number of members in K varies from two to seven. (Since the size of coalition M is held fixed at three in this exercise, additions to coalition K come at the expense of the set of independents, S.)

[8] The authors acknowledge the use of the software package *Mathematica*, Version 2, copyright Wolfram Research, Inc., for facilitating the derivation of analytic expressions for one-period profits in this specification.

FIGURE 1

CRITICAL DISCOUNT FACTORS NEEDED TO SUPPORT TECHNOLOGY TRADING IN COALITION K
PARAMETER VALUES: $\alpha = 1$, $\beta = 1$, $C_1 = 1$, $n = 10$, AND $m = 3$

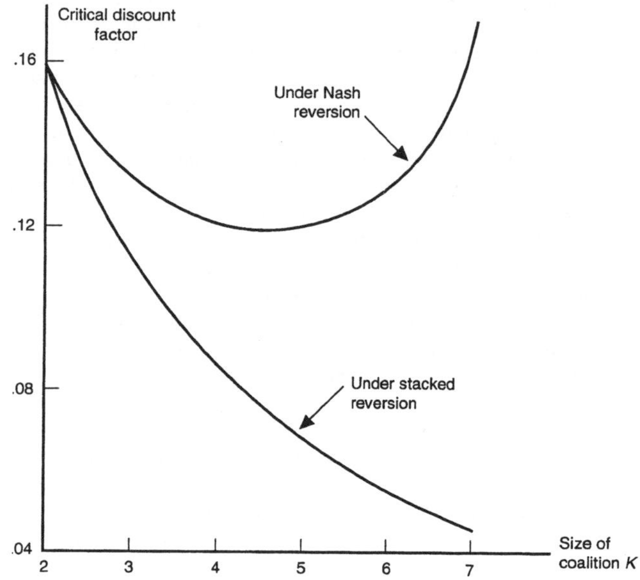

There are several features worthy of note in Figure 1. First, when $k \geq 3$, the schedule for the critical discount factor is everywhere lower for the stacked reversion case, compared to the Nash reversion case, as would be expected. Second, the critical discount factor for the Nash reversion case first declines in k and then increases. In other words, initially it is easier to support technology trading with larger coalitions even under Nash reversion. This happens because the cost advantage to forming larger coalitions generates for its members high profits that they are unwilling to relinquish by cheating. This advantage is particularly strong when the coalition is initially small. For larger coalition sizes, the marginal-cost reduction brought about by an additional member is relatively small. And this small advantage to increasing the coalition size is overwhelmed by the deleterious output effect of drastically lowering the cost of outside members by bringing them into the coalition. (This example provides an illustration of a scenario in which the sufficient condition in Proposition 4 is not necessarily satisfied.)

If the discount factor is in the vicinity of .160, coalition K is supportable under Nash reversion as long as the coalition has no more than six members. Under stacked reversion, however, all coalition sizes up to seven are supportable. If the discount factor is .150, say, coalition K is supportable under Nash reversion as long as it has between three and six members. However, the coalition will not be supportable under stacked reversion for any size $k \geq 2$ because $k = 2$ is not viable. Under stacked reversion, all subcoalitions of K have to be supportable if K is to be supportable as an equilbrium coalition. (In this case, coalition M, which is assumed to have three members, also will not be viable.)

The above example in which the discount factor is assumed to be .150 illustrates the possibility of using a hybrid of Nash reversion and stacked reversion strategies in order to support more technology trading than would have been possible otherwise. Suppose the members of coalition K agree that in the event of cheating they will resort to stacked reversion if $k \geq 4$ but to Nash reversion if the coalition size is three. This strategy will support K as a technology-trading coalition even when it has seven members. The same would be true even if the agreement is that the switch to Nash reversion is to occur at $k = 4$, for example. Thus there is a variety of strategies more sophisticated than Nash reversion that can support cooperation.

References

ABREU, D. "External Equilibria of Oligopolistic Supergames." *Journal of Economic Theory*, Vol. 39 (1986), pp. 191–225.

ALLEN, R.C. "Collective Invention." *Journal of Economic Behavior and Organization*, Vol. 4 (1983), pp. 1–24.

BAUMOL, W.J. *Entrepreneurship, Management, and the Structure of Payoffs*. Cambridge, Mass.: MIT Press, 1993.

CARTER, A.P. "Knowhow Trading as Economic Exchange." *Research Policy*, Vol. 18 (1989), pp. 155–163.

FRIED, D. "Incentives for Information Production and Disclosure in a Duopolistic Environment." *Quarterly Journal of Economics*, Vol. 99 (1984), pp. 367-381.

FRIEDMAN, J.W. "A Non-Cooperative Equilibrium for Supergames." *Review of Economic Studies*, Vol. 38 (1971), pp. 1–12.

GALLINI, N.T. "Deterrence by Market Sharing: A Strategic Incentive for Licensing." *American Economic Review*, Vol. 74 (1984), pp. 931–941.

GAL-OR, E. "Information Sharing in Oligopoly." *Econometrica*, Vol. 53 (1985), pp. 329–343.

———. "Information Transmission—Cournot and Bertrand Equilibria." *Review of Economic Studies*, Vol. 53 (1986), pp. 85–92.

NOVSHEK, W. AND SONNENSCHEIN, H. "Fulfilled Expectations Cournot Duopoly with Information Acquisition and Release." *Bell Journal of Economics*, Vol. 12 (1982), pp. 214–218.

OKUNO-FUJIWARA, M., POSTLEWAITE, A., AND SUZUMURA, K. "Strategic Information Revelation." *Review of Economic Studies*, Vol. 57 (1990), pp. 25–47.

SHAPIRO, C. "Exchange of Cost Information in Oligopoly." *Review of Economic Studies*, Vol. 53 (1986), pp. 433–446.

VIVES, X. "Duopoly Information Equilibrium: Cournot and Bertrand." *Journal of Economic Theory*, Vol. 34 (1984), pp. 71–94.

VON HIPPEL, E. *The Sources of Innovation*. New York: Oxford University Press, 1988.

ELSEVIER

Journal of Economic Behavior & Organization
Vol. 32 (1997) 457–470

JOURNAL OF
Economic Behavior
& Organization

Co-specific investments, hold-up and self-enforcing contracts

P.A. Koss[a,*], B.Curtis Eaton[b]

[a] *Concordia University, 1455 de Maisonneuve Bld. W., Montreal, P.Q., H3G 1M8, Canada*
[b] *Simon Fraser University, Burnaby, B.C., Canada*

Received 21 February 1996; accepted 12 March 1996

Abstract

This paper offers a general model of the hold-up problem when investments are co-specific. Agents are risk-neutral and there are no information asymmetries. Nash bargaining with outside options determines the division of the surplus arising from exchange. The model formally demonstrates that reciprocal exposure to specific assets achieved via the partial redistribution of specific investment costs to the potentially opportunistic party serves as a credible commitment to mutually advantageous exchange.

JEL classification: D21; D23

Keywords: Hold-up ; Specific investments; Self-enforcing contracts

1. Introduction

Klein et al. (1978) (KCA) illustrate the effect of the potential for post-contractual 'hold-up' upon the efficacy with which different governance structures permit the completion of a transaction. They appear to have been the first to emphasize the importance of the presence of transaction-specific investments upon the potential for ex post hold-up. The literature now recognizes the existence of the *hold-up problem*, "the general business problem in which each party to a contract worries about being forced to accept disadvantageous terms later, after it has sunk an investment, or worries that its

* Corresponding author. Tel.: (514)848-3936; fax: (514)848-4536; e-mail: pkoss@vax2.concordia.ca.

PII S0167-2681(96)00031-5

investment may be devalued by the actions of others...."[1] If either of the parties refuses to undertake the initial requisite investment(s), a potentially Pareto-improving exchange will not obtain; thus market failure occurs.

Formal modelling of the hold-up problem has been undertaken by Williamson (1983), Grossman and Hart (1986) and Tirole (1988, Chap. 1). Williamson considers a bilateral vertical exchange where the identity of the supplier is determined through a competitive bidding process. Efficiency considerations dictate that the supplier undertake an investment which is *purely* specific to the transaction. Ex ante competitive bidding ensures that the entire surplus accrues to the buyer. Tirole also considers one-sided specific investment but allows for a non-zero salvage value.[2] Nash bargaining with outside options then determines the division of the surplus. The model offered in this paper differs from those of Williamson and Tirole in that we allow for the possibility of *co-specialized* investments. That is, initial investments undertaken by both parties to an exchange are specific to the same use.[3] We retain, however, Tirole's allowance for outside options and the corresponding Nash bargaining solution. Grossman and Hart (1986) formally recognize the possibility of *co-specific* investments. Their model allows for two possible sources of market failure: inefficient choices regarding the level of specific investment(s); or an inefficient allocation of the rights of control to some other activity affecting the value of the exchange. We demonstrate the conditions under which the potential for ex post hold-up in a much simpler model exists. Moreover, we formalize a different solution to the hold-up problem than that proposed by Grossman and Hart.

The above literature recognizes several potential ways in which market failure arising from potential ex post hold-up can be avoided. Tirole considers the formation of an ex ante contract which specifies penalties for breach and is legally (and costlessly) enforceable by a third party.[4] Grossman and Hart (1986), using their model of co-specific investments, demonstrate that ex ante investment distortions can be minimized through vertical or lateral integration. KCA submit that one way to deal with the problem of post-contractual opportunism is by the formation of an implicit long-term contract enforced via the imposition of a capital loss on the opportunistic party by the withdrawal of future business.[5] Williamson (1983) recognizes that the threat of termination alone may be insufficient to uphold the contract. Specifically, the one-time gain from contractual deviation may exceed the expected future net benefits from the trading relationship. Moreover, the threat of termination may not be credible. If it is in the best interest of the wronged party to renew the contract in the following period, even after accounting for the possibility of future hold-up, the termination threat may not be viewed as credible by the potentially offending party.

---

[1] Milgrom and Roberts (1992, p.136)

[2] Note that Tirole recognizes the possibility of two-sided specific invesment but this is not formalized in his model.

[3] KCA (1978) recognize the possibility of co-specific investments through exemplification. In particular they cite the example of a marriage in which each party to the marriage incurs 'highly specfic investments in affection and children.'

[4] See also Joskow (1987), Crocker and Masten (1988) and Masten and Crocker (1985).

[5] Consider also the well-known 'folk theorem' which indicates that in an infinitely repeated game, and given a sufficiently small and positive rate of time preference, a cooperative outcome can be enforced via the threat of punishments (Friedman, 1971, 1977; Aumann and Shapley, 1976).

Williamson (1983), in developing his 'hostage model,' examines an intermediate product market in which self-enforcing agreements involve 'credible commitments.' He maintains that one way to avoid market failure is to expand the contractual relation by devising a *mutual reliance relation*. That is, the buyer may reciprocally invest in specific capital that has value only in servicing the final demands for the product in question. If the non-salvageable value of the advance commitment undertaken by the buyer equals that of the supplier, an efficient exchange result will emerge. This paper *formally* demonstrates Williamson's contention that the efficiency of a contract may be endogenously enforced by a mutual reliance relation.

2. Examples of hold-up

At the core of market failure arising from hold-up is the existence of transaction-specific investments, that is, investments which have a lower value in an alternative transaction. The transactions cost literature cites many examples of situations in which asset specificity has ramifications for transacting behavior. Joskow (1987), for example, discusses asset specificity in coal supply relationships in the US. Some power plants locate next to specific mines in anticipation of taking most of their requirements from that mine. The value of the power plant owners' site-specific investments is much lower in transactions with other mines. Physical asset specificity arises in this market when plants are designed to burn a specific type of coal: thus, alternative types of coal may be less efficient in generating electricity.

Koss (1993) observes the potential for hold-up in the British Columbia fishing industry. On the supply side of the market for raw fish, physical asset and human asset specificity (resulting from learning-by-doing) arise with the harvesting technology employed: these investments sometimes result in an intermediate product that is of higher value to one processor or to a small number of processors than to others. Similarly, processors may train some portion of their labour force to employ a processing technology that is specific to only one type of intermediate product; for example, the brining process used by processors on the British Columbia coast is specific to the production of herring and salmon roe. Moreover, processing plants may locate in remote areas in anticipation of deliveries from local fishers. Similarly, fishers may invest in licences that are area-specific; owing to the perishability of the intermediate product, delivery outside of this area may be not be feasible. The B.C. intermediate fish market is particularly well-suited to provide a real-world exemplification of the model presented in this paper because co-specific investments are involved (i.e. specific investments are often undertaken by both parties to a transaction).

3. Modeling the hold-up problem

Consider the following potential transaction, T: in stage 1, parties A and B are approached by a third party to produce good X, which requires both parties A and B to undertake *relation-specific* ex ante investments, the costs of which are I_A and I_B. Sale of the product to the third party takes place in stage 2 at the price R; thus, R denotes the *relation-specific gross revenue*. It is assumed throughout that $R > 0$ and that both parties know with certainty the value R. Given risk neutrality on the part of A and B, ex ante efficiency considerations dictate that the investments I_A and I_B should be undertaken if $R \geq I_A + I_B$. It is assumed throughout that $R > I_A + I_B$.

In stage 2, each party must decide whether to complete the exchange of good X under transaction T, or to employ their investments in the next best alternative exchange. Denote the ex post opportunity costs arising from the ex ante specific investments I_A and I_B by C_A and C_B, respectively. Party A's ex post opportunity cost, C_A, of his/her initial specific investment, I_A, is equal to the return he/she would receive in an alternative transaction. This implies that I_A and I_B serve to not only augment the value of X to parties A and B, but will also be valuable investments in alternative transactions as long as $C_i > 0$. When $C_i = 0$, the initial investments are *purely specific* to transaction T. It is assumed that both parties know with certainty the values of their own and each other's ex post opportunity costs. It is also convenient to impose the restrictions, $I_A \geq C_A$ and $I_B \geq C_B$, indicating that the relation-specific investments earn a non-positive return when undertaken independently of one another.

Ex post efficiency (i.e. maximization of the quasi-rent[6]) dictates that transaction T be undertaken, rather than the next bext alternative ex post exchanges, as long as $R > C_A + C_B$. That is, an ex post exchange between the parties should occur if that exchange generates a larger quasi-rent than any alternative exchange. It is assumed throughout that $R > C_A + C_B$.

Given that ex ante investments have been made, the incentives to complete the ex post exchange depends upon the division of the ex post quasi-rent.[7] In order to determine the division of any surplus, a theory of bargaining is required. We adopt the Nash theory of bargaining which implies that the parties will equally divide the ex post gains from trade (Nash, 1953). That is, the ex post returns to parties A and B, R_A and R_B, are determined endogenously as follows:

$$R_A = C_A + \theta/2 \tag{1}$$

$$R_B = C_B + \theta/2 \tag{2}$$

where $\theta = R - C_A - C_B$. Eq. (1) defines party A's ex post return from the transaction: party A must receive at least the amount C_A in order to complete the ex post exchange; in addition, he/she will extract one-half of the ex post quasi-rent. Similarly, party B receives his/her option value, C_B, plus one-half of the ex post quasi-rent, as indicated in Eq. (2).[8] Note that ex post performance is ensured under Nash bargaining as each party receives a higher return under transaction T than would be forthcoming in the next best alternative exchange.

[6] "The quasirent value of the asset is the excess of its value over its... value in its next best *use* to another (user)." (KCA). In this application, the value of the quasirent is given by $QR = R - C_S - C_B$.

[7] Transaction T is assumed to be a one-shot exchange; that is, none of these parties will have future dealings with one another. This negates the possibility that reputational considerations affect the decisions made with respect to transaction T.

[8] Note that it is assumed that the cost of arriving at the Nash bargaining solution is zero. That is, none of the quasi-rent is dissipated through ex post haggling over the distribution of the quasi-rent.

3.1. Ex ante efficiency

There are two conditions necessary in order for the initial specific investments, I_A and I_B, to be undertaken: the endogenously determined *real* rents to each party (i.e. returns in excess of ex ante investments), N_A and N_B, must be non-negative. That is,

$$N_A = R_A - I_A = C_A + \frac{1}{2}\theta - I_A = C_A + \frac{1}{2}(R - C_A - C_B) - I_A \geq 0 \tag{3}$$

$$N_B = R_B - I_B = C_B + \frac{1}{2}\theta - I_B = C_B + \frac{1}{2}(R - C_A - C_B) - I_B \geq 0 \tag{4}$$

Eq. (3) states that, in order to agree to the transaction, party A must earn a return, R_A, sufficient to recover the initial specific investment cost, I_A. Similarly, Eq. (4) states that party B will agree to the transaction if he/she earns a return, R_B, sufficient to recover the initial specific investment cost, I_B.

Fig. 1 depicts a situation in which the above ex ante efficiency conditions hold. The relation-specific gross revenue from the transaction, R, is given by the distance $0_A 0_B$. The ex ante specific investment cost incurred by party A is given by the distance $0_A I_A$, and that by party B, $0_B I_B$. The real rent from the transaction is then given by the distance $R - I_A - I_B$. Similarly, ex post opportunity costs to parties A and B are given by the distances $0_A C_A$ and $0_B C_B$, respectively. Note that in this illustration, $I_A = C_A$. The ex post return accruing to party A is given by the distance $0_A R_A$, where R_A is located half-way between C_A and C_B. Similarly, the ex post return accruing to party B is given by $R_B = R - R_A$, which is given by the distance $0_B R_A$. Since there exist ex post gains from trade from transaction T, (i.e. $R - C_A - C_B > 0$), and each party recovers their initial investment costs (i.e. $R_A > I_A$ and $R_B = R - R_A > I_B$), the ex ante specific investments will be undertaken, as efficiency dictates.

3.2. Market failure arising from ex post hold-up

Consider the effect of reducing party A's ex post opportunity cost. For each one unit reduction in C_A, R_A falls by one-half.[9] This is because party A's bargaining power is reduced when his/her ex post alternative(s) become less valuable. The smaller the ex post opportunity cost relative to the initial investment, the less likely that party A's Nash division of the quasi-rent will cover the initial investment. Fig. 2 illustrates the circumstances under which party A is subject to a potential hold-up by party B. If party A's ex post opportunity cost is reduced to C'_A, party A's ex post return will correspondingly fall to $0R'_A$. Thus, transaction T generates a net loss for party A. This loss, however, equal to $I_A - R'_A$, is smaller than the loss he/she would incur in the next best alternative transaction, equal to $I_A - C'_A$. Given the ex ante undertaking of the initial specific investment, party A would choose to complete transaction T in order to minimize his/her loss. Our assumption of both parties having perfect foresight, however, negates the possibility that a rational individual will undertake the ex ante investment at all. Party A will recognize the potential for ex post hold-up and will be unwilling to incur the ex ante

[9] $\partial R_A/\partial C_A = \partial(C_A + \frac{1}{2}(R - C_A - C_B))/\partial C_A = \frac{1}{2}$

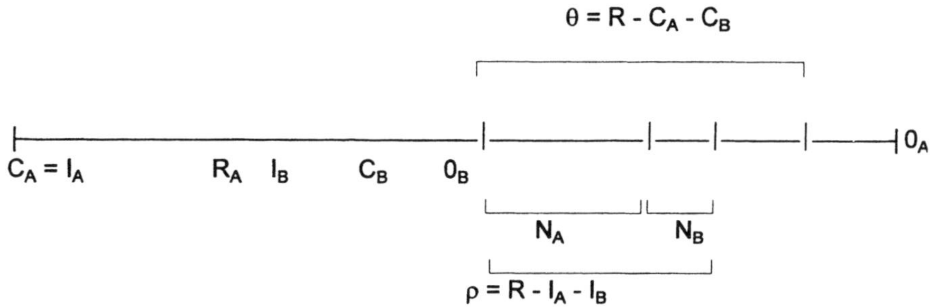

Fig. 1.

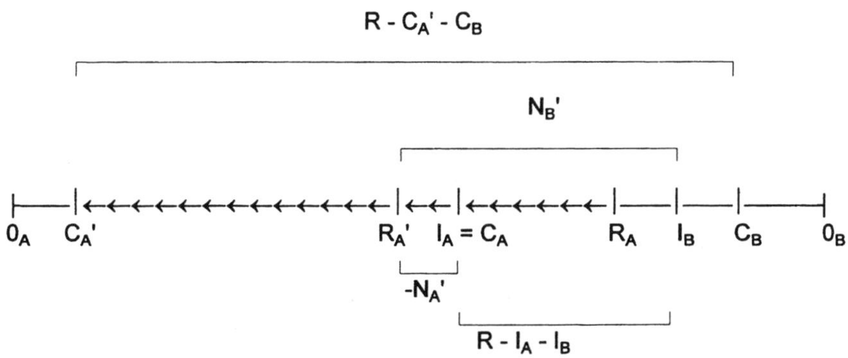

Fig. 2.

investment cost. We identify this as market failure, since transaction T is *Pareto* superior to all alternative transactions.

Circumstances may also, of course, permit party A to hold up party B. This will occur when party B's ex post opportunity cost, C_B, is such that his/her ex post bargaining strength does not allow recovery of the intitial investment, I_B (i.e. when $R_B < I_B$).

Fig. 3 summarizes graphically the conditions under which ex post hold-up is anticipated. In order to realize a given ex post return, R, the production of good X requires an initial specific investment, $I = I_S + I_B$, the size of which is given by the horizontal dimension of the box. Party A's contribution to the ex ante investment, I_A, is measured from left to right, while party B's contribution, I_B, is measured from right to left. The vertical dimension of the box measures the sum of the ex post opportunity costs faced by parties A and B (i.e. $C = C_A + C_B$).

The line labelled AA represents all combinations of I_A and C_A for which party A is just willing to undertake the ex ante specific investment and complete the ex post exchange. That is, for all points on line AA, the following condition is satisfied: $C_A + 1/2(\theta) = I_A$.

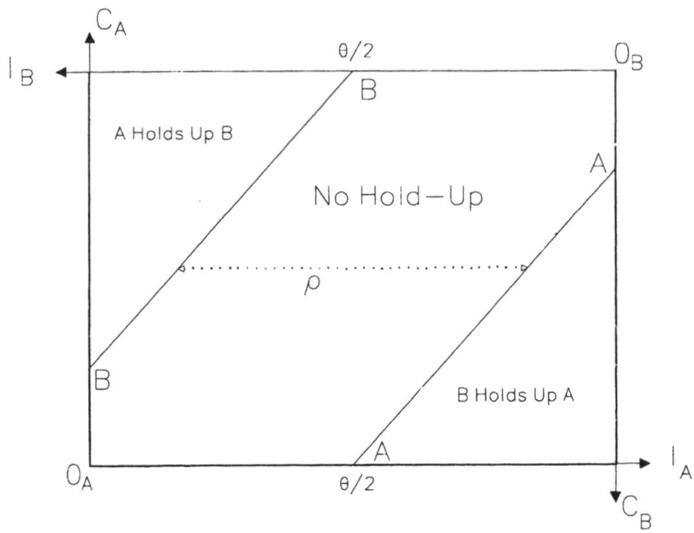

Fig. 3.

Similarly, the line labelled BB represents all combinations of I_B and C_B for which party *B* is indifferent between investing in the requisite specific asset(s) and refusing to participate in the transaction. That is, for all points on line BB, the following condition is satisfied: $C_B + 1/2(\theta) = I_B$.

For all points to the right of line AA, the following inequalities hold:

$$I_A > C_A + 1/2(\theta); \quad I_B < C_B + 1/2(\theta)$$

That is, party *A* anticipates being held up by party *B* and will refuse to undertake the ex ante investment, I_A. For all points to the left of line BB, the above inequalities are reversed; that is, party *B* anticipates being held up by party *A* and will refuse to undertake the ex ante investment, I_B. Thus, if the extent of either party's initial specific investment is high enough relative to their respective ex post opportunity costs, the initial investment will not be undertaken by that party and market failure will occur.

The area bounded by lines AA and BB represents combinations of C_A, C_B, I_A, and I_B for which hold-up is not anticipated by either party. Within this region, then, both parties recover their initial investments ex post and the transaction will be entered into as efficiency dicatates. The horizontal distance between these two lines is equal to the rent generated by the transaction (i.e. $\rho = R - I$).

An increase in the relation-specific revenue, *R*, will shift line AA to the right and line BB to the left, thereby increasing the size of the bounded area, ρ; thus, the higher the return to a given co-specific investment, *I*, the smaller the likelihood of ex post hold-up and, therefore, market failure. A reduction in the size of co-specific investment has the same effect, as this also increases the real rent to the transaction, ρ. Conversely, a reduction in R, or an increase in I will shrink the size of the bounded area indicating an increased likelihood of market failure.

4. Promoting efficient exchange

Given the potential for ex post hold-up, market failure occurs because potential gains from trade arising from ex ante relation-specific investment are unexploited. The potential victim refuses to undertake ex ante relation-specific investments because he/she anticipates that, given the opportunity, the other party will engage in ex post hold-up. Formally, market failure results if either: (i) $C_A + \frac{1}{2}\theta < I_A$, or (ii) $C_B + \frac{1}{2}\theta < I_B$.

Does there exist a contract which promotes efficient exchange when one of the above situations presents itself? In Case (i), the potentially opportunistic party is party B. Since the transaction T generates at least as much rent as any alternative transaction, it is in party B's best interest to convince party A that the latter *will not* be the victim of ex post hold-up. The converse is true if Case (ii) presents itself: party A has an incentive to convince party B that hold-up will not occur. Note, however, that the promise of a higher ex post compensation package is not credible. That is, although the potentially opportunistic party could *promise* that the other party would earn a positive real return, it is not in his/her best interest to abide by this promise ex post, nor is it necessary to induce the potential victim's ex post contractual performance. Thus, a positive expected return to the potential victim can only result if he/she receives some form of ex ante payment (or incurs a lower ex ante investment cost).

There are a number of ways in which market failure arising from potential hold-up can be avoided. Williamson (1983, p. 526) states that common ownership (i.e. vertical integration) is the preponderant response to site specificity. For example, in dealing with the potential hold-up that results from highly immobile assets and the consequent large setup and/or relocation costs, site-specific power plants have been observed to vertically integrate with coal mining operations. In the model presented here, vertical integration between parties A and B would result in one party undertaking both investments I_A and I_B. The entire real rent would then accrue to one party and no hold-up problem would exist. The vertical integration solution to hold-up implies, of course, that at least one of the parties is as adept as the other in undertaking the investment of the other. If we assume that only party A can undertake investment I_A and only party B can undertake investment I_B, vertical integration does not constitute a viable solution to the hold-up problem.

Joskow (1987) observes that in dealing with many types of asset specificity, the parties to the exchange enter into long-term explicit contracts. Such contracts specify the terms and conditions for some set of future conditions ex ante. Third-party enforcement of such agreements provides a vehicle for safeguarding against ex post performance problems. Thus, both parties would explicitly agree to an ex post division of the relation-specific rent that allowed both to recover their ex ante specific investments. However, the design and enforcement of explicit contracts is often costly; indeed, such transaction costs may exceed the potential rent from the transaction.

We are particularly interested in the implicit, self-enforcing variety of contract. Such an agreement relies on the pursuit of individual self-interest to proscribe the enforcement necessary to prevent contractual breach. Williamson (1983) has observed that transactions that are potentially subject to hold-up are often supported by the potentially opportunistic party making an ex ante credible commitment to the exchange. The following discussion illustrates how an ex ante (implicit) contractual agreement, accompanied by a credible commitment, serves to promote the efficient exchange of a good or service.

4.1. An efficient contract

The remainder of the paper designates party A as the potential victim of hold-up and party B as the potentially opportunistic party. Consider the following ex ante contract between the two parties: Party B agrees to take on \$G of party A's ex ante specific investment, I_A. The contract is efficient if the values of R_A and G are such that the incentive exists for both parties to make the ex ante investments.

Formally, we need to find G such that:

$$R_A + G - I_A \geq 0 \text{ or } \left(C_A + \frac{1}{2}\theta\right) + G - I_A \geq 0 \text{ and}$$

$$R_B - G - I_B \geq 0 \text{ or } \left(C_B + \frac{1}{2}\theta\right) - G - I_B \geq 0$$

Thus,

$$I_A - R_A \leq G \leq R_B - I_B \text{ or}$$

$$I_A - \left(C_A + \frac{1}{2}\theta\right) \leq G \leq \left(C_B + \frac{1}{2}\theta\right) - I_B \tag{5}$$

The viability assumptions (i.e. $R - I_A - I_B > 0$ and $R - C_A - C_B > 0$) ensure that such a G always exists.

Fig. 4 illustrates such a contract when party A is the potential victim of ex post hold-up. The previous assumptions of a given ex post relation-specific return, R, a given co-specific ex ante investment, I, and a given sum of ex post opportunity costs, C, are maintained. The line labelled RR represents all combinations of ex post returns, R_A and R_B, that add to the total relation-specific return, R. The line labelled II represents all possible combinations of individual ex ante specific investments, I_S and I_B that add to I. Similarly, the line labelled CC shows all possible combinations of ex post opportunity costs, C_A and C_B that sum to C. Let the initial requisite specific investments for parties A and B be given by I_A^0 and I_B^0, respectively; and ex post opportunity costs by C_A^0 and C_B^0. In the absence of an ex ante credible commitment, party A's return would be given by R_A^0, a return that is insufficient to entice party A to undertake the initial investment cost, I_A^0. In order to induce party A to partake in the transaction, party B must incur a minimum credible commitment cost of $G^*_{\text{min}} = I_A^0 - R_A^0$; if the ex ante contract is accompanied by such a payment, G^*_{min}, from party B to party A, the latter's return is just sufficient to

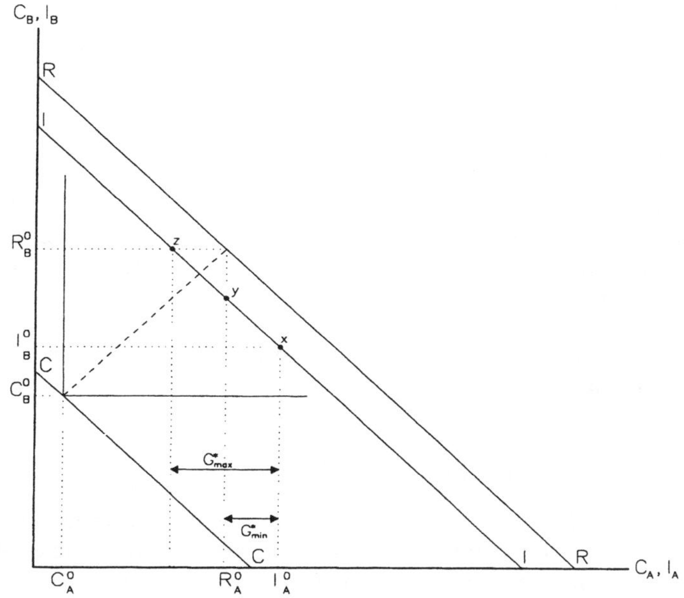

Fig. 4.

induce him/her to undertake the investment I_A^0. While party A would extract none of the relation-specific rent, party B would earn a positive return to his/her initial investment. A credible commitment of size $G^*_{\min}$ effectively alters the distribution of the initial specific investment costs between the two parties from that given at x to that given at y. The maximum commitment cost B is willing to incur is given by $G^*_{\max} = R_B^0 - I_B^0$. Under these conditions, party A earns a positive return to his/her specific investment, while party B earns zero rent. The credible commitment of $G^*_{\max}$ results in an effective distribution of ex ante investment costs denoted by z.

The contract accompanied by the credible commitment $G^*_{\min}$ may be thought of as that which would obtain if B had all the ex ante bargaining power. Conversely, if A had all the ex ante bargaining power, an agreement in which $G^*_{\max}$ constituted the credible commitment undertaken by party B would obtain.

It is extremely important to characterize the precise nature of the credible commitment, G, in this model. It is Williamson's contention that the credible commitment must serve to reciprocate exposure to specialized assets. Thus, the ex ante transfer itself must constitute an investment which is specific to the transaction. Consider the response of party A, the potential victim of hold-up, to a cash transfer of \$G from party B. Since the transfer has the same value outside of the transaction as within the transaction, it does not serve to reduce the level of specific investment required by A. That is, A must still incur a specific investment cost of I_A^0, the ex post return on which is still anticipated to be negative. In order that A's anticipated return is non-negative, it suffices to assume that the opportunity cost of G is zero; that is, that the transfer has no value in a use other than transaction T.[10]

5. The ex ante Nash bargaining solution

The previous discussion indicates that there exists a range of ex ante credible commitments that would serve to ensure that efficient transactions are undertaken in the face of anticipated ex post hold-up. The actual size of the ex ante credible commitment depends upon the relative bargaining strengths of the two parties. If we impose the Nash theory of bargaining ex ante as well as ex post, we arrive at a unique contractual solution to the hold-up problem. In the case of party B potentially holding up party A, ex ante Nash bargaining would lead to a contract, β, in which the relation-specific gross return is distributed as follows:

$$R_A^\beta = (I_A^0 - G^\beta) + \frac{1}{2}\rho; \quad R_B^\beta = (I_B^0 + G^\beta) + \frac{1}{2}\rho,$$

where $\rho = R - I$, R_A^β denotes the relation-specific return accruing to party A under contract β, R_B^β denotes that which accrues to party B, and G_β is the credible commitment necessary to meet the ex ante efficiency conditions.

Under what circumstances will $G^\beta = 0$? In the absence of an ex ante credible commitment (or third party enforcement), it is the distribution of the quasi-rent that will be negotiated in the ex post exchange, regardless of the terms of the contract β. Recall that ex post Nash bargaining leads to the following distribution of the quasi-rent:

$$R_A^0 = C_A^0 + \frac{1}{2}\theta; \quad R_B^0 = C_B^0 + \frac{1}{2}\theta$$

The contractually agreed upon division of the rent will obtain only if the following conditions are satisfied simultaneously:

$$R_A^0 = R_A^\beta; \quad R_B^0 = R_B^\beta$$

That is: $C_A^0 + \frac{1}{2}\theta = I_A^0 + \frac{1}{2}\rho$; $C_B^0 + \frac{1}{2}\theta = I_B^0 + \frac{1}{2}\rho$

or,

$$C_A^0 - I_A^0 = C_B^0 - I_B^0$$

Thus, if the difference between specific investment cost and ex post opportunity cost is equal across parties, no self-enforcement capital is required to uphold the contract. Such a contract is illustrated in Fig. 5. The division of the rent specified in contract β does not require ex ante investment in enforcement capital since the contractually agreed upon

[10] Thus, G might be a transfer of inputs that have value only when used in producing the investment good, I_A. Alternatively, G may be a transfer that can be liquidated subsequent to A's undertaking of the specific investment. Under these circumstances the transfer is a (costlessly enforceable) 'contract' as it is contingent on A's investment.

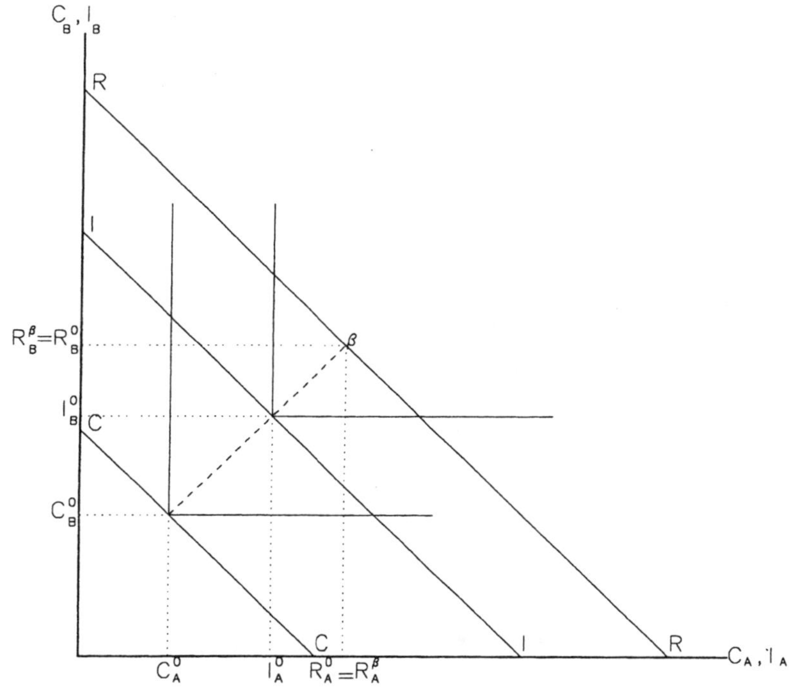

Fig. 5.

distribution of the gross relation-specific return, R_A^β and R_B^β, is identical to the anticipated ex post distribution, R_A^0 and R_B^0.

In general, however, the above condition for zero self-enforcement capital does not hold and an ex ante credible commitment is required to uphold the terms any transaction which requires investment in specific assets. Fig. 6 illustrates the contract β when the ex ante Nash bargaining agreement is upheld by party B investing in self-enforcement capital equal to G^β, where

$$G^\beta = I_A^0 - R_A^0 + \frac{1}{2}\rho = R_B^0 - I_B^0 + \frac{1}{2}\rho$$

More generally, under both ex ante and ex post Nash bargaining, the size of credible commitment, G, that would induce efficient transactions is given by:

$$G = \frac{1}{2}[(I_i^0 - C_i^0) - (I_j^0 - C_j^0)], \tag{6}$$

where $i,j = A,B, i \neq j$, and i is the potential victim of hold-up. Note that $G = 0$ for $C_i^0 - I_i^0 = C_j^0 - I_j^0$.

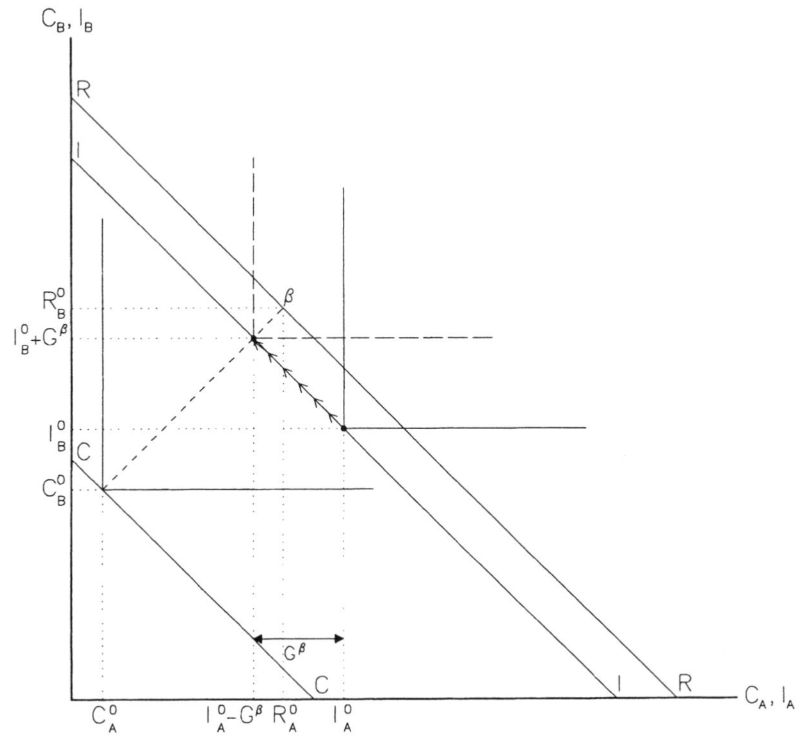

Fig. 6.

6. Concluding remarks

The literature to date has recognized the relationship between the specificity of investments and market failure arising from potential ex post hold-up. Formal expositions of hold-up have been supplied by Williamson (1983), Tirole (1988) and Grossman and Hart (1986). The model of hold-up presented in this paper approaches that offered by Tirole (1988) in terms of its simplicity as well as in the nature of bargaining between parties to a transaction. It is, however, somewhat more general in that parties to an exchange are allowed to co-invest in specific assets.

The literature has also taken account of market responses to potential hold-up. Such responses include the formation of third-party enforceable contracts and vertical or lateral integration of operations. The most significant contribution of the paper is the formal exposition of Williamson's 'reciprocal exposure' solution to the hold-up problem.

An important direction for future research involves the consideration of a more dynamic bargaining structure within the basic framework of the model offered in this paper. Does ex ante reciprocal exposure serve to induce efficient levels of specific investments in repeated exchanges where information is revealed over time and contracts are subject to renegotiation?[11] It would also be useful to consider the consequences of information asymmetries in both static and dynamic frameworks.[12]

References

Aghion, P.,M. Dewatripont and P. Rey, 1994, Renegotiation design with unverifiable information, Econometrica, 62(2), 257–282.

Beaudry, P. and M. Poitevin, 1993, Signalling and renegotiation in contractual relationships, Econometrica, 61(4), 745–782.

Crocker, K.J. and S.E. Masten, 1988, Mitigating contractual hazards: Unilateral options and contract length, Rand Journal of Economics, 19, 327–343.

Grossman, S.J. and O.D. Hart, 1986, The costs and benefits of ownership: A theory of vertical and lateral integration, Journal of Political Economy, 94(4), 691–719.

Klein, B.,R.G. Crawford and A.A. Alchian, 1978, Vertical integration, appropriable rents, and the competitive contracting process, Journal of Law and Economics, 21, 297–326.

Koss, Patricia, 1993, Contractual arrangements in the British Columbia intermediate market for raw fish: An empirical analysis, Ph.D dissertation, Simon Fraser University, Burnaby B.C.

Joskow, P.L., 1987, Contract duration and relationship-specific investments: Empirical evidence from coal markets, American Economic Review, 77(1), 168–185.

Masten, S.E. and K.J. Crocker, 1985, Efficient adaptation in long-term contracts, American Economic Review, 75, 1083–1093.

Milgrom, Paul R. and John D. Roberts, 1992, Economics of Organization and Management, (Prentice-Hall, Englewood Cliffs, NJ).

Nash, J., 1953, Two-person cooperative games, Econometrica, 21, 128–140.

Tirole, Jean, 1988, The Theory of Industrial Organization, (MIT Press, Cambridge, MA).

Williamson, O.E., 1983, Credible commitments: Using hostages to support exchange, American Economic Review, 83, 519–540.

[11]For example, Aghion et al. (1994), by modelling renogotiation as a standard infinite horizon bargaining model, demonstrate that efficient investments can be achieved both through the initial transfer of hostages and the imposition of per diem penalties to be paid by one party to the other until agreement is reached.

[12]Beaudry and Poitevin (1993), for example, consider a situation in which an informed party may propose renegotiation after a specific allocation has been agreed upon. They examine the impact of renegotiation possibilities on contractual outcomes when the environment is characterized by an adverse selection problem.

ELSEVIER

Journal of Economic Dynamics and Control
22 (1998) 1187–1207

JOURNAL OF
Economic
Dynamics
& Control

The evolution of type communication in a sender/ receiver game of common interest with cheap talk

Jasmina Arifovic, B. Curtis Eaton*

Department of Economics, Simon Fraser University, Burnaby, BC, Canada V5A 1S6

Accepted 19 January 1998

Abstract

We use a genetic algorithm to simulate play of a sender/receiver game of common interest in which players engage in anonymous, pairwise interactions. The order of an equilibrium is the number of player types that are communicated. There are many equilibria of each order, equilibria of the same order are Pareto-equivalent, and equilibria of different orders are Pareto-ranked by their order. We discover a dynamic process in which the population climbs an equilibrium payoff ladder, successively moving from an equilibrium of one order to an equilibrium of the next highest order, eventually converging on an equilibrium of the highest order. © 1998 Published by Elsevier Science B.V. All rights reserved.

JEL classification: C63; C70; C72; D82; D83

Keywords: Evolution; Signalling; Communication; Genetic algorithms

1. Introduction

We are interested in the evolution of communication in sender/receiver games of common interest with cheap talk.[1] In the most elementary sender/receiver game, there are two players (sender and receiver), two player types (t_1,t_2), two costless messages, (m_1,m_2), and two actions (A_1,A_2). Play of the game is

* Corresponding author. Tel.: + 1 604 291 3508; fax: + 1 604 291 5944.

[1] The paper that is most closely related to ours is 'Cheap Talk, Coordination, and Evolutionary Stability' by Karl Warneryd (1993). There are, however, a number of other important papers on sender/receiver games, including Crawford and Sobel (1982), Kim and Sobel (1990), Matsui (1991), and Blume et al. (1993). Lewis (1969) is the seminal work on the communication problem addressed in this literature.

0165-1889/98/$19.00 © 1998 Published by Elsevier Science B.V. All rights reserved.
PII S0165-1889(98)00009-8

sequential: first, nature assigns sender a type; then, sender chooses a message and communicates it to receiver; finally, receiver takes an action. Payoffs depend only on sender's type and receiver's action. Given that sender's type is t_i, action A_i is payoff maximizing for both players. Hence, given sender's type, there is a unique Pareto-optimal action. In this regard, the game is one of *common interest* in the sense of Aumann and Sorin (1989). Since messages are costless, communication involves *cheap talk* in the sense of Farrell and Gibbons (1989).

To unerringly achieve the Pareto-optimal equilibrium, sender must perfectly signal or communicate its type to receiver, and successful signalling requires that the players solve a coordination problem – that they somehow arrive at a common vocabulary of types. In the elementary game there are two possible vocabularies, and hence two solutions to this coordination problem, corresponding to the two ways in which the two messages can be assigned to the two player types.

Warneryd (1993) uses this elementary game to construct an asymmetric contest. He shows that in addition to the equilibria that involve perfect communication, there are equilibria that involve no communication, but that only the equilibria with perfect signalling are evolutionarily stable. Hence, evolutionary stability favors perfect signalling.

In this paper we explore a more elaborate game of common interest with cheap talk. We incorporate many player types and many messages, and suppose that the number of messages is at least as large as the number of player types. Our game is bilateral in the sense that both players send and receive messages and take actions. Of more interest, perhaps, we enrich the action space. In the elementary game one can interpret action A_1 as the action that is *appropriate* in an encounter in which sender is type 1, and *inappropriate* in an encounter in which sender is type 2. Similarly, A_2 is appropriate when sender is type 2 and inappropriate when sender is type 1. Intuitively, receiver's decision problem is then a two stage problem: first form a subjective probability as to sender's type and then choose an action. Receiver will have no trouble choosing an action when the subjective probability that sender is of type 1 is close to 1, or when it is close to 0. If, however, receiver is uncertain as to sender's type, we might imagine that receiver would search for some third, *neutral action*, an action that is neither appropriate nor inappropriate for either player type. We enrich the action space by incorporating a neutral action of this sort.

This more elaborate game has a number of features in common with the elementary game: perfect signalling is Pareto optimal; there are many equilibria, only some of which are Pareto optimal; evolutionary stability favors perfect signalling; to achieve perfect signalling the players must evolve a common vocabulary of types.

We study the process by which the common vocabulary of types evolves. Our players use a *genetic algorithm* (GA) to evolve their strategies. The GA was first developed by Holland (1975) as a stochastic search algorithm. In economic modelling, the GA drives the evolution of a population of agents' decision rules represented by binary strings. The performance of the decision rules in a given economic environment is evaluated through their fitness function which is equal to the value of the objective function. The rules are updated using the set of three genetic operators, reproduction, crossover and mutation. Reproduction makes copies of individual strings. Strings with higher fitness values have higher probabilities of being reproduced. The creation of new rules is accomplished through the application of crossover and mutation. Crossover performs randomized partial string exchanges, while mutation changes a bit value on a randomly chosen position in a binary string.[2]

We interpret the genetic algorithm as a useful model of trial-and-error learning. This approach to learning has some important advantages relative to other models in the literature. For one thing, potentially there is considerable heterogeneity across agents, a feature not often modelled in the learning literature to date. Out of equilibrium, some agents are trying one decision rule while other agents are trying other decision rules, with the better decision rules propagating and the poorer ones dying out. For another, the information requirements on agents are minimal. Finally, genetic algorithm learning has been shown in other research (e.g. Arifovic, 1994, 1995, 1996) to successfully mimic the behavior of human subjects in controlled laboratory settings.

The game used in our simulations is introduced, and the equilibria and stability properties briefly discussed, in Section 2. The simulation algorithm is described in Section 3. Results are presented in Section 4.

2. A bilateral sender/receiver game

Our game can be described as a *bilateral* sender/receiver game of common interest with cheap talk and a *neutral* action. There are n players, where n is an even integer. In each period, nature creates $n/2$ pairs of players by a process of random matching. The players in any pair are called *partners* and the game they play is called an *encounter*. Using a uniform distribution, nature randomly assigns one of T types to each partner. Each partner then sends one of M messages. We assume that $M \geq T$, so that the number of messages is no smaller than the number of types. Having received the other partner's message, each partner then chooses one of $T+1$ actions from the set $\{A_1, \dots, A_T, N\}$.

[2] Genetic algorithms and other computational techniques involving artificial intelligence are increasingly being employed by economists as a way of modelling the behavior of economic agents. A partial list of recent references includes Andreoni and Miller (1995), Arifovic (1994, 1996), Arifovic and Eaton (1995), Bullard and Duffy (1994,1995), Marimon et al. (1989), Miller (1996), Routledge (1994) Sargent (1993) and Tesfatsion (1995).

Action A_i is said to be *appropriate* for a partner of type i and *inappropriate* for any other type of partner, and action N is said to be *neutral*. The sense in which an action is appropriate, inappropriate, or neutral will be clear once we have considered payoffs.

Payoffs in the encounter depend on the partners' types and on their actions, but not on their messages. Consider a game involving players i and j, and denote their actions by $a_i \in \{A_1, \ldots, A_T, N\}$ and $a_j \in \{A_1, \ldots, A_T, N\}$. The payoff to player i is

$$\Pi_i(a_i, a_j) = v + w$$

where v is determined by i's own action and w is determined by j's action.

$$v = \begin{cases} y & \text{if } a_i \text{ is appropriate} \\ z & \text{if } a_i \text{ is neutral} \\ 0 & \text{if } a_i \text{ is inappropriate} \end{cases}, \qquad w = \begin{cases} g & \text{if } a_j \text{ is appropriate} \\ h & \text{if } a_j \text{ is neutral} \\ 0 & \text{if } a_j \text{ is inappropriate} \end{cases}.$$

We assume that

$$y > z > 0 \quad \text{and} \quad g > h > 0.$$

Action A_i is appropriate for a partner of type T_i because it generates the largest possible payoff for each partner, and is inappropriate for any other type of partner because it generates the smallest possible payoff for each partner. Action N is neutral because it generates an intermediate payoff for each player.

A player's strategy involves one of $T + 1$ actions for each of the M messages the player might receive, and one of M messages for each of the T types that nature might assign to the player. Here we describe the equilibria and report on their stability properties. Derivations are elementary and therefore not included. There are T different sorts of equilibria distinguished by the number of player types for which signalling is perfect, and we refer to the number of types that are perfectly signalled as the *order* of the equilibrium.

At one extreme are all the *perfect signalling equilibria* – that is, all the equilibria of order T. In an equilibrium of order T, for each player type t there is at least one message that is sent only by players of type t, all players send such a message when they are assigned type t, and all players respond to such a message with action A_t. In a perfect signalling equilibrium, each player gets the highest possible payoff, $y + g$, in each encounter.

At the other extreme are the equilibria of order 0. In these *no-signalling equilibria*, for all messages m, the conditional probability that the sender is of type t is less than z/y for all player types t, and all players respond to all messages with action N. In an equilibrium of order 0, each player gets payoff $z + h$ in all encounters, which is less than $y + g$.

In between the perfect and the no-signalling equilibria are equilibria of order ϕ, $0 < \phi < T - 1$, in which ϕ player types are perfectly signalled and $T - \phi$ player types are not signalled. Consider, for example an equilibrium of order 1, in which player type 1 is perfectly signalled. In such an equilibrium, there is a non-empty set of messages Ω which elicit action A_1 from all receivers, and all players send a message $m \in \Omega$ when they are assigned type 1. In addition, for all messages $m \notin \Omega$, and for all types $t \neq 1$, the conditional probability that the sender is type t is less than z/y. Notice that equilibria of order $T - 1$ are not possible, since if $T - 1$ player types are perfectly signalled, then so too is the one remaining player type.[3] A player's expected payoff in an equilibrium of order ϕ is $(\phi/T)(y + g) + (1 - (\phi/T))(z + h)$.

Notice that equilibria are Pareto-ranked by their order. Suppose we compare two equilibria. If the orders of the equilibria differ, the equilibrium with the higher order is Pareto-preferred. If the orders of the equilibria are the same, the equilibria are Pareto-equivalent.

Regardless of parameter values, perfect signalling equilibria are always possible. However, depending on the values of parameters M, T, z, and y, equilibria of order $\phi \leq T - 2$ may or may not be possible. For example, if $z/y < 1/2$ and $T = 2$, N is never a best response to a message; consequently, only equilibria of order T are possible. However, if $z/y > 1/2$, then equilibria of all orders less than $T - 1$ are possible. Hence, in our simulations, we assume that $z/y > 1/2$.

Finally, if we focus for the moment on monomorphic equilibria, we can say something of interest about the stability properties of these equilibria. Although equilibria of order ϕ, $0 < \phi < T - 1$ are neutrally evolutionarily stable, they are not evolutionarily stable, nor are there evolutionarily stable sets of order ϕ, $0 < \phi < T - 1$. In contrast, when $M = T$, equilibria of order T are evolutionarily stable, and when $M > T$, any equilibrium of order T is an element of an evolutionarily stable set. Hence, standard selection criteria favor the perfect-signalling equilibria.

3. Description of the algorithm

In this section we first provide an overview of the entire algorithm that we use for our simulations, and then describe in more detail its crucial elements.

3.1. Overview

A player is a chromosome, written as a binary string, that dictates (a) for each possible type, the message the player sends in any encounter, (b) for each possible message received from a partner, the action the player takes.

[3] Suppose that the first $T - 1$ types are perfectly signalled. This means that there is at least one message used for each type. Consider the set of messages not used by the $T - 1$ perfectly signalled types. Type T has to be using one of the messages from this set. Thus, if $T - 1$ types are perfectly signalled, type T will also be perfectly signalled and equilibria of order $T - 1$ do not exist.

1. *Initial conditions*: Initially, a chromosome for each player is chosen randomly.
2. A *generation*: A generation is composed of R time periods. In each time period $r \in [1,R]$, each of the n players is randomly assigned a type and a partner. Thus, in each time period, each player has one encounter, and in each generation, each player has R encounters.
3. *Updating*: In stage 3 the chromosomes are updated using the following genetic operators – reproduction, crossover and mutation. Given the updated set of chromosomes, the algorithm loops back to stage 2.

3.2. Chromosomes

There are two parts of the chromosome which are used for decision making. The first part will be referred to as *message sending*, MS, and the second part will be referred to as *message reading*, MR.

MS is used for the choice of message given the type assignment. This is a mapping from types to messages. It contains Tl_1 bits where T is the number of types and l_1 is the number of bits used for the binary number representation of a message m, $m \in [1,M]$. For example, if a player is of type 3 in an encounter, the player will use bits in the range $2l_1 + 1$ to $3l_1$ to determine its message.

MR consists of two subparts MR_1 and MR_2. MR_1 determines whether the player will take a type specific action or a neutral action. If a type specific action is called for, MR_2 determines the mapping from messages to type specific actions. MR_1 contains M bits. If the partner sends message m in a given encounter, the player will use bit m of MR_1 to decide on its action. If this bit is equal to 1, the player takes a type specific action and if it is equal to 0, the player takes a neutral action.

MR_2 is a mapping from the partner's potential messages to type specific actions. It contains Ml_2 bits where l_2 is the number of bits used for the binary number encoding of a type. For example, if message 3 is received, then the bits in the range $2l_2 + 1$ to $3l_2$ are used to determine the type specific action.

Here is an example of a chromosome and its decoding for $T = 4$ and $M = 4$:

	MS	MR	
		MR_1	MR_2
chromosome			
	01 00 11 10	10 1 1	01 00 11 10
decoded values			
	2 1 4 3	10 1 1	2 1 4 3

MS instructs the player to send message 2 when it is of type 1,[4] message 1 when it is of type 2, message 4 when it is of type 3, and message 3 when it is of type 4. MR_1 directs the player to take a type specific action when the partner sends messages 1, 3 or 4 and to take the neutral action when the partner sends message 2. Finally, conditional on MR_1, MR_2 instructs the player to take action A_2 if it receives message 1, action A_1 if it receives message 2, action A_4 if it receives message 3, and action A_3 if it receives message 4.

3.3. *An encounter*

In a given time period r, $r \in [1,R]$, $n/2$ pairs of players are randomly matched. Now consider an encounter of players i and j, when i is assigned type 3 and j is assigned type 4, and suppose the above chromosome describes player i and the following chromosome describes player j:

	MS	MR	
		MR_1	MR_2
	01 10 11 00	01 10	10 01 11 00
decoded values			
	2 3 4 1	01 10	3 2 4 1

Player i, assigned type 3, sends message 4 to signal its type. Since the fourth bit of its MR_1 is equal to 0, player j takes the neutral action when it receives message 4. Thus, player i receives payoff h as a result of its partner's neutral action and player j receives payoff z as a result of its own neutral action. Player j, assigned type 4, sends message 1 to signal its type. When player i receives message 1, it takes a type specific action since the first bit of its MR_1 is equal to 1. Using its MR_2, player i takes action A_2. Since j is, in fact, type 4, i's action is inappropriate. Both players i and j receive payoff equal to 0 as a result of i's inappropriate action. The total payoff in the encounter for player i is $0 + h$, and for player j it is $z + 0$.

3.4. *Updating*

After each generation (composed of R time periods) the players' decision rules are updated using the GA. The GA updating is applied for *maxgen* generations. The genetic operators that are used for the updating are *reproduction, crossover* and *mutation.* The parameters of the genetic algorithm were set using the

---

[4] For $M = 4$ and $T = 4$, two bits are required to code integer numbers between 1 and 4. Thus, 00 is decoded as 1, 01 is decoded as 2, 10 is decoded as 3, and 11 is decoded as 4.

recommended values found in the artificial intelligence literature. Let us denote the pool of players from the previous generation as $pool_0$. The creation of a new generation involves 3 steps.

In the first step, we use reproduction to create a new pool of chromosomes, $pool_1$. Reproduction makes copies of individual chromosomes. The objective is to promote well performing chromosomes and create a pool of n copies of chromosomes in which chromosomes with higher fitness values receive, on average, larger number of copies. The criterion used for copying is the value of a fitness function, which is equal to the average payoff over the R encounters in the current generation,

$$\mu_{i,gen} = \frac{\sum_{r=1}^{R} \Pi_{i,r}}{R},$$

where $\mu_{i,\,gen}$ is the fitness value of chromosome i at generation gen, and $\Pi_{i,\,r}$ is the payoff of player i in an encounter in time period r. The version of the reproduction operator that we use is called *tournament selection.* It is performed in the following way. A pair of chromosomes is randomly selected with replacement, and their fitness values are compared. The chromosome with the higher fitness value contributes a copy to $pool_1$. In case of a tie, the contributing chromosome is randomly selected. This procedure is repeated n times. In the artificial intelligence literature, there are several different ways in which the reproduction operator can be implemented, for example, proportional selection, linear ranking and tournament selection. When applying the reproduction operator, there is a tradeoff between exploration of the strategy space versus exploitation of information gained so far. Some versions of reproduction exhibit strong selective pressure by putting more weight on exploitative search while others exhibit weaker selective pressure putting more weight on exploratory search. Based on extensive simulation studies, Back, 1996 argues that tournament selection nicely balances these two effects.

Applying the crossover operator on $pool_1$, we create another pool of n chromosomes which we call $pool_2$. The n players from $pool_1$ are randomly paired and each pair is treated sequentially. With probability 0.4 both members of the pair go directly into $pool_2$. With probability 0.6, two new chromosomes for inclusion into $pool_2$ are created using crossover. This operator is applied in the following way. A number k is randomly selected from $(1, \ldots, l-1)$, where l is the length of a chromosome, and two new chromosomes are formed by swapping the set of binary values to the right of the position k. An example of the crossover between two chromosomes for $l = 10$ and $k = 5$ is given below:

$$\begin{cases} 1\,1\,0\,0\,1\,|\,0\,1\,1\,0\,0 \\ 0\,0\,0\,1\,0\,|\,1\,0\,0\,1\,1 \end{cases}$$

The resulting two new chromosomes are

$$\begin{cases} 1100110011 \\ 0001001100 \end{cases}$$

Finally, using $pool_2$, a new pool of chromosomes, which we call $pool_3$, is created via mutation. Each binary digit within each chromosome is changed to the other value of the binary alphabet with probability 0.0033. This value of the mutation rate is one of those recommended in the artificial intelligence literature (see Back, 1996). In addition, we also conducted a number of simulations with rates of mutation of 0.033 and 0.0011. With mutation rate 0.033, we did not obtain convergence in the simulations which were conducted for 100,000 generations. This rate of mutation was obviously too high for our genetic algorithm setup and was introducing too much dirsruptive noise into the evolving environment. Mutation rate 0.0011 resulted in convergence times similar to those that were recorded for the rate of mutation of 0.0033.

Applicaton of reproduction, crossover and mutation determines the members of the new population of decision rules that players use during the R social interactions that take place in generation $gen + 1$. The purpose of the reproduction operator is to promote chromosomes that have been shown to be relatively more successful. It can be interpreted as imitation of successful strategies. The crossover and mutation operators advance the search for chromosomes that will yield higher fitness values, while maintaining parts of chromosomes or even entire chromosomes that have performed well in the past. These two operators can be interpreted as players' experimentation with new strategies. Simulation results reported in this paper do not depend qualitatively on the use of the crossover operator. The difference in simulations with and without the crossover operator is in the speed of convergence to perfect signalling equilibria. Simulations that were conducted with the use of crossover converged, on average, 7 to 8 times faster than simulations that were conducted without crossover.

4. Results of the simulations

In this section we discuss the results of our computer simulations. We first study how the process of convergence takes place. Then we present comparative statics results with respect to the number of types, number of messages, and payoff parameter values.

We use three measures to examine the behavior of the algorithm over the course of a simulation. The first is the average payoff, $\bar{\Pi}_{gen}$ per generation and is given by

$$\bar{\Pi}gen = \frac{\sum_{i=1}^{n}\sum_{r=1}^{R}\Pi_{i,r,gen}}{Rn}.$$

The second is what we call a *recognition coefficient*, $rc_{t,gen}$, and is specific to player types. It is defined as the proportion of times that partners of players of type t chose action A_t in generation gen ($0 \leq rc_{t,gen} \leq 1$). It is given by

$$rc_{t,gen} = \frac{r_{t,gen}}{ap_{t,gen}},$$

where $ap_{t,gen}$ is the number of times that type t has appeared in the $(n/2)R$ encounters in generation gen, and $r_{t,gen}$ is the number of times that a partner of a player of type t chose action A_t. In an equilibrium of order ϕ, the recognition coefficient is equal to 1 for ϕ player types and is equal to 0 for the remaining player types.

The third is a metric defined on the strategy space which we call a *best response metric*. This measure is computed in the following way. Since a player must choose a message for each of T types and an action for each of M messages, a player's strategy has $(T + M)$ elements. Each element can be a best response to the environment. The environment, at generation gen, is given by the set of all other players' strategies. We compute a best response for each element of the player's strategy in the current environment. Then we check each element of each player's strategy. We add 0 to our measure if an element is a best response, and we add 1 if it is not. Finally, we normalize the sum calculated in this manner by $(T + M)n$ in order to obtain a distance measure which takes values in the interval [0, 1]. Thus, the best response distance at generation gen, br_{gen}, is given by

$$br_{gen} = \frac{\sum_{i=1}^{n}\sum_{s=1}^{T+M} I_{i,s}}{n(T + M)},$$

where $I_{i,s}$ is the index variable whose value is equal to one if an element s of player i's strategy is a best response and zero otherwise. In calculating $I_{i,s}$, for convenience, we assume that player i operates in an environment described by the set of all players' strategies. The best response metric gives a distance between two points in the strategy space. One is the point which represents players' best responses to the environment in a given generation. The other is the players' actual responses to that environment. In equilibrium, these two points coincide, and $br_{gen} = 0$.

We start our analysis with the examination of the behavior observed in the simulation conducted for $T = 4$ and $M = 4$, $g = 16$, $h = 12$, $y = 16$, and $z = 12$. Fig. 1 presents the average payoff over the course of this simulation. Figs. 2–5 show the four recognition coefficients. The best response metric for the entire simulation which consisted of 400 generations is presented in Fig. 6.

Snapshots of players' strategies at generations 26, 59, 112, and 422 are given in Table 1. There are two matrices, α and β, for each of the four generations. The

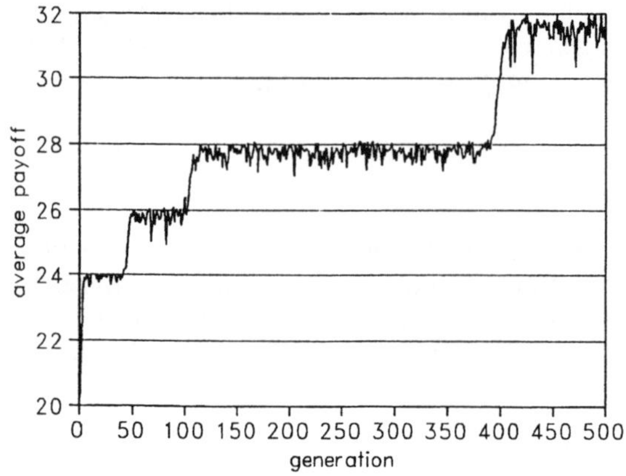

Fig. 1. Average payoff; $T = 4$; $M = 4$.

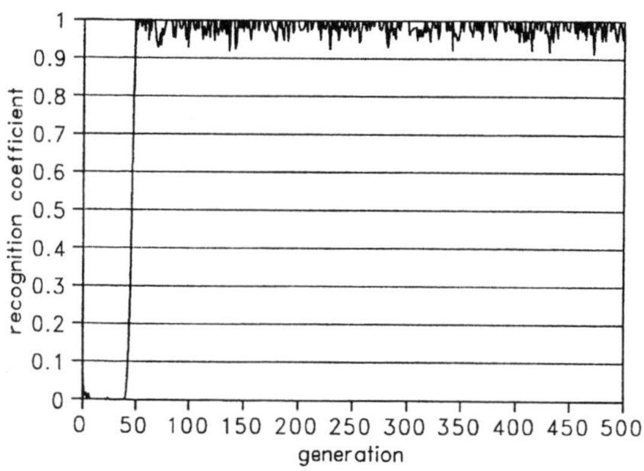

Fig. 2. Recognition coefficient – type 1.

first four rows of matrix α present population frequencies of mappings from types to messages. The fifth row gives the values of a *maximal type-message frequency*, $f_{t_{\max},m_j}$, for each message m_j. This value is given by

$$f_{t_{\max},m_j} = \max\{f_{t_1,m_j}, f_{t_2,m_j}, \ldots, f_{t_i,m_j}, \ldots, f_{t_T,m_j}\}$$

where f_{t_i,m_j} is the ratio of the element $\alpha_{i,j}$ of matrix α ($i = 1, \ldots, T$; $j = 1, \ldots, M$) and the sum of all the elements of column j, $\sum_{i=1}^{T} \alpha_{i,j}$. The player type that has

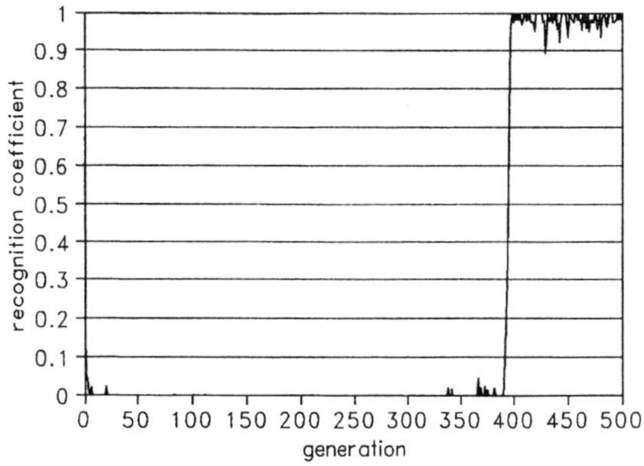

Fig. 3. Recognition coefficient – type 2.

the highest column frequency is denoted by $t_{\max}$. If the value of $f_{t_{\max},m_j}$ exceeds z/y, then the best response to message m_j is a type specific action $A_{t_{\max}}$. On the other hand, if $f_{t_{\max},m_j} < z/y$, then the best response to message m_j is a neutral action, N. The elements of matrix β show population frequencies of mappings from messages to type specific (first four rows) and neutral actions (fifth row).

Our results show that the simulation goes through four stages. Each stage corresponds to one of the four equilibria of different orders ($\phi = 0$, $\phi = 1$, $\phi = 2$, and $\phi = 4$). Initially, the simulation is close to an equilibrium of order $\phi = 0$. During the second stage, the simulation is in the neighborhood of an equilibrium of order $\phi = 1$, and during the third stage it is close to an equilibrium of order $\phi = 2$. Finally, the simulation spends the fourth stage in the neighborhood of a perfect signalling equilibrium of order $\phi = 4$. (Note that an equilibrium of order 3, order $T - 1$, does not exist.) Transition periods between any two stages are very short, not longer than 10 generations. Thus, the proportion of time spent near an equilibrium is high, and the population of players is climbing an *equilibrium payoff ladder*. We give a brief description of what happens in each of the four stages.

Stage 1: *Neighborhood of equilibrium of order* 0.

The simulation approaches a no-signalling equilibrium of order $\phi = 0$ around generation 10. The expected payoff for this equilibrium is $g + z$ and is equal to 24 for the specified set of payoff values. Fig. 1 shows that, around generation 10, the simulation average payoff approaches this value and oscillates around it for 40 generations (until generation 50). The figures of recognition coefficients show that during this period values of all of the four recognition coefficients remain close to zero.

Table 1
Selected populations or strategies

	α					β			
	m_1	m_2	m_3	m_4		m_1	m_2	m_3	m_4
Generation 26									
t_1	0	0	40	0	t_1	0	0	0	0
t_2	0	0	12	28	t_2	0	0	0	0
t_3	0	0	18	22	t_3	0	0	0	0
t_4	0	29	0	11	t_4	0	0	0	0
$f_{t_{max}}$	0	1	0.57	0.44	N	40	40	40	40
Generation 59									
t_1	40	0	0	0	t_1	40	0	0	0
t_2	0	0	40	0	t_2	0	1	0	0
t_3	0	20	15	5	t_3	0	0	0	0
t_4	0	40	0	0	t_4	0	0	0	0
$f_{t_{max}}$	1	0.66	0.73	1	N	0	39	40	40
Generation 112									
t_1	40	0	0	0	t_1	40	0	0	0
t_2	1	0	35	4	t_2	0	0	0	0
t_3	0	0	40	0	t_3	0	0	0	0
t_4	0	40	0	0	t_4	0	40	0	0
$f_{t_{max}}$	0.97	1	0.53	1	N	0	0	40	40
Generation 422									
t_1	39	1	0	0	t_1	40	0	0	0
t_2	0	0	40	0	t_2	0	0	40	0
t_3	0	0	0	40	t_3	0	0	0	40
t_4	0	40	0	0	t_4	0	40	0	0
$f_{t_{max}}$	1	0.97	1	1	N	0	0	0	0

A snapshot of players' strategies at generation 26 is given in Table 1. The elements of matrix α show the frequencies of mappings from types to messages. For example, the element $\alpha_{2,3}$ shows that 12 players use message m_3 to signal type t_2, the element α_{24} shows that 28 players use message m_4 to signal type t_2, etc. Row 5 of matrix α indicates that the values of f_{t_{max},m_1}, f_{t_{max},m_3}, and f_{t_{max},m_4} are less than $z/y = 0.75$. This means that a best response to messages m_1, m_3, and m_4 are neutral actions. On the other hand, the value of f_{t_{max},m_2} is equal to 1 with $t_{max} = 4$. Therefore, a best response to message m_2 is a type specific action A_4.

The elements of matrix β, which show the frequencies of mappings from messages to type specific and neutral actions, indicate that all players respond to all messages with neutral actions. For messages m_1, m_3 and m_4 neutral actions

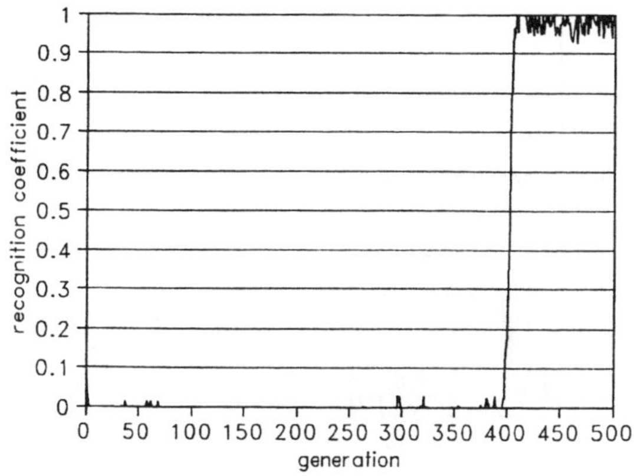

Fig. 4. Recognition coefficient – type 3.

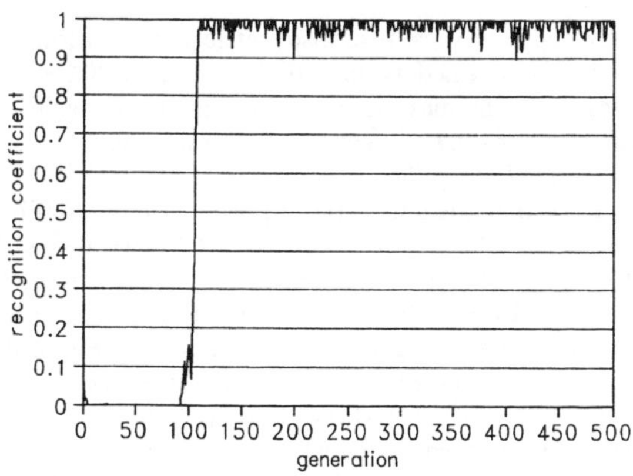

Fig. 5. Recognition coefficient – type 4.

are best responses, but they are not best responses for m_2. Since all 40 players take neutral action in response to message m_2, the message receiving parts of strategies contain 40 elements that are not best responses. Let us examine whether actions in the message sending part of strategies are best responses. Since all players take neutral actions regardless of the message sent, from the message sending part of the strategy any message sent to signal each of the four types is a best response. Thus, in the message sending part of the entire population of strategies there are no elements that are not best responses.

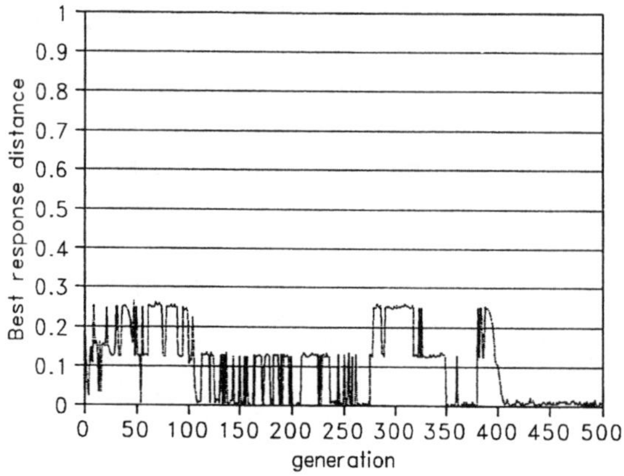

Fig. 6. Best response distance; $T = 4$; $M = 4$.

As a result, the value of the best response metric at generation 26 is 0.125. The value of $br_{26} = 0.125$ is obtained as the ratio between the 40 elements which are not best responses (from the message receiving part of strategies) and the total number of possible actions, nTM, which is equal to 320.

Stage 2: *Neighborhood of equilibirum of order* 1.

From Fig. 1 we see that the simulation approaches an equilibrium of order 1 around generation 50. Stage 2 lasts for about 60 generations. The expected payoff of the equilibrium of order 1 is given by $(g + 3h + y + 3z)/4$ and is equal to 26 for our set of payoff values. Fig. 1 shows that the simulation average payoff takes values close to 26 between generations 50 and 110. Fig. 2 shows that the value of the recognition coefficient for type 1, rc_1, starts taking values close to 1 around generation 50. Figs. 3–5 show that the values of other recognition coefficients remain close to zero. A snapshot of players' strategies at generation 59 is given in Table 1. Matrices α and β indicate that all 160 elements of the message sending strategies are best responses to the message receiving strategies, while 41 of the 160 elements of the message receiving strategies are not best responses to message sending strategies. Hence, the value of the best responses metric is 0.128 (41/320).

Stage 3: *Neighborhood of equilibrium of order* 2.

The simulation approaches the neighborhood of an equilibrium of order 2 around generation 112. The simulation average payoff is close to 28 which is the expected payoff of the equilibrium of order 2 ($(1/2)(g + h + y + z)$). Fig. 1 shows that the simulation average payoff remains close to this value for about 300 generations. Fig. 5 reveals that rc_4 reaches the values close to 1 after generation 100. Recognition coefficients for types 2 and 3 are still close to zero.

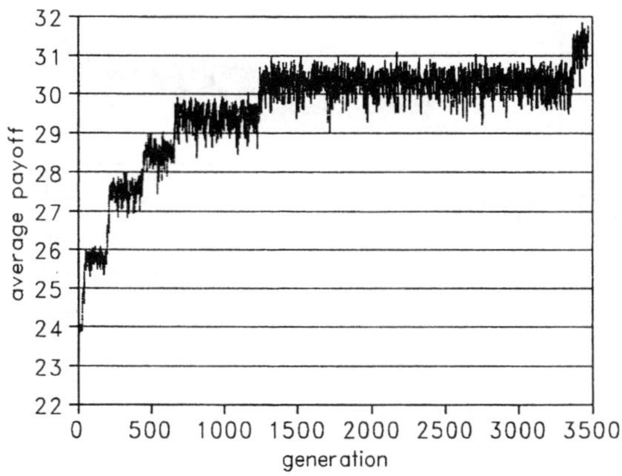

Fig. 7. Average payoff; $T = 8$, $M = 8$.

A snapshot of players' strategies at generation 112 is given in Table 1. At generation 112, all 160 elements of the sending strategies are best responses to the message receiving strategies, while 40 of the 160 elements of the message receiving strategies are not best responses to the message sending strategies. Hence, the best response metric at generation 112 is equal to 0.125 (40/320).

Stage 4: *Neighborhood of equilibrium of order* 4.

Fig. 1 shows that, after generation 400, the simulation average payoff climbs to the levels close to 32. This number is, for our payoff values, the expected payoff in a perfect signalling equilibrium $(g + y)$, an equilibrium of order $\phi = 4$. Fig. 3 shows that rc_2 rises to values close to 1 around generation 390. A few generations later (generation 396) rc_3 starts taking values close to 1 (Fig. 4). Thus, the simulation transits from an equilibrium of order $\phi = 2$ directly to an equilibrium of order $\phi = 4$. A snapshot of strategies at generation 422 (Table 1) indicates that one of the 160 elements of the message sending strategies is not a best response to the message receiving strategies, while all 160 elements of the message receiving strategies are best responses to the message sending strategies. Hence, the value of the best response metric at generation 422 is 0.0031 (1/320).[5]

The above described properties of the evolutionary process characterized all computer simulations. For example, Figs. 7 and 8 show the average payoff for the simulations conducted for $T = 8$, $M = 8$, $g = 16$, $h = 12$, $y = 16$, and

[5] The one element that is not a best response is a result of random mutation. A positive rate of mutation prevents the exact convergence of a simulation to a perfect signalling equilibrium. Instead, as a result of continuing effects of mutation, there will always be a small number of elements that are not best responses as in the neighborhood of a perfect signalling equilibria.

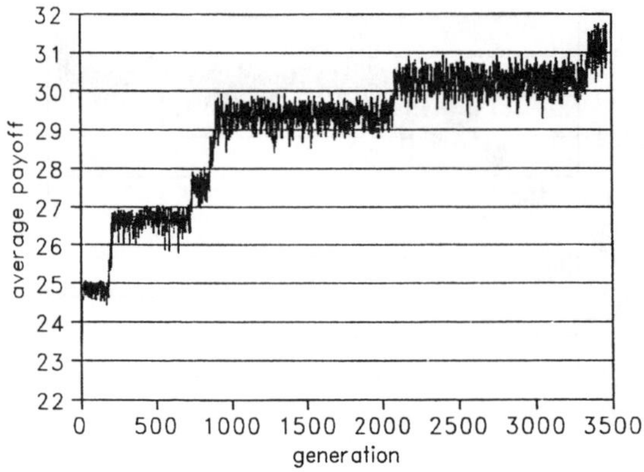

Fig. 8. Average payoff; $T = 8$, $M = 8$.

$z = 12$ and two different random seed numbers. The main feature of the dynamic observed in these simulations is very similar to the ladder climbing dynamic of the simulation with $T = 4$ and $M = 4$. The simulations first approach an equilibrium of order 1, and then, step by step, approach equilibria of increasing orders, 2, 3, 4, 5, and 6. Once they leave the neighborhood of the equilibrium of order 6, the average payoffs in both simulations spend a relatively long time close to the value which would correspond to the expected payoff of the equilibrium of order 7. (As noted earlier, the equilibria of order $T - 1$ are not possible.) Finally both simulations approach the neighborhood of a perfect signalling equilibrium around generation 3400. The difference between the simulations with 8 types and the one with 4 types is that the ones with 8 types take much longer to get close to a perfect signalling equilibrium (It takes the simulations with 8 types 3500 generations to reach the neighborhood of a perfect signalling equilibrium which is seven times more than the simulation with 4 types.) In order to save space, patterns of recognition coefficients for $T = 8$ and $M = 8$ are not shown, but they are consistent with the patterns observed in the simulation for $T = 4$ and $M = 4$.

In Table 2, we present the results of simulations conducted for the number of types, T, equal to 4 and 8 (with the uniform distribution of types) and the number of messages, M, equal to 4, 8, 16 and 32. The GA parameter values were: $n = 40$, $pmut = 0.0033$, $pcross = 0.6$ and $maxgen = 20{,}000$. The values of the parameters g and y were kept constant at $g = y = 16$, and the values of the parameters z and h varied in the interval [12,15.5]. Each set of the payoff parameter values had $z = h$. Thus, the ratios of z/y and h/g varied in the interval [0.75, 0.994]. Five simulations were conducted for a given combination of payoff ratios, number of types and number of messages using different random seed

Table 2
Average number of generations for convergence

$h/g,y/z$ gen	0.75	0.937	0.968	0.975	0.981	0.987	0.994
$T = 4, M = 4$	759	3321	3898	1245	733	3034	6109
$T = 4, M = 8$	171	312	323	647	536	253	617
$T = 4, M = 16$	132	138	358	162	193	155	581
$T = 4, M = 32$	100	123	193	233	164	170	168
$T = 8, M = 8$	2289	5825	ns	ns	ns	ns	ns
$T = 8, M = 16$	1175	3031	4032	8956	ns	ns	ns
$T = 8, M = 32$	517	906	5035	ns	ns	ns	ns

ns – no-signaling equilibrium at generation 20,000.

numbers. Each entry in this table is an average number of generations it took for the convergence to the perfect signalling equilibrium in the five simulations conducted for a given set of h/g, z/y, T and M.[6] Entries in the table that contain the symbol *ns* refer to the simulations which remained at the no-signalling equilibrium for 20,000 generations, with average payoffs close to the equilibrium payoffs of no-signalling equilibria and recognition coefficients values close to 0.

The results of our simulations exhibit the following patterns. For a given number of types and messages, increases in the payoff ratios (values closer to 1) result in a slower convergence to a perfect signalling equilibrium. Higher values of payoff ratios make the evolution of communication harder. For $h/g = z/y \geq 0.975$ and $T = 8$, equilibrium ladder climbing is not even initiated during 20,000 generations.

For a given number of types, increases in the number of messages that can be used result in faster convergence. Increased number of messages facilitates the evolution of communication for the following reason. A population of players moves from an equilibrium of one order to an equilibrium of the next highest order at the time when the genetic drift creates enough players who use the same message when they are one of non-signalled types and who respond to this message with this particular type. The probability of this event increases, for any given order of equilibrium, with the increases in the number of messages that can

[6] In order to save on computer time, we slightly modified the above described algorithm. In generation in which $rc_{t,gen} \geq 0.8$ for all T and $rc_{t,gen} \geq 0.9$ for $T/2$ types, the algorithm starts decreasing the rate of mutation. The effect of this modification was to decrease and eventually turn off the mutation at the time when a simulation reached the perfect signalling equilibrium. This enabled the exact convergence of the algorithm to the perfect signalling equilibrium. A simulation was terminated at the point when the values of all recognition coefficients were equal to 1 for 100 generations.

be used for communication. The higher probability results in, on average, shorter times required for the ladder climbing evolution.

For a given number of messages, $M \geq T$, an increase in the number of types increases the amount of time required for the convergence. As was discussed above, a larger number of types results in longer time required for the evolution of effective communication. (Holding the number of messages that are used constant, the time required increases, with the increase in the number of types, between five and twenty times.)

5. Conclusion

In our model of the sender/receiver problem there are two layers of multiple equilibria. First, there are different types of equilibrium, distinguished by the number of player types that successfully communicate in equilibrium, and this number is called the order of the equilibrium. In an equilibrium of order ϕ,ϕ player types are successfully communicated (messages sent by these types elicit an appropriate response from partners), and $T - \phi$ player types are not communicated (messages sent by these types elicit a neutral action from partners). Second, holding order constant, within any order there are many equilibria, distinguished by the mapping from types to messages for the types that are successfully communicated, and by the different messages that different players send when they are assigned a type for which there is no effective communication. Equilibria of the same order are Pareto equivalent, and equilibria of different orders are Pareto ranked by their order.

We describe players as chromosomes – binary strings that specify a message to be sent for each player type, and an action to be taken for each message received. We begin with a population of random chromosomes. We create payoff histories by a sucession of random pairings of players, allowing each pair of players to play a sender/receiver game in which types are randomly assigned to the players. (Actually, each pair plays two games so that, for each pairing, both players have a chance to be a sender and a receiver.) At regular intervals the chromosomes in the population are updated using a genetic algorithm. Our focus in this paper is on process – how does the population evolve over simulation time.

The process has a number of regular, pleasing features. Although we did not anticipate these features, they are quite intuitive. First, the proportion of time spent near an equilibrium is very high.[7] Second, the population of players can be

[7] There is one exception to this generalization. Equilibria of order $T - 1$ are not possible, yet in our simulations, for significant stretches of time the population hovers near what looks very much like such an equilibrium.

seen as climbing an equilibrium payoff ladder. That is, over time the population moves from an equilibrium of one order to an equilibrium of the next highest order.

Digging deeper, the following intuitive story seems to be roughly consistent with the observed equilibrium ladder climbing pattern. Given the initial, random distribution of the players' mappings from types to messages, for many (most) messages the best response is the neutral action because the messages contains insufficient information to justify a type specific action. For a small number (perhaps none) of the messages the best response is a type specific action. The pressure of selection favors players who respond to the first sort of message with the neutral action, who respond to the second sort of message with the appropriate type specific action, and who choose the appropriate message when their assigned type is one for which there is an effective message. As a result, the model quickly evolves to a low order equilibrium in which: (1) a small number (perhaps 0) of types are effectively communicated – for these types, in their role as senders of messages, all players use the same mapping from types to messages, and in their role as receivers of messages, all players use the inverse mapping from messages to types (actually type specific actions); (2) for the remaining types, different players use different messages, none of these messages contains enough information to justify a type specific action, and these messages elicit a neutral action. Importantly, since there is no unique mapping from player types that are not effectively signalled to messages in this low order equilibrium, there is scope for drift within the set of equilibria of this particular order. Eventually, this drift creates a disequilibrium situation in which enough players use the same message when they are one of the non-signaled types that the population is ripe for invasion by a new type, that both uses this particular message when it is this particular type, and responds to this particular message with this particular type specific action. Such a player (mutation) eventually occurs and, via the force of selection, the population quickly evolves to an equilibrium of the next highest order.

References

Andreoni, J., Miller, J.H., 1995. Auctions with artificial adaptive agents. Games and Economic Behavior 10, 39–51.

Arifovic, J., 1994. Genetic algorithm learning and the cobweb model. Journal of Economic Dynamics and Control 18, 3–28.

Arifovic, J., Eaton, C., 1995. Coordination via genetic learning. Computational Economics 8, 181–203.

Arifovic, J., 1996. The behavior of the exchange rate in genetic algorithm and experimental economies. Journal of Political Economy, 104, 510–541.

Aumann, R., Sorin, S., 1989. Cooperation and bounded recall. Games and Economic Behavior 1, 5–39.

Back, T., 1996. Evolutionary Algorithms in Theory and Practice. Oxford University Press, Oxford.

Blume, A., Kim, Y., Sobel, J., 1993. Evolutionary stability in games of communication. Games and Economic Behavior 5, 547–575.

Crawford, V., Sobel, J., 1982. Evolutionary stability in games of communication. Games and Economic Behavior 5, 547–575.

Farrell J., Gibbons, R., 1989. Cheap talk can matter in bargaining. Journal of Economic Theory 48 221–37

Holland, J.H., 1975. Adaptation in Natural and Artificial Systems. The University of Michigan Press, Ann Arbor.

Kim Y., Sobel, J., 1990. An evolutionary approach to pre-play communication.

Lewis, D.K., 1969. Convention: A Philosophical Study. Basil Blackwell, Oxford.

Marimon, R., McGrattan, E., Sargent, T.J., 1989. Money as a medium of exchange in an economy with artificially intelligent agents. Journal of Economic Dynamics and Control 14, 329–373.

Matsui, A., 1991. Cheap-talk and cooperation in a society. Journal of Economic Theory 54, 245–258.

Miller, J., 1996. The coevolution of automata in the repeated prisoner's dilemma. Journal of Economic Behavior and Organization 29, 87–112.

Tesfatsion L., 1995. A trade network game with endogenous partner selection. Economic Report Series No. 36, Iowa State University.

Warneryd, K., 1993. Cheap talk, coordination, and evolutionary stability. Games and Economic Behavior 5, 532–546.

ENDOGENOUS CARTEL FORMATION*

CURTIS EATON
Simon Fraser University

MUKESH ESWARAN
University of British Columbia

This paper investigates the endogenous formation of cartels in a supergame framework in which cheating on the cartel agreement results in the ejection of only the defector from the cartel while collusion continues amongst the non-cheating members. A more sophisticated notion of cartel stability than has been analysed hitherto is developed here, and it is shown that cartels are even less stable than they are generally believed to be. When firms produce heterogeneous goods and set prices, cartels comprising a small fraction of the industry's firms are shown to be viable. The emergence of two or more cartels within the same industry is seen not only to be a distinct possibility but also to be quite likely.

I. Introduction and Summary

It is well-known that cartels tend to be unstable because their members have incentives to free-ride on the profit-enhancing efforts of other members. However, it has been demonstrated that, despite this, finite cartels can be stable: their size has to be such that the members (insiders) have no incentive to leave the cartel and the non-members (outsiders) have no incentive to join the cartel. This has been shown largely in the framework of a dominant firm facing a competitive fringe, where the cartel acts as a Stackelberg leader with respect to price-taking fringe firms.[1] The issue of cartel stability can also be considered in a supergame framework where cooperation amongst cartel members is facilitated by trigger strategies.[2] Not surprisingly, cartels that are otherwise unstable may be rendered stable by the expedient of repeated interaction. The purpose of this paper is to consider the issue of cartel stability in a supergame when the consequences of cheating by members are different from those usually assumed. It is assumed here that, in the event of cheating, only the cheater is ejected from the cartel in all subsequent periods and that the non-cheating members continue operating as a cartel. This assumption, which leads to a more sophisticated notion of cartel stability than has been developed hitherto in the literature, has

* We would like to thank two anonymous referees for comments on an earlier draft.

[1] This was first demonstrated by D'Aspremont, Jacquemin, Gabszewicz and Weymark (1983), and then also by Donsimini, Economides and Polemarchakis (1986). There exist a few attempts that have treated the outsiders as Cournot players instead of price takers (see, for example, Martin, 1990 and Shaffer, 1995).

[2] Martin (1990) makes an attempt in this direction.

interesting implications for cartel stability. Cartels are seen to be even less stable than they are generally believed to be. The paper, for the most part, considers the stability of cartels in which members produce differentiated products and set prices. Such cartels are seen to have robustness properties that sharply contrast those of cartels in a quantity-setting scenario.

What happens to a cartel in the event a member cheats is a question which has received little attention.[3] Rather than dissolve the entire cartel, the non-cheating members may find it in their self-interest to continue to operate as a cartel. Indeed, if this is so, the members may be unable to credibly commit themselves to dissolving the cartel in the event of cheating. Suppose there are no cost advantages to forming a cartel. Then, relative to the situation in which the cartel dissolves in the event of cheating, the punishment inflicted on a cheater when only the cheater is ejected is not as high - because outsiders benefit from the continued operation of the cartel. This undermines the possibility of supporting the cartel as a viable entity in supergames. Thus repeated interaction - which usually mitigates the incentives to cheat - will be of limited value in promoting cartel stability.[4]

The implementation of the idea that collusion is supported by the presumption that only cheaters get purged from a cartel warrants a fairly sophisticated notion of stability, as will be seen here. For, the continuation of collusion by the non-cheating members presumes that this smaller cartel is itself robust against cheating - a presumption which, in its turn, needs to be tested. Thus the idea that cheaters are sequentially purged from cartels as and when they cheat implies that the stability of a cartel of a given size requires the stability of *all* cartels of a smaller size.

When the product is homogeneous and firms choose quantities, the above result arises for two reasons. First, as is well known in the literature of horizontal mergers, a sufficiently large fraction of firms in an industry must be involved in a merger if the firms are to find it profitable.[5] Even if mergers are profitable, if the member firms are to behave as a cartel rather than simply as a monolithic merged entity, producing the allotted quota of the cartel output may not be even a remotely incentive compatible action for each member. The discount factor required to prevent cheating in a supergame, consequently, would be relatively high - thereby undermining the efficacy of repeated interaction in enhancing stability.

When the products produced by the different firms are differentiated, as is assumed to be the case in this paper, the issues of cartel formation and stability offer some interesting possibilities. The case considered here is one where the demand curves are linear and the marginal costs are constant (zero). With price-setting, the choice variables of the different firms are strategic complements. As a result, mergers are always profitable, irrespective of the number of firms involved; the larger the number of firms involved, the more profitable the merger. In this case, the upper bound on the size of viable cartels is determined entirely by the incentives to cheat. It is seen here that, depending on the discount factor, cartels of relatively small sizes can be stable. Furthermore, since the continued operation by the non-cheating members as a cartel in the event of cheating undermines the stability of cartels, it is very likely that cartels comprising a small fraction of the industry would be observed in

[3] D'Aspremont and Gabszewicz (1985) is an exception.
[4] When firms form coalitions which trade technological information that lowers each member's production costs, the outcome is in sharp contrast to this. There, the threat of ejection of the cheater accompanied by continued trading of technologies by the non-cheating members of the coalition prevents cheating more effectively than the dissolution of the coalition (Eaton and Eswaran, 1997).
[5] See Salant, Switzer and Reynolds (1983) for a demonstration of this.

reality. It is shown here that these same forces can result in two stable cartels simultaneously operating within an industry.[6]

D'Aspremont and Gabszewicz (1985) have argued that the usual incentive on the part of firms in an industry to chisel at the monopoly price set by a cartel may result in a market structure in which there are two cartels. They show that this outcome can arise when the number of deviant firms is small and there are capacity constraints which restrict the output of the firms. Since the capacity-constrained, deviant firms cannot appropriate the entire market, chiselling need not completely undermine collusion possibilities. Thus what can emerge are market structures the authors refer to as 'quasi-monopolies', in which the equilibrium price is close to the monopoly price.

The approach and results of this paper differ from those of D'Aspremont and Gabszewicz (1985) in some important ways. First, their result depends crucially on the existence of binding capacity constraints. We do not invoke capacity constraints on the output of firms. Indeed, we assume that the marginal cost of production is constant (zero) at all output levels. Second, in D'Aspremont and Gabszewicz (1985) collusion is modelled in a static framework. This is feasible there since it is implicitly assumed that the cartel can strictly enforce the quotas of its member firms; firms essentially decide whether they wish to belong to the cartel or to the group of deviant firms. In contrast, it is assumed in this paper that cartels cannot enforce quotas in this manner; collusion is sustained in a supergame. Third, while we demonstrate the possibility of two cartels (of same or different sizes) emerging in an industry, the same principle can result in the emergence of several cartels. In D'Aspremont and Gabszewicz (1985), there can be only two cartels, and these must necessarily be of different sizes. The essential mechanisms leading to multiple cartels are very different in the two papers.

A drawback of much of the existing literature on cartel stability is that the cartel is invariably assumed to be a Stackelberg leader (D'Aspremont *et al.*, 1983; Donsimini *et al.*, 1986, Shaffer, 1995). This assumption is somewhat unsatisfactory, since it confounds the effects of cartel formation *per se* with those associated with a special status given to the cartel, namely Stackelberg leadership. As a result, the comparative static properties of the equilibrium with respect to cartel size are difficult to interpret. To be more precise, the natural base case for comparison would be the Nash equilibrium that obtains when all the firms in the industry behave as independents. Now if two firms opt to merge and behave as a cartel, the conferring of Stackelberg leadership status to the cartel makes the equilibrium outcome somewhat uncomparable to the base case. To avoid this, in this paper, we assume that all entities in the industry behave as Nash players *vis-à-vis* all other entities. The rule by which the oligopoly game is resolved is therefore invariant with respect to the cartel size.

The following section sets out a simple model which describes the evolution of a cartel as members possibly cheat and get ejected. Next, in an industry in which firms produce differentiated products and set prices, the sustainable collusive outcomes that obtain when only cheaters are ejected from the cartel are compared with those that obtain when the entire cartel is dissolved in the event of cheating. The analogous scenario for quantity-setting firms is briefly considered. Finally, the paper demonstrates that the possibility of more than one cartel operating in an industry is very real.

[6] In theory, there can be several stable cartels operating in an industry.

II. THE MODEL AND RESULTS

Consider an industry comprising n firms, which confront each other over an infinite number of periods. The firms face stationary market demand curves. Suppose that a cartel spontaneously emerges in period 0. Cartelisation here means that the member firms agree to choose their decision variables (price) in order to maximise the joint profits of the members of the cartel in that period, while entertaining Nash conjectures with respect to all firms outside the cartel.[7] The outsiders, if there are any, maximise their individual profits by playing Nash with respect to all firms in the industry.

Cartel members are required to set their choice variables at levels that are Nash best responses to the choices of all *outsider* firms, not to the choices of *all* the firms in the industry. From this arises the incentive for individual cartel members to cheat on the cartel agreement. We assume that the choices are monitorable *ex post* and that cheating is detected at the end of the defection period. The gain from defection accrues to the cheater for only one period; from the next period on, the defector is permanently ejected from the cartel. Operationally, this means that the non-cheating cartel members no longer include the defector's profit as a part of the objective function they maximise, and that they play Nash with respect to this firm's choices. The ejected firm operates forever as an outsider, while the non-cheating members continue their collusion. If defection occurs again, the new cheater is ejected from the cartel, and so the process continues. The assumption that only cheaters are ejected from the cartel is one of our points of departure from the standard assumption that the entire cartel dissolves when cheating occurs and that all firms revert to Nash behaviour with respect to all other firms.[8]

The above idea may be formalised as follows. Consider a cartel which initially in period 0 starts out as coalition Z^0, and which evolves over time as Z^t, $t = 0, 1, 2 \ldots$, as firms possibly cheat and get ejected from the cartel. The essence of cartel behaviour is that each member recognises the external effects of its decisions on other members of the cartel, and internalises these effects in choosing its decision variable. Denote by s_{ij}^t the decision of member firm i of the cartel with regard to member firm j in period t: s_{ij}^t is equal to one if firm i internalises the effect on firm j's profit in setting its choice variable in period t and zero if it does not. The coalition Z^t comprises the members of the original cartel who have never cheated up until period $t-1$

$$Z^t = \{i \in Z^0 | s_{ij}^{t-1} = 1 \forall j \in Z^{t-1}\} \qquad t = 1, 2, \ldots \tag{1}$$

The kind of strategy S_{ij}^t that is being envisaged here for an arbitrary firm i in the industry in period t is characterised by

$$s_{ij}^t = \begin{cases} 1 & \text{if } i \in Z^t \text{ and } j \in Z^t \\ 0 & \text{otherwise} \end{cases} \tag{2}$$

The above characterisation says, in effect, that

a) Firm i chooses its decision variable to maximise the joint profit of all the cartel members in period t only if it has itself never cheated in the past. If it has, it is an

[7] For a comparison of the stability of price-setting cartels with those of quantity-setting ones in terms of the degree of substitutability or complementarity of the products produced by the firms see Denekere (1983).
[8] Abreu (1986) is a notable exception to treatments following the standard assumption.

outsider and remains so for ever.

b) If firm i has never cheated, in period t it will incorporate the profit of another firm j into its objective function only if firm j also has never cheated in the past.

a) *A single cartel*

We now consider the possibility of endogenous formation of a single cartel when the firms are selling differentiated products. This allows us to consider price as the choice variable of firms, without eliminating pure profits. As we shall see, using prices as choice variables helps avoid some technical complications and also introduces some interesting features of cartel formation that are missed when the choice variables are quantities.[9] In particular, in the former case we will tend to observe the emergence of small, stable cartels.

It is assumed that there are n firms in the industry producing differentiated products exhibiting Chamberlinian symmetry. The quantity demanded, q_i, from firm i, $i = 1, 2 \ldots, n$, is assumed to be given in terms of the prices p_j, $j = 1, 2, \ldots, n$, by

$$q_i = \alpha - \beta p_i - \sum_{j \in N_{-i}} \gamma p_j \qquad \alpha > 0, \beta > 0, \gamma < 0, \beta + (\mathrm{n} - 1)\gamma > 0 \tag{3}$$

where N_{-i}, denotes the set of all firms in the industry other than i. The negative value of the parameter γ implies that consumers view the goods as substitutes. We assume that the marginal production costs are constant at zero for all firms.

Now suppose m firms, $i = 1, 2, \ldots, m$, form a single cartel, M, and the rest of the firms act as independents. The one period optimisation problem confronting an outsider $i \notin M$ is

$$\max_{p_i} \left(\alpha - \beta p_i - \sum_{j \in N_{-i}} \gamma p_j \right) p_i \tag{4}$$

The problem confronting the firms of the cartel is one of joint profit maximisation

$$\max_{p_1, p_2 \ldots, p_m} \sum_{i \in M} \left[\alpha - \beta p_i - \sum_{j \in N_{-\mathrm{i}}} \gamma p_j \right] pi \tag{5}$$

It is readily verified that the prices set by the various producing entities are strategic complements: an increase in one price raises the best response prices of the others. Let $\mathrm{P}_o(m)$ and $P_c(\mathrm{m})$ denote the Bertrand-Nash prices of an outsider and insider, respectively. Likewise, let $\Pi_o(m)$ and $(\Pi_c(m)$ denote their respective Bertrand-Nash profits. Since an insider explicitly recognises that an increase in its price benefits other cartel members by increasing the demand they face, it follows that $P_c(m) > P_o(m)$.[10]

The m firms here, of course, will contemplate forming a cartel only if their aggregate profit exceeds that when a cartel does not form. Thus a necessary condition for the formation of an m-firm cartel is that an m-firm merger be profitable

$$\Pi_c(m) \geqslant m\Pi_c(1) \tag{6}$$

where $\Pi_c(1)$ is the profit of a firm when all firms behave as independent Bertrand-Nash players. For a homogeneous good industry, Salant *et al.* (1982) have demonstrated that,

[9] More precisely, when the choice variables are strategic substitutes.

[10] A formal demonstration of this is given in the proof of Proposition 1 below.

typically, a large fraction of the firms in the industry must merge for the merger to be profitable. For homogeneous good industries with only a few firms, profitable merger may require the entire industry to participate.[11]

Consider, first, the incentive for mergers in the model constructed above. Suppose an m-firm cartel inducts an outsider into the cartel, thereby increasing the new member's price from $P_o(m)$ to $P_c(m)$. If the $(m+1)$ insiders hold fixed their prices at $P_c(m)$, the outsiders will find it in their interest to raise prices above $P_o(m)$, in view of the facts that the prices are strategic complements and the firm that was admitted into the cartel increased its price. This increase in the price of outsiders benefits the insiders, and invites a higher best response from them. This, in turn, benefits the outsiders, and invites an increase in their prices, and so on. This is the intuition for the following result.

Proposition 1: The equilibrium prices and profits of all firms (insiders as well as outsiders) are increasing in the size of the cartel.

Proof: See the Appendix

In the standard, homogeneous good, dominant firm-competitive fringe model, an increase in the cartel size increases the equilibrium price because of the reduction in the size of the free-riding fringe (see D'Aspremont *et al.*, 1983). Here, the strategic complementarity of the prices plays an important role in generating the result in Proposition 1: it reinforces the effect of reduced free-riding as the cartel size increases. An immediate implication of the above proposition is the corollary recorded below; this result stands in sharp contrast to what obtains in the homogeneous good case.

Corollary 1: All mergers involving two or more firms are profitable.

The satisfaction of condition (6), while necessary, is not sufficient for an m-firm cartel to be viable, since a member of the cartel has an incentive to cheat on the allotted output $q_c(m)$ and earn more than the member profit $\Pi_c(m)$. The one-period profit, $\Pi_d(m)$ of a defector is given by

$$\Pi_d(m) = \max_{p_d} [\alpha - \beta p_d - (m-1)\gamma P_c(m) - (n-m)\gamma P_o(m)] p_d \tag{7}$$

where p_d is the defection period price of the cheater, the optimal value of which we denote by $P_d(m)$.

Under the standard presumption that the cartel will dissolve and a reversion to Nash behaviour will obtain in the event of cheating, the incentive compatibility condition that must be satisfied if the cartel is to be robust is

$$\frac{1}{(1-\delta)}\Pi_c(m) \geqslant \Pi_d(m) + \frac{\delta}{(1-\delta)}\Pi(1) \tag{8}$$

where $\delta (0 \leqslant \delta < 1)$ is the common discount factor for all firms.

Now consider the scenario in which defection from the cartel results only in the ejection of the cheater from the cartel; the non-cheating members continue collusion. The defector operates as an outsider from the next period on. In this case, the incentive compatibility condition (8) is replaced by

[11] The same result would obtain in the present model if the firms' choice variables are quantities.

$$\frac{1}{(1-\delta)}\Pi_c(m) \geqslant \Pi_d(m) + \frac{\delta}{(1-\delta)}\Pi_o(m-1) \tag{9}$$

In the second term on the right hand side of the above inequality, $\Pi_o(m-1)$ denotes the profit of an outsider in the presence of a cartel of size $(m-1)$. It is through this term that the profitability to outsiders of continued collusion by the non-cheating cartel members impinges on the incentives to cheat.

Now if the incentive compatibility condition (9) is to be meaningful, it must be the case that the cartel of the $(m-1)$ non-cheating members is itself robust against cheating. Thus a condition analogous to (9) must hold for the cartel with $(m-1)$ firms, and so on. Thus credibility requires that the following stack of necessary and sufficient incentive compatibility conditions must all be satisfied

$$\frac{1}{(1-\delta)}\Pi_c(l) \geqslant \Pi_d(l) + \frac{\delta}{(1-\delta)}\Pi_o(l-1) \qquad l = 2, 3, \ldots, m \tag{10}$$

We refer to the scenario where only the cheater is ejected from the cartel and the non-cheating members revert to collusion as 'stacked reversion'.

In Table I we illustrate how the profits of insiders and outsiders, and the feasibility of cartel formation vary when the cartel size changes. The parameter values in this exercise are assumed to be: $n = 5$ and $\alpha = 1$, $\beta = 0.5$, $\gamma = -0.1$.

Table I presents the one-period profits of the insiders and outsiders for various cartel sizes. Notice that the profit of an insider of an m-firm cartel always exceeds the profit of a firm that is an outsider to an $(m-1)$ firm cartel. Thus, were it not for the one-period defection profit that might tempt a cartel member to defect, a firm would always choose to be an insider as opposed to being an outsider. (For a given cartel size, of course, a firm would prefer to be an outsider as opposed to being an insider.)

Table I also presents what are termed as the critical discount factors under Nash and stacked reversion, respectively. These are the smallest values of the discount factors for which a cartel is robust against defection. Clearly, the smaller this discount factor the more robust is the cartel likely to be against defection. We observe from the table that, relative to the Nash reversion case, the critical discount factor rises much more rapidly in the size of the cartel under stacked reversion. If the actual discount factor is 0.700, for example, the entire industry could cartelise under Nash reversion but only three firms could cartelise under stacked reversion. Thus we see from Table I that, when the strategy variables are

Table I

	One period Bertrand-Nash profit		*Critical discount factor*	
Cartel size	*Insider*	*Outsider*	*Nash reversion*	*Stacked reversion*
1	1.389	1.389	n/a	n/a
2	1.439	1.486	0.265	0.265
3	1.576	1.758	0.360	0.541
4	1.867	2.469	0.468	0.793
5	2.500	-	0.643	0.985

prices, small cartels can not only form profitably but that they are also likely to be robust against defection.[12]

It is interesting to compare the above numerical results, which are typical of what obtains when prices are the choice variables, to the typical numerical results that obtain when quantities are the choice variables. Inverting the demand system (3), we obtain a linear inverse demand system. The demand price, p_t, facing firm i, $i = 1, 2, \ldots, n$, is given in terms of the quantities q_j, $j = 1, 2, \ldots, n$, by

$$p_i = \hat{\alpha} - \hat{\beta} q_i - \sum_{j \in N_{-i}} \hat{\gamma} q_j \quad \hat{\alpha} > 0, \hat{\beta} > 0, \hat{\gamma} > 0 \tag{11}$$

where the parameters $\hat{\alpha}$, $\hat{\beta}$ and $\hat{\gamma}$ are related in a straightforward way to α, β, γ and n.

Table II presents, for quantity setting, results that are the analogues of those in Table I. The parameter values used for the simulations of Table II are: $n = 5$, $\hat{\alpha} = 1$, $\hat{\beta} = 0.5$, $\hat{\gamma} = 0.2$. (A blank entry in the last column of the table means that there exists no discount factor for which the cartel is stable.)

The picture portrayed by Table II is in sharp contrast to that conveyed by Table I. The difference arises from the fact that the prices are strategic complements, whereas quantities are strategic substitutes. In the latter case, a reduction in the aggregate output of two firms following cartelisation would invite an increase in the outputs of the outsiders - which would impinge adversely on the profits of the cartel members. In fact, for the simulations presented in Table II, it is not even profitable for two firms to merge, since by doing so the merging firms do worse than they would when they remain separate. This is merely an example of the result of Salant *et al.* (1983), where it is shown that a significant proportion of the firms within an industry would need to merge if the merger is to be profitable. For $m \geqslant 3$, mergers are profitable in Table II but, under stacked reversion, they are not sustainable as cartels for any value of the discount factor. This is because the tendency to free ride is so large here that a firm would prefer to be an outsider to an $(m-1)$-firm cartel than an insider of an m-firm cartel. In this case, under stacked reversion, a defector would earn higher profit than an insider not only in the defection period but also in all subsequent periods. Thus, in this example, there are *no cartels* which are stable under stacked reversion.

Under Nash reversion (still with quantity-setting), the problem of free-riding is less severe, since the defector does not benefit from the continued collusion by the non-cheaters.

Table II

	One period Cournot-Nash profit		*Critical discount factor*	
Cartel size	*Insider*	*Outsider*	*Nash reversion*	*Stacked reversion*
1	0.154	0.154	n/a	n/a
2	0.151	0.169	-	-
3	0.156	0.195	0.878	-
4	0.169	0.235	0.651	-
5	0.192	-	0.555	-

[12]The robustness of the intuition for these and other numerical results to follow suggest that they are not artefacts of special parameter values but, rather, that they are likely to be very real possibilities in general.

For $m = 2$, the cartel is of course not viable because even a merger is not profitable. However, as long as a merger is profitable, a sufficiently high discount factor will always render the cartel robust. There are two opposing forces at work here determining the robustness of a cartel. On the one hand, the profitability of mergers increases as a larger and larger fraction of the firms in the industry merge (Salant *et al.*, 1983). On the other hand, a firm's incentive to cheat on the cartel agreement is greater for cartels of larger size. The net effect of these two forces, in the simulation presented in Table II, is such that the critical discount factor actually *decreases* in the cartel size under Nash reversions.[13]

The above discussion rationalises our focus on prices as choice variables in the bulk of this paper. With quantity-setting, the problem of free-riding by non-cartel members and by cheating cartel members is too severe for cartels to be viable under stacked reversion.[14] This renders difficult a simple exposition of the essential points of this paper. There is a further complication that potentially arises with quantity-setting. It is quite possible that mergers with many firms are profitable but those with only a few firms are not. Consequently, under Nash reversion, cartels with many firms can be sustained for sufficiently high discount factors whereas those with only a few firms (two, in the simulations of Table II) can never be sustained. Under stacked reversion, this possibility raises a significant problem in the determination of equilibrium cartel configurations. For here, to determine the viability of an m-firm cartel the viability of an $(m-1)$-firm cartel needs to be assured. In the absence of this assurance, the cartel structure that would obtain in the event of defection is unclear. The construction of a full-blown theory that would address this issue is beyond the scope of this paper. In what follows, we revert to the case in which firms set prices.

b) *Two cartels*

The fact that incentive compatibility requirements can stop cartels short of absorbing all the firms in the industry invites the questions: Will the firms which are excluded from the cartel have an incentive to form a separate cartel? If so, what effect will the emergence of a second cartel have on the robustness of the first? To investigate this, we now briefly consider a scenario in which there are two cartels M and K, with m and k members, respectively. A firm can now be a member of one of the cartels or be an outsider to both cartels. There are $(n - m - k)$ outsiders, and we denote the (possibly empty) set of these outsiders by O. Denote by $\Pi_M(m, k)$, $\Pi_K(m, k)$, and $\Pi_o(m, k)$ the respective one-period Bertrand-Nash profit of a typical member of M, K and set O. Also, denote by $\Pi^d_M(m, k)$ the optimal one-period defection profit of a firm belonging to cartel M.[15]

Assuming that cartel K is robust against defection, the incentive compatibility condition for cartel m under Nash reversion is

$$\frac{1}{(1-\delta)}\Pi_M(m, k) \geqslant \Pi^d_M(m, k) + \frac{\delta}{(1-\delta)}\Pi_O(1, k) \tag{12}$$

and those under stacked reversion are

[13] Similar results would obtain if the good is homogeneous and firms choose quantities.
[14] This suggests that if firms could somehow collectively commit themselves to choosing either prices or quantities as their decision variables, they would opt for prices.
[15] Explicit expressions for these profits are readily obtained but are not presented here because they are not particularly illuminating.

$$\frac{1}{(1-\delta)}\Pi_M(l, k) \geqslant \Pi_M^d(l, k) + \frac{\delta}{(1-\delta)}\Pi_O(l-1, k) \qquad l = 2, 3, \ldots, m \qquad (13)$$

Conditions analogous to those written down above will apply to cartel K. Clearly, the incentive compatibility conditions for both cartels have to be simultaneously satisfied if the assumed configuration of two cartels is to be observable.

In Table III we present the results of a numerical simulation for the case when there are five firms in the industry. When $n = 5$, we can get at most two non-trivial cartels. All parameter values for the simulations presented in Table III are the same as those used in generating Table I. The difference is that in Table III the size of cartel K is parametrically varied, and the effects on cartel M and the outsiders are observed.

The numbers for the cases $k = 0$ or $k = 1$ are the same as those given in Table I, since for these values of k there is no non-trivial second cartel. In other words, the profits of the members of K and M are given, respectively, by those of the outsiders and the insiders in Table I. From Table III we observe that the profit of the members of one cartel and the profits of the outsiders are increasing in the size of the second cartel. More to the point, a cartel would rather have its non-members form a separate cartel than see them remain as independents. This is because by forming a separate cartel, the non-members of one cartel raise their prices in the new equilibrium, which benefits the members of the first cartel. In effect, from the point of view of one cartel, there is less free-riding by its non-members when they cartelise separately. What is more, it is in the self-interest of the non-members to form a separate cartel. While similar forces operate when the firms set quantities, two (or more) cartels within an industry are less like to be observed in that case since, as we have seen, a viable cartel requires participation by a substantial fraction of the industry firms.

Under the presumption that only one cartel can exist, when the actual discount rate is assumed to be 0.700 Table I reveals that, under stacked reversion, only three of the five firms could belong to the cartel. The remaining two firms now have an incentive to form a separate cartel. Table III reveals that, by so doing, each of these two firms raises its profit from 1.758 to 1.837, while raising the profit of each of the first cartel's members from 1.576 to 1.701. Furthermore, the formation of the second cartel makes the first one more robust against defection. This is seen from the fact that, under stacked reversion, the critical discount factor for the first three-firm cartel falls from 0.541 (Table I) to 0.516 (Table III) when a second cartel emerges. (In the case of quantity-setting in contrast, the formation of a second cartel would undermine the stability of the first by increasing the incentive of a cartel member to defect.)

Table III

		One period Bertrand-Nash profit			*Critical discount factor for cartel M*	
Cartel size		*M*	*Member of K*	*Outsider*	*Nash reversion*	*Stacked reversion*
M	K					
1	2	1.486	1.439	1.486	–	
2	2	1.543	1.543	1.594	0.253	0.253
3	2	1.701	1.837	–	0.346	0.516
1	3	1.758	1.576	1.758	–	–
2	3	1.837	1.701	–	0.225	0.225
1	4	2.469	1.867	–	–	–

Table IV

Cartel structure	*Discount factor*	
	Nash reversion	*Stacked reversion*
Cartels infeasible	$\delta < 0.253$	$\delta < 0.253$
Two two-firm cartels	$0.253 \leqslant \delta < 0.346$	$0.253 \leqslant \delta < 0.516$
One three-firm and one two-firm cartel	$0.346 \leqslant \delta < 0.468$	$0.516 \leqslant \delta < 0.793$
One four-firm cartel	$0.468 \leqslant \delta < 0.643$	$0.793 \leqslant \delta < 0.985$
One five-firm cartel	$\delta \geqslant 0.643$	$\delta \geqslant 0.985$

Table IV above shows the cartel structures that would obtain in the five-firm industry considered in Tables I and III at various levels of the discount factor.

In the literature, analyses of cartel formation have invariably presumed the possibility of only a single cartel within an industry.[16] The model constructed in this paper demonstrates that the very considerations that lead to the breakdown of cartels may also be responsible for the formation of multiple cartels . The fragmentation of the industry into two or more cartels is more likely for intermediate values of the discount factor. Multiple cartels can be ruled out only when the discount factor is either so low that even two firms can not successfully cartelise, or so high that the entire industry can successfully cartelise. From Table IV, we see that for the parameters chosen, in the five-firm industry we shall observe two non-trivial cartels when the discount factor falls in the considerable range $0.253 \leqslant \delta < 0.793$ under stacked reversion. Thus the emergence of multiple cartels, in fact, may be the rule rather than the exception.

To be sure, the simultaneous emergence of two or more cartels within an industry can obtain also under the standard presumption of Nash reversion. In Table IV, this occurs when the discount factor falls in the range $0.253 \leqslant \delta < 0.468$. We see that the emergence of multiple cartels is more likely under stacked reversion. The rational presumption of continued collusion by the noncheating members of a cartel makes defection more attractive. This is a greater liability for large cartels than for small ones, since in the former case a defector will view its defection as having only a small adverse effect on the cartel's ability to benefit outsiders. For example, if the discount factor is 0.5, Table IV reveals that, under Nash reversion, a single cartel with four members would obtain and the remaining firm would operate as an outsider. Under stacked reversion, however, a four-firm cartel is unviable; instead, two two-firm cartels would obtain and the remaining firm would operate as an outsider.

Appendix

Proof of Proposition 1

The best response, $\overline{p}_o$, of an outsider to a perceived price p_o of other outsiders and a price p_c of the cartel members is given by the first order condition to (4) in the text as

[16] As noted in the Introduction, the reasons for which two cartels can emerge in the model of D'Aspremont and Gabszewicz (1985) - an exception in this literature - are different from the reasons generating this outcome here.

$$\overline{p}_o = \frac{\alpha}{2\beta} - \frac{\gamma}{2\beta}[mp_c + (n-m-1)p_o] \equiv F(p_o, p_c, m) \tag{A.1}$$

where

$$F_1 = \frac{-\gamma(n-m-1)}{2\beta} > 0;\ F_2 = \frac{-\gamma}{2\beta} > 0;\ F_3 = \frac{-\gamma}{2\beta}(p_c - p_o) \tag{A.2}$$

Likewise, the best response, $\overline{p}_c$, of a cartel member to perceived prices p_o of outsiders and p_c of other cartel members is given by the first order condition

$$\overline{p}_c = \frac{\alpha}{2\beta} - \frac{\gamma}{2\beta}[(n-m)p_o + 2(m-1)p_c] \equiv G(p_o, p_c, m) \tag{A.3}$$

where

$$G_1 = \frac{-\gamma(n-m)}{2\beta} > 0;\ G_2 = \frac{-2\gamma(m-1)}{2\beta} > 0;\ G_3 = \frac{-\gamma}{2\beta}(-p_o + 2p_c) \tag{4}$$

Since $\beta + \gamma(n-1) > 0$ by assumption, we have $\beta > -\gamma(n-1) > -\gamma(n-m-1)$ for $1 \leqslant m \leqslant n$. It follows that

$$0 < F_1 < 1 \text{ and } 0 < G_2 < 1 \tag{A.5}$$

It is clear from the best response functions written down above that each firm views the prices of all other firms as strategic complements to its own: higher prices charged by others elicit a higher price as a best response.

In equilibrium, $\overline{p}_o = p_o$ and $\overline{p}_c = p_c$ so that we have

$$p_o = F(p_o, p_c, m) \tag{A.6a}$$

$$p_c = G(p_o, p_c, m) \tag{A.6b}$$

Denote equilibrium prices of outsiders and cartel members (the solution to (A.6)) by $p_o(m)$ and $p_c(m)$, respectively. The explicit solution to the equilibrium conditions (A.6) are given by

$$p_o(m) = \alpha(2\beta + (m-2)\gamma)/\Delta(m) \tag{A.7a}$$

$$p_c(m) = \alpha(2\beta - \gamma)/\Delta(m) \tag{A.7b}$$

where

$$\Delta(m) \equiv (1 - F_1)(1 - G_2) - F_2 G_1 \tag{A.9}$$

It can be verified, with some algebra, that $\Delta(m)$ is positive for all m in the range $1 \leqslant m \leqslant n$. Since $\gamma < 0$, it follows from (A.10) that the price of cartel members is higher than that of the outsiders

$$p_c(m) > p_o(m) \qquad \text{for } 2 \leqslant m \leqslant (n-1) \tag{A.9}$$

Totally differentiating (A.6) with respect to m and using Cramer's rule we obtain the derivatives of these prices (denoted by primes) as

$$p_o'(m) = [F_3(1 - G_2) + F_2 G_3]/\Delta(m) \tag{A.10a}$$

$$p_c'(m) = [G_3(1 - F_1) + F_3 G_1]/\Delta(m) \tag{A.10b}$$

Using (A.2), (A.4), (A.5) and (A.9) we see that

$$sign\ p_o(m) = sign\ p_c'(m) = sign\ \Delta(m) > 0 \tag{A.9}$$

Thus the equilibrium prices of both the cartel members and of the outsiders increase in m.

It can now be seen that the profits of both outsiders and insiders increase with the cartel size. Consider the profit of an outsider, j. Suppose the cartel size increases from m to $m+1$ and the other outsiders increase their prices from $p_o(m)$ to $p_o(m+1)$ and the insiders increase theirs from p_c(m) to $p_c(m+1)$. This increases the quantity demanded of firm j's product at every price level for this product. Thus at firm *j*'s Nash best response price, which is also $p_o(m+1)$, firm *j*'s profit will necessarily be higher than when the cartel has only m members. A similar argument applies to an insider, say firm i. Suppose that, when the $(m+1)$st member is added to the cartel, all other insiders hold their price level fixed at $p_c(m)$ and the outsiders raise theirs from $p_o(m)$ to $p_o(m+1)$. The increase in the latest cartel member's price from $p_o(m)$ to $p_c(m)$ increases the old cartel members' profits, as do the increase in outsiders' prices from $p_o(m)$ to $p_o(m+1)$. The profits of insiders will clearly increase even more when they, in turn, increase their prices to their collective Nash best response price, $p_c(m+1)$.

References

Abreu, D. (1986), 'Extremal Equilibria of Oligopolistic Games', *Journal of Economic Theory*, vol. 39, pp, 191–225.

D'Aspremont, C. and Gabszewicz, J.J. (1985), 'Quasi-Monopolies', *Econometrica*, vol. 52, pp. 141–151.

D'Aspremont, C., Jacquemin, A., Gabszewicz, J.J. and Weymark, J.A. (1983), 'On the Stability of Collusive Price Leadership', *Canadian Journal of Economics*, vol. XVI, pp. 17–25.

Denekere, R. (1983), 'Duopoly Supergames with Product Differentiation', *Economics Letters*, vol. 11, pp. 37–42.

Donsimini, M.-P., Economides, N.S. and Polemarchakis, H.M. (1986), 'Stable Cartels', *International Economic Review*, vol. 27, pp. 317–327.

Eaton, B.C. and Eswaran, M. (1997), 'Technology-Trading Coalitions in Supergames', *Rand Journal of Economics*, vol. 28, Spring, pp. 135–149.

Martin, S. (1990), 'Fringe Size and Cartel Stability', European University Institute, June (mimeo).

Salant, S.W., Switzer, S. and Reynolds, R.J. (1983), 'Losses From Horizontal Merger: The Effects of an Exogenous Change in Industry Structure on Cournot-Nash Equilibrium', *Quarterly Journal of Economics*, vol. XCVIII, pp. 185–199.

Shaffer, S. (I995), 'Stable Cartels with a Cournot Fringe', *Southern Economic Review*, vol. 61, pp. 744–754.

[31]

Know-how sharing with stochastic innovations

B. Curtis Eaton *Department of Economics, University of Calgary*
Mukesh Eswaran *Department of Economics, University of British Columbia*

Abstract. We provide a model of know-how sharing between competing firms in which each of two firms gets a stochastic innovation in its stock of know-how in every period. Separately considering the cases when innovations are indivisible and divisible, we examine the nature of the subgame perfect sharing agreements that can obtain. We discover that both stochasticity and indivisibility undermine the ability to support sharing. Furthermore, we find that there are equilibria in which know-how sharing can be intermittent and that small innovations are more likely to be shared than large ones, when innovations are divisible but not necessarily when they are indivisible. JEL Classification: O30, O33

Partage du savoir faire quand les innovations sont stochastiques. Les auteurs proposent un modèle de partage du savoir-faire entre entreprises concurrentes dans lequel chacune des deux entreprises obtient une innovation stochastique dans son stock of savoir-faire à chaque période. En considérant séparément les cas où les innovations sont divisibles et non-divisibles, on examine la nature des accords de partage parfait qui peuvent se produire dans le sous-jeu. On montre que la stochasticité et l'indivisibilité minent la possibilité de maintenir le partage. De plus, on découvre que des solutions d'équilibre avec partage de savoir-faire peuvent jouer par intermittence, et qu'on est davantage susceptible de partager les fruits des petites innovations plus que des grandes quand les innovations sont divisibles, mais pas nécessairement quand elles sont indivisibles.

1. Introduction

The phenomenon of know-how sharing among firms that are competitors has been documented by a number of analysts. Two of the most interesting cases come from the steel industry. In his study of the evolution of the blast furnace between 1859

We would like to thank Ralph Winter, two anonymous referees, and the participants of the Economic Theory Workshop at The University of British Columbia for useful comments on an earlier draft. All remaining errors are our own doing.

Canadian Journal of Economics / Revue canadienne d'Economique, Vol. 34, No. 2
May / mai 2001. Printed in Canada / Imprimé au Canada

0008-4085 / 01 / 525–548 / © Canadian Economics Association

and 1875, Allen (1983) found pervasive know-how sharing, which he dubbed 'collective invention.' More recently, in his study of the steel minimill industry in the United States, von Hippel (1988) found that rival firms routinely exchanged technical information. This sometimes went so far as firms setting up entire plants for their rivals. Carter (1989) explores some of the features that make trade in know-how different from ordinary trade.

To explain what he observed in the steel minimill and other industries, von Hippel (1988) proposed a theory of know-how sharing based on the idea that it is cost reducing. In any one period, two firms can be seen as playing a game in which they choose to share or not to share the innovations to the know-how that arise in that period. In these circumstances, it is reasonable to suppose that strategy profile (*not share*, *not share*) is a dominant strategy equilibrium in each period, while strategy profile (*share*, *share*) Pareto-dominates it. Further, if we assume that the game does not change from period to period, know-how sharing can be seen as taking place in a supergame, and standard results can be invoked to explain such sharing. In particular, if firms do not discount future profits too heavily, it is possible to support (*always share*, *always share*) as a subgame perfect Nash equilibrium by using trigger strategies that call for reversion to the dominant strategy equilibrium in the event of defection. Baumol (1993) both surveys the existing empirical evidence on the phenomenon of know-how sharing and articulates and extends the theory proposed by von Hippel (1988). In this, as in a related paper (Eaton and Eswaran 1997), we build on the pioneering efforts of von Hippel and Baumol.[1]

At the heart of this theory of know-know sharing is an exogenous process that drives innovations in know-how. This innovation-generating process is intended to loosely capture learning-by-doing. An important feature of the real process of learning-by-doing that is not incorporated in the theory sketched by von Hippel (1988) and Baumol (1993) is stochasticity. From the perspective of a firm's managers, innovations to know-how are surely stochastic. One objective in this paper is the exploration of how the properties of a stochastic innovation-generating process affect the possibilities for equilibrium know-how sharing.

An important property of know-how is indivisibility. If A discovers some clever idea, she can share it with B or keep it from B, but A may not be able to share a part of her idea. Another of our objectives is to explore the implications of indivisibility for equilibrium know-how sharing. We do this by comparing the set of equilibrium know-how sharing agreements when know-how is indivisible with the corresponding set when know-how is assumed to be perfectly divisible.

By its very nature, know-how is non-rivalrous, and we assume that it is excludable. Thus, firms can choose to share their know-how or to not share it. In addition, we assume that patenting and/or licensing is not feasible. Thus, standard property

1 In a different context, Gallini (1984) has demonstrated that it may be in the interest of a firm to share its technology with a rival, if by doing so the rival is deterred from doing R&D that would prove damaging to the former. The underlying motivation for know-how sharing is quite different in this scenario.

rights arrangements cannot be used to control and direct the diffusion of know-how. We make these assumptions because we think they are appropriate for many real-world situations and because they allow us to isolate the phenomenon of interest: voluntary know-how sharing. The central question of interest here is this: Under what circumstances can voluntary know-how sharing effect an efficient diffusion of know-how?

In our model, in each period two risk neutral firms get independent draws of know-how from a common probability distribution. A firm's profit in any period is an increasing function of its own stock of know-how and a decreasing function of the stock of know-how of its competitor. Hence, in any period, (*not share*, *not share*) is a dominant strategy equilibrium. But the marginal effect on profit of own and competitor's stocks of know-how are such that (*always share*, *always share*) is Pareto-efficient. We look at sharing agreements that are supported by reversion to the no-sharing equilibrium.

Our analysis generates two results that are especially interesting. First, we find that stochasticity inhibits the ability to cooperate, especially in situations where the distribution of innovations has a long, thin, right-hand tail; in these situations, full sharing is difficult to support because a firm that gets an exceptionally valuable, and rare, draw from the distribution must anticipate that the other firm will not be in position to reciprocate for a very long time. More generally, a mean-preserving spread in the distribution of innovations renders full know-how sharing more difficult to support. Second, an interesting feature of the equilibrium of our model is that, when know-how is indivisible, it is possible that sharing is intermittent even when a sharing agreement is in effect. That is, we will observe periods during which no information is being exchanged and cooperation has not broken down: the sharing agreements are still in force. This stands in contrast with the usual scenarios in oligopoly, where absence of cooperation for any length of time in a supergame indicates that a punishment phase is in effect.

We find that relative to the case of perfect divisibility, indivisibility of know-how inhibits the ability to cooperate. We uncover a surprising result here: when innovations are indivisible, it is very difficult to support a small amount of cooperation and impossible in the limit as the amount of cooperation goes to zero. Together, these results mean that, when innovations are stochastic and know-how is indivisible, it may be impossible to support any cooperation where full cooperation in the corresponding deterministic scenario may well have been possible.

In the context of oligopoly theory, it is well known that stochasticity makes collusion difficult, as seen in Green and Porter (1984) and Rotemberg and Saloner (1986). The mechanism in Green and Porter (1984) is very different from that proposed here. There, randomness in the demand facing the industry makes it difficult for firms to ascertain whether cheating has taken place; so, as a way of enforcing collusion, firms automatically go into a punishment mode (a price war) for some length of time if the price falls below some critical level. Closer in spirit to our analysis is that of Rotemberg and Saloner (1986), who argue that the incentive for a firm to cheat is greater during booms than during recessions. However, there are peculiarities associated with know-how (indivisibility, in particular) that interact with stochasticity in a manner that precludes this argument from being carried over to the context of know-how sharing. As we demonstrate, it is with perfectly divisible know-how that stochasticity yields results similar to those in oligopoly theory. It might be thought that results from the literature on Folk Theorems are applicable to our model (see, for example, Fudenberg, Levine, and Maskin 1994). This is not the case, since our model, in fact, is not a repeated game. In each period, the action sets of the firms, and hence their payoff functions, are determined by stochastic realizations of know-how, so that what might loosely be called the stage game in our model changes from period to period.

There are a number of other situations to which our model is applicable. Informal mutual insurance schemes of the sort that are widespread in countries with undeveloped insurance markets have some (but not all) important features in common with our model. The informal pooling of spare parts by firms that are competitors in their output markets is another phenomenon that our model helps to explain. Thus, while exploring the specific issue of know-how sharing, we suggest insights that are potentially relevant in more general scenarios.

The paper is organized as follows. In the next section, we spell out the basic model we use throughout. In section 3, we examine the incentive compatibility conditions that must be satisfied by know-how sharing agreements, and in section 4, we determine the optimal form of sharing agreements when know-how is indivisible. In sections 5 and 6, we derive the results our model generates for the polar cases where know-how is indivisible and perfectly divisible, respectively. We present our concluding remarks in the last section.

2. The model

Assume that there are two identical firms repeatedly confronting each other over an infinite number of periods. In every period each firm receives an exogenous, private innovation which impinges on its own profit and that of its rival. We shall take it that the larger the innovation of a firm, the better it is for the firm and, in the absence of sharing, the worse it is for its rival. The innovations for both firms are drawn from a time-invariant probability distribution, and they are assumed to be independent. Each firm's innovation, x, has a density function $f(x)$ defined on the support $[\underline{x}, \bar{x}]$, denoted hereafter by the set Y. We assume that $0 \leq \underline{x} < \bar{x} < \infty$, and that $f(x) > 0$ on the open interval $(\underline{x}, \bar{x})$. We denote the mean value of the innovations by μ:

$$\mu = \int_{\underline{x}}^{\bar{x}} xf(x)\, dx.$$

We denote firm i's innovation in any period by x_i, $i = 1,2$. (In what follows, firm j will denote the firm other than i.) The density function, $h(x_i, x_j)$, associated with the joint distribution is given by $h(x_i, x_j) = f(x_i)f(x_j)$.

Let g_i denote the transfer ('gift') of innovation received *by* firm i from firm j, and g_j that received *by* firm j from firm i. We assume that sharing entails zero transactions cost if undertaken in the period in which the innovation materializes and that current innovations are infinitely costly to share in a later period. Equivalently, we may assume that last period's information has no value this period. This allows us to ignore the possibility that firms share in some period an innovation that they acquired but witheld in an earlier period. We can then assume that $0 \leq g_i \leq x_j$ and $0 \leq g_j \leq x_i$. For simplicity, we further assume that the payoff to each firm depends only on the innovations and gifts (received and given) of this period: there is no stock dependence.[2] The payoff to firm i in any period is denoted by the function $\Pi^i(x_i, x_j; g_i, g_j)$, continuous and differentiable in all its arguments. We assume that the partial derivatives of this function, denoted by the respective subscripts, have the following signs:

$$\begin{aligned} &\Pi_1^i(x_i, x_j; g_i, g_j) > 0; \qquad \Pi_2^i(x_i, x_j; g_i, g_j) < 0 \\ &\Pi_3^i(x_i, x_j; g_i, g_j) > 0; \qquad \Pi_4^i(x_i, x_j; g_i, g_j) < 0. \end{aligned} \tag{1}$$

These inequalities say that, from the point of view of firm i: larger innovations of x_i are better; larger innovations of x_j are worse; larger gifts received from firm j are better; and larger gifts made to firm j are worse. However, we shall posit that small equal exchanges between firms are necessarily beneficial on balance; that is,

$$\Pi_3^i(x_i, x_j; 0,0) + \Pi_4^i(x_i, x_j; 0,0) > 0 \qquad \text{for any } (x_i, x_j). \tag{2}$$

The last inequality in (1) is the source of the potential for cheating: in a one-period scenario, each firm will find it rational to withold information from its rival. However, the inequality in (2) indicates that a small reciprocal exchange of information, on balance, benefits both firms. This provides the long-term motivation for sharing.

Define the function

$$\Psi^i(x_i, x_j, g_i) \equiv \Pi^i(x_i, x_j; g_i, 0) - \Pi^i(x_i, x_j; g_i, x_i), \tag{3}$$

which represents the immediate *gain* to firm i when it transfers no information to its rival relative to when it transfers all of its information. From the last inequality in (1), it follows that $\Psi^i(x_i, x_j, g_i) > 0$ when $x_i > 0$. We assume that

$$\frac{\partial \Psi^i(x_i, x_j, g_i)}{\partial x_i} \geq 0; \qquad \frac{\partial \Psi^i(x_i, x_j, g_i)}{\partial g_i} \leq 0. \tag{4}$$

2 We are following Eaton and Eswaran (1997) in invoking these simplifying assumptions. However, it is possible to accommodate the case where this period's realizations and gifts contribute to stocks, which, in turn, determine the payoffs. The associated analysis for the special case where the payoffs are linear in the stocks may be obtained from the authors. The essential points of this paper are not changed by the introduction of this complication, and this is why we opt for the simpler model without stocks.

The first inequality in (4) says that the immediate gain to firm i from witholding information is non-decreasing in the size of its innovation. That is, witholding information is more profitable (in the current period) when there is a lot to withold. The second inequality says that the gain to firm i from witholding information is non-increasing in the size of the gift it receives from its rival. Loosely speaking, there are 'non-increasing returns' to cheating in the amount of know-how the firm has access to. That is, the larger the gift received from the rival, the less the advantage a firm's own innovation bestows.

We suppose, first, that innovations are indivisible. Accordingly, in any period a firm can either share its innovation or not share it, but partial sharing is not possible. For purposes of comparison, in a subsequent section we replace this assumption with its opposite extreme: innovations are perfectly divisible.

A *sharing agreement* is a closed set $\Omega \subseteq \Upsilon$ of innovations: the agreement calls for firm i to share its innovation x_i with firm j if and only if $x_i \in \Omega$. We restrict ourselves to symmetric sharing agreements for the two firms. The set Ω (which we will loosely refer to as the agreement set) is not necessarily convex; that is, it may have 'holes' in which innovations are not expected to be shared. Let Λ denote the complement of Ω; Λ is the set of innovations that are not called for by the agreement to be shared.

Support for the sharing agreement is provided by a grim trigger strategy of the sort first used by Friedman (1971) that calls for reversion to no sharing in the event of defection. The strategy profile (*never share, never share*) clearly constitutes a subgame perfect equilibrium (SPNE) since, by (1), each firm's one-period payoff is decreasing in the gift it gives the rival. Notice that the reversion strategy posited here entails the severest possible punishment for defection in this game.

The timing of the events is as follows. Prior to the first period of an infinitely repeated game, the firms come to an understanding regarding a sharing agreement. In each period of the game, innovations materialize and are privately revealed to the two firms. Then, each firm has the opportunity to share its innovation with the other firm. Finally, payoffs for the current period are realized.

Since firm i knows the function $\Pi^i(x_i, x_j; g_i, g_j)$, it can invert this function to infer the innovation of its rival in this period. Hence, at the beginning of a period, each firm knows whether the other has violated the sharing agreement in the previous period. Since the innovations are privately received by each firm and can be only indirectly inferred by the rival, we assume that the firms cannot write explicit contracts that are binding in a court of law.

We can think of a sharing agreement in terms of the reciprocal expected gifts that are exchanged under it. Let G denote the expected gift one firm receives from (and gives to) the other under sharing agreement Ω:

$$G_\Omega = \int_\Omega xf(x)\,dx. \tag{5}$$

From an economic perspective, this *reciprocal gift* – as G_Ω will be referred to hereafter – is of considerable interest. Because the reversion strategy that supports sharing agreements in our model entails the severest possible punishment for defection, our analysis fully delineates the set of reciprocal gifts that can be supported as an SPNE of our sharing game. Since full sharing will be Pareto optimal in our model, it would be interesting to delineate the circumstances in which full sharing (that is, when G is equal to μ) is supportable.

For brevity, we introduce the following notation for arbitrary sets $A \subseteq \Upsilon, B \subseteq \Upsilon$:

$$\langle \Pi^i(x_i, x_j; g_i, g_j) \rangle_{A,B} \equiv \int_A \int_B \Pi^i(x_i, x_j; g_i, g_j) h(x_i, x_j)\, dx_i\, dx_j, \tag{6}$$

with the convention that the left-hand integral is that for x_i over the set A and the right hand integral is that for x_j over the set B. The expected one-period, ex ante payoff to firm i under the agreement, $E\Pi^i_\Omega$, may then be written as

$$E\Pi^i_\Omega = \langle \Pi^i(x_i, x_j; x_j, x_i) \rangle_{\Omega,\Omega} + \langle \Pi^i(x_i, x_j; 0, x_i) \rangle_{\Omega,\Lambda} + \langle \Pi^i(x_i, x_j; x_j, 0) \rangle_{\Lambda,\Omega} + \langle \Pi^i(x_i, x_j; 0, 0) \rangle_{\Lambda,\Lambda}. \tag{7}$$

The four terms on the right-hand side of (7) represent, respectively, the contributions to the expected payoff of firm i in the current period when the innovations are such that the agreement requires (i) both firms to share; (ii) firm i to share but not firm j; (iii) firm j but not firm i to share; and (iv) neither firm to share.

Consider any two sharing agreements characterized, respectively, by the sets Ω and $\tilde{\Omega}$, such that $\Omega \subseteq \tilde{\Omega} \subseteq \Upsilon$. We shall assume that

$$E\Pi^i_{\tilde{\Omega}} \geq E\Pi^i_\Omega, \tag{8}$$

with the inequality being strict if the Lebesgue measure of $\tilde{\Omega}$ is strictly greater than that of Ω. This is a reasonable requirement: it posits that the ex ante expected payoff to a firm does not decrease if the agreement set is expanded. In particular, full sharing is Pareto optimal. The assumptions stated in (1), (2), (4), and (8) will be maintained throughout this paper. (It may be noted as an example that a simple, linear payoff function to be considered later in this paper readily satisfies all of these assumptions.) It may be noted that, when $\underline{x} = 0$, (2) may be derived from (8) by choosing Ω to be the null set and $\tilde{\Omega}$ to be a set of non-zero measure comprising small innovations.

3. Incentive compatibility

In view of (8), any agreement that generates a positive reciprocal gift, G_Ω, will be strictly preferred to no sharing. Hence, both firms would willingly participate in an enforceable agreement Ω with $G_\Omega > 0$. We restrict attention to such agreement sets (that is, those with non-zero measure).

Since the sharing of a firm's innovation with the rival reduces the former's payoff in the current period, however, each firm has an incentive to cheat when its innovation falls in the set Ω. As mentioned earlier, each firm's innovation can be inferred by its rival at the beginning of the next period. Thus, any gains from cheating accrue for only one period. In the event of cheating, both firms will revert to a punishment mode that entails no sharing for ever.

Let δ $(0 \leq \delta < 1)$ denote the common discount factor of the two firms. Innovations $x_i \in \Lambda$ do not raise issues of cheating, since such innovations are not called upon by the agreement to be shared. Suppose, however, that firm i has obtained an innovation $x_i \in \Omega$ in this period and does not yet know firm j's innovation. In the event that neither firm cheats, firm i's expected present value payoff, given its current period innovation, is

$$\int_{\Omega} \Pi^i(x_i, x_j; x_j, x_i) f(x_j)\, dx_j + \int_{\Lambda} \Pi^i(x_i, x_j; 0, x_i) f(x_j)\, dx_j + \frac{\delta}{1-\delta} E\Pi^i_{\Omega}. \tag{9}$$

If, however, firm i decides to cheat in the current period, its expected present value payoff, given its current period innovation, is

$$\int_{\Omega} \Pi^i(x_i, x_j; x_j, 0) f(x_j)\, dx_j + \int_{\Lambda} \Pi^i(x_i, x_j; 0, 0) f(x_j)\, dx_j + \frac{\delta}{1-\delta} E\Pi^i_{\Phi}, \tag{10}$$

where the subscript Φ in the third term denotes the null set, and thus

$$E\Pi^i_{\Phi} \equiv \langle \Pi^i(x_i, x_j; 0, 0) \rangle_{\Upsilon, \Upsilon} \tag{11}$$

denotes the one-period ex ante expected payoff to firm i when there is no sharing agreement in place.

If firm i is not to cheat, the expression in (9) must be at least as large as that in (10). This incentive compatibility constraint may be written

$$P^i_{\Omega}(\delta) \geq T^i_{\Omega}(x_i), \tag{12}$$

where $P^i_{\Omega}(\delta)$, the expected 'punishment' to firm i for cheating, is given by

$$P^i_{\Omega}(\delta) = \frac{\delta}{1-\delta} [E\Pi^i_{\Omega} - E\Pi^i_{\Phi}], \tag{13}$$

and $T^i_{\Omega}(x_i)$, firm i's 'temptation' to cheat, is given by

$$T^i_{\Omega}(x_i) = \int_{\Omega} \Psi^i(x_i, x_j; x_j) f(x_j) dx_j + \int_{\Lambda} \Psi^i(x_i, x_j; 0) f(x_j) dx_j, \tag{14}$$

where the function Ψ^i is defined in (3). The first (second) term on the right-hand side of (14) represents the expected gain to firm i of cheating when firm j's innovation is such that it is obliged (not obliged) by the agreement to share its innovation with firm i. Both the integrands on the right-hand side of the expression in (14) are non-decreasing in the magnitude of the innovation x_i by the first inequality in (4). The punishment for cheating is simply the present value of the difference between the expected future profit to firm i with and without sharing. This is obviously independent of the current-period innovations of the firms. Let X denote this largest element of Ω. Since the temptation to cheat is greatest when firm i's innovation is equal to the largest element of Ω, from (12) the incentive compatibility constraint that is necessary and sufficient for Ω to be supportable is given by

$$P^i_\Omega(\delta) \geq T^i_\Omega(X). \tag{15}$$

This incentive compatibility condition is the same in all periods, since the game under consideration is stationary.

4. The optimal form of sharing agreements

We now will invoke the Pareto criterion to characterize the optimal form of sharing agreements. As mentioned earlier, the set Ω does not necessarily include all innovations smaller than X; that is, the set Ω is not necessarily convex. We now demonstrate that Pareto-optimal agreements must be characterized by convex sharing sets. We call sharing agreement Ω *form-optimal* if it has the following form: $\Omega = \{x : \underline{x} \leq x \leq X\}$, where $\underline{x} < X \leq \bar{x}$. That is, the set of shared innovations is form optimal if it can be described by a real number X lying in the support of the distribution such that an innovation is to be shared if and only if it is no larger than X. The essential feature of a form-optimal agreement is that if, according to the agreement, a particular innovation is to be shared then all smaller innovations are also to be shared: the set of shared innovations is convex. In proposition 1, below, we show that Pareto optimality requires form optimality.

PROPOSITION 1. *If a supportable sharing agreement is not form optimal, there is a supportable form-optimal agreement that (weakly) Pareto-dominates it.*

To prove this proposition, suppose Ω is a non-form-optimal sharing agreement, with X as its largest element. Consider what happens when the sharing set is expanded to $\tilde{\Omega} \supseteq \Omega$ while maintaining X as the largest element of $\tilde{\Omega}$ also. We can write $\tilde{\Omega} = \Omega \cup \Theta$, where Ω and Θ are mutually exclusive sets. The change in the expected current period payoff to firm i for cheating, $\Delta T^i(x_i)$, is

$$\Delta T^i(x_i) = \int_\Theta [\Psi^i(x_i, x_j; x_j) - \Psi^i(x_i, x_j; 0)] f(x_j) dx_j,$$

which is the expected gain in cheating to firm i when firm j is obliged to share its innovation in Θ less the expected gain when firm j is not thus obliged. Since, by the second inequality in (4), the gain to a firm from cheating is non-increasing in the gift received from its rival (owing to 'non-increasing returns' to information), the term in the square bracket in the integrand is always non-positive. Hence, $\Delta T^i(x_i) \leq 0$; that is, the temptation to cheat does not increase when the sharing agreement is expanded from Ω to $\tilde{\Omega}$.

The change in the punishment to cheating, $\Delta P^i(\delta)$, when Θ is added to the sharing set is given by

$$\Delta P^i(\delta) = P^i_{\tilde{\Omega}}(\delta) - P^i_{\Omega}(\delta),$$

which, from (8) and (13), is non-negative, since the expected payoff under the agreement set Ω is no larger than that under the agreement set $\tilde{\Omega}$. Thus, if the agreement set Ω is supportable, so is $\tilde{\Omega}$. Furthermore, since $E\Pi^i_{\tilde{\Omega}} \geq E\Pi^i_{\Omega}$, $\tilde{\Omega}$ (weakly) Pareto-dominates Ω, and the dominance is strict if the Lebesgue measure of $\tilde{\Omega}$ is strictly greater than that of Ω.

In general, we can conceive of the sharing agreements being asymmetric, despite the firms' being identical. In the interest of simplicity, however, we will restrict ourselves to symmetric agreements.[3] This is consistent with von Hippel's observation in the steel minimill industry that 'in an informal way, participants [of a know-how sharing arrangement] appeared to keep a balance in the value given and received' (1988, 82).

According to proposition 1, in effect we can learn everything there is to know about the set of supportable reciprocal gift exchanges by restricting attention to form-optimal sharing agreements. So we confine ourselves to such agreements. Given that a sharing agreement is form optimal, there is a one-to-one relationship between sharing agreements and their associated reciprocal gift exchanges, and this relationship can be expressed in two ways. First, if X is the largest element in a form-optimal sharing set, the expected gift exchange can be denoted (with a slight abuse of notation) by $G(X)$. Second, if the reciprocal gift is G, the largest element in the form-optimal agreement that yields this expected reciprocal gift can be written as $X(G)$. Obviously, $X(G)$ is the inverse of $G(X)$. The relationship between X and G is defined by the following:

$$G = \int_{\underline{x}}^{X} xf(x)\,dx. \tag{16}$$

For any G, the form-optimal sharing agreement, $\Omega(G)$, that generates this gift exchange is clearly defined by

$$\Omega(G) \equiv \{x : \underline{x} \leq x \leq X(G)\}. \tag{17}$$

We denote the complement of this set by $\Lambda(G)$.

3 When the payoffs are linear in know-how, however, it can be shown that if the sharing agreements for identical firms are not symmetric (contrary to our assumption), it can be weakly Pareto-dominated by a symmetric sharing agreement, with the dominance being strict if the agreement sets have different Lesbegue measures. The reason is that unequal reciprocal gifts dilute the incentives for sharing of the firm receiving the smaller reciprocal gift – a situation that can be remedied by making the sharing agreement symmetric.

5. Indivisible innovations

It might appear that agreements requiring the sharing of large innovations will not likely be supported, since these require firms to give away substantial innovations that arrive infrequently. On the other hand, it might appear that agreements restricted to the sharing of small innovations are less prone to this problem and hence would be supportable. It is surprising that when innovations are indivisible, the latter conjecture is incorrect, as proposition 2 demonstrates. In fact, we shall see in this section that there are scenarios in which the ease with which form-optimal agreements can be supported increases monotonically with the size of the largest innovation in the sharing set, with full sharing agreements being the easiest to support.

PROPOSITION 2. *For any $\delta \in [0,1)$ and $\underline{x} > 0$, it is impossible to support as SPNE agreements with sufficiently small reciprocal gift exchanges.*[4]

To prove this notice that, if $G \to 0$, it follows from (16) that $X(G) \to \underline{x}$ and $\Omega \to \Phi$. Thus, from (13),

$$\lim_{G \to 0} \quad P^i_{\Omega(G)}(\delta) = 0. \tag{18}$$

The punishment for cheating on agreements with low gift exchanges is vanishingly small. This is because most of the time in the future the rival will obtain innovations exceeding $X(G)$, which it is not obliged to share in any case. Now from (14),

$$\begin{aligned} \lim_{G \to 0} \quad T^i_{\Omega(G)}(X(G)) &= \int_{\underline{x}}^{\bar{x}} \Psi^i(\underline{x}, x_j;0) f(x_j)\, dx_j \\ &> 0, \end{aligned} \tag{19}$$

since $\Psi^i(\underline{x}, x_j;0) > 0$. The temptation to cheat remains strictly bounded away from zero even as the gift exchange approaches zero. Thus, the incentive compatibility condition (15) is necessarily violated in the limit $G \to 0$. Since $P^i_{\Omega(G)}(\delta)$ and $T^i_{\Omega(G)}(X(G))$ are continuous in G, it follows that there is a range of small values of G for which (15) is violated.

This result does not say that small innovations will never be shared. In fact, if sharing agreement $\Omega(G)$ is supportable, all innovations smaller than $X(G)$ will be shared. What the result does say is that if the expected reciprocal gift G associated with a sharing agreement is sufficiently small, the agreement is not supportable. That is, agreements that share only small innovations cannot be supported. Intuitively, this result is just a variation on an old aphorism: 'A bird in the hand is worth two in the bush,' because the probability that one will actually catch the two birds is small. In the present

4 In the case of linear payoffs considered below, this result holds even when $\underline{x} = 0$.

scenario, the bird in the hand is, of course, $X(G)$, the innovation that a firm must share with its competitor if the sharing agreement is to be supportable. The birds in the bush are the future gifts that, given the agreement, the rival will share with the firm. Should the firm share $X(G)$ today to get these future gifts? None of these future gifts is larger than $X(G)$, since the sharing set is $[\underline{x}, X(G)]$, and, when G is small, the probability that the firm will actually receive a gift in any future period is quite small, since the competitor is required to share only those innovations that fall in the sharing set. According to the proposition, when G is small, not sharing $X(G)$ with the competitor has a higher value than the expected future gifts from the competitor – the bird in the hand is worth more than the birds in the bush.

5.1. An example with linear payoffs

A special case that is instructive to consider is one in which the payoff function has the following linear structure:

$$\Pi^i(x_i, x_j; g_i, g_j) = \alpha(x_i + g_i) - \beta(x_j + g_j), \qquad \alpha > \beta > 0. \tag{20}$$

When the parameter β is zero or negative, the question of sharing has no interesting economic implications, since in each period (*share, share*) is both Pareto optimal and a dominant strategy equilibrium. So we assume that $\beta > 0$. Conversely, when $\beta > \alpha$, in each period (*not share, not share*) is both Pareto optimal and a dominant strategy equilibrium, and there is no economic incentive to share innovations. So we posit that $\alpha > \beta > 0$. This linear payoff function satisfies all of the restrictions we placed earlier on the payoff functions.

The incentive compatibility condition (15) can be readily shown in this case to reduce to

$$\frac{\delta}{1-\delta}(\alpha - \beta)G \geq \beta X(G). \tag{21}$$

This inequality is easily interpreted. According to the payoff function, an increase in a firm's own innovation by one unit increases its payoff by α, while an increase in the rival's innovation by one unit decreases the firm's payoff by β. Thus, if a firm's innovation is the largest one, $X(G)$, within the agreement set, the current period gain from witholding this from the competitor is given by the right-hand side of (21). This is the largest temptation to cheat the firm has to counter. If the firm succumbs, it will lose profits in all future periods. The expected value of the gift expected to be *received and given* in any period is G, and the net profit expected in any period due to this gift exchange is $(\alpha - \beta)G$. Since this is forgone in every future period, the present value of these forgone expected profits – the punishment – is given by the left-hand side of (21). The above incentive compatibility condition may be rewritten as

$$\frac{X(G)}{G} \leq \frac{\delta}{1-\delta}\,\frac{(\alpha - \beta)}{\beta}. \tag{22}$$

Inequality (22) is a necessary and sufficient condition for agreement $\Omega(G)$ to be supportable as a SPNE of the know-how sharing game. Since the benefit of cheating is proportional to $X(G)$, while the cost to cheating is proportional to G, the left-hand side of (22) is a measure of the largest benefit-cost ratio of cheating when payoffs are linear in know-how.

As we observed earlier, efficiency demands full sharing. For the form-optimal agreement that generates full sharing (that is, $\Omega = \Upsilon$), we have $G = \mu$ or $X(\mu) = \bar{x}$. Thus, (22) implies that full sharing is supportable in the linear case if and only if

$$\frac{\bar{x}}{\mu} \leq \frac{\delta}{1-\delta} \frac{(\alpha - \beta)}{\beta}.$$

It is apparent from the above inequality that if the upper support of the distribution, $\bar{x}$, is sufficiently large relative to the mean of the distribution, μ, it will be impossible to support full sharing. Full sharing cannot be supported for distributions with long tails.

If the innovations were certain, that is, if the probability density function $f(x)$ had all its mass at one point, then $X(G)$ would be equal to G, and the incentive compatibility condition would reduce to $1 \leq \delta(\alpha - \beta)/[\beta(1-\delta)]$. But innovations are stochastic in our model, with the result that $X(G) > G$, because G is the density-weighted average of x between $\underline{x}$ and $X(G)$. It is then clear that stochasticity undermines the ability to support voluntary sharing arrangements.[5] It is also clear that the following is a necessary condition that must hold for any sharing to be possible when innovations are stochastic:

$$1 \leq \frac{\delta}{1-\delta} \frac{(\alpha - \beta)}{\beta}. \tag{23}$$

We assume this condition holds.

Suppose, further, that the innovations are uniformly distributed and that the density function is given by

$$f(x) = \begin{cases} 1/(2s) & \text{for } \mu - s \leq x \leq \mu + s, \\ 0 & \text{otherwise,} \end{cases} \tag{24}$$

where it is assumed that $\mu \geq s \geq 0$. This distribution has two parameters: the mean, μ, and what we can think of as the spread parameter, s. (The parameter restrictions $\mu \geq s \geq 0$ are necessry to ensure that $x \geq 0$.) For this distribution, it can easily be shown that

$$X(G)/G = [(\mu - s)^2 + 4sG]^{1/2}/G.$$

5 This is somewhat reminiscent of the insight, in a different context, of Rotemberg and Saloner (1986) that price-fixing cartels are harder to sustain in periods of high demand than in periods of low demand.

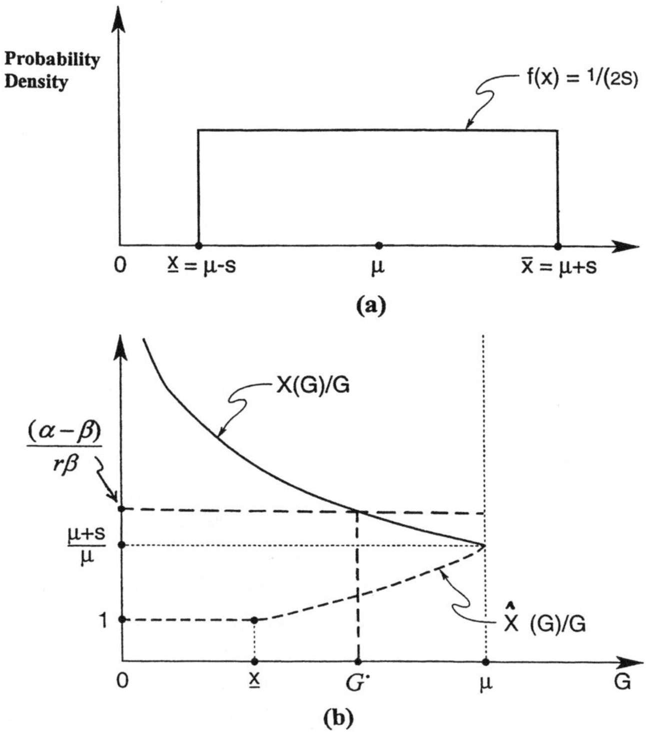

FIGURE 1 The uniform distribution

The density function for the uniform distribution is illustrated in figure 1 (a), and the function $X(G)/G$ is illustrated by the solid line in figure 1 (b). The latter function is downward sloping, is equal to $(1 + s/\mu)$ when G is equal to μ, and shoots off to infinity as G approaches 0. In the case illustrated in the figure, only reciprocal gifts larger than G^* are supportable. Two remarkable conclusions follow regarding the sharing game when the payoff function is linear and the distribution of innovations is uniform. First, if an agreement with some reciprocal gift G can be supported as an SPNE, then so can all agreements with larger expected gifts. Indeed, for any sharing agreement to be supportable, full sharing must be supportable. Second, reciprocal gifts smaller than some critical value cannot be supported. This second feature is a special case of the general result demonstrated earlier in this section.

Given what we know from more familiar oligopoly applications, these results are surprising. When firms produce substitutes and compete in quantities, it is easier to support outcomes that are closer to the Nash equilibrium of the stage game than it is to support solutions that are near the joint profit-maximizing outcome of the stage game. On the other hand, if producers of a homogeneous good compete in

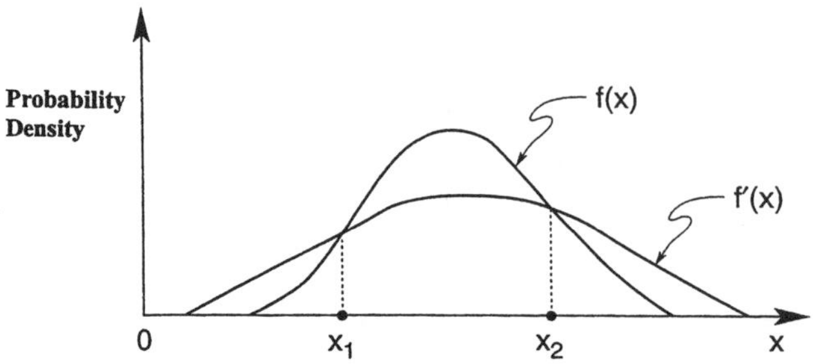

FIGURE 2 A mean preserving spread

prices, the ability to support collusion is independent of the 'distance' of the collusive outcome from either the Nash equilibrium or the joint profit-maximizing outcome of the stage game. In contrast, for the sharing game considered here with linear payoffs and a uniform distribution of innovations, the fully collusive solution (in which $G = \mu$) is the easiest to support, and minimally collusive solutions (in which G is close to 0) are impossible to support. The peculiarity of this result arises from the assumed indivisible nature of the innovations, as we shall see.

If we hold the mean, μ, of the uniform distribution constant and increase the spread parameter, s, we have a mean-preserving spread of the distribution. Such a spread twists the $X(G)/G$ schedule so as to make it easier to support small reciprocal gifts and harder to support large ones. In fact, the derivative of $X(G)/G$ with respect to s is negative or positive as G is smaller or larger, respectively, than $(\mu - s)/2$. (As we argue below, this 'twist' is a general result for the linear payoff model.) Since, for the case of linear payoffs and a uniform distribution, for any sharing agreement to be feasible full sharing must be supportable, it follows that a sufficiently drastic increase in the spread parameter could render unviable all sharing agreements.

In figure 2, we illustrate a mean-preserving spread of the distribution $f(x)$, that produces a new distribution $f'(x)$. The spread transfers mass from $f(x)$ within the interval shown as (x_1, x_2) to the tails of $f'(x)$, while preserving the mean. Let $X'(G)$ denote the largest element of the form-optimal sharing agreement that delivers the reciprocal gift exchange G under distribution $f'(x)$. Clearly, for reciprocal gifts G such that $X'(G) \leq x_1$, it is the case that $X'(G) < X(G)$ because $f'(x) > f(x)$ for innovations $x \leq x_1$. It follows immediately that these 'small' reciprocal gifts are easier to support under $f'(x)$ than under $f(x)$. Conversely, for reciprocal gifts G such that $X(G) \geq x_2$, it is the case that $X'(G) > X(G)$ and these 'large' gifts are easier to support under $f(x)$ than under $f'(x)$. In fact, for this sort of mean-preserving spread, it is easily shown that there is a reciprocal gift $\tilde{G}$ and a corresponding largest element $X(\tilde{G})$ of the associated form-optimal agreement satisfying $x_1 < X(\tilde{G}) < x_2$, such that $X'(G) < X(G)$ for $G < \tilde{G}$ and $X'(G) > X(G)$ for $G > \tilde{G}$. Consequently, a mean-preserving spread generally makes it easier to

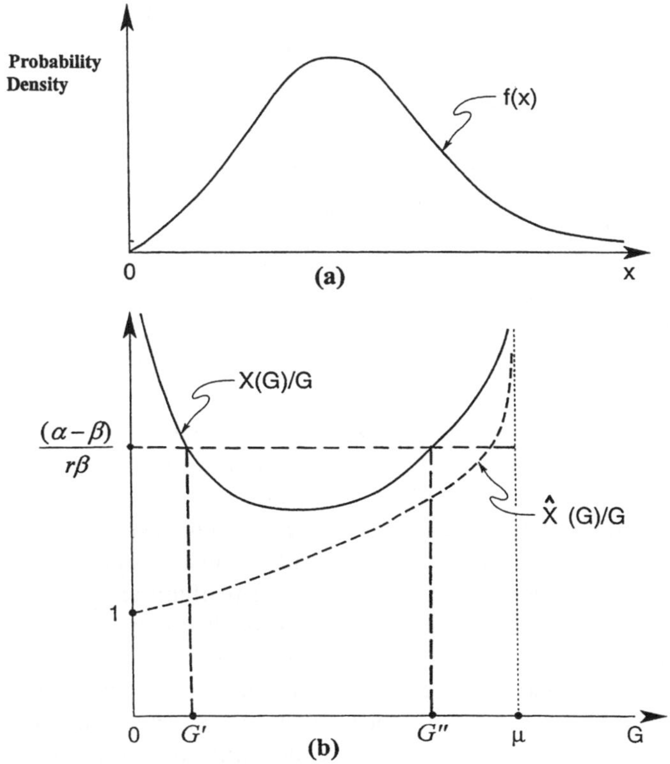

FIGURE 3 The gamma distribution

support relatively small reciprocal gifts and more difficult to support relatively large ones.

We saw in figure 1 (b) that, for the uniform distribution, $X(G)/G$ is downward sloping. However, this is not a general feature of sharing arrangements. To see this, suppose now that the innovations are drawn from a gamma distribution:

$$f(x) = \frac{1}{\Gamma(b)} a^b x^{b-1} e^{-ax} \quad \text{for} \quad x \geq 0, a > 0, b > 0, \tag{25}$$

where $\Gamma(.)$ is the gamma function. The mean and variance of this distribution are b/a and b/a^2, respectively. Figure 3 (a) illustrates the density function associated with the gamma distribution, and the solid line in figure 3 (b) displays the corresponding $X(G)/G$ function. The assumed values for both parameters a and b are equal to 5 in the figure. For these parameter values, the density function rises steeply for very low innovations and falls rapidly for very high innovations, and this feature leads to the U-shape of the $X(G)/G$ function. Consequently, very small and very large reciprocal gifts are both unsupportable; only intermediate valued reciprocal gifts – those in the interval $[G', G'']$ in the figure – are supportable.

In the example with a uniform distribution, larger reciprocal gifts were easier to sustain than smaller ones, whereas with the gamma distribution we see that this is not necessarily so. Why is there this indeterminacy regarding the ease or difficulty of supporting larger reciprocal gifts? We have seen that the ratio $X(G)/G$ is a measure of the largest benefit-cost ratio of cheating on the given agreement. This ratio needs to be below the critical value given on the right-hand side of (22) if the sharing agreement is to be supportable. If the reciprocal gift is increased by a certain amount, the amount by which $X(G)$ has to increase to generate the required increase in G clearly depends on the value of the density function at $X(G)$, that is, on $f(X(G))$: if this density is large (small), the required increase in $X(G)$ will be small (large). Thus, depending on the value of the density at $X(G)$, the ratio $X(G)/G$ could either increase or decrease as G increases. In other words, larger reciprocal gifts may be either harder or easier to support.

6. Perfectly divisible innovations

To get a deeper understanding of the role of indivisibility in our results, in this section we explore the set of supportable sharing agreements when innovations are *perfectly divisible*. Thus, in any period, a firm can choose to share an arbitrary fraction of its innovation with its rival. The development of the analysis closely parallels that for indivisible innovations.

Given perfect divisibility, a sharing agreement is described by a function $g(x)$ with domain $[\underline{x}, \bar{x}]$ satisfying the restriction that $0 \le g(x) \le x$. This is the gift bestowed on its rival by a firm whose innovation is x. A *form-optimal* sharing agreement is characterized by a variable, $\hat{X}$, with $0 < \hat{X} \le \bar{x}$, and has the following form:

$$g(x) = \begin{cases} x & \text{if } x < \hat{X} \\ \hat{X} & \text{if } x \ge \hat{X}. \end{cases} \tag{26}$$

Under a form-optimal agreement, if a firm's innovation is less than $\hat{X}$, the firm's gift to its competitor is its entire innovation; but if its innovation exceeds $\hat{X}$, the firm's gift to its competitor is equal to $\hat{X}$. When innovations are indivisible, the sharing is inevitably all-or-nothing. Here, in sharp contrast, as long as $\hat{X} > 0$ the agreement always calls for *some* sharing, regardless of the size of the firm's innovation.

When the payoff function is linear in know-how, it can readily be shown that agreements that are not form optimal can be (weakly) Pareto-dominated by a form-optimal agreement. However, this cannot be demonstrated for general functional forms. Nevertheless, in what follows we shall focus only on form-optimal sharing agreements – which we denote by $\hat{\Omega}(G)$ – and we shall characterize them by the maximal element, $\hat{X}(G)$, of the set $\hat{\Omega}(G)$ associated with the reciprocal gift, G. There is a one-to-one relationship between $\hat{X}(G)$ and G, and the former is that value of X that solves the following:

$$G = \int_{\underline{x}}^{\hat{X}} x f(x)\, dx + \int_{\hat{X}}^{\bar{x}} \hat{X} f(x)\, dx. \tag{27}$$

Similarly, for any X the implied reciprocal gift exchange, $\hat{G}(X)$, is given by the right-hand side of (27). Note that in the case of indivisible innovations, the maximal element, $X(G)$, of the agreement set associated with any positive G, however small, was bounded below by $\underline{x}$. In contrast, in the case of perfectly divisible innovations, $\hat{X}(G)$ can take on any value in the interval $[0, \bar{x}]$, depending on the value of G.

The set $\hat{\Omega}(G)$ is defined by

$$\hat{\Omega}(G) \equiv \{x : \underline{x} \leq x \leq \hat{X}(G)\},$$

and the complement of $\hat{\Omega}(G)$ will be denoted by the set $\hat{\Lambda}(G)$. By construction, an agreement that requires a firm to share all of its innovations if it falls within $\hat{\Omega}(G)$, and an amount $\hat{X}(G)$ if it falls in $\hat{\Lambda}(G)$ will generate a reciprocal gift exchange equal to G. If $G < \underline{x}$, then by (27) we must have $\hat{X}(G) = G$. In this case, $\hat{\Omega}(G)$ is the null set Φ and $\hat{\Lambda}(G)$ is Υ.

The expressions for the expected ex ante profit per period, $E\hat{\Pi}^i_{\hat{\Omega}}$, and the temptation to cheat, $\hat{T}^i_{\hat{\Omega}}(x_i)$, in the case of perfect divisibility of innovations are, of course, different from those under indivisibility but are readily written down. Suppressing the arguments of $\hat{X}(G), \hat{\Omega}(G)$, and $\hat{\Lambda}(G)$ for brevity, if $\underline{x} \leq \hat{X} \leq \bar{x}$, for example,

$$E\hat{\Pi}^i_{\hat{\Omega}} = \langle \Pi^i(x_i, x_j; x_j, x_i) \rangle_{\hat{\Omega},\hat{\Omega}} + \langle \Pi^i(x_i, x_j; \hat{X}, x_i) \rangle_{\hat{\Omega},\hat{\Lambda}} + \langle \Pi^i(x_i, x_j; x_j, \hat{X}) \rangle_{\hat{\Lambda},\hat{\Omega}} + \langle \Pi^i(x_i, x_j; \hat{X}, \hat{X}) \rangle_{\hat{\Lambda},\hat{\Lambda}}, \tag{28}$$

and if, in addition, $x_i \leq \hat{X}$,

$$\hat{T}^i_{\hat{\Omega}}(x_i) = \int_{\underline{x}}^{\hat{X}} \Psi^i(x_i, x_j; x_j) f(x_j)\, dx_j + \int_{\hat{X}}^{\bar{x}} \Psi^i(x_i, x_j; \hat{X}) f(x_j)\, dx_j. \tag{29}$$

The temptation to cheat when $x_i > \hat{X}$ can be analogously written down. If, on the other hand, $0 \leq \hat{X} \leq \underline{x}$, then

$$E\hat{\Pi}^i_{\hat{\Omega}} = \langle \Pi^i(x_i, x_j; \hat{X}, \hat{X}) \rangle_{\Upsilon,\Upsilon}, \tag{30}$$

and

$$\hat{T}^i_{\hat{\Omega}}(x_i) = \int_{\underline{x}}^{\bar{x}} [\Pi^i(x_i, x_j; \hat{X}, 0) - \Pi^i(x_i, x_j; \hat{X}, \hat{X})] f(x_j)\, dx_j. \tag{31}$$

For the agreement set $\hat{\Omega}(G)$ to be supportable as a SPNE, the following inequality must hold for all $x_i \in \Upsilon$:

$$\hat{P}^i_{\hat{\Omega}}(\delta) \geq \hat{T}^i_{\hat{\Omega}}(x_i), \tag{32}$$

where the left-hand side is the expected punishment for cheating, given by

$$\hat{P}^i_{\hat{\Omega}}(\delta) = \frac{\delta}{1-\delta} [E\hat{\Pi}^i_{\hat{\Omega}} - E\Pi^i_{\Phi}], \tag{33}$$

with $E\Pi^i_\Phi$ denoting, as before, the expected ex ante payoff per period to firm i when no sharing agreement is in place.

Note that for full sharing (that is, $G = \mu$ or $\hat{\Omega}(G) = \Upsilon$), we must have $\hat{X} = \bar{x}$; so the necessary and sufficient condition for full sharing is the same for perfect divisibility as for the indivisibility case. (When there is to be full sharing, it does not matter whether innovations are divisible or indivisible, since the agreements call for the sharing of every innovation in full.) The following proposition looks at sharing possibilities for small reciprocal gift exchanges when innovations are perfectly divisible.

PROPOSITION 3. *When innovations are perfectly divisible, there exists a sufficiently large discount factor bounded away from one above which sharing agreements with small gift exchanges are always supportable.*

To prove this result, note that when $G \to 0$, from (27) it follows that $\hat{X}(G) \to 0$. Thus, if $\underline{x} > 0$, the relevant scenario is that with $0 < \hat{X} \leq \underline{x}$. Expanding the integrand in (30) in a Taylor series around $\hat{X}(G) = 0$ and retaining only terms upto the first order in $\hat{X}(G)$, we obtain

$$E\hat{\Pi}^i_{\hat{\Omega}} = E\Pi^i_\Phi + \hat{X}(G)\gamma, \tag{34}$$

where

$$\gamma \equiv \int_{\underline{x}}^{\bar{x}}\int_{\underline{x}}^{\bar{x}} [\Pi^i_3(x_i, x_j;0,0) + \Pi^i_4(x_i, x_j;0,0)]h(x_i, x_j)\, dx_i\, dx_j, \tag{35}$$

in which the subscripts of the payoff functions, as before, denote derivatives with respect to the respective arguments. Note that, using inequality (2), it immediately follows that $\gamma > 0$. From (33) and (34), it follows that the punishment for cheating on small agreements is given by

$$\hat{P}^i_\Omega(\delta) = \frac{\delta}{1-\delta}\hat{X}(G)\gamma. \tag{36}$$

Similarly, expanding the integrand in (31) in a Taylor series around $\hat{X}(G) = 0$ and retaining only terms up to the first order in $\hat{X}(G)$, we obtain

$$\hat{T}^i_\Omega(x_i) = \hat{X}(G)S^i(x_i), \tag{37}$$

where

$$S^i(x_i) \equiv \int_{\underline{x}}^{\bar{x}} [-\Pi^i_4(x_i, x_j;0,0)\}f(x_j)\, dx_j \tag{38}$$

$$> 0,$$

using the last inequality in (1). Using (36), (37), and (38) in (32), the necessary and sufficient incentive compatibility condition that must be satisfied for agreements with very small gift exchanges to be supportable as SPNE can be written

$$\frac{\delta}{1-\delta}\gamma \geq \max_{x_i} S^i(x_i). \tag{39}$$

Since the right-hand side is finite, there is always a δ sufficiently close to (but strictly smaller than) unity for which the above inequality is satisfied. This establishes the proposition.

The difference between proposition 2 for indivisible innovations and proposition 3 for perfectly divisible ones is that the discount factor required to support agreements with arbitrarily small reciprocal gifts, G, is unity in the limit when $G = 0$. In the case of perfectly divisible innovations, however, the required discount factor remains strictly bounded away from unity even in the limit when $G = 0$.

To get an intuitive grasp of proposition 3, we need the converse of the aphorism we used to discuss proposition 2: 'A bird in the hand is never worth many in the bush, when the birds in the bush are caught with high probability.' Again, the bird in the hand is $\hat{X}(G)$, the largest gift the firm must share with its competitor if the sharing agreement is to be supportable, and the birds in the bush are the gifts that the competitor will share in the future with the firm if the sharing agreement is in place. When G is small, in each future period, there is a high probability that the competitor will bestow a gift equal to $\hat{X}(G)$ because most innovations will exceed $\hat{X}(G)$, and this probability approaches 1 as G approaches zero. Hence, for all practical purposes, not sharing $\hat{X}(G)$ today means foregoing a gift of the same magnitude in most future periods. According to proposition 3, as long as the discount factor is large enough to ensure that (39) is satisfied, the birds in the bush are worth more than the bird in the hand when G is small.

6.1. The example with linear payoffs again

Pursuing the earlier example with linear payoffs, we note that when innovations are perfectly divisible a form-optimal agreement $\hat{\Omega}(G)$ is supportable as an SPNE if and only if

$$\frac{\hat{X}(G)}{G} \leq \frac{\delta}{1-\delta}\frac{(\alpha-\beta)}{\beta}. \tag{40}$$

When the innovations are distributed uniformly according to (24), it is readily verified that

$$\hat{X}(G)/G = \begin{cases} [(\mu+s) - 2s^{1/2}(\mu-G)^{1/2}]/G & \text{if } G \geq \mu - s, \\ 1 & \text{if } G < \mu - s. \end{cases} \tag{41}$$

This function is illustrated by the dashed curve in figure 1 (b). When G is equal to μ, the values of $\hat{X}(G)/G$ and $X(G)/G$ are identical, and when G is less than μ, $\hat{X}(G)/G$ lies below $X(G)/G$. As noted earlier, under the assumption of perfect divisibility, even though the smallest innovation is $\underline{x}$, the amount of information to be shared can be smaller than $\underline{x}$. We have noted earlier that for $G \leq \underline{x}$, we necessarily have $\hat{X}(G)/G = 1$. With the uniform distribution and divisible innovations, the necessary and sufficient condition for small reciprocal gifts to be supportable is $1 \leq \delta(\alpha - \beta)/[\beta(1 - \delta)]$. This is a special case of the general condition (39), since in this linear payoff case $\gamma = (\alpha - \beta)$ and $S^i(x_i) = \beta$ for all x_i.

A feature worth noting is that it is never easier to support larger gifts than smaller ones because, as can be seen from figure 1 (b), the slope of $\hat{X}(G)/G$ is non-negative. This feature is now shown to obtain for arbitrary density functions. Differentiating the function $\hat{X}(G)/G$ with respect to G reveals that this function is increasing in G for $G > \underline{x}$ if $d\hat{X}(G)/dG > \hat{X}(G)/G$ or, equivalently, if $\hat{G}(X)/X > d\hat{G}(X)/dX$. But from (27),

$$\frac{d\hat{G}(X)}{dX} = 1 - F(X),$$

where $F(.)$ is the cumulative distribution function associated with $f(.)$, and

$$\hat{G}(X)/X = (1/X)\int_{\underline{x}}^{X} xf(x)\,dx + 1 - F(X)$$

$$> \frac{d\hat{G}(X)}{dX}.$$

Hence, for $G > \underline{x}$, $\hat{X}(G)/G$ is an increasing function of G. Furthermore, we have seen above that for $G \leq \underline{x}$, $\hat{X}(G)/G = 1$. This establishes our last result, stated below.

PROPOSITION 4. *When innovations are perfectly divisible and the payoff function is linear, it is never easier to support larger reciprocal gifts than smaller.*

In figures 1 (b) and 3 (b), respectively, the dashed curves display the function $\hat{X}(G)/G$ for the uniform and gamma distributions introduced earlier. The non-negative slope of this function confirms, for these special cases, the validity of the result in proposition 4.

When innovations were indivisible we have seen that, depending on the probability distribution for innovations, larger reciprocal gift exchanges may be easier or harder to support than smaller ones. Why is it that, with divisible innovations, larger reciprocal gift exchanges are never easier to support than smaller ones? When innovations are divisible, a firm is called upon to share $\hat{X}(G)$ even when its realization exceeds $\hat{X}(G)$, and this occurs with a probability $1 - F(\hat{X}(G))$, where $F(.)$ is the cumulative distribution function. When the reciprocal gift exchange is increased by a small amount ΔG, the increase $\Delta\hat{X}$ in $\hat{X}(G)$ needed to generate this increase in G is simply given by $[1 - F(\hat{X}(G))]\Delta\hat{X} = \Delta G$. Since the probability in the square bracket is never greater than unity, it follows that $\Delta\hat{X}$ must be at least as large as ΔG. This means that the ratio $\hat{X}(G)/G$, which measures the maximum temptation to cheat relative to the punishment, cannot decline when G increases.

According to this proposition, firms in equilibrium are likely to share small innovations but not very large ones. This is because large innovations come infrequently and the sharing of such an innovation is not likely to be reciprocated soon. The above proposition is consistent with a liberal interpretation of some anecdotal evidence from the aerospace industry. von Hippel (1988, 86) reports that, according to an aerospace engineer, 'they freely exchange most know-how under normal circumstances. But, when competition for an important government contract is in the offing, the situation changes, and trading of information between rivals that might affect who wins the contract stops. Later, after the contract has been awarded, the same know-how that was recently closely guarded will apparently again be traded.' In other words, know-how that is potentially of high value is witheld.[6]

7. Conclusions

In this paper, in a repeated game framework, we have modelled the phenomenon of know-how sharing between two firms when they stochastically realize innovations of various sizes. We separately considered the cases in which the innovations are divisible and those in which they are indivisible, a distinction that turns out to be important. We have shown that both stochasticity and indivisibility of innovations inhibit sharing. We have demonstrated that, in equilibrium, sharing may be observed to be intermittent even when the sharing agreement has not been violated. When innovations are divisible, we have found that small innovations are more likely to be shared than larger ones. When innovations are indivisible, however, we have shown that agreements to share only small innovations are never supportable.

Inspired by Axelrod's (1984) book, a great deal has been written in the past fifteen years about the possibilities of achieving cooperation in the iterated Prisoners' Dilemma (IPD) game. The problem is significant because many – perhaps most – social and economic interactions have the flavour of the IPD game. If the players are not careful to devise clever strategies in these games, they will find themselves locked in a low-level Nash equilibrium trap. Our results suggest that, in the realm of know-how sharing, one cannot be overly optimistic about the prospects for cooperation. If the stochastic innovations of firms are indivisible – in which case, sharing is an all-or-nothing proposition – even the sharing of small innovations cannot easily be supported as subgame perfect Nash equilibria. There is room for optimism only for the case in which the innovations are divisible, a feature that is not generic to many scenarios. Ideas, for example, are often indivisible; one cannot easily share half an idea. Thus, in the realm of know-how sharing between competing firms, for example, the indivisibility of ideas or innovations militates against the possibility of cooperation. Given the fact that knowledge is a nonrivalrous public good, these results suggest that governments might consider eliminating the menace of anti-trust action against competing firms that trade in know-

6 Though this quote seems to contradict one of our assumptions of convenience (namely, that firms cannot pass on know-how that they had earlier witheld), its thrust is nevertheless consistent with the spirit of our analysis.

how. Otherwise, since tacit agreements are unenforceable in the courts, the public interest may not be well served.

In this paper, we took the firms to be identical. This simplified the analysis, since we could conduct our investigation by examining only one incentive compatibility constraint. We briefly remark here on the effects of asymmetry on sharing possibilities. Suppose we render the firms asymmetric by reducing the discount factor of one of them. Their incentive compatibility constraints would differ now, but the binding one would be that of the firm with the lower discount factor (since it is this firm that would be more tempted to cheat). Clearly, the greater impatience of this firm would undermine the extent of sharing. What is more interesting, we could also speculate on the effect of introducing asymmetry in the distribution of the innovations. Suppose we reduce the expected value of innovations for one firm but hold the variance constant. We would expect the distribution of this firm to be the constraining factor in limiting the extent of sharing, since its rival would be less willing than before to part with its information. For small asymmetries sharing would still be possible, especially if information is divisible. In the presence of extreme asymmetry, however, sharing is likely to break down. In general, since sharing presumes reciprocity, asymmetry in the distribution of innovations would tend to militate against the possibility of sharing.

The more differentiated the products that firms produce, the less know-how trading we would expect. This is because the know-how of such firms is more specialized. Know-how that these firms would willingly trade is probably of little use to others, whereas know-how that is particularly important to a firm is likely to be of the kind that differentiates this firm from others and so will likely be witheld. This would explain why one of the firms (Quanex) in von Hippel's (1988) study of the steel minimill industry did not engage in know-how trading. Unlike the other firms in his sample, Quanex produced specialty steel products.

We now briefly discuss an issue we did not raise in the paper so far, namely, that of renegotiation. There are really two issues here. The first is whether the optimal sharing agreement, which we have taken to be independent of time, is really so, or whether the firms will want to renegotiate the agreement sets as the game proceeds. The answer to this is immediate: the sharing agreement deemed optimal by the firms will not change from period to period, since the game considered here is stationary.[7] Secondly, as is frequently the case in repeated games, the game considered here is open to a more standard objection. In the event of cheating, the firms might consider renegotiating in order to avoid the costly no-sharing punishment phase, and this possibility would undermine their attempts at sharing information. We do not address this issue here. We may point out, however, that our earlier work (Eaton and Eswaran 1997), where we considered a scenario in which n firms ($n \geq 3$) trade technologies in a supergame, is relevant to this issue. We argued that cheating on a technology-sharing agreement may be interpreted by the non-

7 Even in the model with stocks, alluded to in footnote 1, this remains true. It will also be true in the event the firms are asymmetric. If the degree of asymmetry changes over time, however, the optimal sharing agreement will also change.

cheaters as a display of bad faith by the cheater and that they might subsequently eject the cheater from the trading coalition while continuing to trade technologies among themselves. We demonstrated that pursuing this strategy instead of dissolving the coalition in the event of cheating by a member not only would be in the self-interest of the honest members but also would inflict the largest punishment on the cheater. While this does not render the supergame equilibrium renegotiation proof, it is less open to this objection than is the standard presumption that cooperation is completely discontinued in the event of cheating. In future research, a similar approach might be worthy of consideration in the context of the present paper. However, the thrust of our results is likely to be robust: indivisibility and stochasticity render information less conducive to sharing in repeated games.

Finally, we observe that the degree of cooperation between firms, in general, might be expected to vary from time to time. Our model suggests two possible reasons for this. In a form optimal agreement, firms see in advance that the sharing of really important and rare ideas and innovations cannot be supported. Hence, in those periods when such innovations occur, the lucky firm will not share its good fortune with its competitor. To see the other explanation, suppose, for simplicity, that firms have inelastic expectations with respect to the interest rate. The set of supportable sharing agreements will then be a function of the interest rate and, in any circumstance where full sharing is not supportable but partial sharing is supportable, a decrease in the interest rate will unambiguously increase the set of supportable sharing agreements. This is because the punishments for defection that occur in future periods are given a higher weight in the firms' intertemporal profit calculation. Then, presuming that firms pick the most profitable sharing agreement for each interest rate, we should expect to see more sharing on average in those periods in which the interest rate is low.

References

Allen, R.C. (1983) 'Collective invention,' *Journal of Economic Behavior and Organization* 4, 1–24

Axelrod, R. (1984) *The Evolution of Cooperation* (New York: Basic Books)

Baumol, W.J. (1993) *Entrepreneurship, Management and Technical Progress*, chapter 10 (Cambridge, MA: MIT Press)

Carter, A.P. (1989) 'Knowhow trading as economic exchange,' *Research Policy* 18, 155–63

Eaton, B.C., and M. Eswaran (1997) 'Technology trading coalitions in supergames,' *RAND Journal of Economics* Spring, 135–49

Friedman, J.W. (1971) 'A non-cooperative equilibrium for supergames,' *Review of Economic Studies* 28, 1–12

Fudenberg, D., D. Levine, and E. Maskin (1994) 'The folk theorem with imperfect public information,' *Econometrica* 62, 997–1039

Gallini, N.T. (1984) 'Deterrence through market sharing: a strategic incentive for licensing,' *American Economic Review* 74, 931–41

Green, E., and R. Porter (1984) 'Noncooperative collusion under imperfect price information,' *Econometrica* 52, 87–100

Rotemberg, J., and G. Saloner (1986) 'A supergame-theoretic model of business cycles and price wars during booms,' *American Economic Review* 76, 390–407

von Hippel, E. (1988) *The Sources of Innovation* (New York: Oxford University Press)

Name index

Abreu, D. 390, 442
Aghion, P. 417
Allen, R.C. 389, 453
Andreoni, J. 420
Aquilano, N.J. 150
Archibald, G.C. 28,80
Arifovic, J. 378, 420
Aumann 405
Aumann, R. 419
Avriel, M. 46, 280, 290–91
Axelrod, R. 473

Back, T. 425–6
Badenhöfer, H.-J. 265
Bain, J.S. 51, 96–7
Barzel, Y. 285
Baumol, W.J. 304, 313, 389–91, 453
Bear, D.V.T. 293
Beaudry, P. 417
Becker, G. 188–9, 206, 226, 265–6, 273, 288
Becker, R.A. 78
Beckmann, M. 4–5, 14, 16, 332
Benjamin. D.K. 189, 195
Benoit, J.P. 227
Berkowitz, M.K. 354–5
Bernheim, B.D. 97
Bertrand 315–16, 321, 329
Blackorby, C. 290
Blume, A. 418
Böventer *see* Von Böventer
Bowles, S. 209, 224
Brander, J.A. 63, 78, 148, 155, 157
Brunt, S. 373
Bucovetsky, S. 78
Bullard 420
Bulow, J. 78, 100, 148
Bush, W.C. 227

Cafferata, P. 373
Carleton, D.W. 182
Carr, J.L. 373
Carter, A.P. 389, 453
Caves, R.E. 41, 48, 50
Chamberlin 13, 15
Chamberlin, J. 16
Chase, R.B. 150
Cheung, S. 227
Chiang, A.C. 86
Chilton, J. 78
Chin, J.C. 355
Clark, C.S. 288
Clark, K.B. 150
Cooper, T. 148
Cournot, A.A. 302, 315–17, 329
Crawford, V. 418
Crocker, K.J. 405

Darby, M.R. 188
D'Aspremont,C. 82, 317, 439–41, 444, 449
Deardorff, A.V. 355
Demsetz, H. 28
Denekere, R. 442
Denike, K.G. 16
Diewert, E. 244, 262
Diewert, W.E. 46, 280, 290–91
DiFranza, J.R. 387
Diwan, I. 355
Dixit, A. 41–2, 50–52, 59–60, 78, 96, 107, 109, 113, 115
Doeringer, P. 289
Domsimini, M.-P. 439, 441
Donaldson, D. 148, 288
Duffy 420

Eaton, B.C. 3, 5, 14, 16–18, 24, 35, 37–41, 45, 50–51, 58, 77–8, 80–81, 86–7, 91, 96, 117, 153–4, 195, 206, 212, 227, 288, 315, 378, 420, 440, 453, 456, 474
Eaton, J. 148, 155–7
Economides, N.S. 439
Edgeworth 316–17
Ehrlich, I. 227, 239
Eswaran, M. 209, 224, 440, 453, 456, 474
Evans, R.G. 181

Farrell, J. 419
Fei, J.C.H. 244
Feldstein, M.S. 290
Frank, R.H. 373
Fried, D. 391
Friedman 405
Friedman, J. 99, 164, 390, 457
Fudenberg, D. 96, 455

Gabszewicz, J.J. 82, 150, 317, 439–41, 449

Gallini, N.T. 391, 453
Gal-Or, E. 391
Gannon, C.A. 14
Geanakoplos, J. 100
Gibbons, R. 419
Gilbert, R. 96–7, 157
Goldberg, I. 188
Grace, S.H. 10
Green, E. 454
Green, J. 354
Greenhut, M. 16
Greenhut, M.L. 16
Greenwood, N.R. 150
Gronberg, T. 332
Grossman, G. 148, 355
Grossman, S.J. 405, 416

Hand, L. 31
Harberger, A.C. 244–5
Harris, J.R. 244
Harris, M. 201
Hart, O. 89, 405, 416
Hartwick, J.M. 5
Hartwick, P.G. 5
Hay, D.A. 77
Herrnstein, R.J. 226
Hicks, J.R. 252
Holland, J.H. 419
Holmstrom, B. 187, 201
Holt, C.C. 244
Hoover, E. 154, 350–51
Hotelling, H. 34, 77, 150–51, 153, 333, 351–3, 356, 369
Hurter, A.P. 154

Jacquemin, A. 439
Jensen, M. 188, 206
Johnson, D.B. 227, 240
Johnson, H.G. 244, 262
Johnston, J. 16
Jones, L.E. 89
Jones, S.R.G. 373
Joskow, P.L. 405–6, 411
Judd, K.L. 156–7

Kahn, A.E. 258
Kahn, L.R. 199
Kaldor, N. 15–17
Karni, E. 188
Karpoff, J.M. 240
Katz, P. 199
Kihlstrom, R.E. 373
Kim, Y. 418
Klein, B. 188–9, 199, 373, 404
Klemperer, P. 100, 354–5
Koopmans, T. 4, 16
Koss, P. 406
Kotowitz, Y. 354–5
Kotwal, A. 209, 224
Kreps, D.M. 316
Kress, A. 189
Kuhn, H. 98

Laitner, J. 297, 302
Landa, J.T. 373
Lav, M.R. 14, 16
Lazear, E. 188
Lederer, P.J. 154
Leffler, K. 188–9, 199, 383
Levine, D. 455
Lewis, D.K. 418
Lewis, W.A. 244
Libecap, G.D. 240
Lipsey, R.G. 3, 5, 14, 16–18, 24, 35, 37–41, 45, 50–51, 58, 77–8, 80–81, 96, 154, 315
Losche, A. 16
Lovell 286
Lucas, R. 289

MacDonald, G.M. 304, 308
Machlup, F. 276
MacLeod, W.B. 151, 154–5, 160–61
Maloney, M.T. 182
Mangasarian, O.L. 291
Marimon, R. 420
Martin, S. 439
Maskin, E. 455
Masten, S.E. 405
Matsui, A. 418
McCormick, R.E. 182
McLean, R. 97, 107
Meckling, W. 188, 206
Meredith, J.R. 150
Meyer, J. 332
Mieszkowski, P. 244, 262
Milgrom, P. 150–51, 405
Miller, J. 420
Mills, E.S. 14, 16
Mincer, J. 265
Mirrlees, J. 201
Modigliani, F. 96
Moore, W.E. 199
Mortensen, D.T. 244, 248
Myer, C. 189

Nash, J. 407
Neher, P.A. 226
Nelson, P. 373
Nichols, D. 286
Nordhaus, W.D. 354

Novshek, W. 80–81, 391

Ohta, H. 16
Oi, W. 265, 288, 295
Okuno-Fujiwara, M. 391
Osborne, M.J. 227

Parr, J.B. 16
Parsons, D.O. 265, 288
Parsons, T. 199
Perloff, J.M. 182
Perrakis, S. 112
Perry, G.L. 260
Perry, M.K. 302
Pierce, J.P. 387
Pigors, P. 189
Pigou, A.C. 276
Piore, M. 289
Poitevin, M. 417
Polemarchakis, H.M. 439
Polinsky, A.M. 189
Porter, M.E. 41, 48, 50
Porter, R. 454
Posner, R. 212, 224
Postlewaite, A. 391
Prescott, E.C. 77, 97, 157, 160
Primont, D. 290

Ranis, G. 244
Rasmusen, E. 156
Raviv, A. 201
Rees, A. 265
Reynolds, R.J. 440
Riordan, M.H. 97, 108, 373
Roberts, J. 150–51, 405
Robinson, J. 243, 245
Rodrik, D. 355
Röller, L.-H. 151
Rosen, H. 372–3
Rosen, J.B. 99
Rosenbluth, G. 28
Rosenstein-Rodan, P.N. 244
Rosovsky, H. 274
Ross, S.A. 187
Rotemberg, J. 182, 454, 464
Routledge 420
Russell, R. 290

Salant, D.J. 317
Salant, S.W. 440, 443, 446–7
Saloner, G. 182, 454, 464
Salop, S. 80–82, 88, 276
Samuelson 12
Sappington, D. 209
Sargent 420
Scheinkman, J.A. 316
Schelling, T. 41,43, 50–51, 62, 76, 148
Schmalensee, R. 28, 41, 51, 76, 78
Schmitt, N. 153
Schultz, T. 258
Schultze, C.L. 260
Schumpeter, J. 145, 176
Scotchmer, S. 354
Selten, R. 76–7, 98
Shaffer, S. 439, 441
Shaked, A. 24, 317
Shapiro, C. 212, 391
Shapley 405
Shavell, S. 189
Shinohora, M. 274
Singh, N. 317, 330
Slivinski, A. 304, 308
Smith, A. 187
Smithies, A. 34
Smolensky, E. 286
Sobel, J. 418
Sonnenschein, H. 391
Sorin, S. 419
Southey, C. 16
Spence, A.M. 41–2, 50, 78, 96, 107, 109
Spence, M. 276
Spence, M.A. 373
Spencer, B.J. 63, 78, 148
Spengler, J. 148
Spulber, D.F. 78, 112
Stalk, G. 150
Starr, R. 16
Stigler, G. 151, 156, 188–9, 206, 230
Stiglitz, J. 188, 209, 212, 276
Stokey, N. 276
Sutton, J. 317
Suzumura, K. 391
Sweezy, P. 297, 301–2
Switzer, S. 440
Sylos-Labini, P. 96

Telser, L. 5, 13–14, 16, 188, 265
Tesfatsion, L. 420
Thisse, J.-F. 82, 150, 317
Thurow, L. 289
Tideman, T. 286
Tirole, J. 96, 405, 416
Tobin, J. 257
Todaro, M.P. 244, 247–8
Tollison, R.D. 182
Tombak, M.M. 151
Tullock, G. 16, 127, 130
Twain, M. 199
Tybout, A.M. 373

Umbeck, J. 227
Usher, D. 226

Veblen, T. 131–2
Visscher, M. 77, 97, 157, 160
Vives, X. 97, 157, 317, 330, 391
Von Böventer, E. 16
Von Hippel, E. 389, 453, 461, 473–4
Von Weizsäcker, C.C. 245, 262

Ware, R. 78, 96–7, 106–7, 117
Warneryd, K. 418–19
Warskett, G. 112
Weizsäcker *see* Von Weizsäcker
Weymark, J.A. 439
White, W. 188, 195, 206, 212, 227
Wiggins, S.N. 240
Williamson, O.E. 405–6, 411–13, 416
Wilson, J.Q. 226
Wintrobe, R. 373
Wood, A. 187
Wooders, M.H. 86–7, 91

Yellen, J. 209, 227

Zang, I. 46, 280, 290–91
Zarembka, P. 248
Zeuthen, F. 16

Economists of the Twentieth Century

Monetarism and Macroeconomic Policy
Thomas Mayer

Studies in Fiscal Federalism
Wallace E. Oates

The World Economy in Perspective
Essays in International Trade and European Integration
Herbert Giersch

Towards a New Economics
Critical Essays on Ecology, Distribution and Other Themes
Kenneth E. Boulding

Studies in Positive and Normative Economics
Martin J. Bailey

The Collected Essays of Richard E. Quandt (2 volumes)
Richard E. Quandt

International Trade Theory and Policy
Selected Essays of W. Max Corden
W. Max Corden

Organization and Technology in Capitalist Development
William Lazonick

Studies in Human Capital
Collected Essays of Jacob Mincer, Volume 1
Jacob Mincer

Studies in Labor Supply
Collected Essays of Jacob Mincer, Volume 2
Jacob Mincer

Macroeconomics and Economic Policy
The Selected Essays of Assar Lindbeck
Volume I
Assar Lindbeck

The Welfare State
The Selected Essays of Assar Lindbeck
Volume II
Assar Lindbeck

Classical Economics, Public Expenditure and Growth
Walter Eltis

Money, Interest Rates and Inflation
Frederic S. Mishkin

The Public Choice Approach to Politics
Dennis C. Mueller

The Liberal Economic Order
Volume I Essays on International Economics
Volume II Money, Cycles and Related Themes
Gottfried Haberler
Edited by Anthony Y.C. Koo

Economic Growth and Business Cycles
Prices and the Process of Cyclical Development
Paolo Sylos Labini

International Adjustment, Money and Trade
Theory and Measurement for Economic Policy
Volume I
Herbert G. Grubel

International Capital and Service Flows
Theory and Measurement for Economic Policy
Volume II
Herbert G. Grubel

Unintended Effects of Government Policies
Theory and Measurement for Economic Policy
Volume III
Herbert G. Grubel

The Economics of Competitive Enterprise
Selected Essays of P.W.S. Andrews
Edited by Frederic S. Lee and Peter E. Earl

The Repressed Economy
Causes, Consequences, Reform
Deepak Lal

Economic Theory and Market Socialism
Selected Essays of Oskar Lange
Edited by Tadeusz Kowalik

Trade, Development and Political Economy
Selected Essays of Ronald Findlay
Ronald Findlay

General Equilibrium Theory
The Collected Essays of Takashi Negishi
Volume I
Takashi Negishi

The History of Economics
The Collected Essays of Takashi Negishi
Volume II
Takashi Negishi

Studies in Econometric Theory
The Collected Essays of Takeshi Amemiya
Takeshi Amemiya

Exchange Rates and the Monetary System
Selected Essays of Peter B. Kenen
Peter B. Kenen

Econometric Methods and Applications
(2 volumes)
G.S. Maddala

National Accounting and Economic Theory
The Collected Papers of Dan Usher, Volume I
Dan Usher

Welfare Economics and Public Finance
The Collected Papers of Dan Usher, Volume II
Dan Usher

Economic Theory and Capitalist Society
The Selected Essays of Shigeto Tsuru, Volume I
Shigeto Tsuru

Methodology, Money and the Firm
The Collected Essays of D.P. O'Brien
(2 volumes)
D.P. O'Brien

Economic Theory and Financial Policy
The Selected Essays of Jacques J. Polak
(2 volumes)
Jacques J. Polak

Sturdy Econometrics
Edward E. Leamer

The Emergence of Economic Ideas
Essays in the History of Economics
Nathan Rosenberg

Productivity Change, Public Goods and Transaction Costs
Essays at the Boundaries of Microeconomics
Yoram Barzel

Reflections on Economic Development
The Selected Essays of Michael P. Todaro
Michael P. Todaro

The Economic Development of Modern Japan
The Selected Essays of Shigeto Tsuru
Volume II
Shigeto Tsuru

Money, Credit and Policy
Allan H. Meltzer

Macroeconomics and Monetary Theory
The Selected Essays of Meghnad Desai
Volume I
Meghnad Desai

Poverty, Famine and Economic Development
The Selected Essays of Meghnad Desai
Volume II
Meghnad Desai

Explaining the Economic Performance of Nations
Essays in Time and Space
Angus Maddison

Economic Doctrine and Method
Selected Papers of R.W. Clower
Robert W. Clower

Economic Theory and Reality
Selected Essays on their Disparities and Reconciliation
Tibor Scitovsky

Doing Economic Research
Essays on the Applied Methodology of Economics
Thomas Mayer

Institutions and Development Strategies
The Selected Essays of Irma Adelman
Volume I
Irma Adelman

Dynamics and Income Distribution
The Selected Essays of Irma Adelman
Volume II
Irma Adelman

The Economics of Growth and Development
Selected Essays of A.P. Thirlwall
A.P. Thirlwall

Theoretical and Applied Econometrics
The Selected Papers of Phoebus J. Dhrymes
Phoebus J. Dhrymes

Innovation, Technology and the Economy
The Selected Essays of Edwin Mansfield
(2 volumes)
Edwin Mansfield

Economic Theory and Policy in Context
The Selected Essays of R.D. Collison Black
R.D. Collison Black

Location Economics
Theoretical Underpinnings and Applications
Melvin L. Greenhut

Spatial Microeconomics
Theoretical Underpinnings and Applications
Melvin L. Greenhut

Capitalism, Socialism and Post-Keynesianism
Selected Essays of G.C. Harcourt
G.C. Harcourt

Time Series Analysis and Macroeconometric Modelling
The Collected Papers of Kenneth F. Wallis
Kenneth F. Wallis

Foundations of Modern Econometrics
The Selected Essays of Ragnar Frisch
(2 volumes)
Edited by Olav Bjerkholt

Growth, the Environment and the Distribution of Incomes
Essays by a Sceptical Optimist
Wilfred Beckerman

The Economics of Environmental Regulation
Wallace E. Oates

Econometrics, Macroeconomics and Economic Policy
Selected Papers of Carl F. Christ
Carl F. Christ

Strategic Approaches to the International Economy
Selected Essays of Koichi Hamada
Koichi Hamada

Economic Analysis and Political Ideology
The Selected Essays of Karl Brunner
Volume One
Edited by Thomas Lys

Growth Theory and Technical Change
The Selected Essays of Ryuzo Sato
Volume One
Ryuzo Sato

Industrialization, Inequality and Economic Growth
Jeffrey G. Williamson

Economic Theory and Public Decisions
Selected Essays of Robert Dorfman
Robert Dorfman

The Logic of Action One
Method, Money, and the Austrian School
Murray N. Rothbard

The Logic of Action Two
Applications and Criticism from the Austrian School
Murray N. Rothbard

Bayesian Analysis in Econometrics and Statistics
The Zellner View and Papers
Arnold Zellner

On the Foundations of Monopolistic Competition and Economic Geography
The Selected Essays of B. Curtis Eaton and Richard G. Lipsey
B. Curtis Eaton and Richard G. Lipsey

Microeconomics, Growth and Political Economy
The Selected Essays of Richard G. Lipsey
Volume One
Richard G. Lipsey

Macroeconomic Theory and Policy
The Selected Essays of Richard G. Lipsey
Volume Two
Richard G. Lipsey

Employment, Labor Unions and Wages
The Collected Essays of Orley Ashenfelter
Volume One
Edited by Kevin F. Hallock

Education, Training and Discrimination
The Collected Essays of Orley Ashenfelter
Volume Two
Edited by Kevin F. Hallock

Economic Institutions and the Demand and Supply of Labour
The Collected Essays of Orley Ashenfelter
Volume Three
Edited by Kevin F. Hallock

Monetary Theory and Monetary Policy
The Selected Essays of Karl Brunner
Volume Two
Edited by Thomas Lys

Macroeconomic Issues from a Keynesian Perspective
Selected Essays of A.P. Thirlwall
Volume Two
A.P. Thirlwall

Money and Macroeconomics
The Selected Essays of David Laidler
David Laidler

The Economics and Politics of Money
The Selected Essays of Alan Walters
Edited by Kent Matthews

Economics and Social Justice
Essays on Power, Labor and Institutional Change
David M. Gordon
Edited by Thomas E. Weisskopf and Samuel Bowles

Practicing Econometrics
Essays in Method and Application
Zvi Griliches

Economics Against the Grain
Volume One
Microeconomics, Industrial Organization and Related Themes
Julian L. Simon

Economics Against the Grain
Volume Two
Population Economics, Natural Resources and Related Themes
Julian L. Simon

Advances in Econometric Theory
The Selected Works of Halbert White
Halbert White

The Economics of Imperfect Knowledge
Collected Papers of G.B. Richardson
G.B. Richardson

Economic Performance and the Theory of the Firm
The Selected Papers of David J. Teece
Volume One
David J. Teece

Strategy, Technology and Public Policy
The Selected Papers of David J. Teece
Volume Two
David J. Teece

The Keynesian Revolution, Then and Now
The Selected Essays of Robert Eisner
Volume One
Robert Eisner

Investment, National Income and Economic Policy
The Selected Essays of Robert Eisner
Volume Two
Robert Eisner

International Trade Opening and the Formation of the Global Economy
Selected Essays of P. J. Lloyd
P. J. Lloyd

Production, Stability and Dynamic Symmetry
The Selected Essays of Ryuzo Sato
Volume Two
Ryuzo Sato

Variants in Economic Theory
Selected Works of Hal R. Varian
Hal R. Varian

Political Economy, Oligopoly and Experimental Games
The Selected Essays of Martin Shubik
Volume One
Martin Shubik

Money and Financial Institutions
A GAME THEORETIC APPROACH
The Selected Essays of Martin Shubik
Volume Two
Martin Shubik

Competition Policy, Domestic and International
F.M. Scherer

Macroeconomic Instability and Coordination
Selected Essays of Axel Leijonhufvud
Axel Leijonhufvud

Economic Thought from Smith to Keynes
The Collected Essays of Takashi Negishi
Volume III
Takashi Negishi

Education Matters
Selected Essays by Alan B. Krueger
Alan B. Krueger

The Economic Structure of the Law
The Collected Economic Esssays of Richard A. Posner
Volume One
Richard A. Posner
Edited by Francesco Parisi

Measurement and Meaning in Economics
The Essential Deirdre McCloskey
Deirdre McCloskey
Edited and introduced by Stephen Thomas Ziliak

The Economics of Private Law
The Collected Economic Esssays of
Richard A. Posner
Volume Two
Richard A. Posner
Edited by Francesco Parisi

The Economics of Public Law
The Collected Economic Esssays of
Richard A. Posner
Volume Three
Richard A. Posner
Edited by Francesco Parisi

Public Economics, Political Processes and Policy Applications
Collected Papers on the Experimental Foundations of Economics and Political Science
Volume One
Charles R. Plott

Market Institutions and Price Discovery
Collected Papers on the Experimental Foundations of Economics and Political Science
Volume Two
Charles R. Plott

Information, Finance and General Equilibrium
Collected Papers on the Experimental Foundations of Economics and Political Science
Volume Three
Charles R. Plott

Growth Theory, Nonlinear Dynamics and Economic Modelling
Scientific Essays of William Allen Brock
William Allen Brock
Edited by W. Davis Dechert